ENIGMΛ:
David Puttnam
THE STORY SO FAR...

ANDREW YULE

MAINSTREAM
PUBLISHING

For Patricia, Pamela and Judith

Copyright © by Andrew Yule 1988

First published in Great Britain in 1988 by
MAINSTREAM PUBLISHING COMPANY (EDINBURGH) LTD
7 Albany Street, Edinburgh EH1 3UG

ISBN 1 85158 127 8 (cloth)

British Library Cataloguing in Publication Data
Yule, Andrew
   Enigma: David Puttnam – a biography
   the story so far.
   1. British cinema films. Production.
Puttnam, David, 1941
   1. Title
791.43′0232′0924

ISBN 1-85158-127-8

Typeset in Ehrhardt by
Richard Clay Ltd, Bungay, Suffolk
Printed in Great Britain by Billings & Sons, Worcester

Contents

Acknowledgements

Grateful thanks are extended to the following interviewees (and to the others who preferred to remain anonymous), whose kind cooperation helped to make this book possible:

David Bailey, Andrew Birkin, Roy Battersby, Fred Bernstein, Frank Bloom, Robert Bolt, Don Boyd, Lenore Cantor, Jim Clark, Nat Cohen, Robert Colesberry, Philip Collins, Ray Connolly, Bob Dingilian, Terence Donovan, Robin Douet, Brian Duffy, Jake Eberts, Adam Faith, Bill Forsyth, Brian Gilbert, Hara San, Gilly Hodgson, Hugh Hudson, Derek Hussey, Roland Joffe, Anthony Jones, Valerie Kemp, James Lee, Tom Lewyn, Sandy Lieberson, Robert Littman, Lord Low of Tribeca, Margaret Maguire, Alan Marshall, Sarah Miles, David Montgomery, Robert Montgomery, Lynda Myles, Michael Nathanson, David Norris, Steve Norris, James Park, Alan Parker, Uberto Pasolini, David Picker, Patsy Pollock, Lyndsey Posner, Susan Richards, John Ritchie, Bruce, Sophie & Lily India Robinson, Stanley Robinson, Marion Rosenberg, Alan Sapper, Anthony Smith, Iain Smith, Lynda Smith, Michael Stoddart, Jeremy Thomas, Francis T. Vincent, Paul Weiland, Colin Welland, Alan Yentob, Alex Ying.

Particular thanks also to the Puttnams – David, Patsy, Marie, Debbie and Sacha, and to Alan Parker for his (eventual) permission to use his brilliant cartoons (one trek to Los Angeles later!).

The following books were consulted in the research process: *National Heroes* by Alexander Walker (Harrap), *Reel Power* by Mark Litwak (Sidgwick & Jackson), *Dustin Hoffman* by Iain Johnstone (Spellmount), *The Real Coke, The Real Story*, by Thomas Oliver (Random House) and *Indecent Exposure* by David McClintick (Corgi). *Variety*, *Hollywood Reporter* and *Screen International* all provided useful background information.

Wherever dialogue is quoted, this represents the recollection of at least one person present when the conversation took place.

A special 'thank you' to all the critics and their journals mentioned in the book, together with my indefatigable secretaries Hattie Forrest and Eunice Sweenie.

Chapter 1

Sweet Chariots

David and Patsy Puttnam arrived unheralded at Los Angeles Airport on Saturday, 27 March 1982, weary after the long journey from London. As for everyone else on the flight, there was a long delay before their luggage could be collected, customs cleared, and their journey resumed with a 45-minute taxi ride to the Bel-Air hotel. Here they were spotted as they registered – hardly surprising, since they made a striking couple: they were both of medium height with blue eyes, she with shoulder-length flaxen hair and classical cheek-bone structure emphasizing her Nordic beauty, he handsome and dark, his barely 40 years belied by an increasingly grizzled beard.

Everyone knew what they had come for and soon after they had settled into their terracotta-floored room at the Bel-Air, with its exotic Jacaranda tree and jungle ferns framing the window, the telephone began ringing. David chose not to attend any of the pre-Oscar parties to which they had been invited. Instead, after resting for a while, the couple dressed and dined quietly in the hotel that evening. Next day David hired a car and they drove to Malibu beach. They revelled in the brief respite they were sharing, for the pressures and separation of the last few months had been almost overwhelming. Still there was an underlying tension that could not be shaken off, as they anticipated the Oscar awards ceremony to be held the following evening at the Dorothy Chandler Pavilion. They strolled together around Malibu, then ate a light lunch as they talked quietly of their chances of bringing back a coveted Oscar to Britain. *Chariots of Fire* had been nominated in seven categories – Best Supporting Actor for Ian Holm, Best Original Score for Vangelis, Best Film Editing for Terry Rawling, Best Script for Colin Welland, Best Costume for Milena Canonero, Best Director for Hugh Hudson and most coveted of all, Best Film.

Until a few days before, the Hugh Hudson-directed picture had been considered a rank outsider in the Best Film stakes. Warren Beatty's three-hour, $43-million *Reds* was the favourite for Best Film, backed by an enormous campaign launched by Beatty – as producer, director, co-writer and star – together with his distributor, Paramount Pictures. '*Reds* is going to win' had been the buzz on the grapevine for weeks, although both David and Patsy were gradually beginning to realize that *Chariots* was *liked* so much more. They had largely shrugged off the few 'I voted for you' calls with 'Oh, yes, but they'll be saying that to everybody!' although there was a growing feeling that these people actually meant it. Strangers approached them with phrases like 'I can't tell you how wonderful your film is', but they still couldn't believe it was seriously a contender, although the British Academy of Film and Television Artists (BAFTA) had honoured *Chariots* by presenting their Best Supporting Actor accolade to Ian Holm as well as the Best Film award to David as producer. Another honour in the same evening was the presentation to David of the Michael Balcon award for his cumulative body of work in the industry, culminating in the *Chariots* triumph. This was especially fitting since Balcon was David's hero, and had become a close friend since their introduction at Cannes in 1975. On the debit side, Hugh Hudson had been passed over for Best Director in favour of Louis Malle for *Atlantic City*, causing considerable resentment from the Hudson camp.

'We've been nominated and that's an honour in itself,' David had rationalized on his return from the States just days earlier, where he had been involved in tough negotiations with Warner Brothers. Patsy had seldom seen him so worn out. 'Oh, God,' he told her. 'I can't get on another plane and go back there.' For once the normally placid Patsy exploded. She had shared with her husband his years of struggle and gargantuan battles to bring *Chariots* into being. 'You're damned well *going*,' she told him. 'If all else fails, I'm going to drag you on to that plane, because *of course* we're not going to win, but it doesn't matter, you have to be there. You have to learn to be a good loser. We're going for everyone who's worked so hard to make the film. We're going for *them*.' Smilingly, David acquiesced, as he had intended to all along.

In the absence of any stars in the movie and since Hugh Hudson was still an unknown first-time director, the media focus had been heavily on David Puttnam as producer. He had, after all, been an increasingly visible presence on the film scene for more than a decade. David *became* the story, as the press finally put it all together. His biography had registered.

Hugh Hudson had begged his producer to take over the promotional interviews, which he reckoned he couldn't handle himself, making it all the more unexpected when he complained later that David had seized all the limelight. The friendship between the two had cooled in earnest after Hugh had been passed over at BAFTA, and it had been further breached in recent weeks with David's announcement that he had decided against producing *Greystoke – Tarzan, Lord of the Apes*, which Hugh had been waiting to direct.

Considered by many to be a brilliantly creative visual director, the tall, aristocratic, somewhat distracted and fairly distracting Hugh Hudson was seen on a personal level as a decidedly complex individual, perhaps a legacy from an apparently perplexing parental relationship. He and his producer had first met in the sixties when David was running a photographic agency and Hugh was a partner with Robert Brownjohn and David Cammell in a company making commercials and documentaries. When Cammell's brother Donald co-directed *Performance* in the late sixties, the film was produced out of their offices. Hugh later joined Ridley Scott Associates as a director in partnership with Ridley, then left after a few years to work on his own, meeting David again in Alan Parker's Soho headquarters, where Hugh rented a back office. David saw Hugh's commercial work and asked him to do surreptitious second-unit work in Turkey on *Midnight Express*, initially under cover of making a cigarette commercial.

When they were joined at the Bel-Air by Hugh and Sue Hudson, the atmosphere was decidedly strained. The four of them travelled together through the baking California sunshine in a hired air-conditioned limousine to arrive promptly at 5 pm at the Dorothy Chandler Pavilion complex, where they took their seats for the Awards ceremony. To their right, in the front row, sat Warren Beatty, their main rival in several categories, including Best Director and Best Film, accompanied by Diane Keaton and Barry Diller, the head of Paramount Pictures.

The electric atmosphere in the huge theatre, and the knowledge that the entire evening would be watched by millions of viewers throughout the world, heightened the tension for the contending participants. There was no clean sweep as the evening wore on for any one film, but Patsy was struck by a remark David made to her right at the beginning. She knew how he loved to calculate percentages for the sheer exhilaration of seeing how numbers work. He had been going through the programme while Patsy was busy looking round at the celebrities in the throng. 'I'll tell you something,' he said. 'If we win Best Costume, that will be the deciding factor.'

'What do you mean? How do you know?' Patsy asked. 'Because,' he replied, 'a lot of Academy members simply fill up the rest of their card once they've decided on Best Picture. Since we're up against *Reds* for costume, I think if we win that, we'll win with the picture.'

'But why costume? Why not production design?' Patsy asked. 'No, it's *costume*,' David replied. When Patsy checked the programme and the other contenders for costume she could see his point, for they were indeed up against particularly stiff competition in this category.

The favourite was *Reds*, but there was also *The French Lieutenant's Woman*, *Pennies from Heaven* and *Ragtime* to contend with. At one of the intervals David observed Warren Beatty and Barry Diller deep in animated conversation. Warren was jabbing away at the programme to illustrate his point and David felt certain that the actor had reached the same conclusion that he had.

Patsy could not help but feel how ironic it was, for *Reds* was in production at the same time as *Chariots of Fire* and Shirley Russell had been able to commandeer most of the period costumes in London for Beatty. An entire aircraft hangar was packed with clothes. Milena Canonero had had to scour the country for any remaining costumes of the same period, then had resorted to her native Italy to have the bulk of the clothes made. The joke in the *Chariots* company was that if Milena had broken into *Reds'* hangar and stolen the costumes she required, they would not even have been missed. David conceded that Shirley Russell, who was an old friend, had carried out a mammoth task with extraordinary skill for Warren's huge-budget production, as Milena had for *Chariots*, bringing him to the conclusion that costume would be the crucial battleground. Later he learned that Warren had indeed been arguing the same point with Diller, but for now both Patsy and he were only too aware that, while *Chariots* was the popular Best Film favourite, the smart money from both cineastes and the industry was on *Reds*.

The excitement mounted as the first of the seven *Chariots*-nominated categories was reached – Terry Rawlings for Best Film Editing – but this was won by Michael Kahn for *Raiders of the Lost Ark*. For Best Supporting Actor Ian Holm lost out to Sir John Gielgud for the Dudley Moore vehicle, *Arthur*. Five categories to go, and the all-important Best Costume was next. Feelings ran high as the announcement was made that the winner was Milena Canonero for *Chariots of Fire*! If David was correct the rest of the evening belonged to *Chariots*! Sure enough, Vangelis won Best Original Score against competition from *Dragonslayer*, *On Golden Pond*, *Ragtime* and *Raiders of the Lost Ark*. Next to win was Colin Welland's *Chariots* screenplay, triumphing over *Absence of Malice*, *Arthur*, *Atlantic City* and *Reds*. 'Look out, the British are coming!' Colin declared as he held his award high.

Warren Beatty's win as Best Director for *Reds* was a crushing disappointment for Hugh which he was unable to hide. Now if *Chariots* won Best Film it would be a virtual re-run of what he saw as the BAFTA injustice.

Sentiment won the day as Best Actor and Actress was awarded to Henry Fonda and Katherine Hepburn for *On Golden Pond*, then the Best Film was next, and last, to be announced. Having scooped the earlier technical awards, Steven Spielberg knew he was not in the running for Best Film, although *Raiders of the Lost Ark* had in fact been nominated in that category. He leaned forward to David and Patsy, squeezing David's shoulder. 'It's going to be you, I *know* it's going to be you,' he exclaimed, as veteran movie star Loretta Young came on to make the announcement. All eyes were on her as she opened the envelope and looked at the name of the winner. As she appeared to hesitate, David's heart was in his mouth. If he did win, even the announcement was delayed! Was the odyssey that *Chariots* had turned into about to end in an unprecedented triumph, or a shattering disappointment?

Loretta Young had been asked many times before to present the Best Film award, but had turned down every request. There hadn't been any film she wanted to give the prize to until the arrival of *Chariots*, which she adored. 'I prayed for it to win,' she told the Puttnams after the ceremony. 'That's the only reason I came here tonight.' The reason for her hesitation in making the announcement when she first saw the film's name on the card was simple. It was indeed *Chariots*, but she had to re-focus in case she had imagined it, *willed* its name to be there. 'Can you imagine an actress making that mistake?' she laughed, and her hesitation was plain for all to see on the video of the event. 'I had to take a breath and look again before I said it!'

After her announcement, the theatre erupted into applause and cheers as David got to his feet to collect the award. His legs promptly buckled under him and he fell into the lap of a priest in the adjacent seat, whom he hadn't even noticed until that moment. As she watched her husband helped back to his feet by the priest, then briskly make his way towards the stage to receive the coveted Award, all Patsy could think as tears blinded her eyes was, 'No, no, it's too *soon*, you can't win things like this yet, you're too young!'

Their first meeting flashed into her mind, she a 13-year-old slip of a girl, transplanted from Westminster Girls' School in St James to Minchenden Grammar School with her parents' move to Southgate. He was three years older and on his last two terms at school. She had felt incongruous in Westminster's grey and pale blue outfit to everyone else's Minchenden green. As she was standing in line with a friend one day waiting to get into the geography room, a boy had come over and said, 'Hi!' as he walked past. Patsy took no notice. She had come from an all-girls school, didn't know who the boy was and concluded that he must have been addressing her companion whom Patsy considered far prettier than she was. Now here in Hollywood she was watching the same boy, her husband of twenty years and father of her two children, bounding towards Loretta Young and an Oscar Award.

Exhilaration was still far away as Patsy's mind continued to race. Oscars were for superstars like Marlon Brando and Barbra Streisand, this was too *early*. She was brought down to earth with a thud as the next thought struck her. 'Oh, God, he hasn't thought of anything to say!' Then she was calm, for she knew he would have something sorted out – that was David.

He later remembered walking up the stairs, terrified of tripping up, as they looked very slippery. On reaching the top he walked towards the gracious, elderly actress who waited to present him with his award. It was like a scene in slow motion. Everyone had been kissing each other all night and he thought, 'That's not right for this woman; she's a very dignified lady and I don't really know her. I can't just shake her hand, though, that'd be too pompous . . .'

As he walked forward the solution presented itself as she held out her hand, which he promptly took and kissed. Then he was standing there, looking at what appeared to be a rather tatty velvet cover on the stand, quite different from the glittering façade presented to the audience. He thought to himself, 'God, these thousands of people here with everything looking so great from the front, if only they knew how extraordinarily tatty the podium looks from here.' He felt that he was unable to enjoy it as much as he wanted, because it was like revenge after the dreadful time the film had gone through in crawling into being. A tiny part of David was saying, 'About fucking time – and thanks for nothing!' Horrible, he knew, but it was something he felt at least a little bit, for there were at least a dozen people out there smiling and applauding – and later rushing up to pump his hand – who had done everything in their power to stop the film.

He could hear every word he was saying as he started his speech, but it was like a movie soundtrack he was listening to, as if someone else was doing the talking. It was a short speech, with only one person singled out, as in an unprecedented departure from the Academy's protocol he declared, 'Hugh is the director and I'd like to have him standing here with me now. I'd like Hugh to come up.' Only when

Hugh joined him and the Oscar was held high by the two of them did he conclude with, 'You're the most generous nation. You've taken this little Cinderella picture to your hearts.' (And he thought to himself, 'Cinderella picture? Where did that come from? Why did I say *Cinderella* picture?') His sense of disassociation was complete. The words were echoing in his head, but it was as if someone else had written the script.

When the couple woke up next morning it seemed that the world and his wife wanted to interview David. Off he went, promising to be back by lunchtime. Patsy sat bemused in their hotel room, 'gob-smacked', in her Cockney parlance, at the patently fraudulent sentiments behind the stream of gifts, cards, balloons, teddy-bears and flowers that jostled with the congratulatory telegrams. It all seemed so vulgar and out of place. Fine to have a little note from friends and associates, but all these gee-gaws from total strangers struck a decidedly false note.

So choked up did she feel, that when David rang to say he was having lunch with someone, she burst into tears. 'What's the *matter?*' he asked, astonished at her reaction. 'What on *earth* is the *matter* with you?' Patsy blurted out, 'I can't cope with this, I don't *understand* this.' The struggle was one thing, the fight to achieve the breakthrough, but not what she saw as this incredible display of Hollywoodian bullshit at the end of it all. That was just too much for her to take.

Underneath the delicate porcelain conformity that Patsy presents to the world is a fascinating mixture of personality shading. When talking about David she is a she-wolf, guarding her brood with a protectiveness bordering on the feral. In debate she can be dogmatic and utterly unyielding, forthright and uncompromising – to Patsy a spade will forever be a spade. The kicker is that all this strength comes over with a disconcertingly effervescent sense of humour, allied to a touching vulnerability. But let no one shortchange this woman.

David has many strengths of his own, all of them enhanced by Patsy's unflinching – but not uncritical – support. Although he has ostensibly taken on the mantle of the high ethical standards of both sets of parents, Patsy is the true keeper of the flame. David chooses to maintain an edge of dissent in their relationship, often shunning the cosy option, giving Patsy the satisfaction of being heeded while effectively removing any question of domination. Patsy remains the single chink in David's armour. If anyone wanted to get to David, Patsy would be the single route.

After the Oscars ceremony Hugh Hudson had been very glum, and at a dinner party the following evening held by Paula Weinstein and attended by the David Pickers and the Michael Apteds, Hugh turned up on his own without Sue. On the photographs of the occasion he can be seen smiling, but the struggle was obvious. Patsy had her view of Hugh's reaction and felt certain he was thinking that if only David had given him his head, he would have been up there on the stand collecting the Best Director Award, not Warren Beatty. If he'd been allowed to spend the sort of money Beatty had, he would have had a real chance at his goal. Paula Weinstein gave her guests a beautiful dinner, but Hugh's attitude put an uncomfortable edge on the whole evening.

Next day Hugh and David said their goodbyes and embraced emotionally. Hugh was off on holiday with Sue to the West Indies while the Puttnams were returning to London, since David had an appointment in a field in Scotland to start work on his next movie, *Local Hero*. On the plane someone gave Patsy a present with a Union Jack on it. 'Wouldn't it be wonderful to attach it to the Oscar for the press photographers at London airport?' she suggested. David smilingly agreed. 'O K Billy,' he said, using his very private pet name for her.

When the photographs were printed Hugh's comment was relayed to them that the Union Jack gesture tied to the Oscar was a typical Puttnam manoeuvre to get all the glory. Patsy's innocent suggestion held no resonance for Hugh beyond the implication of another small betrayal.

As the film continued its successful run, boosted considerably by the Oscar awards, another personality conflict was to emerge as Dodi Fayed's Allied Stars grew decidedly miffed with the constant tagline that accompanied *Chariots'* mention in the press – the Goldcrest connection.

They took the unprecedented step of taking out trade and magazine advertisements, highlighting Goldcrest's minute investment of seed money into the project. 'People honestly believe Goldcrest produced the film,' protested Jack Weiner, Allied Star's president, 'all thanks to their original £17,000 investment.' Allied Stars, he pointed out, had invested $3 million in the $6 million film and co-produced it with 20th Century Fox – not Goldcrest. 'This is *not* a vendetta,' he continued, 'but we would like a little recognition now and again for our 50 per cent backing on the picture.' Dodi Fayed in fact seemed to want more, and to many passed himself off as the film's producer. Although half the money had been put up by his father, Mohammed Al Fayed, with an executive producer credit for his son, David maintained that at no time had Dodi been part of the actual production process.

David was far too busy working out the new eventual rentals in the wake of the awards to worry about fracas. 'We reckon the Oscars will bump them up by about $11 million,' he stated exuberantly. In the event *Chariots* went on to exceed everyone's estimates, and harvested total rental in the USA of over $30 million, making it the most successful foreign film in US box-office history. (It is important to differentiate between money taken at cinema's box-offices and 'net rentals', which represent about 40% of gross box-office takings, the rest being retained by the cinemas. Also to be deducted before the production team sees any money is a one-third charge levied by the distributor to cover his overhead and expenses, together with print and advertising costs on top.)

Far from letting go after *Chariots'* release, David often visited cinemas showing the movie. 'I regard going to my own films as one of the marvellous things about the job,' he declared. 'You really can be in contact with your audience in a way the writer, faced with a printed page, can never be. I don't know or care if other producers do the same thing, but if they don't they're fools because I get so much pleasure out of it.'

Another sour note was to later emerge, though it was not widely reported, as the film encountered hefty criticism from Olympic historians which revealed that most of the dramatic high points in the film were total invention. 'Despite its claim to be a true story,' David Wallechinsky wrote, 'the film contains factual distortions.

'Abrahams did *not* race around the great courtyard of Trinity College at Cambridge. Lord Burghley did that. Neither did he look at the 100 metres contest as a chance to redeem himself after his failure in the 200 metres, since the running of the 100 actually preceded the 200 in real life. Although Abrahams did feel himself something of an outsider because he was Jewish, a much more important motivating factor in his quest for victory was his desire to do better than his two older brothers, both of whom were well-known athletes.'

There was more, remembering that the major dramatic dilemma of the film had come from Liddell's last-minute, agonizing discovery that his 100-metre event was set for the Sabbath.

'It is true,' Wallechinsky stated, 'that Liddell withdrew from the 100 metres because he wouldn't run on a Sunday. However, he did *not* find out about the Olympic schedule at the last minute. In real life Liddell learned the schedule *over six months in advance* and was able to concentrate his training for the alternative race.'

Another invention had Jackson Scholz, played by Brad Davis, offering Liddell a note with a religious message on it before the race.

When contacted, 84-year-old Scholz had no recollection of such an incident, admitting, 'I'm afraid my religious background was rather casual.'

Uriel Simri, a history professor at Israel's Physical Education Institute near Tel Aviv, was so irritated by the film that he assigned his students a term paper on the mistakes in *Chariots of Fire*. 'They came up with about 50 factual errors,' he reported, adding, 'I understand the needs of a movie producer to make a good film, but there were too many historical inaccuracies.'

One can only speculate how successful the film might have proven had it been assembled by academicians. There is no doubt that the basic story of Liddell and Abrahams' remarkable achievements had been 'dramatized' to work as a movie, but the film had to stand or fall on how well that had been achieved. David had at one time compared the situation with that of German documentary film-maker Leni Riefenstahl, who was charged with the propagandizing of the 1936 Olympic Games for the Fatherland's greater glorification. 'As an artist she could not have made a very different film,' he claimed. 'Even if she had been a Marxist, there might have been the odd scene or frame here or there added or cut, but she couldn't have basically changed the film. Film is a very emotive medium to work in and if you accept that and you're steeped in it, as I am, then all your instincts are urging you to make it emotional. Everything tells you, here's a scene where if we hold that shot a bit longer, it will have more impact. It's a very hard thing to control.'

As writer of the script, with total responsibility for the poetic licences taken, Colin Welland defends the factual distortions. 'We never attempted to make a documentary,' he says. 'I never made any character do what they wouldn't have done anyway. Abrahams didn't actually meet his wife until after the Olympics, but what was the point in having him fall in love after the bloody film was finished? The only one I made do something different, and I did it with her permission, was his [Liddell's] sister. I wanted a mouthpiece for the opposition that the students' evangelical movement had against his involving himself too much in athletics to the detriment of evangelism. The other one was the fact that it wasn't the American runner who gave him the note, it was the coach. I wrote to Jackson Scholz and asked him if he minded and he replied he was a writer of sports stories himself and that would be OK. In order to make a film a success you've got to tell a story in two hours to an audience who are totally uninformed. We can't just tell it all correctly – even Shakespeare didn't. People don't understand the business of writing for entertainment.

'I still get flak today for my utterance at the Oscar ceremony, "The British are coming!" but this was completely misunderstood. I wasn't being patriotic or jingoistic. I'd been researching *Twice in a Lifetime* in Pennsylvania and I got to know a lot of the steelworkers there. Whenever I'd walk into a bar they'd say, "Watch your wallets, the British are coming!" It's like, "The bogeyman's coming" over there. When I got onto the rostrum at the Oscar ceremony, I thought it would be a marvellous crack to make. It was never meant as a patriotic gesture, but a lot of people didn't realize that.'

Colin pictures David as 'an imp who leaps from toadstool to toadstool. He'll throw five hats in the ring and pick one of them and be quite happy. The trouble is he tends to throw thousands of hats in lots of writers' directions and they all pick one up and they never hear any more about it.'

In the wake of *Chariots'* success an old friend and colleague attended a party with David. He was staggered at the difference already in the attitude of many who had worked with him in the past, and at David's tacit acceptance of this. 'People queued up to talk to him,' recalled the friend. 'They all wanted his ear, needed him to fix some problems, make an arrangement, read a script, sort out an agent or a director. They all whispered. He listened carefully and courteously to them all and kept saying, "Leave it to me and I'll see to it," and "I'll get back to you."'

A terrible sadness marred the Academy Awards ceremony for David – the death of his beloved father, Len. There was a small consolation in that he had attended *Chariots'* Royal Première and seen how successful the film was proving to be before his fatal heart attack in December 1981, but David was inconsolable. 'The tragedy of my life is that my father died before the Oscars,' he mourned. 'He'd have been over the moon.'

Chapter 2

Blitz Baby

Len Puttnam met a pretty Jewish girl, Marie Goldman, in 1931. Two years later they had married and settled down to domesticity in the North London suburb of Southgate. Both Len and Marie were children of broken homes, each set of parents having separated during the twenties. The couple longed for a family and were heartbroken when Marie miscarried with their first child. So desperate were they that adoption was being seriously considered before David Terence Puttnam's eventual arrival on 25 February 1941. Their joy was completed when a sister, Lesley, was born two years later into the same cosy lower middle-class environment, if you listen to David (or upper middle-class, as his mum would have it). 'David in fact likes to think of himself as working-class, but that wasn't the case at all,' she insists. Marie fondly remembers that when David first arrived 'I didn't want to put him down when I'd fed him. I just wanted to hold him all the time.'

David's maternal grandmother, Marie Angelina, a large, perpetually jolly woman, moved in with the Puttnams at the outbreak of World War II. Shortly after came the news of the death of her long-estranged husband, Samuel. Len's father, George, died just before David was born, after years of separation from his long-suffering wife, Alice Koziah. His intemperate habits had reduced their modest fortunes to such an extent that Alice was reduced to acting as charlady for her own sister to make ends meet. On her own she brought up her three sons and a daughter during the twenties. Len had a morning paper round at 12 years of age, doubling in the evenings as the diminutive tuxedo-clad spotlight lad at the National Sporting Club. On leaving school at 13, he started work full-time as a photographer's assistant. Len's older brother, Bert, designed an aircraft in the thirties, affectionately dubbed 'Puttnam's Flying Flea' and died in action in 1943. A younger brother, Percy, survived until the mid-fifties together with Len's mother. To David and Lesley, Alice Koziah was forever Granny Puttnam, Marie Angelina always Granny Goldman.

Len had become a top Fleet Street photographer by the thirties, and was one of the first five photo-journalists to enlist as a War Correspondent when war was declared. Of these five, three were killed. Only David's father and one other survived.

Marie recalls David's second Christmas at home. She was expecting Lesley in three weeks' time and, miracle of miracles, Len managed to get leave. Having her husband domiciled for the holiday was an event unheard of in the Puttnam household even in peacetime, for Marie was used to spending Christmas alone every year, with Len away from mid-December to end-January in Switzerland covering the winter sports scene. The idyll was rudely interrupted when Len received word to phone the War Office and was ordered to leave for Algiers immediately, where the troop landings had begun.

He had been with the British Expeditionary Forces evacuated from the port of Brest at the time of Dunkirk, before being promoted to the rank of Captain and seconded to the Commandos, photographing half a dozen Commando raids for the Army Film Photo Unit. Posted to Alexandria with Field Marshal Montgomery, Len moved up to Italy with the invading Eighth Army as head of the film and photo section, and spent the last two and a half years of the war there.

The strain of coping with two young children during the blitz took its toll on Marie. Before the war Len had bought and erected a corrugated Anderson air-raid shelter in the garden, which Marie soon brought indoors when she found it packed out with neighbours on crucial occasions. In any case, it seemed forever horribly damp, readily filling up with water and needing to be pumped out. It was set up in the dining-room with a bed inside for the two children, with a totally inappropriate, if cosy touch of a gas fire at the end of it.

'I don't know what I was thinking about,' Marie laughs, 'but Len soon got me sorted out. When he came back briefly that Christmas he obtained a Morrison shelter, this huge cast-iron table with wire mesh round it, with a steel mattress inside big enough for us all to sleep on. We used to sit and listen to the buzzbombs, with their horrible grating noise like a dentist's drill. After they cut out I'd just pray, 'Please, God, let it carry on over the house', as the deafening silence seemed to go on and on. Someone said it was as if the whole world stood and held its breath. People laugh at the expression "doodlebug", but a cold shiver goes through me every time I think about it. It was a trying time. They were after the Enfield Small Arms Factory nearby, so we were badly affected.' For two years it seemed to David that the world was forever framed by the shelter's wire mesh.

Still Marie managed to give the children a holiday, driving them

down to Droitwich Spa in the family's black Ford 10. The couple
who ran the guest house had a greengrocer's shop in which David
would happily play all day when it rained, until the peace of their
holiday in 1944 was shattered by a phone call from Marie Angelina to
say that a bomb had dropped near their street, blasting part of the
roof off their house. Marie remembers anxiously sitting it out in
Droitwich overnight before starting the journey back in the morning
in torrential rain, dreading the damage she might find. Three-year-
old David asked to accompany her, while infant Lesley was left behind
in the guest house. To Marie's enormous relief, the council had
covered the roof with a tarpaulin, so although half the slates were
missing, at least the house had been weatherproofed. For the next
three months the entire Puttnam family were evacuated to Droitwich
while the damage was repaired.

On Len's demob he was decorated with four bronze Oak Leaf
emblems to add to his Medal of Honour, in recognition of his mentions
in despatches. His eyesight had been damaged during his service and
he had to spend some time in hospital before resuming his career, but
first there was an emotional homecoming at midnight, with David
given permission to stay up to welcome his father. When Marie and
the children finally heard Len's footsteps coming round the corner,
David rushed out of the front door and jumped into his father's arms,
burying his head in his father's chest. It is a memory he still cherishes.

A colleague of his war years described Len as 'an extremely glamorous, good-looking, vivacious individual, the life and soul of any party.
If he'd gone to Hollywood, he'd have given the likes of Bill Holden a
run for his money.'

Now the toll of the war years was exacted on Marie, who was
diagnosed as suffering from nervous exhaustion before being confined
to bed for six weeks with an ulcer. Len was the soul of comfort and
concern. 'He was the very essence of kindness,' says Marie. 'We used
to call him, "I'll do it", since that's what he'd say whenever anyone
else went to do a job in the house.' She had occasion, however, to
recall Len's wartime promise, 'When I get home, we'll go everywhere,
we'll have a wonderful time together,' for it was an effort to coax him
to even visit neighbours for a coffee once Marie was back on her feet.
'He came back anti-social, it was the effect of all he'd been through in
the war,' says Marie. 'It took me years to get him to go out; he just
wanted to be quiet at home for a long time. Of course that was all
right with me, my husband and children were always the most important thing in the world. It was just that Len was so well liked by
everybody, it seemed a shame we didn't get round more.'

Like many of his wartime comrades, Len was suffering to a degree from shellshock, aggravated by the impotence he had felt in his position as war correspondent. Recording the evidence of man's inhumanity to man was not a role Len had relished. He felt diminished and scarred by the experience and needed time before regaining the spark Marie had known in him in the thirties. What helped to speed the healing process was the tight-knit, loving family circle to which he returned. As David shrilly demanded to hear every last detail of his dad's wartime exploits, Len found that recounting the happier memories of camaraderie, humour and even of shared danger, had the therapeutic effect of masking the others. Then there was David's apparently limitless joy of just being in his father's company. Marie had to smile as she watched Len making David's coins vanish, to magically reappear as chocolate bars from behind his ear. David would watch open-mouthed, then grin broadly as he was handed the chocolate. There were lots of things only Dads were good for, he had discovered.

He attended kindergarten for a few years until he was seven, before being enrolled at a collegiate boys' school, then transferred to the local Oakwood primary after Marie took one look at what she considered the hooligan element at the fee-paying collegiate school. His grades at Oakwood were good enough to lead to a scholarship to Minchenden co-educational, considered the foremost grammar school in North London.

When Len and Marie went out in the evenings, they would hire a baby-sitter, whom David and Lesley would promptly terrorize. 'David would chase them with his pet mouse,' says Lesley, 'and we were both absolutely horrid to them. We'd do everything to ensure they'd never come back. It was probably that we resented our parents going out.'

David had as many schemes and scams going from the age of four or five onwards as he has now. Oakwood Park was great for fishing for tiddlers or collecting frogspawn. Roller-skates and bicycles got you around. There was cricket in the driveway between David and his next-door pal Colin's house. Subbuteo, with full league and fixture tables. The adventure playground that a bombsite represented. Singing sessions with his pals in the shed at the bottom of the garden, doing impressions of Dean Martin, Bing Crosby and Johnnie Ray. He remembers belting himself painfully in the ear with a golf club during a practice swing. Smashing Mrs Parkhouse's treasured china vase with a football through an open window. War games with toy soldiers, then getting his dad to photograph them in situ. Len blacked out the window in the loo and used it as a dark room to teach David how to develop photographs. Tin-can and string intercoms rigged up between the houses in the street and phoning each other up in the middle of the night. And soon – chatting up the girls.

At the age of seven David saw his first film, *Pinnochio*, at the Classic Cinema in London's Baker Street, just round the corner from Madame Tussauds. He was absolutely entranced and remembers consciously thinking what an amazing way of spending one's life filmmaking would be, although for a while David thought *all* films were animated cartoons. Soon he learned differently as he became a fanatical filmgoer, imagining when a name came up on the screen that one day it would be his. The main theme from *Pinnochio*, 'When You Wish upon a Star', remains one of David's favourite pieces of music, epitomizing for him the cinema and his dream of breaking into its world. From then on his Saturday mornings were divided between two great loves, visiting his father in Fleet Street during the late forties and early fifties, with the occasional Saturday morning matinée as an alternative.

David remembers the Saturday matinées at the local Odeon not so much for what he saw but just for the mere fact of being there. He loved the bouncing ball spelling out the lyrics and tempo to 'Come along . . . on Saturday morning . . .' His busy Saturdays were rounded off either accompanying Len as he took wedding pictures to supplement the family income, or in a local shop selling tea towels for a friend of Marie's, a Mr Grendon. 'Anything to keep him away from the local Saturday hangout, the Mayfair Café,' sighs Marie. 'It wasn't the right place for him to be.'

Despite Marie's strictures, the Mayfair was still where David invariably ended up whenever he could. Lesley remembers him from the age of 10 trying to commandeer the best-looking girls. 'He always had a twinkle in his eye and liked female companionship,' she says, 'and the back room of the Mayfair, where the glamorous crowd congregated round the juke box was like mecca for him. He was always the smallest boy of his crowd, but quite able to keep up with his glam pals.'

In Fleet Street he was drawn to the heady atmosphere of excitement in journalism and photography, which to him were closely aligned with the magic of the cinema. He was given messages to shoot round the building on the air machine at Associated Press, a device that held endless fascination. When news of the assassination of Count Bernadotte, the UN's mediator in Palestine, was relayed to Len by telephone, he watched as his father broke down in tears. David was deeply affected; it was the first time he had ever seen his father so moved. When he himself began to cry, his father comforted him gently, explaining the high regard in which he had held the terrorists' victim. Bernadotte, nephew of Gustav V of Sweden, had been a true man of peace, Len told his son, having acted in two world wars in the same role of mediator. Len had met him often and taken his picture many times. 'People like that,' he declared, 'we can't afford to lose.'

Aspects of Len's Fleet Street career which David found his father hated were the dreaded 'No comment' and celebrities who refused to be photographed. They were the bane of his life. The converse of this was his warm relationship with George Bernard Shaw. GBS would often call Len when he intended to visit London so that he would be there to photograph him. If 'I'll be getting into King's Cross at 4 pm' was the message, Len would rush to meet the train. David learned early on from his father that a newspaper was a living, organic thing with good editions and bad editions. Len would say, 'Look, son, here's a really terrific edition today. They've led with this story, held back this other one . . .' He analysed the use of every photograph – whether it was 'well used' or not – in his new capacity of picture editor.

'Here's a picture that's been *really well used*' was an expression David often heard at Len's breakfast seminars. The next item for discussion was whether the 'organic' nature of that day's paper was a good one or not, then whether the newspaper itself was improving or in decline. Len's heroes included Arthur Christiansen of the *Daily Express* and Hugh Cudlipp of the *Daily Mirror*, with whom he had served in the Army. 'They've led with the wrong story,' he would say, shaking his head in disapproval, handing David the paper. 'Tsk, tsk,' David would agree between mouthfuls of cornflakes.

While Len's role as a banker provided by nature for his son was complete, Marie could claim no such distinction. David, surrounded exclusively by women for the first two years of his life, now felt the first stirrings of male chauvinism. He adored his mother, but as he later described her, she was 'a mum, like other peoples' mums, serving slices of cake and pots of tea'.

Family holidays in these post-war years were switched first to Cliftonville, near Margate, then to Bournemouth, with Len's availability the only problem, due to his hectic Fleet Street career. In 1951 he astonished everyone by leaving Associated Press and taking a job as branch manager with the Anglo-Iranian Oil Company, later BP. Disillusion had set in with Fleet Street and the cynicism that now abounded. 'The unions have taken control and ruined it,' he told his son, 'and the quality and excitement of the papers is being killed.'

Len's initial brief at BP was to establish a photographic library and a photo-service to the press. His first two years were spent regretting the move, for at Fleet Street he had led a glamorous life, travelling all round the world in his profession, a privilege otherwise reserved for the rich and famous.

David was upset when his father sold his camera soon after the move, for it was considered a 'magic' camera, with something very special and different about the lens, credited as it was with having captured a series of stunning photographic images over the years. 'What's past is past,' was Len's comment. 'One door closes, another opens.' For young David it was still the end of an era, although he had learned that nothing was for ever; one must never make assumptions. Things can change, he had found, and people have to change with them.

At the age of ten David was sent home halfway through his Sunday School lesson, the least favourite part of his week. 'What happened?' Marie asked. 'Oh, the teacher said I was a disturbing influence, and never to come back,' David breezily replied. The following week, after David had meticulously followed this instruction to the letter, an extremely contrite teacher called round to see Marie. Once her gamp and Bible were set down, she began her explanation.

'He did behave very badly, Mrs Puttnam. He fidgets and talks through the lesson all the time, deliberately sings off-key during the hymns and torments the girls. I still feel ever so guilty, though, for casting him out of God's house.'

Marie choked back a smile. 'I wouldn't worry about it,' she consoled her benighted guest. 'Believe me, you only did exactly what he wanted you to do.'

Marie enrolled David and Lesley for ballroom dancing lessons, then watched as they earned bronze and silver medals, before retiring when David was twelve. 'I was upset at the time. I wanted them to go for their gold,' she says, 'but the dancing school wanted them to give demonstrations and they were both too shy, so that was that.'

David remembers the end of his ballroom dancing days a little differently. 'I didn't want to be thought of as a pansy,' he laughs. For Lesley it solved the problem of getting back from the classes. 'David wouldn't take me home. He was too busy meeting his girlfriends and I had to phone my parents to collect me.'

David took up tennis at thirteen for his school. He represented Minchenden on the summer circuit when everyone else he was up against was three or four years older. Hopes were nurtured that one day he might represent England at the game.

An older cousin, Michael Darling, who was as movie crazy as David, introduced him to soccer when he started taking him to see Tottenham Hotspur. Since Granny Puttnam lived near the Spurs' ground with Len's younger brother, Percy, this was often the venue for David and his pals after the match. He would take them back for tea there and while away the time for the crowds to disperse by listening to the Sports Report on the wireless before heading home.

David's favourite movies for a long time were musicals, and if they were from MGM and in Technicolor, so much the better. Marie knew the manager of the Odeon in Southgate, where she would occasionally arrange to meet her son after school to have tea in the cinema's restaurant before catching the 4.30 pm show. He began to visit the movies two or three times a week. 'When choosing which ones to see,' he recalls, 'and this is really pathetic, I would first of all go for the Technicolor pictures. "Is it in colour? Right, that's the one we'll see." Then if that left two black and whites, we went to the American one. I remember when I finally met Micky Balcon of Ealing, I told him. "I'm one of the people who killed you!" I would see an Ealing film only if I'd already seen two other films that week. I would always go for a *Hondo* or a *Flame and Arrow* – no contest. I remember being *amazed* that *Genevieve* was any good; it came right out of the blue. That an Earl St John or Rank film could be any good seemed like a total miracle.'

Even the girls in British films compared unfavourably with the American and Continental variety, the young critic observed. 'Shirley Eaton was pretty,' he concedes, 'but outside of her, the English actresses used to be plain. They have these funny-looking bras that always seemed a bit unnatural under their frocks.' Until he was 15 he idolized Debbie Reynolds, but all that was to change with *And God Created Woman* and his first earth-shaking glimpse of Brigitte Bardot. 'I was never quite the same again,' he laughs. 'I *died*. Let's just say I spent a lot of time "studying" Brigitte, who was plastered all over the walls of my bedroom, together with Mylene Demongeot, whom I also fancied. That was when I started creeping up to London each Saturday. How we got away with it, I don't know. We'd get in the back of the cinema to all these 'X' films. We used to stand outside the exit with their push-bar doors and when someone came out, bang, foot jammed in the door.'

This was exciting stuff indeed, but then the world he was living in really changed. 'There was one nude I knew of in the world that you could look at and it was in Charing Cross Road: it was the Marilyn

Monroe calendar. There was a bookshop that kept it in the window, high up in the corner. My pals and I used to hang about there a fair bit: it was the only photograph of a completely naked woman that any of us knew of.'

David's best friend at school, Derek Hussey, remembers their trips into the metropolis, in particular one occasion where they sat through three films in one day – *White Christmas*, *And God Created Woman* (again!) and *Rebel without a Cause*. In between shows they found time to visit the 2-i's and Heaven And Hell coffee bars, where a little discreet jiving was allowed.

David had begun to add singles by Elvis Presley and Buddy Holly to his treasured 10-inch Frank Sinatra albums, *This is Sinatra* and *Songs for Young Lovers*. Being perpetually in and out of love from a very early age, he found it amazing, as kids do, how romantic ballads always sounded as if they had been specifically written with him in mind.

When he was in his early teens he started to be aware that there was such a thing as serious quality films. Movies like Fred Zinnemann's *The Search*, Elia Kazan's *On the Waterfront* and, later, Stanley Kramer's *Inherit the Wind* made a deep and lasting impression on him.

'I guess I was pretty lazy at school,' David admits, 'and I certainly wasn't too bright, but I would always get a relationship going with the teachers so they didn't come down on me as hard as they did on others as indolent as I was. I got away with murder.' One of his old teachers confirmed this. 'I told him one day that he wouldn't always get away with it,' she laughs. 'Whenever I reprimanded him he'd look at me with those big blue eyes and my heart would melt, but I told him he couldn't go through life like that.'

Much to Marie's disapproval, Len read out a passage from his friend George Bernard Shaw's *Man and Superman* for David's benefit. ' "What we call education and culture is for the most part nothing but substitution of reading for experience, of literature for life, of the obsolete fictitious for the contemporary real." So there!'

The strategist in David was pushing to the fore even then. Neither the brightest, nor in terms of height the biggest of his contemporaries, he nevertheless managed to be extremely popular. He had inherited his father's charm and attractive personality and this, combined with a ready wit and quicksilver tongue, was more than enough to see him through. 'A charming wangler' is how one of his school pals sums him up, 'someone you wanted to run with. He knew how to look out for himself, not with his fists, he was too small for that, but by using his wits. And there was never anything ulterior about his little manoeuvres; they were all straight and instinctive.'

At fifteen his school report concluded, 'David is cheerfully ignorant.' He read the intended admonition in the playground, and burst out laughing when his pals asked to see the source of his mirth. Soon half the playground was in stitches. For weeks afterwards it was a joke shared with his pals.

'You know what your trouble is, David?'

'What?'

'You're *cheerfully ignorant*, my son!'

Up to this point David had always assumed he would follow in his father's footsteps to Fleet Street, but Len was implacable, his disenchantment with Fleet Street complete. David could take up photography, he decided, but not in the field of journalism. He found David was less than keen on this idea, although his hankering to enter the movie industry was as yet some kind of vague, unrealizable dream. What Len managed to instil in his son was the ability to recognize and understand the elements that constituted a good photograph, something that would stand David in good stead further down the line.

Patricia Mary Jones – Patsy – together with her twin brother Richard, moved to Southgate with their parents from Islington as thirteen-year-olds. Despite Patsy's pleas to be allowed to continue at Westminster School, the journey turned out to be so arduous that she was forced eventually to accept the inevitability of a transfer to Minchenden, where she stood out like a sore thumb for weeks until her new uniform was obtained. Sixteen-year-old David spotted the new arrival, and walked briskly by, greeting her. 'It can't be me he's talking to,' Patsy thought. This progressed to meetings in the playground and school corridor between classes, then soon after the couple started dating in earnest, outside of school hours.

'Babysnatcher!' his friends teased him, which bothered David not one whit. He was far more concerned with the enormous gap in their musical taste, for Patsy was exclusively a rock 'n' roll child – Frank Sinatra was strictly for parents. David watched proudly as Patsy would do a solo jive in the Mayfair, touching the doorknob in the back room with the tips of her fingers, the better to spin herself round to the beat of The Crickets' 'That'll be the Day' or Elvis's 'Hound Dog'.

Patsy was in the tube station with a friend one night, waiting for her train, when two of the most glamorous, well-dressed people she had ever seen came on to the platform. 'They look like film stars,' she said to her friend. 'Don't you know who that is?' came the reply. 'That's David Puttnam's parents. They're probably off to see a West End show.'

'There's ever such a pretty girl started at our school,' was the first mention Marie had of Patsy. When David had a party at home the following New Year's Eve, Marie and Len went out to spend the evening with friends. The party was still going on when they returned and were introduced to Patsy. After she left David asked his parents, 'What did you think of my new girlfriend?' He had already described Patsy to them as 'sort of like a cross between Brigitte Bardot and Mylene Demongeot.' They were suitably impressed.

David's amorous advances were noted by one of his teachers. 'He preferred girls to work,' was the despairing but entirely accurate verdict. There was a general feeling of exasperation that he was not fully applying himself, at least, not to his studies. David had expected to return to school after the Christmas, 1957 holidays, but was sent home on the first day. He reported to his stunned parents that the headmaster had told him he was wasting their time.

'How stupid we were to have just accepted that verdict,' Marie says. 'Looking back later, we realized that we should have at least protested. The bottom just dropped out of our world!' On David's final report his headmaster wrote, 'After five years I find this boy a *total enigma*.' David rushed to look up the word in a dictionary. To his relief he read he was a person who was mysterious, puzzling and ambiguous. Unsure of ambiguous, he happily settled for mysterious and puzzling. Two out of three wasn't bad, he reckoned.

When David decided to try to get into movies, it was confirmed to him just how vague and unrealizable his dream was promising to be. For months his applications hit a brick-wall of indifference, forcing him to the conclusion that film-making was a completely nepotistic business. With an uncle working at Elstree, the possibility of a break-in existed, but not, it seemed, otherwise.

Off his own bat David bought a copy of the *Evening News* and combed the job opportunities section. He applied for a job with Hutchinsons the publishers, where he was interviewed and began work early in 1958 as a messenger boy, 'the quintessential Dickensian job', as he describes it. His duties started with making tea for everyone in the general office, then he had to load up a huge suitcase full of books and lug them from Great Portland Street to Ireland Yard in the City. 'The damned thing was invariably so heavy that when I got off the tube or bus I took three steps and had to put it down, then another three and so on. That's how heavy it was. By the time I had left things had improved a lot, I'd strengthened to the point I could take *five* steps.' His arrival at Ireland Yard was timed to enable him to make tea for the staff there before swallowing a cup and devouring one of Marie's lovingly-prepared sandwiches while his case was unloaded and reloaded with another ton and a half of books to be returned to Great Portland Street. After struggling back, it was unload and prepare tea again for everybody, then if there was an hour left he was expected to fill in the sales reps' reports on a master chart. It was months before he was able to find another job, courtesy of his dad's influence, this time with an agency called Service Advertising in Brook Street.

'I worked in the basement initially. I was a *mole*,' David recalls. 'I must be the only person in the world who was ever *promoted* to being a messenger!' To this day he hasn't been able to work out just what his job in the basement was, but one of his tasks was to rewind and log commercials. These used to lie in long reels of black-and-white 15-second commercials, which had to be cut into strips, logged, labelled and tinned − film filing of sorts. Another responsibility was working on an early precursor of a Xerox machine, using a wet-print process with light and sensitized paper. A translucent negative had to be prepared first, then positive copies turned out.

'I never saw daylight in this basement,' says David, 'except when I was allowed upstairs every Friday as a special treat to scrub out this damned photocopier in the men's loo. It used to corrode up, like the insides of a battery when it's gone and I had to scrub it out with Vim. I still remember the *stink*! I got militant enough to *insist* on a cover-all coat for this job, because it kept on destroying my suits. There was a big row over this − they reckoned I wasn't entitled − but I got a pair of overalls in the end.'

What was noted, and admired, was the zeal with which he applied himself to every task, no matter how unpleasant. If he was cleaning the photocopier, there was no question it was going to be the cleanest and most efficient photocopier in the business. When Len casually enquired of his contact at the agency how David was getting on, the reply was a somewhat exasperated: 'He drives me mad; he's only been in the bloody department five minutes and already he says he knows it all and wants to move on. He's like the ship's cat, full of piss and vinegar!'

Patsy would hear of his exploits on their occasional dates and at the Sunday teas to which she was invited at the Puttnams'. Still at school, to her it was another world.

The Puttnams moved in 1958 across Southgate to a classic semi-detached house (if you listen to David) or detached at one side and semi-detached at the other (as Marie has it). There was a small garden at the front, with flowerbeds framed by paving stones. The front door was opaque glass, which set the keynote for sliding glass doors inside. The house rule was that if one of the sliding doors leading to the comfortable sitting-room was closed, there was no admittance, for Ma and Pa Puttnam would be having a conversation and were not to be disturbed. If the doors were left a little bit open, it was all right to enter. A dining-room which was hardly used led off from the kitchen, then upstairs there were three bedrooms and the focal point of the house, Marie's pride and joy, a magnificent art-deco black glass and pink tile bathroom.

David discovered, now that he was out in the world, how loved and respected his father was by all who knew him. When he was asked, 'You're Len Puttnam's lad, aren't you?' he would nod his head furiously, accepting the definition with pleasure and pride.

The energetic young man enrolled himself in a three-year night-school course covering company and copyright law, together with psychology as applied to advertising. Promotion to messenger, despite the apparent contradiction in terms noted by David, coincided with the firm's move to Knightsbridge, where he used to delight in competing with himself on a regular run he did to the blockmaker in Fleet Street. He bought a stopwatch and tried to shave a few seconds here and there from the run. To his surprise this was noted by the hierarchy, who got to know he could do the fastest run and picked him out for the urgent errands and late runs. David noted that it was possible to make his own 'luck'. The stopwatch carried out two functions, getting him noticed and giving him something to think about.

When things were really urgent, the taking of a taxi was permitted. David soon opened an account at Austin Reed in Regent Street, making his first purchase a smart black-and-white dogstooth-check suit. Dressed as he was, he would often fantasize during those taxi rides that he was an executive. The briefcase that Marie had given him at Christmas helped him look the part, he reckoned, at 17. 'I used to sit in the cab behind the driver and pretend. I would have these absolutely ludicrous conversations with myself: "It's up to you to save the account, Puttnam!"'

Now the books from the publishing house had been replaced by four-colour blocks. 'They were so heavy my arms felt like they were breaking. It was all I could do to *hold* the case it was so heavy, but in my role as executive I had to pretend it was full of paper, although it weighed a ton!'

Len and Marie were disappointed when David declined to accompany the family for their annual holiday that year. 'I'm off to Butlin's with my mates,' the 17-year-old announced, revelling in his new-found freedom. The pattern of family holidays was broken, although Marie did not give up easily. The following year she booked the whole family on a trip to Italy, which David nevertheless dropped out of at the last minute in favour of a return to Butlin's.

David and Patsy's regular Saturday night outing at this time was a drive to London airport in Len's car. They would have a meal in the cafeteria an hour or two before the evening flight to New York was due to leave.

'Another lemonade?' David would ask.

'No, we're sure to get bags of lemonade on the plane,' Patsy would reply.

'Now, you did remember to book our hotel on Broadway, didn't you?'

'No, I thought we'd try somewhere different this time. I found one on Fifth Avenue handy for the shops.'

'That sounds all right. Is it near the Empire State Building?'

'Not really.'

When the flight was finally announced, the young couple would get up with the real passengers, still playing to the gallery, and make for the departure gate. Then they would turn at the last minute with a regretful smile and head for the exit. David's constant diet of American movies was having its effect. He wanted to visit the States so badly he could taste it.

A career break came when an assistant account executive at the agency went on holiday and a relief was sought. Given the job for two weeks, David then had a further stroke of luck when the second assistant went off for three weeks to get married as soon as the other returned. David thus worked for the same senior account executive for five full weeks. They got on so well together that David was recommended to another account executive as his assistant.

The year was 1959, the Macmillan era was in full swing and there was an air of sociological change in the air. Like all the other agencies, David's employers had what was known as a graduate trainee scheme. For a multitude of reasons, possibly because he was known as the fastest, most alert, and *only* messenger who wore a suit, or because of the extraordinary era it was, someone decided that it would be interesting to have a *non*-graduate on the graduate trainee scheme. To David's amazement and to his employer's gratification, David did as well on the course as any of the graduates. Had he been hiding his light under a bushel at school? The difference was simple. David had been bursting to get out of the starting gate at Minchenden, which he considered a boring preamble to his *real* world.

The hopes of representing England which David had harboured in his tennis career came to an end with a crushing defeat in the first-round juniors at Wimbledon. 'I really loved tennis,' he recalls, his voice even now tinged with regret. 'Each year I found myself beating people who had beaten me the year before. Then at 17 I got *thrashed* by a 15-year-old Spanish boy in a very important tournament. I realized that I would never be any good and never picked up a racket again. It's absolutely the worst thing in the world to lose to someone you should have been able to beat. If I played now, it would be an exercise in frustration, for I'd remember how good I used to feel. If I can't be really good, I'd rather not do it at all. That's *it* through and through; I don't feel there's any point. I don't *have* to win, but I *have* to be a contender. I could never tolerate that I hadn't *competed*.'

After a brief stint as assistant account executive, David was transferred to the marketing department, which turned out to be interesting if a bit dreary. He was responsible for the compilation of television ratings, basically logging what was happening to products in the marketplace. He was diligent enough in the job, however, and after six months found himself promoted to a proper, fully fledged assistant account executive. It was then he made his discovery that his sacrifice of further years in the groves of academe might yet prove a very positive advantage, at least in the short term. 'I suddenly found that the other assistants were all *five years* older than me. They'd done national service, which I just missed by six months and I hadn't been to university, so at 18 I was looking at the next-youngest person in the same job at 23. By accident I'd got this tremendous five-year jump.'

He made another discovery at the same time, that he didn't care much for the work the agency was doing. He had been dating Patsy for the last couple of years and they were talking about getting married, but on £8 a week this was out of the question. A successful application for a vacancy as an assistant account executive at Greenly's agency brought about a huge salary increase to £14 a week. Here he worked on the John Collier's account, together with a few others. Again, his question was what *extra* can I do? His answer was to report to a John Collier branch every Saturday morning so he could find out for himself what it was actually like to *sell* things, to reinforce his earlier tea-towel experience. All this, plus the continuing three nights a week at night classes.

Patsy left school at 17 and briefly joined British Petroleum as a trainee, then soon after discovered she was pregnant. 'Are you sure?' David asked. 'Pretty sure,' Patsy replied a little bit tearfully, 'What are we going to do?'

'Why, get married of course,' David replied, without hesitation. He had known Patsy was the only girl for him since the very first moment he had set eyes on her. At Patsy's suggestion a trip to her doctor's was organized. With the news confirmed, the couple's next task was to break it to their parents. 'We'll do my mum and dad first, then yours,' said David as he drove back home in his father's car. Patsy agreed in between snuffles, her courage rapidly failing her.

Marie remembers she was just about to sit down to dinner with Len and her daughter when Lesley announced, 'Patsy and David are sitting in the car, Mum – and Patsy's crying.' Marie remembers looking at Len. 'Leave them,' she said. 'Maybe they've had an argument or something.' When David came into the house, with a very soggy Patsy beside him, he was white as a sheet. 'Mum, Dad, I need to speak to you . . .'

The couple were ushered upstairs to David's bedroom, which he had laid out like a bed-sit so that he could hold court with his friends. With Brigitte and Mylene looking on, David explained the situation to his parents. Marie held David's hands and felt him trembling. Len squeezed his shoulder, then put his arms round Patsy, who stood on the sidelines in an apparent attempt to merge with the background. 'It's going to be all right, it's going to be fine,' he comforted her. 'This is marvellous. I've really wanted to be a grandfather. Come on, Patsy, sit down.' Marie declared she was off to make some tea, then returned with the steaming mugs a few minutes later. 'I made it extra strong,' she remembers, 'and I put a good dollop of glucose in there as well. Well, they were in a state of shock, the poor things, and I knew that glucose would help.'

Later Marie asked the couple if they could face a bite of dinner. As the meal was finishing she put an arm round Patsy. 'You really should tell your parents now,' she said, sending Patsy into new floods of tears. 'I don't want to,' she sobbed. 'I feel as if I've let them down so dreadfully.' David took her hand in his. 'Look, Patsy,' he urged, 'I've got to. And I've got to do it alone.'

Borrowing his father's car again, David drove to Patsy's home – and a somewhat different reception. As would be the case almost invariably with the parents of the *girl* concerned, there was a degree of shock and outrage. To exacerbate matters Patsy had not been getting on too well with her father for a while, for which she blamed herself.

It was not because they were so different, rather that they were so alike in that they both had a huge stubborn streak. Now she felt she had caused her parents all this distress.

'The thing with Patsy's parents was agony,' David recalls. 'Understandably, in view of the circumstances, they thought it was a disaster, but we didn't. I really wanted to get married. I loved Patsy and that was that.'

He was not allowed to see her the next day and sent a dozen red roses round to the Jones's household. After the initial shock, Patsy's mother soon rallied round and her father contributed a list of no-nonsense, dead-set logical options which his daughter had to choose from. 'You can *not* get married and have the baby; you can *not* get married and we'll see if you needn't have the baby; you can have the baby *adopted*. Or you can get *married*.'

Still the rebel, Patsy resented the options even being spelt out and her father's ex-army major way of dealing with 'the problem', as he referred to it. Unlike David, Patsy had been brought up in a deeply religious Church-of-England household and was very close to her Methodist grandmother. If she was with her granny she would go off to the Methodist Church, while at home she attended the local Church of England as well as Sunday School.

Strangely enough, it was David, who had never known his parents go to church, who wanted a church marriage, while Patsy's attitude was that it really didn't matter. David said, 'No, we're doing this the proper way, this is going to last *forever* and we're going to be married in church.' Their plan was to stay with David's parents after the wedding until they could find a place of their own, the main restriction being the relatively modest £16 a week David now earned at Greenly's.

After a quiet holiday in Bournemouth with David and his parents, Patsy moved in with the Puttnams while David went off to confer with the local vicar, who agreed to conduct a special church service for them. Marie remembers David and Patsy coming home from a meeting with him, absolutely elated. 'I said prayers,' he had told them, 'and God has forgiven you.' His ejection from 'God's house' at the age of nine was all behind him, David reflected.

Patsy's parents, now fully reconciled to the situation, provided a hearty reception for the guests after the couple's wedding in St Paul's Church, Winchmore Hill. Their best man, Derek Hussey, drove them straight to the West End of London, where they were booked into the Cumberland Hotel at Marble Arch. They had a night out at the pictures, visiting the Plaza in the Haymarket, where they saw Zizi

Jeanmaire in *Black Stockings*. Next morning it was breakfast at Lyon's Corner House, then back home to Southgate by tube, the honeymoon over.

David had asked his boss for the day off. When asked the reason, David explained he had to get married. His employer looked at him incredulously for a moment, then fell about laughing.

At about this time David became aware of a series of new and exciting advertisements that had recently emerged, and learned that they originated from a new agency, Collet, Dickinson and Pearce (CDP). A friend, Robert Rendell, had moved from Service Advertising to CDP and the two often met round the corner from the agency in the local Wimpy bar to compare notes. With Robert's help David drafted a letter of application to the agency. He and Patsy worked out that they could pay their way, if only just, on £12 a week, and decided that the sacrifice would be worth it just to get a foot in the door at this new and innovative agency.

After a couple of turndowns, he was finally given a series of interviews. They had never taken on an assistant account executive before, but listened to David's explanation that he was prepared to take on a lesser job if necessary. When the issue of money came up, and they asked how much he was getting at Greenly's, he replied, 'Sixteen,' adding that it would be hard for him to get by on much less than that. David then took the bull by the horns and asked, 'What would you pay?' They replied that they really didn't want to go 'more than 11.' 'I don't see how I can make that work,' said David. 'All right, here's what we'll do,' they said. 'How about 11 for three months and then up to 12?' David agreed rather wanly, then shook hands and went home with his story to Patsy.

'There's good news and bad news,' he told her. 'I've got the job, but only for £11 a week, going up to £12 after three months. At least it's a start, Patsy.' Their calculations showed that they would have to borrow a fiver from each of the parents to see them through the month, so there was little celebration, although they were both pleased he had at least been successful in his application. The next day the letter from CDP arrived confirming David's position. It ran, 'We are pleased to tell you that you will be joining the agency as an assistant account executive and as agreed, your salary will be eleven hundred pounds per annum for the first three months, rising to twelve hundred pounds per annum thereafter.'

David read the letter, then re-read it, the most enormous smile spreading across his face. He had been talking pounds a week, they had been talking hundreds per annum. It was a *giant* rise, from £16 to

£22 a week. 'Patsy!' he cried. 'Come and look at this! We're fucking *rich*! I've broken the grand!' He handed her the letter and watched her blue eyes grow larger as she read it. With a 'Whoopee!' she flung the letter in the air as David hugged her tightly, before literally dancing with joy.

Chapter 3

Jack the Lad

When a daughter, Deborah, was born on 25 January 1962, in the Royal Free Hospital, Hampstead, the Jewish mum in Marie was rekindled with a vengeance. 'She was determined to take us all over,' Patsy smiles at the recollection, then laughs warmly. 'And I was *equally* determined that this was not for me. I could see quickly that Debbie would be spoiled rotten, for her granny absolutely doted on her.' ('Of *course* I did,' Marie declares proudly. 'Debbie was my life! For that matter, I doted on Patsy too. I felt so sorry for her, she was so young and vulnerable, a year younger even than Lesley; they were like sisters.')

Both David and Patsy retain wonderful memories of their first year with Len and Marie, but still they longed for a place of their own, finally finding one in a nearby thirties-built tenement for £6-10s a week. Fourteen stone steps led to the grass-plateaued entrance to their tiny two-bedroom, ground-floor flat. Debbie was left behind with David's parents while they moved in. 'It was in a bit of a state, as a blind couple had lived there before us,' David recalls. 'Again Patsy's parents turned up trumps, coming in to help us scrub the whole place out. Our friends had saved up our wedding presents until we got our own place and we'd furnished it as well as we could. I even did my own plumbing later, which lasted precisely one winter!'

After installing themselves in their new home, the couple walked back to David's parents to collect Debbie. Marie was desolate as the family waved them off. 'They were only going a few hundred yards, but it might have been miles,' she says. 'When they'd disappeared from sight we all went back into the house. I couldn't settle, the whole place seemed so empty without them. Finally Len, bless him, suggested we all go out for a run in the car which helped. I cried for weeks over losing Debbie, though. It hit me hard at a bad age.'

David had seen a whole series of events happen at CDP soon after his arrival there. He was asked to take over Robert Rendell's job while his friend took a holiday. Unknown to him there had been friction between Robert and the management before he went off. On his return he was fired and David given the job. If Robert was shattered, so was David, for it was one of his first experiences of dirty tricks. When Robert was still out of work months later at Christmas, David and other colleagues took him round a hamper of food and gifts.

David had discovered the hard way that all was not as it seemed at CDP in those days. Things were very 'nip and tuck' at the time and the company was just scraping by. An edict was issued that the staff had to write memos on the back of other memos in an attempt to keep costs down. Although the agency had a few prestige accounts like Harvey's Bristol Cream, the payroll money was coming out of Major Collins' Headquarters and General Supplies, a mail-order company which was by far their biggest account, and there was always the fear that this could go elsewhere at the drop of a hat. David realized that Robert had been the victim of the worst kind of economy drive. CDP had discovered they could get someone at £1200 a year to do the job of someone at £1600. It was his first real jolt.

After longing for a place of their own, disaster struck after a few months in their flat, when Patsy developed a painful and unsightly allergy on her hands. She lost the use of them as they turned into open wounds. Gradually the allergy began to spread to her neck and face.

Despite visits to a specialist in Harley Street and treatments of all kinds, nothing seemed to help. In the depths of her discomfort and misery Patsy was aware that probably, although nobody knows for certain to this day, it was just the strain of being eighteen years old and on her own all day with her baby. Until then she had relied on the support of Marie, Len and her own parents. Now she felt on trial. She realizes now how irrational that feeling was, how it was one she alone had created. 'Now prove how clever you are,' she taunted herself. 'You were *full* of it, now let's see how you do.'

The flat lasted a year before the couple had to give in to the inevitable. Patsy had become incapable of looking after Debbie. With their mortifying decision made, everyone concerned made their return to the bosom of the Puttnam household into a sympathetic and loving occasion. Patsy initially saw the retreat as an ignominious one, a further extension of having let the side down in the first place. 'Can you imagine their just taking us back like that?' she asks. 'All my silly notions were banished immediately. There was no fuss, no strain, nothing except a lovely welcome. I couldn't even take a bath on my own at the time, let alone bathe Debbie or look after her, so Marie bathed both of us. Nothing was too much trouble for her.' ('Of course

I did, Marie declares. 'Same as I would have for Lesley, or anyone else I loved.')

With his parents' love freshly illuminated in the light of his own new-found parenthood, David looked anew at his father. The shadows accumulated in the war-time years had all but lifted and he could now see a man who was enormously content. To Patsy, Len was the most amusing man she had ever known. He had her in stitches when she was able to coax him into telling more of his war stories, although he was still reluctant at times to talk about his experiences. When he did, Len always made himself the butt of the story.

David reckons their time back with the family was the happiest year of his parents' lives. With his Dad he would go for long walks in nearby Oakwood park each Sunday, continually getting to know him better, but now as a fellow adult. Even after they moved away, the Sunday walks remained a fixture.

Len could take him back to all the major events, like the drama and politics that had seethed behind the scenes of the Duke and Duchess of Windsor's marriage and abdication, and Chamberlain's return from Berlin with his triumphant declaration of peace, soon to ring so hideously hollow. David was given a unique historical perspective, as Len was able to recall his boyhood's First-World-War period, which David found utterly fascinating. If the past was another country, David found he was able to visit it in the company of his father each Sunday. A feeling that he had irresponsibly taken his father for granted in earlier years began to take hold, yet a dawning maturity and wisdom accompanied the feeling. He began to appreciate how self-obsessed he had been, how narrow his horizons.

'Why do you refer to your dad as a photographer?' Marie would often ask. 'He's a B P executive.'

'That's all right,' David would say, 'there's nothing *wrong* with being a B P executive, but I'm *proud* he was a photographer.'

Marie was caught just a little in the eternal paradox inherent in a mother-and-son relationship, watching as the very love that helped David grow contributed to his independence. On the odd occasion there was any disagreement between them, David was yet able to defuse the situation in a trice. Marie was reduced to helpless laughter at the rejoinder he coined, to become a standard family joke: 'You are, of course,' he would admonish her, 'the woman who had me circumcised in 1941 when this country was losing the war. None too bright, was it?'

As her allergy slowly began to recede, and finally disappear, Patsy announced she was expecting again. David decided this time their new home would be bought instead of rented, and found a flat at Elstree costing £4000. Patsy's banker father did a few calculations and expressed his doubts that they could afford it. 'Oh, we'll manage, Pa,' David airily replied. 'Yes, but do you realize that if you even have a pair of shoes that need mending, you won't be able to afford that? You've absolutely no cover for such things.' David swallowed. 'Well, you see, Pa, I'm pretty certain there's a bit of a rise coming that will make it OK,' he explained, convincing precisely nobody.

After they had found the flat and were waiting to move in, Patsy set out one day to walk Debbie down to the local DIY store to pick up some linoleum tiles for their new home. The tiles were heavy, but she felt she could manage, and carried them back to David's parents. Just as soon as she put the tiles down, she knew there was something wrong – very wrong. When David was sent for and came rushing home it was to the news that Patsy had lost their baby. When she saw him approach her in the hospital bed, her heart turned over. Words came tumbling out in a torrent before he put his arms around her and soothed her. 'It doesn't matter,' he whispered gently. 'You're all right and that's all that matters.'

When Patsy was fully recovered, there was another tearful parting from Len, Marie and Lesley as the couple moved to Elstree and their new flat. It turned out that David had had good reason to believe in the rise at CDP, for after the disillusioning start he had gone from strength to strength.

The creative head at the agency, Colin Millward, had proved an enormous influence on his new recruit. Although Colin normally took against account executives, he was not only tolerant of David, but allowed him to hang about on his floor, and actually encouraged him. David had never met anyone with such rigorously high standards. He was asked to re-do material over and over again. After many nights of revision, something that David worked on might finally be accepted. When he got to know Millward better, David blurted out, 'You know, you're a real bastard. You never gave me any encouragement, never even told me what I was doing wrong!' Millward's reply was, 'No, I taught you to bloody *think*!' He made his charges sit there and rack their brains until they could think of a way to make their copy better, make it right, make it *live*. After the steady diet of gruel David had endured at school, Millward's approach was like caviar. David learned from him that competency was a point of *departure*, not arrival. 'It's very good,' he would say, 'but is it *brilliant*?' He taught the young man standards; how to be critical of his own work. He gave him confidence in his judgement and taught him to push himself further and further. David absorbed Millward's almost religious dedication to the 'original idea', how that was worth everything, how not to over-embellish it but stick to its original purity.

Now a contented painter, whose pastel of Alan Parker hung for years in David's office, Millward declares of his emerging protégé, 'He was very good. He was marked indelibly by the sixties, a brilliant sort of "fixer". He had an extraordinary gift for putting things together, a very, very high mission and a clear-cut idea of what he liked.'

At Service Advertising David's plum account had been Personnel Administration (P.A.). This started with billings of £18,000 a year, then quickly became that much a month. There was a move to take it away from him and give it to a more senior person, despite the fact David had nurtured it from its humble beginnings. His answer was to take the invaluable experience to Greenly's with him. At CDP he was given the Chemstrand account and history repeated itself, as it too grew like topsy. At the start Chemstrand was billing about £100,000 a year. Two years later it was over the million mark and the biggest account in the agency. The fibre wars of attrition had broken out, Chemstrand versus Courtaulds and ICI, each vying for their share of the lucrative synthetic fibres market, with the Woolmark people fighting back gamely.

David started to wear his hair long, in line with the swinging sixties, but despite his success at CDP old traditions died hard. When a client was brought in to be shown round the agency, David and John Vaughan, considered a flamboyant dresser then, used to get a note from the managing director. This was brief and to the point. 'Disappear!' it said.

'We had to go and sit in the Wimpy bar for an hour,' David smiles, 'while the new client was shown around. The interesting thing is that I had done one helluva job doing out my office with all these Chemstrand Acrilan ads that had won every award. It became the showcase of the agency's creativity, a must-see on the client's guided tour. But me and my hair were not allowed to be seen!'

Within a year of joining CDP David's greatest defect was suddenly transformed into his greatest asset. The arrival of the Beatles had changed everything, as long hair became the thing and David's 'problem' disappeared. He suddenly found himself being promoted for the length of his hair rather than being held back by it. He became the company's token 'now' man, their conduit to what was happening in the street. He was the guy who *understood* the new phrases like 'disposable teenage income'. He was plugged in, switched on and tuned in.

His life at CDP altered significantly. Now *he, together* with his office, was on the office tour's scenic route.

When the rise he had predicted did come, it was a suitably dramatic one. He phoned the news through to Patsy at their Elstree flat. 'How much do you think I've got?' he asked.

'Three pounds?'

'No, keep going.'

'Four pounds?'

'Keep going.'

'Six pounds?'

'Still go on.'

When it was established that the increase took his salary from £1200 a year to £3000, it seemed to Patsy that the world was their oyster. She could scarcely believe it; could their days of scrimping and saving be over? David elatedly confirmed he would soon be looking for their first car and that they could look forward to a holiday abroad. With the car, a pale blue Sunbeam Alpine drophead sports model, their life was indeed transformed as they experienced the luxury of mobility for the first time.

Together they drove that summer to the South of France, where they had been offered the use of Colin Millward's rented apartment near St Tropez. Debbie was the model of the perfectly-behaved child in the back of the car during the long drive, just as long as she was close to her mum. Comparatively flush though they were, Patsy still had to work their expenditure out to the nearest franc. Lunch was a picnic with baguettes and cheese or ham. For dinner a marvellous prix fixe menu at a local bistro was discovered that set the family back nine francs each for a four-course meal. Patsy thought she had died and gone to heaven.

According to the *Guardian* who did an analysis, David was one of the first well-paid young executives, in fact the highest-paid executive in his age bracket in the country. A senior colleague, John Ritchie, about to leave the agency for pastures new, was told by Ronnie Dickinson, 'if you ever want to come back, you're welcome. I think by then you might find someone like David Puttnam is managing director.' Ritchie remembers being astonished. Those were the days when managing directors were in their fifties. David was still in his twenties!

'He *was* jolly good,' says Ritchie, 'if a bit strident. What took the edge off his stridency and made it quite acceptable was his willingness to always seek advice and listen to older colleagues. It was an endearing trait unusual in a young man.'

When a rival agency, Pritchard Wood, tried to poach David from CDP to take care of their Woolmark campaign (and David admits he was enough of a whore to go and talk to them), the conversation naturally got round to salaries. David told them he was now earning £3500 a year, at which point the director in charge of the interview turned ashen and exclaimed 'That's more than me!' The interview was over.

In 1962 David had picked up David Bailey from *Vogue*'s studios for dinner. Bailey said, 'I've got these four blokes from Liverpool, a pop group I've promised to photograph for the magazine. They're supposed to be quite good.' The group turned out to be the Beatles. While David was waiting around, he struck up a conversation with Paul McCartney. Later he went off to dinner with Bailey, who remarked, 'They played me their record. They *are* pretty good.'

After that David used to often bump into Paul, more often than not accompanied by Jane Asher, and they continued the running conversation and friendship they had begun in *Vogue*'s studios. Between 1962 and 1964 the whole scene exploded, together with the cast of characters at its epicentre. David had established contact with the up-and-coming young Turks in photography – David Bailey, Brian Duffy and Terence Donovan, all of whom had made it within a year or so of each other. As well as becoming one of the biggest buyers of photography around, he rapidly began to establish himself as the master of the bold stroke. When someone suggested how fantastic it would be to get some work done by Richard Avedon, David left the room for 15 minutes. On his return he told his astonished colleagues, 'I've got Avedon for $1000.' He explained that he had simply picked up the phone and put a call through to New York, fixing the deal there and then.

Since Brian Duffy had convincingly passed David off as Paul McCartney when he had introduced him to Terence Donovan, for David bore a distinct resemblance to the Beatle, Brian could not resist the temptation to take this a stage further during a trip to Paris. He was one of a large group of photographers there to cover the fashion shows, together with David in his capacity of fashion adviser to CDP, through the Chemstrand connection. 'In the hotel we were staying in I introduced David as Paul to all these French models,' Brian recalls with some amusement. 'The Beatles were just breaking through then, and we all watched as the models' attitudes changed from one of haughtiness into absolutely obsequious fans. The Beatles were playing at the Olympia then – Trini Lopez was top of the bill – and we all got fabulous seats near the stage. When we looked around, though, there were all these models sat near us. David had to leave his seat before the Beatles came on and go and stand at the back of the hall to keep our little deception going.'

'He *was* similar to Paul,' another of David's colleagues chuckles, 'except earthier.'

The next move for the couple was to look for a home nearer the centre of London. A terraced house was found in Ranelagh Grove, Pimlico, to be their home for the next seven years. Patsy was again pregnant when the move was made in September 1965, and a son, Alexander, promptly nicknamed Sacha, was born the following April in the house. David was present at the birth. 'Not that he wanted to be,' Patsy smiles,' 'because he was meant to be going out with Paul McCartney. But he did stay.' It was as well he did, because the doctor they called never turned up, leaving David to help the assistant mid-wife to deliver the baby after a nerve-racking all-night vigil.

Offered a change of pace by being temporarily seconded to the Thompson Organization, David was aware that CDP's desire to shift him from the Chemstrand account did not derive entirely from the purest of motives. He went along with the idea anyway, glad of the change and extra experience. Unfortunately, the assignment quickly turned into a nightmare as the launch of a new magazine, *London Life*, ran aground. It was David's first encounter with corporate politics.

He had been loaned out as managing editor to Mark Boxer, founder of *The Sunday Times* colour magazine. The situation turned farcical as the weekly editorial budget of £1200 was cut three weeks before the magazine started functioning to £750. David became convinced that the whole assignment was a political set-up to 'get' Mark Boxer, then a great friend and confidant of Denis Hamilton, editor of *The Sunday Times* and managing director of the Thompson Group, to whom Boxer was seen by many as a threatening heir-apparent. David at one point was even asked to go in and give evidence that Boxer, of whom he was very fond, 'was showing signs of clinical paranoia'. It was back to CDP, sadder and wiser, having glimpsed the lengths to which powerful figures will go to achieve their ends.

In the odd way that situations often work themselves out, the next year at the agency was a wonderful time for David. With colleagues Charles Saatchi, Ross Cramer and Alan Parker, CDP had an enviable run of highly successful and award-winning campaigns. With the energy level high and the adrenalin pumping, for a while the young man was content. Not for long, as David soon reached the point where there was nothing more to do at CDP. Despite their success, he was – in his terms – going round and round the same track, a notion that was to be a recurring motif in his life.

An agency had been formed by Mary Welles that had taken the seemingly precedential step of deigning to advise its clients on the nature of their products. This radical departure, which was to extend the brief of the advertising agent dramatically, was anticipated by David while at CDP with a client belonging to the Thomas Tilling group, Pretty Polly. David reckons he owes Brian Meekin, the managing director of this group, a favour following an argument they got into one day in Nottingham.

'We were having a discussion about a price campaign. It was 8/11d versus 9/11d and in the middle of it all I said, "You're selling the wrong product." There was a huge silence. "Everybody's selling stockings. You should be selling panty hose. Get out of this price war."

'On the train home I got such a bollocking from my managing director: how dare I talk to a customer like that? I argued back, pointing out that in America that was the way it was going, more and more getting involved in and advising their clients on the manner in which they could change their products. I'd done my research, I was very confident, cocky even, like any other feisty 26-year-old. I knew there'd be several other agencies more than happy to take me on, and I was on a year's contract, so I had good job security.

'So the argument continued and a few days later they came round and said, "Look, we can't afford to run the risk of having you arguing with clients in that manner, but you've got a good point. Why don't we start a new unit, where you actually look at client's products, and look at the packaging, and we could offer that as another service." I said, "Great, that would be marvellous." So we sorted it out, how many more staff we'd need – I was on £4,500 a year, this was 1967 and I was about to be put up to £5000 – and I said, "I'd like 10 per cent of any profits that come in. There could be a big breakthrough."' A profit percentage was out of the question, I was told, it wasn't company policy, blah, blah, blah. They just weren't interested in giving me 10 per cent in *anything*. I was an employee, be grateful and all that. For me, that was the beginning of the end.'

The *end* of the end came when David was asked to take on the Benson and Hedges cigarette account. 'That caused a lot of unhappiness too,' David says. 'They didn't feel I should have the ability to choose what I worked on. I'm sure they thought I was being very pretentious, but I've never smoked, I don't agree with smoking and I just wasn't prepared to spend my life urging other people to smoke. I'd had a similar row at Greenly's when they encouraged us to use suits tailored at Kilgour, French and Stanbury in Savile Row and photograph them as John Collier's suits. I said that it seemed to me

completely reasonable to have suits made at John Collier, even if they
had to employ a special tailor to do it. But to have them made by an
eminent Savile Row tailor and purport they were John Collier, no.
You know, when you've had all those rows, the gilt goes off the
gingerbread. I said, "Well, I think, I'd like to go." They didn't rush
to disagree.'

He was made to sign an extraordinarily restrictive termination
contract, stipulating that he would refrain from joining any other
agency for a minimum of five years. In return, CDP would put up
£2000 of the £3000 David reckoned he needed to start up his own
business. He left many good friends behind, like his erstwhile mentor
Colin Millward, together with copy writers Alan Parker and Charles
Saatchi.

David had never lost his ambition to break into films and had
always regarded anything else he did as a means to that eventual end –
but how to break in and in what capacity? A clue came from another
colleague at CDP, a true English eccentric named David Reynolds,
whose advice was 'Be like Diaghilev'. David had been complaining to
him one day that while he had many interests, he couldn't actually *do*
anything. 'Look,' Reynolds said, '*Diaghilev* couldn't do anything.'
David said, 'Oh, really?'

There was only one problem – he had no idea who Diaghilev was.
Reynolds explained he was the greatest influence on ballet and music
this century, although he himself could neither play a note nor dance
a step. David went straight to the library to get a book about him and
gradually became obsessed with Diaghilev. Around the same time he
read a biography of Irving Thalberg, photocopying a portrait of him
in the book which showed him as a 21-year-old starting at Universal
Studios with Carl Laemmle. He was terribly taken by Thalberg's
story. He found the idea of someone of that age making such an
impact both exciting and challenging. As with Diaghilev, it was the
idea that he didn't actually *do* anything himself, rather he *caused* it to
be done. He didn't write, he didn't direct, but he inspired those that
could. David had other heroes, and acquired more over the years, but
these two men and their careers summed up exactly what he wanted
to achieve.

With the money from CDP and a £1000 overdraft facility from his
father-in-law, David set himself up in business as a photographer's
agent. Almost from the very beginning it was a phenomenal success,
as Lord Snowdon, David Bailey, Richard Avedon, David Montgomery, Clive Arrowsmith and Brian Duffy were signed up in rapid
succession. The culture craving for pop fashion exploded as the sixties

went into overdrive and David and his clients rapidly became the new
'old boy' network, the new élite. The one thing they all had in common
was limitless energy and the courage to risk failure. David Montgomery's brother, Robert, was drafted in to help at 'David Puttnam
Associates' as the workload grew rapidly.

Richard Avedon turned out a superb series of Beatles photographs,
to which David acquired merchandising rights. Posters were produced
from Avedon's photographs and since the group was enormously
successful in Japan, David flew out to Tokyo to make a merchandising
deal. While out there he was trapped in a snow blizzard which brought
the city to a standstill. The deal done, he made his way home via
Bangkok. Here he stopped for a few days, drawn to the country for
reasons he hardly understood at the time. With his luggage lost by the
airline, he spent three days in the tropical heat in Thailand dressed in
the thick wool suit he had sported during the Tokyo blizzard. He
would return to Thailand 15 years later on the first reconnaissance
trip for *The Killing Fields*. Something called Vietnam had come in
between and David found the country virtually unrecognizable. In
1967 it had been a beautiful water city where the klongs were a way of
life. In 1983 they barely existed.

His first visit to New York was a magic time for David. It was like
coming home at last after all the years of anticipation. He still remembers his first sight of the Manhattan skyline and the thrill of
picking out the landmarks he had dreamt about for so long, such as
the Empire State and Chrysler buildings. He felt himself responding
to the buzz and excitement on the streets, and being galvanized by the
electric atmosphere. Nothing had prepared him for the heady injection
of adrenalin New York produced.

During business meetings held overlooking the Avenue of the Americas, he could see the lights of the Radio City Music Hall blinking 34
floors before him. He was struck by the informal way business was
conducted, the lack of the starched-collar approach. Everybody, from
the head of the agency down, looked relaxed in their shirt sleeves. If
anyone deigned to loosen a tie, there were no disapproving glances.
David's feeling that the rigid British class system had never taken
hold here seemed to be confirmed when the head man distributed the
lunchtime sandwiches and coffee. In the evening he saw the sun set
down the Avenue as the discussions continued until the natural conclusion of the agenda. Wasn't this what it was all about? he asked himself.
Once back in Britain, David buttonholed everyone he could find,
preaching the gospel of the new age he had glimpsed.

Still the main business of David Puttnam Associates was in Europe, taking him away from home for long spells. One working week a month was spent in Germany, where the agency was doing an enormous amount of business, David having opened up British and American photographers to German art directors. The explosion of advertising in Germany made the country a goldmine for David and his company. For one other spell each month David would do another city, Stockholm, Paris or Madrid, trying to open up business there. This left two weeks out of every month at home, frantically trying to catch up with the work accumulated in his absence. 'And there I was again,' David recalls with a rueful grin, 'lugging these huge fucking cases about; that's what made it so killingly exhausting. I'd invented these sample boxes and each photographer had one, all the samples in plastic, which made them extremely heavy. I'm not joking – I swear my arms got longer! All my life, looking back, I've been carrying heavy objects – books, lead colour sets, then photographic cases and eventually film cans. Always carrying something heavy!

'There was one enormous compensation: I was earning a helluva lot of money. From five grand when I left advertising I was making £30,000 a year eighteen months later in 1968. Patsy and I couldn't even spend it. We saved a year's money in double quick time.'

David Bailey remembers this period well. 'David was extremely hard to pin down, always dashing about, always on the move. If he had a fault, it was his tendency to pick people up and drop them. There's a lot of that about, of course.

'He was the first person I knew who was anti-smoking. We had to go out on the balcony of his house to smoke. I'd always thought of him as straighforward until then. This was the first sign of eccentricity. That, and the fact that he disapproved of my drinking. He's always been a couple of glasses of wine man at the most and was shocked at what I used to shift. Then he was forever dragging me off to clubs. Once it was a reggae club in Southall, where we had an absolutely terrifying night. There was a dreadful atmosphere of menace about the place, ours were the only white faces there. "We'll be murdered," I told him. I really didn't think we were going to get out alive, but he seemed oblivious to the danger. Perhaps because I was born in the East End, I was more sensitive to the vibes than he was, and in the end I managed to talk him into leaving early, thank God.'

When asked about his much repeated 'Hello, he lied' remark about David, Bailey smiles and shrugs. 'You say a lot of things when you're young. It seemed a funny, amusing thing to say at the time, nothing more than that. Who knows why you say things?'

A few years later, in the early seventies, David would tell a colleague, 'You know, one thing I *never* do is lie.' When this produced a raised eyebrow, he immediately qualified the remark, adding, 'Well, I always tell at least *half* the truth.' Then he grinned disarmingly. 'The only problem I have later is remembering which half I've told.'

'Photography is quite a bitchy business,' says Robert Montgomery, 'but I've never heard David actually *lie*. He *could* take certain things and twist them, but you have to remember he was a negotiator. You've got to listen quite carefully to what he has to say, but he never lies. To get where he did in photography, you've got to pull a few tricks, that's for sure.

'There's so much misconception about the business. People think you're having it off right, left and centre. David was involved with nude models, but only through his work. He coaxed one girl into being the first nude advertising model; they wanted a stylish model, not a downmarket one and lots of girls didn't want to do it in case it ruined their career. Then we were involved in the Jimi Hendrix album cover where inside it was full of nudes. My brother David shot that. When you're actually in the studio shooting, it's very hard work. It's great to work with nice-looking girls, but it's more often than not all very straight. You'd probably get more monkey business, Jack the Lad stuff, going on in factories or insurance companies, where it's more hidden.

'David was a total workaholic, even on holiday. He never drank, apart from an odd glass of wine. He never took any drugs. And he always had so much energy he'd charge you up as well.'

Despite his enormous financial success, the problem with the agency was David's acute awareness that it wasn't what he wanted to do. He still nurtured ambitions to enter the film business. But how? On its own, being a sixties' yuppy was simply not enough. Despite the examples of Diaghilev and Thalberg, what was desperately needed was a catalyst.

For Patsy things were not going at all well. There were no money worries, but she was seeing less and less of David, and when she did he was invariably surrounded by a clutch of photographers and their models. The move to Pimlico had been into a badly-built modern townhouse, with paper-thin walls that afforded little privacy.

With David up to his neck in work, there was simply no time for such trifles as illness, Patsy discovered. After feeling unwell for several days, she went along for a check-up. The doctor could find nothing wrong and told her to come back for further examination the following week.

'Sounds like appendicitis,' Patsy's mother told her that evening.

'Don't be silly, Mum.'

'All right, but you've got all the symptoms.'

'Well, I'm going to see the doctor again soon; he'll tell me.'

Next time the doctor had no doubts.

'You've got a *terrible* appendix,' Patsy was told. 'We'll need to get you straight into hospital.'

'You can't,' Patsy informed him. 'My children are coming home from school.'

The doctor exploded. 'Your *children* are coming home? What are you *talking* about? You've got –'

'Listen!' Patsy interrupted. 'I've lasted this long. Just give me a few more hours.'

Debbie and Sacha were duly picked up and handed over to an au pair girl Patsy quickly found. After a lightning tour of the house, with the state of the larder surveyed and a few £5 notes flung at the startled girl, Patsy drove herself to hospital and was readied for the operation. Since David could not be traced, the decision was made to go ahead without his authority.

During Patsy's 10-day sojourn in hospital, David visited once with the children, and once in the company of Richard Avedon. Patsy knew there was a big campaign underway and appreciated the pressure David was under. Still there was a feeling she had somehow or other ended up with the short straw. She felt shunted into the sidings. Even the *fiction* that she was at the hub of things was an unthinkable dream, let alone the reality.

One saving grace about Ranelagh Grove was that the kids loved it, for they were surrounded by lots of children of their own age. Sacha and Debbie occupied one of the bedrooms in bunk beds. David and Patsy were in another and there were two spares, soon to be in almost constant use. What made it difficult for Patsy to cope was the fact that she felt disorientated, totally left behind by the tremendous change that had taken place in society. Four years earlier, she was relegated to the status of a non-person because of her pregnancy outside marriage. Now here she was at 22, feeling as old as Methuselah, with David traipsing through the house at all hours with these bright young things.

'People were living together, weren't getting married. We had David Bailey and the other photographers in and out: I never knew who they were going to bring. There were pop people and stars coming and going. The madness of photography at that time: models, fantastic amounts of money, great Rolls-Royces and everyone behaving in the most extraordinary way.

'We didn't have their sort of money, the sort of money all these personalities had, but we were mixing with them. They *loved* coming round, being around us. We had a very, *very* open house. If any of the photographers was kicked out by one of their models, they would be in one of our two spare bedrooms or if the model was kicked out, she'd be in there. David Montgomery's assistant, a lovely girl, lived with us for a couple of years. David brought over Bert Bell, a very talented Canadian photographer and he lived with us. I was running a *hotel!*'

David represented a photographer named Michael Joseph. When he needed someone to do modelling for him at the last minute, Patsy and the children found themselves roped in. At Christmas she cooked dinner for her parents and family, then left on Boxing Day for the Canary Islands with Debbie and Sacha, a case filled with her own clothes. They met Joseph, the pictures were taken and they flew home. David Montgomery sent for Patsy to model when he was dissatisfied with the girl he was using. David Bailey used her; and Sacha, all of three years old, was drafted in to pose for Salvation Army posters. 'It was a madhouse,' says Patsy. 'and I was only prepared to go up to a certain point with it.'

Everyone has their breaking point and Patsy felt that she was close to hers. She was seeing less and less of David and was bitterly aware that he was the sole begetter of the whole situation. 'He *could* stop it,' Patsy told herself, 'but he doesn't seem to want to.'

David is unequivocal about this period in his life. 'The whole post-Carnaby thing, I really did think I was Jack the Lad. I did it all and I had it all. If I met the person I was then, I'd loathe him,' he says bitterly. 'I fell out with most of my clients. There was a feeling around I was just using them, and they were absolutely right. I became a very unpleasant person.'

Brian Duffy reasoned that if David and his agency were collecting 25 per cent of his fee, more than just a phone-call was called for. 'I was at London airport and discovered the airline tickets hadn't been arranged – nothing. This had already happened a few other times, so we had a disagreement. I was furious and told David I wouldn't speak to him for 10 years. My wife June and Patsy remained friendly and they were always trying to get us together, but I was determined to sit out the 10 years.'

Another monumental row erupted with Richard Avedon, partly over fees for the Beatles posters. Avedon formed the view that the sales figures had been understated, 'He was wrong,' says Robert Montgomery. 'The Beatles posters were not the sell-out we had expected.'

Then there was a confrontation over £17,000 worth of expenses Avedon claimed for a series of Twiggy posters representing spring, summer, autumn, and winter. 'Look,' David exploded, 'our agreement is I do the deals, you provide the pictures. I don't charge you for my flying around and overheads, why should you charge me for your expenses?' That was the end of the Avedon association.

Patsy began to feel she was losing every last vestige of confidence in herself. Everyone around her seemed to be *doing* something. Except her. She felt like a sponge for everything that was coming at her. A whole new world had opened up from which she felt shut out, which was typified by the swinging sixties scene that danced unbidden nightly through her parlour. Gradually she could feel her life, and marriage, begin to unravel

She had been brought up in a family where everything had been orderly and methodical – now she was in the middle of this maelstrom. She felt jolted from one extreme to the other, at home in neither situation. 'I am a total non-person,' she convinced herself. 'I actually don't exist, or if I do, it's merely as an extension of David's mother. He knows his children are well; he knows his house is fine. I take care of absolutely everything and I am now completely faceless.'

Although photographer Terence Donovan was one of the few not on David's books, he had known him since his CDP days. A burly, genial Cockney, Terence owes David a fairly large debt of gratitude for the introduction to his 'trouble and strife'. He tried to return the compliment by making Patsy feel part of the world from which David excluded her. Often he would pop round on a Sunday in his Roller. 'Come on,' he'd yell, 'get the kids inside. We're going down the East End.'

Debbie and Sacha fondly remember the outings with Donovan. 'He was the nicest of the lot,' says Debbie. 'He really liked kids, not like some of them. Bailey, for example, couldn't be bothered with us – now he's got two of his own, of course, he's besotted. Terence Donovan was a lovely man, a great treat-giver, with a son the same age as me. One Christmas he gave us a whole day out. We ate hamburgers, then we went to Hamleys to choose a toy. He took us to the Magic Circle, we got to stay out *late*, then we got fish and chips on the way home.'

One night their father brought two guests up to meet the kids in their bedroom, when Debbie was barely six years old. 'This is George Harrison and Paul McCartney,' he announced. Debbie was impressed – one half of the Beatles in her bedroom! Sacha just looked up from his Noddy annual, smiled and went back to his book. As she got older

Debbie began to see their home as a halfway house for everybody, a place where love affairs were started, and a rest home for the victims of broken love affairs. One particular memory lingers.

'I'd sometimes go downstairs for no particular reason late at night, maybe for a glass of water or something, and there was this little marble table in the kitchen big enough to sit and have a cup of tea at. Mum would often be sitting there talking to someone who'd be doing their heart-on-the-table act. She mothered everybody. She was always there. Dad was rarely at home for any length of time. We really were brought up by our mother in a very straightforward way, despite the fact we lived in such an unconventional house.'

One day a friend of David's stopped by for a word at the office. 'Make it quick, I'm in a hurry,' David snapped, scribbling away at his notes.

'All right, I'll make it quick,' his friend replied. 'Are you aware, or even particularly concerned, that if you carry on as you're doing, there might not be a family to go back home to?'

David paused and put his pen down, and then looked up at his colleague. 'What the fuck are you talking about?' he asked.

'You and Patsy. And take that edge out of your voice. Listen to me as a *friend*. You're going to lose her, David, if you carry on as you're doing.'

'Go on.'

'She can't see past you at the moment, mate, but that's not going to last much longer unless you start to bring her into things more. Take her along with you, and stop playing the field, or someone's going to nab that girl.'

David stared hard at his friend, trying hard to remember that he *was* his friend.

'I know it,' he finally admitted quietly, 'only I don't allow myself to think about it. Isn't that stupid?'

'For an otherwise pretty sharp cookie, yes, it is,' his friend agreed. 'Patsy is one hell of an attractive girl, David. It's only a matter of time before someone makes a move unless you start now to make her a full partner in your marriage. Look, David, call it the old antennae, call it what you will. *My* lesson had to be learned the hard way and I think enough of you as a bloke not to stand idly by and watch history repeat itself.'

'If I can help it,' David vowed, 'it won't.'

Chapter 4

Getting to the Goldfish

The first experience Sanford 'Sandy' Lieberson had of the entertainment business was as a press agent in the States. He had served in the Navy and was readying himself for college in 1958 and working part-time in a restaurant, parking cars in Los Angeles to support his income, when an old school-friend drove up in a Cadillac with a gorgeous blonde on his arm. Sandy hadn't met his friend for over two years and was somewhat taken aback at the very considerable improvement in his lifestyle. How come? His friend explained that he had become an agent. With one eye on the Caddy and another on the blonde, 'Me, too!' Sandy thought.

His friend, astutely noting the gleam in Sandy's eye, told him that if he was serious he would introduce him to someone who wanted a junior press agent, whereupon Sandy decided he had parked his last car and to hell with academic considerations – college, too, was out. His rakish good looks and tremendous enthusiasm, engagingly laced with just a hint of soulful larceny, were endearing qualities. The twin desires to succeed and have some fun at the same time thus brought Sandy smack into the film and entertainment business.

After he joined the William Morris agency and represented actors there for a year, he obtained another job as an agent in Rome. Here he worked for two years between 1961 and 1962, with six months in London tacked on the end before returning home.

Back in the USA he joined the CMA Agency in Hollywood, later merged with ICM. They had just signed Peter Sellers and decided they wanted to open an office in England. Sandy agreed to do it for a limited period of time and returned to London in 1965, where he represented the Rolling Stones. He first met David when Avedon's Beatles posters were being touted, and in a way the contrast between the two groups truly represents the difference in style between the two men, who felt drawn to each other both because of the mutuality and the duality of their interests. David didn't know it then but he had just met the catalyst he had been looking for.

Sandy was constantly astonished at the quality of individuals connected with the British film business he came across. 'There's so many idiots making movies,' it occurred to him. 'I might as well have a go at it myself.' He began by producing a film with clients he represented, co-directors Donald Cammell and Nicolas Roeg, Mick Jagger of the Rolling Stones and James Fox. The film was called *Performance*. The rushes didn't please Warners. It was nothing to do with the quality of the film, which on its release was reckoned by many to be both brilliant and the seminal sixties' movie, but a feeling that the whole thing was somehow totally immoral, as well as the even more cardinal sin, totally uncommercial.

Sandy's next venture was to be *Mary, Queen of Scots*, with director Alexander Mackendrick. Unfortunately, Universal were in the middle of management changes and the movie was cancelled. With *Performance* still in trouble at Warners, then the cancellation of *Mary*, for which stars Mia Farrow and Oliver Reed had been lined up, life swiftly became something of a nightmare for Sandy. When he had to relinquish the rights to *Mary*, Hal Wallis picked them up and produced the movie. Sandy was well and truly stranded. Resourceful, resilient, but undeniably stranded.

His friend's counselling had left David in a turmoil. 'I'm absolutely going to lose everything,' he convinced himself. 'So much for the right little mover . . . getting it all, only to blow it all away.' Although he wanted to talk to Patsy quickly, still he held back for a few days, inventing all sorts of excuses for not taking the plunge before finally admitting it was only the fear of failure that was stopping him. He began to focus specifically on the Friday evening for what he saw as the make-or-break discussion. When the kids were safely in bed, he promised himself, that would be the time.

On the fateful day he worked steadily through the considerable workload he had to finish before the weekend break, then at 4 pm there was a call from Germany to say that one of his clients was already in transit from Frankfurt and could David arrange to have him picked up at the airport and join him for dinner later? 'Fine,' David heard himself say mechanically. 'The Dorchester at 8.30? Fine, no problem.' Here was a perfect example of his good intentions being temporarily thwarted, he told himself, as he picked up the phone to call home.

'Patsy? Just to let you know I'll be back late tonight, so don't wait up for me.' There was no reply.

'Patsy?'

'I heard you, David,' she said quietly. 'I'll see you at breakfast, then.'

After dinner with his client that evening, David opened the front door at Ranelagh Grove quietly and made to go upstairs, before noticing someone appeared to have left the light on in the kitchen. He tiptoed over to put the light out, then froze as he saw Patsy sitting at the marble table there, an empty cup of tea in front of her. Her head was buried in her hands. She was sobbing quietly, then started as she heard him approach.

'Oh, Patsy, I'm so sorry,' he said.

'It's not your fault,' she told him. 'Business comes first.'

'Not any more,' he said, and to her amazement got up and took the telephone extension off the hook.

'What on *earth* are you doing?' she asked incredulously.

'I want to talk to my wife,' David replied with a nervous smile. 'I've been an idiot, Patsy,' he continued as he seated himself opposite her at the little table, and gently squeezed her hands, 'but everybody in life deserves a second chance. From now on I'm going to change, because if I lose you I've lost everything, and I can't let that happen.'

'There have been offers –' Patsy stammered bemusedly, not quite knowing what else to say.

'Really?' he asked.

'– one in particular, but none that I entertained for one split second.'

'Patsy, I'll do whatever's necessary. My priorities have been idiotically wrong. Jack the Lad's finished.'

'David,' Patsy now grasped her husband's hands in hers, 'I don't *care* what you do. I *understand* you're a creative man. You've got more energy than anyone else I've ever met, but you must understand one thing about me if we're going to go the course. I need to be with you every step of the way, not as an afterthought. I don't *care* what risks you take, I don't *care* what hardships we go through, but you have to take me with you in *every way*. I'm not bothered about anything else, I mean *anything*, but we have to get our lives back together again once and for all.'

In that moment David's mind became crystal-clear. He had become so full of self-loathing at the agency it had distorted his judgement. He realized that now was the time to make the break and do what he had wanted to all along.

Patsy saw that if everyone has their moments of madness, David's time at the agency was his, enjoying the youth he never had. She could see how tied down he had felt, having risen to his obligations and responsibilities at twenty. He had been knocked sideways by what was happening at the agency, the swirling hedonism that was going on around him, and the temptations constantly thrown in his path.

For Patsy the episode brought to her the realization that she did after all have a vote, that she was not a complete non-person as she had begun to think. As the weeks and months passed she found David following through in a multitude of ways that would have seemed unimaginable before. With this the clouds of inadequacy slowly began to lift. Patsy was eventually able to look back even on the appendicitis episode with a smile. 'My God, now he'll phone me twenty times a day to make sure I'm all right. But *then* –!

'He realized eventually that everything I said, rightly or wrongly, was how I saw it. I had no axe to grind, I wasn't making points, I had nothing to win or lose with the advice I was giving. I would never tell him something was good, not then, not now, if I didn't think so, because I think he's better than that. I've always treated him like that, because I've always felt him to be very special. I still do, I really do think he's extraordinary.'

If it is true that there are six requisites in every happy marriage, Patsy had learned that for her the first was faith and the remaining five were confidence. The couple were back from the brink.

Resolved to leave the agency and pursue his ambition of breaking into movies, David joined his two ex-colleagues, Ross Cramer and Charles Saatchi, in forming Cramer Puttnam Saatchi. This began unpromisingly with a couple of false starts. With American film producer Elliott Kastner's £1000 investment, David wanted to make an animated cartoon, *The Man Who Was Magic*, to be drawn by illustrator Alan Aldridge from a Paul Gallico book. Of the £1000, £750 was spent on drawings and the balance on a screenplay before the venture was scrapped. Charles Saatchi had written a script he called *The Carpet Man*, with which he provided the company gratis. David thought it was a terrific treatment, based on Jim Webb's 'Fifth Dimension' song, and the plan was to turn it into a movie with Gene Wilder.

'We're going to get into the film industry,' they told an astonished Alan Parker, who retorted, 'Don't be stupid!'

'And you're going to write us a couple of scripts,' they added.

'But I've never written anything longer than 30 seconds in my life.'

'That doesn't matter. Alan. Look, we believe in you. We know you can do it and we're going to try and sell it!'

After a visit to New York in an attempt to raise money, Alan remembers their return and Charles's instant disillusionment with the film business. 'I'm going to open an advertising agency,' he told Alan, who has often wondered since what would have happened if Charles's script had been accepted. 'Maybe he'd be a film director and I'd now own the biggest advertising agency in the world,' he muses. 'We knew nothing. My first script looked like a rejected novel scribbled in an old exercise book.'

David wanted it to at least look professional and after a glance at Alan's first efforts, he announced, 'It doesn't even *look* like a script. I'm never going to sell it if it doesn't look like a proper script.' He promptly gave Alan a pile of old movie scripts to copy the presentation.

Alan tackled David one day. 'Look,' he said, 'are you *really* serious about this, because it's a lot of work, me scribbling away on the kitchen table, if you're going to be on to something else next week.' What he had in mind was David's reputation, deserved or otherwise, as a bit of a butterfly, trying everything out. 'No,' David replied vehemently. 'I promise you this is it, I'm going to devote all my time to this. I've never been more serious about anything in my life. Any time you want to spend with me is fine.' To make himself even more serious, a beard was developed which David saw as suiting his new film-producer image.

His next move was to phone Sandy Lieberson and invite him round for a meeting to discuss the possibility of a collaboration. As soon as Sandy entered his office, David took a polaroid picture of him, which his visitor thought was a neat, appropriate gesture from a photographer's agent. Then they got down to a general kicking around of ideas, the ultimate purpose of which from David's point of view was to discover how to gain entry into the movies.

During David and Sandy's follow-up meeting over lunch at the Terrazza in Soho, they agreed upon basically a partnership to make things happen, an association summed up eloquently by friends as: Sandy brought the phone book, David supplied the cash. Sandy did indeed have the contacts, while David had a little over £30,000 to invest in films. He still retained a 60 per cent interest in the agency, which he left an old friend and a colleague, Peter Russell, and Robert Montgomery, to run. Its headquarters were moved to plusher premises in Goodge Street, while the old Tilney Street office was retained to house the film company. They dubbed their joint entity V P S (Visual Programmes System)/Goodtimes Enterprises Production Company (*Performance* having been Sandy's first Goodtimes enterprise on his own). David's hope was that the photographic agency would keep them in funds while they made their first tentative steps into film production.

Since Sandy was still involved with *Performance*, David duly went along with him to see Kenneth Hyman, the new head of Warners' London office, expecting nothing more than a routine meeting. After rushes of the movie were shown the Warners' contingent started fuming. 'Who's that ugly guy up there on the screen?' they demanded to know. Sandy gently explained that it was Mick Jagger, whom the previous administration had approved. 'Get him off the picture!' was the response. David watched open-mouthed as Sandy defied them.

'It's impossible,' he declared.

Hyman erupted. 'You'll never work in this industry again!' he roared.

David could hardly believe his ears. His brand-new partner would never work in the industry again? The volatility of the film business was brought home to him when Sandy and Hyman cordially shook hands no more than 30 minutes later. One of Hyman's aides had rushed in with a fact sheet attesting to Jagger's worldwide popularity. It was a nerve-racking start to the partnership.

Sandy and David had set themselves up at a peculiar time and constituted their company in an unusual manner, since most producers tended to align themselves with film distributors who provided the funds. As for the timing – 'Sandy and I just happened to choose exactly the same month as the American studios pulled all their money out of England,' David recalls.

In a sense, this would turn out to be to their advantage. For years American investment in British films had been running at full throttle, following the success of Woodfall and their *Tom Jones* hit. British film-makers had grown pampered in the cash flood from the US that followed. David's experiences would always be in a period of comparative stricture. Lean and hungry would work better than fat and spoiled.

In addition to film development David and Sandy were convinced that with the home video cassette business set for an explosion in the future (it was 10 years away, not the five they had estimated), the way to manoeuvre themselves into a uniquely advantageous position was not only to initiate new product, but also to acquire existing libraries. David introduced a friend of his, Jocelyn Stevens, to Sandy and together they enthused Stevens with their plan. He offered to subscribe some of the capital they needed himself, and put them in touch with Evelyn de Rothschild, a business and personal acquaintance of his.

Through him they gained a further introduction to Lord Westmoreland at Sotheby's. Rothschild helped the partners put together a financial plan, subsequently endorsed by an Economic Intelligence Report.

When Rothschild and Sotheby's saw the report, they agreed to capitalize the company. Unfortunately, David and Sandy could not afford to buy the 23 per cent stake due to each of them. Technically they had to put up the money, since they apparently could not just be *given* the shares. The answer was a loan from the Rothschild bank, rendering them virtual employees.

Goodtimes was in business, for any and all opportunities that arose, but primarily interested in the making and acquiring of product. Consultancies came their way through some of Sandy's contacts. They represented one of the early companies in the video business and did some consultancy work for CBS and Philips. Sotheby's put them in touch with W. H. Smith, who were keen to watch the development of the cassette side. Generally, business began to bubble. At an early stage, however, Rothschild saw there was not going to be any kind of large, substantial revenue from the video side of the business to pay for David and Sandy's salaries, script development and product acquisition. Although allegedly enthused about the video side of the business in the long term, they now decided not to pursue library acquisition. 'The very things we wanted them to do, they wouldn't do,' says David. 'We wanted them to take a long position on video cassettes. Frankly, if they'd listened to us, we'd all have made a great deal of money. In 1970, for a million quid, you could have owned the video cassette rights to every film ever made in Britain, from every library, Korda's London Films, Rank, EMI – everything, the *lot*.'

Despite his ambition to break into movies, David actually felt at that point there was no real long-term future in mainstream moviemaking. However since this was the side of the company which Rothschild decided should be pursued in the interests of cash flow, David went back to Alan Parker.

Between the two men they came up with the idea for a film called *Melody*, a love story of two young kids who meet at school. 'We had also acquired the rights to seven Bee Gees songs and I had to incorporate them into this story,' Alan recalls. 'One song was called "Melody Fair", hence the title and the name of the young girl in the story. There was also a song called "First of May", my starting point for a love story involving two children. You have to remember this was 10 years before the new Bee Gees music was used so successfully in *Saturday Night Fever*. David was ahead of his time in many ways, not least in the use of music in films. He knew every fifties' song, had every current record and even surprised Ken Russell later by knowing so much about classical music. In fact, music is his greatest passion and still the area of his greatest strength.'

Although based on Alan's old school in Islington, David insisted that they travel to Southgate as well to visit Minchenden one afternoon. 'We just walked around,' Alan remembers. 'It was a typical middle-class suburban school, no tarmac playground, just a pretty grass field. Kids were sitting around in groups and we just walked up to them and started talking about ideas we had for the film. We were also invited for tea in the teachers' common-room which gave David a kick as they'd written him off as a "no-hoper" when he left school. He stood there sipping tea with the headmaster, as if he'd been the head boy with a "first" at Cambridge.' Something to be borne in mind at all times about Alan Parker is that his comments on David must be distilled through several layers of puckish malice and deeply-felt affection, wickedly and perfectly conveyed in his cartoons. In person he is an overgrown Puck, expecially with the page-boy bob he sported for a while, who dresses up and serves his bile-ridden epithets with the deepest, most satisfying chuckle you could ever wish to hear.

David took Alan's script of *Melody* to Marion Rosenberg, a producer's assistant he had befriended at the photographic agency. 'We bumped into each other a lot,' she recalls, 'both socially and professionally. I *loved* his energy and brassiness and cockiness. He asked me, as I expect he asked umpteen others, how he could best break into films. I asked David to bring his treatment of *Melody* to us. We loaned him £3000 for development money and he came back with this absolutely amazing presentation. It was more than a screenplay, it had visuals and all sorts of beautiful art work, a wonderful visual presentation. We tried to get the project moving, but didn't put all that much energy into it. It was, after all, a very small film and didn't seem to have any great potential in it.'

A few months later David phoned Marion. 'Look, can I give you the £3000 back? I want a go at flogging it myself now.' Marion could see that he was just bursting to get out of the starting gate. 'Of course you can,' she agreed. Producer Ron Kass had offered to send the script to Edgar Bronfman, boss of Seagram the Distillers, in his Connecticut home. Although Bronfman was interested in a modest investment in film projects, he was less than keen on *Melody*. Luckily his 15-year-old son was very taken with it. Bronfman reconsidered, giving in to the irreducible logic that in show business one's offspring represents a microcosm of world taste. He put up £400,000 of the budget, with Hemdale, run by David Hemmings and John Daly, topping it up by another £200,000.

Alan Parker remembers a meeting at David's house with *Melody*'s production manager and first assistant director to discuss the film's production. Since Alan had been involved with commercials, David had invited him along to help out at the session. 'He sat down and went through the schedule and the budget with such assurance and thoroughness, like someone who'd been doing it for 30 years, with absolutely instant, intuitive understanding of every detail of the process. When the two of them finally left, he leaned over to me and said, "It's a good way to learn, isn't it?"

'*Melody* had an agonizingly slow beginning and really got going in the scene where the girl buys a goldfish. This was a phrase we continued to use ever since, that in a film you're all right once you've got to the "goldfish", meaning that the narrative has finally gathered enough momentum to carry you through to the end.'

The characters in the movie were transparently autobiographical, although it was as if Alan and David had poured themselves into a bottle and given it a light shake. Alan Parker might be seen as the extrovert schoolboy in a South London comprehensive school with David as his quieter, introverted pal, who falls for young Tracy Hyde as Melody/Patsy. David and Sandy secured the services of Jack Wild and Mark Lester to play the two boys, following the success of *Oliver!*, in which Wild had played the Artful Dodger to Mark Lester's title role. *Melody* was Hemdale's first movie investment, the decision being clinched when they figured that with the amount they were getting from their commission on Jack Wild, Mark Lester and others in the movie, all of them Hemdale clients, they could have a chunk of the picture itself for very little more. David produced *Melody*, with Ron Kass as executive producer, and Waris Hussein was chosen to direct, following his film, *A Touch of Love*, which David had seen and enjoyed. He also signed *Touch of Love*'s photographer, Peter Suchitsky. As well as the Bee Gees music, there was a single contribution to the soundtrack from Crosby, Stills and Nash.

Alan offered to take the second camera and film some of the activities going on in the centre of the field for a school sports day scene, while Waris Hussein directed the main unit. Although his filming only lasted a day, Alan admits, 'I did get carried away at the long jump and got the directing bug for the first time!' Until this point in his career Alan had never directed anything, not even commercials, but now it occurred to David that perhaps his talents lay here as well as in writing.

Melody opened in the States in 1971 just one week before its British début, to good reviews, but non-existent business. In Britain the film was dreadfully renamed *S.W.A.L.K.* (*Sealed With A Loving Kiss*) by the Boultings' British Lion distributors. This time it was largely attacked by the critics, and again did no business.

Portions of Alan Parker's Script were conceded by some to have a real sense of school humour and style, as when *Melody* declares to her family that she likes being with her boyfriend more than she likes doing geography. Her father asks, 'Why don't you wait until you're older?' 'How old?' Melody replies. 'In your twenties,' her dad tells her. 'But that's *twice* as old as I am now,' Melody replies indignantly.

At another point Alan has a teacher ask his class if they can name any of Jesus's disciples. No response. Does anyone know what a disciple is, then? Blank stares. Finally, in total exasperation, the teacher asks, 'Does anybody know who Jesus was?'

George Melly in the *Observer* strongly objected to the soundtrack David had packaged the film in, complaining about current fashions of 'pouring pop music over every film as if it were hot chocolate sauce over ice cream. This practice has been carried to hideous excess in *Melody*,' he wrote, in which there were 'no less than eight songs of the utmost banality, performed by the Bee Gees, whose only effect is to soften an already soft-centred film' (Parker on Melly: 'If you've ever heard George Melly murdering a Bessie Smith song, you'll know not to take his criticism of the music in films too seriously.') Still, Margaret Hinxman in the *Sunday Telegraph* found the film 'an engagingly true and detailed picture of junior school life'.

John Russell Taylor was to prove somewhat more acerbic as he wrote that nothing at all happened in the movie for the first 45 minutes, which were 'devoted mainly to a repetitious exploration of a school like nothing at all in our present educational system'. Tracy Hyde and Mark Lester were 'required turn and turn about to be excessively knowing and unbelievably innocent, according to the dictates of the story, which goes to show that the director, Waris Hussein, is perfectly able to do well by good material (as in *A Touch of Love*), but is not yet able to make something out of nothing.'

The ending seemed to alienate even critics who found some of the early scenes charming. When the young couple are refused permission to marry, the whole school erupts in an explosion of violence. 'You can see,' Davina Robinson wrote in the *Financial Times*, 'that the distributors thought they were getting the best of *If* (juvenile anarchy) and *Kes* (comedy and pathos of school days); inevitably they get the worst of all worlds.'

David regarded the critical mauling *Melody* received in Britain as unthinking. 'I know it wasn't a *Kes* or an *If*,' he railed, taking his cue from the *Financial Times* review and starting his often hilarious habit of scattering instant-comparison titles around, 'and we didn't want to make Coronation Street-on-wheels. But we will have succeeded if some of the people who watch Coronation Street go and see that film. It may not have been as good as they say it was in New York, but I don't think it was as bad as they said it was here.'

David agreed to an interview with a feature writer on the London *Evening Standard*, Ray Connolly, to defend the film against the British critics' reaction. He quickly established a rapport with the tall, soft-spoken young journalist. ('Soft-spoken, but funky,' says Ray. It is necessary to imagine the sound of a top-of-the-range CD player with the volume at a whisper.) Both men were fully-paid-up rock 'n' roll addicts, an affinity that would lead David to his breakthrough picture soon after.

Resigned to a financial flop with their first venture, an unexpected bonus came to Goodtimes with news that the film had gone through the roof in Japan, following its sale at Cannes to Nippon Herald Films. David visited Tokyo for the second time, to be greeted by another windfall. The negotiator of the Japanese contract had awarded Goodtimes a percentage of the Japanese *gross* revenues, rather than the *net* they had expected. The resultant cheques from Japan kept Sandy and David solvent for some time to come.

Nippon Herald had an enormous success with *Melody*, selling an astonishing three million tickets. With the soundtrack album nestling at No 1 on the Japanese charts for months, the film was re-issued soon after and has been in almost continuous circulation ever since. David was greeted at Nippon Herald by the company president, Mr Furukawa. He was introduced to Furukawa's young assistant, Hara San, now one of the most respected names in Japanese movie-making and distribution. An enduring friendship was formed.

Patsy watched as David basked in the Japanese success of 'the Jules and Jim of the nappy set', as he chose to further dub *Melody*. It was but a modest start, yet David had his feet wet and the fledgling Goodtimes had taken its first faltering steps. '*Melody* was what it was,' Alan Parker summarizes, 'a beginning for all of us.'

Patsy sagely described her husband as a gambler who played everything to the edge. If he falls over, she reckoned, his attitude was that he could always start again. At the same time she was keenly aware of his desire for respectability, which placed the success of the cassette venture even higher than the production of feature films. 'If he does make a lot of money,' she declared, 'and he hardly thinks he can fail, he'll be very glad if he's done it out of his educational cassette thing, rather than making a film like *Love Story*, when he might have felt a bit ashamed to take it.'

Patsy's point was well made as, to the bafflement of many of his friends and colleagues, David continued to insist that cassettes were going to be his main career, not the production of feature films. He explained to anyone who would listen that videos would work in just the same way as an ordinary sound cassette except that they could be slotted into the back of a television set. As is often the case with visionaries, his views were treated as those of a crank. His boundless youthful enthusiasm became a turn-off for many, perhaps unsurprisingly in view of his somewhat Orwellian vision. Magazines, he reckoned, were doomed. When asked to give a lecture to students at the London School of Printing, he calmly informed them they were being trained for redundancy. Newspapers? He conceded they would survive a while longer, but forecast that eventually evening papers would be on large screens on commuter trains.

One of the reasons for David's enthusiasm for cassettes was the depressing conviction that it would be a long time, if ever, before he could begin to emulate the great film-makers whose movies had made such an impression on him over the years. He regarded the likes of Fred Zinneman, Elia Kazan and Stanley Kramer as having dealt with the big issues, forging on the screen searing, recognizable areas of life that probed and illuminated the problems of the little man, but always in an entertaining way. Apart from his father's influence, he was aware that much of the ethical basis in his life had been implanted by these films. He had wanted to *be* Montgomery Clift in Zinneman's *The Search* and James Dean in Kazan's *East of Eden*. Although these pictures had been critical of society, to David they illustrated the American's capacity for infinite hopefulness, a quality that held great appeal for him both as a man and as a film-maker.

As a new producer on the British film scene, David was flattered to be singled out even then for some press attention. How did he account for the measure of success he had so far achieved? 'Well, I'm 30,' said David, 'which is an incredibly good age to be at the present moment, it's perfect timing. Then I've always been married, so I've never had to go out chasing after birds. When you're single, that's all you do. I hear blokes in the office constantly on the phone fixing themselves up for the night and all that. Their lives revolve around it.'

For Goodtimes' next venture, David and Sandy wanted to do a version of *The Pied Piper* legend. The financial deal was similar to that worked out on *Melody*, with Seagram and Hemdale putting up the cash. Milos Forman was approached to direct the project and was undecided. On the principle of nothing ventured, nothing gained, David approached Fred Zinnemann, who courteously but firmly turned him down when David phoned from Prague for a final decision. He was on his way in any event to see director Jiri Menzel, whose *Closely Observed Trains* he had much admired. Menzel was keen, but David could not obtain permission from the Czech authorities for the film-maker to leave the country, so it was back to Forman. Unfortunately in the meantime his backers had viewed Forman's first American film, *Taking Off*, and loathed it. The conversations with Milos were terminated – a matter of great regret to David.

The scriptwriter on the project was Andrew Birkin, a tall, gangly, somewhat emaciated-looking individual with a marvellously self-deprecating sense of humour. At 19 he had worked with Stanley Kubrick on *2001* in a variety of jobs, before doing research on the director's Napoleon project, later abandoned when the MGM management folded. He remembers first meeting David, Patsy and the family in 1969, when he saw David poised to enter films rather in the role of a happy amateur who was at last being allowed to treat a hobby seriously. Andrew, working as a location manager, was recruited for some second-unit work on *Melody*. ('He was responsible for the bang at the end,' says Alan Parker crisply.) Even so, the apparently diligent execution of the bang led to an offer to write *The Pied Piper*. This represented an important advance, the first time he had been offered actual payment for writing. He was despatched to a hotel in Rothenburg, where the film was to be shot, and soon had a finished script. David saw the results when he joined him in Rothenburg with associate producer Gavrik Losey, son of Joseph, and declared himself pleased.

A fine cast had been assembled to support Scottish folksinger Donovan Leitch in the title role, including Donald Pleasence, Jack Wild, Diana Dors, John Hurt and Michael Hordern, together with 200 rats on whom £7000 was expended. It was essential that the film be started on schedule, since the money was dependent on Donovan's participation, and he was squeezing the film in between absolutely unalterable tour dates. If the movie failed to go ahead, all the money Goodtimes had spent on development would be lost.

In desperation after Milos Forman was turned down by the money men, David flew off to New York to see French director Jacques (*Umbrellas of Cherburg*) Demy, who seemed taken with the project. When he returned with Demy signed, Andrew Birkin was invited to

dinner to discuss the movie. During the meal they talked about manifold subjects, but not the script. In the end Andrew could contain
himself no longer. 'Well, what do you think of the script?' he asked
Demy, as casually as he could. In his measured Gallic tones the
Frenchman replied, 'Oh, I like it very much. A few problems here
and there, but I like it very much.' As the conversation then drifted
back to the weather, Andrew persisted. 'Well, what *don't* you like
about the script?' he asked, to which Demy enigmatically replied,
with a charming smile, 'Oh, nothing, it's fine.'

With dinner over and Demy despatched to Browns hotel, David
asked Andrew what he thought. 'I can only assume,' Andrew replied,
'that the man's doing it purely for the money, because it doesn't seem
to me that he has any interest in the subject at all.' David was miffed
at what he saw as Andrew's developing 'attitude' to a director who
was, after all, an Academy-award winner. And hadn't Andrew admitted that he was keen to direct himself? Their discussion concluded
with Andrew being asked if he would still knuckle down and work
with Demy. Of course he would, he replied.

During the sessions that followed at Browns hotel, Demy began to
question everything in the script. Andrew felt he was being extremely
accommodating, but the script soon arrived at the stage where it was
no longer the picture he had set out to write. He had seen the film as
being light on the surface and dark underneath, where Demy seemed
to want change for the sake of change and the whole thing to be much
more sentimental. He penned a 'Soliloquy to a Rat' in French, then
got a friend, Mark Peploe, to translate it into English. Andrew had
had enough. To David he declared, 'I just can't work with Demy. For
the sake of the project and my sanity, it's better we part company.'
Since Demy had more or less delivered the same ultimatum, there
was no contest. Andrew went.

David still had the temerity to ask him to read Demy's finished
shooting script. Andrew thought it was dreadful and said so. When
David asked if he could make a few changes here and there, he replied
that there was no point, it would be like putting new wine into old
bottles. Still David invited Andrew to fly out to the German location.
His decision to choose Demy over Andrew, dictated by economic
necessity, had not diminished his enthusiasm for Andrew's ability.

From his German visit another project would later spring, but for
the moment Andrew was left wondering precisely why he was there.
However he was pleased to see Patsy and the kids, who had been
drafted into the picture themselves as unpaid extras.

Demy proved to be a charming dinner companion and remains

friends with the Puttnams to this day, despite their subsequent experience on *The Pied Piper*. They would watch as Jacques lingered over such life-and-death decisions as the choosing of the wine, before echoing their approval of his choice. If he had but known, the Puttnams' budget was such that a bottle of wine was a rarity, while Patsy's mealtime specialities often consisted of a heaped plate of thickly-cut sandwiches.

When David introduced Jacques to Donovan, the whole affair really turned ugly. Demy semed to lose faith completely in Andrew's original screenplay, then became more and more dismissive about Donovan's songs. Of 10 submitted, he said he only cared for two of them. As the production lurched along, David stood by as Demy changed the film from being scriptural to a production designer's movie. Soon Andrew's script, which David had considered dense but extremely playable, had long since gone by the board. David realized he was watching a disaster in the making, but had not the faintest notion how to stop it.

When the film was assembled in rough cut back in London, Andrew was asked along. What did he think of it? David wanted to know. 'Appalling,' Andrew replied, 'and moreover, I want my name taken off it.' This proved impractical, since in those days to get payment on determination of credit it was necessary to have one's name affixed.

Andrew could see that David was angry at his reaction, but was unrepentant. He had been asked for his opinion and had given it. David was in the unhappy position of having to sell the film and continued to delude himself it had some redeeming features. Even when the self-deception could no longer be sustained, he had to maintain a front with outsiders and put his best face on it.

For the first time David was in the unhappy position of having a film run away from him. *Melody* had been an easy shoot, by the same token earning no spurs for David. On *The Pied Piper* at least some lessons had been learned and some spurs earned.

David and Patsy rented a Soho preview theatre and ran the film for a group of close friends to mark the tenth anniversary of their wedding in 1971. After the final credits rolled the lights went up in the little cinema. Alan Parker got to his feet. 'That's the worst film I've ever seen,' he muttered. Terence Donovan was shocked at Alan's tactlessness, taking the view that such criticism was inappropriate for the occasion. While David accepted his friend's outburst philosophically ('He was right,' he said later, 'it *is* a piece of shit.'), Terence and Alan have not spoken again since. 'I hadn't realized back then the emotional investment anyone has in making a film,' says Alan, 'so, as his friend, I tended to speak before I thought.'

The film had been run with the first reel missing. 'Even in those days,' Alan chuckles, 'David was *such* a mover. *The Pied Piper* had this terrible first reel, absolutely dreadful, and because this first reel was so awful, every time he showed it to people he'd claim that the missing reel was still in the lab. He did this on at least twenty different occasions. People would say to one another, "Has anyone *ever* seen the first reel?" No one ever did, I think, until the first night!'

Paramount in the US initially planned a Christmas 1971 release for what they perceived as a kiddies' fable. When they viewed the finished movie, there was a swift change of mind. It finally surfaced eight months later as the bottom half of a double-bill in a few playdates. *Village Voice* described the picture as being 'virtually unmarketable', adding that 'very little can be said about Donovan, who performs a few of his typically tiresome songs', the ones that Jacques Demy had allowed to remain, 'and who has considerably less personality than his rodent adversaries'. However, there was one saving grace, the *Voice* reckoned: 'Demy seems to have understood his star's limitation,' they said, 'because the camera generally tracks away from Donovan as soon as he begins singing.'

The film's varnished tones and doom-laden scenario, including not only the swarming rats, but poverty, infanticide and the Black Death, baffled many other reviewers, who wondered for whom the alleged kiddies' fable had ever been intended.

The failure of *The Pied Piper* was a bitter pill for David to swallow and it taught him a lesson he was never to forget. He had been made to compromise from his original choice of director and paid the price by hiring someone established on the international market of whom he was somewhat in awe. Intimidated by Demy's reputation, he had given in to him every step of the way. He vowed that in future as a producer he would remain in charge of each project, for he could see that the alternative would be one disastrous compromise after another.

Thoroughly disabused as to the film's commercial prospects, Goodtimes' hope was that Hemdale would shelve it completely and save the company the embarrassment of a press showing in Britain. Four months passed after its Stateside opening before Hemdale took it down from the shelf in Britain in time for Christmas 1972, with an 'A' certificate affixed. Alexander Walker in the *Evening Standard* dubbed it 'A migraine-inducing film. The one good laugh occurs at the start when a title announcing that the period is "The years of the Black

Death" is followed immediately by the trademark, "A Goodtimes Enterprises Film".'

Andrew Birkin had to swallow hard at the notice one critic gave the film, which basically said what a ghastly script Andrew and the others had written, and that it was a measure of Demy's genius the film still had some style. One example cited was almost the only Birkin touch left in the picture depicting rats emerging from a wedding cake. (*Time Out* would later refer to *The Pied Piper* as one of the great undiscovered masterpieces of British cinema, a review that David reckons tells us more about the *Time Out* critic than it does about the movie.) It was clearly time for the Goodtimes' partners to move on, heads bloody but unbowed.

To Debbie and Sacha, Sandy was firmly established as the indulgent uncle every child should have. His breezy, buccaneering attitude to life manifested itself to them in the most likable way imaginable. If he baby-sat for David and Patsy, the kids knew Sandy could be relied upon to let them sit up that bit later and enjoy midnight snacks – all the things their wicked parents denied them in fact! He had joined the Terence Donovan 'good guys' club.

By the time *The Pied Piper* had completed production in 1971, David was running pell-mell after a third property, whose scale dwarfed anything the company had tackled before. *Melody*, and even *The Pied Piper*, would look like easy calls beside the monumental problems *Inside the Third Reich* would provide.

Chapter 5

David at War

While Andrew Birkin was on the plane to Germany to visit *The Pied Piper* location, he came across a fascinating interview with Albert Speer in *Playboy* magazine. The author of *Inside the Third Reich* expanded openly on how he had joined the Nazi Party as a young man. A product of the middle classes, not particularly a Nazi, not particularly a Communist, he recognized his was a second-rate talent as an architect and that if he was going to succeed, he would need a patron.

At dinner that evening with David, Andrew declared he had just found the next subject he wanted to do. 'So have I,' replied David. They both then produced the same copy of *Playboy* and the Speer article. The identical point in the Speer interview had struck David, where Speer stated: 'The following day I joined what became the Nazi Party and a week later it was my twenty-third birthday.' David thought, 'To spend the rest of your life haunted by a decision you made at 23 . . .' That interested him very much, for he had always wanted to make a film about second chances in life. After all, he had been given one, hadn't he? The next step was to read the book itself, which took Andrew three days and nights, his copy emerging prolifically annotated.

When the book was brought to Sandy's attention, it was to make a tremendous impression on him as well. 'I saw it as an amazing revelation about Nazi Germany,' he says. 'It was the first thing I'd ever read that brought into focus the mentality behind the Nazi movement and the fascists. There was nothing I'd ever been exposed to that had such a powerful effect on me, particularly being Jewish. We all of us ended up with a passion to make a movie of Speer's book.'

With Andrew engaged to write a screenplay, the three associates flew to Germany to talk with Speer's publishers. Following this, David and Andrew flew to Heidelberg to see Speer himself, to discuss their hopes of adapting his book for the screen. Every major company in the world had also made a bid for the book, it seemed, but it was Goodtimes that Speer selected.

70

The acquisition was a great coup for the small company. David swore he could feel the earth move under his feet. Could they rise to the occasion? While Andrew continued to develop his script, David hammered out a deal with Paramount – for a fee of $150,000, Goodtimes would produce the film for worldwide release. This represented the first whiff of big money for the team, together with an awesome responsibility.

In the process of script development, David and Andrew came to know Speer well. Andrew's relationship with the author went deeper, for he saw a parallel between Speer's relationship and unswerving devotion to the Führer, and his own allegiance to Stanley Kubrick. 'I would have done almost anything for Stanley,' he says, 'and just about did! I could put myself in Speer's shoes if I was a writer or director and this character came along and said, "You make the films you want to make, and turn a blind eye to what else is going on." When I first met Speer, I was very much in awe of the situation, that old routine that you're shaking the hand of the man who shook hands with the Führer, but Speer was utterly charming in his slightly Machiavellian way and I think he rather took to us. He'd only been let out of Spandau three or four years earlier, where he'd been since the Nuremberg trials, and the only people he'd seen were learned historians like Trevor Roper and Bulloch. David and I were a couple of rather naïve Englishmen, asking the kind of questions a kid would ask. I think our ingenuousness appealed to him. He told me later that he rather looked upon me as one of his sons, for although he had five of his own, none of them ever wanted to talk about Nazi Germany.'

During one of the early meetings between David, Andrew and the tall, saturnine, distinguished-looking German, Speer suddenly halted in mid-conversation. 'Oh,' he said, 'I think I've got some old 16mm home movies we took in those days somewhere in the cellar. I've never looked at them, since I don't have a projector. I'll go and get them anyway.'

The excitement David and Andrew felt when Speer left was almost a tangible thing, which mounted as he reappeared with a pile of boxes, neatly labelled 'Agfa'. 'Here they are, but there's no projector unfortunately,' he said. Quickly excusing themselves, David and Andrew drove into Heidelberg and hired a 16mm projector from the only photographic shop they could find. Back at Speer's home they carefully fed the fragile history they held in their hands into the gate, terrified they might scratch or break it. Then they sat back to watch the show, projected against a white pillowcase pinned to some curtains.

A girl came up and waved at the camera. 'That's Eva,' said Speer. Then Adolf Hitler came out, smiling broadly and waving. David turned to look at Andrew, his mouth open. This was film that had never seen the light of day in 30 years. With hindsight, there was something repellent about it, yet on the screen it was utterly fascinating. David and Andrew became convinced that this very ambivalence held the key to their adaptation of Speer's book.

Andrew stayed on to work with Speer, who referred to him by his first name, while reverentially referring to David at all times as 'Mr Puttnam'. Speer was in the habit, at the end of each day, of putting on a piece of music, usually something by Strauss, which Andrew was obliged to listen to for about an hour and a half before he left, with no talking permitted. When one day Speer selected Mahler's Ninth Symphony, Andrew was sure something was on his mind. As the music ended, Speer turned to him.

'I have to tell you that there's just been an article published in America that states I knew everything about the Nazi extermination problem. I feel that after this you and Mr Puttnam will no longer wish to continue making the movie.'

He then showed Andrew the article, which had been telexed to him from New York. Such was Speer's sense of self-importance, that he felt the story would make the front page of the *New York Times* and the world press the following day, and that therefore Andrew and 'Mr Puttnam' would inevitably see it. In fact, it failed to spread beyond the pages of a small Zionist magazine, but it did purport to quote chapter and verse of the various meetings Speer had attended where the mechanics of the infamous final solution were discussed.

Andrew's attitude was expressed directly to Speer as he explained in all honesty, 'Speaking personally, it doesn't make any difference to me at all, since I always assumed that you *did* know all about it and turned a blind eye to it.'

'Well, yes, that may well be correct,' Speer admitted. 'Perhaps I did. But –' he hesitated and frowned '– how will Mr Puttnam take it?'

Andrew decided to call David up there and then to explain the situation to him in Speer's presence. 'I've assured him it won't make any difference to how *I* feel about it as *we* always assumed that, to a greater or lesser extent, he was aware of what was happening, didn't *we?*' was the gist of the guidance he gave David. 'Is Speer in the room?' David wanted to know. Andrew nodded furiously, replying, 'Yes, yes, very much so.' There was a brief pause during which Andrew swears he could hear his colleague's brain weighing up the information.

'Well,' said David finally, 'what can we do about it? Is this good news or bad news?'

'Very good news,' Andrew replied, 'for it gives us the licence to confront the situation in the film.'

At the end of the conversation Speer's mind seemed to be at rest regarding 'Mr Puttnam's' reaction. Andrew asked for his agreement that a scene should now be inserted of a gathering of officials, Speer included, listening to Himmler in 1942 as he told them, 'We all know of the *problem*. We have to face it and do something about it.'

Many months later David received a vitriolic letter from Speer's publisher, asking how they had dared to put the scene in. 'Herr Speer,' they wrote, 'never knew anything about an extermination programme.' Andrew and David were summoned to Berlin, where Speer had indeed amended his position. Somehow or other, agreement was still reached to leave the scene in. Andrew's point to Speer was, 'You can always say this is only a movie. It's a painting, not a photograph, and I think it's far better to err on the side of your knowing more than you did.' It turned out that Speer had been worried about another aspect of the news even more than 'Mr Puttnam's' reaction: that it was his protestations of ignorance that let him off so lightly at Nuremberg.

When the finished script was in their hands, Paramount was divided between those who thought they had a wonderful project and the contingent who considered the film either anti-Semitic, or at the very least 'soft on the Nazis'. Andrew would submit that he tried to reflect Speer's point of view that if Hitler was painted as the Devil, no one would recognize other Hitlers as they came along, since they were only human beings and not necessarily given to chewing carpets. Andrew received a considerable set-back when he proudly submitted his script to film director Carol Reed, his cousin and mentor.

'Andrew,' Reed told him on the phone, 'it's wonderful, you've done a *wonderful* job. You've shown us what it was like to live in the Depression after the Great War, inflation rampant and the rest of it, and this young man, with his head full of dreams, meeting Hitler. They plan for a new Germany together – it's just tremendous and it's all going so well for them too, it's all going *so* well – and then *tragedy*! They lose the war.'

There was silence on the line as Reed stopped talking and Andrew gathered his startled thoughts. 'Well, is that how you see it?' he asked, rather lamely. 'Look, Andrew,' said Reed, 'you can't have a scene with Hitler and a dog without the audience loving him. You painted him as a human being, and if that was your intention, great! You've done it wonderfully.' If Andrew had intended to portray Hitler as a slightly misguided human who just had this one thing about Jews (rather like Neville Chamberlain, Reed pointed out, who was renowned for saying, 'Yes, it's ghastly about the Jews in Germany, but have you ever met a Jew you could trust?') then he had succeeded.

Andrew felt his bellows well and truly punctured. David shared his concern, for they both realized the enormous responsibility they were carrying. This was a film which in theory would be seen by middle-class America, precisely for whom David intended it in one way. Yet because a lot of it was in Andrew's oblique and understated style, there was a real danger it might come out and lead a vast section of America to think Hitler was right in many respects. Not about the Jews, but that the man had an interesting – and, from a German point of view – defensible position. Speer himself provided the perfect example, receiving hundreds of letters from Americans, including many eminent people, saying they felt he was a splendid individual and that it was a pity things hadn't worked out. This fuelled the argument from those factions at Paramount who hated the film.

Then there was the problem of a suitable director. Sandy had sent the script to Stanley Kubrick, thinking he would be fascinated by the challenge of the subject. Andrew had recalled being on location in German South West Africa for Kubrick on *2001*, where for a couple of marks Nazi magazines could be procured, still fresh in their boxes from Berlin. Andrew had purchased a trunk-load of the stuff, all of which Kubrick had kept. At the same time Sandy, of all of them, might have anticipated Kubrick's eventual response: 'I'm Jewish. I can't – *don't* see how I can make it.' He obviously felt it was an impossible subject, for how indeed did one arrive at the *right* approach?

After Kubrick the man everyone, except Paramount, was most enthusiastic about was Nicolas Roeg, who had co-directed Sandy's earlier *Performance*. When he came round for a meeting with David he seemed to be in favour of a Bertolucci-esque approach. He said, 'Well, I see this film opening with a boxing match, for instance.'

David egged him on.

'Great! But why a boxing match?'

Roeg shrugged. 'Dunno,' he replied. 'Anyway – something symbolic.'

Andrew was so enthused that he told David he was prepared to rewrite the entire script if necessary, to accommodate Roeg's vision. Paramount plumped for the safer choice of Peter Yates, from whom a somewhat more pedestrian reading of the project was relayed, while

David fought to have Costa Garvas considered. After six months this was squelched when Costa Garvas himself lost his enthusiasm.

While David and Andrew were in Vienna, looking for suitable Austrian locations they could use in the increasingly unlikely event they would ever be required, a girl was despatched from a London newspaper to report on their progress. David was allocated the task of showing her around and came to Andrew later in desperation. 'What the hell am I going to do?' he asked. 'From the first moment we met she's been coming on to me, she's obviously looking for the quick pick-up. So anyway, I've told her that you and I are having an affair. Andrew, you've got to follow up for me.'

Birkin looked at his friend incredulously. 'You've told her *what?*' he asked. David grinned. 'Don't get carried away,' he said. 'I don't *really* fancy you. I just need you to corroborate my story to get this girl off my back.'

A few moments after David's departure Andrew was visited by an extremely penitent reporter, clearly on the verge of tears. 'Gosh, Andrew, I'm so sorry,' she declared. 'I didn't realize that you and David – I mean, that I was coming between a beautiful relationship. I just want you to know I think gay love is wonderful.'

All the acutely embarrassed Andrew could utter was, 'Oh, well – *yes*. Quite. Thank you very much.' Then he put his arms around her comfortingly, but not for too long, in case she got the wrong idea. She left for London on the next plane.

David's intuition had for some time told him that the film was in decline at Paramount. It was off the boil, no longer the hottest subject around, or perhaps too hot. It was one of those pictures that never had an actual death-knell. There never was a time when anyone would say the project was shelved, but time passed without a resolution to the manifold problems. In the end the option on the book ran out.

Sandy was left to deal with an extremely irate publisher, who had been promised Goodtimes would make a film of his client's book. Now other war books had come out and the heat was off. David's regret was the loss of what could have been a reputation-making project, one that had sustained him daily since first reading the original *Playboy* interview. Rather like the best way of getting over the death of a beloved pet is to quickly find another, practicality now told him it was time to cool the passion that had burned for *Inside the Third Reich*. Goodtimes had bitten off more than it could chew. The file had to be closed and he had to move on.

In one of Speer's letters to Andrew he wrote fairly emotionally to say how fond he was of him and how much their relationship meant, which Andrew largely put down to his showing the interest Speer longed for from his sons. Then, aware that David would be reading the letter also, he concluded, 'I won't continue because I know Mr Puttnam would not approve.'

Andrew could see the point at which David's antennae told him it was time to put his eggs in other baskets. Many of his friends uncharitably suggested he had been taken advantage of by David, then dumped, first on *The Pied Piper*, now on *Inside the Third Reich*. The fact that Andrew had risen in the process from dogsbody to an accredited and respected screenwriter appeared to have been somewhat overlooked. Andrew's feeling was that while David may have seduced, it had never been the case of rape. It was a mark of the esteem in which David held Andrew that he now offered him a guaranteed £10,000 a year to write two scripts. When Andrew held back and asked for some time to think, David misinterpreted his hesitation.

'Look,' he said, 'that's all *I* make and I don't work any less hard than you do. So why should you make more than me?'

In fact, it had been the idea of having to turn out two scripts a year that had made Andrew hesitate. *Inside the Third Reich* had taken 15 months to write, and if that counted as one script, the Birkin household would be in deep trouble. Since David had focused on the question of money, however, Andrew chose to question what he saw as the astonishing revelation of David's own earnings. Although David was being utterly honest, Andrew decided against taking up the contract.

An unexpected cash boost was soon delivered to the beleaguered Birkin, as he was introduced to another producer desperate for a quick rewrite on a project. Although everyone, except the producer himself, recognized the material for the junk it was, Andrew obliged with his rewrite and for a few weeks' work received four times the payment he had for *Inside the Third Reich*. The introduction was made by one David Terence Puttnam.

David and Sandy were still determined to make something of the research material they had come up with during the long delays on *Inside the Third Reich*, despite their loss of the rights to the book itself. When Paramount behaved impeccably and handed over their $150,000, it was decided to use the money to produce what became two documentaries. Two directors had been involved in the research, Lutz Becker and Phillipe Mora, and although they got along, each wanted to make his own film. Then there was the sheer amount of material garnered, far too much for a single project, including as it did further incredible home movies taken by Hitler and Eva Braun themselves which Becker had unearthed. In archival terms it was a tremendous scoop, and Goodtimes had exclusive rights to the footage, established after a tough legal battle with the German Government.

The Double-headed Eagle and *Swastika* were widely praised, with David deciding on a bold experiment with *The Double-headed Eagle*, booking it into London's West End. When he and Patsy went along to see it on the Friday after it opened, they were in for what they now describe as 'a lonely experience'. While David still believes in the potential of feature-film documentaries, in this case the public did not want to know. Rights to both films were sold at home and abroad and they became very successful ventures. Of the two David prefers *The Double-headed Eagle*, covering Germany in the years 1918–1939, which he considers a more thoughtful film. With *Swastika* there was tremendous controversy, mainly stemming from the use of the Hitler/Eva Braun footage. In the wake of a *Time* magazine article the movie became a cause célèbre in the media. With the money Goodtimes realized from the two films, another documentary, *Brother, Can You Spare a Dime?* was commissioned from Phillipe Mora, covering the American depression of the thirties. It was to prove another fine piece of work.

David and Sandy next found themselves approached by Tony Elliott, who ran the London listings magazine, *Time Out*. With the advent of TV and instant news nightly, the old Movietone and Pathé newsreels shown in the cinemas had disappeared. Elliott's idea was to produce a *Time Out* newsreel, something along the lines of the old *March of Time* series, tackling subjects the media normally shied away from, for theatrical release. In the wake of Bloody Sunday, the proposed first subject was internment in Northern Ireland.

'I've got just the guy to pull it all together for you,' David told Elliott, 'name of Andrew Birkin.'

Andrew went on to research and co-produce the venture, travelling to Northern Ireland with Clinton Cavers of Goodtimes. Together they joined the Newry march, getting heavily involved and arguing with anyone that would take them on, to establish attitudes and feelings firsthand.

David himself decided to accompany Andrew on his next visit, which was to coincide with another march, this time protesting against conditions in the McGilligan internment camp. Patsy packed their sandwiches before they caught the morning flight over and counselled them both, 'Do be careful, for God's sake. Don't do anything stupid.'

On the march, David got into a heated argument with an R U C man who ordered him back in line. Andrew could scarcely believe his eyes and ears as he watched a new side to David, utterly defiant and fearless. He felt both intensely proud of him, and sick with fear at the same time, as David stood up to the officer, by now ominously beating time into his palm with his billy club. He was a citizen of the United Kingdom, David pointed out, there was no law that said he couldn't stand there, and he wasn't going to budge. Andrew saw the officer take in David's *Time Out* press badge, not the RUC's favourite, and groaned inwardly. All he could think was, 'Back off, David. For *God's* sake, back off!' Luckily the officer's attention was diverted by a scuffle taking place further down the line and the incident passed off, leaving David white-faced and shaking with rage and Andrew even whiter and shaking with relief and admiration.

Since the proposed *Time Out* feature at the end of the day had to be newsworthy, the idea was to gather as much background material as they could, with their hopes pinned on a slam-bang finalé from the anti-internment march scheduled for London in two weeks' time. Nine camera crews were assembled for this event so that absolutely nothing would be missed. 'If a fly shits, film it,' was the instruction. David asked Don McCullin, the Vietnam war photographer, to come along as a favour and take some stills in Trafalgar Square, where the march was due to end at three in the afternoon.

The expectation, and it was a reasonable one, was that there would be rioting instead of a peaceful demonstration. Some even predicted a bloodbath. In any event, it was a highly volatile situation that the *Time Out* newsreel unit was well placed to record for posterity. Any footage that did emerge could certainly be sold to ITN or BBC for their news broadcasts that evening, which would alone cover the costs of the venture; then they would be home free with their picture for national cinema release.

What happened instead, with nine movie cameras and one war photographer standing by, was one of the quietest and most orderly gatherings ever seen in London. 'I'm fucking off,' said a disgruntled Don McCullin after a couple of uneventful hours had passed. One of the cameramen came up to David and Tony Elliott and said, 'We've got absolutely fuck-all footage. Hasn't anyone got some marbles we could chuck under the police horses?' He received twin glares for his pains. The demonstration ended as peaceably as it had begun. There was no sale to the BBC or ITN, who mentioned the demonstration only in passing.

What *Time Out* was left with was many hours' film of the anatomy of a demonstration, exhibiting all the excitement and suspense of a

Sunday School picnic. The footage would have been useful for a police training programme, but proved an unexciting climax to *Bringing It All Back Home*, as the movie was called, which exploded across the nation's screens, (well, two or three of them at any rate) with all the impact of a box of waterlogged squibs. *Time Out*'s plan for a series of such ventures was promptly aborted.

The next project in which the rather unlucky combination of Andrew and David was involved was a proposed remake of *The Secret Garden*, for which Andrew wrote the script. David was very enthusiastic and threw his full support behind it, but M G M turned out to be the spanner in the works. They owned the rights, or claimed they did, and asked for an enormous sum to let them go, considering that their version of it, in 1949, had found little public acceptance. This children's classic, by the author of Little Lord Fauntleroy, Frances Hodgson Burnett, David saw as a small film which would be inexpensive to shoot. He worked out that the book was out of copyright, but M G M's attitude was that if he made the film they would meet him in court. M G M were not, however, prepared to guarantee that they even had anything to sell, so this was the rock the project foundered on.

Although it wasn't David's fault, Andrew still felt a certain distancing, a clear indication that the subject was no longer David's flavour of the month. It reminded him a little of his days with the author of *Inside the Third Reich*. 'Speer told me that he might join a line of ten people on any given morning waiting to see the Führer. If he had a roll of architect's plans in his hand and Hitler saw them, he would summon him to the head of the line, treating him with especial favour. When Speer became armaments minister or was slightly out of favour, he just had to join the line. He still got the half hour of the Führer's time, but it wasn't the same. That was rather the way with David, and I imagine remains the way. If it's something that's his number-one project at the time, you get to jump the line, whereas if he's moved to something else, he's still very kind and polite, but you join the line.'

For Andrew the *bottom* line with David, is this: 'I criticize him sometimes, yes, and we haven't always seen eye to eye. But if someone else criticizes him in my presence, I *leap* to his defence!'

When Sandy re-established contact with the London lawyer he had worked with at C M A, Frank Bloom agreed to represent Goodtimes. He was immediately struck by the new partner Sandy introduced.

'When I first met David,' says Frank, 'he obviously loved being a film producer, and was in love with the *idea* of being a film producer.

I'm not sure he ever structured his career, setting out with any positive ideas or goals. What he had instead was boundless, infectious enthusiasm and the energy to carry his ideas through.'

Once they were in business together, Frank discovered that David was also an extremely competent desk man. With his company sending a plethora of letters to Goodtimes on expensively-printed paper replete with full lists of his partners and other recurrent data, Frank suggested to David that a plain memo-pad system be devised. 'He wouldn't hear of it,' laughs Frank, 'reckoning the idea was cold and unfeeling. He loved the pomp and circumstance of the prestige letter-heading.'

To keep the pot boiling during the delays on *Inside the Third Reich*, and still searching for that elusive mainstream hit, David gave Alan Parker a choice of two sources from which he wanted scripts developed. One was a book, *Calf Love*, the other a song, '1941', from a Nilsson album. Alan chose *Calf Love*. When Ray Connolly called round early in 1972 to borrow a book on Elvis that he needed, David found that Ray knew and liked the Nillson album, and '1941' in particular.

'OK, you're a writer,' he said. 'Do you want to take a crack at writing the film?'

Ray looked at him disbelievingly. 'That'll be the day,' he replied.

'That'll do for the title,' David retorted.

With the expiry of their lease in Ranelagh Grove rapidly approaching, Patsy decided that a spot of househunting was in order. Someone had to do it, she knew. If it was left to David, the Puttnams would be out on the street.

Chapter 6

'They'll Demand A Sequel'

Now David was in films he seemed to have even less time with his family than before. The saving grace was that he was happy doing what he wanted to do – and Patsy was involved in his every decision. She would explain patiently to him that they only had a year and a half to go on their lease, then a year, then that they really had to think about a move. Finally she was given several options. She could look for a house, in SW1, SW10, SW3 or SW7. The problem was that every time some money came in, David wanted to buy the rights to another book. In the end, Patsy had to say, 'Look, *I* need a bit of that!'

Patsy looked at everything that sounded remotely suitable in the approved areas. Her search ended in Queensgate Place Mews in South Kensington, although it hardly looked like the house of anyone's dreams. Except to Patsy.

There was a huge garage on the ground floor, full of old cars. Someone had been making a vain attempt to carve out a living-room on the first floor. The top flat was a magnificent drawing-room – or rather Patsy could see that it might be, once its beautiful glass cupola ceiling was de-gunged. She could see how it would all work – an enormous kitchen on the ground floor, big enough for the whole family to eat in, separate bedrooms on the next floor and the sumptuous drawing-room above.

She described it to David, who listened distractedly in between phone calls. It sounded to him like hell on wheels, but he reluctantly agreed to at least go along and see it. On the great day she stood back while he surveyed it from the outside, then picked his way through the floors inside. When he came out he looked at it again and Patsy noticed that this time he had an odd, somewhat baffled expression on his face. 'You must be totally mad,' he told her. 'You are now absolutely, totally mad.' Then he smiled and looked at her. 'You're a hopeless case.' Patsy saw her chance.

'*Believe* me,' she pleaded. '*Trust* me, I can turn this into something.'

He thought for a few seconds and turned to look at the property again. 'I've got no time,' he said. 'You'd have to do everything yourself.'

Patsy felt she was at the point of victory. 'I won't ask for anything, I will do everything,' she promised, and hugged him.

The key to the success of the entire venture was Patsy obtaining planning permission to turn the garage into living-quarters, for she quickly discovered that the adopted plan for Kensington was to lure families back into the inner city. With the vital permission obtained, the house was purchased on a mortgage, with further money borrowed to pay architects' fees. Patsy practically lived in the mews by day, nipping back home just in time to pick up the children, who were in a rebellious frame of mind at the thought of the impending move. Debbie was ten, Sacha was six and for them their stay in Pimlico had been one of blissful content, for the cul-de-sac was full of children their own age with whom they attended the local school, and they both had masses of chums they would now have to leave behind. They became reconciled to it in the end, but it was a close-run thing, with many a mutinous murmur heard beneath the normal family banter.

Patsy reckons that the scene on the day of the move from Pimlico sums up David's involvement. She had the removal men in and was as organized as she could be although aware that they were moving into absolute shambles at the mews, where the builder had let her down. David was about to depart for three months to the Isle of Wight to do *That'll Be the Day*. No problem, she thought, everything can be sorted out by the time he returns.

As David sat in their bedroom, deeply engrossed in a phone call, Patsy told the removal men to clear every other room first. When they finally had nothing left but the bedroom, David was still on the phone.

'Excuse me, ma'am, we've got to go in there now,' they appealed to Patsy.

'OK, take everything except the bed. Take the dressing-table, then the chairs.'

Slowly the men removed each item of furniture as David, on the phone the whole time, moved from chair to chair to bed. Either he moved or the men moved him, until everything else was gone except the bed.

'Ma'am, we've got to take the bed now,' they told Patsy, who nodded hesitantly, then watched as they delicately started by picking up the pillows. As soon as they began to move the bed itself, David got up, staring at them as if they had just broken into the house. In his best North London Cockney, with the phone still held in his hand, he yelled,

'*Wot's* happening here? Wot *is* going on?'

'Bye, David,' Patsy said, watching her husband returning to his phone conversation. She then got into the van with the removal men, Debbie and Sacha and drove to their new home where she helped with the unloading. David locked up the house and left for the Isle of Wight. It was the last Patsy saw of him for two months.

On David's return he was accompanied by Andrew Birkin, who had glimpsed the property in its original state. A Christmas tree with lights ablaze welcomed them from the ground-floor window. Patsy had worked nothing less than a loving miracle on the house, filling it with colour, light and warmth, and furnishing it exquisitely. Andrew stood at the door, looked in, gasped and muttered something about how wonderful it was, clearly moved. Then he disarmingly burst into tears, the emotion sparked by a potent mixture of self-pity and outright envy. Still a single man then, he saw David as the guy who had everything. For David it was, 'Fine! We're here now. Great! The family's still going on.'

Further large chunks of autobiography were stirred into the mix that became *That'll Be the Day*. The two colleagues worked closely together, David beating a path to Ray's house for breakfast every morning to collect the pages Ray had written the previous day. Next morning he would return with any revisions and take away another batch. Within six weeks the script was complete.

The main character was Jim MacLaine, a school drop-out whose adventures the plot chronicled. Ray acknowledges that the wet, sensible character in the film was based on him, whereas Jim MacLaine was far more David, the tearaway who dumps his schoolbooks.

David had the idea to incorporate his father's magical return from World War II at midnight into the movie, thus seizing the opportunity to frame and preserve the scene for all time. As if to underline the thought, he cast Sacha as the child he had been, adding a surrealistic three-generational touch, the first occasion on which David had etched his signature on the screen.

Ray was particularly taken with one scene, which had the Jim MacLaine character initiated into the joys of sex during his stay at a holiday camp. 'I wouldn't let anyone else,' the allegedly inexperienced girl he takes back to his chalet tells him. 'You're the only one.' After making love, in fairly rapid time, there is a pause before the girl asks, with a rather disappointed expression in her voice. 'Do you always come so quickly?'

This tickled Ray so much he had to share it with David, who fell about laughing as well when his colleague popped over to the house with the new pages. Patsy came into the kitchen. 'What's so funny?' she asked.

'It's this scene Ray's written,' David explained. 'Go on, Ray, tell her –'

Ray duly obliged, but could soon deduce from Patsy's disapproving demeanour that she was less than amused. David and Ray felt like two grubby schoolboys caught out doing something unsavoury by the head-mistress.

Sandy took David along to meet Nat Cohen of E M I Films, a man whose name was already a legend in the film business. David had the feeling Nat would see him as someone from the brash world of advertising who had hustled his way into movies. After all, it was Sandy Nat knew and trusted.

At the end of their meeting with Nat, together with his assistant Philip Collins, a handshake deal was struck. 'I'm going to give you half the money you need for *That'll Be the Day*,' Nat told the partners, 'Now find the other half and you're in business.'

'I think he liked you,' Sandy whispered on the way out.

What neither of them knew was that Evelyn de Rothschild had cannily asked Nat for a reference on Sandy's business acumen before making his original investment in Goodtimes. Nat had given Sandy a first-class report, but after the company's various setbacks, he had begun to wonder if he had misled his friend. It certainly sweetened the pot for Rothschild when Nat agreed to help with *That'll Be the Day*'s finance, although Nat was genuinely taken with the idea for the film – and its presenters.

'They were both very charming, bright young boys,' said Nat. 'Sandy I'd known, David was new to me, but I was struck immediately. He sold himself and sold his goods too. Very commendable.'

Philip Collins recalls the meeting and the subsequent relationship between Nat, David and Sandy. 'He had a great affection for them both and took a real paternal interest in them. He regarded them as two of the brightest guys around.'

Faced with the challenge of finding the other half of the budget, David rose superbly to the occasion. Although he makes no claims to be an inventor, that is just what he became with the record tie-in idea he originated. When the record division of E M I turned him down, David went to Ronco, offering a bizarre deal. If they put up £100,000 for the film, he would guarantee to feature a minimum amount of rock classics on the soundtrack, which Ronco could then release on a double-album. Flush with cash from their compilations of forties' and fifties' music, Ronco agreed and added a further guarantee of a minimum sum they would spend on cross-promotion of the album and movie. David and Ray went through the script, marking it every so often where they could put a record player or radio in the scene. Characters took to wandering along beaches and through fairgrounds, *anything* to squeeze in the necessary tracks.

Pop star David Essex was hired to play the self-confessed 'Puttnam role' of Jim Maclaine, the school dropout trying to make his way in the world, with Ringo Starr cast as the streetwise friend he encounters. David and Ray had made an appointment with Ringo at the Beatles' Apple offices, thinking they could draw on the experience of someone who had been through the Jim MacLaine trip. Their talk with him went so well that David suggested that he should accept the part in the movie.

A director new to films, Claude Whatham, was hired to pilot what had become an extremely personal Puttnam project. In many ways it was too personal a vision for David simply to stand back and watch someone else's interpretation. After all, this was David's first mainstream film since *The Pied Piper* fiasco. He had sworn never to allow a situation like that to develop again.

'With Claude I had to get a little bit muscular; that was quite clear very early on,' he says. 'We'd originally offered it to Michael Apted, who turned it down, so we went to Claude because I'd seen *Cider with Rosie* and he obviously had a wonderful sense of period which was important to our movie. Ray and I were also concerned that we were too rock 'n' roll orientated and there may be other values in the film that could and should be stressed, so we went to Claude specifically because he was patently disinterested in rock 'n' roll.

'This was an intelligent idea, until it became very clear that not only was he not unfamiliar with rock 'n' roll but there were whole sub-texts to the story that he absolutely didn't understand. This became evident once we'd started shooting and it caused a lot of distress. There was one extraordinary sequence where David Essex is wandering round a fairground at night, which we shot one night in Southsea. Dawn was coming up, and we still hadn't shot the boy on the whip. I said to Claude, "We haven't got to the really pivotal thing, which is the kid on the whip." He said, "Well, if we get to it, we get to it; it's just another fairground thing." And I said, "It is *not* just another fairground thing. The whole point of this scene is that it shows Maclaine's original stirrings of why there is a class structure operating within this society. He sees that the guy on the whip, the most dangerous piece of equipment, is the one who pulls the two girls and is the most glamorous figure in the fairground." Claude said, "I didn't realize that."

'Here we were, at four o'clock in the morning with the sun coming up, he's never even *cast* the kid, it turned out. We had to find some guy in the crowd who was prepared to have his hair cut short. It was like a bloody nightmare and there was a tremendous row over that. For other things Claude did very well, but then he threw a wobbly one day and said he wasn't coming in, didn't feel very well. I called Alan Parker and I said. "Al, I don't have a director. Would you come in?" And Alan came in and directed for two days. Claude got better *very* fast. I'm certainly not saying that he hadn't felt ill in the first place, but the insurance company were unhappy. The idea that we hadn't closed down and waited for Claude just *freaked* him.'

With the film in the can, and his producer muscles well and truly flexed, David found he had underspent. Proudly he went back to Nat Cohen and handed him a cheque. 'What's this?' demanded the doughty Nat. 'It's money we saved on the budget,' David explained. Nat handed him the cheque back. 'I allocated the full amount for *That'll Be the Day*; use it for some aspect of the movie, its promotion, whatever you choose.'

That Goodtimes were on the verge of their biggest success was confirmed when the film opened well in 1973, and to good reviews. Ray Connolly remembers David coming to his house on the Saturday evening following its opening at the ABC cinema in Shaftesbury Avenue and driving him to Fleet Street to wait for the Sunday papers to get the reviews. They were worth waiting for.

George Melly reckoned the film was not to be missed on several counts, like the amazing fifties' accuracy and David Essex and Ringo Starr's fine performances. 'Satisfyingly intelligent work from England,' noted Gavin Miller, adding, 'the film has a great deal of the atmosphere of *The Last Picture Show* without the American movie's faint air of affectation.'

'A study of adolescence, at once honest and harsh, persuasive and sad, and sometimes very funny,' enthused Eric Shorter in the *Daily Telegraph*. While of the opinion it was a very slight story, amounting to something less than the sum of its parts, Derek Malcolm in the *Guardian* found the film consistently enjoyable. 'Well written by Ray Connolly, directed with some imagination by Claude Whatham and splendidly acted,' was his summing up.

Alexander Walker in the London *Evening Standard* was unstinting in his praise, claiming that the film opened a floodgate of memories for him, with its reproduction of the era of Elvis, James Dean, Sandra Dee, teddy-boys, stiletto heels, Tony Curtis haircuts and coffee-bars.

Ray Connolly had succeeded, Walker reckoned, because he had not set out to exploit the era. 'The thing I like most about this very enjoyable film is its honesty,' he wrote. 'It doesn't cheapen what it sets out to recall, but illustrates it with a kindly, charitable light that explains without excusing, analyses without endorsing.' His mention of the men behind the film was unusual for a review in those days, but clearly Walker felt them worth noting, as he added, 'Producers David Puttnam and Sanford Lieberson have made something freshly native and all of a piece.'

'They'll demand a sequel,' David informed Ray before *That'll Be the Day* had even opened. Nat Cohen called David three weeks after the première. 'This film of yours is *unbelievable*,' he told him. 'It's doing more business the third week than it did in the first. What about a sequel?'

David used to stand outside the ABC in Shaftesbury Avenue on Friday nights and buy any remaining seats, for he had found out that the manager only used to notify 'Sold Out' houses to head office. Their method of judging the following week's bookings and level of promotion was based on the Thursday and Friday night's returns, so if a house sold out on these nights, the film was retained for a further week, with additional advertising money pumped in. For weeks after making this discovery David would spend £20 or so to ensure a 'Sold Out' return. He regarded it as money well spent. On one occasion David took Ray along to the ABC to watch the queues. Gesturing at the crowd, he turned to his friend. 'I've waited four years for this sight, Ray,' he said.

The film came over quite differently from the cheap exploitation effort that might have been expected by anyone unfamiliar with David. Despite Goodtimes' need for cash flow (and indeed the cash did subsequently flow in) obvious commercial angles were ignored in favour of Ray Connolly's biting acerbity and wit. The film never talked down to its audience for one second and recreated the fifties' era without resorting to the use of rose-tinted spectacles. David acknowledges it was the first film he made where he really knew what he was doing, a film he had believed in from the beginning. At last he felt master of his own destiny. If until now the jury had been out on his ability to succeed in films, after *That'll Be the Day* the verdict was in. By the nature of things, the question now was – would the film turn out to be the one good book everyone is said to have inside them?

The movie's success was accelerated by the release and T V promotion of Ronco's double album of soundtrack hits, the company going on to sell over 600,000 units. Despite a disappointing lack of business in the U S, *That'll Be the Day* went on to yield a net profit of over £400,000 against a cost of less than £300,000.

David and Ray worked in the same way on the sequel, *Stardust*. David wanted the story set in the early sixties, while Ray wanted to update it to the seventies. A compromise was reached that the film would cover all of the sixties, tracking the rise and fall of Jim MacLaine, pop superstar. When David took a house for the summer south of Rome, he was joined by Ray. *Stardust*'s storyline was laid down in a week.

Ray acknowledges that working with David on the two films was unlike any other experience he has had with producers. So many ideas came tumbling out of David that even if Ray knocked several of them back, there were plenty to spare and no offence taken. Instead it was, 'Fine, O K, now what if we did this instead?' The credit on both films, Ray reckons, should read, 'Story by Ray Connolly and David Puttnam'.

Their first choice to direct *Stardust* was Alan Parker, but he turned it down in favour of Jack Rosenthal's play *The Evacuees*, which he directed for television in 1973. It was back to their first choice for *That'll Be the Day*, Michael Apted, a man whose work they had admired on the big screen with *Triple Echo* and on television with *Another Sunday* and *Sweet F A*.

Alan Parker continued to watch, fascinated, as David applied himself to his areas of limited knowledge. After attending their first union meeting together, Alan declared, 'We're babies. Political babies.' Walking back to their car they discussed how little of the union's general meeting they had understood. On many issues they had failed even to grasp how to vote, let alone understand how the entire procedure seemed to be manipulated by people with diametrically opposed views to theirs.

'You're right,' David agreed. 'I never realized until today how little I knew about this lot, but I promise I'm going to learn.'

And learn he did, as Alan saw. David proceeded to absorb every detail of the union process. His secretary, Lynda Smith, would often see her boss at the end of a long working day, loading up his briefcase for a union meeting. 'He spent years going to them,' she observed. 'How he could be bothered half the time I don't know. Other men would be off for a drink or rushing home. David would be off to a meeting.'

Rank tried to woo David away from his original backer, but he chose to stay with Nat Cohen, with the American end sewn up with Columbia. 'Nat used to do a very sensible thing,' says David. 'That is only work out what his *downside* risk was, the *most* he would lose, so consequently he would never turn down a project that was remotely interesting. What he would say was "I'll give you £150,000", knowing that the film costs £250,000. It was *your* problem how you found the other £100,000.'

Sandy agrees. 'Nat Cohen was a great supporter, someone I'd worked with as an agent. Quite a character. He gave us a blank cheque in effect, but always kept the reins on. The man had a real flair for movies and was such an underrated figure in the British Film Industry in the sixties and seventies, probably the most underrated. He made a tremendous contribution, not only for the films that David and I made, but also for Joseph Janni, John Schlesinger and Ken Loach. He backed *people*. If he liked you, he'd back you. He hated failure, that was the one thing Nat couldn't stand to be associated with.'

With David Essex lined up to play Jim MacLaine once again, Ringo Starr declined a role in the sequel. 'I lived through it,' he told David. 'I don't want to act it.'

David turned his sights on ex-pop singer Adam Faith after watching him on television playing a small-time Cockney crook in Budgie. 'I haven't even got time to read the script, let alone play the part,' was Adam's response.

'Look,' said David, 'read it. It's the greatest part you'll ever get offered; it's exactly what you should do. If you don't like it, I'll send you a crate of any champagne you care to name.'

Adam eventually read the first few pages in bed on Christmas morning, and decided he had to phone David immediately.

'Dave, OK, I'm definitely going to do it. It's *fabulous*.'

'Marvellous, Adam. Have you read it all?'

'Only four pages. It's enough.'

Ray Connolly and Michael Apted thought Adam was an interesting choice, but were less than totally enthusiastic. David arranged a meeting in a recording studio with the singer. Following an adjournment to a nearby Italian restaurant in Holborn, Ray and Michael were sold – although Ray was convinced then, and remains convinced, he was merrily flogged a bill of goods by the Puttnam/Faith alliance, or Faith at least.

'He conned us again and again,' Ray recalls with a broad grin, 'just like the character I'd written for the film, exhibiting all the collusive crumminess and cunning I'd put in. I thought – well, that was quite an act! It could be that David clued him in, that I'm not sure about, but I knew from his performance Adam was perfect.'

All David will admit now, with an impish smile, is 'I pushed very hard for Adam.' As far as Adam himself is concerned, 'I'm only glad Ray hadn't written the part for a one-legged guy. I think Puttnam would have had my leg off!'

Nor was the battle yet over, as the financiers dug their heels in.

'Adam, they insist you do a test,' was the message.

'I'm not testing, David,' Adam replied.

'You've got to. They want to see how you fit in with David Essex.'

'I'm *not testing*. Tell you what – do a test on David Essex and see how he fits with me!'

'We can't do that. He's already on the board; he did the first film. Don't be daft, Adam, it's *his* movie.'

'OK, I know that's impossible, but I'm still not testing.'

One week later David was back on the phone.

'Adam, you know I want you, but they are absolutely adamant. They're talking about pulling the movie if you don't test.'

'Don't lose the movie because of me, David. You're better off finding another actor.'

'I'm not going to do that. I'm going to go back and tell them we'll look for the money elsewhere.'

The ultimatum delivered to the money men was crisp and to the point, for David was indeed prepared to forfeit their backing and start all over again if necessary. 'It's my choice or no movie,' the studio were told.

'OK, sign Adam Faith,' was the eventual grudging response.

A veteran then of four movies, all made during his pop idol days – *Beat Girl*, *Mix Me a Person*, *Never Let Go*, and for Nat Cohen, the epic *What a Whopper!* – Adam was left owing David a debt of gratitude for the rest of his life.

David took his interest in the music for *Stardust* even more seriously than before, producing and recording the score with Dave Edmunds. 'It was the one time I really indulged myself,' he says. 'I got on really well with Dave; he didn't want to do it on his own and I certainly couldn't do it without him, so we did it together.'

While all the film activity was going on, Sandy Lieberson was taking care of the business and video side of Goodtimes. '*That'll Be the Day* and *Stardust* were David's visions,' he says. 'We discussed things; we talked over problems. I might have given suggestions. We talked about casting and such, but more as a counsellor than to do with the actual producing. Of course, I was involved in the deals on all of them. I worked harder on the deal side while David had a much closer artistic involvement. I was off doing *Romantic and Classical Art* with Kenneth Clark, trying to build the whole video side of it and using my contacts in the film business to sustain David in terms of deals, distribution and financing.'

Ray had written the part of MacLaine's unscrupulous American manager for a New York Italian type, Francis Di Gillio, and had Tony Curtis cast in the role. When Curtis dropped out a few weeks before shooting began, Columbia Pictures, demanding input, wanted to replace him with Larry Hagman. Larry was particularly keen to clinch the role, since for years he had been cast as the wholesome boy-next-door character. He spent weeks in his study in Malibu learning his lines with a New York Italian accent before flying to London to meet David, Ray and Michael Apted. Since no one knew what Larry looked like, it was left to a waiter at the Terrazza to point him out. They looked at each other perplexedly. 'He doesn't look a bit like a New York Italian,' was the unspoken thought.

During the lunch he was transmogrified into a Texan named Porter Lee Austin, Porter from Larry's best friend, Lee after Lee Harvey Oswald and Austin after Larry's hometown in Texas. Ray did some fast rewriting on the character, while Larry quietly put away his hard acquired Italian accent without a murmur. Ray recalls Larry's entry into the production halfway through the shooting schedule, and the galvanizing effect it had on cast and crew. 'He was an injection of super professionalism, a real pleasure to work with. He had the longest speech in the movie, which he had to deliver walking down a flight of stairs, followed by an escalator ride. Every time he was absolutely word-perfect, then Adam Faith, who had one single solitary line to deliver at the end of it all, kept changing it.' Having laboured long and hard to get the perfect pay-off line worked out for Adam's character, Ray was not about to see it thrown away. He finally managed to convince Adam it really was important that the line be delivered exactly *as written*.

'Larry had the effect of encouraging the rest of the cast to treat the script with greater respect,' says Ray, somewhat tersely. 'He made not one single complaint throughout the many retakes necessary on the escalator scene and remained word-perfect every single time.'

Larry told David later that his role as Porter Lee led directly to his getting the part of J. R. Ewing in Dallas. If the character had remained di Gillio, who knows?

Adam smiles today at Ray's recollection. What *was* the line? 'I *still* can't remember it!' he laughs. What he does recall is the worried conference called after a few days' shooting by David, Ray and Michael.

'We're a bit worried about your performance,' the imperturbable Adam was told. 'There doesn't seem to be too much happening.'

'I see. Can I ask how long this movie is going to be?'

'Two hours plus.'

'Well, it depends what you want. Do you want me to act the whole movie in the first two minutes? Or do you want a balanced performance all the way through?'

The complaint was promptly withdrawn.

David was upset when the British Board of Film Censors awarded *Stardust* an '18' certificate, for he saw this as potentially decimating the target audience of under eighteens. Unit publicist Gilly Hodgson was hastily contacted. 'If we could assemble a representative audience in, say, Reading, and convince the censor to come along to the screening, it might change his mind. We'd issue a questionnaire afterwards that hopefully would confirm what we think, that the ruling's ridiculous.' Gilly was duly despatched to Reading, musing that her boss was not one to take other people's arbitrary decisions lying down. It took her a week to assemble the audience from as wide a range of the population as she could muster, including police, nurses, shop assistants, refuse collectors and housewives.

What had brought about the award of the unwanted '18' was the scene with David Essex in bed with two women (the 'eenie, meenie, minie, mo' scene.) The local newspaper picked up the story and on the day of the screening David and the censor turned up at the cinema to be met by newspaper hoardings that ran, 'Reading Housewives to Judge Sex Scenes'. Gilly observed rather ruefully that the cinema promptly filled up with what looked like a wholly undesirable element off the streets, which she reckoned might throw the whole study out of kilter. In the event, the screening passed off quietly and the censor agreed to downgrade the certificate after studying the results of the questionnaire.

Although the feeling in the air was that they had another hit, David was there as usual on the film's Thursday-night opening at the ABC in Shaftesbury Avenue, where it was showing at both ABC 1 and 2. He had to buy a few seats to get the 'Sold Out' return for the night. Friday was sold out without any help, which was a relief, for Ronco Records, again releasing a double album of tracks from the movie, had messed up on their television promotion. Planned to start the Saturday *prior* to the film's opening, it didn't start until the Saturday *after*. 'It was a real disaster, a real worry,' says David, 'for there was no major advertising. We'd relied completely on Ronco's TV advertising, which started at 8 pm on the Saturday after opening.'

By that time the film had gone out to 80 cinemas, a much broader release than for *That'll Be the Day*. Without the benefit of advertising the film went on to break 73 of the 80 house records that Saturday. It struck David that somehow or other the audience *knew*. 'I was staring at a complete marketing fuck-up – and it hardly seemed to matter!' When David went to see the manager of the ABC in Shaftesbury Avenue, he was told, 'Your movie's doing great! I love your film, but I can't say the same about the people that are coming to see it.' It seemed his box-office window had been accidentally smashed in by the crowds.

'What surprised me most about *Stardust*,' wrote Derek Malcolm in the *Guardian*, 'is that most people I know who have already seen this much-previewed sequel to *That'll Be the Day*, are so surprised by it. It shouldn't be all that dumbfounding that an English film could be lively, thoroughly well-made and capable of achieving a resounding commercial success . . . Ray Connolly's sharp, forthright screenplay and Apted's economical and sometimes imaginative direction back up a series of first-class performances, notably that of Adam Faith, whose portrait of a rough diamond on the make could scarcely be more authentic.'

Alexander Walker was equally enthusiastic. 'It is the truest, most ruthless dissection of an era through its phenomena that I have ever seen. Moreover, it is quite the best British film so far this year. Adam Faith is outstanding. He plays the role the way he knows it – and he knows it all the way.'

Dilys Powell in *The Sunday Times* was less persuaded by the movie, but equally lyrical about Faith. 'The trouble is that one should laugh, perhaps sourly. But some tiny element of the ridiculous has been left out. There is, however, a remarkable performance by Adam Faith as the scheming, possessive road manager.'

Richard Barkley in the *Sunday Express* wrote, 'It is to the credit of the film, pungently written by Ray Connolly and directed with skill and sensitivity by Michael Apted, that you're not invited to feel sorry for its hero. Adam Faith's contribution, so redolent of the era, is magnificent.'

Tom Hutchinson admired Ray Connolly's 'literate muck-raker of a script', but added, 'while David Essex is convincingly good as the lightweight made significant by fame, it is in all conscience Adam Faith's movie; a remarkable study of a manipulator whose invitation, "Fancy a drink?" is an offer his enemies wish they could refuse.'

In the States there was an equally enthusiastic reception from the critics. Jay Cocks in *Time* described the movie as 'fast, canny, tough-minded, brightly acted – especially by Hagman, Faith, Ines Des Longchamp (as a girlfriend of MacLaine's) and Keith Moon of The Who.' Jim MacLaine himself, they noted, was played with 'charm and chill' by Essex.

'Faith is the best thing about this picture,' wrote Judith Simon in *Rolling Stone*. 'While everything else – plot, script, and actors, credibility – occasionally sags into boredom, Faith prevails.'

David's faith in Adam had paid off for both men. 'When people know what they're doing, they recognize talent for what it is,' Adam reckons. 'They don't need it proved to them. A diamond is a diamond. Whether it's uncut or a bit rough is irrelevant.' Although Adam is not talking immodestly of his selection for the role, but about David's giving chances to new directors, the remark pays tribute equally to the way his producer stood up, even to the point of losing his finance, to get the actor he wanted.

Stardust went on to make a net profit of over half a million pounds against costs of about the same, despite another disappointing US outing. It was previewed in a snow blizzard in Boston in the winter of 1974, and promptly dropped.

'We had done very well with films about ourselves,' Ray Connolly summarized. For David the film was much more to him than just a look back at the era he had lived through. He admits that *Stardust* was a kind of wish fulfilment. 'I've always felt that at one moment in my life, if I'd been able to play the guitar, I might have taken that particular route.' Instead he had seized the opportunity to emulate his film-making heroes, who had often taken supposedly exploitative subjects, then imbued them with revealing insights illuminating particular eras of contemporary history. *Stardust* was an extremely brave film to make, with the budget of *That'll Be the Day* doubled and many of the elements that normally spell 'smash hit' eschewed in favour of a deeper, bleaker statement that anyone could have foreseen. David had done it again.

Although *Stardust* was not a second 'good book', with its final descent into parody and satire, it was certainly an interesting extension of *That'll Be the Day*. If he had been fortunate in achieving two hit films in a row in his own country, the friend who had previously given him the benefit of his own marital experience reckons he was also fortunate in other respects. 'His finally getting into movies saved him, yes,' he agrees, '*together* with Patsy's tolerance and influence. When he came to his senses, she was still there for him.'

Now Goodtimes began to expand in all directions. Sandy finished the twelve-part series with Kenneth Clark, and a distribution company was formed, run by Philip Strick and Gilly Hodgson, to release product acquired, like the Andrei Tarkovsky masterpiece, *Solaris*. The company was into production, distribution, movies, video and television. It was truly multi-faceted, with an ever-increasing staff and overheads. The name 'David Puttnam,' on a movie had begun to have real meaning.

Chapter 7

Tricks and Treats

A series of six films was planned, to be based on the life of musicians, starting with Gustav Mahler and to include George Gershwin, Franz Liszt and Ralph Vaughan-Williams, all with the controversial 'enfant terrible' of the British movie industry, Ken Russell, at the helm. Many felt that Russell had already said it all in his reputation-making television features on musicians such as Delius, which had not proved to everyone's taste. When Alexander Walker first heard that Russell was being let loose on Mahler he wrote, 'This man must be stopped. Bring me an elephant gun!'

David read the request and felt it was his bounden duty to oblige. Borrowing the weapon for a lark from a gunsmith, he confronted the startled critic as he was dining one lunchtime in a crowded Covent Garden restaurant and ceremoniously handed the elephant gun over.

When a complicated finance package collapsed on the first day of shooting, and the National Film Finance Corporation withdrew their support, Mahler's budget had to be slashed there and then from £400,000 to £180,000. 'Ken was wonderful,' says David. 'He made the film for less than half the budget we'd planned; he was superb.'

The critics did not find the movie anything like superb when VPS/Goodtimes handled the release on their own in 1974. 'The more one sees of Ken Russell's work,' write Nigel Andrews in the *Financial Times*, 'the more convinced one becomes it is the product of a man bent on some crazily ingenious form of self-glorification.' Conceding there were some eye-catching moments, Andrews declared himself baffled that the film had been chosen as Britain's entry in 1975's Cannes Film Festival. 'This is an intensely vulgar film,' wrote John Coleman in the *New Statesman*, while Philip Hope-Wallace found 'a great deal meretricious, lurid, even offensive. It seems to me flawed, pretentious and regrettable.' To David's acute embarrassment Russell Davies wrote in the *Observer*: 'What Ken Russell needs is someone to say nay to him occasionally.' The implication was clearly that David was too much of a bantam-weight to make any impression on the likes of Ken Russell.

David defends the film to this day. 'I happen to like *Mahler*, I think it's good,' he insists, 'not flawless, but a bloody good picture. Given what Ken put on screen for £180,000, a remarkable piece of work.'

When he heard that the president of 20th Century Fox wanted to see the movie he jumped on the first plane for Los Angeles, clutching the precious reels of film, beside himself with excitement. He drove straight from the airport to the studio and arrived five minutes late, to find the president and his colleagues already seated in the screening room. 'We ran it,' says David, 'and it turned out that the guy was just a big Mahler fan, who wanted to show the movie to some friends. I'd thought of course that he wanted to *buy* the bloody thing. It was the most dreadful disappointment, a good example of why I sometimes get bitter.' Dejected, he caught the first flight home next day.

An agent named Robert Littman negotiated the deal for the US release of *Mahler*. Bobby had been keen to finance *Melody* in his capacity in the late sixties as head of MGM in Europe, before the idea had been squashed by head office. He then moved to Columbia, where he helped in setting up the *Stardust* deal for David, before branching out as an independent agent based in Hollywood, in 1974.

Mahler's US outing was brief. If the British reviews had been bad, the American verdict was even harsher, the field led by John Simon in *Esquire*. 'Collectors of supreme cinematic monstrosities,' he railed, 'had better keep a sharp lookout for Ken Russell's *Mahler*, which may yet set a quick disappearance record even for a Russell film. This one surpasses *The Music Lovers* and *The Devils*, though in sheer loathesomeness it may fall just a bit short of that emetic duo. The film is of such demented and rotten taste that I do not wish to waste much space on it.'

For his part Ken Russell saw the production as perfectly of a piece. 'My film,' he wrote, 'is simply about some of the things I feel when I think of Mahler's life and listen to his music. It is by no means a definitive view. There are many facets to the mystery of Mahler's music as there are lovers of it, and of which I am happy to say, I am one. When every second counts it is often necessary to say two things at once, which is why I frequently introduce symbolism into scenes of reality.' If that wasn't ominous enough, try this: 'In one fantasy sequence Mahler appears to be cremated by SS men. When I first planned this, his pall bearers were not conceived as being anything other than the usual mourners, albeit military ones. But in depicting the nightmare in which the dead Mahler sees his wife desecrating his memory of her lovers in the future . . . it becomes inevitable; put an

Austrian Officer of 1900 into a uniform of mourning and you have an SS man. Take a Jew pretending not to be a Jew, project him a few years into the future and you have Mahler, or someone like him, being carried off to the crematorium. Alive!'

Oddly enough, Goodtimes had the last laugh. 'In the end *Mahler* was sold everywhere,' says Sandy, 'and made me a tidy profit.'

The life of George Gershwin was to be Russell's next outing, with Al Pacino hopefully cast as the composer, but Ken decided otherwise. He had filmed The Who rock opera, *Tommy*, after *Mahler*, and was full of his own ideas for the second Goodtimes venture, as David discovered to his cost. 'He *insisted* he wanted to do Liszt next, with Roger Daltrey. We agreed. The problem is he never really finished the screenplay and frankly, he just seemed to go off his rocker.'

Rather like a host at a runaway party constantly running out of liquid refreshment, David had to beat a path to his 'off-licence' in California no fewer than five times in twelve weeks. 'The film was rocketing over-budget and every time I got back from raising money, the budget had gone up again. I did my best, but it was a nightmare, impossible to keep up with.'

Sandy watched as the unstoppable Russell continued. 'It was such an unhappy experience for David and myself,' he says, 'and a real betrayal. He just went off the deep end. Instead of having the film taken over by the completion guarantor, we had to put up our own money to let Ken complete the film the way he wanted to. We decided we didn't want to work with him any more after that.'

The final cost of the *Lisztomania* folly, nicknamed *Duelling Pianos* and *Blazing Piano-Stools* at various times in the production by David and Sandy. ('We had to find *something* to laugh about'), was £1.2 million. *Mahler* had performed satisfactorily on its £180,000 budget, but £1.2 million was insupportable. This time the losses were significant, despite the Warners distribution deal Bobby Littman negotiated for the film's US release in 1975. Ironically, the process introduced David to a group of Warners' executives, which would lead later to the 'first-look' deal they struck with him at the end of the seventies.

'The reason *Lisztomania* became what it did,' says Bobby, 'was this potty idea Ken had of emulating the success of *Tommy*. Comedy and musicale were mixed in willy-nilly. I saw the finished version for the first time with Ken. He stood up at the end of it and said, "The man who made that should not be allowed to work in movies."'

David had to swallow hard to rationalize the brush with Russell. 'My experience with Ken,' he claimed, 'was a learning process. I learned in that job what I would have had no other way of acquiring –

that no producer can afford the luxury of respecting a director over-much. He was the most naturally gifted director I'd ever worked with, so far as the look of the film was concerned. When he was at his best, he was on the Himalayas, but too often he lost sight of the end to which all this had to be applied. I am a very old-fashioned boy. I believe in the text, the script, the blueprint. Ken took pride in his ability to juggle without these fundamental disciplines.'

Lynda Smith saw the dispute from the sidelines in a more down-to-earth manner as 'Ken got a grip on David and got him to do it his way.'

Once again, despite his Jacques Demy experience, David had al-lowed control of *Lisztomania* to slip through his fingers. Both films were pure Russell through and through, devoid of even the most modest Puttnam influence. Goodtimes were strained to the limit by the subsequent financial drain, although David would insist, 'It was a partnership I got a lot out of personally,' before going on to admit that his association with Russell had 'emotionally and financially cruci-fied me'.

Unknown to Ken Russell, David had shown his script independ-ently to Andrew Birkin and Ray Connolly before shooting started. Andrew pronounced it 'dreadful', but followed David's plan to have dinner with Ray and talk about it between the two of them in an attempt to come up with solutions. Both writers could see few, if any, redeeming features in it and Andrew commented that David and his crew should just go the whole hog and open the film with a metronome ticking away and Liszt screwing in time. 'Blow me down,' he says, 'that's what they did! So I guess I earned the dinner!'

Sandy was relieved beyond measure that they didn't proceed with the George Gershwin project. 'We were far better not doing it,' he explains, 'because Russell's interpretation of Gershwin would have been so contentious, the man's personal life filled with innuendoes and suppositions. I'm sure it would have backfired. America would never have accepted that; we'd have been slaughtered.'

Despite Patsy's interest and contribution to David's business deals, there was one aspect he never discussed with her. 'He knew that, being a bank manager's daughter, I always worried about borrowing money and he never told me how much money it was costing us to finance our business until eventually he came to me and said, "We're just not going forward; it's crazy." Then I realized the extent of the burden he'd been carrying and kept to himself. I first read in an interview he gave, how he sat in this hotel room in Hollywood and cried his eyes out. He couldn't leave because he couldn't justify having got there and staying there and he couldn't afford to stay. Now I never *knew* that. To this day, he doesn't believe in burdening his family when things go wrong.'

An offer of a £30,000 advance from Chas Chandler, the manager of pop group Slade, encouraged Goodtimes, now in grave danger of becoming a misnomer, to produce *Slade in Flame*. Andrew Birkin was asked to write the screenplay and noted David's lack of involvement. When he asked to see his producer about several script problems, David clearly didn't want to know, making no secret of the fact he was only doing it for the money. The film was well enough received, but proved to be strictly for hard-core Slade fans.

The next contribution, a strange sci-fi fantasy hybrid, *The Final Programme*, did not help matters either. 'It was my idea to do this one,' says Sandy. 'I loved Michael Moorcock's writing and I really liked the Jerry Cornelius character. David acted as executive producer. I thought there was a chance to do something very different, so I got Moorcock to let me have the rights to it and I signed Robert Fuest to direct. He'd just made *The Abominable Dr Phibes*, which had been a huge success, and EMI said if I got Fuest it was a deal. So we got him, but he insisted on not only directing but also designing it. I think he wrote it as well, I mean he got completely out of hand. He just became another person and decided he was going to be an auteur. Nice man, but he really went off the deep end on the movie.' Sandy smiles laconically. 'I thought it was an interesting film, though it lost me toward the end.' EMI released the movie in a double bill with *Confessions of a Chinese Courtesan*, perhaps a worse fate than it actually deserved, for it has its devotees.

David struck up a friendship with David Picker, president of United Artists, in the early seventies. 'He'd seen *That'll Be the Day* and asked if we could meet,' David recalls. 'We had lunch at The Dumpling Inn in Soho and got on great. He used to pump me for information, like who's doing what and which directors to watch and such. A couple of months later he rang again and we had another lunch. I showed him a rough cut of *Stardust* and the relationship grew, with him flying in every other month. I couldn't figure out why he showed any interest in me, I'd never approached UA for any pictures, we just got on tremendously well. When he left UA and became an independent producer himself with *Juggernaut*, *Royal Flash*, *Lenny* and *Smile*, he would occasionally ask for my help and advice, and could I put him on to some people? and of course I did.' For the moment that was it, but Picker and Puttnam's paths were to cross many more times in the future.

David worked on a documentary with Ray Connolly that was to prove highly profitable, considering its modest cost. *James Dean: The First American Teenager* was a natural for the two of them, for they were both fascinated by the late actor and acknowledged his iconographic influence on the character of Jim MacLaine in *That'll Be the Day*. David astutely bought up the rights to a documentary Robert Altman had already produced, *The James Dean Story*, while Ray conducted interviews in America with as many of Dean's contemporaries as he could find. These included Corey Allan (Buzz in *Rebel without a Cause*), Dennis Hopper, Sal Mineo, Rebel director Nicholas Ray and Leslie Caron. Together with clips from Dean's films, courtesy of Warners, stills, Dean's original five-minute screen test, a Natalie Wood interview that was bought in and excerpts from Altman's film, the raw material of the documentary was gathered together.

'A lot of Dean was in *That'll Be the Day*,' Ray acknowledges. 'That was a secretive kind of bond David and I had. We echoed the scene in *East of Eden* where Dean slumps into his jacket as the train carries him home from Salinas with our scene of David Essex hunched up in the back of a truck. We took Dean's red jacket from *Rebel without a Cause* and gave Essex one that was identical, then when Essex went into a cinema, it was showing a James Dean film. Although we changed it, we paralleled the *East of Eden* scene in which Dean releases the ice blocks when MacLaine throws his school books over a bridge into the river.'

Although making a documentary on their hero was fun, David and Ray got too near the real James Dean. 'We both came to the conclusion that if we'd ever actually met him, we'd probably never have liked him,' says David. He again gave the job of selling the film in the States to Bobby Littman, who sweated for months in 1976 to find a distributor. When he did, they paid more than the entire production had cost. 'If I'd known how cheaply it had been made, I'd never have had the balls to ask for what I did,' Bobby laughs. 'David was desperate to get a deal and get some money in, but neither he nor I expected what we got.'

David and Sandy continued to search for the next mainstream hit film that had eluded them since the heady days of *That'll Be the Day* and *Stardust*; compared to these two 'the collection of oddities' they had turned out since, as a competitor gleefully referred to them, paled into insignificance.

They looked first at a property called *Trick or Treat*, a script written by Ray Connolly, based on a novel he had published in 1974, telling the story of two lesbians who want to have a baby and how they become tragically involved with a married couple. To get the right mood of the piece, Ray had gone to Paris, originally the setting, to work on the novel.

David recalls even the beginnings of the picture as an embarrassment. 'What has never been said is that I turned it down when it was first written as a book, then while I was away on holiday Sandy read it and really liked it. "Look," he said, "this is terrific," so it started off with this extraordinary awkwardness between me and Ray, because he knew I didn't like it and that Sandy did. So I stayed back. Not that it would have changed anything if I hadn't.'

'I thought it was a good idea,' says Sandy. 'Certainly if we cast it right and everything, it could be very commercial. David's contribution was to bring in Michael Apted to direct.' The film rights were handed to Goodtimes as a favour from Ray to David, for Warners were keen and might well have provided full financing. The casting called for three Europeans and one American. Nigel Davenport and Stephane Audran were to be the married couple, and for one of the girls Californian Jan Smithers was cast.

Since the film involved nudity and one fairly graphic sex scene between the two girls, Jan Smithers expressed concern that a scar on one of her breasts would show up on camera. A screen test was arranged, with a mightily embarrassed Michael Apted in charge, at 9.30 one morning. 'Smithers' tit passed with flying colours,' one of the crew declared. For the part of the other girl many European beauties were discussed, like Isabelle Adjani, Maria Schneider and Ray's favourite, Bulle Ogier. Then Sandy had a novel idea – Bianca Jagger, whom he had known for years.

When Ray located Bianca and showed her his draft script and novel, she seemed co-operative and enthusiastic. After David and Michael Apted had a meeting with her in Rome, they requested a screen test. While this was going on, Ray continued to work on the script, which was still considered somewhat lacking.

Michael Apted flew to New York to do the test, to suit Bianca's timetable. She came over impressively, but even then the warning bells were ringing behind the scenes. 'She *insisted* on a helicopter to pick her up for the test,' says Lynda Smith. 'She absolutely wouldn't do it unless the helicopter was produced. At the office we told each other, "*This* is crazy. This girl is going to be *trouble*." We knew it before it even started.'

Unfortunately Bianca had now become not just a part of the whole package but the most important part. Finance for the film was in place through Nat Cohen at E M I, the National Film Finance Corporation (NFFC) and an Italian company, Rizzoli, but then NFFC withdrew its support when a new budget was submitted asking for an extra £50,000. Hugh Hefner of *Playboy* stepped into the breach, making Bianca's starring role an absolute condition of his investment.

The pressure now focused on Ray and his script, which he knew was still not properly realized. Now that Bianca was firmly installed, she indicated that she wanted a woman writer to help Ray achieve the correct nuances of the relationship between the two girls. With the delay this caused, Stephane Audran was obliged to drop out. Her place was taken by Elsa Martinelli. As more and more script changes were demanded by Bianca, rejecting the new writer's contribution with a dismissive 'It's *shit*,' Ray visibly demonstrated the strain he was under as his hair began to fall out. At this point he decided to stand up to Bianca and proceeded to give her what for him, a gentle and caring man, was a thorough dressing-down. She listened demurely enough, then as soon as the interview was over telephoned Sandy Lieberson to complain of Ray's behaviour, threatening to walk off the picture. Sandy promptly called Ray and asked him what the hell he had been playing at. Bianca's threat to leave was withdrawn only after she was satisfied that Ray had been suitably chastened.

As the action moved to Rome in the autumn of 1985, and shooting started, Bianca became costume-obsessed, arguing constantly with Marit Lieberson, Sandy's wife and costume director. With a heavy heart Ray, now working with Michael Apted, began the sixth draft of the screenplay. Because Sandy had worked in Rome and spoke Italian, he took on the role of producer, together with Gavrik Losey.

'As soon as we got there,' he says, 'things went from bad to worse. Bianca Jagger was just a pain in the ass from beginning to end. She was absolutely schizoid and hysterical and decided she couldn't possibly take her clothes off in the film and couldn't be seen in bed with another girl. I mean, all the reasons she'd wanted to *do* the movie initially! Mick Jagger was flying down to Rome and telling her she was crazy to do it. They'd just been married and why does she want to be involved with this lesbian movie? And it came to an impasse. I mean, we couldn't get her to take her goddam clothes off, an essential part of the movie and the highly erotic love scenes between Jan Smithers and her.'

Now Jan Smithers got into the act and indicated that she too was not prepared to do the nude scenes, while Gavrik Losey set to work on his calculator, figuring it would cost at least a quarter of a million pounds to scrap the film. Michael Apted came to a complete dead-end when he found both Bianca and Jan Smithers refusing to take direction. There was suddenly a crying need for a sacrificial goat, who turned out to be Ray Connolly. 'One of us has to go,' Apted told him. Ray got the message and left for London.

As the situation continued to deteriorate Sandy saw that something had to be done. 'I decided to stop shooting on the movie for a while. David promptly came over to Rome. *Everybody* came over, except Hugh Hefner, who sent his emissaries. The decision was made to bring everything back to London, and David was going to take charge.' With Christmas approaching the plan was to shoot in London for three weeks, then break for the holidays, when a new script, the *seventh* draft, would be produced by Kathleen Tynan and Michael Apted.

Patsy looked at the situation that had developed from a woman's point of view. 'In Bianca we had a girl who I know in certain areas is very timid, and she had to take her clothes off. I figured she was stopping the film for one reason, that she was frightened to do that one scene. She'd lost her bottle. Since Bianca had brought Hefner's money, it was a terribly difficult situation. As far as Michael Apted was concerned, he was very insecure at this time, which didn't help. He felt *very* intimidated.'

In the crucial last scenes to be shot before the break, Jan Smithers at last complied with Apted's request to bare her all, while Bianca remained demurely under a sheet. After the holiday, with filming resumed in January 1976, David was informed that Jan Smithers had no intention of returning to complete the movie. Then came word from Bianca's lawyers that a renegotiation of both actresses' terms was required, together with the small matter of final cut approval. For many this was the straw that broke the camel's back. There was pressure from every side. Costs were mounting, there was less than 40 minutes of usable film to show for their efforts, and the press was filled daily with the latest horror stories from the set.

Sandy was one of those who held out for carrying on. His argument was 'Look, EMI and *Playboy* have this huge amount of money invested in it, let's finish it and deliver them a movie at least. We'll use doubles, and *screw* Bianca Jagger and Jan Smithers!'

David was in agreement with Nat Cohen that the whole thing was an embarrassment that should be terminated quickly before more money was wasted. 'Let's just bury it,' was their attitude, opening up a considerable area of disagreement with Sandy.

David rapidly made the discovery that it was as difficult to stop a movie that was underway as it was to start one up. An encounter he had with Hugh Hefner took place in the basement of Hefner's house.

'Stopping the film is an admission of failure,' Hefner intoned. David's reply was, 'Yes, but this could go on *forever*; there's no *telling* what it might end up costing.'

'I thought it could go on and on,' says David. 'I saw no end to it. The awful thing is that I think Nat Cohen had pretty well lined us up to move into E M I, at the time of all their company changes. One of the tragedies of *Trick or Treat*, from our point of view, is that the deal was made instead with Michael Deeley and Barry Spikings.'

When the decision was finally made to pull the plug, with £400,000 expended. Sandy was all for taking things further. 'I wanted to sue Jagger. I think we had an incredible case against her. She was in complete breach of her contract, she was resident in the United Kingdom and she had a tremendous amount of assets. Just to let someone away with capriciously deciding to do a movie and halfway through breaking her contract and every agreement – I was all for taking action.'

In the event the question of whether to sue or not was taken out of Goodtimes' hands.

'Unless Goodtimes sues Jagger, we'll hold Goodtimes responsible,' Frank Bloom was told by the *Playboy* organisation. A writ was promptly issued against Bianca and Jan Smithers.

'Jagger defended the writ,' Frank recalls, 'while Jan Smithers just disappeared into obscurity and never even answered hers. We obtained judgement in default against her, which was worth precisely nothing. The case against Jagger was that she was contracted to play the part and failed to perform, all to do with the nudity involved. The burden of proof lay on us to show that Jagger and Smithers had been in no doubt as to the explicit sexual nature of some of the scenes. The action went on for over a year. I did all the spade work and must be one of the very few people in the country to have actually viewed the footage, 40-odd minutes of it, and quite pretty as far as it goes. I found out more about the art of film-making than I learned in the rest of my life put together. I got all the dailies, all the notes, the annotated screenplay. David provided me with reels of tape from the final day's shooting, before the shutdown took place, which he'd seen fit to make in his wisdom. He had kept the sound rolling throughout the day.

'Apted was complaining to David that Jagger and Smithers wouldn't perform the nude scenes required, then David came on, his voice tight as if being held in by a great effort of will. He said something like, "I understand from Michael that you're refusing to play this scene." Then I remember Smithers' voice saying, "Oh, *David*!" before she burst into tears. He then read the riot act to both of them and told them if they didn't perform to Michael's direction, they'd be suspended.

'As it got nearer to the trial, costs were mounting fast. Goodtimes were on a hiding to nothing, only suing in order to repay *Playboy* and EMI and to avoid the distinct possibility of being sued themselves. All the players featured were going to have to be wheeled into the witness box – Jagger, Puttnam, Lieberson, Apted, Connolly – and it was clearly going to be a big tabloid splash. David isn't very keen on that sort of thing and I gather he quietly began to set the scene for an abandonment of the action. The more I spelled out what was going to happen, the more he didn't like it. Somehow or other, I never discovered how, he managed to persuade EMI to pressure *Playboy* into dropping the threat of legal action against Goodtimes. And that's what happened. The action was abandoned and each party paid its own costs. There was no payment by Jagger to us. She had a counter claim against us, but neither of us ended up paying the other anything.'

There was no recriminations from Nat Cohen. 'It was a pity,' was all he said. 'The film could have been all right. The abandonment came as a great shock to me, the first and last time that had happened. It wasn't their fault, it was Bianca Jagger's. In the end we all felt there was no future in it and decided to end it and stop the expense. For David and Sandy it was obviously a terrible set-back. They'd created an overhead which had to be fed, quite why, I don't know. I saw them as a young, dynamic couple who needed no more than a chair, a desk, a telephone and their wits.'

For Ray Connolly there was no satisfaction in seeing the project abandoned. He had laboured over it in one form or another for more than two years and lived with it until his removal from Rome. There was, however, one consolation. His hair stopped falling out and began to grow back.

Did he hold David responsible for his treatment on the movie? 'Yes, partly,' he admits, 'but we were all responsible for the damn thing, every one of us. I am, because I wrote it and never really got it right; Michael Apted couldn't control the actresses, so it was partly his fault. The trouble with David is he did his job *too* well – he got the money too early, before we were ready to go. Then there was the small matter of Bewanker – sorry, Bianca. I did feel hurt by David because I felt he should have given me more support than he did when things were going badly wrong, but he didn't. That may be the *other* side of David.

'When you work with him, he seduces you and you think he's your very best friend. You're incredibly fond of each other and you think this is wonderful; it's a great relationship. Then, when things go wrong he withdraws slightly and tends to lose interest a little bit, and if there's something else he'll go off and do that. When *Trick or Treat* was falling apart, he had something else to go to. He senses the ground is shaky underneath him and he's off, edging away. You feel really hurt because you've regarded him as your best friend. The truth is he's friendly, but he isn't your *best* friend. He's a producer and you're a writer or director, so when things go wrong, there's no answer, no way out, except animosity.'

With the benefit of hindsight David saw that *Trick or Treat* was a film that should never have been made. 'We did it because there's this innate pressure on producers to produce. At the time Sandy and I were in desperate straits for enough money just to pay the staff wage bill at Goodtimes and we worked out that if we didn't collect the producer's fee for *Trick or Treat*, we couldn't keep going for another six months. Since we'd other things in the pipeline we thought were really worth making, we made it very much as an expedient picture. When it got into trouble in Rome, I made a very, very stupid error. I tried to be a boy scout and thought, having produced a few films, that if I went to Rome, it would be all right.

'When I got there I quickly found I was dealing with an absolutely irreconcilable situation, an actress who didn't want to act in a lead role and every other unfortunate thing happening. It would have been a clean and quick decision to have stopped at that point, but it took a long time to persuade the financiers that this could go on for ever and could cost them an unlimited amount of money.

'If I were Ray, I'd feel exactly the way he feels, but I really don't think I had any alternative at all. You know, over the years there are certain people I really owe, and Ray is one of them. I've tried to repay my debt to him and I'd like to think that maybe I have, but there's no question, the time I really needed help, he wrote two important films in my life.'

The summer before the family's move to Queensgate Place Mews in South Kensington, Patsy had begun to accept that she would never be free from mild recurrences of the allergy she had suffered early in their marriage, together with hay fever and on occasions, asthma. When she took the children abroad with her to Italy or to Corsica, everything seemed to get better. She was talking one day to Terence Stamp who was living in the Albany on his own in his post-Jean Shrimpton period, when the subject of acupuncture came up.

'You're such an idiot,' he told her. 'All right, I'm sure acupuncture could *help* you, but why don't you look at the *real* problem?'

'What do you mean?'

'What you *eat*. You *are* what you eat.'

'Well, what am I doing wrong?'

'*Everything*. You've got to begin again, stop eating meat, stop eating *all* the rubbish you're eating at the moment.'

'Will you teach me?'

'Of course I will. If you're *really* serious.'

Patsy was immediately put on a 10-day brown rice diet, from which no deviation was allowed. It was brown rice and *nothing else* but brown rice for 10 whole days. 'At first it was *terrible*,' says Patsy, 'then all the toxins started coming out and I felt amazing. I couldn't believe how good I felt. Terry, my master and guru in the whole thing, had been learning this stuff for years in Tibet. He was a great teacher, but boy, was I a great convert! From then on I wouldn't touch an ordinary cup of tea or dairy products. When I made porridge, I would buy the oats and cook them for hours and hours.'

Debbie shudders at the recollection. 'It was Mum's major hippie phase. All that stuff was *horror* food for children – *real* porridge with *bits* in it, ugh! If we weren't eating lentils and rice, Mum had decided life wasn't worth living. Sacha and I felt really badly done by. We called it Mum's kaftan, beads and brown rice period.'

Meat, of course, was completely ruled out. For his part David refused outright to have anything to do with the new régime and took sides with the children. 'They are for ever dancing to whatever your latest *thing* is,' he told his supremely unrepentant wife.

Patsy has never gone back to eating meat, is very selective in her diet and still feels the benefit to this day. 'To the kids it must have seemed like years,' she laughs. 'If *only* they could have sold their mother! My dad would come round and say, "A good steak-and-kidney pudding would do you the world of good, my girl," when he saw what I was eating. At the same time he had to admit I'd never looked better. I knew I'd gone too far, though, when I went on to nothing but rosehip and herbal teas and my mother started bringing her own teabags round!'

Patsy's education was furthered in another direction when Terry Stamp introduced her to an interior decorator and antique shop owner, Geoffrey Bennison. While picturesquely describing his own special-ized field of furniture as 'fucked-over vicarage', he was none-the-less able to instil in Patsy a further appreciation of the decorator's art. She was one of several friends who hung out in the back of Bennison's Pimlico shop, comparing finds with each other and learning all the time.

Soon after *Trick or Treat's* conception Sandy and David had come across another project as they sat in Lew Grade's outer office waiting for an appointment. Sandy had known Lew since his agency days and had asked for a meeting to see if they could work together. As they sat there, a mutual acquaintance, Peter Fetterman, emerged from Lew's office, clutching an armful of storyboards for a film Alan Parker wanted to do.

'Let's have a look at them, Peter,' Sandy coaxed. After a quick scrutiny he turned to David, 'Jesus, why aren't *we* doing that?' he asked. 'It's a *great* idea!'

'Well,' David said, 'Alan obviously wants to work on his own, otherwise he'd have brought it to us, so *fuck* him.' Sandy looked at his partner in surprise, then grinned as he saw the smile on David's face. The storyboards were for *Bugsy Malone*.

Chapter 8

April 1st, 1974.

Good Times, Bad Times

A young entertainment lawyer, David Norris, was hired in 1975 by French documentary film-maker Marcel Ophuls, son of the legendary Max, to bring an action against Goodtimes and their financial partners, the BBC and Polytel. It was an encounter that would establish the subsequently spiky Norris-and-Puttnam friendship.

Ophuls' contention was that *Memory of Justice*, his documentary on the Nuremberg trials, had been 'taken away' from him by the Goodtimes/BBC/Polytel triumvirate. Their joint defence was that Ophuls had repeatedly ran over his delivery dates and budget, then ended up handing over a version that exceeded the agreed maximum length.

Norris regarded Ophuls as one of his most difficult clients, a highly emotional man who had threatened to commit suicide more than once. He was pursuing the action under the Continental concept of 'droit morale', the 'moral rights' clause embodied in the Berne Convention. This upholds an author's right to protect the integrity of his work from the surgeon's knife, drastic cutting and alteration, or any form of vulgarization, even though he may have assigned copyright to the work in question. Norris had looked for a way to apply this to Ophuls' case to beat the triumvirate over the head and bring them to the negotiating table. His fear was that if the case went to the High Court in London, which did not recognize 'droit morale', his client might lose.

After hectic discussions between David and Norris, both men believed they had reached an agreement that would be acceptable to Ophuls. Eagerly Norris put the proposition to his client, and was staggered when Ophuls refused to accept. Tearing his hair out, Norris was obliged to go back to David and relay Ophuls' unexpected resistance. David was furious and accused Norris of reneging on their 'deal'. Norris argued that while they had discussed a solution, the final decision had of course to be made by Ophuls himself. David stuck to his guns and insisted that Norris had given him the impression it was a fait accompli.

Zeroing in now on the fact that Polytel was German based, Norris took Ophuls case to Germany where the 'droit morale' clause applied, and obtained an injunction against them. Ophuls' position was saved by the threat of pending litigation, as the BBC, Polytel, David and Goodtimes were forced back to the negotiating table, where the dispute was settled to Ophuls' satisfaction.

Goodtimes found their coffers impoverished to the tune of £150,000, bringing the company dangerously close to bankruptcy. Worse, the Rothschilds' confidence in David and Sandy's judgement was further eroded. The partners had discovered the 'moral rights' concept the hard way.

David felt strongly that they had been justified in removing the film from Ophuls and that the decision of the court had impugned his integrity. To sustain what he saw as a blot on his innocent escutcheon was galling indeed. All the judgement proved as far as he was concerned was that morality is a matter of geography. Or – as Robert Bolt had written in *A Man for All Seasons*, 'Morality's not practical. Morality's a gesture. A complicated gesture learned from books.' Patsy held her own counsel. Whatever else morality was, for her it could never be a matter of expediency.

'Ophuls' is an example of a first-rate mind in a second-rate person,' David muttered darkly, 'a man condemned to living in the creative shadow of his father. He's attempted to put together a career as a man too gifted to be properly understood.' The word Norris got back was, 'Puttnam thinks you're a shit.' Norris found he could live with this, especially since there was no further contact between the two men for four more years.

The interview David and Sandy had with Lew Grade was a pleasant one, but no deals were done. Lew basically wanted people to deliver his projects, while Goodtimes sought backing for their own ideas. Since David had come across the *Bugsy Malone* project in Lew's outside office, although he had known full well that Alan was trying to fund the project, he still felt honour bound to take it back and offer it to the impressario, who again turned it down.

Alan Parker had moved on after *Melody* to direct television commercials, before producing a television play, *No Hard Feelings*. Although taken up by the BBC, it was produced independently, just to prove, in Alan's words, 'We could make something longer than 30 seconds.' This in turn led to a Jack Rosenthal television play, *The Evacuees*, which went on to win him a British Academy Award. The hundreds of commercials he had turned out for his own 'Alan Parker

Film Company' had earned him a reputation as a keen scene-setter, with a sharp eye for period and character detail, together with a sly sense of humour. Not only that, but together with Hugh Hudson, Ridley Scott and Adrian Lyne, Alan had completely revolutionized the small-screen commercials art form. Out were the pedestrian, clichéd, 'You'll wonder where the yellow went' jingles; in were luminous images and mini-features, using real people and real stories and treating humour in a way it had never been put across before. It was a case of brain rather than brash; for the first time the commercials were in many cases more interesting than the programmes around them.

Alan's partner in the company, a no-nonsense Cockney named Alan Marshall, had started in the film business as a message boy, quickly going on to cutting-room assistant, editor, then picture-editor on commercials. He produced commercials at CDP for a while, meeting David and Alan Parker in the process. 'I wrote *Bugsy* as a script as a pragmatic exercise to try to do an American subject,' says Alan. 'Everything that I'd written up to that point kept coming back with a rubber stamp on it marked "too parochial". So I decided to take an American genre in order to make an American success. I didn't know about America, but I knew about American movies, so I took a gangster genre and an American musical and had this idea of maybe doing it all with children. I had four kids of my own and I'd done a lot of work with kids. Alan Marshall and I had our own little company going, so I told David, with whom I'd become quite good friends at that point, that I badly wanted to do it on my own. We asked everybody, took on Peter Fetterman to try and tie the finances together. David was into his own stuff at Goodtimes in any case, but I just couldn't get it going on my own. We had the money from our commercials to finance the pre-production of the movie. I had this elaborate presentation, the only time I'd ever story-boarded anything. No one could conceive what it would look like; I had photos of kids taken all made up. We didn't just try Lew Grade, we tried *everybody*. Out of sheer frustration I grudgingly asked David to get involved. He offered me one piece of advice: 'I urge you not to do it with children.' 'If I don't do that, David', I told him, 'I don't know what we've got!' He was *always* full of ideas, most of them crackpot, but he could never be defeated. If David had one thing knocked down, he'd be on to the next thing, there was always something else up his sleeve. His energy and ability to be whacked over the head and climb up again were extraordinary.

'It was never easy for him in these early days; in Britain it was a depressed industry and the people who were running it were pretty pathetic. It was mostly run by narrow-minded chartered accountants and Wardour Street bookies in Burton suits and dandruff, who *knew* absolutely nothing, but couldn't be *told* anything, even though the industry was a disaster. In David's trips to America, it was even more humiliating for him. He was treated like a carpet salesman coming from nowhere and no one knowing who he was. They were contemptuous of us being English because our Industry had been peopled for so long by second-rate losers. They were very hard times for him and they left a mark on him.

'He was very unforgiving of how badly he was treated by our own Industry, but more so the Americans. He was always thought of as a sort of swift-of-foot spiv, an energetic loonie, and no one would ever acknowledge that he might actually be any good, let alone brilliant. The way in which business is done in Hollywood, the fact that you come thousands of miles and the fact that you can't afford the air fare or the hotel room doesn't count. You've got to sit there at the Beverly Wilshire, as he often did, waiting for days for someone to return your call. Then you find out they haven't even bothered to read your script!'

Once David accepted that Alan was determined to press ahead with his cast of kids, he went on to sell the film with all the zeal of someone who thought his partner had come up with the best idea in the world. He had convinced himself to enable him to convince others.

He was sure all he had to do was go to Rank for finance on *Bugsy Malone*. Since they had tried to woo *Stardust* away from Nat Cohen, surely they would look favourably on his new project? He could not have been more wrong. 'It was *murderous*,' he recalls. 'Worse than raising the money for *Melody*. I would telephone people I'd already dealt with and I'd say we're going to be doing this terrific picture and it's all about gangsters, and they'd say, "Oh yes?" And it's a musical, and they'd say, "That sounds interesting." Then I'd say that what's really wonderful about it is that all the cast are 12-year-olds. And the line would go dead or they'd say, "Are you feeling all right?" It was a very painful experience.'

Alan had started on the *Bugsy* script in November 1973, finishing it during the summer of 1974, then spending nine months touring US bases looking for 12-year-olds he could cast. He made three visits to the States for more interviews, while David made no less than four money-raising trips. The film had to be produced during the summer holidays to ensure the kids' availability and by the spring of 1975, only £100,000 of the £500,000 budget was in place, from the NFFC, conditional on a major US distributor coming in for around £200,000.

Alan had three choices of singer/songwriters in mind for the *Bugsy Malone* score, all of them Pauls – McCartney, Simon and Williams. During his next US trip David ran into Paul Williams in A & M Records' office (they were releasing the *Lisztomania* soundtrack at the time). Williams was promptly force-fed the script. With William's agreement that he would compose original songs for the movie, David steered Alan Parker and the project to Paramount through Bobby Littman. 'We both went round to the studio and met Richard Sylbert,' Alan recalls, 'a rather unique bod, an Oscar-winning production designer who'd taken the job for a couple of years at Paramount before Barry Diller, who arrived soon after.'

They were offered $300,000 in exchange for the US negative pickup rights. 'A terrible deal,' Alan Marshall says, 'although if it hadn't been brought off, the film would never have been made at all. But Paramount had no commitment to promote the movie or support it in any way. The studio spent more money on their clients' lunches than they did on *Bugsy*.'

The balance of the budget still had to be found, so it was back to Britain, where David read an interview with Rank's boss, Graham Dowson, in which he had been asked, 'Why aren't you making more movies?' His reply had been that they weren't being brought anything that conformed to their criterion of what makes a good movie. When pressed as to what this constituted in their terms, Dawson had come out with 'family entertainment at the right price'.

Quick as a flash David was on the phone to Evelyn de Rothschild – did he know Graham Dowson? Very well, was the reply. OK, can you get me to him quickly? The next day David was in Dowson's South Street office with a yarn that he was about to be interviewed by the press and one of the questions to be put to him was 'Why aren't you working with Rank?' He explained that he thought he knew the answer until he read Dowson's interview, but what was clear to him now was that the film he was working on did in fact fulfil all the criteria listed, so the answer no longer applied. 'I have no wish to embarrass either one of us,' he concluded, presenting Dowson with *Bugsy*, and a dilemma. 'Someone will contact you,' Dowson declared as David left his office. For months past David had been trying to contact Frank Poole at Rank to reconsider *Bugsy*. Now, by the time he got back to Goodtimes' headquarters from the Dowson interview, Poole had phoned three times. The deal was tortuously concluded, somewhat hoisting Graham Dowson on his own petard.

An extra $100,000 was required, Polydor Records stumping up half for the soundtrack album rights, then for the rest it was back to

Hollywood. 'We needed a last $50,000,' David explains. 'With it we could make *Bugsy* and without it we couldn't. I sat in a damned hotel room waiting for the new head of Paramount, Mr Barry Diller, to make up his mind whether to put in the extra or not. When the message came through that the answer was yes, that was it. The amount of money was so finite I was actually able to make that "eureka" phone call to Alan Parker.'

The whole exercise planted a growing disenchantment in David's mind. The NFFC, Rank, Paramount and Polydor, all had contributed to *Bugsy*, but he felt increasingly that the often unspoken question as he sought outside investment was, where did the Rothschilds stand in all this? 'I was hassling around,' David points out, 'raising money privately from different sources, when the people who held the bulk of the company's equity weren't prepared to come up with some of it. It was the fight for the last $50,000 that really crazed me. I was running about all over the place, when the directors of the company, who had millions, didn't have the courage to come up with it.'

There was one more problem to overcome before the film could proceed, the signing of Tatum O'Neal for the leading role of the junior gangster moll. Her terms were expensive, a major budgetary consideration. Bobby Littman sped to the rescue after viewing an independently produced picture called *End of Summer* starring Richard Harris. David was contacted in London as soon as Bobby could get to a phone.

'David, forget Tatum O'Neal. I've just seen an absolutely extraordinary girl who's perfect for *Bugsy*,' Bobby enthused.

Alan Parker was promptly flown over to Hollywood where Bobby Littman met him off the plane. 'Before you go to your hotel,' Bobby said, 'we are going to Fox, where I've arranged a screening of *Edge of Summer*'. Next day Jodie Foster's agent and mother were assembled in Bobby's Beverly Hills offices to meet Alan. Jodie would film *Taxi Driver* before starting work with Alan, but the deal for *Bugsy* was struck there and then. Ironically, Jodie had already scored a big hit in an American television series playing Tatum O'Neal's original big-screen role in *Paper Moon*.

In August 1975, with the film shooting at Pinewood for producer Alan Marshall (and with David as executive producer), *Variety* trotted out one of its most deadpan headlines ever, 'Gangster Pic With 200 Kids In Cast And No Adult Rolls In UK', a 'no hope' message if ever there was one.

Almost as soon as shooting at Pinewood had started, David recalls the unit being presented with Rank's first surprise. 'They would only give us the studio resources to build *one* side of the street on our main set,' he maintains. 'It was a terrible betrayal; they knew we needed *both* sides. We had to put it up ourselves. Alan Parker had to mortgage his house to cover it, £80,000. Then there were the hydraulics. Everything was built on hydraulics because we needed cellars for people to vanish into and Alan Marshall had made a deal with the studio that since these hydraulics were lying idle, they would let us have them free. Two weeks after we started shooting, they told us they were afraid they were going to have to charge us for the hydraulics. When Alan Marshall and I asked why, they explained it was because there was another film that wanted them and either we agreed to pay their charges or they would have to remove them. We said, "You can't do that, our fucking sets will collapse!" They said, "Well, we'll need to charge you for them." We settled it in the end, but only after a terrible row. From start to finish their involvement was a nightmare. They were totally negative, and the money was always late. Thank God they stopped production. They've saved people a lot of pain and unhappiness.'

Alan Parker, with a wicked chuckle, says this is not entirely true; indeed that David was hardly involved at all in the physical production of *Bugsy*. 'With David, he gets a bee in his bonnet about someone, in this case Rank, and he never forgives. They were a pain in the ass about their share of the money because David wouldn't agree to their ridiculously unfair production and distribution agreement and it caused us a lot of anxiety. But I didn't mortgage my house! Not unless Alan Marshall did it without telling me! There were no hydraulics or trap doors either; that's all anecdotal. He wasn't there for most of the filming so he probably is confusing it with Alan Marshall telling him about a problem we had with scaffolding rostrums that the whole set was build on. We'd built this incredible New York street set on four-foot rostrums inside the studio so that we could get real New York steam coming out of manholes. Pinewood Studios threatened to take them away for a *Cinderella* set that was shooting at the same time so our set would have to be struck. In the end they relented. This is David half-hearing things reported to him second-hand. It's anecdotal, *theatre*, not true. What's the expression, "In the end, history is the unreliable, fantasized memories of old men." And movie stories are that much richer. A half a joke at lunch about what happened in the morning is recounted in the evening as dinner conversation, which gets repeated in a month's time as an anecdote about the making of that movie. Then it becomes the truth.

'During the shoot David was away in the States vainly trying to get

Warner Bros to get behind *Lisztomania*, a pretty well impossible task. It was a terribly hard time for him and I remember him lying on the couch in our office and putting his head in his hands; he'd had enough of movies and Americans. I think he only got involved with *Bugsy* to help me and in a way he was probably surprised it worked at all. His own movies were his priority.'

'Later they wouldn't put up any advertising money,' says David, 'so we did all the ads ourselves. Then we had to do our own posters. How we financed that caused the biggest row of the lot. I'd made the deal with a Japanese distributor for *Bugsy*, the deal was directly with Goodtimes for an advance of $75,000. The money would come to us and we'd pass it on to Rank. So when Rank wouldn't give us any money to advertise the picture, I very meticulously put this advance into a different account called *Bugsy Malone* Promotion and started spending *their* money, *their* $75,000, on the advertising and promotion of the picture. They were going to sue me, take me to the High Court; I mean, they just went berserk. Once the film was a hit, of course, everything became fine.'

David's efforts to get *Bugsy* entered at Cannes were thwarted at first when he was told it was not 'esoteric' enough for the festival. 'It's a film for *everyone*,' he raged, 'that just happens to feature a cast of kids.' After a storm of publicity, some of it skilfully engineered by David, the film was accepted and put forward as the British entry to Cannes in May 1976. It received one of the most enthusiastic receptions of any film that year. Rank provided not a penny for the Cannes outing, which consisted of a carload of posters and billboards, driven down by David and the Alans Parker and Marshall. 'We did our own billposting,' David recalls. 'We took our own press kits and copies of the record we'd got from Polydor. Alan Parker still talks about getting into his tuxedo in the loo of the Carlton Hotel on the night of the Festival screening. We couldn't actually afford to stay there; we were in a small place way up in the hills outside.'

After *Bugsy* had begun shooting, David Picker was appointed head of Paramount. He flew to Cannes to see *Bugsy* and enthusiastically renewed his relationship with David. 'Now maybe we can work together,' he told him. 'That would be marvellous,' was David's grateful reply. Cannes was suddenly beginning to turn out well. Of *Bugsy*'s screening he recalls, 'It was just an unbelievable triumph. Alan Parker was literally chaired shoulder high. It had been a particularly bloody Cannes; there'd been violent movies all over the place. That evening a special dinner was held in honour of Michael Balcon's eightieth birthday, attended by Mick, himself, and Aileen, his wife, given by the whole of the British film industry. So *Bugsy* became more than just another movie at Cannes – it became Mick Balcon's birthday present. David Picker gave a speech and said something lovely about *Bugsy*, that he'd been waiting to see a film like that for the last 15 years.

'Later that evening he said to me, "Have you got any more guys like this? I mean, Parker really knows how to shoot a film." I said, "Well, as a matter of fact I have." It was Ridley Scott I had in mind. So I phoned Rid as soon as I could get away and said, "Get on a plane first thing tomorrow morning." He did, he got the 8 o'clock plane, so by lunchtime we were eating on the beach at the Carlton – David, Rid and I. We were pitching a picture called *The Duellists* and another called *The Gunpowder Plot*. Picker said, "Which do you feel more strongly about?" I said, "Well, basically we prefer *The Gunpowder Plot*, but it's going to cost at least $2 million, but we can make *The Duellists* for $1 million." He said $2 million was too much; he preferred what he called "the $1 million one". That was my first deal with David after our years of friendship.'

Rank unenthusiastically arranged a West End première for *Bugsy* at the Leicester Square Theatre in July and sat back, sceptically, to await results. David continued to foot the publicity bill with their money. The only unpleasant memory David has of *Bugsy*'s London première was its coinciding with his father's first attack of arthritis, an ailment from which he would suffer terribly for the next five years.

Overall the critics loved the film, as did the paying public. 'Original, perilous and marvellously entertaining,' said John Coleman in the *New Statesman*. Ian Cameron in the *Spectator* was not won over, but had the wit to take his two children along, from whom he reported 'almost unqualified enthusiasm. Both had a great time, as apparently did all the children in the audience.'

Despite personal reservations, Derek Malcolm in the *Guardian* concurred with this view, 'but I can't quite go along with all the eulogies so far,' he wrote. 'There are times when the movie loses its way, when the invention sags and when the essential artificiality of the concept becomes apparent.' However, Malcolm felt that a lot of people were going to be entertained and not even critics would feel patronized. 'This is a very considerable achievement,' he wrote, 'and an unusual one.' He felt Alan Parker had gained from directing as well as scripting. 'The added responsibility of seeing the job through before the cameras has clearly made him twice the man.'

Still not man enough for Pauline Kael in the States, however, who lay in ambush when the film opened. 'He has made an elaborate version of an "Our Gang" comedy,' she wrote, 'stuffed with stale whipped cream. Without irony ... *Bugsy Malone* is nothing but its godawful idea ... the movie stays on the level of refined, wholesome grotesqueness, like Disney without the energy, and never takes up the underlying suggestiveness and creepiness of its own material.' No one, it seemed, would have caught Miss Kael standing up and cheering the film on at Cannes. The American public gave the film the thumbs-down also, but worldwide the bottom line was a gratifying net profit close to £2 million.

When impresario Robert Stigwood had earlier viewed a rough cut of the movie, he expressed enormous enthusiasm. He predicted a gross of $100 million and offered to buy into the movie. This suited both David and Sandy at Goodtimes, alleviating their financial position, as well as that of the two Alans, although it naturally reduced their upside potential. While in America for the première, David was extremely upset when he saw the posters, which read 'Paramount and Robert Stigwood presents –' Since he felt that Stigwood had stolen the film, his plane seat for the journey home was booked in short order.

For Bobby Littman's contribution, the introduction of David to Paramount and the discovery of Jodie Foster, he was given the impression he was on a percentage of the movie's profits. So far he has seen around $2000. 'My deal was on a profit percentage, then when further finance had to be brought in, the terms were altered to a gross deal. Evelyn de Rothschild didn't pay me any money on the gross. I was very upset. It wasn't David's fault. I never resented David for it. I did occasionally feel he could have tried a little harder for me with the Rothschilds, however.'

David chose to agonize publicly on his feelings about Goodtimes. As always, he was putting out signals for anyone who cared to pick them up, in this case an advance requiem for Goodtimes.

'We have failed,' he declared, 'because we don't seem to have hit on a style of film-making.' No one rushed to disagree with him for the only films that could be said to have offered anything like a personal statement and an indication of what might yet emerge had been *That'll Be the Day* and *Stardust*.

'Had we been the kind of success we wanted to be, there would be five other Goodtimes operating here,' he continued. 'We've also failed because we haven't created an energy. And that pisses me off because it hasn't been for lack of trying. We'll go on, according to our own lights, because I'm too selfish to do it any other way, and hopefully by a process of natural selection there'll come a time, if we keep hanging in there, when what we make will also be popular.'

The parting of the ways had in fact taken place for David and Sandy while *Bugsy* was enjoying its triumph at Cannes. 'We didn't part with any animosity at all,' says Sandy, 'but with *Trick or Treat* and everything, it just seemed all too much. We were making so little money out of the company; we were by now collecting a £12,000 salary each and all the real profits weren't coming through to us since Rothschilds invested in the movies *personally*, rather than through Goodtimes. We got *nothing* from it, we were in debt, both of us owed money to the tax collector, David had a huge overdraft and I think the banks were worried about him being able to pay it off. We both still owed Rothschilds the money they'd loaned us for our stock in VPS, so with *Trick or Treat* and all, we just thought, "Christ, we'd better cut and run."'

'I didn't feel I was doing what I wanted to do,' David stated, admitting he had been the one to precipitate the split, while rather glossing over the fact that Rothschilds, after the shock of the Marcel Ophuls settlement, the *Lisztomania* disaster and the *Trick or Treat* fiasco, were about to abandon ship in any event. To them Goodtimes had run the gamut, from out-of-control budgets to court actions and project abandonment, incidents not best calculated to comply with their conception of prudent management.

'The company always lived, it seemed to me, from crisis to crisis,' says Frank Bloom. 'David had to fight tooth and claw for everything he got. He developed good relationships with Thorn-EMI and some of the American majors, but it was always a one-off battle. My own theory was that because of the continuing office overhead and the difficulty of making enough productions to pay for this overhead and the salaries, they were always on a treadmill. What happened was they would often make things and then try to sell them in a hurry, like the speculative television ventures. They were under tremendous pressure to sell and that was more significant when it came to selling off bits of their profits of a film, where they couldn't afford to wait. Of course when they produced for the majors, the majors made the investment and the company earned a producer's fee. But that was all they got unless the film went into profit, which could take a long time, if ever. Even then David refused to compromise. On *Stardust* he needed to boost American scenes and went along to the financiers and begged them to give him another £150,000. He had to cut his own fee to get it, but that's the man – he won't compromise on the screen. He will wreck his own finances first to get the results he wants.

'In the end the venture just fizzled out because they weren't getting any money. Patsy's strength helped him enormously through that difficult time when he had to pick himself up and start again. She didn't show it then, but she's very strong. She hid that from me for a long time. I remember the Aga cooker she had in the kitchen at Queensgate at least 10 years before they were rediscovered. I hadn't seen one for years and I mentioned something about it. She just said, "Oh, Frank, it's like me, it's slow, but dependable." She tried to give the impression of slow thinking, but I've since realized it's really not quite like that.'

'She's everybody's mother,' is Andrew Birkin's affectionate view of Patsy. For a while her concern was for her own childrens' feelings. In the last few years, Patsy found herself occasionally straining to keep up with her husband's growth. She watched in dismay as acquaintances were jettisoned and left behind. 'The children used to worry about that a little bit,' she admits. 'Suppose their dad did that to them? David never acknowledged the fact they were children. When he played Monopoly with them he played to win. Maybe it brought out the best in them; then again maybe it made them a little unsure of their ground. Both of them have this thing never to let him down. Nowadays David never finishes a phone-call to them without saying, "You know I love you, don't you?"'

David was fully aware of the situation with Patsy and the children and smiles a little contritely. 'Patsy would fall behind, become frightened and then suddenly get it together again. Debbie and Patsy took over Sacha; he didn't have anything to do for himself. When Patsy wasn't bringing him up, Debbie was. He had an enormously rough time when Debbie first went off to school. For him it was an incredible jolt. But yes, I plead guilty to always treating the kids as people.'

Sandy's plan was to continue independent movie-making under his own original Goodtimes banner, while David formed a new entity, the appropriately named Enigma Productions, in May 1976. The company already had its starter in *The Duellists*, with Ridley Scott making his directorial début on the big screen after five gruelling years of struggle.

He had originally adapted the Joseph Conrad short story, *A Point of Honour*, for television. The story followed the fortunes of two men involved in constant duelling over many years during the Napoleonic Wars, to satisfy an increasingly vague idea of honour. When David came on board, the screenplay had been reworked with Gerald Vaughan-Hughes and spun out to feature-film length. 'This was one of three pieces of material that were in development as potential directorial débuts for Ridley,' David recalls, 'but I found that having harnessed David Picker at Paramount and his enthusiasm for Ridley's talents,

The Duellists was the only one of the three projects that could be made within the parameters that were set. The point worth reiterating here is that the final decision was not a creative one, but budgetary!'

David had located Enigma's offices above the N F F C in Dean Street, prior to the acquisition of adjoining property in Queensgate Place Mews that would enable him to have his office virtually at home. Dean Street was small and run down and his only staff was his secretary from Goodtimes, Lynda Smith. Low overheads were the order of the day for the new régime, together with spartan stringency. When the move to Queensgate did take place, David found a tenant in a literary agent, Ed Victor, to whom he rented Dean Street.

Some months later a dispute arose over a telephone bill for £600. Victor refused to pay it, maintaining it had been run up by Enigma before they vacated the premises. David took the view, after carefully checking the matter with Lynda, that this was not the case. With the dispute in stalemate, Frank Bloom's advice was sought.

'What do you want?' asked Frank. 'Do I sue?'

David went whitefaced with anger. 'If I can't prove it, I'm not going to sue him,' he declared. 'But – I'll get even.'

David duly paid the bill and Frank heard no more of the matter until almost ten years later when he arrived at Los Angeles airport. On the way to collect his hired car from the Avis desk, he saw Ed Victor in the line in front and reintroduced himself.

'How's David?' Victor asked.

'He's fine,' said Frank. 'I'm sorry about that dispute over the phone.'

'Me, too,' said Victor, still obviously smarting. 'I put a client of mine onto David and he turned him down. He told him that while he was represented by Ed Victor he didn't want anything to do with him. He shouldn't have done that. My dispute with David had nothing to do with my client or his abilities.'

As Frank drove into Los Angeles he reflected on Victor's story and the occasionally vindictive, unforgiving side of David it revealed. The agent had crossed the invisible line David kept in his head. Once crossed, there was no going back.

Location shooting for *The Duellists* was to take place in France, followed by the north of Scotland in late 1976. When Terence Stamp, Patsy's erstwhile dietician, turned down one of the lead roles, David was urged by Paramount to consider Keith Carradine. He had admired

Harvey Keitel's performance in *Alice Doesn't Live Here Anymore* and was able to strike a good deal for both actors on discovering they were represented by the same agent. A strong supporting cast included Edward Fox, Christina Raines, Robert Stephens, Tom Conti, John McEnery, Diana Quick and Albert Finney. 'Finney was wonderful,' says Patsy. 'He'd just fallen in love with Diana and agreed to do a week for David for actors' minimum. It made it possible for David to go back to Paramount and ask for the bit of extra money he needed: $50,000.'

Money was still tight and the price extracted from Ridley Scott was his agreement to do the picture for next to nothing. David took a leaf out of quickie king Roger Corman's book here, that you learn as you work – for free. David himself was on a potential hiding to nothing. 'We had to make these conditions because we budgeted the picture in March and when we were ready to start shooting it was October. By then Technicolor prices and Kodak stock prices had gone up and it was going to cost another $60,000. In the end, if you're a producer who wants to make a *good* film, the amount of money you make at the end of the day can't be your main criterion.'

David discussed with Ridley the sort of picture they wanted from *The Duellists* long before shooting began, summarized in his typical verbal shorthand as a mixture of Stanley Kubrick's *Barry Lyndon*, with a touch of Clint Eastwood's *The Outlaw Josey Wales* thrown in for good measure. They searched for the perfect settings in the French countryside for the film, settling eventually in the Perigord area. This had the kind of geography Ridley was looking for, with dozens of castles and villages that had remained unchanged and unspoilt since the early 19th century. The unit stationed themselves at the village of Sarlat for the 10-week shoot before the final scenes in the north of Scotland.

Fencing director William Hobbs was engaged to work with Ridley to ensure realism in the duelling scenes. 'It was as if we were choreographing a ballet and each move had to look right. This was not an Errol Flynn film, though, and we had to make sure the actors didn't get hurt.' Despite this vow, Harvey Keitel had a close call when a sabre blow by Keith Carradine that was meant to hit him in the chest landed too high and caught him under his left eye. Only after the scene was wrapped did Ridley and David realize that the blood on Keitel's face was the real thing. The actor shrugged off the scratch and insisted that filming continue. David stood watching Ridley admiringly while location shooting went ahead. 'He is making us a great film,' he observed.

Towards the end the unit had terrible problems with the weather, as France was buffeted by wind and rain for 16 straight days, the wind at times reaching hurricane force. David presided anxiously over this period, encouraging his director to keep on shooting whenever possible. The mediaeval town of Sarlat had never seen anything like the unit's invasion, but seemed to cheerfully absorb the convoy of lorries that positioned themselves at strategic points around the area. Three separate buses served as kitchen and canteen for the unit. The day Ridley filmed the final scene showing Harvey Keitel on a hill overlooking a village along the Dordogne, the river overflowed its banks, flooding part of the village and its access roads. The team were provided with some matchless footage. The unit left on the last road that was passable, with the waters still rising.

David flew to Scotland to set up further location filming, armed with a large pile of scripts he was considering for the future. He refused to see himself as altruistic in his choice of new directors, regarding it instead as pure common sense to work with his contemporaries. He had seen how ill-equipped he had been to bring anything to a Ken Russell or a Jacques Demy, let alone control them. Doing it his way, he reckoned, he would produce a team of five or six directors to work with in the future. 'He'd recognized the pool of talent that lay in commercial advertising,' says Alan Parker. 'He was brilliant to do that, the one person who recognized that potential. He'd started by taking the conventional route, then after *Bugsy* the penny dropped. We were never taken seriously as a group of directors by the British critics, our pedigree was wrong; none of us had made documentaries for the BBC!'

While shooting for *The Duellists* was taking place in freezing conditions at Scotland's Aviemore Ski Centre, Alan Parker was in New York on a two-fold mission; to promote *Bugsy Malone* and to check out the stage musical, *The Wiz*, which Universal were interested in having him adapt for the screen. He saw the show and decided against accepting the assignment. One day as he was passing by Columbia's 711 Fifth Avenue offices Peter Guber emerged from the revolving doors. 'He's the only man I've ever met who talks faster than David Puttnam,' Alan laughs. Guber had left Columbia Pictures with a golden handshake and had teamed up with Neil Bogart of the highly successful US record label, Casablanca. The resultant Bogart/Guber concern was known as Casablanca Records and Filmworks, fulfilling Bogart's ambitions to break into motion pictures. Guber explained to Alan they had been trying to reach him to consider directing a new project they had acquired, *Midnight Express*.

David says he got a call from Guber around the same time. 'Very typical of Peter, he tracked me down,' says David. 'I was in the Rank Hotel in Aviemore and a message arrived while I was on location, there was a call coming in and it was very important. I assumed it was something to do with *The Duellists*. I'd known Guber, because he'd been at Columbia when they had *Stardust*. He called and asked what I was doing and I said, "What do you mean, what am I doing? I'm doing a film." And he asked me when I was going to finish and I said two weeks. He said, well, did I want to come to Los Angeles and work with him? "To do what?" I asked. He explained they had a story which Columbia had agreed to do, called *Midnight Express*. I said I would need to read it first. He said he'd send me the book.'

When Alan phoned David later to tell him his news of the meeting with Guber David said, 'You're never going to believe this. Peter's asked me to produce it!'

Peter Guber does not entirely agree with David's version of this story. After meeting Alan and giving him the galleys of *Midnight Express*, he says he then hired Oliver Stone to work on the screenplay, 'and agreed with Judy Scott-Fox, Alan Parker's agent, that Alan Marshall would produce the film for me. Sometime after that I hired David Puttnam to be the president of Casablanca Filmworks, to develop his own films through us. Later he came to me and said he would like to produce *Midnight Express* with Alan Marshall, because he wanted to work with Alan Parker, who he was very close to and because he very much liked Oliver's screenplay.'

Although the offer – either to be president of Casablanca, produce *Midnight Express*, or both – was made in January, the Puttnams deliberated for fully six weeks before making their minds up in March. There were two elements to consider, one being the production of a film called *Agatha*, for which Kathleen Tynan had provided a screenplay and which had Julie Christie and Vanessa Redgrave lined up to star in. This was set to be David's follow-up to *The Duellists* for Enigma. Could he now mastermind this long-distance when it rolled in the autumn?

The other element was plain necessity. To all outward appearances, David was a successful film producer who had made the proverbial packet out of hits like *Melody*, *That'll Be the Day*, *Stardust*, *James Dean: The First American Teenager*, the German documentaries and *Bugsy Malone*. The truth was quite different, for David had been paying himself a pittance. As producer of *That'll Be the Day* he had taken a salary of £10,000, then for *Stardust* £12,000. From *Mahler* he had taken nothing and from *Bugsy Malone* he had extracted precisely

£6,000 for two years' work. Although additional income was anticipated from some of these films as well, David and Sandy had to face
the prospect of paying 83 per cent of anything that came in over
£21,000 in tax. David was in hock to the bank, and the two years out
of the country the Casablanca offer represented – and the opportunity
to make a tax-free half a million dollars – was the perfect answer.

'What had happened,' David ruefully explains, 'is that I was 10
years into my film career, I'd spent the £30,000 we'd saved through
the agency and I'd been living on an overdraft of £68,000, at the
Natwest. (Thank God Patsy's father had retired by this time!) We
were totally boracic, and worse, I had a tax bill looming on top.'

The decision to accept the Hollywood offer may not have been
instant, but it was inevitable.

Chapter 9

Tales of Hoffman

'I won't go unless you come out too,' David declared, to which Patsy did what she now calls her best spoiled-brat act, answering that she simply didn't want to live in America and agonizing, fairly understandably, about the disruption that Debbie and Sacha's education would face. What won the day was the acknowledgement that the way they were living was becoming intolerable, with David on and off planes and hardly ever settled at home for as long as they could remember. 'You've *got* to come to America,' David told her. 'I can't stand all these plane journeys. You've *got* to come. It's the only way we're ever going to crack it!'

David moved out on his own in April 1976, while Patsy stayed at home and held the fort until the summer-holiday break arrived and Debbie and Sacha could be organized. Debbie was packed off to France on holiday, then was to stay in England with Patsy's parents to enable her to take her O-levels the following year, while Sacha found himself sitting the American Scholastic Aptitude Test, roughly the equivalent of the common entrance in England, which would enable him to apply for a place at Harvard Prep School in Coldwater Canyon. David had arranged to rent an attractive house overlooking the sea at Aderno Way, Pacific Palisades, which was available from the end of June, and on his advice Patsy and Sacha travelled out a week early, staying at the Bel Air hotel before taking over the house. 'You're going to be exhausted and you'll need to get acclimatized,' he had told Patsy, who was grateful indeed for his consideration, for she felt badly jet-lagged for days.

'We moved in on Friday, 30 June,' she recalls, 'and on Saturday, 1 July, we were all three sitting on the bed together, I'd just made a cup of tea and some breakfast, when it was announced on television that Virginia Wade had won in the finals at Wimbledon. I suddenly felt so homesick, I just started crying. "What the *hell* am I doing here?" I asked myself. Then that was it over and done with and I got down to the daily business of organizing the thousand and one so-called petty things necessary to ensure that life continues.'

Sacha was duly enrolled at school. 'It was so ironic,' Patsy reckons. 'He was there against our adjusted financial situation. Just a few months earlier we'd told both children's headmasters that we might have to take them out of school, since we didn't think we could meet the fees. Now things had certainly changed, but the future was still a blank piece of paper.'

With the start of production on *Midnight Express* constantly put back and now due to start in September, a couple of months were spent in Aderno Way that were relatively carefree. 'Alan Marshall, Alan Parker, Ridley Scott, Jack Rosenthal, Mike Apted – everyone – they all came to stay with us at one time or another during that period. I was back to running a hotel again, but it couldn't have felt more different from Ranelagh Grove. I was *part* of a creative community, we were in *California*, I had *help*, it was *totally* different. We all used to sit around at these breakfasts, nobody wanted to go to work, while endless supplies of English muffins and tea and coffee were wheeled in. The best ideas would come out then; there was this tremendous atmosphere. David was flying back and forth, but was still there a lot of the time. At night we were the kids in the candy store again; every night it was hysterical as people came in and told their stories of the day. On Saturdays we all sat outside in the sunshine, reading endless scripts and being complete hooligans. We sat in the garden overlooking the sea with the Santa Monica mountains behind us. "I can't get into this one at all," one of us would yell, "fling us another script over." *Hooligans!*'

For David the daily routine at Casablanca, in between location scouting trips, was somewhat different. He hated the constant rounds of committees and decisions eventually taken that were then subject to change by further committees. At what precise point he became firmly aligned with and co-producer of the *Midnight Express* project must remain a matter of dispute between David and Peter Guber, but when he returned from one particular session Patsy could tell immediately from his demeanour that something was wrong. 'I've got some news,' he began, shifting his weight from one foot to the other, tugging away at his beard and coughing nervously, 'and I just don't know how to break it to you.' Patsy stared hard at him. 'Just blurt it out quickly,' she said, thinking she was ready for anything; Britain could take it. After all, what could it be that was so bad?

David looked very unhappy. 'The company has decided, I mean, we thought about it a lot and looked at every other option, but at the end of the day we're making *Midnight Express* in Malta.'

As his words sank in (Malta? *Malta?*) all Patsy could think was,

'But I could be at *home*!' All the move had been for nothing, it seemed.

'In the end it was good,' Patsy now sees, 'because it reconciled me to living in Los Angeles and I got to know my way around with David gone, and got to like it. For Sacha it was not so good; he started in Harvard and had a dreadful time. They put him in a class with older boys; this small English boy with the funny accent amid all these hulking blondes, who used to call him "fag" every time he opened his mouth. He kept the whole miserable thing to himself for months.'

Since Sacha's school was a 30-odd mile return trip night and morning, Patsy fell in with a car pool, and rather than return home during her on-duty days, took a job in the school library. 'I felt better being close to Sacha in this way,' she says, 'not that he ever ran complaining to me, but I still felt better. As for the rest, we had a great house and I decided just to get on with it. In some ways it was better, for when you're on your own you have no alternative, so although it was a dreadful blow to start with, in the end it turned out to be rather good.' Patsy had learned how to roll with the punches.

During David's first couple of months in Los Angeles, Oliver Stone was working in Alan Parker's London office on the script for *Midnight Express*. 'On the whole it was a very professional relationship,' Alan recalls with a wry little smile. '*All right*, it wasn't a bundle of laughs, I didn't necessarily want him to be my *best pal*, in fact initially I told David and Alan Marshall I didn't know if I was going to be able to work with this guy. "Don't worry," they said, "let him deliver the script and that'll be it." We got the script and within half an hour of reading it we were all on the phone to each other saying how brilliant it was. There was a brief time in Los Angeles later after it had all been written when David had to step in between the two of us, but there was no problem on the set since Oliver wasn't there when we made the movie. The next time I saw him was after he had a look at the finished film, then after that when he won the Oscar.'

When Alan had come out to Los Angeles to start pre-production, he found David installed in lavish offices at Casablanca's headquarters overlooking Sunset Strip. Less impressive was the office Alan was allowed, virtually a windowless cupboard next door to David. Alan soon had the walls decorated with pictures of the hundreds of applicants for the key roles in *Midnight Express*. Patsy noted that David's office was as usual furnished and equipped to his very exacting requirements, complete with all the accoutrements that accompany him wherever he goes. 'He has to have one desk against a wall, where he can work quietly facing the wall. Around the desk are his photographs, of Diaghilev, Irving Thalberg, photographs of the family, all strategically placed. An art-deco lamp, pristine and perfect, illuminates the desk, on which sit neatly-stacked pads of stationery, pens, pencils, sharpeners, erasers. Then he has another desk in the middle of the floor, various chairs and bookcases, his music unit. Then, and *only* then, can he work. The man's a self-confessed tidiness freak.' (One of Marie's favourite sayings at home had been 'A place for everything and everything in its place.')

One day Alan was due to interview an actor for the leading role. Ostensibly the film was to be the true story of Billy Hayes, a young American drifter who was held captive and brutalized in a Turkish prison, following a drug-smuggling attempt. The press dubbed him 'the pawn in the poppy game between Nixon and the Turks'. Hayes had maintained that the two kilos of hashish found on him had just been for his friends back home. The punishment had been an initial four-year sentence, later extended to a horrifying 30 years.

Since Alan had made a lunchtime appointment and David was out of the studio for an hour, he decided to conduct the interview in David's rather more impressive quarters. 'Sit down,' he told the actor, who was wandering about all wired-up and speedy-looking. Alan gestured towards the seat opposite him at David's desk in the middle of the floor. 'Do you mind if I take my jacket off?' Alan was asked. 'Of course not,' he replied. 'Now, the scene I want you to play is the one in which Billy, who thinks he's only got a few weeks left of his sentence, is informed by the Turkish judge that it has in fact been extended to 30 years. All right?'

'Uh, huh. Fine. Look, do you mind if I loosen my tie?'

Alan looked up from his script. 'No, whatever makes you feel more comfortable . . .'

'Well, how about if I take my shirt off as well?'

'Fine, I mean, whatever . . .'

'Look. Would you mind if I just took the whole lot off. It'll help me to get into the part.'

'Go ahead . . .' (Alan was by now sinking into his seat as the actor sat naked across from him.)

'It's just that, before I can do this scene, I have to humiliate myself in front of you.'

'Sure, sure, I understand. Off you go,' Alan managed. He had picked the scene deliberately for its emotional content, reasoning that if the actor could handle it he could certainly cope with the rest of the picture. What he hadn't reckoned with was this particular applicant's enthusiasm, for as soon as he got into his speech, he began picking up various items from David's immaculately laid-out desk and hurling them to the far corners of the room as he reacted to the new sentence imposed by the Turkish judge that Alan was playing.

'How can I expect you to understand how I feel? It's like asking a bear to shit in a toilet!', he yelled as David's pen and pencil set went flying, then as the scene reached its pitch of intensity (and Alan was thinking, 'Oh, dear God, how will I explain this to David?') the actor bodily hauled Alan across the desk.

'I hate you, I hate your nation, I hate your people. I fuck your sons and daughters because they're pigs,' he spat out, then jolted him back into his seat.

An alarmed Lynda Smith, hearing the disturbance inside David's room, opened the door just in time to see the naked actor, bellowing '30 *years*! 30 fucking *years*!' at the top of his voice, overturn the desk and all its contents, sending them crashing to the parquet floor. Quick as a flash she banged the door shut again. 'Film people!' she muttered, while all Alan could think, facing total panic, was 'What's the time? David will be back any minute. I've got to get this bugger's clothes on and get him out of here before he comes back and sees his office in this state!'

'Thanks very much. We'll let you know,' he informed the actor, professional to the last, then Lynda was promptly roped into the frantic effort to restore David's office to its former glory. What slightly gave the game away was the art-deco lamp Patsy had lovingly chosen for her husband, which was smashed to pieces.

David expressed concern to Oliver Stone that certain sequences in his script, notably those featuring the Turkish prison warden, could not be satisfactorily transferred to film. Even if they were, David argued, they would never get past the censor. Stone sensed it was compromise time, and took another look at his script. He wrote to Alan Parker, the emergent director inside him straining to the forefront on some scenes that would indeed never see the light of day:

Dear Alan,
David suggests that I take another look at the script. I hadn't done so in 2 months . . . so I read it all in one sitting A.M. a few days ago and thought about it. I have made some minor last-minute notes which follow, to do with as you please:

P. 20 Scene 138: . . . if your actor is blond, obviously you know a large

part of the sexual tension is the blond hair and what it means to the
Turks, and you must play this up with Hamidou's feeling his hair to
make sure it *is* blond as is what happened to the real Billy (he told
me).

P. 91 Scene 600: . . . one night, in the earlier prison, you may do a brief
visual of Billy going to the toilet at night and seeing two guys banging
each other and turning away disgusted (then he finds himself with
Erich in that same toilet later) . . . when Billy goes into the stalls with
the (photo) album, two guys are fucking openly on the floor . . . he
ignores them, freaking out only when the three loonies are looking at
him while masturbating . . . the nuthouse is a whorehouse! and in
this atmosphere the audience will know that ANYTHING GOES,
as Billy is dragged up to the steam bath (where the visuals could be
great, Alan!).

Note those words – anything goes – and don't go the opposite way.
Don't *limit that* . . . I am totally against Melnick's theory of the bribe –
this is precisely the logical limitation you should fight against (and
David too, if he agrees with it) . . . I hope you stand by the backbone of
my script. All my love in this undertaking.

Yours,
Oliver.

The modifications Alan made to many of Oliver Stone's conceptions
are ironic in view of the subsequent abuse he had heaped on his
shoulders for the film's excesses. Alan was making what he regarded
as an Alan Parker movie, nothing more, nothing less. 'I'm very strong
when it comes to making a movie,' he says, 'and *nobody* tells me what
to do. Nobody. I don't remember seeing Oliver's letter and if I had,
I'd probably have torn it up. One of the frustrations that David has
working with me and why he'll probably never work with me again –
it's *my* film and no one else's. I'm very egocentric and megalomaniac
about that. I believe that the director is the one who makes the film
and no one else, not the studio executives, not the producer, no one.
The scriptwriter has a contribution to make, but only up to a certain
point.'

With filming about to start in Malta, the set-up consisted of David
and Alan Marshall as co-producers for Alan Parker, the two Alans
having worked closely together to prepare the film. Their joint en-
deavours were supervised from Los Angeles by executive producer
Peter Guber of Casablanca and Dan Melnick, Columbia's production
head. Alan decided that a note to the crew would be in order, outlining
the way he saw the film they were about to make.

Dear Everybody,

We are about to embark on a new film, most of us not for the first time together, and I thought it would be nice to drop you a line before we begin.

The reason for the letter is firstly to say something *before* we start, secondly to warn you about a very difficult film and thirdly because I heard Ingmar Bergman always did it.

As you have gathered from the script it is my intention to make a very violent, uncompromisingly brutal film, the subject matter of which will no doubt take its toll on all of us. (That's assuming sunstroke, cheap Maltese wine, Mr Marshall's scowls and the service at the Excelsior don't do it first.)

The screenplay is 80% truthful to the original autobiography, as it happened to the real Billy Hayes; but I think we are creating something else which will match reality with a slightly bizarre theatrical edge. It's difficult to put into words, but I would like the audience to be shaken and shocked that such things happen, almost to the point of disbelief – but never to lose them.

The shooting will naturally be very strenuous on our actors, and where possible we have tried to schedule things in a sequential order to accommodate this.

Our film will not moralize about the rights and wrongs of drugs but will hopefully bring attention to the inconsistencies of sentences from country to country – and in the USA even from state to state. In California, possession of marijuana is in the process of being de-criminalized, yet in Texas it still carries a life sentence. In Turkey it can be punishable by death.

In short, Midnight Express is a film about the hypocrisies of drug offence penalties, brutalities of prison life, the nearer verges of insanity, growing up, and above all, about never losing hope.

I wish us all well.

Yours,

Alan.

The *Duellists* had meanwhile opened to negligible box-office on its Paramount release. In the *Sunday Times* Alan Brien put his finger on what he saw as the film's malaise. 'What appears to be needed is some deeper sense of personal, social and historical seeds from which the duellists' bizarre enmity must spring.' He reckoned that Joseph Conrad had set it all out in his book, but the film-makers had seemed to assume the situation could be accepted just as it was, without any need for further enlightenment. 'What we mainly retain,' Brien concluded, 'is the impression of two clockwork protagonists wound up for a series of rattling good bouts of swordplay, with little more idea than we have who turned the keys.' This very lack of flesh on the bones of reason seemed to lie behind the film's dispiriting failure. It appeared that David and Ridley Scott had failed to ensure there was some meaningful background and subtext beneath the highly polished veneer. No warmth had been allowed near the chilly heart of the film, although it certainly *looked* magnificent.

With *Midnight Express* being shot in Malta, David now felt able to supervise the pre-production of *Agatha* in England at the same time. Kathleen Tynan's screenplay speculated on the reasons for Agatha Christie's real-life disappearance from her home in 1926, when she was in the middle of her unhappy first marriage. The film had first seen finance in place through the dreaded Rank Organization, David's sparring partners from *Bugsy Malone*. Rank were in the throes of once again reactivating their only recently-abandoned production programme, but the liaison came to an end when it was discovered that Colonel Christie, from whom Agatha had been fleeing in some mental distress according to the screenplay, had been a director of Rank at one time. The old boy network put paid soon thereafter to Rank's potentially embarrassing involvement and a company called First Artists entered the picture, together with their distributors, Warners. Through his British agent, Jarvis Astaire, the talents of Dustin Hoffman were brought to the project.

The actor was having marital problems at the time. This, combined with the need to deliver First Artists their final picture under his contract, made filming on *Agatha* in Britain an attractive proposition. David already had Vanessa Redgrave, Helen Morse (in place of Julie Christie, who had broken her wrist) and Timothy Dalton lined up to star.

'Out of the blue he phoned me,' says David. 'I just picked up the phone and someone said it was Dustin Hoffman. He told me he'd read the screenplay and thought it was a wonderful piece of work. He said he badly wanted to work in England for personal reasons for a week or so, and was there any chance he could become involved? I thought, well, that doesn't seem too onerous. There was a role for a journalist and we worked out that we could make the proprietor of the newspaper a Canadian, give him a nephew with an accent and make the thing work.

'Dustin then literally arrived in England with a writer, a very nice man named Murray Schisgal, who proceeded to rewrite the script! Now that wasn't the deal. On the other hand, as I was very quickly encouraged to understand, the reason that Warners were twice as pleased was that they now had a film starring Dustin Hoffman and felt they had a real bargain. And no matter what Dustin did it became very clear that he was running the film.'

The problems on *Agatha* quickly escalated, with Dustin Hoffman's role expanded overnight from a cameo to co-billing with Vanessa Redgrave. Someone else's part had to be reduced, and it was the unfortunate Helen Morse who emerged as the main victim. Yet again David found himself in the position of having a picture careering away from him. He recognized that *Agatha* was no longer going to be the production he had planned. It was being transformed into a Dustin Hoffman vehicle. Since Dustin's name meant far more than his, it was clear which one Warners would back. David saw himself hopelessly squeezed out between the star and the studio.

He decided the only way out was to terminate his involvement with the film, and wrote to Jarvis Astaire accordingly. 'I went through agonizing and cajoling,' David told a reporter, 'and found myself asking if I really wanted to work with this worrisome American pest when I could be having a productive time in Malta on *Midnight Express*.' It was a quote that would be repeated with relish over the years.

'I gave up a year's development work on a screenplay I had loved very much indeed,' says David. 'I realize now that someone had found the "leading man" clause in Dustin's contract and a cameo was no good for his purposes. But he didn't *tell* anybody. Instead of telling us the truth, he just took over the set with his own writer. Nobody understood what was going on.'

Michael Apted stayed on and had to put up with endless delays due to the constant script rewriting. Having originally described the picture elatedly as his 'passport to Hollywood', grave doubts were now setting in. Here was one individual who did not appreciate David's point that there can only ever be one head of a successful enterprise: 'As soon as Hoffman arrived as producer on the film David just *ran*. I don't think David wanted the competition, he didn't want the fact that he was not going to be the sole producer influence.

'I think this was a ridiculous thing for him to do, for he had been responsible for bringing Dustin into the project. I think if you are taking on a major American star who is bringing the finance with him you have to acknowledge his existence in other ways than he's just going to turn up in the morning and act. He's going to have his own people round him and his own demands. David would never acknowledge that.

'So there was one horrendous punch-up and David left the film and left me and Vanessa and the project stranded in the hands of

Hoffman, who is very difficult to deal with. It was a very dreadful state of affairs. There is a slight element to David that unless he can run the show, unless he can be the full captain of the ship, then he'd rather not be in it at all.'

Alan Parker could see the other side of the coin. While conceding that if he had been in Michael Apted's position, he would have felt let down as well, he still felt David had made the only sensible move. 'If, after a certain point, he sees it's not going to work, he doesn't hang around, he moves very quickly. He *moves*. Now the rest of the people couldn't move, they had to stay with it, so you can see why they're a little bit resentful. On the other hand, I understand exactly what David was doing, because *we* were saying, "Don't bother with *that*, come over to us. We're having a lot of fun." So it was comfortable for him to walk away from *Agatha*. Alan Marshall being the producer he is, the Malta side of it would be left to him. David would handle the Hollywood end for us. Selfishly, I was quite pleased.'

In view of subsequent events, David's decision to leave can be seen as not only eminently sensible, but absolutely inevitable. Dustin Hoffman claims he found to his horror that the revised script, which he was responsible for initiating, was unfinished when shooting began. 'I literally went down on my knees and begged them not to start the film,' he maintained. 'Once you go on the floor to make a movie, it's crazy time. It's painting a picture on a railroad track, with the train getting closer. *Agatha* was every actor's nightmare. The script was literally being written every day.'

With Murray Schisgal attending to Dustin's lines, Vanessa Redgrave asked Michael Apted to get Arthur Hopcraft for her. Communication between the two stars was non-existent, since Dustin refused to talk to Vanessa. Since someone had to make the two sets of dialogues mesh, the task fell to the enterprising script girl, Zelda Barron. When amalgamation proved downright impossible, Zelda would add a few lines of her own to smooth the joins. The entire cast found themselves with fresh script pages being thrust at them each day just before shooting was due to start. At one point, in absolute desperation, Vanessa Redgrave insisted that shooting be held up to give her time to absorb the new lines and make sense of where her character was going.

Meantime, a unit publicist observed that Dustin himself was taking a hand in the script changes. 'Dustin won't have anything to do with publicity now,' he stated, 'he's too busy rewriting the script!' Dustin himself referred to it as a 'rainbow of green, yellow and pink revision pages.' When a visiting journalist asked Dustin how the movie was progressing, the star replied, 'I'm fulfilling my contract with First Artists and then I'm going to get *the fuck* out of here!' The journalist described the atmosphere on the *Agatha* set as the most bitter and frenzied he had ever encountered.

With Christmas approaching, First Artists decided enough was enough. Although Jarvis Astaire and Gavrik Losey were officially the film's producers since David's departure, the company nevertheless let Dustin know of their decision directly. 'They gave me a letter that it was to be finished in three days,' he groaned. 'I *begged* to be allowed to use my own money to shoot the final scene. I was refused.'

He himself later refused to do post-production dubs on the movie, then backed down, realizing only too well that First Artists would not hesitate to engage another actor to complete the chore if he refused. Recriminations flew between the two parties, with First Artists claiming that Dustin had acted 'in bad faith and with improper motives out of a desire to dispose of his commitment to First Artists with the least possible inconvenience to him and in the shortest possible time in order to move on to work which would be more lucrative and personally rewarding to him.'

Multi-million dollar lawsuits promptly flew in the Hollywood manner between Dustin and First Artists. Dustin claimed $2 million in lost salary on the two First Artists' films and $66 million in damages in breach of contract, $3 million of that directed against First Artists' president Phil Feldman and his own business manager, Jarvis Astaire. Much of this bombast was to pressure First Artists into giving him final edit on *Agatha* and *Straight Time*.

'When Dustin found out that as producer I was agreeing with First Artists and not with him, our business arrangement and our friendship were over,' said Jarvis Astaire. 'It's just a shame that the Hoffman of today isn't the Hoffman I've known in the past nine years. Puttnam was complaining that Hoffman had too much power. He was lucky. Hoffman didn't have as much as he wanted. Hoffman also accused Vanessa Redgrave of refusing to act certain scenes. It's just untrue. It was *he* who refused to act in the film as originally written.'

Many years later Astaire came up with his own version of David's 'feud' with Hoffman. 'David Puttnam created this myth,' he claimed, 'but Dustin was not the reason David didn't produce *Agatha*. He couldn't produce the picture because he could only come to England 20 days the rest of the year. He was in Malta finishing *Midnight Express* and he said his tax accountant gave him the tax reason for not coming to England. He was getting what is called a "tax breather".' Astaire had known David since his photographic agency days. 'I can tell you that butter wouldn't melt in his mouth,' he said, 'but don't stick your finger in it!'

David stuck to his guns and denied Astaire's version. 'I didn't produce *Agatha*,' he insisted, 'because it became a movie out of control. *That* was the reason. I saw, in that film, how *not* to make a movie. How *any* star can't be allowed to decide what's right for a movie.'

In a seven-page opinion handed down by Judge David A. Thomas on Hoffman's request for a preliminary injunction to halt distribution of *Agatha*, he ruled, 'There is no expectation that depriving him of the job of editing the picture will be harmful to him. There is no assurance that if Mr Hoffman is given the right to approve the cutting and editing of the picture, it will be done skilfully or expeditiously.'

In a fairly incisive footnote the Judge pointedly noted that Hoffman had attained his present position as a 'prominent, well-recognized actor' by playing in movies 'which are edited by others and in which he has no particular voice beyond acting'.

When the lawsuits were finally abandoned and defeat was conceded, Dustin had no alternative but to put the *Agatha* episode down to experience. 'I got the shit kicked out of me,' he declared, 'and that can be very valuable in going through life. I learned to not trust anybody.'

Michael Apted and Jim Clark, the editor who had worked with him through the entire travails on the movie, were left to deliver the final cut – or, to be more precise, the last but one final cut, since at the last minute First Artists threw out the film's strong dramatic score and substituted a lusher, softer soundtrack. '*Not one single word* was left of the original script by the time we'd finished,' Jim says. 'We restructured the whole thing in the cutting-room, since it didn't seem to make too much sense as it was. We had to invent various devices, like the writing of the diary, to explain things and keep them moving.' Despite everything, he has good memories of Dustin. 'I was fond of him. You can't *not* love Dustin. He's a monster with directors, though. He's a perfectionist – quixotic, difficult, bright, a great guy – but not to direct, I think!' As for David, '*Of course* he did the right thing, he was right to leave. Yes, Michael and I were left in the lurch – but I think everyone got over that a long time ago.'

David was indeed well out of it, but in the light of all the circumstances, could be seen as harsh in his judgement on Dustin. It seems a pity that the hatchet has not yet been buried, for both David and Dustin have proved time and again, in their own different ways, their talent and commitment to quality film-making. Computerized press cuttings have endlessly repeated the 'worrisome American pest' jibe.

Life imitated art as Dustin lunched one day with writer/director Bruce Robinson. 'Why is David Puttnam saying these awful things about me? What's *with* the guy?' he asked – rather echoing the title of his earlier movie, *Who Is Harry Kellerman and Why Is He Saying These Terrible Things about Me?*

Chapter 10

'You're off the Picture'

With Brad Davis in the role of Billy Hayes, supported by an international cast including Randy Quaid, Paul Smith, John Hurt, Peter
Jeffreys and Bo Hopkins, work on *Midnight Express* in Valletta, Malta
proceeded smoothly and on schedule.

As Alan Parker went off to work every day in the hot Maltese sun,
he would often humorously refer to David and Alan Marshall, within
their earshot, as the 'bloody table-tennis brigade'. Sure enough, there
was a table-tennis room in their headquarters and it was indeed a
game at which David excelled. With Alan's inference that the table
was being well and truly used by certain parties while he was sweating
his guts out on location, David has it that he simply could not resist
the temptation to take Alan on. As soon as they heard the unit returning each day from their location filming, the two producers dashed
into the table-tennis room and started batting the ball back and forth.
As Parker passed by, David would yell, 'What does that make the
score now? Forty sets to me and 30 to you? Oh – hello, Alan. God,
you look *exhausted*!'

Alan Parker had his own version of this story. 'I think it's the fact I
actually caught them playing in the first place' (this accompanied by
his deepest chuckle) 'he was so filled with guilt that he came out with
that story as an explanation – I mean, as always, David has an explanation, he's the fastest tapdancer in the movie music-hall. I immediately
did a cartoon where the film unit is lost in these underground caves,
up to their waists in water; this guy's just managing to hold the
camera above the water level. They're lost, then finally one of them
(me) says, "I think this must be the way out. I can hear the producers
playing table-tennis!" In fact, David didn't have a lot to do on the
movie as Alan Marshall was doing the leg work, so he had a lot of free
time.'

Many another gentle tussle was seen between David and Alan
Parker on the movie, each fighting their own corner in their different
ways. 'The costume designer on the picture, Milena Canonero, used

145

to call me 'The Maestro', which really used to get up David's nose,'
Alan recalls with not a little glee. 'David said, "The trouble with
Milena is that, being Italian, there's the director and everyone else is
other ranks, including the producer!" After the film was over David
gave me this beautiful silver cigarette lighter that he had inscribed,
"To the Maestro – from the *Master*", just to point out that he had a
different view of how he saw producers.'

It is unrecorded whether David accepts that one measure of a
master is his success in bringing all men round to his opinions 20
years later. If he does, there yet remains time for Alan and him to
reach complete unanimity. What is recorded is the support Alan
received on the film from both David and Alan Marshall.

'The two of them made the film as effortless for me as they could.
We had this problem with Columbia with regard to the homosexuality
in the shower scene, which they didn't want and we had to fight them
over it. What happened was that David took the footage to Paris and
Dan Melnick was not very happy. He went berserk when he saw the
guys kissing with the tongues down the throat. In fact, I believe he
used somewhat more colourful language to describe the scene. Melnick
was shocked at how it had been done and I was shocked he should
react that way. He didn't mind any of the other excesses in the film,
but he wasn't going to take a couple of faggots doing that. I thought I
had articulated how I was going to do it, but apparently I hadn't got
through to him. But there was no way I was going to change it or
drop it. It was a very tender and beautiful moment in an otherwise
relentlessly violent film.'

Melnick was under enormous pressure back at Columbia where the
David Begelman cheque-forging chaos was erupting. In Paris he felt
isolated and vulnerable and went into a paroxysm of rage when David
refused to doctor or remove the scene.

'You may have lost me my job,' he yelled at David, then jabbed
him in the chest with his forefinger. 'You're *suspended*, buster. You're
off the picture.'

When Peter Guber failed to return David's calls, a telex was despatched from Paris that David reckons turned the international lines
blue. The polite version of what David had to say to Peter was, 'Every
time I need any help, you vanish on me.'

Things back in Hollywood turned very ugly, with armed guards
being placed on his office door at Casablanca. 'It was farcical,' says
Lynda Smith. 'I wasn't allowed to take any papers out of David's
room. They must have thought I was going to try and smuggle
David's files away or something; it was just too silly. The armed

guards became friendly and used to sit and chat to me because it was so boring for them. What was so crazy was that the mail boys used to come in and out unimpeded and empty David's out-tray. We could have posted the entire office back home if we'd chosen to. It was unpleasant, but funny as well.'

This situation continued for over a week and was only finally resolved by Dan Melnick's girlfriend, who voiced the opinion that the shower scene was great and should definitely be kept in. David was reinstated and the armed guards back in LA were dispensed with. With such unpaid technical advisers, who needs highly-paid professionals?

There was further conflict, when Alan Parker decided to delete some final scenes Oliver Stone had written showing Hayes running to the border after his release and being chased by the militia, in favour of a simple freeze frame immediately upon his release. The plan had been to go to Greece to film this last act, but to Alan it seemed like a waste of time and money. As far as he was concerned the film was over. David was duly despatched with this news to Columbia. 'No, you can't do that,' he was told. 'If you do, you're in breach of contract. You promised you'd go away and film the script *as written*, now you're not filming that script!'

Well aware that he might be facing another suspension, and with Lynda only moments away from having further hordes of armed guards surrounding her, David made a compromise suggestion. 'Look,' he said, 'allow us to finish it the way we want to: we'll cut it together and if you still think that's not the right ending, then we'll go back and shoot it in full as originally written.'

While David returned to Hollywood, Alan Parker took the film back to Britain to do an initial rough mix, on which he dubbed music from Vangelis' albums, before the score by Giorgio Moroder was finally added. At the vital first showing to Columbia executives, with David Begelman, Dan Melnick and Sherry Lansing present, together with Peter Guber, Alan and David, the projectionist managed to mix up the reels, which had been marked in alphabetical order. Since one of the main concerns was to win over Columbia to their ending, Alan Parker was horrified to find the penultimate reel and the last reel had been switched. He can laugh about it now. 'David *screamed* at the projectionist for not knowing his alphabet. He's been angry at projectionists ever since. But we got it sorted out, and when it was all over and the lights went up, they were in tears. They loved the movie. David squeezed my hand. "Al," he said, "we've finally cracked it".'

Alan recalls with much amusement some of their joint meetings with the Columbia brass. 'David used to wind me up – he'd always take me along to bite people's legs. If ever we had a difficult meeting, he always made sure we went in a bar opposite Burbank, so I'd have at least four kirs before we went in to see the bosses there. He wasn't nearly as aggressive as he is now, so he used to enjoy watching me scream and shout.'

The prankster side of David was equally irrepressible. On a visit to Columbia's Fifth Avenue headquarters to discuss publicity strategy for *Midnight Express*, he entered the building accompanied by Alan Parker, Alan Marshall and Bobby Littman. At the reception desk sat a truly spectacular blonde, who directed them to the eleventh floor – once they were able to tear their eyes away from her.

After a day of meetings they emerged once more from the lift. The blonde sashayed over to David. 'Are we still all right for tonight?' she cooed. 'Sure,' he replied. '8.30 pm at the Sherry Netherland, Room 324.'

His astonished friends staggered outside with him. This was a side to David they had never fully appreciated before. Bobby was first to break the silence as they strolled up Fifth Avenue. 'Two questions, David. First, are you out of your mind? Second, how the hell did you manage it, you lucky sod?'

David continued to string his friends along until they were sitting having coffee later. 'It's 8.20, hadn't you better be moseying along?' Bobby asked him. Only then did David admit to having nipped down to Columbia's reception during a visit to the rest-room. 'Just ask if we're still all right for tonight on our way out,' he had asked the bewildered girl, who meekly agreed before David rushed back into the meeting.

Midnight Express was entered at Cannes in May 1978, signalling another cost-cutting visit by David and the two Alans. Incredibly, with a Columbia delegation of eleven booked into the plush Hotel Carlton, including Peter Guber, Brad Davis, John Hurt and Billy Hayes, the producers/director team was isolated in the distant Hotel Mas Candille. 'We had just this little Citroën to get us up and down the hill,' says Alan, 'and couldn't afford to stay in the town. The only way we could do the press stuff and change into our tuxedos for the evening was in our usual venue of the men's loo at the Carlton Hotel. We laughed all the way changing in there, then when we were driving along to the movie's first showing, suddenly I just went berserk. I saw this enormous limousine passing us with a chauffeur and a single passenger. 'That's bloody Muller from Columbia!' I yelled. 'What is he doing in that fucking great limousine?'

'It was Columbia's German distributor. Eric Muller,' David confirms, 'sitting in this stretch limo and here's three of us stuck in this little deux chevaux, including Alan Marshall, who at that time made two of any normal human being. Parker just went *crazy*!'

Although the film had a tremendous reception at Cannes, the following morning the press seemed to take against the whole enterprise, hurling question after question at Alan Parker regarding the excesses shown in the picture. At one point Alan was photographed yelling back defiantly at the marauding journalists, with David caught in the background tugging away worriedly at his beard.

On the same day David was despatched a letter from the British section of Amnesty International;

'Dear David Puttnam,
    'You may remember at your preview of *Midnight Express* a few weeks ago, you were kind enough to mention to my colleagues that you would be happy to consider giving the première of *Midnight Express* to Amnesty International. We were, needless to say, over the moon about your kind offer . . . I thought I would send you this note just to register our great excitement at the thought of having the première . . .'

The film subsequently opened in London first, at David's favourite cinema, the Odeon, Haymarket. The critics lay in wait, ready to echo the hostile reception at Cannes. David Robinson in *The Times* reckoned that Oliver Stone and Alan Parker had clearly felt a need to compensate for their somewhat negative hero and their solution had been to turn Hayes's story into a drama of degradation and subsequent retribution. The sodomizing of Hayes by the Turkish chief warden had been added on only one assumption, Robinson felt, that if it were a Turkish jail, wasn't this de rigueur? In Hayes account his escape involved bribing a guard and rowing away in a fishing boat; in the film he kills the chief guard before he can be sodomized again. 'The film is more violent as a national-hate film than anything I remember even from the Second World War. The worst trouble is that Alan Parker's direction is facile enough, Michael Seresin's photography picturesque enough and Giorgio Moroder's music soupy enough to give an innocent spectator the impression that this unpleasant film has some sort of class.'

Geoff Brown in the *Financial Times* concurred: 'It is a story to invoke hot anger and outrage,' he wrote, 'but Parker handles his material in so perverse a way that one's anger and outrage becomes directed at the film itself . . . and the script is as unthinking as the camera style.'

A bewildered Felix Barker in the *Evening News* wrote that the prison scenes were like something out of Hogarth, while the whole tone of the film, together with the appalling brutality shown, rendered him incredulous. To underline this he reported that he had received a communiqué from the Turkish embassy protesting that the film was 'unjust and callous and attempts to de-humanise the Turkish people'. Barker continued, 'I am assured by the producer, David Puttnam, that according to Hayes the film actually understates the squalor of the prison and his treatment. This is a serious matter. Dramatic licence hardly excuses so tendentious and damaging a picture of conditions if they have been grossly exaggerated . . . I don't know how the matter can be resolved, but if they are as innocent as they assert, I think the Turks should immediately invite an independent investigation.'

Amnesty International found themselves in the middle of a storm for having accepted the proceeds from the film's première, for a disclaimer had been inserted at the end of the film that all the characters and events were fictional *despite* the first line on the credits which stated 'The following is based on a true story'. For once it seemed this was more than a mere legal convenience in view of the fact that Hayes's own account was so different from that of the film makers.

Alan Parker's view is quite unequivocal. 'For me, it was a film that was fictionalized anyway. The truth had been moved away from at so many stages. The boy had written the book, and I'm sure some things happened to other people he suddenly claimed had happened to him. He was suddenly in the spotlight and he liked being a celebrity. Then it was ghost-written by a writer who had to change things from a literary point of view and make it a good read. Then Oliver Stone changed things and I changed things. So each time truth was moved away from and what was left was a movie. *Not* a documentary. That was never my intention.'

Ted Whitehead wrote in the *Spectator* that 'Since the film doesn't even claim to be authentic, it's disturbing to see Amnesty International accepting a benefit performance, as if the piece were a moral protest on behalf of imprisoned innocents.' If this was enough to give David and his team a twinge, so were Whitehead's next comments: 'In its beady-eyed horror at homosexuality and its sadistic exultation, it's actually one of the nastiest and most hypocritical films ever made.'

Within a month Amnesty International gave in to the mounting pressure and publicly disassociated itself from the movie and its proceeds, in a tersely worded statement:

The association of Amnesty International through its British Section with the London première of the film Midnight Express has led to misunderstanding both inside and outside the Amnesty International movement. This has happened despite the fact that the London Section of Amnesty International had nothing to do with the production of the film.

To clarify this situation the Amnesty International Executive Committee has decided to disassociate Amnesty International from this film, in particular from any tendency which could be interpreted as a generalized denigration of Turkey and the Turkish people, and from its proceeds.'

Alan Parker has his own view on Amnesty's defection: 'There were different groups involved. We'd worked with the London office, who very much liked the film and we very much wanted to help them by giving them the money. Then another branch of Amnesty International decided they didn't like it, because it was too critical of the Turks.'

To everyone's relief the American opening went ahead as planned, though to predictable critical reaction. Richard Schickel wrote in *Time* that 'What we have here is one of the ugliest sadomasochistic trips, with heavy homosexual overtones, that our thoroughly nasty movie age has yet produced.'

Variety found the film 'sordid and ostensibly true. Alan Parker's direction and other credits are admirable, once you swallow the specious and hypocritical story.' *Hollywood Reporter* took one of the few totally positive views, describing the film as 'harrowing, yet filled with hope. Major credit must go to Alan Parker, who controls every inch of the footage.'

It seemed that the public had stronger stomachs than the majority of the critics as the film went on to become a huge international success. Nor was it ignored in the honours stakes, garnering six Golden Globe Awards, three British Academy Awards and two Hollywood Oscars, Best Score for Giorgio Moroder and Best Screenplay Adaptation for Oliver Stone. On a total cost of just over £2.5 million, *Midnight Express* went on to return net profits of almost £8.5 million. David had achieved his international commercial breakthrough at the cost of a humiliating climbdown. This could be seen as having been handled by him with either admirable candour or the distancing evident over the years.

'I discovered too late that Billy had, shall we say, a much more "complex" background than I'd been led to believe,' he stated. 'At the time it was supposed to be the story of a basically good boy who behaved stupidly and brought inordinate punishment on himself. I think we film makers were conned over that one. I went into shock; I thought it was a really good, well-made picture until I saw it with an audience, and then I suddenly realized that as much as anything else, we'd been ripped off. We thought we'd made one film but in the end we'd made exactly the film Columbia Pictures wanted us to make, a very commercial film where the audience is actually on its feet saying "Go on!" during the scene in which Billy Hayes bites the tongue off one of his captors. We thought they'd be under their seats, but instead they were cheering! That's the depth of misjudgement I realized I was capable of.'

Today he describes *Midnight Express* as a 'career movie, made with a certain cynicism which is inescapable. We conned *ourselves*. There had been love in *Bugsy Malone*; there was not much love in *Midnight Express*.'

'Conned?' Alan Parker asks. 'It's irrelevant. That was just David doing his tapdance to justify the criticism we got for it, but I don't run away from that. We didn't meet the boy until afterwards, when he was certainly less than he had seemed, but it didn't matter. If the film doesn't succeed it's absolutely my fault and I certainly wouldn't blame it on being conned by anybody. I am immensely proud of it and much of the criticism has since been seen to be alarmist nonsense. It's one of the most important films in many young people's lives and I stand by every frame of it. Maybe I'm more protective of it than David because it's more my film than his. He is more critical of it and the attitudes within it because he doesn't necessarily see it as part of his body of work. It was something he helped me to do, but it's very much part of *my* body of work, so obviously I'm infinitely more defensive of it.'

David's ex-partner Sandy Lieberson, who by this time had gone on to produce Terry Gilliam's *Jabberwocky*, has his own views on the *Midnight Express* controversy. 'I thought the criticism of the film was a load of crap,' he declares. 'I saw it simply as an outstanding movie on every level, with amazing performances. I think that what you did was you sympathized with Billy Hayes's fate; of course, he was a drug smuggler, he was breaking the law, but I don't think that was the point in question; it was his treatment as a criminal and it was an indictment of the system. It was a powerful movie that worked for me. I didn't agree at all with the political bullshit.'

Something David did gain from the movie came out of his relationship with Peter Guber. Although their journey together was a bumpy one, this reflects to a large degree the enormous value David places on his independence. 'I don't like working for anybody,' he admits, 'and Peter and I have totally different styles. We often rubbed up against each other the wrong way and Alan and I got aggravated in that we felt he put little into the actual production of the picture while disproportionately rowing himself in on its success. Where I did learn a lot from him was in terms of the subsequent promotion of the film and the energy he put into it. I was influenced a lot by Peter in that respect. I hadn't realized the extraordinary lengths before that you can go to in order to push a film. I watched the degree to which he was able to utilize reviews, making each critic feel as if they had the inside track. He was brilliant at that.'

Andrew Birkin had spent three years writing his J. M. Barrie play cycle, *The Lost Boys*, for BBC-TV and at the same time composing a biography of the writer. 'Sacha Puttnam was my technical adviser on boyhood,' he acknowledges, 'and unwitting author of the best lines in the script.'

> 'You're old, but you're not grown up,
> You're one of us.'
> Alexander Puttnam, aged 11

This dedication appears in the introduction to the biography, which Andrew wrote despite the author's admonition in one of his last notes, 'May God blast anyone who writes a biography of me!' Andrew filmed Sacha on an 8mm sound interview in Kensington Gardens. 'He came up with some wonderful lines, all of which I nicked, using them as if spoken to Barrie.

'David was very helpful while I was on Barrie, but concerned I was turning into an academic researcher in a basement. Although it killed me financially, it was my favourite project. I'd like to think the book will be on the shelves of the British Museum long after the movies have degenerated into dust. When we ran into money trouble with the BBC, while David was making *Midnight Express*, I asked the Beeb if I got some American money, could we use these better locations I wanted. The answer was yes, so I got David up to it; he was great. What he did was a delaying tactic of money being promised to the BBC, then the BBC spending the money, which they never subsequently received, through some loophole in the deal that I believe was their own fault, but that only David fully understood.'

*

David returned to Los Angeles in 1978 for Casablanca's new movie, also planned for Columbia release, the subject of which was teenage suicide. 'I found it very interesting that Beverly Hills, which for many people represents the apotheosis of hundreds of years of human striving, should have the highest level of teenage suicide in the world. In looking into it, I stumbled across a tough script by Gerald Ayres about children living in single-parent homes, *Foxes*. I worked on that for about four months, and after several false starts got it off the ground, but again I found myself in that old situation. I was working with Casablanca who had a "special relationship" with Columbia. After dithering with the film Columbia didn't want to do it and Casablanca didn't have the nerve to go it alone. So, I was left cobbling together a half-arsed deal with United Artists, having got the script in turnaround from 20th Century Fox. It was the Goodtimes situation all over again. What on earth was I doing raising funds for a film, when I was supposed to be having my salary paid and working with a company that had money?'

For *Foxes* yet another director had been recruited by David from the ranks of television commercials, this time Adrian Lyne, who in Britain had independently turned out a 40-minute dark comedy, *Mr Smith*. Much as David admired Adrian's talent, the feature and its setting seemed to defeat them both. Jodie Foster and Scott Baio from *Bugsy Malone* were cast, together with Sally Kellerman. 'We made a hash of it for all the obvious reasons,' he later admitted. 'The first thing we jettisoned was being sensible. I should never have done it in the first place, because I didn't know anything about the subject. The Beverly Hills setting was changed to San Fernando Valley then Sally Kellerman came in one day before we started to shoot and asked if I liked some earrings she proposed to wear. She thought they were perfect for the character she was playing. I hadn't a clue and asked the wardrobe mistress, then realized what I was doing. If the wardrobe lady was any good, I was going to be all right, but if she was less than good, I was in deep trouble. And that's the way the entire film was produced. It was always, I felt, like producing through glass. I was only as good as the people I was checking with. They wouldn't always tell the truth, because in many cases they were more interested in telling Adrian and me what they assumed we wanted to hear. I'd never met the woman that Sally Kellerman was depicting, nor even anyone like her, so I was absolutely impotent in that conversation.'

Lynda Smith remembers David's feelings on this and the frequent arguments they had on the subject. 'I really got quite cross with him,' she says. 'My view is that it wouldn't take anybody long to fill themselves in on any location. The feeling should be in the script to begin with and after that it's a matter of observation. A couple of hours sitting in bars and visiting a supermarket, or just listening to local radio, would do it. No, David's main problem on that film lay with the terrible indiscipline of those around him. He hoped they would all respond to Jodie Foster's level of professionalism. They didn't.'

When, halfway through the production, Casablanca was bought by Polygram Pictures, a division of the record company that was to prove short-lived, David found himself subjected more than ever to front-office interference. 'Why does she have to commit suicide?' he was asked. 'I mean, I can see your point, but couldn't she just die self-destructively?' Then it was, 'Couldn't we spice it up a bit, make it more exciting?' and 'How about a big rock soundtrack?' Filming was held up while would-be film executives and their wives were photo-graphed with the actors on the set, and David was obliged, much against his will, to include a skateboard chase scene.

Still looking for an actor to play Jodie Foster's ex-rock star father, David met Adam Faith in the Polo Lounge of the Beverly Hills hotel. 'We're in terrible trouble,' David told him. 'Would you play the part?'

'I can't,' said Adam. 'I've got to go back home next week.'

'Please, Adam, it's a cameo and will only take a day.'

Adam smiled, 'You sod. After what you did for me on *Stardust*, how can I say no?'

United Artists sat on the picture for a year after its completion, then rushed it out in 1980 in the glare of publicity for Jodie Foster after the assassination attempt by John Hinckley on Ronald Reagan. The reviews were mixed, the *Newark Star* reckoning that 'Gross is the word for most of this heavy-breathing movie.' In *New York* magazine David Denby wrote, 'After a promising beginning, *Foxes* becomes a maudlin com-mercial for unhappy youth.' In the New York *Daily News*, Katherine Cornell found it a 'murky-looking teenybopper soap opera'. As against that, David Ansen in *Newsweek* found *Foxes* a 'funny, rueful, sexy little movie about coming of age. The first real sleeper of the season.'

Rex Reed dubbed it '*A Rebel without a Cause* for the 1980s, an oddly moving experience.' In the LA *Times* Charles Champlin de-scribed it as 'an astonishing and powerful film'. Martin Mitchell in *After Dark* singled out both the director and writer's contribution: 'Adrian Lyne not only captures and conveys the realism of the charac-ters and events, but also makes them matter. He merits high praise for working wonders with a superlative cast. Gerald Ayres' screenplay is a marvel of authenticity.'

Nicolas Wapshott in Britain perhaps reviewed the timing of the film's release, rather than the film itself, when he wrote, '*Foxes* is a shabby film which does not deserve to be saved from obscurity by such naked opportunism.' His verdict that the film had 'no material audience' regrettably proved only too accurate on both sides of the Atlantic.

One small glimmer of daylight for David came in the shape of a reconciliation with Brian Duffy. Nine years and ten months into his 10-year vow of silence, Brian was in Hollywood when he had a note slipped under his hotel door. 'I'm down the road,' David wrote, 'why don't you phone me if you get a moment?' Brian's first reaction was, 'The cheeky bastard!' even as he conceded the tremendous style the message displayed. 'He's making sure I don't get my full 10 years in,' Brian ruminated, on his way to make the call.

Towards the end of his first Hollywood tenure David found himself counting the days until he could return home. His visit to the movie mecca had started off badly with the side trip to Malta, then ended disastrously with the *Foxes* débâcle. He felt tired, disgusted and thoroughly disillusioned.

With Dan Melnick anxious to move on after his holding operation at Columbia, following the departure of David Begelman, David was offered the job of head of production at the studio, first informally by Melnick, then formally by Frank Price. Producer Ray Stark asked him to produce a film with Alan Parker. David found it easy to turn both offers down. Hollywood had been a dispiriting experience and he felt the need to return home and resume independent production. 'I wasn't tough enough to deal with it,' he declared. 'It was *always* going to beat me. Running a studio would have cost me my domestic life and that would have been a ridiculous price to pay.'

Back in Britain many were of the opinion that the real root of David's unhappiness in Hollywood was his being reduced once again to the small fish, in relative terms, that he had been in the days of *Melody*. At least in Britain he had grown to be one of the bigger fish around, albeit in a smaller pond.

'Of all of us, we thought he would take Hollywood by storm,' said Michael Apted. 'I think David met a lot of people in Hollywood who were just like him, people who were just as aggressive, but who loved film a lot less and had far fewer scruples than he has.'

Alan Parker was far more sanguine about it. 'What happened was this: half of him liked it a lot, more than he would admit. And he hated himself for it. I remember him happily driving down Sunset Strip in his big flash BMW. In many ways, I've never seen him happier. It would have been infinitely easier for him to work there than it is in Britain in terms of the kind of money that's available – if he'd been prepared to make certain compromises, which of course he wasn't.'

Several months before his departure David felt distinctly unwell and decided to spend a few days at home. He and Patsy had moved from Pacific Palisades, following the expiration of their lease, to another furnished residence near the studio in Doheny Road. The normally kind Los Angeles climate had turned temporarily inclement, with violent rains, which had caused numerous mud slides and damage, subsiding after a few days into a miserable steady drizzle. As Patsy went to light a fire to cheer the place up one February morning, David looked around at the pile of scripts he had spent the last few days reading and decided he needed a break. Searching around in a bookcase, he came across a bound volume on the history of the Olympic Games. In the chapter on 1924, it became clear, just by reading down the lists of medals and times, that the British runners had done extraordinarily well. The dark horse was Scot Eric Liddell. Having refused to run in the finals of the 100 metres event, he had amazed everyone by breaking the world record on his way to a Gold Medal in the 400 metres. David decided to find out more by getting a researcher on the job back in Britain.

It turned out that Liddell had died in a prisoner-of-war camp during the Second World War, while another Gold Medallist, Harold Abrahams, was still alive and living in Southgate, just a few streets from David's parents. The more he read about the characters and events that came from the research notes, the more enthusiastic he became. Soon he knew he had found nothing less than his next project. Telephoning Colin Welland, he said, 'Listen, Colin, this could really be something . . .'

When Alan Parker called round, he was treated to a résumé of this story about two competing British Olympic runners in the twenties, and the conflict one of them had with running on a Sunday.

'I thought it was a terrible idea,' says Alan, 'about a load of pompous English twits. I told him to forget it. That's how much I know!'

Chapter 11

David, you have to understand about Hollywood. A couple of dopey upper class English twits running the hundred yards in slow motion for an hour and a half is not what people pay their five bucks to see...

To Learn Twice Over

On David's return to Britain in 1979 he felt all at sea, although he had come back with a bonus in the form of a Warner Bros contract. In exchange for picking up his overhead, they were to get first look at any projects he would develop. (In fact, this enabled them to close down their London office and still left them with a toe-hold in the market.) Patsy began to realize the whole effect of his working in Los Angeles had been much worse for him and gone deeper than she had understood. 'I knew that he didn't like it, but he had to see his term out. It was brought home to him that when he's not on his own territory, he isn't as strong as he should be. He came back to Britain needing to exorcize the whole process.' David felt he had been seriously 'out of sync'. 'You're mad if you don't reflect on that,' he says. 'How do I avoid that misjudgement again?'

His answer was to spend a year teaching – perhaps on the basis that to teach is to learn twice over – while Colin Welland laboured away on the Olympics script. David was invited by the Australian Film Commission to lecture for six weeks as a script consultant, and travelled round eight universities in Britain. 'I'd come back with a lot of opinions,' he says, 'and wanted to test them. It was also a test for me, the first time I'd spoken in public.' If in the speech of men there is more agonizing than dumbness in the eyes of animals, it seemed that David had found one way at least of striving for solutions.

A worrying aspect of David's dark night of the soul was his asthma-like attacks of being unable to breathe that left him pale and exhausted. On his doctor's recommendation David briefly put himself in the hands of a psychoanalyst. Since David felt he spent more time listening to the doctor than he did talking, this idea was quickly abandoned. Still he recognized his need for help. Through friends he was introduced to a Jesuit priest, Father Jack Mahoney, with whom he talked for several hours and whose counselling was to prove a considerable influence.

Patsy could see her husband was crying out to find a way forward.

After a visit to Father Mahoney he brought home some books, which Patsy would see him take to bed. Since David had never been a churchgoer, his studies clearly fulfilled a need and stimulated the dedication he sought.

David maintains he is extremely self-analytical and constantly questions his own nature, a process which, he concedes, can be painful at times. Father Mahoney confirmed this when he told David he was 10 times harder on himself than any objective observer would be. He pointed out at the same time that censure of a man's self was considered oblique praise in Samuel Johnston's definition. Was David's indulgence partly to show how much he could spare?

David gives much credit to Jack Mahoney for rebuilding his shattered confidence. It was to a great extent through his guidance that David was able to press on with *Chariots of Fire*.

There was no further movement towards Catholicism, despite David's acceptance of Jack Mahoney's influence. 'It wasn't the Catholicism in particular,' Patsy reckons; 'it could have been Buddhism, he just needed someone who was making sense to him, cleansing him, asking him questions and helping him to answer these questions without the usual dogma, just talking the truth. That's when he felt he should stop and take stock of where he was and where he was going.'

Alan Parker, totally established in his alter ego role of Lennon to David's McCartney, saw it in his usual down-to-earth manner: 'He was suffering from a touch of the Americas but was embarrassed to go to a shrink like everyone else does there. It was easier to go to a Jesuit priest, probably cheaper too. In his early days, because he was so swift of foot, he wasn't taken as seriously by the establishment as he maybe should have been, which makes him very wary of the establishment now. He'd dress strangely or whatever; someone said he was the second person in London after Paul McCartney to have a fairisle jumper. In those days he was really thought of as being much more of a spiv, not to be believed for one second or taken seriously for a moment. On the other hand, that's why we all loved him.'

In the striving for deeper understanding, the realization of the awesome power of movies as a means of mass communication hit David forcefully during his sabbatical. The welter of criticism for the way *Midnight Express* was slanted had gone deep. He still felt conned and swallowed the accusations of political naivety, but the acceptance was not a happy one and he knew this was something that had to be dealt with.

For the first time David was truly beinning to understand the

Len and Marie, Isle of Wight, 1933
(David Puttnam)

Len, 1939
(David Puttnam)

Marie, 1940
(David Puttnam)

David, 1944
(photographed by Jack Esten *of* Illustrated Weekly *to send out to Len in* Africa)

'There's ever such a pretty girl started at our school.' Patsy and her twin brother, Richard, aged 13
(David Puttnam)

Len, Lesley, Marie and David
(David Puttnam)

Patsy and Debbie
(David Puttnam)

Debbie
(David Puttnam)

Sacha
(David Puttnam)

Mark Lester, director Waris Hussein, Jack Wild and David on Melody *location*
(National Film Archive, London)

'Look, kids, don't give me a hard time': Alan Parker demonstrating the Mussolini school of film-making — Scott Baio/Alan Parker/Florrie Digger on the Bugsy Malone *set*
(National Film Archive, London)

Harvey Keitel, David and director Ridley Scott on location for The Duellists
(National Film Archive, London)

Bill Forsyth and David on Local Hero *location*
(National Film Archive, London)

Director Pat O'Connor on location for Cal
(National Film Archive, London)

Director Roland Joffe and David on location for The Killing Fields
(National Film Archive, London)

David and Fernando Ghia on location for The Mission
(National Film Archive, London)

Director Roland Joffe and Robert de Niro on location for The Mission
(National Film Archive, London)

impact of communications, and the damage messages of a negative kind could bring. With this dawned awareness of the responsibility he held in his hands as a film-maker. No longer could it just be a question of finding a commercial project, getting it financed, shooting it and putting it out. From now on there had to be a broader canvas, with wider issues addressed. Cause and effect began to preoccupy his mind, together with the nagging realization that nothing comes from nothing. He saw that while anyone could get from one point to another, it was *how* it was done that was important. For every 'why' there had to be a 'wherefore'.

The process of learning, and teaching, performed another function. It helped to ease the feeling of inferiority David had suffered ever since from prematurely leaving school. While the 'total enigma' description had rather tickled him at the time, what emerged later was the impression that he had disadvantaged himself by leaving school so early, as more and more of his contemporaries turned out to have benefitted from a period at university. The same feeling that he had lost out on the academic front, however, had the positive effect of fuelling the desire to prove himself through his natural ability. Alan Parker watched the process. 'All this flirtation with teaching and universities was to find an educational and intellectual respectability that he always felt he didn't have. He had an enormous inferiority complex about not being better educated; in fact he's still sensitive in some areas. What he did was make sure he made up for it. He's incredibly well-read and self-taught. It was a spur for him. The greatest thing to come along in that respect were the honorary doctorates he was given. When he got his second one I said to him, 'Just think, you've almost got the same number of doctorates as you have O-levels!'

Now Alan soars into the realms of the apocryphal. 'At the drop of a hat he'll put on his gown and ermine fur hat just to make a speech; he loves dressing up in his gowns. He doesn't care how ridiculous he looks – it's just that he wants the whole world to know he's got a degree after all.'

In 1973 David Norris, who would have the run-in with David two years later over the Marcel Ophuls court case, was involved in the setting up of a contract between one John D. 'Jake' Eberts and producer Martin Rosen, that advanced $50,000 development money to start an animated version of Richard Adam's runaway success, *Watership Down*.

Jake might have seemed a surprising recruit to the ranks of film financiers, for his dynamism is completely lacking in flamboyance. Tall, sandy-haired and possessed of scholarly good looks, the earnest be-spectacled Jake had started off as a chemical engineer in his native Canada before going on to work in various factories around the world. He came to the UK with a US investment bank, Oppenheimer. He saw his organizational factory experience as his greatest strength, all too often having watched as agents and lawyers attempted to create structures in the British film industry which they little understood.

He raised *Watership Down*'s $50,000 of development money by going round 10 friends who gave $5000 each against a percentage of any profits that came from the venture. This led Jake to fund raising for the actual production of the movie, since after a year his friends' money was spent with very little to show for it. He was introduced by Rosen to *Watership Down*'s paperback publishers, Penguin Books, owned by the Pearson group. Rosen was able to convince Pearson and their affiliates, Lazards, that this might be an opportunity to invest in the project, on the basis that if it were at all successful, they would see a dramatic increase in the sales of the book. Through this introduction, and after spending some time in the city, Jake went on to raise a total of £1 million to make the film.

One unfortunate diversion almost stopped Jake in his tracks. On the understanding that a movie called *Zulu Dawn* had a completion guarantor, Jake persuaded a friend to put £100,000 into the film. When the movie soared over budget, it emerged that Jake had been mistaken; no completion guarantor had been involved. With this friend's investment down the drain, Jake borrowed the sum from a Swiss bank and repaid his friend in full, leaving himself with a crippling debt burden.

When production on *Watership Down* was about to start, Jake found himself involved with a baptism of fire. He knew nothing whatever about film documentation and from the outset Murphy's law seemed to apply, as everything that could go wrong did go wrong. When the film's director, a brilliant animator named John Hubley, was months into the picture, he was rushed to hospital requiring open-heart surgery and died on the operating table. Martin Rosen himself stepped in at this point and finished the picture with Hubley's assistants. The unit had to build their own studio, there were legal problems and completion guarantee problems, all of which had to be tackled by Jake as they arose. He was learning on the hoof, and had the growing feeling that if he could bring this one home, he could do it again. And again.

His next step was to approach Pearson with the idea of their putting up £100,000 as the initial seed capital for a new company whose principal objective would be to develop projects with an eye to the Penguin library as a primary source of material. Pearson were happy to consider it, on condition Jake could find another partner for half the action.

Electra House, run by Michael Stoddart, was one of the largest outside shareholders in Oppenheimer. Since Michael had already put up some of *Watership Down*'s cash, he seemed like an obvious person to see. He took up a 49 per cent position to Pearsons 51 per cent. Jake got the £100,000 he had asked for and resigned from Oppenheimer in 1976. He was to be paid £10,000 a year by the new company to cover all his operating costs, including travel, secretary, rent, and telephone, which amounted to no salary and £10,000 in expenses. However, he was also to receive 10 per cent of the profits in the partnership, once Pearson and Electra recouped their money. They named their new company, Goldcrest Films International.

Jake's first meeting with David Puttnam, whose antennae had been alerted to this new source of finance, was sought by David on the basis that no stone be left unturned. 'He was a great one for sniffing out new sources of finance, a *tremendous* hustler, a *relentless* pounder of the pavements,' says Jake. 'He heard I'd put money into some picture and boy, he was on that phone! He was exactly the same as he is now, nervously pulling at his beard, that slight nervous cough, but you could just feel the *energy* coming out of this guy. I was terribly taken with him, for I could see exactly the sort of problems he was facing, having done the same thing myself a few months earlier. At the time he wasn't asking for money for anything specific, just generally trying to discover what I was doing and whether my contacts were really serious about putting money into the film business. He came right to the point and was *very* impressive.'

Jake was hooked. He had just spoken to the man who would launch Goldcrest's fortunes with *Chariots of Fire* and return the tiny company a staggering windfall of a million pounds on their minute investment of £17,000 in the film.

The next step came when David invited Jake to the first screening of *Midnight Express* in 1978. Jake was struck by the fact that David recognized him among the hundreds of people at the première. He told David he had Goldcrest organized, and some money raised, and invited him to sit down and talk to his committee when he was ready.

When David phoned to make the appointment he described his

idea for *Chariots*. Jake was not about to start asking him to prove that
it was a good idea. His immediate gut feeling was that it was a *great*
idea. David duly turned up at Jake's tiny office in Mayfair and was
introduced to his committee. This consisted of a lady from Penguin
Books, the head of Pearson, and an octogenarian lawyer who, by an
amazing coincidence, had been an Olympic runner in the thirties.
Was there anything Puttnam would like to put forward? There was,
David replied, and began to describe *Chariots*. Jake watched him in
action on the committee and noted his almost uncanny ability to
anticipate objections and answer them before they could ever be
voiced. He wanted £17,000 for script and development money, he
explained, rocking the committee back on its heels. That was, after
all, a big percentage of their total capital! With Jake and the lawyer
firmly behind the idea, the deal eventually agreed was that he got his
£17,000 on condition it was repaid on the day the film started principal
photography – with interest. Goldcrest would get 10 per cent of
David's profits as producer of the film, which, after it proved successful, he later allowed to be altered to seven and a half per cent of
the gross profit, increasing Goldcrest's windfall still further. The
payback on the initial £17,000 loan came to £25,000 once interest was
added, before a foot of film was shot.

In the meantime, prior to the formal loan agreement being prepared, David wanted to despatch writer Colin Welland to New York
to do research work on Jackson Scholz, the US Olympic runner. Jake
still has the correspondence explaining to David that while he'd *like*
to advance the £500 requested for this purpose, that under the rules,
since the deal was still to be promulgated, this was not possible.
'That's how naïve and inexperienced we both were at doing this kind
of deal,' Jake laughs, 'that I still had to go to the board of directors to
get a £500 approval. The £17,000 doesn't sound like much now, but
it was a big part then of our total capital and when you're scratching
around for £1000, £17,000 is a lot of money. With most films you
make nothing, so you need a percentage on the ones that turn out to
be winners.'

Now, for David, there was just the small matter of *Chariots*' $6
million budget to be found. He wrote and spoke to every major source
of finance – banks, city institutions, film companies and TV networks,
failing to elicit even a glimmer of interest. What particularly depressed
him was the reason he was turned away. The subject of the film, he
was told, was 'too British for the international market'.

'Sir Harold Wilson once said to me that compared with the film
industry, running the country was a doddle,' David told a reporter.

'At no point did anyone ask to see the balance sheets of my previous films, where in most cases I could have demonstrated levels of profit ranging from the satisfactory to the sublime. No one seemed anxious or willing to treat the making of the film as a serious business proposition.' (Clearly 'most cases' did not include *Lisztomania*, *Memory of Justice* or *Trick or Treat*, three items David preferred to forget.)

He conceded that he did not blame the banks too much for being reluctant to lend on something whose risk they were unable to evaluate. 'But they can surely be blamed for not having the expertise about an industry that's been around in this country for the past sixty years. I can't go and have a knowledgable conversation about films with many people in the City. This lack of knowledge continually encourages the wrong people into the film industry. They have given it a bad name – and in turn, made financiers unwilling to invest.' What he did manage to get, during Sandy Lieberson's hold-the-fort stint as head of production of 20th Century Fox, was an agreement to put up half the budget for *Chariots* in return for world rights outside the US and Canada. Now all he needed was another $3 million.

In fairly rapid succession David had taken on the job of governor of the National Film School in 1975, become chairman of the Producers' and Directors' Section of the ACTT Union in 1976, a founder member of the National Film Development Fund in 1977, a member of the Cinema Films Council in 1978, a director of the National Film Finance Corporation (NFFC) in 1980 and joined the Governing Council of the British Academy of Film and Television Arts (BAFTA) in the same year. In addition, he had been a member of Harold Wilson's Interim Action Committee since the mid-seventies. 'Hell bent on gaining honours,' sourly commented a bemused competitor. 'A kamikaze attack on his knighthood,' was the irrepressible Alan Parker's way of putting it. 'Every time Patsy brought out the butter knife, he gets down on one knee!'

David still managed to find time for his family and never lost his sense of humour, no matter how frustrating money-raising trips proved. Debbie remembers her dad coming back from an American visit, bursting to tell everybody about this incredibly funny British film he had seen, the Monty Python team's *Life of Brian*. At breakfast, to an enrapt audience of Patsy, Debbie, Sacha and their housekeeper, Margaret Maguire, he insisted on acting out the movie, putting on all the different voices – Eric Idle said this, Michael Palin did that. When the family eventually saw the film, none of them thought it was half as funny as David's version. The last lines of one particular story raised many a laugh with the Puttnams over the years as they recalled David's animated recital: 'Brian's mum catches him in bed with Mary. People outside the window are chanting, "The Messiah! The Messiah!" And his mum flings the window wide open and says, "*He's* not the Messiah. He's a *very* naughty boy!"'

David Norris came into the Goldcrest picture in 1979 when he was asked to look after an Egyptian shipping millionaire, Mohammed Al Fayed, who wanted to invest in films. Since his son Dodi was a film fanatic, his father's idea in forming the Allied Stars film company was to launch his film career. The first film they invested in under Norris's guidance was a British musical, *Breaking Glass*, which proved unsuccessful at the box office but returned all its production money from pre-sales. When Jake Eberts suggested to David that Allied might be a source of production finance for *Chariots*, he was naturally enthusiastic, but concerned that the project might be rejected on the same grounds of parochialism already levelled by so many individuals and institutions.

'You must be out of you mind,' a Warners executive had told him when commenting on the draft screenplay he had prepared. He held the folder over the wastepaper basket as he spoke. 'I don't *understand* you,' he berated David. 'You get an opportunity to produce mainstream commercial movies and you bring along *this*' – so saying the outline was dropped in the bucket. 'Go away and *grow up*,' was the final admonition, 'and don't waste our time again in the future.'

The encounter would normally have gone beyond humiliation, but even as David's cheeks burned he remained utterly convinced he was right, and that in the end he would be vindicated. He nevertheless decided to establish a fall-back position with the submission to the Fayeds, by offering them the option of a second project, an East–West drama entitled *October Circle*.

If *Chariots* had not been picked by Allied Stars' Timothy Burrell, David and his chosen director, Hugh Hudson, would have been content to make *October Circle* instead, although at least in David's case there was no doubt which film his heart was in. '*Chariots of Fire*,' he declared, 'is about winning on your own terms.' Over the years many would become romantically convinced that David had seen a parallel in his own life.

After a conciliatory talk between David and David Norris, their first since the Ophuls contretemps, a meeting with the Fayeds was set up. From the point of view of self-interest Jake wanted *Chariots* to be picked, since he had no money invested in *October Circle* and Gold-

crest would receive nothing beyond a token 'thank-you' for the introduction. To Jake's intense relief, Allied Stars confirmed their preference for *Chariots* and a meeting was set up to discuss the terms of the
Fayeds' support. One of Norris's primary concerns with the film was
the validity of Sandy Lieberson's 20th Century Fox commitment,
since this consisted of a two-line letter which Norris felt could never
for one moment be regarded as a binding contract. He decided a trip
to Los Angeles to seek confirmation was in order, especially since
Sandy had left by this time to join the Ladd Co.

On the day before his departure, Fayed's Allied Stars advisory
committee met to finally decide whether or not to back *Chariots of
Fire*. Present were Tim Burrell, Mohammed and Dodi Fayed,
Bernard Coote, Norris himself – and David, very much in the position
of a supplicant. 'Should I make this film?' was the question which
Mohammed addressed to each of his advisers, while David had to sit
and listen. Everyone except Norris had read the script and voted to
back it. 'Should I make this film?' Mohammed boomed at Norris,
who replied, 'You've heard all these opinions, all from professional
people, you don't need mine.' Mohammed glared at him. 'I'm not
going to make this film unless you tell me to,' he thundered.

'But I'm your lawyer,' Norris protested. 'I can't –'

'I'm *not* going to make this film unless you tell me.'

'But –'

'Have you read it?'

'No, I haven't, and I'm leaving to negotiate with 20th Century Fox
in Los Angeles tomorrow morning.'

'Fine, phone me when you've read the script. You can do this on
the plane.'

For David, who had hoped for a quick decision, the meeting ended
in a shattering disappointment. Now it was all up to Norris, who duly
phoned Mohammed as soon as he arrived in Los Angeles.

'What is your decision? Do I make the film?'

'Yes.'

'*Why* should I make the film?'

'O K, Mohammed, I'll tell you a story. The script is about these two
athletes, one of whom is Eric Liddell, who's been a hero of mine since
I was 10. I went to the same school as he did, both of my children are
there now, and I'm a governor of the school. The second athlete
involved is Harold Abrahams. My father-in-law was his doctor for 35
years and he was a guest at my wedding.'

'What am I to think?'

'Well, quite apart from all that, I have to tell you the script is one of the most literate I have ever read, or am ever likely to read. I think it's terrific.'

'Do you think I'll get my money back?'

'Look, I can't tell you that, but it's something I think, for £3 million, you've got to have a good chance just on network television alone.'

There the matter was left, with Mohammed saying that he would have to give it more thought. With Alan Ladd Jr, Jay Kanter, Ashley Boone and Sandy gone, 20th Century Fox had virtually no management left to talk to, Norris quickly found. There was only a business affairs individual who proceeded to stonewall him for a full week before agreeing to the deal on *Chariots*, subject to a check on the strength of Fayed's finances. When Norris produced a telex from Fayed's bank to say he was good for up to $100 million for the deal, Fox insisted they still wanted a deposit of Allied's half share of the budget, plus an extra one third. When Norris told Fox they would be required to do the same, they were outraged. 'We're 20th Century Fox!' they protested, then capitulated and deposited the money. At last the finance was in place and the green light was given, but still without a guaranteed US release or an advance from that market, which can account for 70 per cent of the world total.

David's cash flow, expended on pre-production essentials, had run dangerously low, and he had second-mortgaged his house to keep things going. Bob Towne came to see him, oddly enough with his own script about two runners, *Personal Best*, which he wanted to direct and David to produce. David was torn until the Fayeds' decision was made and Fox were nailed down, for he had confided to Patsy only days before that their cash would run out completely within a week or so. 'I'll have to take that offer of going to work with Bob Towne,' he told her. 'It's a good script . . .'

'Hang on,' she advised.

Although Andrew Birkin experienced a disturbing cash drain on the J. M. Barrie projects, he met a girl named Bee, a photographer who helped him with the illustrations on Barrie's biography, *The Lost Boys*. He can now claim three boys of his own ('*Not* lost, I trust,' he says happily), named David, Alexander and Ned. The next project he was offered led again to an association with Sacha Puttnam, now gratefully re-absorbed into the English educational system.

'When I agreed to do the script for Omen III – *The Final Conflict* – David said it was a ludicrous thing for me to do, but I had to sort myself out financially and pay off my overdraft. *The Final Conflict* paid for *The Lost Boys*, is the way I viewed it. The producer was Harvey Bernhard, a man more unlike Puttnam would be hard to imagine. We got on well, but he was a bit like Richard Nixon: we argued about *everything*. However, there was Eady money available for shorts accompanying main features at the time and I talked Bernhard into giving me the money to make an adaptation of a Saki short story, *Sredni Vashtar*, on the basis that he'd get all his money back and a profit as well providing 20th Century Fox showed the film alongside *The Final Conflict* on the circuit.

'He agreed, and I wrote, produced and directed the picture, using Sacha as the boy and my mother, the actress Judy Campbell.' (One gets the distinct impression that Andrew's sister, Jane Birkin, would have been in there as well, had Hector Munro woven a few more characters into his story.)

'When I first asked Sacha, he naturally went to David for advice. I think David was a bit odd about it, because he wasn't producing it. I was coming to David to ask for his help, but not financially. I wanted his son, not his money. He told Sacha that if he wanted to be an actor in the future, he shouldn't do it. If he didn't want to be an actor, he should. So Sacha did it.

'We got a B A F T A award for Best Short and an Oscar nomination. David saw some of the rushes and the finished film, but to this day he hasn't told me what he thought about it. I heard that a few people have come up to him and said, "You know, your son was wonderful in that", and he says, "Yes, yes" and promptly changes the subject. He's never been one, in my experience, who's taken a profound interest in something that wasn't directly to do with him. He'll take an interest, but not a profound one.'

Actor/writer Colin Welland soon became exposed to the Puttnam perfection ethic. 'Colin did five drafts for *Chariots*,' David recalls. 'A couple of times he was fed up and I'm sure he thought I was either pedantic or wrong, but we staggered through it. Some people aren't that lunatic. I suppose you could say I'm exceptionally tenacious.' He stoutly defended his choice of newcomer Hugh Hudson for the movie. 'I don't see it as taking chances. Hugh had made hundreds of commercials, thousands and thousands of feet of film going through a camera, the equivalent of two or three feature films, learning his trade. Other people don't seem to see that. The real gamble to me is if you just *buy* name directors or stars, because films should be cast technically as well as for the performance. The reason *Midnight Express* worked was that Alan Parker was coming off *Bugsy Malone* and his greatest desire was to prove he didn't just make kiddies' films. He wanted to make a "hard" film, so he was ideal casting. My feeling with directors is that each film is an absolute "horses for courses", where the best director in the world for one story could easily be the worst director for another. I've never worked, to my mind, with an unproven director; I've always seen something they've done before. I think that film is a very special language, where within five minutes you'll know whether that man speaks the same language or not. Someone can have a shot for 20 years and never have understood the language of film, while another man can pick it up in a year. It seemed to be self-evident that Hugh Hudson was perfect for this as a director, for his attitude and mine towards the script were very much the same. Hugh understands class, he understands England and he has an incredible visual sense.'

Patsy looks back on the film's casting with some amusement. 'We did all the tests in the mews, which was in an uproar at the time due to alterations we were carrying out; there were builders and chaos everywhere. There was no staircase from the house to the office, so all the actors had to come into my kitchen and collect the bit they had to read. I had to make them all sign for it, since we were so short of money that we couldn't afford any unnecessary photocopying. One day, into all this chaos, walked this extraordinarily arrogant guy. He pushed past Margaret, who was dusting. 'Where do you think you're going?' she asked him. Oh, he was an actor and he'd come to read for a part, he told her, but hadn't expected to find this two-bit dump. Margaret sent him through to the kitchen, very upset, whereupon I doled out his piece. He signed for it with a sniff and marched off. Margaret was livid; for two pins she'd have *thumped* him.'

A week later, after David invited Patsy to watch the screen tests with Hugh and his wife, the arrogant individual suddenly appeared on the screen. '*That* fucker!' Patsy yelled. '*He's* not going in the film!'

'But Patsy —'

'Over my dead body! We don't want people like that here. He had Margaret in tears; he has no manners whatever. He'd never be able to play someone upperclass, he's got no class at all!'

Sue Hudson turned to her husband. 'She's right, Hugh. This is going to be difficult enough; you don't want to work with people like that; you don't want people who are arrogant.'

'But you know it's very hard for actors —' David offered, before being roundly shouted down. He nevertheless stuck to his guns and decided to talk to the actor concerned.

'You've really upset my old lady,' he told a bemused Nigel Havers. 'What on earth made you act that way?' Then it all came out. Nigel had been told by his agent he was auditioning for the part of Abrahams and to act abrasively in character from the moment he set his foot through the door. In actual fact, he was being auditioned for the part of Lord Andrew Lindsay!

'Poor Nigel, he really wanted the part desperately,' says Patsy, 'and had gone out of his way to change his whole personality. As we've discovered since, he's the nicest, most easy-going person you could find, with time for everybody. We're great friends now and still laugh about it!'

Chapter 12

Cannie Laddie, Handy Sandy, Acquire Fire

David was thus poised, in 1980, to begin production on *Chariots of Fire*, with two unknown actors heading the cast, Ian Charleson in the role of Scots Presbyterian Eric Liddell and Ben Cross as the Cambridge-educated Jew, Harold Abrahams. Brad Davis (Billy Hayes in *Midnight Express*) was back as US athlete Jackson Scholz. Ian Holm was set to play the part of Liddell's trainer, Sam Mussabini, with Sir John Gielgud as the Master of Trinity and Lindsay Anderson as the Master of Caius.

The considerable drama in Welland's script revolved around twin climaxes in the film. In one, sabbatarian Liddell discovers at the last moment that the 100-metres event for which he had been training was being run on a Sunday and withdraws after much agonizing. He then enters the 400 metres instead and triumphs. For Abrahams the climax comes after his failure in the 200-metres event, where he redeems himself by winning the 100-metres event, the very race Liddell had dropped out of on religious grounds. The film ends on a note of double triumph with the two men, though fiercely competitive in spirit, never actually competing against each other. The contrast between the pushy, abrasive Abrahams and the dour, modest Liddell were reflections of how totally personalized the film had become, for its conflicts seemed to strike at the very depths of David's psyche and take him back to the values his father had instilled in him.

'There were elements of *Chariots of Fire* that were deliberately there to exorcize the type of life I feel I've led for the past ten years,' David declared at the time. 'The film is about people who do not behave in an expedient manner. And for the past ten years my career has led me to behave rather expediently. So it is a wishful film, trying to examine both sides of the coin of my personality. Eric Liddell, an evangelical Scot whose motivation on the track was entirely unselfish, is the kind of person I dream of being. Harold Abrahams, a somewhat aloof, unpopular figure who ran in order to satisfy his personal ambition, is more similar to the kind of person I find myself, a pragmatist, rather than an idealist.

173

'*Chariots of Fire* attempted to tackle a whole range of issues, class, race, religion and the question of gentlemen and players which has plagued me all my life. For my money, the difference between the 20s and the 80s lies in terms of expectations. I think that in my adulthood I have found myself living within a totally expedient society. Yet the values I was given as a child were not expedient, they were real values, the differences between good and evil, right and wrong, truth and untruth. All those values, it seems to me, have taken a terrible battering in the last twenty years. I believe men like Liddell and Abrahams were not instinctively corrupt. They were instinctively *honourable* and that's the important difference. Their instinct was to do the right thing, ours is very often to do that which is most convenient.

'There's no question that *Chariots* is, as much as anything, a reaction to having been the producer of *Midnight Express*, a film in which I found no sense of identity other than the craftsmanship with which it was made.'

The location manager on *Chariots of Fire* was a tall, boyishly good-looking young Scot named Iain Smith. He had worked on a variety of documentaries and commercials before the opportunity came to work with David, whom he had known for several years in his position on the National Film School board of governors. Since they only met every three months or so their relationship was fairly distant, but Iain was aware of David and the fact he was considered a bit of a renegade, with a reputation for toughness stretching almost to the point of unfairness. He was familiar with David's background in advertising, where the motto was 'all or nothing' to achieve the desired ends, and was therefore pleasantly surprised when he got to know David better. He discovered that, while he was indeed all he had heard, there was a great deal more on offer besides.

Despite the travails of *Chariots'* filming, for there were problems in getting money released despite the joint account that had been set up, Iain quickly saw that David never allowed these problems to pervade the main structure of the film. There was one point in the production stage when David concluded on Wednesday that the unit would be unable to continue beyond Friday. 'What he was actually dealing with was a nightmare,' said Iain, 'which was one of the features I began to realize is one of his several unusual qualities. He can keep a lot of secrets, particularly ones which will destroy the confidence or morale of the crew.'

Iain observed there were two sides to David, amounting almost to two entirely separate people. There was the child, the romantic who dreamed about the stars. Then there was the toughest, hardest man anyone was ever likely to meet, who was totally uncompromising. 'I'm absolutely fascinated by this peculiar balance of the devil and the total innocent,' Iain admits; 'this person who will start a project and will at that point literally not see any of the problems or obstacles, but will only see what is ultimately possible and will go forward making that film happen with an energy which is born of pure innocence and a kind of naïvety. By the same token, and without damaging that innocence, he is able to understand that he needs leverage in order to get things done, he needs more than just sheer talent and energy. He needs to *engineer* it, so that the financiers actually get round a table and finally, reluctantly, *actually* put money down to make films.'

Iain learned from David that financing films was not about going to ask for money and hoping to get it; rather that it involved the creation of an osmosis, a natural flow of energy from A to B, making an irresistible force to finance a film. David *created* publicity; he *created* a sense of people losing out if they missed the bandwagon. He would constantly be tap-dancing around these different components with great speed and dexterity, creating the osmosis that would make everything possible.

On the set Iain would see David stand back, observing the many things that had been well achieved, but well aware this was not his main function as producer. Instead he was constantly on the look-out for danger spots, the elements that were out of synchronization or about to head that way.

David put Iain in mind of the story of Samuel Goldwyn and the soapdish. Goldwyn had never taken an interest in having a home of his own and lived in rented quarters until fairly late in life. His wife finally coaxed him into letting her build a home for them, which he left entirely to her. Two years later the beautiful Goldwyn home in Beverly Hills was ready. His wife arrived at the studio to pick him up and take him out there. She had moved all his favourite furniture, pictures and ornaments into this splendid mansion and as she showed him around, he was absolutely flabbergasted at what she had achieved. She pushed the door open into the private suite of rooms that comprised his bedroom, bathroom and dressing-room. He could scarcely credit the miracle she had wrought; everything was just perfect. She left him behind to have a look round and as she was making her way downstairs she heard a bellow of rage.

'For Christ's sake!'

'What's the matter?' she asked, running back up the stairs.

'I'm trying to wash my hands,' he replied, 'and there's no goddam soap in the goddam soapdish.'

Although apocryphal, this story still seemed to sum David up, in Iain's view.

'He throws people in at the deep end and if they swim they're fine,' says Iain, 'but if they sink, they sink. That's the hard side to David; he expects the very best and you've got to give it to him. If you don't, you are never forgiven. It's a mafia thing, that's the best example I can give. He'll draw a circle of influence, and if you stay in that circle, he'll treat you like a brother. You'll never starve. But if you step out of there you'll probably never work again with him. Of course, he never says that, but behind him there's this sense of the great depth he'd go to to push his point. I once met a murderer in jail in Glasgow and I was very disturbed by this meeting. The man was very bright and wasn't your average thug. He was articulate, and the chances are he wouldn't do it again, but I was still very disturbed by something and it took me a long time to work out what it was. In any argument there might be with this character, I realized that *my* ultimate recourse would be to walk away, feeling annoyed. *His* ultimate recourse would be to kill me.

'That's a very extreme example of what I mean. Power of that sort is to do with how far you're prepared to go to emphasize your viewpoint. Now David has an *incredible* power, and it's to do with the face-off – it's to do with the fight or flee. He's a fighter. And how! So again you come to another duality. On one side you've got this real streetfighter, yet wearing the face of an angel. Those beautiful big eyes of his, his nice little cardigans are such comfortable symbols. They emanate an image of something he's not, a sort of comfortable Englishness. David's *international*, and his whole background is *international*, his whole *being* is to do with the *bigger* world. He emanates this nice sort of Englishness as a device, no doubt about it.

'Underneath the comfort he's a man who is very, very determined. Of course there are aspects to David that I don't like, there are sides to him which have annoyed me enormously, but in the main he's always taken me by surprise. And I like that. He's interested in the making of films as a concept, not as a process in itself. The actual *making* of a film is uninteresting to David, the detail and minute planning are of no interest. He finds the technicalities uninteresting. He's interested in the "why" of a film, not the "how" of it.'

For a while all was harmony between David and Hugh Hudson. 'The sun literally rose and set out of Hugh's arse,' is how an irreverent studio observer put it. Iain was one of the eyewitnesses to the differences that soon developed, with Hugh rebelling against what he saw as David's rank pulling. Since total control was such an integral part of David's ethos, there could be only one outcome.

'He creates for himself a totally autocratic power base,' says Iain, 'where he will rule *absolutely* and there is no one to second-guess him. Particularly directors. Having achieved that position, he will then rule with enormous kindness and wisdom. That doesn't always work, and certainly didn't always work with Hugh, for occasionally situations which crossed came up, then the dragon arose and terrible conflict resulted. David turns muscular in these situations, *horrifyingly* muscular, and can become very unkind.'

At an oyster bar location in Edinburgh, David came in overnight from London and turned up on the set expecting to see progress confirming that the whole scene could be completed within the day, since the alternative was killingly expensive weekend overtime payments. What he found instead was the entire set at a standstill with Hugh occupied in cutting out pictures from a magazine, then framing them to hang on the restaurant walls.

It seemed that art-nouveau prints were supposed to have been organized by the props girl and had been overlooked. David was furious when he heard Hugh's story and demanded that filming start forthwith. He then sacked the props girl and let Hugh know this had been done. Progress was still agonizingly slow and as 'golden time' approached, David peremptorily reached out and killed the lights, plunging the restaurant into darkness. 'We've got enough,' he muttered to Hugh furiously. 'The scene'll play as it is. There'll be *no* overtime.'

Back in England, Hugh covered a running track with water for what was to prove one of the most effective scenes in the film, echoing as it did the pain and frustration of the moment for the runner concerned. David had been absent on an errand and could scarcely believe his eyes when he beheld the wet track on his return. 'He was *furious*,' says Hugh, 'for he thought I'd ruined the track for running the following afternoon. Of course, I might have, but I was prepared to take that risk. I'll *never* forget the sight of David walking towards us across the whole centre of the track. I saw this figure, this lone figure, walking along and you could *feel* the clouds of anger *pulsating* all around him. I turned to the first assistant director and said, "Here comes trouble."' It turned out that Hugh was indulging in one of the great understatements of recent times, but when David saw the finished result he conceded it was a fine scene. He smiles ruefully at the memory and shrugs. 'I was wrong,' he disarmingly admits.

David saw from the start the considerable disadvantages in raising *Chariots of Fire*'s money with neither a name director nor a bankable star and as filming drew to a close he ruminated on the balancing act this represented. 'The trick is in working out what you can give away to the backers without actually ruining the film. What we gave away was not Colin Welland's excellent script, nor the director nor the cast, but a week's badly-needed extra shooting. We had to shoot both Olympic finals on the same day and use every single piece of footage we had. I think it's all right but it might well not have been.'

When filming and post-production were finished, and David departed for the States to show *Chariots* round the majors, David Norris found he had worked for a financier who wanted to wash his hands of the project. Mohammed Al Fayed ordered him to telex 20th Century Fox: 'We are offering you the opportunity to buy our share in this film for our basic costs, plus interest, plus a five per cent net profit share.' Although the Fayeds had decided they wanted out, Fox were not about to oblige them. Instead Sandy Lieberson rode once more to the rescue with Alan Ladd Jr, after the film was shown round the major studios and turned down by all of them, including Warners for the second time. On Sandy's recommendation, Laddie put up half of the $1.2 million advance to acquire the US rights to *Chariots*, which Warners would now release after all, as Laddie's distributors, the *third* time around. *Variety*'s headline might well have read: 'Cannie Laddie, Handy Sandy, Acquire Fire'.

The deal negotiated by Norris was that profits on the picture would go into a single pot after Fox and the Fayeds had recouped, then the balance would be split between Fox, the Fayeds, David and his crew and Goldcrest. Far from being grateful for David Norris's sterling work, the same Mohammed Al Fayed who had vacillated by trying to sell off the movie for a pittance to Fox, now accused Norris of taking a bribe, ending their relationship.

Once again a David Puttnam film was picked to represent Britain at Cannes with *Chariots*' selection, the sixth film of his in eight years to be honoured, in itself probably an unbeatable record, following *Swastika*, *Mahler*, *Bugsy Malone*, *The Duellists* and *Midnight Express*.

As he anxiously awaited the film's opening, David elucidated his theory on how potentially-good movies go bad. 'They are created by people who are making slightly different films. And as silly as that may sound, I see it time and time again. The writer is writing a film 10 per cent different from the one the producer thinks he's commissioned, and the director is directing a film 10 per cent different from the resulting script. Before anyone knows what's happening, you've got a lopsided equation and a film, being a very frail object, can't survive a 20 per cent difference from intent to delivery. So my obsession, if you like, is ensuring that we're all making *exactly* the same movie. Once I'm sure of that, my job is to protect the director and give him everything he needs. This involves a very unique approach as a producer – it's called common sense, the least applied factor in the entire film industry. My greatest problems have come whenever I've strayed from that.'

That David had tried harder than ever to tailor the film to audience expectations was evidenced by his admission that he was 'beaten up' from many quarters about the sex and violence aspects of *Midnight Express*, 'So to an extent, *Chariots of Fire* is a reaction to the film audiences' pleas for family entertainment. It will be fascinating to find out whether the same people who have been complaining vote with their feet and turn up at the film, or whether they are, in fact, inveterate television watchers who are merely complaining about what is effectively an excuse for not going to the cinema at all.'

The film opened in London after being chosen for the Royal film Performance, to enthusiastic reviews over the Easter 1981 holiday weekend. The film reminded Philip French in *The Observer* of the classic essay by George Orwell in 1940 on boys' weeklies and the reply it elicited from Frank Richards. Orwell maintained that *Boys' Own Paper*, *Gem*, *Magnet* et al were snobbish, insular, reactionary, xenophobic, obsessed with sport and dangerously out of touch with the real world. Richards – creator of Greyfriars and St Jims – stoutly defended the genre.

'Even if I were a Socialist,' he wrote, 'or even a Communist, I should still consider it the duty of a boy's author to write without reference to politics; because his business is to entertain the reader, make them as happy as possible, give them a sense of cheerful security, turn their thoughts to healthy pursuits, and above all keep them away from unhealthy introspection, which in early youth can only do harm.'

Hugh Hudson, French pointed out, was the third gifted British director of TV commercials and documentaries introduced by David to feature-film making, 'and like Alan Parker and Ridley Scott, he knows how to achieve the maximum emotional impact with the minimum footage, how to bypass the mind without insulating the intelligence, how to beguile.' He summed the film up as 'immensely attractive, immaculately acted'.

Alan Frank wrote, 'The story is simple, but brilliantly put over. Colin Welland's script is first-rate, and Hugh Hudson could not have done a better job.'

Alexander Walker decided to go for a jingoistic tub-thump. 'It is fresh. It is original. It puts you in direct touch with sentiments so long unexpressed publicly you wonder if they ever existed – love of country, fear of God, loyalty to the time, unselfish pursuit of honour, becoming modesty in victory – and that doesn't by any means exhaust the list.'

David had been coaxed into going on holiday to the Scilly Isles with the family after the première, but phoned the Odeon, Haymarket daily to check the takings. To his horror these collapsed on the all-important Easter Monday. 'It was certainly a time when you'd have figured we'd have had a rock-solid sellout. Instead the audience *vanished* for the Monday afternoon and early evening performances. My world *collapsed*. My doctor says I get myself in the most terrible state prior to a movie opening and for the few days after it's opened, but no wonder. I just saw all these years of effort going down the drain. To think that London couldn't find just 600 fucking people to pack the Odeon out on an Easter Monday. I was devastated. There was this terrible feeling there was *nothing* I could do. Then it was over and by the following weekend we were a sellout, thank God.'

For someone who had nursed and lived with the project from its birth and whose faith in it had never wavered for one fraction of a second, it was a trying time, not just for David, but the whole family. Patsy had never seen him so low. 'If it hadn't picked up,' says David, 'I honestly don't know what I would have done.' Although that was the first hurdle over, he was acutely aware that the real test would come from foreign territories, especially the crucial American market. Openings in Europe were set first and were to prove a crushing disappointment, headlined by *Variety* as 'Chariots Of Fire Scores In Britain – O'Seas Is In Doubt'.

Pointing out that the film was 'going great' in its native market and had won critical applause at the Cannes Festival, they nevertheless had to report poor box-office response to the film's French and Italian openings. In Scandinavia the film had only produced average figures and there was some doubt as to whether there would even be a German release in view of the high dubbing costs and the film's lacklustre performance outside the UK. When 20th Century Fox's Ascanio Branca reported that he expected $2 million in rentals from the UK market, *Variety* conceded that this was an impressive figure for a film with a budget of $6 million, but that it was still a long way behind other 20th Century Fox's blockbuster rentals in the UK, which included $9.5 million for *Star Wars*, $6 million for *The Empire Strikes Back* and $5 million for *Alien*. The article did nothing to shake the Ladd Co. nor Warner Bros' confidence in the film, for their reaction had been overwhelming after finally viewing the finished film.

They busily set about preparing for the movie's autumn 1981 US release.

With the success of the film in Britain, the full emergence of Puttnam as Personality had taken place, as he found himself picked up and adopted by the media. He acknowledged this reluctantly prior to the film's US opening.

'I've learned a lesson with *Chariots of Fire*,' he declared. 'I've spent the last 10 years trying to sell the idea that film making is a collaborative process. The industry knows this to be true, but with the media it's been a long hard slog, for it suits them to believe that a film is one man's vision. It's convenient copy. Up until now one had to go along with the fact that it suited them it was a director's medium. What's happened with *Chariots* is that the media decided I was the most tangible thing to hang their copy on. Suddenly *I'm* the one being interviewed, *I'm* the one having to step forward and do my stuff. And I'm doing it because I want the name of the film in the paper. I don't really care, at least I *think* I don't care, whether they write about me or Hugh Hudson or Colin Welland, so long as they write about the *film*. But the net result is, suddenly it becomes "David Puttnam's *Chariots of Fire*", the awful *possessive*, which I've been fighting against for a decade. The truth is it's Colin Welland's film, it's Hugh Hudson's film and it's my film, in just about equal parts.'

Alan Parker saw the change in David that press attention brought about. 'He suddenly realized that if he said something, somebody wrote it in a newspaper. Ironically, years ago, at the end of *Midnight Express*, after all the interviews I did, he said, "Your trouble is you're becoming a media figure!" Hugh's hero is Stanley Kubrick, who is very private and doesn't shoot his mouth off like the rest of us. David stepped into the breach for the sake of the film and he is extremely articulate, extremely charming, able to manipulate others to his point of view. We had no voices in film-making except the mundane twits at the BFI and suddenly David had a point of view, which gave him incredible respectability. If any member of the press wanted a comment on any aspect of film-making, they came to him. And he began to rather enjoy it. In fact, he began to feed off it. He *needs* respectability to prove that he's no longer a spiv,' Alan chuckles, 'maybe he picked the wrong industry! That's why he spends so much time trying to give it intellectual credibility.'

Hugh Hudson readily acknowledged his producer's contribution in one of his few interviews he gave. 'We all need to identify with certain values,' he asserted, 'not necessarily out of the past. It was David Puttnam who found this subject and had an immediate positive reaction to it. He thought of me as director because I am familiar with the class conflict and religious values found in the subject. And I was fascinated by his enthusiasm and his faith in *Chariots* – we were in perfect agreement and were complementary. He was so enthusiastic and I felt a personal commitment to make his dream come true,' There was certainly no sign in this statement of the backlash from what Hugh would come to see as the media over-kill on David as producer.

There was concern at the Ladd Co. that the G (General) rating the film was initially awarded – meaning anyone, even unaccompanied children, could go and see it – was undesirable and liable to put adults off. An expletive dubbed on to one of the characters took care of this and gained the film a PG (Parental Guidance) tag. The Ladd Co. had yet to have a hit since its formation, although Laddie had left his previous position as boss of 20th Century Fox in a blaze of glory. Not only were mega-hits like *Star Wars* to his credit, but also a whole slew of smaller, quality pictures like *Breaking Away*, *The Turning Point* and Fred Zinneman's *Julia*. David felt the film was being promoted by the right company in the States, but knew he was up against ingrained American prejudice on both the subject matter of the movie and its foreign source, and anxiously awaited the opening reviews.

Andrew Sarris in *The Village Voice* led the band of critics who were against the film, but in case anyone got the wrong impression, he had to first point out that he was not alone. Sure, he acknowledged, there were the guys who stopped him in the street and in elevators to tell him how overwhelmed they had been by the experience of the movie – but there was also the hard-core cognoscenti, who winked knowingly and shrugged their shoulders, both in print and in person. Hadn't Richard Corliss noted in his Cannes report for *Film Comment* that the picture was 'a hymn to the human spirit as if scored by Barry Manilow?'

Sarris found the movie 'a surprisingly skimpy entertainment. True story or not', he argued, 'there are three false starts to the narrative and half a dozen anticlimaxes at the end.' However, one thing he did concede – thanks to David's adroit musical packaging of the picture in an uplifting Vangelis score – 'You do come out humming the movie.' Pauline Kael, doyen of American critics, was another who disappointingly came out against the picture. 'The effects calculated to make your spirits soar,' she wrote, 'are the same effects that send you soaring down to the supermarket to buy a six-pack of Miller or Schlitz or Lowenbrau. The film is bursting with the impersonal, manufactured, go-to-the-mountain poetry that sells products . . . The picture works, though. It's held together by the glue of simple minded heroic sentiments . . . Produced by David Puttnam, who is widely regarded as the major force in the (coming) revivification of the British Film Industry, this movie is in love with simple values and synthesized music . . . I hope *Chariots of Fire* wasn't dedicated, like Liddell's sprinting, to the glory of God, because it looks as if it were thrown together in desperation in the cutting room. It's retrograde moviemaking, presented with fake bravura. The movie has a mildewed high moral tone, and it takes you back; it's probably the best Australian film ever made in England.'

Time Magazine provided welcome balance. 'Like every element in the picture,' they wrote, 'the actors look right, they seem to emerge from the past, instead of being pasted on to it, as so many characters in historical movies seem to be. That quality, finally, is what distinguishes the film.' Jack Kroll of *Newsweek* agreed, adding: 'The large cast provide the kind of sheer acting pleasure you get from Britain's best repertory companies.' Kroll discounted any objection his readers may have. '*Chariots of Fire* is a wonderful film. You'll hear it's about runners, British runners at that, and the 1924 Olympics, and you may think you don't want to see it, but you do. *Chariots of Fire* will thrill you and delight you and very possibly reduce, or exalt, you to tears.'

A healthy trickle of money from the box-office was beginning to roll in from the slow, carefully planned release by Warners. *Variety* ran an article that warmed the cockles of David's heart, headed, 'Chariots: Slow And Steady Will Win The Race, Per Elated Ladd/WB'.

The enterprising Jake Eberts had meantime formed a New York-based company called International Film Investors (IFI) in partnership with Jo Child, raising $10 million in funds from a variety of shareholders. He persuaded Pearson/Electra House, as partners in Goldcrest, to invest $750,000 in IFI, thus making Goldcrest IFI's largest single investor. Jake now had one foot planted firmly on each side of the Atlantic, with a development company in Goldcrest in Britain and a production financing company, IFI, in New York. The arrangement between the two was that each party was required to offer the other an opportunity to invest in their films.

Jake's next task was to find further funds in the city to set up a production-financing wing of Goldcrest in Britain, for he realized that to grow the company would have to move away from purely development finance. Instead of only putting money into one project at a

time, which is how previous entrepreneurs had foundered, Jake drafted a prospectus which explained how the new production-funding
division would spread its risk over a portfolio of films by part-financing them. In this way investors could rest assured they were not being
exposed to any one project on a make-or-break basis. Pearson put
£4 million into the new kitty, Electra contributed £500,000 and
Jake's other representations brought the total up to £8 million.

Chariots had been too late to benefit from this new cash flow, but it
proved the saviour of another project that had struggled along for
almost 20 years trying in vain to find a backer: Richard Attenborough's
Gandhi, to be the next major step in Goldcrest's history.

Jake was also able to offer Goldcrest's new-found financiers the
opportunity to look at projects being separately developed by IFI,
the first of which were *Hopscotch*, *Escape from New York* and *The
Howling*. With the new kitty established and the second stage of
Goldcrest achieved, Pearson decided to second one of their directors,
James Lee, on a part-time basis to be the company's chairman. Jake
continued to act as virtually an unpaid chief executive, with a staff
consisting of himself and Irene Lyons, his secretary – and the interest
mounting on his debt to the bank.

Chariots of Fire went on to take $1.5 million at the box-office in seven
weeks of limited release in the United States in 11 cities and most
important of all, it maintained or actually increased its box-office
performance with each subsequent week. Warners predicted an eventual $10–$15 million rental figure for the movie. Even at this, *Variety*
argued, *Chariots* would be placed far below the more successful pictures in the same year. Why the fuss? 'It's a film everybody loves that
allows us to go back to all the basic elements in the business,' a
Warners spokesman maintained. 'It's hard on this film to tap all of
the resources we're now used to in advertising, for you can't synopsize
a picture about two runners in the 1924 Olympics, you can't come up
with the definitive copyline. What you *can* do is what we've been
doing – that is getting the cooperation of the exhibitors and *showing* it
to the people.'

The *Chariots* campaign had so far relied primarily on newspaper
advertisements and advance publicity screenings, with no television
and a minimal amount of radio time bought. Warners readily credited
the co-operation of exhibitors in arranging advance screenings to
selected interest groups, group sales, and generally 'working' the picture in their particular city in order to build word of mouth.

The Ladd Co. and Warners had decided early on to only book the film into theatres that would play it through Christmas 1981, and adhere to its plan of restricted release no matter how well the picture did. They estimated the slow build-up and the film's legs would see it through until the following February's all-important Oscar nominations. Then the film could go wide.

After Len and Marie had enjoyed a game of bridge on Boxing Day with some friends, Marie was about to make some tea when Len remarked he was feeling ill and was going to have a lie down. She was relieved when he came back after an hour, declaring he felt fighting fit once more. That evening the couple watched *Gone with the Wind* on television.

In the morning Len did not feel at all well. 'Not as bad as yesterday, though,' he assured his anxious wife. 'I thought I was *dying* yesterday.' Marie, now thoroughly alarmed, rushed off to phone their doctor. After Len had been examined the doctor declared he must go straight to hospital. An ambulance was summoned while Len shaved and dressed. Marie remembers the thick snow on the ground outside as Len was helped, very much against his will, into the ambulance.

In the hospital later, Marie was told Len was suffering from angina. When she saw her husband on the machine to regulate his heartbeat, she felt the tears start. As soon as David and Lesley were phoned, they rushed with the whole family, to be by Len's side.

Barely a week earlier, David had taken the first-ever colour photographs of the whole family together at Queensgate Place Mews – Marie, Len, sister Lesley, her husband Jeffrey and their three children, together with Debbie, Sacha and Patsy. They turned out so well that David had them all enlarged and took them along to show his father in hospital. Len had laid them out in front of him like cards in a game of patience and had been unable to keep his eyes off them all through the visit. Even as David left and waved goodbye to his father for what was to be the last time, he remembers Len nodding back happily, then stealing another glance at the photographs, an expression of utter rapture on his face.

Marie was at home on 29 December when David phoned, having received a call from the hospital. 'Dad's worse,' he told her. When Marie arrived at the hospital, her husband of 49 years was dead.

A friend and colleague from BP, Roly Stafford, wrote a moving and eloquent obituary for *The Times*, recording that Len had been 'one of Britain's outstanding news photographers, responsible for much of the Associated Press's most important picture coverage of European events in the 1930s. Although he had a distinguished career in the service of photography, the press and the oil industry, he will be remembered for what he was, a kindly friendly man, proud of his charming wife, his children and his grandchildren, a man with a deep interest in people, particularly the young, with whom he had a remarkable rapport, a man with an irrepressible sense of humour and zest for life.' David organized a memorial service in St Bride's Church, in Fleet Street, that was packed to the doors with a multitude of his father's friends and colleagues.

Len left behind two great legacies. The first was to the nation, forever enshrined in the national archives, of unique, memorable and historic pictures: General Franco's triumphant entry into Madrid; Hitler at the head of his army in Sudetenland; the Royal marriages, coronations and state funerals of the thirties; workers riots in Vienna; hunger marches in Britain; polo at Hurlingham and his exclusive photographs of the wedding of the Duke and Duchess of Windsor.

The second was the best legacy any man can leave his family – the memory of a wonderful, warm, devoted husband and father. Len was one of those extraordinary men who seem during the course of their entire lives to be giving their family reasons for being consoled at their death.

By February 1982 the Hollywood Press Association had awarded *Chariots* a Golden Globe for 'Best Foreign Film'. Warner Bros were in two minds about the accolade, and went out of their way to emphasize to Academy members who would vote on Oscar nomination categories that *Chariots* was eligible for *all* regular Oscars and should not be limited to the 'foreign-language' category. Terry Semel of Warners spelled out the cost of the company's campaign in boosting *Chariots*: 'So far we've spent $1.2 million marketing the film. By the end of February, with the film entering wider release, we will have spent $4 million and we expect the movie will take in a minimum of $10 million in film rental and perhaps as much as $20 million.'

Everything in the US handling of the movie was aimed at making it a commercial success, while spending the minimum amount. The rationale was that in many ways the film would sell itself and become its own best advertisement. 'Let's treat this as if every penny is important,' was the keynote.

With another 196 theatres ready to open the movie almost five months after its début, Warners looked to the 11 February announcement of the Academy Award Nominations. 'We hope to be going into our second wide weekend with lots of nominations,' Semel declared. His hopes turned out to be more than justified, while back home in

Britain David and Patsy Puttnam hugged each other with delight as the news broke that *Chariots* had been nominated in no fewer than seven Academy Awards categories, as well as 11 British Academy nominations.

David felt complete. *Midnight Express* may have been the *breakthrough* film but it had not been *his* breakthrough film. Now he had a movie of his own that he was proud to acknowledge. If elements of his Abrahams persona had made the film possible, it was Liddell who reaped the subsequent Oscar awards.

After the ceremony in Hollywood and the enthusiastic headlines in the dailies, tying in the success of the film with the prevailing Falklands spirit, congratulations from many colleagues were disappointingly muted. Many seemed reluctant to even allude to the film's triumph. Colin Welland's misunderstood 'The British are coming!' declaration at the Oscar ceremony was seen by the prophets of doom as vainglorious and premature. The peculiarly English phenomenon of despising success was quickly setting in.

'I'm very glad for you, David,' Lindsay Anderson told him after the awards. 'You like that sort of thing.'

David Norris invited David, Colin Welland and Hugh Hudson along to be the guests of honour at an Old Boys' Day reunion of Eric Liddell's contemporaries at the South-East London School of which he was a governor. The headmaster had rounded up no fewer than 65 80-year-olds, together with Jenny Somerville, Liddell's sister. 'It was an extraordinary day,' Norris recalls. 'They brought the Oscar along and the whole thing was terrifically emotional, a really genuine moment for all of us. David and Colin came along – it's the sort of thing David would do, he has a tremendous generosity of spirit, while Hugh didn't turn up. I never did get close to Hugh. I'm not sure anybody does.'

Even before the runaway success of *Chariots of Fire*, an invitation for David to join the board of Goldcrest as a non-executive director was widely tipped, so there was little surprise when the appointment was announced in the wake of the windfall *Chariots* had proved to be.

Alan Parker appreciated the transformation in David more than most. 'He'd come back from America and said, "Enough is enough. I'm going to do it on my own terms." I remember that period very strongly at the beginning of the seeding of *Chariots of Fire* when he first met Jake. There was a definite change. We've always had the anger, but from the point of view of having been in Hollywood and getting fucked by the system, our only salvation was that we always laughed at it and always knew we'd get them one day. He came back, he was determined to do it differently, outside the system. He wasn't an evangelist yet, but he was certainly someone who wanted to get back his dignity as a person. He wanted to feel good about himself. It was hard for him, for he didn't exactly come back in a blaze of glory. *Chariots of Fire* was the end of the spiv.'

Many would argue, despite Alan's well-intentioned view, that there was still an element of the barrow-boy approach in *Chariots of Fire*, and indeed viewed the film as being in every way as exploitational as *Midnight Express*. If this film had been manipulatively made, what about *Chariots*, with its quasi-inspirational, jingoistic message and many factual distortions? Had David simply moved on to a classier con-game – but a con-game none the less? As Scarlet O'Hara's mammy had admonished her mistress: 'You ain't nuthin' but a mule in hawses' harness. You kin polish a mule's feet an' shine his hide an' put brass all over his harness an' hitch him ter a fine cah'ige. But he a mule jes' de same.' There was still a way to go.

Margaret Maguire became the Puttnam's housekeeper shortly after their return to Britain and saw the family through their good times, and their not-so-good times.

'I got to know Patsy first more than David,' says Margaret, a handsome, motherly Irish lady in her early fifties. 'I thought he was a quiet person to start with when his office was elsewhere, then they bought the house next door and turned it into an office. That's when I got to know David, and I couldn't get over how sweet and nice he was. I had always been taught to address my people as "Sir" and "Madam", but they said no, we're David and Patsy. And the kids were so sweet. I *love* Debbie and Sacha. Sacha's a little bugger, but I love him.

'I would come in at 7 in the morning and bring David up his tray, a cup of tea at 7.30. "Oh, Mrs Maguire, I can't open my eyes," he'd say, then in five minutes he'd be sitting up, talking and joking and laughing. We'd talk about football. He's Spurs mad and I'm a Queen's Park Rangers fanatic.

'It was the *laughter* in that house, *that's* what I loved best. And they loved to see everyone else laughing. Soon as you'd look unhappy, they'd want to know why. I've been in domestic service since I was 13, over 40 years, and they're the nicest people I've ever been with. They made me one of the family immediately.

'David picks up on everything. As soon as you move something it's, "Oh, Margaret!" One morning I came in and heard Terry Wogan on the wireless say he wasn't going to see *Chariots of Fire* until he got a free ticket. I told David and straight away, he got Lynda to write to Terry saying, "Mrs Maguire's come in and says you're not going to see it unless you get a ticket, so if you go to the box-office, there'll be two tickets there for you." That morning on the radio, Terry says, "*Mrs Maguire*! Saying I'm not going to see it unless I get a ticket!" David got Terry to play the *Chariots* theme music for me, which I loved.

'They used to have these marvellous breakfasts where they'd all meet, the four of them, until the breakfasts stopped when Debbie got a flat of her own for a couple of years before getting married. Then Sacha stopped coming down, this was when he was 15 years old, out half the night, in bed half the day. Patsy was very strict. It was, "Get out of bed. Work!" Sacha rebelled a bit for about six months, you know that period, when everything your parents say is wrong. Sacha had always been musical; he'd go up to the top floor and be in heaven playing his guitar. I think eventually he'll write and produce music. He calls me his London mum now he's got a flat of his own. His dad loves him to death. He adores Debbie too and she's so proud of her dad. But do you know the marvellous thing about David and Patsy? They're still so much in love.'

Debbie remembers waking up early on the morning of the Oscar announcement, convinced that something great had happened. Sure enough, the earliest broadcast reported a sweeping of the boards, without mentioning whether or not the 'Best Film' award was in the bag. Marie phoned at 7 am. 'I think it's won Best Film,' she said excitedly, 'although they haven't actually said so. But from all the song-and-dance they're making, I think it must have done.' Debbie had no sooner put the phone down than her father was on the line from Los Angeles, confirming the top honour. When she told Margaret, they hugged each other and began to dance round the kitchen, shrieking with delight. 'Sacha!' Debbie yelled. 'I've got to go and tell Sacha!'

She rushed upstairs to wake her brother up, severely crashed out as he was after a late night. 'Oh, yeah, great, great,' he said sleepily. Debbie had the feeling she could equally have told him their dad had just landed on the moon and got the same completely unfazed reaction.

As she left to go to work an hour later, there was Sacha on the doorstep chatting to a couple of reporters. 'Oh, yes, we're all delighted,' he was saying. 'Plans for the future? Well, I know he's got quite a few things lined up . . .'

Debbie had to smile as she ran to catch her bus. 'Heaven help us,' she thought. 'Sacha's holding a press conference!'

Chapter 13

Chasing a Dream

The second film David and Hugh Hudson planned together remains unmade, despite numerous re-writes. Iain Smith was asked to get involved as an associate producer on *October Circle*, one of the two projects originally offered to the Fayeds, but found the enterprise oddly lacking in energy. There was insufficient wind in the sails of the ship, which Iain put down to David not being 100 per cent behind it. Andrew Birkin was asked to help, but failed to work up any enthusiasm and promptly dubbed *October Circle* 'Czechoslovakia's Greatest Hits', since he felt it had every East/West element known to mankind folded in there somewhere. It remains Patsy Puttnam's favourite project.

Following *Chariots'* success, Warner Bros were keen for David to produce *Greystoke – Tarzan, Lord of the Apes* a re-telling by Robert Towne of the Edgar Rice Burroughs tale. Hugh was again to direct, but there were many elements of the film which David did not like. A major one was that it would be a Warners production, with David acting as a hired-hand producer. He had realized early on that there are two types of films. One is a studio film, where the studio will provide 100 per cent finance, then insist on having their own people crawling all over the superstructure, compiling reports and demanding progress checks – the proposed *Greystoke* system. The idea of this was anathema to David for a multitude of reasons, *all* of them boiling down to control.

The second type of film is the one David had vowed to make – independently produced, outside the auspices of a studio. Instead of studio interference, raising of finance is the bugbear with this route. All the problems, horrendous though they might be in pursuing this chosen path, are justified in his mind by the one shining light at the end of the tunnel – *total autonomy* over the product. When *Agatha* turned into a Warners/Dustin Hoffman studio effort and autonomy walked out the door, so did David. In many ways his Casablanca period had represented the worst of both worlds, his function there

191

being reduced to acting as hired hand for an independent company, tenuously tied to a major studio.

David had now fully defined his own role, his confidence restored by *Chariots'* success. Following the money-raising traumas, part of which would ideally be the acquisition of his film by a US major as a 'negative pick-up' on completion, his aim would then be to build a wall around his project. At the outset he would try to make the wall large, capacious and impregnable, like a fortress. The wall would perform twin functions, the first and most important of which was the protection of the creative forces inside; it would also restrict, inhibit and prevent leakage. With the wall achieved, and with all his lonely, isolated battles with financiers fought and won, David would now stand back. He would not hang around the camera; he did not have to be seen everywhere.

If there was a dispute to be settled, involving the breaching of the fortress wall, it would usually be in private at the end of the day and only with those concerned. It would be as acrimonious as it was required to be, firm and to the point. There would be no trace of indulgence in the insidious 'blame syndrome', where the people in power take the credit and apportion the blame. Behind this was the wisdom of keeping a balance on the production between the twin demands of the creative and budgetary forces, for David viewed crews on a movie in two ways – the people whose primary responsibility was towards the script and those to whom the budget came first; as he saw it, his job as producer was to ensure that both lungs stayed the same size. Another endeavour would be to ensure that the people whose primary responsibility was for *one* lung, also cared about the *other* lung. A production designer should respect the budget without the feeling his artistic integrity was being compromised, while a production accountant would be expected to make his decisions beyond purely money-orientated thinking.

The sum of all these principles and experience told David one thing – not to get involved in *Greystoke*. Other elements of the film bothered him as well, such as the problem of special effects involved. 'I'm not the producer for this; I can't stand about when I've got a special-effects man telling me he doesn't know if the ape masks will be ready in time,' he told Patsy. 'Who needs it? And I've told them that while it's budgeted at $18 million, they'll be lucky to get it out for $25 million. In fact, it could easily go up to $30 million.'

Despite his reservations, there was one aspect of the *Greystoke* script that held enormous appeal, the delineation of the love of the ape for the human child. The notion that like does not necessarily have to love like totally captured his imagination. This was the single facet of *Greystoke* that attracted him, for it held a powerful, elemental appeal. The question still nagged – was the concept, beguiling as it was, worth the likely $30-million price tag?

David asked Warners to let him have three months to consider the project so that he could have a feasibility study conducted. They agreed to this, while Hugh waited with increasing impatience. What David came up with while the study was going on was an idea to make the ape-men in the film realistic, by using a troupe of Bulgarian acrobats, who would be able to swing convincingly from tree to tree while dressed in their ape costumes.

Once the feasibility study was ready, David took one look at it and concluded that the film's production was going to be a nightmare in which he did not wish to participate. This made Warners angry. In the rule book of Hollywood, the mere fact that someone is doing a study and talking about a project . . . well, for God's sake, he wouldn't turn it *down*, would he? David did, to joint howls of rage from Hollywood and Hugh – whose attitude was that David had left him in the lurch. Hugh then elected to become *Greystoke*'s producer as well as director, letting himself in for the nightmare that the movie's production indeed turned out to be, but still with a $30-million movie in his pocket. When David went to Warners for a fraction of this amount for his own proposed new film, *Local Hero*, they – whether piqued, short sighted or plain downright vindictive – chose to turn him down.

Today Hugh talks freely of his relationship with David over the years, alternately praising and condemning his tormentor/colleague/father-figure/alter-ego: 'He *voraciously* grabbed anything he could for himself from *Chariots of Fire* and denigrated my position many times, to the extent that people wondered what I had to do with the film. He capitalized on misquotes that had him as "director". Of course he had a lot to do with the film. He initiated it – but I directed it, I styled it. I've heard other things he said, like he chose the music. *I* chose the music for the film; Vangelis was my collaborator on many of my projects, someone I'd known for 10 years. It enhances the film; it holds it all together. I've heard David say on the radio that he chose the music and that the film was nothing without the music. That's absolute rubbish and a dishonourable thing to say. It's so patently untrue.

'He should have done everything after the event – as he did during the making of the film and before producing the film – to protect the director. If he is the captain of the ship, his job is to protect and help the people on the ship. He's not a great leader until he can do that. You don't abandon your crew. The great leader, and he may have learnt this now, is one who has to deal with all those human issues. They're part of the deal of life.

'I *would* have done interviews if he had asked me. I was nervous a bit of being on TV, especially in the beginning, but I've learned since. I was new at it. If you're a producer or you're in control, you're a father-figure, therefore you've got to *be* a father. You can't take on the position of father and then run away from it and abandon the child. It's very, very immature to do that, and hurtful. He *has* given people wonderful opportunities all his life, for whatever reason or motivation. It's very admirable, but he has at times abandoned them. He's often run away when things got difficult, so he hasn't grown up; he's not totally mature.

'B A F T A and the Oscars *didn't* worry me; that had nothing to do with him; that's not the reason I was aggravated. The Americans are taught the only important thing is winning, but we're not taught that in England. Participating is. *Chariots* is about that – participating, not winning, because you can't win all the time in your life. We all play to win, but if you lose you've got to learn from your losses. There's that great scene in *Chariots* where Abrahams has won and he breaks down, showing how awful it can be to win. It's worse than losing.

'David was determined to grab everything; didn't want to share the glory – that's the truth. But it's all over now; it really doesn't matter any more. It's only ego and vanity that were bruised, so it doesn't matter. I *made* the film. I know what I did on the film. I know that he initiated it and that a lot of the success and the style of the film was my doing in conjunction with him and all the other people who worked on it – the musicians, the actors, the writer, all of them. *Certainly* he's self-lacerating; I know that. But the reason is *guilt*. There's a *lot* of guilt there.'

Hugh could be confusing guilt with responsibility, since one cannot exist without the other. Certainly David has never shied from taking full responsibility for his actions. A friend of both men can see the 'feud' from both men's perspectives. 'Hugh manoeuvred himself into a position where *Chariots of Fire* was the fall-back subject using *October Circle* as his ticket. He went to David originally, saying he loved the book and had tried to buy the rights before he discovered David held them. Perhaps they could do it together? Remember that Hugh was 40 now, and came from the same background in commercials as the Parkers and the Scotts. He'd even seen Adrian Lyne, who was much younger than him, get his chance. So when David failed to get *October Circle* off the ground, he felt honour bound to give *Chariots* to Hugh, who did a very nice job with it, no question. But if ever a film was one man's vision, that *film* is *Chariots* and that *man* is David Puttnam.'

Hugh stresses he still feels enormous affection for David, while disarmingly admitting, 'I've been bitchy about him, but there's no point in being bitchy. I've felt slighted by him in many ways. We still share a building in the mews next to his house and I feel bound to him in the way my career's gone. I wanted him to produce *Greystoke*, but he didn't, for whatever *real* reason.

'David would *not* just have been a hired producer. Bob Towne approached David to produce it with three-quarters of a script written, and a brilliant one at that. Towne was going to direct it, then he abdicated his directorial role when his film, *Personal Best*, went way over budget. He had to sell *Greystoke* to Warners so they would put more money into *Personal Best*. Warners wanted the David Puttnam/Hugh Hudson partnership to do "something". When *Greystoke* came up, we thought it had wonderful unfinished potential. We said, "Let's do it." We were given a six-month period to decide on the actor, finish the script and find the locations. They paid David and I to work on this development.

'In six months we did all that, then he announced he wasn't going to do it. He phoned me one morning at the Beverly Wilshire Hotel from New York to say he was walking off the film. Naturally I was cool about it. The project could have been scrapped! I told Warners I would look around and try to find another producer with whom I could work. Eventually I had to tackle both jobs myself.

'If David *had* stayed and produced the film, I think it would have been more successful. I'll say that, which is a great compliment to David, because when I took on both functions I had to wear two hats. I remember one fundamental meeting where I was talking about the creative aspects in Claridges with the whole of the Warners' hierarchy, at a moment when it looked like we might be going over budget. They said, "Hugh, we've talked about the script and the acting and all the wonderful things you're doing, now go out and come back again and be the producer." And I had to go out of the room and come back again before I could talk business with them!

'If David had been there it would have been easier. We wouldn't have had the troubles we had, the power battles I had to endure with Warners at the end. They cut the film unnecessarily in the States. If David had been running in partnership with me, he would have persuaded them not to do it. He would have made it work and it would have come out a better film. *Of course* I was annoyed when he walked off, because he was a very good partner to work with. He *shouldn't* have walked off. *That's* my great criticism of him. When you start something, you've got to finish it. It *wasn't* a special-effects picture. The eventual budget was $30 million and we made it for that. By the time we had recceed it he saw it going up. No wonder! There was a $4-million pay-off to Bob Towne and $5 million to pay for the fucking apes. He *could* have dealt with Warners and produced the film – *I* did.'

Alan Parker looked at the *Greystoke* conflict from a distance. 'The Hugh Hudson of *Greystoke* was not the Hugh Hudson who made *Chariots of Fire*. He asserted himself in a way that was not pleasing to David. It was clear that Hugh was going to be very much in the driving seat because of the confidence he had in himself and from Warners after *Chariots of Fire*. David was uncomfortable with that part of it as well as all the other stuff. Hugh had become a *maestro*. There was always something else about Hugh, too – to do with his manner. With him on the set, you absolutely know who the director is. He has that wonderful "born to rule" look, that manner, that stature. On the other hand, someone like me, I'm always frightened someone's going to tap me on the shoulder and say, "Right you, back to Islington, the game's up!" I'm sure David does too. With Hugh, coming from a different background, he would never dream of being anything other than in control. He knew from an early age he was going to be in charge, then Eton presumably reinforced that. After *Chariots* there was no mistake that Hugh would be in charge, which I happen to believe is right. David, on the other hand, hates the auteur theory, but curiously re-invented the idea of the producer as auteur. That's fine for him, but as a theory and a system, it's incredibly dangerous, because there are very few people who have David's ability to understand the mechanics of film and the sensitivities of the creative side. Producers in control are usually a recipe for disaster. Perhaps arguably, for David to be in control it's different, because he is unique and extremely talented – but I call his the Mussolini school of film-making.'

The casting director on *Greystoke* was Patsy Pollock, a chestnut-haired beauty, whose talent and creative ability are only matched by her unbridled use of English ('Blame it on my East End upbringing,' she says cheerfully, 'my Irish gambler father and my six brothers'). Desperate in the mid-sixties to get out of the East End of London, Patsy started work in the typing pool of CDP, but reckons she was far too gorgeous and lippy to last long there. ('I couldn't type anyway, so I used to hang around in the art department.') While she was babysitting for David (Diaghilev) Reynolds and his wife one day, David Puttnam drew up outside the house in his bright red Triumph TR4 sports.

'Fuck me, it's Jack the Kipper,' Patsy thought. 'What a tasty geezer. I wonder who 'e is?'

From then on she listened whenever the two Davids, Reynold and Puttnam, were talking business. 'All that dialogue in my earhole,' says Patsy, 'I knew I had to somehow get into the business.'

From then on her and the 'tasty geezer's' paths crossed frequently. After promotion to photographer's stylist, delicate-as-a-flower Patsy found herself casting commercials at CDP with the rudely-macho crowd of Alan Parker, Alan Marshall, Hugh Hudson and Ridley Scott. Out on her own as a casting agent, she worked first in the theatre, then moved into films with *Quadrophenia*, *Yanks*, *Reds* and *The French Lieutenant's Woman*. For *Greystoke* she discovered Christopher Lambert. ('I sat in a Paris hotel room all day, interviewing loads of lovely crumpet. Christopher had never made a film; I met him straight out of the Conservatoire.')

She found herself on centre court at the *Greystoke* tournament. 'I missed David madly when he left. I was going to achieve what had been my dream, to take a film all the way through from beginning to end and work with him. That dream was dashed. The essence of what the breakdown was amounted to a big and painful emotional scene. In cases like that, I don't think it's a bicycle-repair-kit job, is it? Still, all it boils down to at the end of the day is two geezers falling out.

'If, in his heart, David felt that Hugh was such an unusual and phenomenally gifted film director, I think somehow he would have been able to appease the situation. But he didn't, so fuck it. In any case, Hugh's so bloody devious, clever, subtle-minded and revengeful. He's got the most devious brain of any director I know.' Patsy smiles. 'Not a bad bloke, though.'

Patsy reckons her old mum had the movie businesses all sorted out, prior to her departure to the big Green Room in the sky.

'This is it, Ma?' Patsy asked. 'Off to meet Sir Ralph and Charlie, is it?'

'Who?'

'You know, Sir Ralph Richardson and Charles Laughton.'

'Fuck them! I want the lively ones. I want the ones what sing and kicks their knees up. Anyway, Patsy, I'm getting a bit muddled and confused. What is it you do again? Are you still a photographer?'

'No, Mum, I never was a photographer!'

'Well, all the boys keep saying they've seen your name on the telly. And you don't even like the telly.'

'That's right, Mum, I don't. You see, I cast these films, then they're shown on the telly later.'

'Oh! You're a director, then?'

'No, Mum.'

'Well, I got to tell you, I think I've worked out at last what a director is. 'E's this bloke, see, with all these ideas in 'is bonce and 'e gets the camera and wot 'appens is, all these ideas in 'is bonce go on the film. And if 'e's got fuck all in 'is bonce, nuffink comes out in the film. Any good, P?'

'Excellent, Mum.'

The surprising coda to the *Greystoke* saga illustrates, despite the undoubted sincerity of all the other views expressed, just where the bottom line is finally drawn. In the wake of *Chariots'* success, Hugh Hudson found himself looking for representation in Hollywood. 'Talk to Creative Artists,' David suggested, aware of the already dizzy rise of Mike Ovitz's agency since its foundation in 1975. Hugh was duly taken on as a CAA client.

Originally the deal Warner struck with David and Hugh was for a fee of $500,000 each for *Greystoke*. Shortly after CAA's appointment, Ovitz began to do his job and renegotiate Hugh's fee. Warner agreed to upgrade Hugh to $650,000.

David was informed of this by Warner when the deal was a fait accompli. CAA had done well for Hugh – too well in Warner's view. Would David help them out by reducing his fee to $425,000?

From that moment on, beginning with a burst of outrage that rocked Burbank and the nearby Ventura freeway to their foundations, Warners had effectively blown it. Pride, not money dominated the equation. Goldwyn-isms were again the order of the day: David 'included himself out'.

One of the projects David had in mind for a future collaboration with Hugh was now placed on indefinite hold. His attention had been drawn to the famous polar explorer Ernest Shackleton's advertisement in London newspapers in 1914: 'Men wanted for hazardous journey. Small wages, bitter cold, long months of complete darkness, constant danger, safe return doubtful. Honour and recognition in case of success.' David felt that here lay the true stuff of epics. 'It seemed,' Shackleton had written, 'as though all the men in Great Britain were determined to accompany me, the response was so overwhelming.'

'The story has all the human elements,' David declared. 'It is a success story about failure. Whereas Captain Scott did indeed reach the South Pole, Shackleton's expedition failed because he had to make the momentous decision to turn back before he lost a single man.' With Hugh Hudson no longer possible as one element, the story of Ernest Shackleton was put away for another day.

The disparate talents of David Puttnam, David Norris and Jake Eberts were finally brought together round the Goldcrest boardroom table. The first Norris heard of the plan was in a pub on the evening of *Chariot's* BAFTA awards in 1982. 'I've got some terrific news for you,' David told him. 'Great,' Norris replied, thinking David had been tipped the wink that *Chariots* was going to sweep the BAFTA boards. After the ceremony they met again. 'Great news –' David continued.

'Marvellous,' Norris replied.

'No, not that,' said David, 'we've talked it over and we want you to be business and legal affairs director of Goldcrest. Go talk to James Lee.'

When Norris did, he found himself arraigned before the rest of the board as well, chief executive Jake Eberts, John Chambers and Mike Wooller, with David and now Dickie Attenborough as the other non-executive directors. The company was still in the business of appraising developed product and raising equity against foreign sales. 'A film brokerage operation,' was the rather unglamorous appellation Norris gave it, not an expression that met with widespread approval. In Lee's outline of Goldcrest's future plans to Norris, movies loomed large.

'What do you think of it?' James asked at their initial meeting.

'I think you're mad,' Norris replied, citing the cases of ABC, CBS and NBC in the 1967–70 period, all of whom had tried to enter the theatrical motion picture field; then Mel Simon, Lorimar and Polygram in more recent times. Each had ended up licking their wounds, recording huge losses and writing off the bulk of their venture capital as an irretrievable loss. The one thing they had all lacked was distribution, Norris noted. On this the long-established majors had the stranglehold.

'I *like* your madness,' he added, 'and I can see how you're trying to contain risk, but you can't expect bonanza business.' He nevertheless agreed to join the board, largely because of the presence of film-makers like David. He could see a parallel between the forces which drove his former antagonist and another immense talent that he had represented for several years, Stanley Kubrick. At one stage Norris innocently asked Kubrick if he had gone to university back in the States. He was met with a glowering look and the choked admission, 'I got caught by the GI charter.' Kubrick explained the bill had the effect of flooding universities after the Second World War with ex-servicemen guaranteed the right to a university education. It also had the effect of squeezing out many younger men who would normally have won a place, Kubrick for one. By the time the universities had emptied out, he had moved on.

Norris realized, from Kubrick's demeanour, the enormous nerve he had struck with his casual enquiry, which he reckons accounts for a lot of the darker side of the director's nature and much of the underlying angst in his work. He sees David as similarly vulnerable, with a desperate need to prove himself and an attitude of 'I could have done it – I *know* I could have fucking done it!'

Although non-executive, David ensured his presence on the board was felt from the beginning. 'David was very important to the development of Goldcrest, more important than was fully realized,' James Lee asserts. 'When we first met, just after I'd become chairman, he'd been involved with Jake in an advisory capacity. He was invited to be the first actual film-maker on the Goldcrest Films International Board, the company that was the forerunner of Goldcrest itself. At our very first meeting we had to decide whether or not to invest in a picture called *Hopscotch*, with Walter Matthau and Glenda Jackson. Jake had arrived at an understanding with Jo Child, who seemed to feel the picture would be put through on the nod. Child was present and was absolutely incensed at David's very forceful argument that *Hopscotch* was not a good bet. David made the point that Walter Matthau was not necessarily a sure-fire box-office proposition. His audience was getting older with him. The recent trend in Walter Matthau movies had been down, while the cost of the films had gone up. In summary, he observed that this was an extremely bad investment to make.

'Coming from the only person round the table with any experience on films, since Dickie Attenborough had yet to join, we decided not to back *Hopscotch*. Jo Child raged, but to no avail, and in the end IFI had to back the film themselves.

'For the first time Jake could now see he wasn't going to have it all his own way. The rest of the package we were offered was a partnership

in *Escape from New York* and *The Howling*, the latter especially I was
particularly against making. I said I didn't think it was the sort of film
that Goldcrest had been set up to develop or be associated with. It
went on to do *very* well, much to my chagrin, whereupon I received a
telex from Jo Child after it had opened successfully which said, "In
the light of the fact that you disliked the film so intensely, we are
prepared to take it off your hands at cost." We decided not to allow
him to do that! So David was on the board – and I liked the cut of his
jib, and continued to do so thereafter. He was never afraid to speak
his mind.'

There are as many theories on the reasons for David's modus operandi
as there are variations of the account of Goldcrest's fortunes, but of
one thing there was now no doubt – David's unique ability among
British producers to generate an idea on his own, a process which, by
definition, puts the producer in the driving seat, leaving him free
to enjoy a genuine collaborative intimacy between producer, screenwriter and director. Although criticized by friends and enemies alike
for making his life so public through his press contacts, what David
was telling everyone was, 'Look, I *have* changed. I *will* be taken
seriously!' A reaction to his sixties' period of self-loathing and the
expediency that ruled in the seventies, his attitude was, 'That was
then, now is now.' He was not prepared to tolerate the fractious sort
of relationship he had in the past with the likes of Ken Russell.

That David requires to get pleasure out of films beyond the pleasure
of actually getting a film *made*, or indeed of making money, was
evidenced when he was asked if it wouldn't give him a kick to help a
'real' director to make a chef d'oeuvre – a Visconti, perhaps, or a
Fellini. 'Quite frankly, no,' he replied. 'I don't get any pleasure out of
being a banker and making the money available. What's the thrill in
that?' Thus David stands almost alone among producers as a breed,
who are eager primarily to get *any* film off the ground, especially if
they've managed to collar a certain director or star. David would
maintain that the main thrill is in *loving* the films he makes and the
people he makes them with *at the time*. And, being all too human,
hoping the feeling is reciprocated.

Alan Parker has watched David's system in action, but notes its
flipside. 'His whole way of working is to befriend people. That way he
gets the best from them and creates the most enjoyable kind of environment. The moment a project is finished, though, he's no longer their

friend; he's on to something else. A lot of people have smarted from that friendship not continuing.'

Since their return from the States, Patsy had been chasing a dream nurtured over the years, then quickened by a visit to Ridley Scott's magnificent Gloucestershire country house in 1977. During the discussions she and David had about the pros and cons of the *Midnight Express* trip, he had spoken the magic words: 'Look, it won't be for that long, and when we come back, you can have that house in the country you've always wanted.' Patsy was sold.

In Los Angeles a subscription to *Country Life* was taken out. 'It was my little treat to myself,' she says. 'I would look through it, anticipating the sort of place we might get. Little did I realize we'd be coming home to England *still* boracic! Our tax problem was solved, our overdraft was down, but still the coffers were empty. That hadn't stopped us from looking all the time, and a lot of people we knew back home had helped. Alan Parker was marvellous; he used to go round houses for us. I mean, it was all *bubbling* in our minds.

'When we got back, boracic or not, we still went around looking at houses. Anyone who's done that knows how disappointing it is. We'd go for months not doing it, and then start all over again. We came across a lovely house in Dorset in the Isle of Purbeck, but Edward Fox got to it first, so that was that. After that we weren't going to do any more about houses. We were sick of it and all our friends were sick of us talking about houses. One thing had changed, though, as *Chariots* began its incredible run in America: for the first time there was some real money in prospect.

'One day we were sitting down to dinner with David Westmoreland and his wife Jane, and inevitably the subject turned to houses. I said, "We're not looking any more; that's the end of it and anyway, I'm only interested in something with a river. I must have lots of water." I'd imposed all these extra conditions just to make the hunt even more impossible! Their daughter Camilla said, "My God! I know the very house – and it might be coming up for sale!" She promised to keep track of developments and a few months later it was confirmed that the people she knew were indeed going to put their house on the market. With the *Chariots* explosion continuing, we went off to the Oscar ceremony and on our return I spoke to the owners, who were delighted that we wanted to go down to Wiltshire to see it. We had to be quick, because David was due in Scotland the following Monday.

'We drove from London and arrived early. It was a typical showery April day, then suddenly the sun came out just as we entered the gates. There are the bottom of the drive, flanked on one side by the River Avon, whose banks were lined with hundreds and hundreds of daffodils, lay my dream come true, this beautiful old stone-built mill-house.

'The owners began to show us round, but it didn't matter to me. I was totally hooked. I was just in a daze. David was being practical and looking in all the corners and gazing at the timbers in the roof and such, but I was *hooked*. From then on he had to deal with a woman who was totally in love. I mean, for me it just went out of the realms of practicality and all that nonsense.'

David left at the weekend for Scotland and his rendezvous with Bill Forsyth. He had always been keen on the Scots as a race and had enjoyed location filming on *The Duellists* and *Chariots of Fire* in the past. The assignation also gave him a break from Patsy's entreaties about the house, though if the truth be known these were hardly required, for he had fallen in love with it himself. But for now it was battery-charging time and a complete change of pace. The magic of Scotland was about to weave its spell, as one 'Local Hero' met another.

Chapter *14*

'Awright, It's Not Perfect,
but it Works'

There are few certainties in the film world – there had been none at all for David in his career to date – but at last, following the BAFTA awards for *Chariots*, he was able to announce that on 19 April 1982 he would be standing by a camera, producing a film. For the first time an element of certainty had been introduced, *Local Hero* was about to roll.

David had been recommended by Colin Young, the director of the National Film School, to see Bill Forsyth's *That Sinking Feeling*, following its appearance at the Edinburgh Film Festival. A showing in London was arranged, when Bill handed over the script for *Gregory's Girl*. 'Because I'm such a terrific judge of material I turned it down,' David laughs. 'I had two reasons. I felt that for him *Gregory's Girl* didn't represent a major departure from *That Sinking Feeling* and then I felt it was a regression for me to *That'll Be the Day*. It was a very stupid decision and I regret it deeply, but there it is!'

Bill's film career began in 1964 at the age of 17, when he answered an ad in the paper, 'Lad required for film company'. He had no particular interest in films, but the ad rather stood out among the others. He wrote for an interview, using a green pen to make his letter different, only to be greeted with, 'You're not a *Catholic*, are you?' Then he was asked if he could work a lawnmower, wash a car, and various other key questions. Bill was hired and found himself flung into the world of documentary film-making. Within a week he was writing a shooting script for the Bank of Scotland.

By 1971 he had formed a company, Tree Films, with Charlie Gormley. Their slogan: 'Branches everywhere'. The association ended seven years later in a welter of unproduced screenplays. Bill wrote *Partners*, which he would eventually make as *Comfort and Joy*. He had a rubber stamp cut, the legend reading, "PARTNERS" . . . See it Once To Laugh, Twice To Cry' – this for a film 10 years and a title change down the line!

To raise money for *That Sinking Feeling*, Bill wrote to every source of finance he could find, obtaining the £8,000 budget from William Hill (£25), Marks & Spencers (£25), AUEW (£2), Glasgow District Trades Council (£10), Scottish Television (£250), and scores of others, all of them credited on the end-titles.

'I owe David a great deal,' Bill acknowledges, flicking his dark shoulder-length hair away from his eyes, and looking for all the world a Scottish cross between a likable leprechaun and a benign troll doll. 'Not only did he get me a distribution deal at GTO for *That Sinking Feeling*, but he introduced me to my agent, Anthony Jones. So indirectly through David I found my *Gregory's Girl* producers, Clive Parsons and Davina Belling. Then it was David's brilliant idea to double-bill *Chariots of Fire* with *Gregory's Girl*, which brought in more money for my film than it made on its first release. I associate our meeting with a big change in my life, the start of good things happening.'

A year after the first encounter the two men met again in a tobacconist's shop in Wardour Street. David phoned Bill a few days later. 'He said he wanted to show me a movie,' Bill recalls. 'We arranged to meet at BAFTA at 7 pm where he had *Whisky Galore* run. He didn't talk about it there and then, but I got the idea that maybe he had it in mind we should make a film together and maybe it would be set in Scotland. After a week or so we got more serious and began to talk about it.'

David had found a clipping about a man in the Hebrides who had negotiated a major deal with an American petrochemical company, a better deal than anything the British National Oil Corporation had achieved. The chemistry that produced *Chariots of Fire* from his study of the Paris Olympics was at work again, as David sought to repeat the organic growth that had brought forth *Chariots*. Bill agreed to submit a two-page treatment, pointing the emphasis away from oil rigs and the hardware of the business, while still retaining the concept of an American petrochemical giant being taken to the cleaners by the supposedly naïve inhabitants of a small Scottish fishing village.

He wrote the script between May and September 1981, a year after David's initial approach. 'At first I tried to be funny, which was a bit of a hindrance,' Bill recalls. 'I felt it was expected of me that whatever I did had to be funnier than *Gregory's Girl*, which I didn't see as being all that funny myself when I was writing it. There were one or two false starts when I tried to impose humour on the story line – pratfall humour, which was very easily extracted after I decided that it would just be as funny as it wanted to be.'

Between their meetings David enjoyed his enormous success with

Chariots, while Bill's breakthrough film, *Gregory's Girl*, was released. He had plodded on doggedly after David rejected it and raised the £200,000 necessary to fund the project. Although still a small-budget film, it was a gigantic step up from the £8000 which produced *That Sinking Feeling*. 'The odd thing,' David points out, 'is that when we started working together, neither of us was particularly successful. *Chariots* could easily have been the end of me. You could swap Don Boyd's experience and mine. *Honky Tonk Freeway* at EMI could have been this immense hit and mine could have been the flop.'

From the beginning the major problem with *Local Hero* was the length of the script, which Bill was reluctant to cut down. Nor was it a question of a few pages long, for instead of the ideal 90-page length, it ran to 150 pages. Bill resisted the idea of shortening it, preferring to shoot the whole script, then see which parts worked. 'There were things in the script it was difficult to pin a value on,' Bill explains, 'especially with so many intermediate characters wandering in and out of the main story. It was difficult on the page to tell what was strong and what was weak, so I thought it was sensible to shoot everything we had and then edit it down.'

Bill's screenplay had Felix Happer, the head of Knox Oil and Gas from Houston, Texas, planning to build a massive oil refinery in a remote Scottish coastal village. When Happer sends one of his executives to Scotland to buy up the land, he finds himself up against some harder bargaining than he reckoned on, as well as being seduced by the rather less hectic pace of life. Bill wrote the part of Happer with Burt Lancaster in mind, while accepting there was not the slightest chance of actually obtaining the actor. Still, it was an interesting thought.

David liked Bill's original script, but had grave reservations about its length. A second draft arrived two months later, still roughly the same length. Then the money soundings began in earnest, while Bill and newly-appointed associate producer Iain Smith – retained following his sterling work as location manager on *Chariots of Fire* – went off to Scotland to find suitable locations and to consider casting. Goldcrest initially agreed to put up £100,000 to enable pre-production to proceed on the basis of Bill's treatment, then agreed to fund no less than half the budget of £2 million when they saw the shooting script. David reckoned the other half would not be too difficult to find at the stage he was at in his career, but he was in for a rude shock. First Warners, then EMI turned the project down. Rank made an offer which would have meant financial suicide.

Only weeks were left before principal photography was due to

start. On the night that *Chariots of Fire* won Best Film and Bill
Forsyth was named Best Screenwriter for *Gregory's Girl* at BAFTA,
Goldcrest's chairman, James Lee said, '*Enough* fucking about, *we'll*
put up *all* the money; let's just make the film and worry about it afterwards.'

What followed was a chain of events David understood only too
well, as Warners then hastily bought the US distribution rights for
half the budget – exactly what David had been seeking all along. Why
the change of mind? It's the 'Jesus Christ, it's actually being made!'
syndrome. A project is all too easy to reject in paper form. It's much
simpler to say 'no' and therefore avoid responsibility on the basis that
most scripts never get made anyway. When a project is actually *rolling*
it becomes a different beast entirely, and the same executives who
turned it down are now going to have to live with their possible mistake.

Casting was under way by autumn 1981, with Fulton Mackay,
Peter Riegert, Denis Lawson, Rikki Fulton, John Gordon Sinclair,
Peter Capaldi, Jenny Seagrove and Alex Norton lined up. Bill
broached the subject of the star he had in mind for the role of Felix
Happer, his dream-casting of Burt Lancaster. David was intrigued,
but had qualms about the effect this might have on the film's budget.
At the same time he was aware of the beneficial effect Burt's name
would have on cable and television rights. When the script was sent
out to him in Los Angeles, Burt loved it, then David struck the deal
with him at the BAFTA awards ceremony in London in March
1982. He was riding high with his triumph in *Atlantic City* and had
been captivated by Bill's script, so much so that he agreed to do his
three-week stint on the film for a much-reduced fee upfront in exchange for profit points in the picture. Bill flew out to Rome to meet
Burt after the ceremony and a date in April was set for the start of
filming. Apart from a week in Houston, Texas, the entire film was to
be shot in Scotland over an eight-week period.

Bang on schedule Bill and a party of 17 flew out to Houston to join
the already assembled 15-strong crew. Burt Lancaster flew in from
Los Angeles for the day and a half his scene required. The major set
piece involving the star was a discussion which took place round a
boardroom table as Happer and his directors debated their proposed
major investment in the Scottish village. Happer falls asleep halfway
through the meeting which is then concluded in whispers. The scene
was a nightmare to shoot for a multitude of reasons, and the end
result was something that would lie about the film's shoulders like an
albatross until the later editing process. 'I think it's awright,' Bill

claimed defensively. 'I think it's fine. Awright, it's not *perfect*, but it works.'

Bill's script described a small village with a beach, which proved impossible to find in the one spot. 'We'd been on every single bloody beach in Scotland,' says Iain Smith, 'and there simply wasn't one with a village attached to it as Bill had written it. It was very difficult for him to suddenly come to the point where he had to realize the two had to be separate; we'd have the beach round the headland from the village. Our ideal beach was at Morar, 30 miles west of Fort William – then we found our village, Pennan, up on the Morayshire coast. It's a funny little place . . . it wasn't what Bill had perceived. So myself and Bill and Roger Murray Leach, our set designer, went on down to Pennan. Roger and I knew this was it, that we had no other option in the whole of Scotland – but Bill was a long way off feeling that.

'We drove down this steep little hill at Pennan and walked for a couple of hours observing this and that, while Bill hardly said a word. In the end the pub opened and we just ran out of words to coax him and sat down and had a pint. Then another. We realized we had come to the point where we were just going to sit this out. Bill was most unhappy. Finally he got up and went out onto the front, while Roger and I just stayed. He walked the whole length of the village on his own, turned round and came back and said, "Yeah, I think it might work."

'God, he's so *strong* – David will tell you that he is the most determined and stubborn director he had ever worked with. He's what they call in Scotland "thrawn". If he's not for it, he'll definitely not move. You can send brigades of men with axes and he won't budge!'

Bill combined this characteristic with an acute shyness that prevented him from even shouting 'Action' and 'Cut', relying on assistant director Jonathan Benson to carry out this function. His shyness in no way undermined his determination, as cameraman Chris Menges confirmed: 'He had an interesting way of dealing with the money side of the shooting. Time and again people would come up and say, "We're overshooting" or "The script's too long" and Bill would say yes, and do nothing about it. He's not scared of where he is and recognizes *Gregory's Girl* was OK; he's really pleased it made money. He's quite happy to take money from David to make his new film, because he sees himself as learning. Just like a kid is supposed to come out of school, so Bill wants to find out what this world is all about. Many film people don't think in that way; they think of ambition, conquering their souls, of great drama, fame or the great acclaim of life. Bill's not about that.'

Although the unit had been greeted initially in Scotland by snow and force 9 gales, interrupting what had been beautiful spring weather, the adverse conditions were to prove short-lived and filming was soon well underway. As usual, David was there on day one and for most of the shooting. He saw the film as an ecology piece – a *Mr Smith Goes to Washington* for the eighties. Never having produced a comedy before, he admitted he was nervous about the outcome. 'What we're trying to make is a modest-budget film that looks like a big film with universal implications,' he stated. 'I believe passionately that only by being specific do you become global. I hate these films that aim for some nebulous mid-Atlantic market. Cinema is about the transference of personality to that of someone on the screen and you can only do that if they have a fixed, clearly-rooted identity.'

With a weather eye on the way Bill was shooting the film, aware that it had to be boiled down to a final running of under two hours, David voiced his reservations during filming. 'I think the film does take on a lot,' he admitted. 'Maybe when we come to cutting it, we'll find it has taken on too much. Most films follow a line that is reasonably consistent, whereas *Local Hero*, in common with some of Preston Sturges' films, takes the opposite tack. When a camera would normally come into this room to see what you and I were doing, here it would go next door to see what the secretary's doing. How does one define the film? With *Chariots* that problem was solved in a way because it was so unlike anything else and I didn't have to come up with a parallel. With this film one can talk about the nature of humour itself.'

As David's associate producer, Iain Smith was a key figure on the set, flush with his promotion, and quickly established a working relationship with David which he describes modestly – and hilariously.

'He's a bit like the man on the beach with the dog. He'll pick up a stick from the sand and he'll think, yes, that's a really good stick, it feels the right sort of weight, and he'll hurl it into the sea. The dog will go rushing in and splash about energetically, working hard, whip up a lather, get out there and fight the waves, grab that stick in his jaws, turn around and swim straight back, fighting his way on to the beach.

'David meantime is strolling along the beach. The dog – *me*! – all dripping and wet, knackered, comes rushing up with the stick. And David will say, "Great. Thank you."

'I don't genuinely think David knew what to make of Bill Forsyth. Unlike Alan Parker and Hugh Hudson, Bill was someone who came from another hemisphere altogether, from another planet in fact. Not just because he was Scottish, but because of his mentality. Bill was a man working with David for the first time who was more interested in *content* than he was in *style*. I'm sure David thought about that, as one of the many contributing factors that led to his interest in Bill, that he could see in Bill somebody who went direct through all the conventions to the screen, tell a story straight from my mouth to your ear, and wouldn't get too wrapped up in technique. David was fundamentally dipping into a pool he didn't really understand. It was a new game: Celtic, fey kind of people who didn't respond in quite the way he had been used to. So in that sense he was very smart in getting another Celt – me again! – someone he could trust, or maybe as a kind of enema. The two of them were, in a way, getting into quite a different bed. Bill was being obliged to make a film that was more commercial and glossy and David was being required to make a more ethnic, rough-edged, less thrusting sort of film.

'David's system was to stay well back from the film during the shooting and the first part of cutting. He then allowed the film to take its form and shape between the director and the editor, then only at that stage would he come back in again and start to look at the film, when everyone else was starting to flag. It's a very clever thing to do, because it gives him the ability to tidy up all the things that are wrong, with a kind of objectivity. And he's doing it when everyone else is saying, "Oh, Christ, this isn't going to work," and this is always the case, every single film that's ever made. This always happens after working for 15 weeks of cutting. You're sitting there watching it, you no longer know what you're looking at and you think, "This is really going to bomb, this is terrible." You sit there and you wonder why on earth you ever tried to make the picture in the first place and at this low point David arrives, all dapper and spruce. He notes all the dejection and then he'll say, "Well, I've been thinking about this, and I've made some notes. I think we should take this scene and move it around –"'

David was able in this way to salvage the boardroom scene at the beginning of the film by having Happer asleep all the way through the meeting. The entire scene was overdubbed in whispers. Suddenly, it worked beautifully.

Despite Bill's stubbornness and the occasional friction that had taken place on the set, *Local Hero* was still one of David's happiest filming experiences. He recognized qualities in Bill that he admired tremendously. 'I think he's got a very, very wonderful vision of people. Not so much life as people. Bill has a unique ability to feel out the best in people and he has an innate belief in the best of people. He's a remarkably uncorrupted and unsoured man. From my point of view I'm not sure what I give Bill and wouldn't be presumptious enough to say that it amounts to anything. In terms of what he gives me, I find him an absolutely reliable man, sometimes taciturn so that you're a little unsure as to where you're going or what you're doing, but on the other hand he's always come through. I've grown to trust him more and more, not less and less, and sometimes it can go the other way. I trust his instincts, that's the most important thing. What I like is that he allows me a bit of room to do my job well. He's not an easy person to work with because he's not verbal. Bill, I think, likes to leave stuff on the table and I think probably in his terms rightly so. I think maybe Iain and I were a little unresponsive to his need for room. On the other hand we all created problems by not cutting the script enough and didn't give ourselves the room. However, I know we both have the same dreams and that's crucial.'

Bill in turn was equally appreciative. 'He's been great,' he declared. 'Really supportive. I was very apprehensive. However, it has been a delight to find out how good producers can be. We did not have a lot of problems. It would have been interesting to have had a couple of big problems just to see how we would have got on.

'I know now that we got on famously and it's been a really good relationship. When you're involved in a project there is a chance of becoming a little blinkered, so what a producer does is act as devil's advocate. It's his job to question almost every decision you make, just to make sure you are making it properly and to give you something to bounce off. It also gives the director the chance to see whether he is really serious about something because if there's an objection to an idea, if you really believe in it you'll see it through, if not you'll back off. It clears your own head in a funny sort of way.'

David was sanguine about the film's prospects. 'I think we'll get great reviews and have to fight for an audience like we did with *Chariots*. I think we could have a big hit, it's a film I think the public is waiting for. I've always known it was going to be a good film; recently it moved into the area of maybe it's a great film with cuts and changes we've made. I think we've now got three or four things we did that I think has made an immense difference to the picture. I am now buzzing with excitement over it. I love it, I absolutely love it. Let's put it this way – it's a ship I'm prepared to go down with.'

Mark Knopfler of Dire Straits was drafted in to compose and perform the score for the film. Having turned down earlier movie offers, which he had considered unsuitable, his management wrote to a dozen British producers, indicating Mark's interest in composing a score for the right project. Only two had the courtesy to reply, one of them being David: then a meeting between Mark and Bill cemented the deal. 'Whenever I'm reading a script,' says David, 'it has a tonal quality to it. A few of the tracks on Mark's *Making Movies* album reminded me of *Local Hero*, which I thought had a danger of being a bit too lyrical and needed a punch in it every now and again.'

Patsy and David were both aware that their dream house would go to auction and that although Patsy had got to know the owners, business was business in the final analysis. A friend's advice was to get professionals in to do the bidding, since it would take an expert to bid well. Patsy was all in favour, while David held back on the decision. Finally his response was, 'No, I'm not going to get anybody else in to do it – I'm going to do it myself, because the major things in our life that we've done, we've done ourselves, often against other people saying how mad we were. You're a fatalist, Patsy. You *know* that if you're meant to have the house, you'll have the house. So *I'm* going to bid for it.'

Everyone's advice was that David should hold his bid until as late as possible and to sit at the back of the hall, on his own, without Patsy. ('They were right,' Patsy says. 'I'd have been sitting there with this inane grin on my face in a state of total nervous collapse!') He should also leave his opening bid until the last minute, ran the counsel, using the late entrance as a shock tactic.

When the great day arrived, the couple had a cup of tea in Malmesbury before David proceeded alone to the Bell Hotel, where the auction was being held. Patsy took one look at the hundreds of people milling around and thought, 'Oh, my God! All these people want *my* house!' Even discounting the number who were probably just there to look, there was a whisper that someone had an idea of turning the house into a hotel, still another that kennels were planned.

As David disappeared into the Bell, Patsy began wandering around the nearby church garden as a steady drizzle began to fall. 'Penance in the rain,' she thought grimly. They had been advised that the auction would be over quickly, but as Patsy began her third circumlocution of the garden, she noticed that 20 minutes had elapsed. The only explanation that occurred to her was that the bidding had soared through the roof, eclipsing the top figure they could afford.

As the crowd began to spill out of the auction room, she could see no sign of David. The first face she recognized was that of the owner's wife, who rushed up to her with a cry of, 'Congratulations!' As they embraced she saw David leave the hotel, looking modestly pleased with himself.

'I can't believe it,' Patsy exclaimed happily. 'What held things up?'

'You remember the little cottage on the outskirts of the estate that was being sold separately?' David asked. 'I had to buy that as well to top the other bids.'

For the next two years, as Patsy began her remarkable odyssey with architects, surveyors and craftsmen, her task nothing less than the restoration of the house to its former glory, she would think gratefully a hundred times how fortuitous it was that David had included the cottage in the purchase, for they were to virtually live in it for the duration of the refurbishment.

A few weeks before Christmas 1982, a bizarre lunch conversation took place between David Puttnam, David Norris and James Lee. 'What happens if someone gets a CBE?' David kicked off.

'It depends when they get it in life,' Norris replied. 'If they get it early enough, it means they're pretty well thought of and they're on their way.'

'Can they go higher after that?' David wanted to know.

'Yes, they can.'

'But if they get it late, they're not going any higher?'

'That's it, usually.'

James Lee chipped in at this point. 'My father got the CBE.'

'My mother-in-law got it,' Norris added, 'and now she's a DBE. She didn't get her C until she was in her mid-fifties, then she did more good works and got her D.'

'So if you get the CBE, you might go further?' David persisted.

'*Yes*,' James and Norris chorused; then 'Congratulations, David,' Norris added.

'What do you *mean*?' David asked then promptly changed the subject.

After the lunch, James took Norris aside. 'He's got the CBE,' he said. 'He had to let us know, but couldn't tell us.' Both men reflected on the vulnerable, profoundly human side to David which they had just witnessed – the small boy bursting to share a secret, but having to hold back on the final revelation.

'I hope you're not going to change. Do I have to call you "sir" now?' Margaret Maguire asked David as he went off with Patsy and his mother to collect the honour.

'Mrs Maguire!' he scolded. 'If you ever see me changing, you tell me off!'

Part of the deal with Warners was a commitment by them to spend

$1.5 million on *Local Hero*'s promotion during the first 90 days of its US release in 1983. The movie opened first in the US market, since David had to wait a few extra weeks for the availability of the Haymarket Odeon, with 20th Century Fox in charge of UK distribution. David attended the New York première with Bill and felt they were off to a good start. 'We're on a roll,' he declared exuberantly. 'I don't know yet how big a hit it's going to be, but I know it'll be a hit. I could watch the film, knowing where the laughs should come, and every time they came right on cue.'

Now the heavyweights moved in and many of them were the very critics who liked *Chariots of Fire* least. David was apprehensive as he picked Andrew Sarris's *Village Voice* review, but he needn't have been. Sarris noted that Bill Forsyth had described the film – shades of David – as a combination of *Brigadoon* and *Apocalypse Now*. 'There is nothing in either film,' he reckoned, 'that comes close to matching the assured artistry, charm, finesse, amiability and deadpan hilarity of *Local Hero*. The whole film is so much of a complete surprise that I don't want to spoil it for you by giving away it's exquisitely modernist melodies comprised of bitter-sweet half-notes. This is one film in which money is given its proper weight in the universe, not too little and not too much, but just enough to divert people from their destinies. With *Local Hero* you must forget all your preconceptions and prepare for a joyously grown-up, warm-hearted and clear-headed meditation on the vagaries of contemporary existence.'

It is no easy job to charm the pants off Miss Pauline Kael, but David and Bill came close as she described the movie somewhat bemusedly as 'misleading in the most disarming way imaginable. Experience in movies has led us to expect a whole series of clarifications, but here they don't arrive. After a while, their non-arrival becomes a relief and we may laugh at ourselves for having thought we needed them. *Local Hero* isn't any major achievement, but it has it's own free-form shorthand for jokes and it's true to itself.'

The reaction in Britain was upbeat as well, with Geoff Brown in *The Times* noting a touch of wild natural magic in the film, close to the spirit of some Michael Powell classics 'trying to present the cosmic viewpoint of people, but through the most ordinary things'. Derek Malcolm in the *Guardian* declared, 'If he made no other films but *That Sinking Feeling*, *Gregory's Girl* and *Local Hero*, Bill Forsyth's place would be secure as the most original comic author to emerge within the British cinema.' Nigel Andrews in the *Financial Times* was one of the few dissenters. 'In Scotland itself,' he wrote, 'the pace becomes not so much mystical/hypnotic as snail's pace slow. Some

sequences seem to have stuck to the movie like barnacles. The Russian
fisherman who pops up enigmatically in the village for a scene or two
must have come from a red-herring trawler, for he has no discernible
purpose in either the plot or the allegorical scheme. It's both a sterling
advance and a perplexing hiccup in Forsyth's career, making it another
Scottish mystery no Sassenach can unravel.' Michael Owen had no
such reservations. 'I have only seen it twice and twice is not enough,'
he wrote. 'It is such a joyous experience, bearing the identifiable
pedigree of both men, that I predict worldwide success, awards, dollars and everything else it deserves.'

Regrettably, the outcome was not so glowing, although the film
turned a very tidy profit with cable and TV sales. For some reason,
however, it failed to take off in the unpredictable US market, where
the universality David felt was within his grasp turned out to have
eluded him. Worldwide it was still a successful outing.

The love affair that had started with the Scottish location work on
The Duellists and *Chariots of Fire* was continuing and David even
declared that he felt himself an honorary Scot.

'I loved *Local Hero*,' he said later. 'I loved everything about it.
Making it, being on location with it and seeing it. I *needed* what *Local
Hero* gave me – after leaving Hollywood on the Wednesday with an
Oscar, there I was in a field in Scotland the following Monday,
bargaining with a farmer whose cows we wanted to use. The film is all
of a piece; there is nothing artificial jammed into it; it's the opposite
of a manufactured film.' If the film came over to many as a meander
through the Scottish countryside, at least it was a charming meander,
with no trace of the manipulative strings that had been suspended so
clearly over both *Midnight Express* and *Chariots of Fire*.

Gilly Hodgson contributed as usual to the publicity campaign for
Local Hero, and was now a friend of the family as well as a trusted
colleague. She saw the dedication to detail that David gave to both
pre- and post-release publicity. 'He has fixed ideas for what he wants,
the sort of newspapers, how the films are presented, what television
programmes he goes on, what sort of *look* the film has to achieve. So
far as the design of the film and the posters are concerned, the whole
thing has to have an image of excellence. He doesn't mind what he
spends on good design; he'll push his own people though the system
to achieve exactly what he wants, and that goes for album covers and
the books that are written about the films and the television programmes that are presented. He's ruthless, but in the very best sense of
the word. He's also unusual in that he places great store by the
provincial press, not like some who think London is the universe.

There are lots of reporters he prefers to talk to, the interesting and informed journalists who really know their stuff and are film buffs. He appreciates that.'

Gilly marvelled at the incredible amount of press interest *Local Hero* had engendered from the start. 'The press will grab something that doesn't seem at all likely sometimes,' she says. 'This one grabbed local interest, first in Scotland, then national, then went international. In the end we had a positive embarrassment of films about the *making* of the film, together with the book about its production. That's something else where David was extremely innovative. Most people make the film first, then start to bang the publicity drum a couple of weeks before it opens. Not David. He's always employed someone from the start to do an overall campaign right up to and through the film's release.'

Gilly constantly saw the strength that David draws from Patsy. 'She is what makes David's life *work*. Her really *quiet* strength, very kind, quite tough. She oils the machinery and makes him able to do *anything*. Then when he needs to, she will *make* David relax. She's just like him, really straight down the line.'

There was one regret that came with his Bill Forsyth collaboration – the realization that he could never out-Liddell the canny Scot. Compared to Bill, David realized he was back making the best he could of Abrahams and hoping some of the association with the Scot would rub off. Liddell may have refused to run on a Sunday, but Bill was prepared to go much further than that, as Iain Smith would testify. If events were not moving in the right direction, Bill was quite capable of refusing to run *any* day!

David recalled talking to singer/songwriter Paul Simon some years ago about being properly valued. 'He said there was a moment in a London pub when he was hired for £100 a week and he knew that was just the right value for him. Before that he'd never been paid enough, and afterwards he was always paid too much. And it's like that for me with *Local Hero* – that was the moment at which I felt correctly valued.'

Chapter 15

Now you're absolutely sure you're a friend of David Puttnam's...

' "Bollocks" to Shooting in Cambodia'

Jake Eberts dates his involvement in *The Killing Fields* from a tele-phone call in 1980 from Bob Rehme, then heading the Embassy set-up in Hollywood. 'Look,' Rehme said, 'there is a wonderful article in *Newsweek* about the French Embassy in Phnom Penh and what they did to the Cambodians who tried to leave the country and were denied exit visas. I think the story would make a terrific movie, but as you know, we're not allowed to develop projects of our own under the brief we have from Avco, our parent company. So why don't you guys develop it and when the time comes we'll talk about being your distributor at Embassy?'

Jake was in New York for a week's visit at this time and was sufficiently intrigued to seek the article out. US journalist Sydney Schanberg and various others had gathered in the embassy com-pound with the Cambodians to prepare for the mass departure, before being frustrated by the exit visas demanded for their native colleagues. Rehme was right, Jake felt: there *was* a movie here. His next step was to contact David. 'I called him up and told him the story about Schanberg, explaining that I wouldn't put up the money unless some-one like him was prepared to make the film as the producer, and would he get involved? He already knew about the story, he said, having read the article and heard it from other sources and said, yes, he would like to get involved. The way IFI was constituted, we had to put our funds into someone else's company for development, and an American one at that. So David actually formed a company in Nevada, of all places, called Enigma Nevada Inc. If David had not agreed to go ahead, I would never have got involved with *The Killing Fields*.'

David had read the dramatic wrap-up piece in *Newsweek* and saw at once the combined elements of male friendship that trans-cended cultures and continents, involving crushing guilt and astonish-ing tension, set against the huge backdrop of a country in the agony of genocide. Sydney Schanberg described his relationship with Dith Pran, a Cambodian interpreter who had saved his life, and how he had been forced to leave Pran behind in 1975 in the flight from the Khmer Rouge after the fall of Phnom Penh. Four years had been spent by Schanberg trying to trace Pran, who had survived starvation, incarceration and torture while witnessing the systematic slaughter of his people.

While impressed with Schanberg's account, the ever-canny David sought corroboration of the story from the *Sunday Times* correspondent in Phnom Penh, Jon Swain, who had been with Schanberg the day that Pran had saved both their lives. To David, Swain's confirmation was crucial before he would proceed, although he neglected to make it clear to the correspondent when they met for tea at Fortnum and Mason. 'I couldn't afford to spend time on Schanberg's story and then have it trashed by Swain,' he reasoned. Later, when he met Schanberg in New York over lunch, it turned out the story was already committed to the *New York Times* magazine as 'The Death and Life of Dith Pran'. David indicated he would bid for the rights when the article appeared; Schanberg promised his bid would be considered.

David saw the broad canvas of the subject and the large theme he had long sought. He alerted his American lawyer Tom Lewyn to the fact that he wanted the rights to Schanberg's article. These were subsequently acquired against stiff opposition from other interested parties, some of whom offered considerably more money. Since Schanberg hired Sam Cohn to represent him, an agent who had always been well disposed towards David, this probably helped his case, although he still continued to make exhaustive representations to Schanberg both in person and through Tom Lewyn.

As usual, David had very specific ideas on a writer, director and casting for the film and resisted pressure from Jo Child at IFI, who had separately proceeded to talk to Paddy Chayevsky and Sydney Lumet off his own bat. Not only that, he wanted David to consider Dustin Hoffman to play the role of Schanberg. Clearly, he was unfamiliar with the *Agatha* tale.

The writer David had already assigned to write the script for *The Killing Fields* was Bruce Robinson. Born in 1946, Bruce had initially wanted to be an actor and had enrolled at the Central School of Speech and Drama at 16. The tall, good-looking youngster successfully auditioned for the role of Benvolio in Franco Zeffirelli's *Romeo and Juliet* the year after he graduated, a promising start for any aspiring actor. Unfortunately, Bruce was by now an aspiring *writer*, having decided that acting was not for him. His involvement on the set with Zeffirelli did nothing to rekindle any enthusiasm. 'I had personal problems with Franco,' says Bruce.

Other parts followed, including a movie called *Tam Lin* with Ava Gardner. 'I have two things to thank Ava for,' Bruce believes. 'Meeting Lesley Anne Down and being introduced to the magic of alcohol. I was so terrified when I arrived on the set that Ava called me into her dressing room and said, "Here, have some breakfast", and handed me a large glass of vodka. I felt wonderful straight away; I really felt I could go out there and play Hamlet. I thought, "*This* is the key to acting!" '

With 16-year-old Lesley Anne in residence, Bruce concentrated on pursuing his writing career. Lesley Anne told him not to worry about money, that she would support him – and with a burgeoning career following her success in *Upstairs/Downstairs*, her ability to do this far outweighed his own. The final nail in Bruce's acting coffin was hammered in with François Truffaut's *The Story of Adele H.* The notices were good, but the picture convinced him he should give up acting once and for all. 'If I can't enjoy acting with this talented man,' he reasoned, 'I'll never enjoy it with anyone. Every time Truffaut said, "Action", I was filled with horror.'

Bruce was first introduced to David in 1975 through their mutual acquaintance, Andrew Birkin ('The Bermondsey Undertaker', as Bruce refers to his tall, cadaverously thin friend). Andrew brought Bruce's first novel, *Withnail and I*, to David, thinking he might be interested in doing something with it. 'He didn't like it,' reckons Bruce, 'but thought at least that I could write. He then paid me £200 for a treatment for a planned multi-episode TV series, *Garret's Guitar*, that never got made. The payment worked out to £8.50 an episode! Then I did research for a version of *Treasure Island*, again never made. The first actual film I ever wrote for him was called *The Silver Palace* – never made. There was some bullshit that I didn't even want to do very much, an Elton John thing called *Captain Fantastic* he asked me to write that I never got paid for. Nothing to do with David; it just fell to bits. Then he wanted me to write something about Boris Pasternak, and I just had no fucking *money*, but I went down and bought all these books about Pasternak and the Russian prison camps and all the rest of it, did a massive amount of research, then David decided he didn't want to make that. This happened several times and I got paid fuck all until *The Killing Fields*.

'I had done all these things for David, but for him they were on the back burner of a 15-fucking-hob oven while for me they were right on the front, *blazing*. Sure, he took a chance with me on a big-budget picture like *The Killing Fields*, but he wasn't being the chairman of the Save The Children Fund. He wouldn't have asked me to do it if he hadn't thought I could do it. He has this amazing organic sense that if he puts *this* writer with *this* director he will get what he's after.'

What David liked about Bruce's writing was its power and total commitment. With the kind of pellucidity that characterizes his best decisions, he sensed that the subject cried out for the *edge* he was convinced Bruce could provide. Bruce started with the *New York Times* article and the telexes from Schanberg out of Phnom Penh. 'Although David had this feeling I could do it,' he says, 'he never knew what I was going to come up with. He never interrupted. He trusted me.'

Before Bruce began work on the script he realized that the film would only succeed if he could get a proper handle on the central character of Schanberg. After reading his *New York Times* article he was left wondering, where was the Cambodian point of view? 'I disliked Schanberg on sight,' he admits. 'I found him terribly uptight and defensive. He made me feel very uneasy. He was pungent and authoritarian, like my father. I was disarmed, though, when he told me I must write what I liked.' After meeting Pran, Bruce's misgivings returned and he felt moved to contact David and put his thoughts in writing:

Dear David,
    Still a lot of Vaseline on the lens. Schanberg is coming into focus. It isn't the film we thought we had, it's different. It's better, but there are problems. I'm convinced Sydney needed to hang his dirty linen out. I'm also convinced the linen was a sacrifice of sorts, ie, if we show them this much, nobody will ask to see any more. I've been asking to see a *lot* more. Some of it is really dirty and I feel sorry for Schanberg. I'm sure he didn't expect this, I'm sure you thought it was going to be as simple as adapting his New York Times story. Sydney is a very complex man, motivated by very base emotions – rage, ambition, anger and truth – this last one is a big worry. He treats it like Pran, but it will not go away. Pran and truth are Schanberg's sideshow and they will not go away.
    What I want to write is not flattering. I found a lot out the last two weeks. There's no way I can avoid truth if I am to write this man properly, so what do I do? His wife is very important to the story (and his wife, incidentally, wouldn't be involved in it, they're in the middle of a divorce). His wife hasn't signed the release. His wife is part of this truth, so is his girlfriend. Can't use either of them. If I can't, I can't tell the truth. If I'm not attempting a truth, why don't I just dramatize the whole fucking thing?

I would lay my career on the line that I'm right about Schanberg. Under the circumstances he and Pran were living in day by day, a relationship developed. Intense relationships develop under intense situations, but I think Schanberg exploited Pran. I think his love for him was motivated by an Everest of guilt that never existed until they were separated. All I know is that the New York Times piece is an iceberg floating in a very suspicious sea. As soon as you arrive in Los Angeles we must talk. Someone has to make a decision about what I must do. I'm perfectly prepared to fake it, I'm not a historian and I don't need a Nobel Peace prize (Kissinger) or a Pulitzer Prize (Schanberg) from all this misery.

Love, Robinson.

Bruce thought at this time the whole essence of *The Killing Fields* was a fake. 'David made no response to the letter,' he says, before adding with a wide, toothy grin, 'for the simple reason I decided against sending it in the end.'

The writer's next stop was the Far East. After failing to get into Cambodia he settled for Thailand, arriving in the middle of a military coup. The sight of unburied dead bodies in the countryside provided his sensibilities with a shock they had never before suffered. On his way to the airport he was horrified by the sight of a girl in flames from head to foot. He begged his driver to stop, only to be told they could do nothing to save her and that they themselves would be killed if they stopped. These encounters, together with the grinding, abject poverty he encountered everywhere on his visit made him realize that this was a background to Schanberg's story he had barely understood back in New York. He began to see that Schanberg's behaviour had to be judged against the instability of the terrifying background he had lived in for years. His perceptions of the man changed as Bruce was able to picture himself in similar situations. Slowly, admiration began to develop.

'As a film-maker David was right in essence, that the *greater* truth can come from a few lies. If we'd made the film really truthfully in the sense that Schanberg's relationship with Pran was pure Gunga Din, had we *really* made the film about that kind of relationship, I wonder if people would have been moved to tears by it.'

Bruce remembers a breakfast with David at the Carlyle Hotel in New York, where they discussed with French director Louis Malle the possibility of his involvement with the movie. 'I couldn't believe what this fucker was saying. He's talking about ballets of B52s in the opening sequence – just nonsense, absolute nonsense, just as if he hadn't even bothered to read the script. He said he would want to rewrite it, after I'd worked on it tortuously for a year and a half! We came out of the hotel to get into the limo, David was going back to England on the Concorde and I was going back to Los Angeles where I was living at the time and he asked me what I thought about Malle. I said, 'He's ridiculous, the man's absurd, it's crazy what he's saying.' David listened, then said, 'Look, there's this young English director, never done any films, called Roland Joffe, whom I feel in my balls is right for the film.' I said, 'Yes? Well, for Christ's sake go with him, have him. Go on – have him!'

In turning Malle down, David wrote to the ubiquitous Sam Cohn, who also just happened to be Malle's agent, saying, 'All of my successes have been based on my ability to bring together a group of equals who instinctively wish to make the same movie. Bruce's script, to which I am heavily committed, has gone too far to be turned around and made into what could be termed Louis Malle film.'

In a stinging reply to Childs, David had written earlier, 'In essence, it comes down to this, my enthusiasm for our project stems from the fact that the entire picture exists in my mind, and what I have to find is a writer with whom I can communicate and who can put down on paper the film as I see it. My job has only been worthwhile when I've had along side of me contemporaries whose lives contain the same dreams, resonances and points of departure. This is patently not true of Paddy, and probably not true of Lumet. Further, I have never envisaged the piece as a star vehicle and I think it's fair to say that Dustin Hoffman would be as unprepared to work with me as I most assuredly am to work with him.'

The sequence of events that led David to Roland Joffe started with a play he saw on television, *United Kingdom*. 'This had a row between husband and wife. It's the only time I have watched a television drama and been really frightened. I honestly felt these two people were going to kill each other, until I remembered they were acting, and I knew it must have been an extraordinary bit of direction to have got them up to that pitch. I decided to look at more of his work. Then I wrote to Roland, as I always do with directors, asking him to criticize the screenplay for *The Killing Fields*. His critique was identical to mine, so I knew the things we liked about it were the same and the things that worried both of us were the same. We were either both right or both wrong, but at least we were talking about the same movie. The third thing was a chance remark of Colin Welland's. He said that, in the making of *United Kingdom*, Roland was the best-prepared director he'd ever worked with. And I knew that whoever did direct *The Killing Fields* was going to have to be extraordinarily well-prepared.'

For the part of Sydney Schanberg David and Roland defiantly cast Sam Waterston, whom David had spotted in producer Don Boyd's film, *Sweet William*. 'I don't want a star who will bring with him all sorts of associations with other films,' he declared. 'I want all the audience's attention focused on the story.'

For the part of Dith Pran, Haing S. Ngor was cast. Dr Ngor was working in Los Angeles as an assistant supervisor for the Indo-Chinese Employment programme when Roland discovered him. He had been a gynaecologist in Phnom Penh when the Khmer Rouge had occupied the city and like Dith Pran, had escaped into Thailand four years later. Only his nine-year-old niece had also survived; the rest of his family, mother, father, four brothers, and his fiancée had been exterminated.

David had long since decided that the budget for the movie must be on a scale that matched the natural scope of the project. 'The day I decided to produce *The Killing Fields* for £10 million.' he recalls, 'I knew it had to be a big feature film. You can't borrow £10 million of somebody's money and then bugger off and make a personal statement. All we'd have done in making a film that appealed only to a minority would have been to castrate the film business by proving yet again that you can't make serious films popular.' Nor was *The Killing Fields* to be loaded with below-the-line costs: 'The director's fees, my fee, the rights to Sydney and Pran, the screenplay and two leading actors, totalled less than £900,000.'

Another thread in the developing Goldcrest story, and one in which David became intimately involved, was their television adventure. The origin of this was Pearson's wish to apply for the British breakfast television licence in 1981. To head up the application Pearson hired Mike Wooller, then when Pearson Longman Television failed to acquire the licence, they decided to splice the television entity on to Goldcrest Films as Goldcrest Television.

Despite considerable misgivings, Jake Eberts went along with this scheme. He could see that the possibilities for cable had started to burgeon in the States, while in Britain Channel 4 had been given the go ahead. It was still not a side of the business for which he could work up any enthusiasm, but he set about raising money for a fund called Goldcrest Films and Television Partners, and gathered in £10 million, to which Pearson added a further £5 million. An accountant, John Chambers, Goldcrest's first full-time employee apart from Jake and his secretary, was duly asked to start crunching numbers. Mike Wooller set about assembling his first projects before going along to see Jeremy Isaacs at Channel 4 to glean the level of interest.

With *Gandhi* in post-production, *Local Hero* in production, *The Killing Fields* in development and the foreign sales company Jake had developed with Bill Gavin gathering momentum, things at Goldcrest began to turn hectic. Jake had by now divested himself of his stake in IFI after a monumental falling out with Jo Child, and at Goldcrest suddenly found himself, from being a one-man band, an eight- or nine-man band. 'Mike Wooller came back from seeing Jeremy Isaacs at Channel 4 with an offer for *every single project on our slate*; our timing couldn't have been luckier. I'd also become very friendly with the pay-cable people in the States and managed to sell everything we had to Showtime and HBO. We just happened to hit at a time when everything was getting snapped up. They desperately needed product and *I had product*. I had a sales company, a television company, a film company, then *Chariots* took off, then *Gandhi* – we were going through the roof!'

David's involvement in the television side's initial success story was as the initiator of the *First Love* series, starting in 1981. He had been approached by a colleague with an idea for a single adaptation of a Laurie Lee story on the theme of first love, which he felt was too slight. Instead, his idea was to put together a generic series of such tales under the collective *First Love* logo. This was a large part of the product Jeremy Isaacs snapped up and which Jake Eberts was initially able to sell to cable TV in the States.

Enigma produced the series, the bulk of the finance being put up by Goldcrest and the balance by Channel 4. Initially employed by David as head of development at Enigma, Susan Richards found herself responsible for all the scripts that came pouring into the company. Neither her experience at the ICA, nor her PhD, had prepared her for such a post.

Susan was handed a list of eight people David had had a conversation with about the *First Love* series. 'Ring them up,' she was told; 'none of them know how to write scripts except Ray Connolly. Most of them are writers in different mediums. You'll have to teach them.'

This meant that Susan had to quickly learn how to find her way around scripts herself. 'It was like trying to be ahead of a game I didn't actually know,' she recalls. 'That of course is absolutely characteristic of the man. He gives you 100 per cent trust until you fail him, then he withdraws it. There's a sort of quixotic generosity about the way he allows you in. Whatever the difficulties later on in one's involvements with David, he is the most wonderful apprenticer.'

Lynda Myles, another PhD, who had organized the Edinburgh Film Festival for several years in the seventies, joined Enigma in 1983. Her brief – to find the greatest love story around, today's *Anna Karenina*. It might be argued that both Susan and Lynda, two very cool and sophisticated eighties' ladies, were hardly ideal casting for their respective assignments. Indeed, after meetings with over a hundred writers and putting a handful of items into development, Lynda became side-tracked by a political thriller she would later produce, *Defence of the Realm*.

Armed with the guaranteed sale to cable TV in the States and the high quality of the first couple of films, prospects for the *First Love* series looked good. With the modest budget of the first film, *P'Tang Yang Kipperbang*, and the example set by the professional writer/director team of Jack Rosenthal and Michael Apted, David planned the rest of the series as a nursery slope for new talent. 'It started as such a delight,' says Susan, 'and was an extremely idiosyncratic Puttnam thing to do. The series has totally got David's influence on it – the combination of humour and sentimentality, an innocence which I think is finally overcaptured and overpackaged.'

When market conditions changed as the cable boom in the US turned out to be short-lived – it had been competition rather than viewer-led – Channel 4 were unable to increase their contribution for each film enough to cover the US cable-sale shortfall. To exacerbate matters further for Goldcrest, budgets were on the rise. Some hard thinking was called for at the company if they were not to face a crippling short-term loss on the series. Since one of the films, Peter Duffel's *Experience Preferred but not Essential*, had actually received a US theatrical release through the Samuel Goldwyn Jr Company, encouraging Goldwyn to follow up with Gavin Millar's *Secrets*, David Drury's *Forever Young* and Roy Battersby's *Winter Flight*, David's plan for the rest of the series – after 10 television movies were made – was to gear up for the big screen and expand into full theatrical features.

To illustrate how this might work, David boldly double-billed the first two films in the series, *P'Tang Yang Kipperbang* and *Those Glory, Glory Days* and booked them into London's West End – to disastrously low takings. Criticism which had been levelled at the series in any case mounted, many considering the films too cosy-English and coyly insular to even be acceptable in the local market, let alone abroad. Susan saw David determined to buck the system and still make the rest of the series happen theatrically. 'He can't see why he shouldn't transcend the limits of something he could quite well see objectively and analytically of being true. He felt he could make an exception of it. I don't think you can be a good producer without having some of that, it's the necessary illusion.'

Unfortunately, the series had run away with itself. Costs and the exit of US cable sales were one factor; alarming variations in the quality of the product quite another.

'The *First Love* series turned into a total nightmare,' says Patsy. 'It sounded like a good idea and a cheap way of funding new talent, but David wasn't supposed to be directly involved in it, only as executive producer, then when things started to go wrong he *had* to get involved. There was just too much aggravation. I was against the whole thing from the start. I *fought* him over his involvement in it.'

The pressures David was under at Enigma began to mount. The need to push out more and more product to cover overheads and keep the momentum going, almost to the point where the logic of supply and demand was defied, imposed a strain reminiscent of Goodtimes at its worst. Lynda Smyth had asked David two years earlier, when the Goldcrest association began, 'What are we doing here? Why have you put yourself back in this position? You swore you would never go back to a situation that could run away from you.' He had no answer.

David had been under the impression he was constructing a support mechanism for himself at Enigma, but the bulk of his time was being spent *providing* a support mechanism. *He* was working for Enigma, but the company wasn't working for *him*. The tail was wagging the dog.

Then there was the backlash of David's campaign to become the father-figure of the British Film Industry, and his tacit acceptance of this role. He had created a Frankenstein monster that now rampaged through his life. Even as he tried to raise the drawbridge at Enigma, the creature scaled the battlements and gained access. He was forced to spend endless hours answering correspondence and granting interviews to journalists. No matter what the topic, if it even remotely concerned the British Film Industry, the watchword was – ask Puttnam. His father's 'I'll do it' had become his son's 'I'll say it.' Something was going to have to give.

'David's interest in TV was more an act of desperation,' James Lee says now. 'He reckoned the future lay in making films for television, with a feature film interspersed every three years or so. Unfortunately, his *First Love* series was not a great success either commercially or critically. One or two were at the beginning, but 10, no. With the

initial cable sales David and I were fooled into thinking we'd discovered the future, but it didn't quite work out. Ahead of our time?
Maybe, but if so we made the right decisions, five years too *early*,
which makes them the *wrong* decisions! The driving force in any case
would turn out to be video, not pay-TV. David influenced a lot of the
strategic thinking at Goldcrest behind the scenes, more as an adviser
and a friendly counsel rather than someone who had that responsibility, but I consulted him a lot on a good deal of the changes
that took place. Not everyone was in favour of the leaning towards
TV. Jake and Dickie certainly wanted to concentrate purely on
theatrical films.'

It is characteristic of David that he still defends the *First Love*
series to this day. 'Failure? Not at all, in no way. Firstly, not a
financial failure. I wish I owned them. Half are in profit and every
single one is due for re-licensing. They're a little goldmine, for an
individual they represent an industry. They can be licensed for ever.
Secondly, not unsuccessful in terms of quality. Although this varied,
overall there was a creditable average. Through these films some very
good people broke through into the mainstream of the industry – Roy
Battersby, Brian Gilbert, the list goes on and on.'

He denies that the 'strike rate' on the series was low. While James
Lee reckons that over eighty stories were commissioned to find two
dozen scripts, David puts the success ratio of scripts at around 2–1.

David continued to see *The Killing Fields* from its conception through
to its completion in highly graphic terms. 'Ideas are God-given,' he
declared; 'they don't come from anywhere else. All you have to worry
about initially is whether a particular idea has the right dramatic
curve. What is wonderful about this story is that it starts off with an
exciting relationship which goes down through a kind of visual and
energetic period to reach a crisis, a tragedy, a parting of the ways.
Then the curve flows up again to a reunion. That curve is as good as
you're ever going to get for a movie. You can't ask for more. So long
as you hold true to it you'll end up with something that works emotionally because it's the classic curve of every human being's life,
hope passing through trouble and travail to some form of resolution.'

David recognized the constant theme running through his work.
'All the best of my pictures are, one way or another, about men in
moral crises,' he acknowledged, adding that it was this aspect that
intrigued him most – how people act under sometimes intolerable
pressure; how much the human frame can stand; how moral issues are
argued and resolved, or left hanging to await resolution another day,

maybe another lifetime. Even when treated in a gentle, comic way, as in *Local Hero*, the theme was the same, although for him *Chariots of Fire* had seen its ultimate encapsulation.

Cambodia itself had been under consideration for a possible location, but the initial difficulties, together with the potential problems, soon ruled this out. A memo from Bruce Robinson also helped, running as it did: 'I can't believe that any insurance company will cover a unit of Puttnam and his running dogs. I put this to Anthony Burnett, the left-wing New Statesman writer, a good man who's genuinely interested and wants to help:– Is it at all conceivable that a bunch of Khmer Rouge terrorists would rush up and knock off the producer/director/screenwriter team? It is my duty to tell you that the answer to this question was "yes". That'll do for me, I say "bollocks" to Phnom Penh. He reminds me that there are 300,000 Viet soldiers in Cambodia, that means 100,000 each. Are you prepared to walk around with 100,000 men? You'd never get them into your office, and just imagine taking a cab. I say "*bollocks*" to shooting in Cambodia, Love, B R.'

Thailand, just across the border, presented itself as the logical second choice. There were advantages in that it was not virgin territory as far as filming was concerned and the co-operation of the Thai armed forces was promised.

The budget of £10 million included a hard-won completion guarantee that brought about another verbal punch-up between the two Davids, Puttnam and Norris. 'There was a lot of nervousness that we wouldn't get a completion guarantee on the film,' says Norris. 'They wanted an enormous contingency allowance before they would touch the picture. There was fighting on the border of Thailand and Vietnam and we were dependent on the Thai army providing the equipment, so it was a tricky situation. David kept saying, "Look, you fellows are getting hold of the wrong end of the stick from 6000 miles away; it isn't nearly as bad as the newspapers are telling you." This is in the pre-production stage! I suggested we take out war risk cover for $75,000 as a way round the contingency, and it was finally reduced to an acceptable level.'

Goldcrest put up the entire budget, save for $3 million from I F I, with Warners advancing $4.75 million for North American theatrical rights and a further $4 million for U K, French, German and Japanese territories. With a video sale to Thorn/E M I, the budget was thus comfortingly 80 per cent covered in advance.

The Thai authorities turned out to be sensitive enough about the project to request that the script be translated into their language for their approval, and it subsequently fell to Iain Smith to establish a liaison with the Thai Government's various ministers, bolstered by occasional appearances by David as necessary. Only six weeks before filming was due to begin, and with an irretrievable $1 million already spent, the production was almost shut down before it started as a memo informed them that the movie was considered 'contrary to Thai foreign policy'. In the event, Iain only had to concede a few purely cosmetic changes, but the Thai Government insisted on the right to keep an eye on the production thereafter. Representatives had to be present at all times on the set, they declared, although they would turn out to be mainly concerned with religious matters. Although the script could hardly claim to be above political matters and a point of view in the Cambodian tragedy, it would have been ironic indeed if the film had foundered on this, since David and Roland were carefully following Schanberg's avowed declaration that he and Pran both cared little about local or international politics. 'What propelled us was the human impact,' they had declared.

Iain Smith recalled his first introduction to Roland Joffe. 'There was a young, earnest-looking man sitting in a chair in David's office, looking like a sort of bird. David introduced him jocularly to me as the man who would be my biggest problem on the picture. I'd read *The Killing Fields*; it was one of those scripts that was just breathtaking, but it was a huge problem. It was overly long, it was going to be monumentally expensive and strategically nightmarish. On the other hand it was the best script floating around in Enigma. Roland and I had a long talk before we started the film and at the end of it I knew I was going to work with someone really special, a really talented man with an enormous intellect and a huge heart. So I was very elated by that. I was also shit scared of the responsibility that David had, apparently carelessly, thrust in my direction. The deep end again! With the exception of David, the film was going to be made with people who had *everything* to prove. We were all young and fighting hard to establish our reputations, and David obviously realized this was on energy you can't buy.'

There would be many times when the travellers would stray from their chosen path. With only weeks to go before production began and Roland, Iain and David already out in Thailand, major cuts in the script were ordered by David in an attempt to adhere to the budget. When Roland agreed to lose thirty-five pages of script, David flew home content. At 3 am the following morning, Roland was wakened by Iain in a state of panic. 'What have you done?' he demanded to know. 'You've pulled the wool over David's eyes, you've cut thirty-five pages, but you haven't taken a single major scene out.'

'I know,' said Roland, not at all placating his colleague.

'My worry,' said Iain, 'is that we could lose the film; the plug'll be pulled out.'

Roland's reply was uncompromising. 'It's probably better to lose a really brilliant film that we would all be proud of, than to keep a mediocre one.'

Iain stopped and listened to Roland's words. He knew at that moment he had no reason to worry, certain of the similar response Roland's argument would evoke in David.

'I can trust this guy,' he thought.

One of the people most impressed by David's audacity and courage in casting was Sam Waterston. 'When I arrived in Thailand,' he marvelled, 'it suddenly struck me that here was a producer gambling all this money on a movie of high purpose without a major star to carry it. Not only that, but he was using a first-time director and an Asian as one of the two chief characters. Now *that* takes some guts!'

Roland found out quickly the type of man he would be dealing with for the next few months when his original one-page critique of the script was handed back to him by David a week before shooting was due to start.

'This may amuse you,' was all David said as he passed Roland the document. Roland had written that he saw the movie as being all about people, as opposed to a 'hardware' film; how they had to be careful handling the way they 'used' the war. He saw David's point in producing the letter. 'Look,' he was saying, 'when you weren't under any pressure to make a great Hollywood movie, this is what you said.'

Roland began to realize just how subtle and smart David was.

Chapter 16

So far on this movie, we've had 24 cases of dysentery, four V.D., three malarias, six divorces, two nervous breakdowns all so some woolly woofter film critic can slag off the finished movie in between glasses of Chablis provided free by the film companies..

The season of
the 'Small Monsoon'

David's love of cricket was behind his enthusiasm for *Bodyline*, chosen as one of his projects to follow *The Killing Fields*. The story centred around the infamous 1932 cricket tour of Australia that had featured the notorious tactic of bodyline bowling, a method of attacking batsmen with 100-mph legside bowling. Harold Larwood, England's spearhead bowler, had become a detested figure in Australia as he disposed of their batsmen like ninepins. It seemed there was much more than cricket being played, with widespread rumours that Larwood and his captain, Douglas Jardine, were acting on British Government orders. Sport certainly came out the loser in the tour, which England won by four matches to one.

'An unbelievably cynical series of positions was taken by people, and it was politics – very high politics,' David darkly maintained. 'The political argument was all to do with the depression and the fact that the effects really hit Australia very savagely and rather quickly. Australia felt it was Britain's job to look after it. There was great bitterness in Australia that they were the victims of *our* Depression. A number of people, most notably the Colonial Secretary, had it in for the Australians and it was made very clear to Jardine that it was politically very inconvenient for us to lose the Ashes. It was a war! Jardine's father, who acted as a Government go-between, rammed the message home.'

He planned the film with a sympathetic view of the cricketers, especially in the cases of Larwood and Don Bradman, the Australian captain. 'Larwood had a very real distaste for the whole thing, but he was a kind of classic amateur who did as he was told. He had a great personal antipathy towards the Australians because he had been very badly mauled in the 1928 tour.'

David saw Bradman as a victim of his own character. Determined to prove he was the best batsman in the world, he reacted to the English bodyline tactics by regarding it as a challenge to be answered, rather than the outrage it was. Instead of taking a reasonable attitude and refusing to play under these conditions, both men appeared to have bowed to the situation – one by obeying orders and the other by his determination to cope.

David's projected film of *Bodyline* was soon in trouble with colleagues of Jardine, who felt the script brought his memory into disrepute. When they threatened to withhold their co-operation from the production, David refused to budge. 'At the end of the day,' he declared, 'I am making a drama and not a documentary. We will show Jardine as an immensely complex, troubled and unhappy man. He ends the film as a classic victim of the British Establishment – a career and a reputation destroyed.'

Bob Wyatt, who had been Jardine's vice-captain on the ill-fated tour, read the film script and promptly washed his hands of the project. 'Jardine is made out to be an absolute cad,' 80-year-old Bob fumed. 'Although I never agreed with the method of attack he used, I was very fond of Douglas. The way the film sees him is very wrong and in my loyalty to the man I am quite prepared to stand up for him. It would be awful for his family to have his name smeared like this.'

Another octogenarian ex-colleague of Jardine's, Sir George 'Gubby' Allen, concurred with this view, averring, 'We had many disagreements, but the man was not a cheat, as the script appears to suggest. He was a man of great principle and we must not let him down.'

David hastened to mend fences and was quick to stress, following this reaction, that further revisions of the script had still to take place. 'We have a fine director in Bruce Bersford,' he assured the world at large, 'and we have the money. It won't be made, however, if I feel that it is not a film I can be proud of. I have no intention of producing a cheapskate film.'

One fictional scene had already been deleted as a direct result of Allen and Wyatt's objections. This had shown an Australian batsman being carried from the Adelaide wicket with blood pouring from a head wound, while Jardine lay nonchalantly on the grass. The deletion was not strong enough to still the storm of protest over David's proposed treatment of the subject. Wyatt argued that the whole inference of the script – that the exercise was carried out on Government orders – was incorrect and outrageous. 'That simply is not the way things happened,' he declared. Allen agreed, describing David's treatment as 'rubbish'. David certainly gave the impression of being less sure of his ground after trying for – and signally failing to achieve – Allen and Wyatt's approbation. Allen's final taunt rang in his ears: 'I'm afraid with this script you are going to be laughed at. Technically you've got things wrong and where *Chariots of Fire* was gentle and romantic, this is rather nasty.'

It was almost with a sense of relief that David eventually learned he had been pipped at the post by the Australians themselves, who had gone ahead with their own version of events and fielded a five-hour mini series. An Enigma spokesman reported, 'David is very sad about the film, but he thinks the subject has now been covered properly and there's nothing left to do but forget the idea.' In view of his approach to the project – leaning once again towards 'enhanced reality' – perhaps it was as well.

The Killing Fields' first day of shooting in May, 1983, was fraught with tension. It could well have turned out to be the *last* day of shooting.

One of the many gambles taken by Iain Smith, after studying the weather records, was to plump for shooting during the 'small monsoon' season of April, May and June, before the main rainy season arrived. Contrarily, the first day brought a huge torrential downpour that flooded the streets and film set. Iain thought, 'God, I'll never work in the film business again,' as David strode about, with an expression under his big floppy hat that would have soured milk, adding to the air of terrific tension everyone felt.

As suddenly as the rain had started that morning, it stopped early in the afternoon. Frantic efforts were made to clear the waterlogged set. While David sat fuming, Roland Joffe observed there was probably as much rain pouring inside his soul as there had been from the heavens. He held his breath as the Cambodian interpreter on the set turned to his producer.

'You are very lucky, David,' the brave individual chirped.

Slowly the bedraggled David turned to him, smiling fixedly with as much charm as he could muster.

'In what way am I lucky?' he politely enquired, squeezing every word out.

'Well,' came the reply, 'this is the first day of the monsoons and it's raining very heavily. In a temple area that's three times good luck!'

'Really?' said David, looking at his director with a wry, but amused smile. 'Fancy that!'

With the floods cleared up, shooting at last began. If the monsoon forecast good luck, it was for the future.

The opening scene in the movie had Sam Waterston and Haing Ngor chatting in an outdoor café, their conversation abruptly curtailed when a bomb explodes.

To simulate the explosion, the special-effects men had a pile of Fuller's earth off-screen, together with an air hose connected to a compressed air cylinder. Purely to alert the actors that the 'explosion' was happening – for all that would otherwise be produced was a 'whoosh' followed by large quantities of Fuller's earth flying everywhere – a squib was set to go 'bang'. Unfortunately, a local assistant substituted a calor-gas cylinder for the compressed air. As the squib went off, the gas was ignited, creating a horrific fireball which blazed across the set.

Luckily for Sam Waterston, the action required him to be leaving his table, so that when the big bang came he was already moving. The flames still managed to singe the back of his hand and shoulder, as if he had been caught by a blow torch. His were the only injuries, but there was a terrible moment of shock and horror until this was established.

'It was *unthinkable*,' says Iain, shuddering at the memory, 'and it could have been the *end* of the film. We'd been so pedantically careful with all the safety precautions. But still the accident had happened.'

David is not proud of his reaction. 'I went fucking berserk,' he recalls. 'My instinct, sad to say, was that Roland is one of those hairy-arsed realists and had somehow done it deliberately. I mean, obviously it was a mistake, but that the situation had been created by Roland in his quest for more realism. I tore into him, and he was so bewildered by my attack, he didn't even defend himself, just looked at me. Of course he was in shock as well. I *pounded* home my attack, how irresponsible he had been. Then it turned out to be an unbelievable error by one of the special-effects men.'

Roland's recollection is somewhat at variance with this. He had chosen to forget David's outburst and instead recalls his concern over Sam Waterston's reaction. 'My worry was that Sam might have thought I'd done it deliberately. The first day of shooting is the day you want to gain everybody's confidence. Sam took a lot of convincing that I hadn't set up that scene. The guy was in shock and he was obviously thinking, "Am I going to be walking across real mines with this guy?" It was a problem to regain his confidence. It took time, but I did.'

David immediately had someone else flown out from Britain, specially empowered to watch over all the safety measures for the remainder of the film's duration. When the rushes of the film were subsequently viewed, it was clear there was no need for retakes and a decision was made to incorporate what could have been a tragic accident into the finished film. 'It certainly had the effect of tightening everyone's sphincters. We were all *doubly* alert,' says Iain.

With the weather quickly settling down, and Iain Smith gradually able to breathe again, David saw he had made the right choice in

Roland Joffe as filming proceeded. Even so, he relied heavily on a colleague back in London, editor Jim Clark, to let him know how the rushes were looking, since they were being processed in England owing to the lack of local facilities.

'He basically wanted me to tell him if I thought they could be improved upon,' says Jim. 'He gave me a lot of trust; it was very gracious of him. Specifically I was quite critical of some camera positions in the early days. I thought that Roland was being too loose with his angles; he could have gone in closer. There were a number of things like that which he gradually changed and improved, because he's a very intuitive man and very good with performers. I felt also there was a certain lack of detailed coverage, which I wanted to make a scene work. Like the evacuation scene from the city, shot very largely in long masters with two cameras. What I was looking for were those moments of detail of people who were injured and such. David thought up the idea of the little boy who was lost. The scene needed more highlights, which Roland went out and shot on a separate day. But in general, that film was no problem. It didn't present difficulties of a creative nature, because I was able to put my finger on the problems at an early stage and get them ironed out. I guess David felt I had this ability to "read" the rushes, which is important when you're separated by many thousands of miles.'

A major confrontation took place between David and Roland over a scene set in an opium den, when Roland expressed his wish that real opium be obtained for the actors to give the scene an extra edge. 'David saw the whole thing as potentially enormous trouble,' says Roland. 'He was obviously asking himself what this signified for the rest of the film; was it all going to go like this? I'd been shooting this scene all day, without opium, and hadn't finished. David was terribly worried, because the report would go to Warners on the dailies that we hadn't finished this apparently-easy indoor scene and that I'd want to go on shooting it for ever – which was quite possible. I *might* have said, "No, I'm sorry, I think this scene is so important, I want to keep on shooting it tomorrow *and* the day after."' Who knows what caverns were opening up in David's mind. Understandably.

'David called a production meeting. I knew he would scream and shout; he had to do something to get rid of all that tremendous tension. *So I didn't go.* I figured out that if I went, and David said an awful lot of things he might regret, that would leave a lot of repair work to be done. If I didn't go, he could say whatever he liked, but not to me. So I went to bed instead, whereupon this huge memo arrived. I told the man who brought it, "The best thing you can do with that is take it outside and fling it into the Chao Phraya river." The point I conveyed to David was that in his worry over the scene that day he'd probably put a lot of stuff in his memo that he'd regret. What I would rather he did was take the memo back, read it again next morning and black out the stuff he didn't really want to say, but which was probably necessary to express at the time. The memo duly came back – all eleven pages of it – almost *entirely* blacked out except for the beginning, "Dear Rolie, Yesterday was a very difficult day," and the last line which said, "We are in this together, we are partners. Yours, David."'

The scene was shot in the end without opium, and subsequently dropped in any case from the finished film. Roland had made his point – like the hero of Charlemagne legend, he was clearly determined to at least measure up to David's Oliver.

The crucial evacuation scene was shot during the hottest day in Thailand for 45 years, while the temperatures during the whole location filming averaged 108°F. As the unit sweltered and filming proceeded, David and Iain smoothed the way for the other considerable obstacles which had to be overcome. Several of the Thai Army's officers were killed in an unrelated helicopter crash, whereupon the insurance company who had covered helicopter scenes for the picture promptly escalated their premiums. On top of this, the helicopters themselves became unavailable and those sequences involving their use had to be shot later in San Diego.

Iain describes the scheme he and David adopted for the picture as 'the tiger in the cage': 'David stood right back until I'd pick up on a situation that might be arising, let's say between Roland and the designer. Roy Walker and Roland would zoom off to some place to scout for location and come back saying, "Well, we'll need a wall built along there and we'll have the Armoured Personnel Carriers coming in right here . . ." My philosophy as a line producer was always to get in on these recce trips and I'd immediately inform David if there was a major confrontation coming up. "I'm going to stand against this," I'd tell him, knowing at that point Roland would immediately go over my head. So David and I would strategize in advance. Invariably I'd be the one to make the opening statement like, "We just can't afford to make this scene, *end of story*" – like that. David's role would be much nicer, much the best friend the director's ever had. Part of that would be to give in on some occasions, but never arbitrarily. In being seen to be as warm, embracing and strong a producer he would have the right whenever he *had* to, of saying. "I'm sorry, but no, we can't . . ." This game would go on daily, either when David was there or even when he was back in London: we'd do it on the phone.'

Other worries surfaced during the three months of filming in Thailand, some brought on by visiting reporters. Surely David realized the whole basic stand of the picture was anti-American, suggesting as it did that US involvement in Cambodia was a tragic mistake? Wouldn't this serve to turn off the huge American audience the picture needed to at least earn its cost back? 'We're certainly at risk,' he conceded, 'because of the long gestation period of any picture you can't really consider what the political climate may be when it is eventually shown. But the US is not truly represented by either the left or the right. There is a decent centre and we must hope the film plugs into it.'

One irreverent wit at Warners described the production as a simple 'boy meets boy' story. David spelled out in his own fashion the rather different angle from which he viewed the picture; 'What we're attempting is a film which has the realism of *Battle of Algiers* but with the operatic quality of *Apocalypse Now*, in order to make it work commercially. That's a difficult thing to achieve. It's always been one or the other in the past. I think we have a very substantial base to build on. I admire both *Algiers* and *Apocalypse* enormously but neither had a central relationship with which you could identify. Our film *has* that relationship. But I'm extremely nervous about the ambitions of the project, and it's not made easier by newspaper articles like those which have been appearing recently about *Gandhi*. We're dealing with a factual situation in *Killing Fields* and in preparing the film we've talked to many of the people involved, and read all the books and articles which are available. But in the end we have to tell a long, complicated story in just two hours, and the final criterion is how you make it work as a film. If you get subjected to the undergraduate nitpicking to which *Gandhi* has been subjected, saying this or that is wrong, then you're sunk. The thing I reject is the notion that only newspapers and scholars can make judgement on serious situations, and that film-makers aren't clever enough.

'The kind of thinking that seems to be going on at the moment implies that film-makers shouldn't tackle serious subjects. Are the people who write these articles saying we should make nothing but musicals and fantasies like *ET*? If they are, I think that's very worrying. In my case I've reached the stage in my career when it would be very easy to say, sod it. I don't need this aggravation.'

Was David saying that film makers should be allowed to abdicate responsibility for sticking to facts when making what are claimed to be 'true stories'? Wasn't 'the final criteria is how you make it work as a film' reducing *The Killing Fields* to the level of a melodrama reprehensibly using a tragic backdrop to 'trade up'? Were the manipulative strings *still* showing? Perhaps it is as well *Inside the Third Reich* had never gone ahead when David was 10 years younger, since the result might have been the ultimate buddy movie featuring the double-act of Hitler and Speer, with several million Jewish extras in the background. And was he wilfully confusing any attack on *Gandhi* as an attack on the man, rather than Dickie Attenborough's attempt to portray the man?

If Frank Bloom is right (he sees David's announcements as signals for the future), the purpose of this one appeared to be to pre-empt criticism of *The Killing Fields*. David's message came over as: 'If it works on a visceral and emotional level, suspend reason and forget the rest. And if you don't agree, I'll leave you to Hollywood's tender mercies.'

Sure enough, a first bombshell was dropped at the end-of-shooting party with David's announcement that the movie might be his last as on-the-spot line producer. 'It's probably my swansong,' he declared, 'for it's got to the point where I feel that I'm competing with myself and it's time I started to do other things.'

When David first read Bernard MacLaverty's *Cal*, at Susan Richard's instigation, he saw it initially as part of the ongoing *First Love* series. Further development convinced him that the tender story of a doomed love affair between two Ulster Catholics demanded more lavish treatment suitable for the big screen. With funding in place from Warners, Pat O'Connor was hired to handle the directorial chores after his award-winning *Ballroom of Romance* on television. In an unusual move, David retained the services of Bernard MacLaverty himself to fashion the script. 'I've since been told that David said he'd let me have a go and then he'd get someone in to write a *proper* screenplay,' the novelist laughs. When this was freely admitted by his unrepentant producer, MacLaverty allowed that at the beginning he did not have a clue where to start. 'My characters were speaking paragraphs and we had to get them down to grunts.'

With Helen Mirren and John Lynch cast in the leads, a cast including Donal McCann, John Cavanaugh and Ray McAnally assembled, and filming already underway, David went straight to Ireland from location work in Thailand on *The Killing Fields*. The trip would prove a wonderful antidote to the large-scale problems he had encountered in the Far East. Although *Cal* was a small-scale picture, David felt a genuine excitement as he saw the film being put together. He was particularly enthused by Helen Mirren's performance, predicting it would be the breakthrough film of her career.

With filming completed on *Cal*, David received a letter from Bristol University offering him an honorary doctorate of law. He jokingly wrote back asking if this meant he had to retake his 'O' levels, since he thought the whole thing was nothing more than a prank. It wasn't, and he duly turned up in the standard-issue burgundy cap and gown to receive his doctorate.

Was there a future in the offing in politics, bearing in mind that he had joined the SDP a year earlier? It seemed not. 'I believe I can aid society more effectively by helping people to express their ideas in the films they make,' he declared. He was offended that he was seen as running pell-mell after honours. Referring to his CBE, he stated that he was still wounded that one or two old friends refrained from ever referring to it. 'They seem to think I've done something dirty,' he complained, 'but I was urged by people I trust to accept it on behalf of the industry. And anyway, my mum loved it!'

'SDP,' Alan Parker suggested, 'does *not* stand for Sir David Puttnam!'

Regarding the possibility of further honours, David laughed them off with, 'It doesn't seem at all likely. I see myself as an iconoclast, or, if that's a bit strong, a disturber of society. Any films I plan to make in the future certainly won't endear me to the establishment.' He had already commissioned a script from Hugh Whitemore on the Ponting affair and the trouble at GCHQ, which he termed the 'appalling dominance of government in the 1980s'. 'Whitehall won't like it – and I don't see it as a short cut to a peerage.'

After this statement, David was particularly disturbed throughout much of 1984 to find that his mail appeared to be constantly tampered with. Letters addressed to Enigma had often been opened prior to delivery, before being carefully resealed. Soon after this first discovery he became convinced that telephone calls to his London office were being tapped. This was disturbing enough, but made even more so when he compared notes with Bruce Robinson, who had independently come to the same conclusion and was avoiding the use of the telephone altogether. 'We were definitely tapped without a doubt,' says Bruce, 'and our mail was delivered ripped open, with things hanging out. They made no attempt to be secret about it.'

Had MI5 decided that a little discreet, or not so discreet surveillance was called for? Apart from the two men's involvement with the story of the Khmer Rouge takeover in Cambodia, David had asked Bruce to do some preliminary research on the story of Robert Oppenheimer and the genesis of the atomic bomb, a project confidently expected to unlock many cupboards and release their resident skeletons.

To David's relief there seemed to be no surveillance on his home phone. He made his suspicions known through friends and indicated the further steps he would be prepared to take unless the 'operation' was stopped. Many friends counselled he was over-reacting to what was probably nothing more than a series of coincidences, but David was convinced the establishment had become anxious to know where his sympathies lay. Just as suddenly as the 'surveillance' had begun, it ended. Within a few weeks of the return to normality, David and Patsy began to wonder if they had indeed imagined the whole thing. It lingered afterwards as a disturbing interlude.

The major problem with the length of *The Killing Fields* was never satisfactorily resolved, although on the eve of the film's release David reacted with outrage to rumours that he had censored scenes in the film's extended post-production process. 'Not a frame has been changed,' was the official story. In reality, a tremendous amount *had* been changed. Roland's attitude before filming, 'Yes, it's far too long, but let me shoot the lot. It'll only cost you extra film stock,' had come home to roost, with the result that the first assemblage weighed in at a marathon four hours. Even the eventual rough cut was almost three hours long. All sorts of ideas were mooted, including a re-cut for an eventual TV mini-series that never took place, and an extended version to play in selected cinemas following the release of the cut-down print. The problem was what to drop in order to get the length down to a more manageable two-hours plus. Roland decries the process of editing in the camera, where a director shoots sparingly, having made up his mind in advance exactly the amount of coverage he needs. 'I regard that as insanely macho,' he says, 'rather like a westerner going into a saloon and immediately firing off every round he's got.' Perhaps there is an equal argument against going into a gunfight laden down with six months' ammunition supply.

David agreed to try out the longer version Roland was keen to see released, but they withdrew it after a disastrous initial preview. 'If we'd released that first version, nobody would have gone to see it,' they now agree.

Bruce Robinson was critical of alterations made to his original script, of which he reckoned about 80 per cent survived. He saw himself as exposed to David at his best, and his worst. 'Just imagine, you need $15 million to do an American guilt job, you've got an unknown Cambodian as the star and a scriptwriter financiers have never heard of. He held out for me to do it. Puttnam was marvellous. I don't know how he had that kind of confidence. He did dilute a measure of anti-Americanism in the script because he knows what you can get away with in a very expensive film. Anything I wanted, he got for me immediately. He's great in that sense, bloody brilliant. I'd say, I need this thing that was published in 1971 in an edition of 250 copies in Bangkok, really need a copy – and the fucker got it for me. He's a wonderful uncle until he doesn't want you around any more. Then he's a fucking nightmare. He was always astonishingly kind when I was supplying what he wanted, but as soon as I didn't give him the goods he expected from me, which was acquiescence, being a housewriter, then he wasn't very charming any more. That's just one facet of him, of course. I can be quite unpleasant when I'm doing my job too.'

Patsy could see both sides of the equation. 'David knows Bruce so well and he's totally in awe of his writing talent. He tried to push his scripts for years when nobody wanted them. Ray Connolly was having a moan at me at one time about *Trick or Treat* and how hard it was and I had a go at him. I told him that – believe it or not, Ray, there are people who have written *ten* scripts that have all gone down the toilet and never reached the screen. You've had your first two scripts filmed and you're in trouble with the third, *big deal*! The trouble with Bruce is, he gives you so much, his scripts are so rich and so packed with magnificent descriptive passages. It can be painful working with him, just holding him in. You need to be there constantly, keeping him on the track.'

'David requires 100 per cent loyalty from people,' says Bruce, 'but he doesn't give you it back; he doesn't give you a break. You have to be 100 per cent David Puttnam, not 99 per cent; he won't allow you that 1 per cent: he won't forgive you for anything. You get in line and do what he wants you to do. If you step out of that line, you're in trouble. If I wrote *The Killing Fields* for David and it suited him the day after to turn it into a musical with the Khmer Rouge dancing up the road, and if I said, "David, you can't do this: it's a disaster," he'd just say, "There's the door." I believe that's what he'd do.

'Would I work with him again? Like – tomorrow. Why? Because he's a *brilliant* fucking film producer!'

David again chose to open *The Killing Fields* in the States, in 1984, just a few weeks ahead of its scheduled British opening at Warners' Leicester Square Theatre in London's West End. There were some favourable reviews, but there was also harsh criticism, notably from J. Hoberman of the *Village Voice*. While conceding that the movie was ambitiously adapted from Schanberg's story 'under David Puttnam's auspices' Hoberman found the picture 'murky and undramatic. It suffers from the *Gandhi* syndrome. The film-makers are so convinced of their subject's importance that they don't bother to develop characters, sustain dramatic tension or maintain structural coherence. *The Killing Fields* turns Schanberg and Pran into cartoon figures. As played by Sam Waterston, the reporter is an officious, deadline-obsessed prig, his Cambodian sidekick is one step removed from Gunga Din ... At once overwrought and sketchy, *The Killing Fields* is hectic when it should be still, somnolent when the material demands urgency ... Roland Joffe even bungles the scene in which Schanberg is held captive by the Khmer Rouge and then is saved by Pran. The sequence simply ends – it's as though the camera has run out of film. The film's prosaic shaping of this material is likely the work of David Puttnam.'

Referring to the film's score by Mike (Tubular Bells) Oldfield, Hoberman stated that David's theory seemed to be, when in doubt turn up the volume. He felt that the forced evacuation of Phnom Penh, where Schanberg's original description was not only pithier but more visual, was typical of the film's botched climaxes, hyped up by loud pseudo-Gregorian chanting.

'The Puttnam aesthetic dictates that inspirational music swells as Pran struggles over the mountains to Thailand and the Red Cross camp. Half a world away, the same thundering chords accompany Schanberg's gallop down the hall to tell his editor the news. This is cornball stuff, but what happens next is absolutely shameless. Using "Imagine" on the soundtrack to score the final reunion effectively trivializes Pran, Schanberg, Cambodia and John Lennon all at once.'

Against this, *Variety* found the movie 'Intelligent, sober, perhaps even too austere. The picture is terrifyingly successful in physically evoking its time and place, and is also the sort of tremendously ambitious project that can only be undertaken when an adventurous producer such as David Puttnam has carte blanche to make it his way.'

In Britain Quentin Falk in the *Daily Mail* described it as 'An epic to move us all, a superbly designed, vividly photographed and confidently directed movie, despite a misjudged ending, with John Lennon's "Imagine" blaring intrusively.'

Philip French in the *Observer* felt the film was 'essentially a celebration of the human spirit. In this,' he pointed out, 'it is characteristic of producer David Puttnam, whose films are virtually all inspiring stories of courage in adversity and male friendship, with women relegated to a marginal position or approached from an adolescent perspective.' French was yet another who quarrelled with the way the finale had been scored. 'Pran's reunion with Schanberg in the Thai refugee hospital is puzzling as well as moving,' he wrote, 'but it is muddled and sentimentalized by John Lennon's "Imagine" being played on the soundtrack. How are we supposed to react to this emotionally overwhelming climax?'

There was no doubt about Gavin Martin's reaction in the *New Musical Express*. 'The major structural fault of the film, and it is a glaring one,' Martin felt, 'is the failure to develop anything other than a cursory master/servant relationship in the first half of the film. *The Killing Fields* may be a film of worthy intent, but it is also unbearably ponderous. It seeks hope and refuge in the relationship of the two men, but the inevitable closing shot of Schanberg and Pran embracing to a backing track of John Lennon's "Imagine" is just another sentimentalized disconnected image.'

'Slaughter unexplained,' was Patrick Gibb's headline in the *Daily Telegraph*. 'I found it unsatisfactory as a whole,' he declared. 'Few films have so needed a map and a summary of background facts to enable us to appreciate the foreground it so colourfully presents, facts which the author might well have worked into the narrative. Pran eventually turns up in Thailand, making an ending that would have been more moving had the film suggested better the depth of feeling between the two men.'

Derek Malcolm felt that the film's flaws were 'comfortably transcended by the power and imagination of the film-making and the rare sense that everyone is going for broke to produce something as far away from the merely adequate as possible. Joffe's direction proclaims him to be a film-maker of international class.'

So who *was* responsible for the much-reviled inclusion of John Lennon's 'Imagine' over the film's dramatic reunion scene between Schanberg and Pran? According to Bruce Robinson, he hated the use of the song, but the wishes of David and Roland Joffe prevailed. Not according to editor Jim Clark. 'Bruce must have forgotten,' he says, 'because it was right there in his script that the track was to be played where it was, so we had it on the very first rushes that David saw. David turned round to me and said, "Don't *ever* take that off!"'

Jim is in fact mistaken as to the origins of the song's inclusion. Roland Joffe admits unrepentantly, '*I* wrote that instruction on the script.'

Jon Swain's views on the film are highly relevant, since Dith Pran saved his life as well as that of Schanberg. He confesses to feeling apprehensive when he first heard the film was being made. 'Could the mood of a beautiful South-east Asian country so earnestly and stupidly at war be recaptured in a Western-made film? And, more important, was it possible to make a film about the conflict which would convey the Cambodians' point of view with compassion and understanding and still appeal to Western film audiences?' he asked himself. 'In spite of my uneasiness about these things, I think all of us who lived in the shadow of Cambodia's unimaginable horror wanted this film to be made. For me, personally, *The Killing Fields* represents something which is of great importance, a chance to give recognition to what was a true act of courage by one particular Cambodian. I had been through the war as a journalist and come out safe, where many I knew, Cambodian friends as well as journalists, perished. In the last analysis, I owe my life to Dith Pran, Sydney Schanberg's interpreter. How he saved us from certain execution is scrupulously and flawlessly told in this film.'

Working together with David over such an extended period gave Roland a considerable insight into his producer's mind.

'He's an enormously complex man, that's part of his delight. The strata of David, the levels at which he works, both psychologically and actively in the world, are always interesting because they are nearly always contradictory. David is a man who has six or seven agendas going at any one particular time. The power of most of these agendas is that he has to be massaged with affection.

'He's not combative in a frontal way, although he very much wants to win. He also wants to be liked, and that sets up interesting dynamics. He's got immense charm and as a friend that's absolutely wonderful, but that same skill and charm are put to work when he works. I see it operating on other people and it's wonderful. Then I see it operating on me . . .

'The curiosity side of David is not well understood. You see it in his face sometimes when he's discovering things. Because he never underwent a formal education he's got a marvellous privilege that I don't think he fully appreciates, that his untrained mind is therefore wonderfully flexible and enables him to think laterally. The day I realized that we both have very curious natures is the day I really began to like David. I thought, here's a man who likes to lift the carpet up, peek into the envelope.'

While in America to push the movie, David examined his own role as producer and chose to answer a question for the record which he'd been asked many times. 'I know I *could* direct,' he said, 'but I'd be mediocre. I wouldn't be a bad director in that I would certainly create the illusion of a decent result, but I would be a mediocre director. I like to think I'm a sufficiently good producer to be inclined to fire myself after viewing the first few days' rushes. I really believe that, and if I ever lose that objectivity, then I'll be lost as a producer. I'm proud of my job, and it gives me a satisfactory level of creative employment.'

When it was pointed out to him that his pictures generally depicted people with a sense of values and morals, he explained that this was no coincidence. 'I genuinely believe,' he said, 'that there is wonderful material for film-makers in the area of people's emotional crises. Cinema offers the ability to sit in darkness, to watch people something like five times life-size on the screen, and to lend them your identity. It seems pretty silly to me that one should go through that process only to offer them an identity which they find repellent. I hear extra-ordinary statements like "*On the Waterfront* was really an apologia for the McCarthy era" and "Don't forget that when Brando walks through these gates at the end, they close behind him and any Marxist would tell you that he's sold his workmates out to the system." That's not what I got out of it. I *wanted* Marlon Brando to win, and I *hated* Lee J. Cobb. So what I would put to you is that as a teenager in the mid-fifties, I was effectively living in a Third World environment where America sent its movies. I was looking in on a society that I had no knowledge of, but finding it by and large utterly admirable in purpose, tone and intent.

'I've often wondered what my equivalents who were brought up in the seventies thought, seeing that same society full of self-loathing, violent agression, and an extraordinary ability to trivialize itself. American films of that particular decade must have had a devastating effect on the way that America was viewed by the world. Many in that audience have since left university; they may have jobs in government. Their entire image of America may well be based on films like *Walking Tall*, *Death Wish* and *The Exorcist*, and I wish I were joking. In looking at the nihilistic output of that decade, I can't imagine how anyone could perceive the United States as anything other than a completely insane self-destructive society.

'I have in my office a Norman Rockwell signed print that means a lot to me. It's the one of the runaway kid sitting at a lunch counter, with a policeman. The cop has a gun, but you're pretty sure he's not going to use it on the kid; there is a man gazing at the kid from behind the lunch counter, but you assume he's not going to rape him; and you know that sooner or later the kid is going to go home and everything will be all right. That is the image of America I was brought up with.

'If *The Killing Fields* is a homage to anything, it's a homage to some of the films I saw 20 years ago. The *Battle of Algiers* may not have made back its negative cost, but what it did do was give me the encouragement to produce *The Killing Fields*. Please God, someone will see our picture and be encouraged to make something even better.'

The Killing Fields went on to collect nine British Academy Awards, including one to David for Best Film, to Bruce Robinson for Best Adapted Screenplay, and to Haing Ngor for Best Actor, as well as Outstanding Newcomer, an unprecedented double-honour. The film was then nominated for seven US Oscars and went on to win in three categories, Best Cinematography to Chris Menges, Best Film Editor to Jim Clark (David and Roland's eyes and ears), and Best Supporting Actor to Haing Ngor.

Bruce Robinson had no illusions about the film, although he reckoned it to be a good one in the lexicon of movies. 'The whole essence about the stupidity of the cinema,' he says, 'is that when *The Killing Fields* came out everybody said, "Oh, *great*, an anti-war film," then six weeks later *Rambo* comes out and does 3000 times the business, and it's about this guy with these *huge* tits, killing the Vietnamese and winning the war. Which just reiterates from my point of view that film is nothing, film is entertainment. One television *World in Action* special will do more than $15 million lavished on a screenplay.'

Following the Oscars, David travelled to Japan in May 1984 for the Tokyo International Film Festival. Alex Ying, in charge of Warners' Far East operation, was busy devising a brand-new campaign for the movie. He watched as David flung himself into his hectic schedule of appearances.

'He was doing three things within the week, lectures on film, dialogue with Japanese producers and acting as chairman of the Festival jury. I don't know how he finds the energy; it was amazing to see him work. He would finish one thing, drive somewhere else, get on the stage, take off his jacket and start to talk about film. He did this as if he'd thought the whole thing out, but I know he wasn't always prepared. Many times it was impromptu.

'In August he and Roland came back to Japan for the opening of *The Killing Fields*. They travelled with the film to different cities, not just the main ones of Tokyo and Osaka, but others that never see foreign celebrities, like Sapporo. We had a screening without telling the audience the director and producer were there. When they were told afterwards, they couldn't believe their town had been judged so important. People wouldn't leave the theatre after the picture; they were genuinely moved. Both Roland and David stayed on too; they wouldn't let anyone go without an autograph if they wanted one.

'Another time there were just kids staying on and they were so excited. David sat down and started talking to them. He has a genuine interest in young people. Each person is important to him.

'Japan is a special place for him. People have a great deal of respect for him here, ever since *Melody* in the early seventies. There is much similarity between Hara San and David. They are two people from different continents and culture, both of whom have dedicated their lives to film.'

David's faith in Helen Mirren turned out to be fully justified as she went on to win the Best Actress award at the Cannes Film Festival in 1984 for her performance in *Cal*. The talents of Mark Knopfler had again been employed with tremendous effect, only this time his themes were even more plaintively beautiful and haunting, in keeping with the tragic background to *Cal*'s story. David saw it as, 'Our best-ever score, beautifully integrated.' He set about pushing the film in his forthright manner. 'I love the picture,' he declared. 'If pictures like *Cal* don't work at the box-office, all we'll be left with is *Ghostbusters*.' Rebutting a charge that the storyline required a sophisticated audience to understand *Cal*'s background, he pointed to the example of *Romeo and Juliet*. 'No one asks, what's all this with the Montagues and Capulets, you just accept that there's a dispute. Similarly, here you don't need any special knowledge about Northern Ireland.'

The film was well received and did decent business in Britain and on video release, but failed in the vital US market. 'No disrespect to Warners, but it was just *thrown* out,' said David.

Variety saw it differently, having forecast with deadly accuracy 'limited box-office prospects in arthouse venues' looming for *Cal*'s US release. 'It's difficult to imagine audiences,' they had added, 'particularly outside the British Isles, becoming too excited by this mute tale.'

There were rumours that David would soon be taking a break. He was offered the post of chairman at Saatchi and Saatchi by Charles and Maurice, which he declined, despite the considerable financial inducement that came with it. His wife saw David sink into a terrible 'black dog' depression after *The Killing Fields*' opening. The experience of shooting the film had left a legacy of two ulcers and the feeling he had peaked as a producer.

Patsy was alarmed. 'What happened after the film was that he saw again the huge impact movies can have on people. Despite his earlier agonizing about understanding communications, he still didn't feel he was really qualified to fiddle around in people's brains, since he didn't know that much himself. He was full of self-doubt about everything.

'He felt by this time that *Chariots* was not the film everyone said it was; it was just a nice, honourable picture. He agreed with the people who had called him politically naïve after *Midnight Express*. He was still very much his own severest worst critic. He was now picking on everything and saying, "It's only mediocre and I've gone along with all this glory and all the trumpeting. It's *not* right, *who* am I kidding? I've *got* to stop kidding myself." I think that what was really happening to him was the final stage of growing up.'

Unfortunately, the angst accompanying this process obliterated what should have been elation after what many saw as the triumph he had wrought for Sydney Schanberg's story and the four hours of material Roland had shot. Although victory could be said to have been snatched from the jaws of defeat, the onset of maturity seemed to have made David aware of the ambiguity of success.

Another reason for David's depression was the attitude of others in the British Film Industry, exemplified by the niggardly response of the organization to British Film Year. The much-touted push to bring the missing millions back to the cinema was greeted in many quarters with apathy and scepticism.

David dropped his second bombshell soon after. 'I'm planning a sabbatical once outstanding contracts are out of the way,' he told a stunned press conference, 'and after that, I seriously want to leave the business altogether. Patsy and I may go to New York, then I want to come back to England and possibly teach for five years. I know something about making films and I'd like to pass on what I know.'

Many believe David had just hung a 'For Sale' sign round his neck.

Chapter 17

Never Say Never Again

When *The Killing Fields* had been about to go into production, one of David's most ardent supporters over the years had run himself into a career dead-end. With Goldcrest's success basically founded on his backing of *Chariots of Fire*, then Dickie Attenborough's *Gandhi*, Jake Eberts found himself with very little to show for his efforts. He decided to seek an interview with James Lee and attempt to work out a deal that would give him a slice of the action. When his request to James Lee turned into a mammoth six-month negotiation, and with offers from the States for his services beginning to pile in, notably from Embassy, Jake was torn between the need to pay off his debts – he had taken no salary from Goldcrest until 1981 – and his desire to stay with the company.

It seemed that Lee had become very intrigued with the whole business of Goldcrest and motion-picture production, for although the company only represented 10 per cent of Pearson Longman's assets, he was now spending 90 per cent of his time on Goldcrest business. This suited Jake, who thought Lee was a wonderful chairman capable of coaxing the Pearson board into backing any idea he put up – except, for some reason, the financial package for himself he had proposed. Lee appeared to be thinking in terms of moving to Goldcrest as full-time chairman and had in mind a considerable expansion of the company's activities, starting with a move to larger premises.

When Jerry Perenchio and his partner Norman Lear, the heads of Embassy, indicated to Jake in 1983 that they would not be prepared to wait forever to have their offer accepted, Jake realized the time had come for a career decision. Two things made this easy, the first being the change in the nature of Goldcrest. Jake found he was attending a constant round of board and management committee meetings and was inundated with personnel and pension-plan problems.

'What I'd really loved,' said Jake, 'was my relationship with David and Dickie and John Boorman, whose *Emerald Forest* I'd put in place, and Peter Yates, who was doing *The Dresser* with us. *That's* what was really exciting. All these people didn't want someone who was running a company and was always busy on the phone; they wanted a guy who could be available to them at a moment's notice to help out with a problem with the studio, with the writer, whatever.' The second element that facilitated Jake's decision was Embassy's latest offer. 'The amount of money was absolutely *obscene*, so I decided the time had come. I consulted with David and he was, I think, ambivalent because as long as he got his money, it didn't matter to him whether it came from James Lee or me. David's job was not to run Goldcrest; he used to come to meetings and did his best, but he didn't really care about my leaving. Dickie was probably more emotional, because to him Goldcrest was a chance for the British film business. He was a great flag-waver, but he also knew that I was in debt and at that time I was 43 years old and had been in the business for quite a long time and hadn't got very far. So I went to Jerry's house in Malibu and there as usual were umpteen servants and cars and champagne and God knows what, so I finally said, "Oh, fuck it!"

'Dickie was devastated, but he understood. Once I'd made my mind up he was a complete supporter, in fact he made *Chorus Line*, his next picture, for us at Embassy. To David it was no big deal; we don't have that kind of relationship. If I was happy, he was happy. He wasn't promoting it, but he wasn't going to make a big fuss over it. And furthermore – the guy was *busy* shooting *Killing Fields* in Thailand.

'So I came back. I told James and the staff; it took about one day. Then we had the problem of the shares I'd been given in Goldcrest at the outset, because under the terms of my contract I had the right to put these shares back to the company at so-called fair market value, as if the company were publicly traded. We went into four months of negotiations, they hired Rothschilds to act for Goldcrest in trying to make a settlement for me. I was asking for, let's say 2x and they offered me less than x; less than half of what I felt my shares were worth. And I thought, *enough* already, I've been here all this time, it's not *that* much money after all. Dickie had offered me two and a half per cent profit share in *Gandhi*, which I couldn't take as I was running the company. That couldn't be worked out – James wouldn't do that.

'I hired a stockbroker friend of mine, because I wanted someone who understood the public market, as if Goldcrest was publicly traded. Goldcrest hired Rothschilds and we couldn't agree. We had to call in an arbitrator, whom they had the right to choose. They chose an accountant, someone from Touche Ross. I said, "Oh God, curtains. He'll offer me *point* 2x, he probably thinks the film business is nothing but a bunch of flakes anyway!" So we had these two or three meetings with the arbitrator. My paper was a great thick document listing share price movements, and the impact on Pearson's shares when *Gandhi* won the awards. It was a pretty well-thought-out and documented piece of work. Rothschilds' was nothing more than a hand-written note, which said, "We believe the shares are worth so-and-so." That was it.

'We submitted our stuff and the arbitrator went off to do his little number, and about two weeks later I got a copy of a letter he had sent to James Lee. I was away at the time in the States, but I got it read out to me. It said simply, "Dear Mr Lee, We conclude that Mr Eberts' shares are worth 4*x*." That was it – a *vast* premium over what I had myself been asking for, and no justification. "Yours sincerely, Touche Ross." No background, no nothing, but it was a *fabulous* day for me. I said, "God, they've done *something* right for me, but hey, check out that number, make sure it's not *point* 4*x*!" But no, the number was right, it was several hundred thousand pounds, so I said, "Jesus, cash it before it's too late!" This was 1.20 pm or something, I said, *"Get the money in the bank!"* '

Since her *Greystoke* involvement as casting director, Patsy Pollock had gone on to associate-produce *Wetherby*, written and directed by David Hare, starring Vanessa Redgrave. ('Oh, Al, you will come and see it, won't you?' she had asked Parker. 'Fuck off, P, I ain't got enough GCEs to get in,' the hobgoblin chortled.)

She had gone after Ian Holm for a tiny but important role in the film, and got him. Soon after she was in David's office talking about the possibility of her working at Enigma. All David was offering was involvement in the ongoing *First Love* series.

'I don't want to work for your B-team,' she informed a furious David. 'I'd rather make the tea for the A-team than fuck around with the Bs, thanks very much.'

'How did you get Ian Holm for *Wetherby*?' David asked, when he had cooled off, 'I offered him the lead in one of the *First Loves* and he turned it down.'

Patsy saw her chance. 'Oh', she replied, 'I did what you would have done five years ago. I just *infected* him with the importance of doing it. Took him and his agent to lunch – he said "no". His agent left – he still said "no"! Walked down the road with him – still "no". Bought him a cup of tea – "no" again. Then in the war of attrition, a moment came and he gave in. You know, David, it's so damnably *attractive* when someone wants you that much. Did *you* pick up the phone yourself to Ian?'

'No. But I wasn't producing the film.'

'Did your producer pick up the phone?'

'I don't *know*. But why should I *have* to? I got Ian into *Chariots of Fire* and you know what, P, nobody ever earns their dues. You don't *ever* have any real clout, no matter who you are. You *always* have to go on doing it and fighting. No one ever says, "David, it's a dodgy part, but I owe you one. I'll do it for you." So I'm really proud of you. One up for you, P. Just curious, though, how much did you pay Ian?'

Patsy's eyes blazed.

'*Fuck all*. What's that got to do with it?'

'Nothing, P. *I* know that.' David averted his eyes.

'Right back to business. Look, you're *my* tribe, David – not these fucking blue-stocking tarts you employ. I know you have to listen to my GBH of the earhole about how you've lost touch with what people are doing on the streets, but it's good for you, it's the slut's eye-view of what it's like working in the British Fim Industry. It seems you just don't want to give me an associate-producer credit.'

'You're a financial hooligan, P. Brilliant creatively, but – '

At that moment Patsy Puttnam entered the room, all innocent smiles.

'Cup of tea, anyone? Come on, you two, you're *awful*, shouting the house down. What's it all about?'

'Don't you interfere!' P yelled. 'I'm going to bash him up!' – then the three friends fell about laughing.

David first came across the script for *The Mission* in 1977 in Los Angeles while at Pacific Palisades. Fernando Ghia was in Hollywood trying to raise money for the project and had a finished script by Robert Bolt which David asked to read. He was not only deeply moved by it, but could not get it out of his mind thereafter. Something about it kept coming back to haunt him, although he could see there were deep-rooted problems still to be solved. Oddly, the script about Jesuits in the jungle of South America pre-dated his own brush with the Jesuit faith in the form of Father Mahoney.

He and Ghia met fairly regularly afterwards, when David would invariably find the producer just about to close a deal, or with some prospective deal just broken down.

During his depression after the completion of *The Killing Fields*, his thoughts again turned to *The Mission*. Despite everything he had said about pulling out of films, or at least taking a break, *The Mission* somehow represented unfinished business. And wouldn't Roland Joffe be the ideal director to be involved in the project?

'It was very odd,' David muses. 'The *man* reminded me of the material.' To Ghia he said, 'I feel I'm working with the best big film-maker to come along in many years a sort of natural David Lean figure, and Roland's qualities seem to coincide with some of the things you said you wanted for *The Mission*.'

The theme of the film harked back to the time in the mid-eighteenth century when the Spanish and Portuguese were dividing up Latin-American territories between them. Jesuit missions stood in their way and eventually were overrun and destroyed in the interests of trade and to allow the region's natural resources to be fully exploited. The wholesale slaughter of the Guarani Indians who had joined the missions followed.

The main characters in the story were Gabriel, the Jesuit missionary who had founded the community of Christian Indians in the jungle, and Mendoza, a slave-trader racked with guilt after killing his brother in a duel. Gabriel accepts Mendoza as a novice, then when the mission is attacked the two men take up their own positions, Gabriel opting for passive resistance, Mendoza once more taking up his sword.

David intended only to executive-produce the picture, distancing himself from the vicissitudes he had experienced on *The Killing Fields*, and leaving the actual location and production duties to Fernando Ghia, with Iain Smith hired to repeat the line production he had handled so capably on *Local Hero* and the arduous *Killing Fields* location. David was still concerned about certain aspects of the script and met with Robert Bolt to have these ironed out. .

Patsy has her own idea about David's motives in making *The Mission*. 'I would say that he wanted to do it because he wanted to do another film with Roland, something that had never occurred before with any of the other directors. I think he was feeling that at his age he was absolutely tired of finding new directors all the time, only to have them pillaged by others. He was going to stick with this one. But truthfully, his heart wasn't in that film like it was in *Killing Fields* or *Chariots of Fire*. They'd been his conceptions from the word go. That isn't to say he wouldn't give *The Mission* his best, but it wasn't his own baby.'

With David only on board as executive producer, this was fine, but the position was about to change as pre-production began and Ghia clasped the controls. First he alienated Roland Joffe, then Iain Smith fell foul of him. Word quickly got back to Warners and Goldcrest.

David was left with no alternative, but it was with a very heavy heart that he agreed to step in and take over the production reins

himself, having vowed after *Killing Fields* never to personally produce
a film of that size again, so taxing had that movie been both physically
and mentally. When Roland Joffe declared that he was keen to get
Robert De Niro to play Mendoza, David fought him over the
choice.

'I'd rather go for a non-star, not someone who's going to bring
their own baggage to the part,' he argued, but Roland dug his heels
in, and besides, De Niro was interested. He offered to bring his fee
down and take a larger part of the profits instead. 'It isn't true to say I
didn't want Bobby,' David insists. 'I was just very concerned about
the impact on our schedule, for it was extremely tight on this picture.'

David, Roland and De Niro had a long talk late one night at Blake's
Hotel in London.

'Look, I'm really concerned,' David told the star. 'You have a
reputation for wanting a lot of on-camera rehearsal time. Quite honestly
the film was never set up to accommodate this or the type of actor you
represent.'

'I understand your problem,' De Niro replied gravely, 'and I will
never delay your picture.'

David was surprised at this ready acquiescence, but he had another
bombshell ready.

'I'm also not totally convinced that you are right for the picture.'

This time De Niro was clearly taken aback, but still he politely
replied, 'Nobody has ever said that to me before, David. I'm an actor,
and my feeling is that I'm right for anything that I really sincerely
feel that I can do.'

David felt it was enormously to De Niro's credit that the exchange
at all times was handled with dignity, decorum and a mutual respect
for each other's position for what he had been trying to enunciate
between the lines was, '*I'm* the producer. *These* have to be the rules.
If you're not happy with them, please, for all of our sakes, don't sign
on.'

It was a cool introduction.

The situation was taken a stage further by the signing of Liam
Neeson for the supporting role of one of the priests. 'It was never
enunciated,' Patsy says, 'but I suspect that Liam was in that position
so that if Bobby decided to pull out he would be available to go straight
into his part. Left to David, maybe Liam would have got the job in
the first place. This way, he had his fallback position, his plan "B".'

Now Roland further flexed his casting muscles, David found. 'He
had developed an obsession that he might find a non-actor in the
Haing Nor tradition, and turn them into a star. He had several people

in mind – like Danny Berrigan, a Jesuit priest with whom he spent a lot of time – trying to sincerely convince himself that he would work in the role of Gabriel. When Roland finally decided on Jeremy Irons, it was Bobby's turn to feel unsure. It wasn't really that he did or didn't want Jeremy, but people tend to strike attitudes. He came round marvellously.'

With Jake Eberts' departure there was a flurry of activity at Goldcrest to find someone else the company could bring in as head of production. Although James Lee was familiar with the financial operations of the company, he had no experience in the production area and was anxious to get the post filled with reasonable speed to deflect any criticism that might arise from not having enough of a team there in the first place. David recommended the name of Sandy Lieberson to the board, which really seemed an ideal solution all round, although Sandy himself had grave reservations. For several years he had been enjoying the life of an independent producer again after his studio tenure, and it took a lot of persuasion by David to bring him round to the idea of joining Goldcrest.

After Sandy's spell with the Ladd Co. came to an end, he had formed a company that was meant to act like a film-makers' co-operative, with Alan Marshall, Alan Parker, Michael Apted, John Boorman and Hugh Hudson as the members – a bit, in fact, like a David Puttnam old boys' club. At David's urging, Goldcrest had tried to make a deal with the unit, but there was a dawning realization that the set-up was not going to work. Sandy saw Hugh Hudson and Alan Parker, who were old friends, sit down across the table to read each other's script to decide whether they should be produced. 'They couldn't even agree on that,' says Sandy, 'and Alan Marshall and I looked at each other and we knew that this in no way was ever going to work, so we called it quits.'

Sandy took the job at Goldcrest despite his reservations, only through David's assurances. 'It was a nightmare,' he says, 'one of the worst experiences I ever got involved in. Just from day one when I arrived, the atmosphere of the company was so bad, so hostile that I knew I'd made a dreadful mistake. I saw there was little way out for me, since Jake's departure and my appointment had been announced side by side in the trade press, otherwise I'd have left there and then. David and Dickie kept telling me, "Don't worry, it will all be wonderful in a few month's time." I just *hated* it.'

Today James Lee says, 'Sandy seemed a natural choice, but he was always in an awkward position and was more useful in talking about what direction we should go in and on general ideas, rather than films themselves and individual projects, because he always felt compromised to some extent, pronouncing on someone else's project. Then he often had some indirect interest in the film as well, so that if you were putting something forward, he couldn't be judge and jury as well.'

Many saw the rot setting in with the sudden tremendous change in James Lee, who seemed to go *very* Hollywood *very* fast, the process taking weeks rather than months. Someone said it was when he started to wear pink bow ties that the game was up.

Jake Eberts is uniquely placed to record the shift in philosophy that now took place in the company. 'David and Sandy agreed that the way *I* had run the company was not the way that they would have run the company. They felt that a lot more product should be developed in-house. To do this you need a staff, because you're spending money acquiring options and having scripts written and doing budgets and all the preparations that I used to have done by outside parties. I felt that the film-makers that I wanted to work with were far better at developing product themselves than we ever could do in-house, so my theory of developing product was quite different from David's. And Sandy turned out to be of the David school, so it was suitable all around, for David, for Sandy and for James. The difference in philosophy is quite important when you try to analyse what happened and what David's role was and how Sandy interacted between David and James Lee. When Sandy arrived he decided, with David and James' full support, to staff up the Goldcrest development and production arm so it could develop its own product. I think that was, in retrospect, a mistake – not even in retrospect, for I never believed in doing it that way.

'So the basic change in strategy led to a very substantial increase in staffing, because not only did they have to hire all these people to seek out product and read books and scripts and meet with writers and producers and directors, but they needed to have a whole legal apparatus to go along with that, to write up all the documents and to control all these contracts, and that led to a virtual quintupling of the number of people employed there. It was just a completely different business. I'm not saying it was right or wrong – it might have worked had the product been better – but it *was different*.'

Sandy quickly found he had been thrown in at the deep end, with one of his first decisions having to decide whether or not to continue development of John Boorman's *Emerald Forest*, which Jake had left in an advanced stage of development with Goldcrest. Boorman had

been working on *Emerald Forest* for 18 months, while Jake had tried
to piece together a financial structure, including a substantial contribution from an American major, a large advance from Goldcrest against
the foreign rights and a straightforward tax deal which would in fact
have produced 100 per cent of the financing the picture required. The
main difficulty with *Emerald Forest* had been in trying to establish a
fixed budget, for the movie was to be shot in the jungles of Brazil and
Jake had been proceeding very largely on faith and trust in Boorman,
together with the hope that the project would acquire a good completion guarantee. In the event, the guarantor began to make extremely
nervous noises about the Brazil location shoot.

For John Boorman a mandate to proceed was essential, since he
had committed large sums of money in hiring a crew, building sets
and making down payments on transport and hotel costs. Boorman
had at one time been offered a seat on the Goldcrest board by David
and Dickie Attenborough over lunch at Mr Chow's. 'Come and help
us to make it a company of film-makers,' had been the invitation.
Boorman turned the idea down, although he was more than happy to
ally himself with Goldcrest in a less formal way. The lunch contributed to the film co-operative idea that Sandy later tried to put together.
Boorman found David to be 'an enigmatic character of immense
charm, adroit and skilful as a producer – a little too good to be true'.
As for Dickie, 'One cannot escape the suspicion that Dickie is acting
out all his roles as mediator, peacemaker, director, chairman, businessman, yet he is redeemed by a true goodness of heart, which drives
him to pursue the common good.'

Communications were difficult between Boorman, Sandy and
James Lee, partly because of the fact that Boorman was out there in
the jungle and partly because of Lee's inability to evaluate the problems Boorman was grappling with. Then there was the fact that
David's new picture, *The Mission*, was to be shot in the jungles of
Colombia – wasn't that just too much for one company to take on
board at one time? Sandy was placed in an impossible position. He
had had no opportunity of talking to Boorman before he left for
Brazil, and therefore very little means of making a proper, meaningful
judgement. What emerged from all the uncertainty was less than total
enthusiasm for *Emerald Forest*. Boorman noted in his diary, 'Goldcrest
was adventurous, bold, tough, decisive. Without Jake it's lurching
alarmingly.' The Goldcrest board met and duly decided to pull out of
Emerald Forest.

'I am in a state of shock,' Boorman recorded, '[and] try to speculate
about what happened at the Goldcrest board meeting. We know that

David Norris is on our side. I am sure that Bill Gavin, Head of Sales, would not want the film to founder since he has done the hard work of selling it to distributors all over the world . . . That means that David Puttnam and Dickie Attenborough must have voted with James Lee against me.'

Jake Eberts came to Boorman's rescue, having negotiated with Embassy while still at Goldcrest to acquire the American rights. 'We were pretty far down the road for a deal whereby Goldcrest would keep the foreign rights and all the tax benefits and Embassy would get the American rights,' he recalls. 'And that was an extremely attractive deal for John Boorman because it meant that for a fairly small amount of equity capital this kind of picture could be made, and John could be in profit pretty soon, and in fact if the tax deal had been done, there would have been a profit in the film before it started shooting.

'John was anxious to start shooting and I was anxious to get the picture made, so I approached Goldcrest after it became clear that communication had broken down between John and them, and in the end Embassy acquired *all* Goldcrest's rights in the picture and simply paid Goldcrest the costs which they had invested up to that stage and took over all the foreign sales which had already been done.

'Embassy therefore ended up with worldwide rights in the picture, and for reasons that are too complicated to go into, decided not to do the tax deal – which is unfortunate, because had that been done, Embassy would have made a profit too, but they chose not to. This was all very unsettling for John, who felt he had been badly done by by Sandy and James – and possibly even David, because he was suspicious of the reasons why the picture had ultimately been rejected by Goldcrest; he didn't accept the argument that the completion guarantor couldn't provide a satisfactory guarantee or because John wasn't able to fix the budget because the Brazilian cruzeiro kept on going up or down. I think he was convinced it was because David Puttnam was making a jungle picture in *The Mission* and voted it down, and Sandy was David's pal, so voted it down too, and James was going along with it. I don't know what happened, but I'd be very surprised if that was the reason. But that's why there was very bad blood between all of these people at the time. Personally, I was ecstatic, because it meant that my baby, which I'd been working on with John Boorman for two years by that time, was now fully with me at Embassy.'

David Norris threatened to resign over the *Emerald Forest* row, for he had been in the worst possible position with the project, both as John Boorman's lawyer *and* as a member of the Goldcrest board. 'A couple of us were in favour of continuing with the project, the rest shouted it down,' he says. 'As for David, he was true to himself. He was very out-spoken all the time about how we couldn't have a producer who is also a director, since there was an inherent conflict of interest in his view. In fairness, Terry Clegg, an associate we had sent over to weigh up the situation, came back from Brazil, saying, "Jesus, this thing could go millions over." I know that in John's subsequent book, *Money into Light*, you can see that he misunderstood Terry. He thought Terry was saying how well prepared everything was, that they'd done terrific work. Terry and he had worked together before, they are good mates and he's a friend of mine too. I'm very close to him and John, but John *completely* misread Terry. John brought me his *Money into Light* manuscript before it went to the publisher and said, "Change anything you like." I said, "Well, there's a lot of stuff in there, John . . ." He said, "Change it." I said, "No, this is a diary. This isn't revisionist time, it's what you thought at the time, you must publish it."

'So what David was saying was in effect correct and totally fair, based on Terry's report. But John seemed to feel betrayed by him, if you read his diary. David, you see, had also been part of a much earlier process trying to get John and Mike Apted and Sandy Lieberson and various others on a slightly more formal footing with Goldcrest, to try to get Goldcrest stacked around film-makers, and it hadn't really worked out. So David's views on *Emerald Forest* were perfectly logical, justifiable and honourable.'

David remembers being called in to Goldcrest one evening to pronounce on whether they should go ahead with the project or not, and as usual he had done his homework carefully. 'David Norris was in an awkward position,' he recalls, 'wearing two hats, but when we looked at the thing there was no agreed budget, there was only a national schedule; there was no completion guarantor in place – I mean, all the things you normally put together before you start a picture honestly didn't exist. We discussed it with Terry Clegg, who'd just come back from location and based on that I felt it would be complete madness to encourage them to go ahead. Now there are two kinds of horrible decisions that happen when a film-maker becomes the decision-maker on other people's films. It's a situation that should be avoided. The key caution and the key figure in the debate was Terry Clegg, just returned from the Brazil location. Iain Smith, incidentally, had also visited and thought it was chaos, absolute chaos. I put the question straight to him, "Would *we* go ahead under these circumstances?" He didn't hesitate for one second. "No way," he replied.

'In fairness, there may be different ways of making movies. John Boorman may work one way, and Iain and I and certainly Dickie and Terry Clegg tend to be extremely orderly. But you can't make a financial judgement based on someone else's way of seeing the world. So, based on the way that *we* would have proceeded, it was an easy call, not difficult at all, which was – why don't they get their act together? In the event, to a very great extent they managed it. I think it was probably what we term in the business a kick, bollock and scramble, but they did it and I take my hat off to John Boorman. And frankly, that was one of the reasons why later I really went to bat for him on *Hope and Glory*, the fact that he'd pulled together a chaotic situation into a movie. For all I know that's how he runs his life. It's not the way Patsy and I run our lives and it isn't Dickie's and you can only make judgements based on your own lights. I thought a lot of *Money into Light* was rather self-serving.'

Another reason for Norris's threatened resignation was the new post-Eberts set up and the matter of reorganization for the company's next stage of in-house development. Rothschild were to provide the cash and Noble Grossart were to be working with them. 'I said I was leaving in February 1984 stating that I thought the new set-up was wrongly structured. I didn't agree with the pairing of James and Sandy, who were *bound* not to get on. Rothschilds were alarmed and took me out to lunch. "If you persist with your resignation, we won't proceed with the reorganization and fund-raising," they told me. It was moral blackmail, but I went back against my better judgement. David persuaded me to stay, and I did. Then we disagreed *again*.

'He was developing three – let's call them theatrical *First Loves* – and trying to get Goldcrest to finance them 100 per cent. I said no, John Chambers said no, there was some shilly-shallying among the others. Frankly, none of us had any real enthusiasm for them. He said, "Thorn/EMI have always been wanting me to work with them, let's see if we can bring them in to do this jointly with Goldcrest." So we worked with the Thorn/EMI boys who just looked at us in the end and said, "The numbers don't stack up. We have to stay no, the projects don't make sense financially." Still no one at Goldcrest was prepared to say an outright "no" to David. "Maybe they didn't get their numbers right," David persisted. The buck was then passed to Warners who had the rights of first look at all David's theatrical movies, which these really were intended to be. The feeling at Goldcrest was that Warners would have more sense than to proceed. Then Sandy went over there and said, "We'll back them if you do," which wasn't *strictly* correct. Warners were none too sure, but figured that if

Goldcrest were going in for half . . . So it got into one of these silly situations where the truth is *everyone* was frightened to say "no" to David, corporately and collectively. Thus we got *The Frog Prince*, *Knights and Emeralds* and *Mister Love*. It never soured our relationship, but David knows I said "no".'

What it *did* sour was any further thought in David's mind of continuing on the Enigma treadmill. Susan Richards reckons his decision to convert the balance of the *First Love* TV projects to theatrical, while well-meaning, was based on insuperable illogic. 'David said to us, "Do what you can; go for it. At this price we can't make films for television any more. Do you want to take the opportunity to move these projects to theatrical?" On the other hand, they were a real embarrassment for Warners once they were made, because something had to be done with them. They were Enigma films and they wouldn't let them go to any small distributors, many of whom were longing to get their hands on them. The vice we got caught in was that they wanted to kill them off in the way they were distributed. It was beginning to be the time when little British features could be marketed with skill and success, but Warners were not really wanting to encourage that from David, so it was an unhappy experience. He and I were at war with Warners. David's heart was still with the movies, but he wasn't prepared at the same time to go out on a limb for them.'

David recalls the exasperating phone calls to Terry Semel at Warners, begging him to give the films a chance. For David the final straw came in the autumn of 1984.

'I'd built up this whole structure of script readers, developers and producers at Enigma. Our offices at Queensgate Place Mews were crawling with staff. The whole thing had just run away with itself. Then the bills started pouring in, for lunches, for taxi fares. Some of these people had got it into their head they were working for a big production company. Then I heard we'd lost the chance to acquire J. G. Ballard's *Empire of the Sun*, which one of our staff turned down. The argument was that no Ballard book had been remotely filmic before and there was no reason to assume that this one was any different. I went bananas, for a three-line synopsis which I picked up in a newspaper convinced me it would have been a great picture for Roland and I. There was a tremendous silence. Not only had we passed on it, but the option had been sold for peanuts! For all the size of the monster we'd created, the one thing we'd really looked for had been lost for $10,000. Frankly, I'd have carried the money round to them on my hands and knees.'

He was still fuming when he arrived for lunch that day with

Debbie's boyfriend and fellow-journalist, Loyd Grossman, who, with brilliant timing, had arranged the appointment to ask for Debbie's hand in marriage. Loyd was obliged to sit nodding sympathetically while David went on about losing the book and how he was going to close the company down completely that very afternoon. 'Have I picked the wrong time?' Loyd asked himself, then he thought, 'Oh, to hell with it, in for a penny, in for a pound – if he's going to hit me, he may as well do it now.'

David was thrilled, but had just one piece of advice for Loyd. 'Either go away *quietly* – or we tell Patsy *now* and be prepared to have the wedding taken over. That will be *it*. She's been planning this potential wedding since Debbie was born!' Like the excellent prospect he was, Loyd wisely chose the latter course. He recalls arriving at his flat that night at the usual time of 7 pm. Only micro-seconds later, Patsy was on the line. 'Hello, it's your mother-in-law here!' she greeted him. Later Debbie was asked when she wanted the wedding. 'We haven't really thought about it,' she replied.

'June's the best time,' Patsy had decided. 'A June wedding will be lovely. Leave it all to me'

'Fine,' said Debbie, 'but Mum – isn't Dad still a bit upset about losing the book?'

'Yes, he is a bit cut-up still, but he's managed to rationalize it. He says he may have lost an empire, but he's gained a son.'

For a while the only outward sign of David's intentions was his instruction that no contracts signed should take the company further forward than one year. Soon, however, the Enigma staff were assembled and put on notice. 'We'd known the writing was on the wall for some time,' said one ex-member of the Enigma staff. 'David was deeply unhappy to have to tell us we were closing down and was very generous in his settlements.' Many who had looked to David as the omnipotent great provider still turned bitterly against the hand that would no longer feed them. 'With time to think about it since,' says another ex-staff member, 'one can rationalize that, given the state of the British Film Industry, what David had attempted was the equivalent of building an edifice on constantly shifting sands. In some ways it was admirable, in others foolhardy. We thought he knew something no one else did. We were wrong.' One of David's colleagues on the SDP team, Shirley Williams, had described in glowing terms the nine-month sabbatical she had taken at Harvard University. Once *The Mission* was completed and launched, and with the Enigma monster reduced to pet-size, and on a leash, David announced this would be his next port of call. It was beginning to look as if the cynics had it wrong.

Chapter 18

Rumble in the Jungle

David Norris remembers one particular Friday night late in 1984 that must stand as some sort of landmark moment, when Sandy Lieberson presented a script that he asked each of the board to read over the weekend. 'This has the potential to be the best movie script I've ever read,' he told them, 'and I want the go-ahead on Monday to buy it.'

Norris disdainfully flung his copy on James Lee's desk the following Monday. 'If that's the best script Sandy's ever read, I just fucking well don't know,' he exclaimed. Lee agreed there were far too many coincidental meetings and a rather drifting narrative line, but did not feel so strongly about it. 'It needs a lot of work, but I do think there's something here,' he summarized.

Sandy stands by his initial judgement on *Revolution* and argues that it is not what it *was* but what it *became*, that caused the problems. 'We started with a modest cost movie,' he says, 'very personal, a romantic, heroic story. Robert Dylan wrote a really great, wonderful script.'

Lee does not concur with this. 'Warners and ourselves realized,' he claims, '*very much on Sandy's advice*, that the dialogue in the first draft of the script was inadequate and that there were real flaws in the development of the characters.' Potential *had* been Sandy's key word.

When the discussion on whether or not to proceed with *Revolution* began, with none other than Hugh Hudson slated to direct the movie, David found himself in the most difficult position he had ever encountered on the Goldcrest's board. He voted for the film to be postponed until the script problems were sorted out, pointing out that in any case he did not believe the budget which had been drawn up was realistic. David was saying, 'Look, I'm a film-maker. I've worked with Hugh. We've watched the lesson on *Greystoke* and this is *all* Goldcrest's money. The board's attitude was largely, 'Oh, come on, your fight with Hudson should be over by now. You should be bigger than that. You should be able to be magnanimous.'

David was furious at the implication he was bad-mouthing Hugh.

'I do not doubt,' he told them, 'that Hugh will do the picture brilliantly, but he will *not* do it for that price. He's not that sort of film-maker.' With only Dickie Attenborough supporting him, David felt he had no choice but to react to the jibes of partiality. 'If you won't listen to me as a film-maker, what the hell is the point of my being here?' he railed. 'If you're really foolish enough to believe in this nonsensical vendetta, then I must take myself off the board.'

Dickie was unequivocal. 'If you go, I go too,' he stated. Now the same pressure that had been exerted earlier on Norris was brought to bear on David and Dickie, that Goldcrest couldn't possibly afford to have two major board members leaving at such a *delicate* time. When would it be any different? The two found themselves in a cleft stick, unable to leave in case it rocked the boat as far as the current fund-raising campaign was concerned.

With the decision made to proceed on *Revolution*, and a percentage of the budget in place through a European consortium, James Lee felt confident there was plenty of time to get the script right. 'There was a lot of delay while Hugh Hudson dithered with the casting,' he recalls. 'He was very uncertain about exactly what he wanted and only late in the day got around to Al Pacino. We ended up committed to going into pre-production around November 1984, with February 1985 set as the start of filming in Devon. Sandy was an enthusiast, as I was, as were Warners. *The Mission* was going ahead at the same time, together with *Absolute Beginners* and *Room with a View*. Although we sold Warners the package of *Revolution* and *The Mission*, *Revolution* was the one they really wanted. *The Mission* was carried on *Revolution*'s back, so it was ironical that if David had had his way and halted *Revolution*, he might never have got the go-ahead on *The Mission*. And history would have worked out a little bit differently!'

Once the unit for *The Mission* was settled down in Cartagena, Roland Joffe for one rediscovered the joys and sorrows of location filming. 'In Colombia, you can shove your actors out into the street and say, "I'll see you in two days." And just with that act, something exciting begins to happen for them, by osmosis. Bobby De Niro actually *changed*. His look changed. In three days of walking about with Colombian men and observing their ways, the New York Italian began to disappear and a powerful Hispanic appeared. The key to location shooting is planning. The planning stage is a lovely stage; however, it is also an idealized one. One has to remember that each shooting day will be what it is. I can plan in the morning that I'm going to do 24 shots. That's my ideal day. But I go out and somebody thinks he's stepped on a scorpion, so there's five minutes lost there. Ten minutes, allowing for the nurse to come and collect him and discover it's only an earwig. And then the magazine suddenly gets a wire in it and so in the middle of a take the thing is going *wumph, wumph*. Or the lens gets condensation. Why does it get condensation? It never had condensation yesterday, but it's got condensation today! When you travel back alone at night from location, if you can say to yourself, "I've achieved 80 per cent of what I wanted," that's a good day.

'David and I, we both agreed to totally respect each other's positions. I'm the director and he's the producer, both of us have to create the environment. If the producer and the director find themselves in an adversarial relationship during filming, it's a disaster. Ideally, both men will have agreed on the kind of film they want to make *before* the camera turns. After that, no secrets, unless it's something that would send your partner into terminal shock. I would not say to David, "I had a very complicated dream last night and that means I'm going to shoot the entire thing in Swahili." And about the only thing he wouldn't tell me, I guess, would be, "I'm going to have a heart attack." The rule of the game is that we both want to make a good film, so we've made a deal that says in the small print, "I will not sacrifice him for my pride and he will not sacrifice me for his."

'As much as a I love David, and I do, I have to confess he's unhappy when there isn't a telephone within a hundred yards. He's got a fetish about communication, not one shared with the Colombian Ministry of Communications. So Colombia for him was anguish. "Roland" he said to me one day, "I thought you were sane, but you've now totally taken leave of your senses." And I said, "Why?" He said, "The nearest telephone is 60 kilometres from here. I mean, how can we communicate with the production office?" This is the producer's view of the world. The director's eye is always fixed on what's going right and the producer's on what might go wrong.'

A rule of thumb for the Waunana Indians, playing the Guarani, to sort out important people in the cast and crew on *The Mission*, was to look out for the bearded individuals. Since these included David, together with Robert De Niro, Jeremy Irons, Roland Joffe, Robert Bolt and Chris Menges, director of photography, the system worked pretty well. They could see, however, that De Niro was the most important of all, mainly by the deference paid to him by the rest of the 'beards'. He seemed to keep to himself a lot and avoided looking directly at anyone. 'Bobbie is exactly like them,' David said. 'They believe that when you take a photograph of a man you remove something. Bobby feels that about press photographs and interviews.'

While David and his crew stayed at the local Hilton, the company had built a village of huts on the outskirts of Cartagena to house the Indians. All went well until a plague of rats swept through the village. David decided the whole area had to be fumigated because of the health danger and the fact that vital food supplies were being broken into. The Waunanas persuaded him not to go ahead with this drastic action, their witchdoctor announcing that he himself would talk to the rats. Thereafter the food supplies remained miraculously untouched. David was very impressed. 'Could you,' he asked 'do the same for the mosquitoes that are giving us hell?' The witchdoctor looked at him strangely. 'Talk to the mosquitoes?' he thundered. 'Do you think me mad?'

Unaware of his position as Robert De Niro's stand-in, Liam Neeson suffered like the rest of the crew from the mosquito bites. Liam noted that the pale-faced David, who would have seemed the most likely candidate for the dive-bombing mosquitoes, was completely unaffected.

'How do you do it?' Liam asked. 'What's your secret?'

David smiled. 'Loads of vitamin C,' he replied.

Roland saw the dilemma facing Gabriel and Mendoza, while they sought their own solutions, as the emotional centre of the movie. David was worried about modern audiences' reaction to Gabriel's passive stance. A decision was taken to slightly alter the ending. In the new version, Gabriel's last five minutes were changed from being wholly passive. 'The original version was wonderfully dramatic,' David observed, 'in that Gabriel was burned to death inside the church, basically while praying. It was a very devout ending, but we all became worried that his character would suffer terribly in comparison with the enormous activity of Mendoza. There was a real chance that a young audience would say, "What a wimp! All he can do is sit and pray while people are being burned around him." So instead Gabriel attempts, within the confines of his own non-violent beliefs, to *do* something. We gave him a more Gandhian position.'

Jeremy Irons was fully aware of the contrast in acting styles between himself and his co-star. 'Playing opposite Bob was a great learning experience,' he admitted, 'as he works very differently from me. He's a very instinctive actor and he has an uncanny persistence in finding truthful moments. I think I'm quicker and have more technique, as I'm more of a theatre actor. I'm used to working on pictures that don't have the sort of budget where you can go again and again and again. Bob will tend to do a few takes, but within them come up with extraordinary acting choices, very real choices.'

Roland and David got close to both actors during the shoot, Irons with his training in classical theatre, De Niro the master of the instinctive and improvisional. 'Bobby and Jeremy worked out a relationship over the course of the film,' Roland saw. 'Bobby was holding his own in what was really quite a simple film. It was not a film about New York, in which he can use his street-wiseness.'

David heard one day of a disagreement that had arisen between De Niro and Joffe during shooting. It seemed that De Niro wanted to change not just the lines in one particular area but also to effect a considerable character change. At dinner that evening, diners at adjoining tables were startled to overhear the conversation between David and his star.

'I hear you're unhappy with one of the scenes, Bobby,' David began.

'Yes, I am.'

'Is it the lines?'

'No, it's more than that. I feel the character wouldn't react in the way he does here –'

The offending scene was discussed in detail, then David delivered his thunderbolt. 'Well, Bobby,' he said, 'you may be right, but if you're not, we stand to lose a lot of money. We're walking into a brick wall here. You know, if *The Mission* only takes as much as *your last five films combined*, we'll lose a lot of money.'

'Hey, what do you mean?' De Niro growled.

'Just what I say. You know them as well as I do. *Falling in Love, True Confessions, King of Comedy, Once upon a Time –*'

'What are you saying?'

'I'm saying that the real danger here is that what you've got is a pattern of films where you're quite wonderful, but somehow the film doesn't become the sum of its parts. They've been turned into De Niro *vehicles*. That's why we've got to make sure you fit perfectly in this picture with the overall.'

'Mmm. I'll have to think about that.'

Although the discussion had not been acrimonious, the people around them could feel the crackling tension as the discussion took place. There were no explosions, although there could have been. The rest of the dinner seemed to pass without a return to the topic, with the star and his producer seeming to relax together. The scene was shot as written.

The gamble David had taken had paid off, the consummate artist that De Niro undoubtedly is having been faced by a persuasive argument he was genuinely unable to ignore. As David had stressed from the beginning, if *The Mission* was not a team effort, it was nothing. Still, he had pushed the point to the very edge, the 'face-off', as Iain Smith calls it, of which he is truly a master.

Jeremy Irons acknowledged it had taken some time for him and De Niro to come together on a personal basis. 'When we started the film, Bob was doing some of the early scenes as the slave-trader and working very hard on his relationship with his brother, and I was preparing with Daniel Berrigan, a campaigning American Jesuit who also played a Jesuit in the movie, therefore it didn't seem to be useful to fraternize very much during these first few weeks. Then, during the area of the film where he starts to become a Jesuit, we got to know each other much better. He's a very shy man, and takes a lot of getting to know, so I suppose our off-scene relationship mirrored our on-scene one. For me, it was a very happy shoot. I always find that filming can be a little testing at times, but when you're in such magnificent locations, it's a great spur to your work. I think people like David Puttnam and Iain Smith had a much rougher time, but kept us guarded from it. One was aware that they were having enormous problems sometimes, that things were harder than we actors were allowed to see.'

The 'enormous problems' which Irons sensed behind the scenes were only too real, and genuinely enormous. David was livid when the financial problems generated by Goldcrest's other commitments began to manifest themselves in the most awful way imaginable in Colombia, with funds failing to materialize in time to keep *The Mission*'s large unit going.

'In Thailand with *The Killing Fields*, we were able to lean on a sort of infrastructure that already existed,' says David, 'while in Colombia, there was absolutely nothing. Everything was shipped in from Europe, down to the last sandwich. When it comes to the whole issue of what happened at Goldcrest, there are two things that I still resent. One is that they didn't share with me either the initial problems or the true gravity of the situation, and I was supposed to be a director of the company! That's one thing when you're working round the corner, but when you're working in Colombia and paying a lot of people weekly wages, you cannot mess around with Friday night's cheque. It's not negotiable. I think on more than one occasion we weren't given sufficient opportunity to cover ourselves in ways that we could have prudently organized. That still hurts me. We were given a good deal of unnecessary anxiety because of lack of information and candour.'

With Roland hospitalized for four days, suffering from dehydration,

David was convinced his illness came about when he tried to share the financial pressures his producer was under. Old friendships were put under terminal strain as word filtered through to this difficult location about the apparent extravagances being practised on the far less vulnerable set of *Revolution* back in Britain, and the subsequent cash drain on Goldcrest. This in turn created enormous additional pressure on David and his team thousands of miles away in the stifling heat of the Colombian jungle.

'My resentment,' he declared, 'is that while we caused our director to become quite seriously ill, attempting to conform to the limitations placed on our production, other people were not coping with their crises, not cutting their cloth, not taking responsibility for the seriousness of Goldcrest's financial situation. That's when I got *very* upset indeed. I feel I took it out on someone's health, because another group of people had different priorities. That will always leave me bitter. The break in our friendship came down to the fact that I don't believe Hugh or Irwin Winkler, *Revolution*'s producer, were prepared to take on to their shoulders the compromises and pressures that Roland so magnificently absorbed. That I can never forgive. When our weekly cash flow was arriving late, first of all there was one excuse, then another, then it was the bank's fault, and when it happened for the fourth week I just went berserk. I called Bob Daly at Warners. "How do you feel about advancing money here direct instead of sending it all on to Goldcrest when the film's delivered? Can you advance $200,000? I need some cash – we're using a lot of extras and we have to pay cash." He said, "That's fine, but I have to tell Goldcrest what I'm doing." I said, "Fine, you tell them, but I *need* the money."

'Next thing I have James Lee on the phone shouting and carrying on. It wasn't up to me to get money paid direct. I said, "OK, *you* pay us the money." And only then did it all start to emerge, confirming the stories we'd been hearing. The overrun on *Revolution* and *Absolute Beginners* was killing them. So my argument was, *Revolution* was shooting in *Devon*, *we're* in fucking Cartagena, you *can't* mess around with our cash flow. And that's where it got *very* ugly. In a situation like that I'm probably not at my most tactful. It was *dangerous*, what they were doing was positively *dangerous*. At one point the Colombian authorities threatened to hold Iain Smith hostage until the money came through. I mean, they don't screw around out there. It's not like sitting in High Wycombe. Goldcrest misled us for three solid weeks.'

In addition to this peril, Iain Smith had to grapple with the realities of modern-day Colombia. 'We made the film in *spite* of the Colombians,' he asserted. 'They don't have any sense of their endemic history and they don't have a work ethic. The cost of everything was largely influenced by the United States, and also by the main export, which happens to be cocaine. At the same time, Colombia is one of the kidnapping centres of the world, so I was very concerned about security for the crew.' The 'cocaine capos', it seemed, had just announced that because of the U S Drug Enforcement Agency patrolling the coast for traffickers, they would kill any Americans they found in Colombia – a big worry with Robert De Niro in the film. Iain Smith managed to enlist the help of the Colombian secret service, who provided the unit with bodyguards to protect the crew, but specifically De Niro, for it would have created a major international incident had he been kidnapped, or had any attempt been made on his life.

Uberto Pasolini was another witness to the jungle traumas on *The Mission*. An Italian in his early thirties, tall, slightly manic, sandy-haired and with a penchant for camelhair sweaters, Uberto had been introduced to David by the late Ascanio Branca of 20th Century Fox in 1983. Uberto wanted to break out of the family investment-banking business and get into films, David was told, in an almost non-stop half-hour verbal torrent. At the end of it, David said to the startled Uberto, 'You don't know what you're talking about. And you talk far too much. If you want to learn something about making movies, I'm making a film in Thailand soon. If you get yourself there, we'll find something for you.' Uberto promptly bought a ticket and has worked with David ever since. When he eventually breaks away to produce on his own, Uberto will take with him memories of *The Mission* and its high and low points.

'During Roland's illness,' he recalls, 'David spent those days trying to convince the insurance people that the film would still finish on budget, so that they would make good on the stoppage-time suffered. Like most insurance companies, they were difficult and suspicious, but listened to David's promise that the schedule would continue to be adhered to. With Roland back, we were shooting a scene in the interior of a church, with two galleries upstairs, one looking east, one looking west. The director of photography picked one of them to start the day's shoot of a scene between Bobby De Niro and Ray McInally. Neither the director, nor the director of photography, nor the first assistant, focused on the fact there was a window up there and that the light was going to change, therefore they should have shot everything that looked toward that window first, then turned around and shot all the interior of the church, where the light could be balanced by artificial light.

'At 2 pm, three hours before sundown, we were stuck. Everything

had been shot with the window behind us, then the director of photography turned around and said, "Oh, I can't shoot any more today.
There's a window up there and the sun's going." A call went up to
the office to David that we were wrapping early and that the scene
had not been completed. He went bananas. We all had walkie-talkies
and were told to switch them to channel 3. When we did, we had to
listen to David screaming at us for a full 10 minutes. He was really
terribly upset. Unprofessionalism. Hadn't thought it through. His ass
on the line with Warners and the insurance people. And we were
letting both him and ourselves down. Oh, my God!

'Another day it rained heavily. The location was quite far from our
hotel and could only be reached by walking, and supposedly with some
vehicles provided by the army. David arrived and saw everyone getting
stuck in this muddy road and not getting through fast enough. While
we were shooting the scene, he took the initiative and ordered an
enormous truckload of chips to scatter on the track. He shouldn't have
– it wasn't his job, and he didn't tell anybody. On the way back, the first
truck got stuck and nothing else could get past. We got back hours late,
utterly exhausted – David's "good idea" had made things *more* difficult, not less. What can you do? Some you win, some you don't!'

There are those who maintain that David Puttnam is a maverick in
the British Film Industry, working alone with scant regard for other
producers' well-being. Don Boyd knows differently.

While working on *Gossip* in 1982 – Don had gone back from
producing to his first love, directing – the project, which was fully
financed ('but by a bunch of fraudulent crooks,' says Don), teetered
on the verge of collapse. There was no rush to help from any quarter.

'I'm in a major mess here,' he told David, 'and I don't know what
to do.'

David tried his best to help, but the project sank despite all his
efforts. 'He did everything in his power to re-finance it,' Don recalls,
'including his specific vote at the NFFC to fund the film. The
agreement was to view the footage, but appallingly only one person
turned up to see it. David saw it all. 'Don, it's terrific,' he told me. He
then did his best to provide employment for a lot of people thrown
out of work by the film's collapse.

'For the next three years I was out of work. I told David I was
going to give it all up and become a wedding photographer in the
north of Scotland or somewhere. "Don, we've all been there," he said
– I don't think he meant the north of Scotland – "don't be silly. You're
a producer and you're great at it. You mustn't stop trying."

'In 1985 he agreed to be part of a four-picture agreement with Virgin I set up. One of the films was to be produced by me, one by David, one by Jeremy Thomas and one by Michael Hamlyn. I had it all set up with Virgin and independent money; they were all to be done with French co-producers on very low budgets. David's project, *Real Class*, was a football script to be personally produced by him for my Boyds Co. There was no money whatever in it for David, hardly a penny.

'As soon as the deal was announced, all the people who'd lost money on *Gossip* came back to me, including the two unions, ACTT and Equity. "No, Don, you can't work until you come to an arrangement with us to pay the people off who lost out over *Gossip*." I was heartbroken and scandalized by the attitude of many people in the business, who were most unhelpful. In desperation I rang David in Colombia. I hated doing it because I knew he was having terrible problems of his own on *The Mission*. "David, you're the only person I can think of who can help me here," I told him. "I think the ACTT may come out on my side in the end, but Equity are an impossible stumbling block."

'He sent me a telex, with a copy to the two unions, which read, "I envy your determination. The situation faced by the British Film Industry does not allow for the luxury of recriminatory vengeance, it requires every ounce of goodwill and positivism if it is to survive in the coming year. I hope very much that you are able to urge the Equity members, many of whom I regard as friends and all of whom I regard as colleagues, to see your present position in that light. All the luck in the world with your appeal, David."

'A further telex was despatched to Equity itself. "I've been in this position myself," David wrote. "If I were to be in it again, would you penalise me in this way?" It was such a selfless thing for him to do, and it changed the atmosphere completely. The four-film project itself didn't get off the ground, but I was back in the movie business.'

Within two years Don was indeed back on his feet, with Derek Jarman's *The Last of England* and the multi-segmented *Aria* under his belt. With this background of real affection and gratitude, Don would still feel obliged to become one of David's most vocal critics in the future. Possibly this tells us more about David than it does Don – for, infuriatingly, David can be both far better *and* much worse than he is generally given credit for.

The arrival of the last of Goldcrest's money just before the end of *The Mission*'s shooting brought intense relief, since the authorities had announced their intention of holding Iain Smith hostage if all bills were not settled before the unit's departure. The Waunanas received $80,000 for their work on the film against De Niro's $2 million – and the Indians were also allocated a small percentage of any profits that might emerge. In addition, and at David's behest, Goldcrest and Warner made a substantial contribution to a fund to buy agricultural equipment and finance an education and health programme. 'Having worked with them, we now feel a certain responsibility for their fate,' said David.

Before the difficulties had begun, David had invited Patsy out to the location in the early days of filming to see the breath-taking falls where much of the picture was being shot. Patsy makes it a point never to attend the shooting of any of her husband's films ('That's *his* province'), but David was especially persuasive and finally coaxed her to fly out to Colombia for a few days. He kidded her constantly about the time she was spending on Kingsmead Mill, their country house. 'I can make three films, *Local Hero*, *Killing Fields*, and *Cal*, now I'm on *The Mission*, and you're *still* toiling away on your production,' he laughed.

The unit was taking a break as Iain Smith showed Patsy around, climbing high up on the scaffolding built round the falls. 'We were making our way along all these platforms they had built,' says Patsy, 'and I was marvelling at the incredible beauty, when I spotted a ragged, bearded figure on the rocks below, running and jumping around in his bare feet. "Who on earth's that?" I asked Iain. "It's Bobby De Niro," he replied. "He's got to do that in his scene tomorrow." I winced. "But his *feet* –"

"I know," said Iain.'

This brought it home to Patsy what De Niro is all about, as she glimpsed the other side of the man, the man the cameras never see. 'Everyone talked about how he *never* stopped working, and was *always* totally in character and just worked, worked, *worked*. No wonder David had such an enormous respect for him, although the two had hardly had a conversation at all for the first month after their hotel encounter. That's a typical Puttnam manoeuvre. That's what he does. Bobby is, I think, a man who desperately wants to be loved. He's very shy and insecure. He truly does hate the star system. I mean, most times limousines would be there waiting for him in London and he'd happily have caught the bus. He'd rather do it that way – he'd rather go incognito. That's Bobby – he's a strange, strange guy, but because he loves films so much and cares about his work, when he sees it in others he respects that, which is why in the end they got on so well.

They might have disagreed on certain things, but both of them always respected one another for what they were. He came off the film saying to David and Roland, "Anything you ever want me to do again, I'll be in it." '

Kingsmead Mill had reminded Patsy from the start of a French country house, from the charming original mill-house itself, to the two connected cottages, enormous front lawns and big iron gates. The Bristol Avon divides so that half flows under the mill-house, originally to grind flour, while the other half flows into the mill pond before the river rejoins and makes its way downstream. Part 17th century, part 18th century, the 16-acre estate they had bought now boasts an orchard, a walled garden, a vegetable garden, an Elizabethan knot garden and a laburnum grove and stone courtyard at the back of the house. With David's support, ('I'll make the films, you get Kingsmead sorted out'), Patsy set about restoring the mill to something that would survive a few hundred more years. Their plans also included the acquisition of several surrounding fields, for originally the mill-house had been complete with a 40-acre estate, and it was this proportion relationship between house and land that they wished to recreate. Meanwhile, discussions went on about the renovation of the house and cottages.

A series of builders were interviewed before Patsy took on some local people from Stroud. For the first time in their lives they were not confronted with a client demanding to know how quickly a job could be undertaken, but how well it could be done. Patsy's keynote was simple – the workmanship had to be fully up to the best of the old standards. Materials were a problem, but if it meant waiting for an old barn somewhere to fall down before they could get their hands on some of the magnificent old Tetbury roof tiles they required, then so be it.

The workmen found they were dealing with someone obsessed with getting every single detail correct, and responded accordingly. Endless conferences followed, on such subjects as how to get double-glazing installed without destroying the fenestration that would take the correct period-look away.

With joiners working away inside, builders swarming over the out-side and an estate manager appointed, Patsy saw she was going way over budget. 'I'd have been fired by any producer,' she happily admits. With Debbie and Loyd's marriage looming up – despite the timing of his approach to her father! – David's availability became crucial. Although still out in Colombia, he arranged to fly back, arriving the night before the wedding, while Sandy Lieberson took his place for a few days.

Patsy chose the occasion to unveil Kingsmead Mill, which looked magnificent. She had worked another miracle, although she declared to everyone's astonishment that she hadn't finished yet. There was a bridge to be built over the Avon ('Over the *Avon? All* of it?' David choked). Then there was the mill pond to be stocked, new trees planted, a nature reserve and bird sanctuary to be built. Kingsmead made a truly splendid setting for the happy couple's wedding reception.

Lynda Myles never did manage to get one of her romantic projects past the starting gate. She concentrated instead on *Defence of the Realm*. 'When I read the first draft in 1983 by Marcel Stellman, I thought it was amazing and desperately wanted to do it,' she says. 'Warners didn't want it, nor did Goldcrest and it took two years to get the money. We had half the budget from the NFFC and we finally got the rest of the money from Rank. A large factor was David's name. He had to go and work on *The Mission* and he suggested I co-produced *Defence of the Realm* with Robin Douet, who had done production work on a number of *First Loves* as well as *Local Hero* and *The Killing Fields*. David was tremendously supportive. He saw rushes every day for the first two weeks and then he went off to Colombia where we still sent rushes out on video.'

Lynda and Robin worked on the movie – typically green-lighted by Rank and the NFFC only four weeks before the start of shooting – during March, April and May 1985, then struggled to get a preview cut ready for July when David would be back for a few days for his daughter's wedding. 'I don't think I'll ever make a movie quite like that again,' says Lynda, 'because it was a first proper feature for the director, David Drury, my first feature and Gabriel Byrne's first as a leading actor. We were all totally committed. Then the preview turned out to be one of the most depressing nights of my life.'

'We showed the film to a test audience at Reading,' says Robin Douet, 'one of the most horrendous experiences I've ever known. It had been a rush to get it ready and it was only half done, no music track had been added. When I arrived at the cinema with my wife the audience was queueing up outside and they were all kids! I couldn't believe it – it was meant to be an average cinema audience. Out of about 500 people there were only about 30 adults and since it was certainly not a kids' story, they hated it. They sat there laughing and chattering, going in and out, and the worst thing was at the back of the hall we had representatives from the Rank Organization. After the screening they just got up in a body and walked out. In the morning they were seriously talking about halting everything. David stepped in and pointed out that it had been totally the wrong audience, that two or three days' extra shooting would make all the difference. Thank God he got them to agree.'

Although the film was well received on its release in November 1985, the edge was taken off its success by the closure of Enigma and the end it signalled of so many nurtured hopes and dreams.

Regardless of how firmly-based David and Alan Parker's friendship may be seen, it is not founded on a mutual admiration of each other's product, except in fairly isolated instances. Their separate views on *Midnight Express* are well known, less so how they view their other efforts over the years. 'I don't think I've ever liked anything he's done,' says Alan with an almost perfectly straight face, 'and he certainly hasn't liked anything I've done, but that's why its a healthy relationship. I remember once he attended the Cannes showing of *Pink Floyd – The Wall*. We had the sound turned up so loud there were bits of plaster falling off the ceiling. He left immediately afterwards and didn't talk to me for days! We've still never discussed it. We can rely on one another to hate the other person's work, but that's good.'

Having got that off his chest, Alan admits, 'I *did* like *Local Hero* very much. I like Bill Forsyth. It didn't completely work as a film, but the parts that are Bill's work.' (That chuckle again.) 'Bill's got this incredible humanity – you even like his villains – because he really loves people.

'*The Killing Fields* is David's best film, I think, a terrific, very substantial film, the only film of his I've liked without any criticism, except for the John Lennon error, a *terrible* idea. Come to that, most of his ideas *are* terrible. On the other hand two out of ten are brilliant and these are the ones you have to look out for. *Chariots?* Extremely well made, but a little too pompous and self-righteous, which is the theme of all his work, a theme that many people admire.

'The *First Loves* were not films he was absolutely in control of, he was dissipating his energies by getting involved in them, and a lot of them turned out to be mediocre. It was a way of discovering new writers and directors and he always had more ideas than he could cope with at any one time.

'He's an optimist, David would say, and I'm a pessimist. He wanted to make films which will show how human beings can aspire to being better, while I try to find the things that are wrong by human psyche, and explore what's rotten with the world in order to make it better. In his life he's tended to become more pompous and self-righteous because he's gone evangelical. I much prefer the spiv over Jesus!'

Fifty years earlier – unknown to either David or Alan – Columbia had produced a film with virtually the same title as their joint epic. It was advertised as the third-in-a-row hit for actress Elaine Hammerstein, following her success in *One Glorious Night* and *The Foolish Virgin*:

A Hundred Per Cent Picture
Loudly Proclaimed By The Critics
THE MIDNIGHT EXPRESS
The Story Of A Railroad Man
Who Would Not Be Sidetracked!

Nothing really changes, does it?

Chapter 19

Pseudo-Masochism

Despite the undoubted millionaire status of Jerry Perenchio and Norman Lear, Jake Eberts discovered with his new bosses at Embassy never to confuse personal wealth with money available for movies. He spent a year on the road on the toughest fund-raising operation he had ever faced, a depressing experience after his successes in Britain. There were so many routes for US investors wishing to dabble in movies, such as simply to buy Coca-Cola shares if they wanted a piece of Columbia Pictures, or Gulf and Western for a stake in Paramount. Jake also found that the hits he was associated with, such as *Chariots of Fire* and *Gandhi*, were considered small beer in comparison to the *Star Wars*, *Indiana Jones* and *Tootsie*-scale hits investors were more interested in.

'It was probably the worst year of my life, a discouraging experience,' says Jake. From being the guiding light behind Goldcrest, the great white hope of the British Film Industry, he found himself in the invidious position of fund manager for American millionaires unprepared to risk any of their personal fortune. In February 1985 matters came further unstuck when Perenchio and Lear announced their intention of selling Embassy. To dress the company up before the sale, they intended to appoint a studio head. Jake could see there was no place for him in the new set-up, and negotiated a settlement. Shortly after he left Embassy, the company was sold to Coca-Cola.

Back in Britain Jake began to hear rumours about Goldcrest and their difficulties, but was too busy setting up his own new company, Allied Filmmakers, to pay too much attention. With Allied he was going back to the first principles he had initiated at Goldcrest, a pure development financing operation. Since this was in place when news of Sandy Lieberson's imminent departure from Goldcrest came to his attention, Jake immediately proposed to James Lee that Allied take over Goldcrest's development function – and for a fraction of its running cost. Lee was not prepared to consider this, clearly seeing himself as taking over the production reins, following Sandy's departure.

By June 1985, anxiety being expressed by the Goldcrest board came into the open. Their concern over the commitment to finance *Revolution*, *Absolute Beginners* and *The Mission* all at the same time came to a head with doubts that a co-financier in Europe for *Revolution* would come up with his share of the cash for the film, now seriously over budget. When their worst fears were confirmed, Goldcrest had to replace their ex-partner's share of the budget, and assume total responsibility for the over-runs. The drain on the company's resources began to reach horrendous proportions.

With his offer of help turned down, Jake set about Allied's investment portfolio on his own. The *Emerald Forest* had proved to be a moderate success when released by Embassy and Jake eagerly helped John Boorman's new endeavour, *Hope and Glory*, get off the ground, despite a false start when an intended purchaser of Embassy, André Blay, who had agreed to finance the film after acquiring Embassy, was pipped at the post by Coca-Cola. With typical resourcefulness, Jake managed to get the project financed by Coca-Cola itself, who agreed with him that they were honour bound to do so since that had been part of the André Blay deal. In addition Jake was involved with seed funding for *The Name of the Rose* and Dickie Attenborough's Biko project, *Asking for Trouble*, later redubbed *Cry Freedom*. In a deal similar to David's, Jake's overheads were covered by Warners, in return for first refusal. Incredibly, as David had already found, Warners turned down every single project for 100 per cent funding. *Hope and Glory* eventually went to Columbia very much through David's later good offices, *Name of the Rose* to 20th Century Fox and *Cry Freedom* ended up at Universal. With his relatively small, but crucial seed money investment in these movies, Jake had his cash refunded on the first day of shooting and retained a profit participation in the pictures. Life was beginning to look good again after his chastening experience at Embassy.

While spending some time at his farm in Quebec, he received a call from Michael Stoddart at Goldcrest. 'Look, we've got ourselves in a terrible mess. Would you be prepared to come back?' was the message. Jake replied that he had no wish to be the cause of James Lee's departure, but that if the board had decided to get rid of James in any case, they could talk again when this was accomplished. Back in England a few weeks later, Jake received his usual invitation to attend a lunch given by Australian Kerry Packer's Channel 9 at Wimbledon. All the Goldcrest people were at the table reserved for them, except James Lee, who was conspicuous by his absence. Although one of the board passed it off as a financial problem back at the office that had to be dealt with, Jake realized something fairly dramatic must be going on to make Lee miss the opportunity of meeting one of his major customers. When Michael Stoddart phoned soon after, he explained that James had proposed himself as production head following Sandy's departure, as well as wishing to remain chief executive and chairman. The board had found that unacceptable and in as elegant a way as they could, had made it clear that James had to go.

Knee-deep in problems of his own in Colombia, David was not involved in any of Goldcrest's discussions with Jake, who agreed by mid-July to take over again, negotiating a contract with Allied Film-makers for his services. Jake was led to understand there was nothing more than an interim financial problem at the company, basically brought about by having three expensive films made at the same time. Together with the abdication of the outside investment from *Revolution* and the budget overruns on *Revolution* and *Absolute Beginners*, the whole thing had been further exacerbated by the change in the value of the dollar. Even though the company was technically close to bankruptcy, he saw that the situation could quickly change if any of the movies turned out to be hefty revenue-earners. An anxious viewing of whatever footage he could assemble of Goldcrest's three major projects was promptly arranged.

Jake felt *The Mission* had a chance of being a very good film, but doubted it would recoup its £17 million cost. Warner had only put up $5 million to acquire it for the States, since Goldcrest had decided to go for broke, accepting less in advance in return for a bigger slice of the hoped-for US take.

Jake had no idea how *Revolution* would play and found *Absolute Beginners* a total disaster. He asked Alan Marshall to supervise the completion of the picture and credits him for whatever remnants finally emerged. The budget for this venture ended up at £8.6 million, against an advance from Orion Pictures for the States of only $2.5 million.

There was tremendous pressure to get *Revolution* out in time for the year-end and the Oscar nominations, and Jake was in favour of rushing post-production to make the deadline. 'I didn't see much value in hanging around and recutting it,' he admits. 'There was no way months of post-production was going to make a change in that film. Those who are being blamed now for the film ending up so terrible in turn blamed me for having pushed so hard to get the picture finished. My answer's pretty simple: it's inherently *uncommercial*. I actually don't think it was a terrible picture; I think there are some glorious scenes in it and I think Hugh Hudson's an extremely talented director.'

Hugh Hudson had felt aggrieved from the beginning of the *Revolu-*

tion story. 'Sandy Lieberson refused me a script-writer at the beginning of the film, then gave me one when the film started, when it was too late. I should have known better than to start it when I did, but I was told the film wouldn't be made unless I was in production by March. Then there was the need to get it out. At that point, to give him his due, Sandy said to wait another three months. He was right – wrong at the beginning, but right at the end. The irony is that when Warners saw the film, Bob Daly and Terry Semel thought it was wonderful. They embraced and kissed me. "Hugh, this is the best thing you've ever done, it's wonderful," they told me.'

A few weeks after Warners had screened the movie, Jake and Hugh Hudson were flown out by Concorde to attend the first audience preview. There was a limousine at the Concorde exit, then a helicopter to whisk them over to New Jersey and the theatre. Everything seemed to go well during the screening, with Semel and Daly in attendance, together with Mike Ovitz, head of the powerful Creative Artists Agency (CAA). Only afterwards when adverse comments came in, did everyone realize there was a very real and deep-seated problem. With only three weeks to go before the opening in December 1985, there was time to make only a few cosmetic changes. Most people acknowledged at this stage the film was not going to be a blockbuster, but few were prepared for the savagery of the reviews, and the subsequent public indifference. It came as a resounding shock when the £19-million production was taken off after an embarrassingly brief run with just over one-third of a million dollars in the US box office. Any hopes Goldcrest might have entertained of a cash bonanza that would save the day were well and truly dashed.

Attention focused more than ever on *The Mission*, placing a crushing responsibility on David and his team, still deep in the lengthy post-production process. 'If one swallow doesn't make a summer,' David asked, 'then why should a single flop be held to wreck an industry? Is it really possible that a resurgence of British film has been dealt a mortal blow by the critical and box-office failure of *Revolution*?'

Despite the fact that David had personally produced *The Mission*, at Warners and Goldcrest's insistence, Fernando Ghia dug his heels in and asserted that David should retain executive producer credit only, with himself listed as the film's sole producer. Without David's knowledge, Robert De Niro, Roland Joffe and Jeremy Irons got together and laid down their own ultimatum – that a co-production credit be applied. 'We accept David has to share credit with Ghia,' they told Warners, 'but if he doesn't get that, we want our own credits taken off the film. The whole thing will be a lie.' Terry Semel saw that the billing was promptly altered to 'co-produced by Fernando Ghia and David Puttnam', but only over Ghia's loud protests.

David is philosophical about the affair.'The film industry has a place for its Ghias as well as its Puttnams,' he shrugs. 'He's got very good literary taste, but frankly I don't think he could organize a piss-up in a brewery, and I've told him this many times. In British terms he has no management skills, which in turn breeds a resentment in him. We were getting on with making the picture and he couldn't stand to see what he regarded as his film being made without him. He knows that, and of course it caused tremendous stress.'

A colleague of Ghia defends his fellow countryman: 'This was to be the film of Fernando's life,' he says. 'Everybody wanted to buy him out, but he said no, this is mine, they can't buy me out, I've got all the aces – and for a while Goldcrest played along with this. He was a lonely figure, entering into an already constructed team of Puttnam, Joffe and Smith, who had already worked together on *The Killing Fields*. He didn't mould himself into areas he could have helped in; there were silly disagreements about where his office was to be in London, which hotel he would stay in, things like that. He played his role wrong, but David does not understand the Italian modus oper-andi. Try putting an Englishman among Italians! Ghia recommended Sabatini to do the costumes, which were done in Italy entirely self-sufficiently. And he helped to get Morricone. If Ghia makes a movie on his own, he would make it work. He and David were simply two people at a certain stage demanding space – and there was simply not room enough for both of them. David – being David – prevailed.'

Producer Don Boyd was shocked and disappointed at David's distancing stand over Goldcrest's difficulties. 'He and Dickie Attenborough were, after all, the only experienced film-makers on the Goldcrest board. How can they avoid responsibility? *Revolution* was started without a completion guarantor in place. On *Absolute Beginners* the production team simply weren't properly qualified. On his own *he* would never have gone ahead. A large proportion of the blame for Goldcrest's failure must go to David, Dickie Attenborough and the rest of them. What appalled me also, and appalled Hugh Hudson, was when *Revolution* failed, and all the argy-bargy about Hugh's overspending and wanton behaviour, David washed his hands of it all and blamed Hugh and the management of Goldcrest! *This* was a man who was on the board and partly responsible for the company being able to raise money. I couldn't believe it. I thought it was sheer technical hypocrisy. And I didn't just read about his views, I heard him say it privately and publicly. I know that he read *Revolution*'s script, although he denies it. He must have forgotten. And as a director of Goldcrest, if he didn't read it, *why* didn't he? I'll bet there's not a $25-million project that goes forward at Paramount or Universal without proper script approval.

'And at this point there was so much publicity about David's vital role in the renaissance of British cinema – the one big investment opportunity we've had in Britain for 25 years. I wonder if David's ever addressed himself to that. I was tearing my hair out watching it happen – from my position of being down-and-out and having made the same mistakes myself with much more modest funding. It was a complete mess-up.

'When he began to promote *The Mission*, he profited enormously from the high profile he had. He brilliantly manipulated – he's the most brilliant self-publicist I've ever come across. He does it so innocently, but it's so calculated, including the way he appears on television with his slightly self-deprecating manner – it's genius. It's so good, in fact, I occasionally succumb to copying it on occasions.'

Did David address himself to Goldcrest's predicament? '*I* didn't let them down,' he maintains. 'All *my* films came in on budget. James Lee reckoned there was an American investor coming in. I told him he wouldn't. I met the financier in Los Angeles, had breakfast with him, then phoned James and told him it wouldn't happen. I wrote to James at one point in early 1985, "You can't afford *Revolution* and *The Mission* in the same year. I am in an impossible position, sitting here with two hats. It's my job to do everything I can to get *The Mission* off the ground, then I have to tell you as director of Goldcrest that in my opinion you can't afford to make both films. I find it untenable." Then I came back from the States to find not only *The Mission*, but *Absolute Beginners* given the go-ahead – and with no tangible change to the cash flow. As late as May 1985, I was still telling James we could pull out of *The Mission*. It would have meant an $800,000 write-off, but it could have been done. And don't forget my remit was not to oppose other film-makers' films. Dickie and I fought tooth and nail within that constriction.'

By January 1986 David found himself appointed a trustee of the Tate Gallery, the *Daily Telegraph* rationalizing that the reason for his unusual choice was that he represented the kind of specialized, high-risk man much favoured by Prime Minister Thatcher. Hot on the heels of this came his appointment as president of the Council for the

290 ENIGMA: DAVID PUTTNAM

Preservation of Rural England (CPRE). *The Times* commented, 'Puttnam's appointment may seem incongruous, but arises from a long-
standing interest in the countryside.' One of David's colleagues found
this a mite difficult to swallow. 'Doesn't David's interest in country
matters simply date from his acquisition of a house in the country?'
was the question he disingenuously asked. When Lynda Smith departed to start a family (and she did not go empty-handed, having
been given, like many of David's team on *Chariots of Fire*, a 1 per cent
profit share in the film that yielded her over £100,000), she was
eventually succeeded by Valerie Kemp, who had worked at Goldcrest
with James Lee.

Within weeks David was in action on CPRE's behalf, delivering a
tersely-worded letter to Margaret Thatcher and the three other Party
leaders, outlining his own agenda for the conservation debate and
indicating he would be a far from tame president. Anyone who knew
David's style had already taken this for granted.

David was offered a fellowship for the 1986/87 year in Harvard's
philosophy school, under Professor Stanley Cavell, and was set to
attend in September 1986. The intention was that he would give
eight lectures as a university-visiting artist, and spend one afternoon a
week with the other six Kennedy Fellows.

'If film-makers set the moral agenda, then maybe we aren't clever
enough to deal with that,' he said, appearing to question once again
his qualifications to make films with a responsible message for a
world-wide audience. 'It does seem to me that as someone who instigates
and is at the sharp end of movie production, to expose myself to
different forms of philosophy might well influence my work and then
might be the beginning of something more. It's literally learning to
ask myself the right questions.' Had the cynics been wrong?

David was concerned to learn that Thorn-EMI's Screen Entertainment Division (TESE) was for sale, the assets including their film
library, Elstree studios and the ABC cinema circuit. When the US
Cannon group, headed by Menahem Golan and Yoram Globus, emerged with the Rank Organisation as the front runners, his concern
grew. Cannon already owned the Classic and Star circuits, and their
acquisition of ABC would mean their sharing the vast bulk of cinema
exhibition with Rank. David's other objection to Cannon was their
determinedly down market product and exploitative image, the very
opposite of the kind of film-making he stood for. 'I am an appalled
onlooker,' he declared. 'This is British film year and the legs are being
kicked away from under it.' Whereas Thorn-EMI had made a
£500,000 commitment to British film year, no money whatever had

been received from Cannon, he pointed out. 'It is run,' David declared disdainfully, 'by two guys who spend their lives on planes.'

Nor was Rank exempted from his wrath, as he forecast that if their bid succeeded, they would have no need of Elstree studios, due to their ownership of Pinewood, which would jeopardise the future of one of Britain's main studios.

He was unprepared for the accusations of racism that came from the Cannon side, citing 'prejudice, jealousy and misinformation', truly ironic in view of David's pride in what Terence Donovan wryly calls 'his Jewish streak, the side of him that produces all that angst'.

'Never mind the funny names, David Puttnam,' blasted one of Cannon's acolytes. 'Golam and Globus have got the drive and success in management we sorely need over here.' There were many who doubted the truth of this, viewing the group as an over-leveraged house of cards kept from tumbling down only by numerous trips to the public well, astronomical bank borrowings and supremely optimistic forecasts of film revenue. The entire operation was funded by a huge mountain of debt and unrecognized costs that would rebound on the company within a year – not, however, before they had been allowed to swallow T E S E.

Golan and Globus were taken aback at the vehemence of the British reaction to their bid and invited David to a working breakfast in an effort to mend fences. Globus implied after the meeting that David had seen their point of view, but David was not to be silenced for long. 'I make movies which take a position which is essentially humanist,' he declared. 'It's quite clear to me that the majority of Cannon's work in the past has been work which appealed to the lowest common denominator in the audience.'

One assurance that David received from Globus at the breakfast was that Cannon's apparent refusal to contribute £2000 to the National Film School had been a misunderstanding. When the money still did not appear, David asked, 'How am I supposed to believe these are benign buccaneers? I *have* to be sceptical.' Globus admitted the money still had not been handed over at that point, but replied, side-stepping the principal involved, 'To pick on an issue involving £2000 is just silly.'

It began to look for a while as if a management buy-out might prevail, pipping both Cannon and Rank at the post, as Thorn-E M I agreed to give Gary Dartnall and his team some time to get their funds in place, with the help of their Australian backer, Alan Bond. 'I was worried about aspects of the deal anyway,' Golan claimed, 'and I don't think this is the end of the story either.'

Golan was correct, but later fears that the TESE management buy-out had run into trouble were temporarily put at rest when Alan Bond declared he would fund any shortfall the team experienced. 'We are pleased to have this opportunity to invest in the British Film Industry,' he stoutly maintained. Then on 25 April 1986 he bought TESE for £125 million before promptly selling it outright to the Cannon group one week later for £175 million. It seemed that Dartnall had departed the management team leaving Bond high-and-dry with a company too big for him to handle. He found Cannon eagerly waiting in the wings determined to get TESE at any price. Golan and Globus were thus installed as the new heads of the British Film Industry, controlling 39 per cent of the total UK screens to Rank's 25 per cent. Regarding the possibility of a reference to the Monopolies and Mergers Commission, Golan blithely referred to the settlement as 'a done deal'.

David was distraught, for his had been almost the sole voice raised against Cannon's ownership. He had other things on his mind, however, the most important of which was *The Mission* and the responsibility which now centred around the movie. With the failure at the box-office of *Absolute Beginners*, despite one of the most expensively-hyped openings in UK cinema history, it was now indeed all down to Goldcrest's third big throw of the dice. With five more weeks of post-production still to be completed, David decided to take an incredible gamble with the film and accept an invitation to show it in competition at the Cannes Film Festival in May 1986. While appreciating the tremendous prestige an award at Cannes would bring, he was equally aware of the reflection it would be for the picture in the event of its failing to win a prize. And could the film even be ready for showing in Cannes in its unfinished state?

The ubiquitous Cannon dominated the Cannes Film Festival, having three films entered for the coveted Palme d'Or, in direct competition with *The Mission*. The event was dubbed the 'Cannon Film Festival' by many journalists, in view of the immense Cannon presence, including 'Cannon – the Company of the Future' slogans which were splashed everywhere. It seemed that the company was making a serious effort to shake off its former schlock image, for their three movies represented an impressive line-up: they were Franco Zeffirelli's *Otello*, Robert Altman's *Fool for Love* and Andrei Konchalovsky's *Runaway Train*. The stage was set for a real David versus Goliath contest, as hostilities were resumed by Golan, flush with the success of his 'done deal'.

'I think the British film industry were spitting in their own bowl of soup by trying to keep us out,' he declared, 'but now they have all changed their minds, except Mr Puttnam. He stood up at a meeting of the British Film Producers' Association and said everyone should reject us. He said we didn't back the National Film School, but we're putting up £3 million for new young directors from film schools to make films, a thing Mr Puttnam never did. I think David Puttnam is a very good and talented producer, but he is very stubborn, or maybe he is trying to secure some publicity.'

David resisted the attempts of some of his colleagues to arrange a conciliatory meeting with the Cannon chiefs during the Festival, only too well aware that the gulf between them was too wide to be bridged by a few platitudes.

Against all the odds, what David described as 'the unfinished work-in-progress version of *The Mission*' went on to capture the coveted Palme d'Or from under the noses of the Cannon team, their three entries, and the rest of the very considerable competition. 'My heart pounded and I felt full of horror every time we changed a reel of the film in case it went out of synchronization,' he told a reporter, going on to describe the win as a 'near-miracle'.

Some observers were having none of it, one journalist claiming 'cynical amusement in film circles over the success of the "unfinished" film.' Another declared,'Everyone knows the Cannes rule is that an uncompleted film is ineligible for the competition. In fact, the film the jury saw *was* the completed picture. Calling it a work-in-progress would have been a get-out excuse if the film had fallen flat on its face.'

Bill Rowe, whose last job before *The Mission* for David was as dubbing editor on *The Killing Fields*, but whose association with him goes back to *That'll be the Day*, was not amused by these inferences, having worked night and day to assemble the Cannes version of the movie.

'We did a preview mix first,' Bill recalls, 'to sense if they got things right. Based on that, they had to decide, as with every other movie, if they're going to edit, tighten up or expand, whatever they want to do. Then I got a message they're going to submit it to Cannes double-headed, which means you have two pieces of film, a piece with the soundtrack and a piece with the picture. And you have a synchronization thing of two machines running separately.

'Well, that was a good time to retire, I think, for David's pay-off line was, "And you've got *three days* to do it!" Fortunately, we were into pre-mixing and pre-dubbing, and we made it. It was a lot of fun to do, but having done it, then the adrenalin disappeared and I thought, "Oh, my God, it's got to run at Cannes!" Then they went off, eventually you have to let go of it and you worry then about *where* it's going to be shown, if it's going to *sound* right, if the picture and sound are going to stay in synchronization. I know David felt the same way and so did Roland Joffe, we were a bunch of wrecks.'

So late was the picture in coming out of the labs that David missed the scheduled flight which would have taken him, Roland and Jim Clark to Cannes. A chartered flight had to be quickly organized. 'We ran the film through at 5.30 am with Jim Clark on the morning of the 11 am press screening,' says David, 'this being the only picture as far as I know ever to be run double-headed at Cannes. It stayed in synch, but we only did two screenings instead of the usual three. I felt we just couldn't risk a third.'

Back in England Bill Rowe began to clear up the debris left behind, anything to keep going as he waited on word from the Festival. Finally it came. 'The phone rang and someone said, "We won." And I cried. I really, really cried.' Bill laughs now. 'This rather ruined an image. I mean, my crew tell me I've got to have cardiac arrest to prove I've actually got a heart.'

An even more damaging assertion was still to be levelled by David's critics, this time that the Cannes jury had been bribed to vote for *The Mission*. 'These people are vicious arseholes,' he raged. 'They manufacture the truth that's most convenient for them. When people say things like this, do they realize they are seriously stating that Sydney Pollack and an eminent jury are all actually corrupt? These shibboleths need destroying. It was *anything* but a fiddle. Tarkovsky's *The Sacrifice* was the favourite, but *The Mission* won the Palme d'Or on a 9–2 vote with only Istvan Szabo and Philip French voting against it.'

The controversy surrounding *The Mission*'s passage at Cannes was not ended, as yet another drama unfolded at the presentation of the Palme d'Or. 'I had to *physically* hold Fernando down when Roland went up to collect the prize,' says David. 'He was *screaming* that it was *his* Palme d'Or. He had this conviction that *he* should have collected it. The television cameras were on us and I was trying to pretend it was an affectionate embrace. In truth, I had to physically prevent Fernando from making the biggest arse of himself of all time in front of a million viewers.'

Although buoyed by the news of *The Mission*'s triumph at Cannes, Jake Eberts still did not see the movie as a major revenue earner. Every week he was obliged to issue a new cash-flow report, supervised by an outside director, which often showed the situation at Goldcrest getting worse. The company began to sell everything off – the rights to films, the television library, office space, *anything* that would raise cash and reduce the overhead. Gradually the company staggered to the point where they could just about survive. Then the inevitable search began for a new investor.

'All during that period, David was highly supportive,' says Jake. 'He made every *possible* effort to publicly and privately give us the kind of support we needed. *The Mission* was certainly the reason for even continuing with the holding operation at Goldcrest, because it was clear to us that neither *Revolution* nor *Absolute Beginners* had a chance of even recouping their investment, forget about making money. The problem was the *The Mission* wasn't due to open until later in the year. It was far and away the biggest investment in our portfolio and we just had to hang in there and see what it was going to do. David had a running battle with the press about whether or not the film had gone over budget. That's just the way David is, he's a perfectionist and he kept on getting exercised, quite rightly, about these comments. After all, his whole reputation and his livelihood as a producer, his financial integrity, was at stake. In pounds sterling *The Mission had* stayed with its budget; in dollars of course it had gone up, purely due to the dollar's fluctuating fortunes. The press picked this up, but that was nothing whatsoever to do with David. The problem with *The Mission* was not any budget overrun on the picture itself; it was the basic cost of the picture. It was a very fine movie, but for £17 million *any* picture is going to have trouble recouping its production costs.'

Alan Parker for one could not see why David got himself so agitated over the budget overrun stories, reckoning that the vast body of his work spoke for itself. 'Supposing he *did* go over budget,' Alan argues. 'His reaction was very strange, almost as if his pride was on the line. David's dignity is so important to him, perhaps another legacy from the early days when he didn't feel he was given enough credence. In any case, everyone in the business knew how careful he was with his budgets. In fact, he became famous for always throwing in his own fee to make a point.'

Anthony Jones, who acts as agent for Michael Apted, Iain Smith, Ray Connolly, Colin Welland, Bill Forsyth and others – earning him the name of 'One-stop shopping' by American film-makers – confirms this facet of David with a rueful smile. 'There is a classic pattern on deferments of salary,' he reveals. 'Two weeks before any of David's films are due to start, I'll get the inevitable phone call. *He's* deferring, everyone's deferring together. I *expect* it, I *wait* for the call. Of course I agree. David and I find it very easy to negotiate with each other. We recognize the parameters. His word is his bond, it's yes or no in a phone call in any deal we do – *then* there's that inevitable deferment call!

'David should be a shareholder in our agency – the number of clients he's introduced since I first met him and Sandy over lunch to discuss *That'll Be the Day*. He's taken bigger risks over the years than anyone I know, starting films with his own money before getting the official go-ahead. He's a buccaneer, but he's also a masochist. After *Chariots of Fire* he could have had what he wanted, but consciously he seems to ask himself what project he can put up that the studios will give him a hard time with. *Right*, he seems to say, they all say they want to make pictures with me – let's see how they feel about *this* one!

'He loves all the agonizing, feels it's not worth it if he doesn't suffer a lot. He's really more of an impressario than a producer, and the best salesman I've ever met. He regards selling these projects as a *challenge*. His high-media profile is totally misunderstood – it's not to get a statue erected to him as many imply, but simply to help him make the films he wants to make the way he wants to make them. The man's a workaholic who never stops, and he's got the most incredibly-acute sense of his audience. I remember once he was in my office and I was arguing about who would want to see the picture he was talking about. He was looking out the window at the time and turned to me, pointing to a window-cleaner on a scaffolding across the street. "*That's* who I'm making this picture for," he declared. "*That guy* is my audience. If I didn't honestly think he would come to see the picture, I wouldn't be bothering to produce it!" '

Jones is perhaps only half-correct in summing up David as a masochist, for David can probably lay claim to the invention of a new condition – pseudo-masochism, since much of his agonizing is in fact either to make others fall into line with his way of thinking or to issue a signal for the future. So far as the supposedly masochistic act of shunning obviously commercial subjects is concerned, to David this is a non-issue, with *Chariots of Fire* providing the perfect refutation.

The reactions of the press to *The Mission* and its win at Cannes were mixed. 'Unfinished victory,' heralded the *Sunday Telegraph*'s David Castell, while describing Robert Bolt's screenplay as 'halting'. He found the teaming of De Niro and Irons disappointing and concluded, 'Within it exists the potential for a great movie and it would be wrong to niggle while the opportunity remains to correct the pacing and the emotional temperature of the climatic scenes.'

Derek Malcolm in the *Guardian* reported that the film had received a rapturous reception from the public and a more diffident one by the critics. 'All I should say just now is that whatever the eventual shape it takes, it will have plenty of flaws, but will also be a considerable feat of film-making.' David Robinson for *The Times* found much to praise in what he called the 'admittedly unfinished stage, with the cutting incomplete and grave anxiety about whether the splices would get through the projector without breaking. Clearly awaiting further editing, for the moment the weakest section of the film is paradoxically the climactic battle where the film loses its rhythm and lucidity and the contrivances of Joffe's set-pieces which handicapped *The Killing Fields* are exposed.'

Iain Johnstone in the *Sunday Times* was the film's main champion. 'It is a triumphant success,' he trumpeted. 'Roland Joffe directs with mastery approaching that of David Lean. Thank goodness films like this are still being made.'

Despite his enthusiasm, the jury – in the broader sense – were clearly still out.

With the Cannon deal a fait accompli, reference to the Monopolies Commission having been overruled at Government level, David's sense of isolation within the British Film Industry began to grow. *The Mission* was now expected to do everything in terms of saving Goldcrest, and there were other factors at work, as he began to signal. 'I don't know whether I can afford to remain a line producer of films,' he declared. 'If I do a film every two years, I cannot afford to live at the Mill. I'm going to be 46 next year, I'm self-employed and I have to think about my pension. I'm trying to do a version of *Stars and Bars*, scripted by William Boyd from his own novel. It'll be directed by Pat O'Connor and we'd be in the pre-production process now if it weren't for the *Revolution* drama.'

He had two other projects in mind, a version of André Brink's *The Dry White Season* and a possible third venture with Roland Joffe, *Fat Man and Little Boy*, the atomic bomb story. For this, Bruce Robinson was toiling away on a script.

'All of them might be made,' David told a reporter, 'or none.'

Musical chairs is one of Hollywood's favourite pastimes and after a year of recurring rumours, Guy McElwaine found himself ousted as chairman and chief executive officer of Columbia Pictures. Since no successor was announced, speculation began as to the possible future role of Richard C. Gallop, who was one of the presidents in charge of Coca-Cola's Entertainment Business Sector, the umbrella company that included Columbia, under chairman Francis T. 'Fay' Vincent Jnr. Another equation was under consideration, however, the first move on the table taking place between Vincent and Tom Lewyn. As they lunched together in the spring of 1986, Fay quickly got to the point of their meeting.

'Tom, would David consider taking over the hot seat at Columbia?'
'No way.'
'How can you be so certain?'
'Well, I just happen to have a copy on me of a letter he sent to Paramount, turning down a similar offer.'
'Do you mind if I take a look?'
'Not at all.'

Fay Vincent studied the document for a few minutes, sipping away at his glass of Perrier. Tom surveyed his menu with a poker face, knowing that Fay would be taking in David's minimum conditions and unprecedented autonomy demands. Finally Fay took off his spectacles and looked Tom straight in the face.

'I think we can live with these,' he said quietly. Slow dissolve . . .

Numerous examples must crop up, in any attempt to relate 'factual' events, of the traffic-accident theory that no two witnesses will report identical versions. Akira Kurosawa took this to the filmic limit in his classic *Rashomon*, illustrating that elusive truth exists only peripherally, even in what purports to be 'definitive' versions of any event. To label anything as 'the truth' relies heavily, therefore, on one's attitude to witnesses' credibility. According to Fay Vincent, the preceding version of his meeting with Tom Lewyn – the one that David has allowed to pass into Puttnam mythology – is inaccurate in one vitally important and telling detail. Pity, for it makes a great story. Some would argue that Fay's version makes an even better – and a more revealing – tale.

There was indeed a luncheon meeting with Tom Lewyn, Fay confirms, *but called at Lewyn's request* at Columbia's 711 Fifth Avenue offices, or to be more precise, the Coca-Cola company's offices. 'I've got an interesting idea to talk to you about,' Lewyn told Vincent, who knew him as a fellow-lawyer while being completely unaware that he represented David Puttnam. Lewyn wasted no time as the lunch proceeded. 'How are you doing on the studio job?' he asked. Vincent replied that they had a series of names they were working their way through.

'Have you thought of David Puttnam?' Lewyn asked. Vincent replied that the name had never occurred to him, since he had never felt David would be interested in the job.

'I think he would be,' Lewyn replied. 'I know that he likes you and I think that you like him. He might well be interested.' When Vincent expressed enthusiasm, Lewyn pressed on. 'There would be three conditions. One is he would have to have total authority to make whatever movies he'd want to make.'

'That goes without saying; that's what the job is,' Vincent replied. 'That wouldn't be a problem as long as there's a budget and he stays within the amount of money we allocate to production.'

'Second, he would want to leave the US with $3 million net capital after taxes to take back to England, because he needs that to support his life-style. He has needs to make major capital.'

Vincent could see the lunch proceeding well beyond mere exploratory talks. 'I'm not negotiating with you now,' he told Lewyn, 'but that certainly is possible.'

'The third condition is that he would only want to do it for a limited amount of time. He would only want to live in Los Angeles and be committed to staying in the States for three years.'

'That's all right, too,' Vincent replied, 'provided it doesn't mean he'd be leaving the *company* after three years, and that we can talk about where he lives and how he works after that. In other words, that three years doesn't mean he wants to work for that length of time only and then *leave* Coca-Cola? The three years would only be his *residency* in Los Angeles?'

'I think that's correct, but if you want to pursue the matter further, you'll have to talk to David.'

'Why don't you tell David I'm interested?'

'What you should do, Fay, is go to England and see David.'

Within days Lewyn was on the phone to Vincent. 'David is very excited, but he has a lot of questions and would you meet him in London?'

'Sure,' Vincent agreed. Second slow dissolve . . .

'When David was approached by Paramount,' Tom Lewyn recalls, 'the chief executive officer, understandably enough, said, "I've got to have the final decision on which projects go and which don't. I'll listen to you and I'll probably go with you, but I occasionally won't." Then, later, David and I were talking and it came up – why not Columbia? That's the *perfect* situation. There isn't a finer gentleman than Fay Vincent. He's a man I have a very, very high regard for; he has always kept his word to me. So it was he and I who concocted the idea of bringing David to Columbia. We bear the responsibility, for the good and bad.'

Chapter 20

The Reel Thing

In 1973 producer Ray Stark had become extremely concerned about the financial health of Columbia Pictures, to whom he looked for continuing revenues from his production of *Funny Girl*. He watched with dismay as the price of the stock fell from $9 to $4 and in desperation turned to Herbert A. Allen Jr of Allen & Co., New York investment bankers. Columbia's management had remained unchanged under Abe Schneider and Leo Jaffe's control since co-founder Harry Cohn's death in 1958. Financial control dating back to the mid-sixties had passed into the hands of a pharmaceutical tycoon, Matty Rosenhaus, whom Herbert Allen Jr now approached. With his help, and their banker's promise of a stay of execution until new management could be injected into the ailing company, Allen & Co. gained control of Columbia.

Although Leo Jaffe stayed on, the power source was now Herbert Allen Jr, his appointee Alan Hirschfield – and Ray Stark, who had instigated Allen's takeover. Stark was appointed neither an officer nor a director of Columbia, preferring instead to pull the strings from behind the scenes. A $50-million loss for 1973 was reported, confirming their fears that the problems were deeper-rooted than they had seemed. Almost as deep-rooted, in fact, as the unlikely friendship of Ray Stark and Herbert Allen Jr.

Raymond Otto Stark was born in 1914. After failing to graduate from New Jersey's Rutgers University, he moved to Hollywood in the late thirties, taking a job first as a florist at Forest Lawn cemetery before moving into radio, then Warner Bros publicity department.

The end of the Second World War found Stark working with talent agent Charles Feldman, who introduced him to Charlie and Herbert Allen of Allen & Co. Stark and Charlie Allen immediately struck up a friendship, then the next decade saw Stark's career blossom as a highly successful literary and talent agent. The short, slightly-built Stark, with his sandy-coloured hair, squinted blue eyes and blond eyelashes, began to command respect for his hustling ability on behalf of both himself and his clients.

When Warner Bros ran into insuperable difficulties in 1956, Charlie Allen moved in, joining the board and purchasing large blocks of shares. In a fund-raising exercise the entire pre-1948 Warners Bros library was sold off to Associated Artists Productions (A A), a company run by Eliot Hyman to licence movies for T V. Finance for the purpose was provided by Louis (Uncle Lou) Chesler, A A's chairman, a man with established ties to Mafia boss Meyer Lansky. Nor was this A A's only shady connection – their vice-president, Morris 'Mac' Schwebel, would be later convicted of criminal activity. Through his Charlie Feldman connection, Ray Stark joined the A A's board in 1957.

One year later Stark left with Eliot Hyman to form their own movie production company, Seven Arts. He then departed to produce his first movie, *The World of Suzie Wong*, but rejoined Seven Arts two years later, serving under 'Uncle Lou' Chesler's chairmanship.

Charlie Allen and his associates had meantime bought a 25 per cent interest in Grand Bahama Port Authority Ltd., a company 50 per cent owned by a convicted stock manipulator, Wallace Groves. A subsidiary, Grand Bahama Development Co, was formed, in which Ray Stark, Eliot Hyman and Lou Chesler invested, together with Seven Arts itself, in the company to the tune of a 21 per cent interest for $5 million. 'Uncle Lou' Chesler was named president of Grand Bahama Development, thus teaming up with ex-con Wallace Groves. Together they began payment of several hundred thousands of dollars to Bahamanian government officials for permission to build a gambling casino on Grand Bahama Island. Following a meeting with Mayer Lansky in Miami, the casino was duly built, and staffed with associates of the mobster.

When Jack Warner of Warner Bros retired in 1967, Seven Arts bought his stock for $32 million and formed Warner/Seven Arts. Ray Stark left again at this point, with a large chunk of Warner/Seven Arts stock in his pocket, together with a lucrative agreement from Columbia Pictures to produce a film version of his mother-in-law Fanny Brice's life-story, *Funny Girl*, which Stark had steered to its triumph on Broadway.

At the end of the sixties Warner/Seven Arts were taken over by Steven Ross's Kinney National Services Inc. and Warner Communications was formed. Allen & Co. were the investment bankers involved, the deal yielding a hefty profit for the shareholders, not least the Allens and Ray Stark.

Charlie Allen, Ray Stark and Eliot Hyman had significantly solidified their financial positions, while remaining themselves utterly odour-free throughout all these transactions. Although they had formed questionable associations, there was no implication of any illegality or wrong-doing on their behalf.

Herbert Allen Jr graduated in 1962 from Williams College and was appointed president of Allen & Co. in 1967 as his father and uncle took more of a back seat. Many were sceptical of the young man's ability to run the company and felt their fears justified when allegations of fraud were aired and a Securities and Exchange Commission investigation began. Fraud and manipulation charges against the company were dropped, but Allen & Co. was enjoined from violating other laws. Herbert Jr smarted under the accusations and was reported by the *New York Times* as having defiantly said, 'We trade every day with hustlers, deal makers, shysters, con-men . . . that's the way businesses get started. That's the way this country was built.' Although this statement was not disavowed by him at the time, he chose to do so when he was four years older and wiser.

Just as Ray Stark got on tremendously well with Charlie Allen over the years, so that same friendship now extended to Charlie's urbane nephew. Stark had experienced a terrible tragedy in his life when his 25-year-old son Peter appeared to have taken his own life by jumping 14 floors to his death in February 1970. Possibly in Herbert Jr, Stark found a substitute for his son, although Herbert was in no need of a stand-in father. For whatever reason, the two men survived the gap of 25 years in their ages to form an alliance that was as close as Stark had enjoyed with Charlie Allen before him, a relationship that had benefited both men handsomely.

Stark's first string-pulling at Columbia led to the appointment of his friend, ex-agent David Begelman, to head motion-picture operations in Hollywood under Alan Hirschfield's presidency in New York. So far so good – except for Hirschfield, who dared to question Stark's relationship with Columbia and the fairly spartan returns coming to the company from his productions. It was not that his films were unsuccessful – Stark's films for Columbia included the *Funny Girl* sequel, *Funny Lady*, together with Streisand/Redford's *The Way We Were* and a string of Neil Simon successes – simply that the way his deals were structured, Columbia was the last to see any money.

Hirschfield also felt that Stark's overheads, charged as they were under his contract to Columbia, required pruning. If this attitude of Hirschfield was bound to cause a rift, it was nothing compared to the row over marketing methods that Hirschfield was determined to win. When Hirschfield objected to Stark's appointment of two 'production representatives' to monitor Columbia's marketing campaign for *Funny*

Lady – he saw Stark's move as demeaning to the studio – Stark fired back with, 'Friday the 13th would not necessarily seem the likeliest day for you to write me a memo . . . My support of Columbia in this town has been a helluva lot more important to helping you acquire product than you may realize . . . I believe the success of a picture, Alan, is contingent upon the whole rather than any individual elements. I welcome Columbia's executive advice as to the creative areas of my production . . . I know that after you have read this letter, you will agree there is no Frankenstein replacing the lady holding the torch for Columbia Distribution. All we want to do is help make *Funny Lady* the richest lady in the world.' Still the two managed to stop their differences from boiling over into outright warfare, although each was increasingly wary of the other.

'Why can't Alan just leave David Begelman in charge?' Stark demanded to know. For his part Hirschfield retorted, 'I can't run Columbia and keep looking over my shoulder at Ray Stark all the time.' The stage was set for a split, with David Begelman the catalyst that would bring about the final disagreement.

The Begelman scandal began when actor Cliff Robertson could not recall receiving a cheque from Columbia Pictures for $10,000 in 1975. Nor could he remember having done any work for Columbia that warranted the payment – yet there it was on his 'Statement of Miscellaneous Income' from the US Internal Revenue in 1976. After fighting his way though a tissue of lies, evasions and cover-up attempts, he traced the cheque. It had been made out to him, but cashed by someone else who had forged his signature on the reverse. That someone was David Begelman, Columbia Pictures' president.

The next cheque to surface was for $35,000, made out to Peter Choate, allegedly a technician hired to install special sound equipment in cinemas for the movie *Tommy*, until he turned out to be an architect who had carried out construction work on Begelman's home. Choate himself was a completely innocent party in the deception. When various other bits and pieces were added in, Begelman's embezzlements and misappropriations totalled $75,000.

Where Hirschfield should have been firm on the issue, he vacillated, and was undone as Stark and Herbert Allen excused Begelman's activities as aberrational. Only when the scandal could no longer be contained and exploded across the nation's headlines, rocking first Columbia, then the entire Hollywood community in its shock wave, did Stark and Allen back down and agree that Begelman had to go.

Still Hirschfield had gone much too far, further alienating the formidable trio of Matty Rosenhaus, Stark and Allen by trying to override Allen's chief executive role and seek an outside buyer for Columbia without board authority. 1975's successes *Shampoo* and *Tommy*, 1976's *Murder By Death* and *Taxi Driver* and 1977's smash hits *Close Encounters Of The Third Kind* and *The Deep*, were put to one side. Although Hirschfield had presided, with Begelman's help, over Columbia's return to corporate health, his services were dispensed with. 'A disaster and a disgrace,' was how Leo Jaffe termed Hirschfield's dismissal, although total concurrence with this was tempered by the question of what was seen as Jaffe's own long-passive role.

The new chairman, Herbert Allen Jr, brought in Francis T. 'Fay' Vincent, another graduate of Williams College two years ahead of him, as president of Columbia Pictures Industries in Hirschfield's place. Vincent was counselled by some – *not* Herbert Allen – to fire Victor Kaufman, Columbia's young general counsel through the Begelman contretemps, as part of the stable-cleaning exercise, since Kaufman was widely seen as having supported Hirschfield. Vincent declined to do this – ('I can't fire somebody I don't know; I have to use my own judgement'), enabling Kaufman to emerge in the years ahead as a particularly significant player. Frank Price, late of Universal-TV, succeeded Begelman as head of motion-picture production, being appointed president of Columbia Pictures, in charge of all film activities, by Vincent soon afterwards.

Herbert Allen admitted to Vincent that he had made two mistakes during the Begelman affair; the first in taking Begelman back, the second in not firing Hirschfield sooner. Fay is amused at frequent press references to Allen as Herb or Herbie: 'He hates it. Those who know him least refer to him like that. And the whole issue of the Begelman/Hirschfield era has been wildly over-simplified. It's far more complex than it was made out to be. The company was in worse shape than is generally acknowledged. Hirschfield was simply unwilling to acknowledge Herbert Allen's leadership, and since Herbert's constant theme is loyalty, the end was predictable.'

Columbia had acquired the rights to the Broadway musical, *Annie*, in 1977 for a reported record $9.5 million. Several producers were mooted for the project, generating stiff competition since the fee for such a big-budget movie would be commensurately lush. One of Frank Price's first acts as new head of production at Columbia was to hand over the reins of Annie to – one Raymond Otto Stark.

Columbia's management was looking good again by 1981, the company now a well-drilled unit under Herbert Allen, Fay Vincent and

Frank Price. Hits like *California Suite*, *The Cheap Detective* and *Midnight Express* in 1978, *Kramer Vs Kramer* and *The China Syndrome* in 1979, *Stir Crazy* and *Blue Lagoon* in 1980 and *Stripes* and *Absence of Malice* in the current year, had kept revenues from the film division flowing nicely, many of the earlier titles a legacy from the Hirschfield/ Begelman era. Columbia had purchased Ray Stark's Rastar Company, although this covered revenues and rights only to his previous pictures, for 300,000 Columbia shares, each valued at $32.50, for a total of $9,750,000. The stage was set for the entry of Coca-Cola.

Roberto C. Goizueta, Coke's chairman, a first-generation Cuban immigrant, had joined the company in Cuba before fleeing from Castroism in 1961 and transferring to Coke's technical division in Atlanta as a flavour chemist. Born to wealthy aristocrats, Goizueta speaks English as a second language, albeit with a heavy accent. Reporting to him is president Donald R. Keough, son of a third-generation Irish-American cattleman. As two of the six vice-chairman up for the job of chairman in 1980, the duo had agreed over a few drinks that whoever got the title would make the other his right-hand man.

Goizueta can at times be stiff, patrician and cold, for the most part well able to keep his emotions and instincts tightly under control. Only on rare occasions does his composure slip, allowing his reserve to give way to a temper that can flare up quickly under fire. Keough is the perfect buffer for his chairman – smooth, charming, hail-fellow-well-met – the outgoing, bright salesman personified.

As a team they were resolved from the beginning to make their mark by leaving no new idea unappraised, no potential acquisition unexamined, no business opportunity unexplored. And no formula – not even that of their main product – regarded as sacred. When Coke's consultants, the firm of Arthur D. Little, recommended buying into the entertainment business, Columbia, with its library of 1800 movies, was a natural target.

The preliminary meeting in New York's '21' Club went well, with Don Keough leading the advance Coke party and Herbert Allen and Fay Vincent captaining the Columbia team. Allen adopted the soft-sell approach. While listing Columbia's assets and management strength, he went out of his way to also detail the problems he could foresee.

Coke's board consisted of a large number of elderly, conservative men (and we're talking elderly – average age, 70). How would Coke feel about any sexy movies Columbia might turn out? 'Just so long as they're not X-rated,' he was assured, 'that would not be a problem.'

He next pointed out that Columbia, although only one-tenth the size of Coca-Cola, attracted an inordinate amount of press attention. 'You would think we were A T and T. And if someone in New York sneezes, somebody in California says, "Bless you."'

'We've thought about that aspect,' Allen was told, 'and we can live with it.'

He emphasized that the salaries of Columbia's creative people in Hollywood might be considered out of line by Atlanta standards. Although Frank Price reported to Fay Vincent in New York, he earned twice as much as Vincent.

'We can handle that,' Coke replied. 'We don't mind paying, just so long as these creative people deliver. Otherwise there could be a problem.'

The litany continued with Allen pointing out the advent of David McClintick's book, *Indecent Exposure*, which would chronicle the Begelman episode. 'He was sick,' Allen told the Coke team, 'which the doctors and the courts concurred with – so we penalized him and then tried to make a deal with him as a human. We tried to rehabilitate him, but that was the wrong decision, given the P R of the day post-Watergate.'

'That's in the past,' Allen was assured. (Later, when the book was in galley proofs, Allen sent a copy to Goizueta who claimed he gave up reading it early on, disgusted at McClintick's assertions. Keough has a copy, but claims not to have read it at all.)

In any case, Allen pointed out, Columbia had no particular desire to sell to Coke. If a merger were to take place, a hefty premium would be sought. 'It will knock your eyes out,' he smilingly told Keough.

'Great company,' Vincent told Allen as they left the meeting, with a follow-up set at Columbia's 711 Fifth Avenue offices, 'I bet we make a deal.'

'I don't,' Allen replied, 'because wait until they see the price I'm going to ask.'

With the introduction to Goizueta at Columbia's offices over, a complete listing of the company's assets made, and further emphasis laid on how comfortable they felt with their present independence, Allen again zeroed in on the 'exorbitant' price he would ask. 'I think we are the best in the business,' he told the Coke team, 'and we have to have a price Columbia can't turn down.'

The number-crunchers moved in, prior to a final make-or-break meeting in Atlanta. With Columbia's stock bubbling around the $40 mark, a fair way up from the $2.50 Herbert Allen had paid in 1973 (and most of it bought personally by Allen, rather than through Allen

& Co.), Allen and Vincent discussed the 'number' they would ask. Vincent was convinced that Allen would ask him to go for $100; after all, they had no wish to sell the company. With Vincent designated to do the talking, Allen came out with an asking price just before the meeting started – of a still-hefty $85.

'That's so far off it isn't even funny,' was Coke financial officer, Sam Ayoub's immediate reaction, before the meeting split up for separate discussions.

When they had readjourned, Ayoub declared that the $85 Vincent was asking for simply would not fly. Opening his briefcase, he pulled out a buff-coloured envelope. Vincent had an inspiration that Ayoub had a series of envelopes prepared and decided to back his hunch. 'Forget that first envelope, Sam,' he declared, 'and go to the next one.' Sam Ayoub chuckled ruefully. '$68,' he said. Vincent conceded $82.' '$72,' said Ayoub. '$75,' said Vincent, 'and that's *it*.' Although the Columbia team played it cool, they were stunned when Coke accepted $75, valuing Columbia at nearly $750 million, almost twice the market value of the shares.

Goizueta was displeased with press reports that he had paid far too much for the company and claimed in his defence he had heard a rumour that Time Inc. had also been interested in acquiring Columbia. Within a year however, he was vindicated by the same analysts who had condemned the takeover, as Coca-Cola's stock advanced after the initial slide that had taken place when the news of the takeover broke. What happened next is one of the most astonishing coups in the history of the movies.

If theatrical audiences, people who actually pay to enter cinemas, were the only source of revenue for a production company, very few of them would be in business. In the old days, the only after-life to a theatrical release was a theatrical re-release. Now there's a whole variety of other ancillary uses – network, local, satellite and pay-television, together with the lucrative video market. Just as these end-uses have grown, so have movie budgets.

In response to this all manner of financial arrangements are worked out in advance by both major studios and independent producers. Pre-selling means just that. If a production company has a script and a star, why shouldn't a theatrical distributor in, say, Thailand guarantee to pay on delivery of the completed movie? Then, why shouldn't a bank discount that guarantee and pass the money on to the production company to make the movie? OK, that's 1 per cent of the budget found, now how about the other 99 per cent. Well, if a video company wants the product, they too must pledge a guaranteed amount, ditto the pay-TV company and everyone else who wants a piece of the action. This was the pitch that Time-Life's pay-TV division, Home Box Office (HBO) swallowed from Columbia in 1982.

Together with CBS, a joint-venture deal was entered into by HBO with Columbia. In return for the licence to show Columbia movies exclusively on HBO pay-TV, Time agreed to contribute 25 per cent against the production costs of each movie, without a ceiling, *no matter what the movies cost*. If a Columbia picture costing $12 million made no money at all in its theatrical release, $3 million would *still* have to be paid. The killer was the sliding-scale agreement Time agreed to *on top of this*. If the $12-million movie went on to take $36 million in rentals, HBO's price tag escalated to 25 per cent of $36 million, or a cool $9 million.

On top of this again, Time agreed to finance 25 per cent of the cost of the movie as an equity partner, raising their *total* investment to 50–60 per cent. *Then* CBS chipped in to the Columbia vaults a further $2 million for free-TV rights.

The other enterprise that sprang from this meeting of minds was a new production entity, Tri-Star Pictures – conceived in discussions between Fay Vincent and Victor Kaufman – to be owned one-third each by Columbia, Time Inc. and CBS, and run by the eager, ambitious Kaufman. The same basic terms would apply for all their product, except that Columbia would cream off a *further* 12.5 per cent of the films' rentals in return for distributing Tri-Star product.

The inside joke at the conclusion of this deal was, 'Coke paid $750 million to *buy* Columbia. Time Inc. will pay the same just to *rent* it for three years!' Fay Vincent put it even more succinctly, 'We had a pipeline to Time Inc.'s treasury.'

Ghostbusters was the movie that finally caused a re-negotiation, as its rentals soared to an astronomical $144 million. The cheque that Time Inc. was obliged to write was for $36 million – a cool million more than the entire movie itself had cost to produce.

After this Time Inc. shouted 'enough!' and requested re-negotiation of the deal. After ceilings were put on production costs and licence fees, the deal between the two companies was then extended to 1992. 'We made an incredible deal the first time,' Fay Vincent acknowledges. Who says money can't be made from movies?

As a boy of 18 in 1956, Fay Vincent had been enrolled at Williams, two years ahead of Herbert Allen Jr. With his captaincy of the freshman football team, he was following in the illustrious footsteps of his father, who had been an outstanding player at Yale. Fay was first and foremost a serious student and a devout Catholic, who was considering becoming a Jesuit after Williams, a prospect that was to change one Saturday afternoon when his room-mate locked him in their room as a prank. Fay tried in vain to batter the door down, but the fact that it opened inwards rendered the task impossible. Resignedly, he decided to make the best of it and take a nap. When he awoke two hours later, there was no sign of his room-mate. Anxious to get out, Fay looked to the window. If he could go outside and make his way along the ledge, he figured he could enter another room and be free. It was December and the day had turned icy, something he had failed to realize in the warmth of his room. As he started to edge his way along, he lost his footing on that ice that encrusted the ledge, and plunged four floors to the ground below. What saved his life – but broke his back – were the railings on a balcony halfway down the building. They smashed his vertebrae, before his fall continued. The several inches of shattered backbone were replaced in a later transplant from his hip bone. After being totally paralysed for weeks, he was left with legs that are semi-paralysed to this day. The plucky youngster made the best of it, reckoning he was lucky to be alive, and spent the time that would normally have been taken up with sports to intensify his studies. When he applied in 1960 to join the Jesuits, he was rejected because of his limited mobility.

After graduating from Yale law school in 1963, Vincent practised law in Washington for 15 years, then spent a few months at the Securities and Exchange Commission in Washington. In July 1978 Herbert Allen called up out of the blue and began discussions that would eventually lead to Vincent being offered the job of running Columbia Pictures. After the Begelman scandal and Hirschfield's departure, they needed a 'Mr Clean' – stocky, square-set, straight-as-a-dye Fay Vincent was it. With the value of his Columbia stock multiplied by the enormous success he made of running Columbia, and later by the advent of Coca-Cola's takeover, Fay was made independently wealthy. 'Fay's ability to take Columbia from its lowest period to its peak was vital to the Coke transaction,' Herbert Allen gratefully acknowledges.

A warm friendship grew between Vincent and Don Keough over the years and deals. Urged by Vincent, Herbert Allen – reluctantly – accepted a position on Coke's board in 1982. It was no sinecure. As chairman of the company's compensation committee, he was responsible for the award to Goizueta of a 'performance units' bonus worth over $6 million, in the year of the new Coke launch. (Herbert Allen's prophetic pre-launch advice to Goizueta was to bring in the new drink, but keep the old one.) He has stayed on the board, Vincent feels, purely because of the close relationship he developed with Goizueta. Nowhere near as close, however, as with his surrogate father in Hollywood, Ray Stark.

By May, 1982, Stark had *Annie* set for release after a reported $40 million had been spent. Directed by John Huston, with whom Stark had earlier made *Night of the Iguana*, *Reflections in a Golden Eye* and *Fat City*, *Annie* starred Albert Finney, Carol Burnett and Anne Reinking (soon to become born-again bachelor Herbert Allen's inamorata). 'It's the movie I want on my tombstone,' the producer declared, unprepared for the withering reviews *Annie* would receive.

In the *Los Angeles Times*, Sheila Benson wrote, 'Golly, *Annie*, how could they have put you in the movies and left out your heart?' *Daily Variety*'s Jim Harwood described *Annie* as a 'lumbering, largely uninvolving exercise', while Pauline Kael attacked the screenplay as 'feeble' and 'melodramatic'. Although the film went on to give Columbia a net return of $37 million, it never went into profit because of its huge production and launch costs. Frank Price tried to take the heat out of the situation by describing the film's $40 million budget as 'the hype sums', maintaining that $25 million was nearer the correct total. The price for the rights to the Broadway musical was similarly revised downwards from $9.5 million to $6.5 million. In fact, Price was referring to 'present-value' figures, a common and perfectly legitimate Hollywood numbers game. In Columbia's *Annie* deal, $9.5 million was indeed the purchase price the company was committed to paying – but over a period of years; $6.5 million was the *present-value* amount of money the company was obliged to set aside to provide, with compound interest, the eventual $9.5 million.

Stark's reaction to the adverse criticism his pet project received was truly extraordinary, as he vengefully hired ex-*Village Voice* columnist Stuart Byron as 'creative affairs executive' in June 1982. 'Stark said he wanted to write something about film critics and wondered if I could suggest someone to ghost-write it for him, or at least to give him some ideas,' *New York Times* film critic Vincent Canby recalled. 'I suggested Stuart as one who wanted to get into that side of the business.' When *Newsweek*'s David Ansen maintained that Byron had called him to say he had been hired to pen an article about critics, Byron insisted Ansen had misunderstood and described his first task for Stark as 'finding a writer who can write a script for a "Sweet Smell of Success" – story about a film critic.'

Several were of the opinion that Byron's project was directly inspired by *Time*'s Richard Corliss, who had dared to describe *Annie*'s tone as 'dark, dour, mean-spirited'. His review had ended by quoting Stark's tombstone announcement, adding 'Funeral services may be held starting this week at a theatre near you.'

After a year of breathless anticipation as to what Byron might produce, Stark hired Howard J. Koch, in October 1983, as new head of his Rastar Company. Two months later Koch dismissed the entire production staff of the company – including creative affairs executive Stuart Byron.

Unpredictable, quixotic, a major player and power-broker, Stark had woven an inextricable thread through both the warp and weft of Hollywood legend. Obsessed by the desire for complete confidentiality – many of his telephone calls would begin with a whispered, 'Are you alone?/Are you sure?/And what we say will go no further?/*Swearzy?*' – few in the community could ever hope to escape his byzantine influence, especially those incumbent at Columbia. Despite the bottom line on *Annie*, Stark argued that if all the half-price seats given out to children were doubled up, the film would have ended up as a money-maker. When he brought up the question of a sequel to *Annie* being filmed at Columbia, Fay Vincent was incredulous and turned the motion down. Stark promptly took the proposal to Victor Kaufman at Tri-Star, who approved the project without referring to Vincent. 'We took a loss on the original,' Vincent told Kaufman, 'it makes no sense to make a sequel, especially the price Ray's talking.' Stark was infuriated by what he saw as Vincent's high-handed countermanding of Kaufman's decision and for a while it was open warfare between the two men. Only when Stark re-submitted the project at a much lower cost did Vincent relent and allow Kaufman to OK the deal. 'I didn't fight it again,' he acknowledges, 'I thought, "what the hell".' He watched as Stark went ahead with an ill-fated Neil Simon vehicle, *The Slugger's Wife*, which the producer hubristically chose to shoot in Atlanta under the very noses of the Coke bosses. Stark was mortified by the complete failure of the $25-million project, and bitterly regretted the high profile he had maintained during its production, blaming himself for hiring director Hal Ashby, with whom he fought constantly. 'It embarrassed him so much he would raise it all the time,' Fay recalls. 'He said he was going to make it up to the company. It just turned out to be a very bad movie and he felt very bad about it.'

For a proud man now into his eighth decade, time was running short for Stark if he was to go out on a note of triumph.

Frank Price had been against the forming of Tri-Star and Columbia's alliance with HBO. Although his success had continued with *Gandhi, The Toy* and *Tootsie* in 1982, 1983 had produced only *The Big Chill* and *Blue Thunder*, together with a fair sprinkling of expensive failures like *Krull*. His power struggle with Fay Vincent ended with the announcement of his resignation in October, 1983, and the appointment of his assistant, ex-Ray Stark protégé, Guy McElwaine, in his place. 1984 proved a truly spectacular year for Columbia, including as it did both *Ghostbusters* (a fond farewell from Frank Price) and the *Karate Kid* adventure. 1985's harvest was of a much more modest scale, with the combination of *Silverado, St Elmo's Fire, Jagged Edge, Agnes of God* and *Fright Night* reaching only a fraction of the previous year's revenues. Then there were the manifold embarrassments – *New Kids* (box-office gross: $0.9 million), *Fast Forward* ($3.9 million), *Sylvester* ($0.7 million), *The Slugger's Wife* ($2.8 million), and *The Bride* ($4.9 million) – none of which even recovered their release costs. It was clearly time for a different approach.

'Don't give in on any of your demands,' Patsy counselled before David's meeting with Fay Vincent and his deputy Dick Gallop at Queensgate Place Mews. As he drove to London, he reflected on a memorable phrase Dan Melnick had used when offering him the job of production head at Columbia in the late seventies: 'Don't forget, this job gives you the right to talk to creative people the world over, not just in Hollywood.'

Fay's recollection of the day's events in Queensgate Place Mews is a happy one, although tinged now by the turn events took at Columbia. 'We had a very good day and discussed all of the issues in question and really from then on I believed we had an understanding that we were going to move forward. One of the points David raised was over the movie *Ishtar*, when he told us he and Warren Beatty and Dustin Hoffman didn't get along. He told us why. My view was that the picture was already going forward and I didn't understand the enormity of the hatred. He put it to us very straight. He had had very bad dealings with Dustin during *Agatha*. He had never spoken to Beatty, but they had fought over the Academy Awards and Beatty resented him. He felt that both these people would be very negative about his coming. He was correct. I agreed to deal direct with the *Ishtar* people.'

As for David's avowed insistence on a meeting with Goizueta and Keough to further clarify issues before he would sign, Fay says that by the time that took place, he and David had already reached an agreement. 'The meeting with Roberto and Don,' says Fay, 'was just a case of them getting to know David, since of course they were going to be important to each other, but David and I had already made the deal and they knew David and I had an agreement. They were a little uneasy because he was a British producer and I'm known as an Anglophile and I think they worried that I was using my own personal inclination. He was a strange choice to a lot of people.'

David's residency was to be for three years in Los Angeles, although Columbia had the right to extend this by another six months. Fay felt secure in the knowledge that this would not be the extent of David's service with the company, for he and David had confirmed their understanding that his tenure would extend beyond the three- or three-and-a-half-year point, wherever he was based.

He would have complete autonomy for all projects budgeted at under $30 million. He would report directly to Fay Vincent as head of Coke's Entertainment Business Sector, as the company was presently constituted. The one thing Fay was reluctant to concede immediately to David was control of International Marketing and Distribution, since this was tied in with television and video, which were outside David's brief. He was also aware that Patrick Williamson, who had been in charge of International for many years, was unhappy at the prospect of reporting to David. Fay sensed either a dislike or a distrust between the two.

Williamson, who had joined Columbia in England straight from school during the blitz, went to the length of warning Fay that David's appointment was a mistake. His disturbing prediction was that David would self-destruct. He would not be able to keep his mouth shut, he had a big anti-establishment chip on his shoulder and he would cause trouble for the company. 'How can you say that?' Fay asked. 'I really know him and you don't,' Williamson replied.

Chapter 21

'Have You Taken Leave of Your Senses?'

David solicited 'advice' on the Columbia 'offer' from everyone he could think of. Almost overwhelmingly the reaction was 'Go for it.'

'Hell's bells!' Robert Bolt declared. 'Of course you must take it! You are going to, aren't you?'

'I don't know,' David replied. 'I don't think so. After all I've said about Hollywood, I don't see that I can. Everyone will think I've just sold out for the money.'

'Well,' said Robert, 'you're a better man than I am if you would turn it down for such a high-falutin' reason.'

A few weeks later Robert and Sarah Miles were visiting Kingsmead Mill as guests for the weekend.

'I think I'm going to accept,' David told them, 'although there're lots of detail to be hammered out.'

'Well done,' was Robert's wholehearted reaction. Sarah was not so sure, having swam herself in Hollywood's murky waters in the seventies.

'David's a fighter,' she acknowledges in her delightful, quirkily charming, off-the-wall way. 'He has his enemies and there's a lot of jealousy attached to his name. The English don't like putting themselves forward, they think it lacks humility or something, but David just goes all out. He's the best PR man for David in the world and therefore the best producer we have. That's his ace card. One has to question David's taste in the subject he chooses, of course. We'd love it if he would just open up and forget his class-consciousness.

'There was a time when he wanted to have his cake and eat it too, but one has to take one's hat off to Patsy that she hung in through these rough patches. He's past all that now. I think there comes a time when all these energies go into other things. She held back with great dignity and I think it's all paid off for both of them. They belong together. Many a great man is only great because of his woman and Putters without his Patsy would be like a ship without a sail. She's the balance for him, in every way a well-earthed woman. There's tremendous toughness – you can see it in her eyes; you can see it in her every move. And there's so much loyalty.

'What's always been between the two of us is table-tennis. Putters wants to win more than anybody I know in life. He doesn't see it as sport; it's a life and death struggle. You get to such a pitch with him that you think, "I'd better lose here." Even if you could win, you don't want to. He's *that* keen to win. I think it's a very healthy attitude and I'm very envious of that final toughness. Robert Shaw was the same, on the tennis court, or any other games you were playing with him. He went white with fury if he wasn't winning. David's got that same quality – for him there's only winning and nothing else. I personally find it very attractive; lots of lovely men have it. I'd love to have seen him and Robert Shaw duel to the death.

'The point about Puttnam is if suddenly someone said to him "Look, English tennis is really down the nick; train this year and enter Wimbledon next year; you've got a good chance of getting into the finals," he would. You see, he really cares enough about England to do *anything* for it. Something *impossible* – he'd try to do it for England.'

A combination of factors drove David into the arms of the Columbia lady. One of the notions behind the *First Love* series had been to get a whole slew of projects bubbling rather than depend on one major project every two or three years. The motoring was fine when connected to the Goldcrest bandwagon, but with its fuel supply choked off, Enigma too had ground to a halt.

The type of film-making Cannon stood for was everything he was against – violent, opportunistic, exploitational – yet he had been forced to stand back and watch as colleagues bent their knees to the Cannon invasion. Despite their approaches, if they were to be the financial power source in Britain, it was not for him.

Yet again Warners had humiliatingly turned down his latest Enigma project, William Boyd's own adaptation of his comic novel, *Stars and Bars*. Susan Richards had kept a flame alive in the window for this one, but as he accompanied co-producer Sandy Lieberson round the Hollywood studios in search of alternative finance, David felt back at the beginning of his career, as if he had no track record to his name, a supplicant having to answer a 23-year-old script editor's question, 'What makes you think *you* understand American humour?'

Then there was the main problem – money. Apart from producer's fees, David had seen no appreciable income since *Chariots of Fire* had gone through the roof, while Patsy had soared splendidly and unashamedly into the stratosphere at Kingsmead Mill. The very definite need to replenish the Puttnam coffers would be achieved spectacularly by the Columbia deal. Kingsmead would be rendered invulnerable, a little piece of England that would forever be the Puttnams'. From the $3 million net guaranteed at the end of his term there would be enough to maintain Kingsmead and still give David the luxury of only making the projects he really believed in, free at last from any treadmill.

Even against the necessity of having to live above the store at Columbia for three years and wave a temporary goodbye to Kingsmead, the proposition was beguiling. And if going back to Hollywood had vague echoes of running on a Sunday and a defeat of sorts, David swore the community would soon discover he was no lame duck.

With the meeting in Atlanta organized, David took Patsy along with him, determined she would see her husband in action against the infidel capitalists. Although he had made the initial approach to Columbia, he still coquettishly wanted to be seen to be seduced on his own terms.

David had all his points ready as he and Patsy were driven to Coke's headquarters, an impressive 26 storey concrete, steel and granite skyscraper on North Avenue, set apart from the peach-tree-laden metropolis. With the introduction to Goizueta and Keough made in Keough's office, and with Tom Lewyn flown in from New York for support, David came out with the first of his hypothetical situations – and it was a lulu.

'Suppose,' he asked, 'I wanted to make a film on the People's Power Revolution in the Philippines, where the San Miguel Brewing Co. is both your bottler and a previous Marcos supporter, how would you react?' Assured that the decision would be solely his, David managed to stop short of next canvassing Coke's views on a multi-million dollar epic on the Cola wars.

The Cuban/Irish double act was next handed David's manifesto for Columbia, which they read in reverential silence. 'I was brought up on the movies,' David had written. 'They formed far and away the most powerful cultural, social and ethical impact on my formative years. These were the movies of the fifties and, for the most part, they were American movies. Many of them were made by Columbia Pictures. I was one among millions of young people around the world who basked in the benign, positive and powerful aura of the post-Marshall plan, concerned and responsible America. The first day I came to this country was, in many ways, the most exciting of my life. "Part of me was coming home." That's how powerful the effect of American cinema had been on me.

'Far more than any other influence, more than school, more even than home, my attitudes, dreams, preconceptions, and pre-conditions for life had been irreversibly shaped five and a half thousand miles away in a place called Hollywood. I labour over all of this in order to explain exactly where my passion for cinema stems from, exactly why it hurts me that the movies so frequently sell themselves short; unable or unwilling to step up to the creative and ethical standards the audience is entitled to expect of them.

'The medium is too powerful and too important an influence on the way we live, the way we see ourselves, to be left *solely* to the tyranny of the box office or reduced to the sum of the lowest common denominator of public taste; this "public taste" or appetite being conditioned by a diet capable only of producing mental and emotional malnutrition! Movies are powerful. Good or bad, they tinker around inside your brain. They steal up on you in the darkness of the cinema to form or confirm social attitudes. They can help to create a healthy, informed, concerned, and inquisitive society or, in the alternative, a negative, apathetic, ignorant one – merely a short step away from nihilism. In short, cinema is propaganda. Benign or malign – social or antisocial, the factual nature of its responsibility cannot be avoided. To an almost alarming degree our political and emotional responses rest, for their health, in the quality and integrity of the present and future generation of film and television creators. Accepting this fact, there are only two personal madnesses that film-makers must guard against. One is the belief that they can do everything and the other is the belief that they can do nothing. The former is arrogant in the extreme. But the latter is plainly irresponsible and unacceptable.

'Without doubt, film-makers will continue to stagger from real to imagined crises and back again for years to come. The Film Industry is no place for fainthearted "timeservers". It needs thoroughgoing professionals with a love for cinema and respect for its audience. There can be no place for heroic posturing or overnight reputations. We have a business to nurture and build and that will require patience and a form of application which allows reputations the opportunity to develop and mature. Only those with a long-term interest in the Film Industry can expect to be rewarded. Speaking from experience, the rewards for that patience and faith are enormous.'

Although there was no actual applause when the Coke chiefs had finished reading, there was a considerable clearing of throats. Patsy could see that both men seemed moved – or at the very least be-mused.

'You're right. You're right,' Goizueta volunteered, breaking the silence, 'When I came from Cuba this is what cinema meant to me. I'm ashamed at what we have now.'

'Fine,' said David, 'so you'll understand precisely why I wouldn't make a *Rambo* no matter what the size of the built-in profit guarantee. If someone wrote me a cheque for the total box-office gross, I wouldn't take it.'

His reason for picking on *Rambo* was not ingenuous, for it illustrated the type of film whose values he found abhorrent – and at the same time, perhaps more significantly, had been chosen for distribution by Victor Kaufman at Tri-Star. *Rambo* therefore represented a despised genre *and* provided a convenient close-to-home hypothesis. ('You don't need to make a *Rambo*,' Dick Gallop claims he replied when David raised the same point at an earlier meeting, 'but you sure need to make a broader, more commercial slate of pictures than you made heretofore.')

As he elaborated on the manner in which he would address what he saw as Columbia's exorbitantly expensive 'housekeeping deals', where producers' overheads were paid in return for first pick of their product, Fay Vincent reflected that David was now talking territory in which the Coke bosses were not particularly interested. In any case, a number of deals had already been terminated before David's arrival. Although the housekeeping arrangement was not dissimilar to what David had enjoyed with Warner, the comparison ended with their richness and scale. David had already been briefed enough to be horrified at the terms to which Columbia had surrendered. While Warner remained essentially a studio run from the inside, it was clear to him the 'housekeeping' system at Columbia had become rampant. The studio was no longer a sovereign state, more a princely state which had to appease and mollify a group of barons.

Close on $10 million of Columbia's money was pouring out the door in retainers to a handful of producers. There was a massive accumulated figure of 'General Production Advances' of several times that sum, advances that had been paid out for production that had never taken place, dead money to all intents and purposes. He was staggered at the breadth and interpretation of 'legitimate costs' that Columbia allowed.

'And you are aware of my conditions of complete autonomy over the product I greenlight,' David went on, 'up to a ceiling of $30 million on any one film. Talent packages would be out. If I don't have your support in this, then I'm the wrong person for you.'

'We hear you, David,' was Coke's response, 'and we like it.'

Now the moment of truth had arrived as David asked, 'How about the major producers who may well find their situations altered by these policies?'

'Like who?' Keough asked.

'Well, like Ray Stark,' said David. 'He's certainly going to be one of the producers who'll feel the effect of these changes.'

Fay Vincent stared philosophically out of the window, having known this point was going to come up. Fay's relationship with Ray Stark had for years been a strained one, the *Annie* sequel row simply one of the last of a long line. Following the original *Annie* and the disaster of *The Slugger's Wife*, many of the producer's other pictures had done poorly; even his ex-protégé Guy McElwaine had refused to give several of Stark's movies the greenlight, notably *Biloxi Blues* and *Brighton Beach Memoirs*; these he had been forced to find a home for at Universal, during Frank Price's reign. What had always made Fay's position doubly difficult was Stark's closeness to Herbert Allen, although Allen heroically performed the difficult task of providing a balance between the two men, preventing either one from doing the other great harm. At best it would not take too much to upset the balancing act, as Fay was only too painfully aware. When David had raised the Ray Stark issue earlier with him, Fay had told him he thought Ray was difficult and dangerous. 'The trouble with Ray,' he summed up, 'is that he can't separate a business from a personal judgement, so if you say something to him in a business sense that he doesn't like, he'll say, "How can you say that? You're not being my *friend*." ' Fay told David frankly that Stark would indeed be a big problem, but that that was part of the territory. He would have the job and the authority to do what he wanted with Stark. If he got too close to him, the producer would want to run the whole show. It would be pretty well impossible to maintain a distance, almost a no-win proposition.

'Don't worry about Ray Stark,' the Coke bosses assured David, in an echo of Fay's original comment. 'We'll take his calls, we'll be polite, but Ray has no real currency down here. It'll be your show.'

Now Patsy had her say, adding her own warning about the support David must be given. 'I know my husband,' she told them. 'He'll give you all the blood, sweat and tears you could ever want. But if you don't back him to the hilt, he'll walk away. You'll lose him.'

'At Coke, we back the people we hire,' Patsy was assured.

The shimmering heat on the pavement outside was as nothing to that generated by the outpouring of admiration in Keough's office.

There was one important area to be left for further discussion – the question of David having complete control over International, which Fay had left open. Goizueta sent Fay a note following the meeting to say how thrilled he was with Puttnam and how tremendous it was that he was joining Columbia – and all because of Vincent's good offices. 'I can talk to David and Patsy about movies,' Goizueta enthused. 'I now have somebody I can talk to in California.' The bosses of Coke were elated. Out of the multitude of situations available to David Puttnam, he had chosen *them*.

Patsy and David were both 'gob-smacked' by what they saw as the warmth and sincerity of their reception, although David still felt an advance meeting with Ray Stark was called for. This was arranged at Stark's Mapleton Drive mansion in Hollywood's Holmby Hills, once the home of Humphrey Bogart.

During the meeting David divulged that Fay Vincent was reluctant to concede control of International Marketing and Distribution. Ray was all charm. 'I'll make a call,' he offered, 'leave it to me.'

'The great problem for me,' David continued, 'is the so-called "special relationship" you seem to enjoy at Columbia. Ray, you really can't continue to be both a customer *and* an adviser. You've got to decide just what you want to be.'

There was no immediately discernible chill as the two men sipped their tea in Stark's garden and only a few seconds elapsed before Stark replied, 'Oh, really? That's something I'll have to think about, although all in all I seriously think I'd rather be an adviser. I can get my pictures made at Universal. I've got a good deal there right now and I've got things at Tri-Star. Yes, I'd enjoy being an adviser.'

David felt as if a great weight had been lifted. 'Great, Ray, that's terrific,' he beamed.

As he was leaving, Stark asked if he had considered buying a house in Hollywood for his stay. When David replied he would prefer to rent, Stark insisted it made better sense to buy. If money was a problem, he would lend whatever was necessary. He would help him locate a house. He would help in any way he could. David was unable to escape the sense that he was being 'folded in'.

As he turned the offer down, a warning bell was ringing in his head. David Begelman had a three-year lease back in the seventies on a house in Beverly Hills that was owned by a company called Burton Way. Unknown to Columbia, who were paying the bulk of the bill, Burton was wholly owned by Ray Stark's lawyer, Gerald Lipsky. It seemed the house had been purchased by Lipsky specifically at Begelman's request and leased back to him. When Begelman was being investigated, he was asked if it would not have been more above-board if he had divulged to Columbia his landlord/tenant arrangement with Lipsky, a man with whom he was in constant negotiation over the terms of Ray Stark's pictures. Begelman replied that he saw nothing improper either in the arrangement or Columbia's ignorance of it. Direct financial ties had been found between Stark and Begelman – a loan of $15,000 in 1964/5 and another of $27,500 in 1976, which Begelman had kept in his desk for use as required. Stark had also guaranteed him a loan of $185,000 from the City National Bank. Although all the loans had been repaid and no impropriety had been inferred – 'Thanks a lot, Ray,' David thought, as he drove through Bel Air, 'but honestly, no thanks.'

David recalls that two days later he was informed that Fay had conceded control of International, making it look as if Stark had made the promised phone call. 'Ray never spoke to me about this,' says Fay, 'and David never told me he had raised it with Ray. I had agreed in London that David would ultimately have control of his own films. The main problem was in extricating his product from video and TV, and Williamson's reluctance to report to him.'

Earlier in 1986 David had an angry phone conversation with Bruce Robinson, which the writer recalls in his typically prosaic manner. 'He was pissed off at me for something, probably the fact I'd signed with Warners to do a screenplay of Emile Zola's *Germinale*. I'd been working on bloody rewrites for David until I was green; I had fucking mildew up to my ankles. I was so *fucked* with working for him on the atom bomb project, just *wasted* with work. He looked at it and said it was no longer a movie, what I'd written was a mini-series and I was off the project. As for my ambitions to direct a movie, he yelled, "*You'll* never be a director! You haven't got the emotional *staminá!*" I said, "Well, you're *fucking wrong there, Puttnam!*" and slammed the phone down. Then I carried on the conversation on my own. "That *cunt!*" I yelled. "How *dare* he say that. I'll fucking show *him!*" '

Bruce's long-held ambition to direct was in fact about to be achieved, ironically with the very first project of his that David had been shown by Andrew Birkin, his semi-autobiographical *Withnail and I*. 'David will inspire you,' says Bruce with a perfectly straight face, 'then he'll piss in your mouth.' A toothy grin. 'He's a demagogue, but he has that rare quality of being a leader. And let's face it, all producers are dyed-in-the-wool, sink-in-the-Atlantic cunts. He's not the biggest one around. In fact, all in all, at the end of the day, he's a good man. I still feel an incredible affection for him.'

In Beverly Hills in June 1986, the stage was set for the official announcement of David's appointment as Chairman of Columbia Pictures and senior executive vice-president and director of the main Columbia Pictures Industries Board, the corporate parent, reporting to Fay Vincent. Although not due to start officially at the studio until September 1, David would spend the next few months immersing himself in matters Columbia.

'Wooing the international audience,' was the theme Fay Vincent spelled out. Since 60 per cent of Coca-Cola's business was done outside the US, why should only 30 per cent of Hollywood's revenues come from abroad? All right, one of the products was brown syrup, the other was celluloid, but why let a fact like that stand in the way of such unarguable logic? In fact, increasing revenue from abroad was being discussed more and more at many other Hollywood studios. Fay Vincent's view was that Coke's international strength would be of help in achieving this goal, rather than any notion of Columbia's emulating Coke per se.

'I came here because of the tenacity of Fay, an old friend,' David enthused, 'and of Dick, a new one, who frankly wouldn't take "no" for an answer. I find it incredibly refreshing to be with a company whose outlook by definition is international. When you are a foreigner dealing with the Hollywood system, there is a sense sometimes it is a very parochial society. Coca-Cola is the least parochial company imaginable.'

He paid special tribute to the Warners executives, who had agreed to suspend his first-refusal contract with them, although it still had 20 months to go. The flip side of this coin, not lost upon many in the film community even while the tribute was being paid, was that Warners had refused to pick up in full one *single film* from Enigma throughout the years the contract had run. 'They've simply suspended refusing his films for 20 months,' one cynic wrote, reminding everyone it had been the Warners turn-down of *Stars and Bars* which had proved one of the last straws. Ignoring this, David went further over the top, declaring that Warners' 'generosity and understanding' over his contract, together with his working experience with them over the years, was one of the factors which had persuaded him in the end he might have been too harsh in his criticisms of Hollywood.

'Roberto understood my third-world mentality,' said David, 'about the responsibility of the American cinema and the job that cinema has to do in the rest of the world. This was something I didn't have to convince him of. He was brought up with it in the same way I was. And Don is this marvellous, enthusiastic entrepreneur who likes the idea of the film industry being given a boot up the bottom. When I went to Atlanta I was a neutral sceptic, but I came away a positive apostle.'

Patsy stood by her husband's side, 'I encouraged his idea of taking a sabbatical to Harvard and didn't think the Columbia idea was right, but the Coca-Cola people turned me round. They told us they wanted Columbia to be the best film company there is and I believed what they said. I may look ridiculous in a couple of years, but in any case, I always like the fight better than its resolution.'

Disbelief in Britain turned in many cases to outrage when the open secret of David's move was confirmed. Alexander Walker sent a telegram that read simply, 'Have you taken leave of your senses?' Hugh Hudson said, 'It's everything he said he'd never do.' He was dubbed 'a defector' by the *Daily Mail*. 'So much for Puttnam's patriotism,' a *Daily Telegraph* article ran. One of his ex-Goldcrest colleagues said, 'Hollywood will chew him up and spit him out.'

'I felt like Burgess and MacLean rolled into one,' David chuckled; then added prophetically, 'I may have to eat some of my words, but one thing I'm not is a defector. I see myself in a situation just like an aerospace engineer for Rolls-Royce. Imagine that everybody acknowledges you're producing the best-quality work. Then one day, through no fault of your own, Rolls-Royce closes down, and you get a telephone call from Boeing asking you to join them. Honestly, what would you do?'

Warren Beatty for one was concerned when he heard the news of David's impending arrival, and made it clear that as far as he was concerned there was no question of David getting his hands on *Ishtar*.

'You may have hired a very good person,' said Beatty, 'but I don't get along with him. I don't want to deal with him. He's going to torpedo my picture and he'll do everything possible to kill *Ishtar*. I don't know if we can function; there'll have to be lots of safeguards so he doesn't hurt the film.' Beatty's accusation was that Puttnam had said a number of terrible things about *Reds* in the fight over the Academy Awards, which the star termed 'unacceptable chicken shit'. Fay Vincent, who holds Beatty in great esteem, describing him as 'a clever, sophisticated guy', told him there was no need for concern, that he had already covered that ground with David. 'He has no wish to go anywhere near *Ishtar*,' Beatty was assured.

At the same time he began to wonder if he had underestimated the strength of feeling of the *Ishtar* participants. It would be neither the first, nor the last time he would have mistakenly minimized the bizarre motivations and rampant paranoia endemic in Hollywood. Both Beatty and Hoffman felt *they* should have been consulted about David's appointment.

Patsy Pollock's career continued to interact with that of David's on her next assignment, as co-producer with Sandy Lieberson on his first solo venture after leaving Goldcrest, *Rita, Sue and Bob Too*. Although saddened by the factors that led to David's decision to leave Britain, she could see his rationale.

'He was saying, "I'll get on my bike and go somewhere I don't have to tap dance and do the Mammy act on my knees." *Of course* he was depressed about England; *of course* it was extremely humiliating to be turned down for peanuts for *Stars and Bars*. Then he'd had a lot to put up with over the years, not least me and my GBH of the earhole, or Alan Parker in his cups, in between doing his laser-beam brilliant cartoons.

'He's a good man, Puttnam. He protects people, although his paternalistic sense is reserved purely for his family and his warmth for the family circle. I don't think David's very knowledgeable about women, to be perfectly honest. He's quite shy. Although he respects me professionally, I'm not the sort of person he would work with except as a casting director, although I always hoped that might change.

'Patsy is the classic "great woman"; I think she's quite remarkable. She has a powerful spiritual belief in his talent. She herself has this talent to run lives beautifully. Even when they were skint she managed to do it. David's not really a sociable person, no dinner parties for twelve and all that stuff. Patsy protects him from that. She gives a new dimension to the way you look after a man, but without any hint of subservience. No, it's outward-pushing, rather ambitious in a way. She forms a layer that soaks up the trivial, with tremendous grace and style. She has a talent for the quality of life. If there was a class in this, Patsy would major in it.

'She motivates a climate in which he can thrive, featuring in a *dazzling* way in his life, not as a subtext. Far from being one of the "her indoors" of the film trade, Patsy's got her own life, her own views, while remaining completely absorbed in his life. Everything she does, from ironing a handkerchief to replacing a marble staircase, has been to make a life for them both.'

With her parents' twenty-fifth wedding anniversary looming, Debbie decided something had to be done to mark the occasion. In the past neither David nor Patsy had made a special effort to observe anniversary celebrations. Debbie planned to change all that and combine it with a visit to Venice, which she knew her mother had always longed to see. It would be like the honeymoon they never took. With David, Sacha, Debbie, Valerie and Margaret in the plot, David told Patsy there was no possibility he could return from the States in time for a get-together. Patsy resigned herself to spending the anniversary alone at Kingsmead Mill, until another phone call came from her husband.

'Hello, Billy,' was the greeting. 'Good news, I *can* get back after all.'

'*Marvellous*! Will I arrange something?'

'No, no, let's just have a quiet time at the Mill. It'll be our last chance for a bit of peace before Columbia.'

Debbie leapt into action, spiriting her mother's passport away from the Mill and packing a case for her, subsequently hidden in David's car. David flew in and phoned Patsy from the airport.

'Let's go out for a nice lunch somewhere,' he suggested. 'Let's do it right. Wear something smart. After all, we have got something to celebrate.'

When David arrived at the Mill, Patsy was whisked off in the unexpected direction of Heathrow airport.

'Where are we going for lunch?' Patsy asked.

'Paris,' David replied with a smile.

'*Paris*? Oh, David, don't be so ridiculous. You're only here for a few days – to dash around like this is crazy. And I haven't got my passport with me.'

'That's OK, I've got it.'

As they parked the car at Heathrow, David hailed a porter to take Patsy's bag over to the Alitalia check-in, where he managed to create enough confusion to get through without arousing Patsy's suspicions. It was only on the flight itself, when the captain announced they were passing the French capital on the left, that the cat was out of the bag.

'Venice!' Patsy exclaimed. 'Oh, my God, David!'

The bridal suite at the Hotel Cipriani, standing serenely on its own island, was their destination. Over dinner in the hotel that night, David explained the conspiracy, or part of it, to his delighted wife.

The next day was spent sightseeing, then by early evening the couple were back at the Cipriani. 'I'm going to order a bottle of champagne,' David declared. 'We'll have a drink before we go out for dinner.'

'That's weird,' Patsy thought. 'He's never done that in 25 years.'

Ten minutes later the door chimes rang out.

'Can you get that, darling?' David shouted from the bathroom. Patsy went over to the door and flung it open. There on the doorstep, bearing a huge tray of champagne in an ice bucket between them, were Debbie and Sacha, who had flown over that morning.

Tears – and champagne – flowed before the Puttnams trooped out together to dinner at the sumptuous Gritti Palace, then three wonderful family days in Venice followed, before the trek back to London for the family – and the lonely onward journey to Los Angeles for David.

David and Hugh Hudson, Oscar Night, 1982
(National Film Archive, London)

David Essex and Ringo Starr in
That'll Be The Day
(National Film Archive, London)

Jodie Foster in Bugsy Malone
(National Film Archive, London)

Harvey Keitel, Keith Carradine in The Duellists
(National Film Archive, London)

Scott Baio and Florrie Digger in Bugsy Malone
(National Film Archive, London)

Brad Davis in Midnight Express
(National Film Archive, London)

John Lynch and Helen Mirren in Cal
(National Film Archive, London)

Fulton MacKay, Peter Riegert and Burt Lancaster in Local Hero
(National Film Archive, London)

Ben Cross and Nigel Havers in Chariots of Fire
(National Film Archive, London)

Ian Charleson and Ian Holm in Chariots of Fire
(National Film Archive, London)

Haing S. Ngor in The Killing Fields
(National Film Archive, London)

Sam Waterston and Haing S. Ngor in The Killing Fields
(National Film Archive, London)

Robert de Niro in The Mission
(National Film Archive, London)

Robert de Niro and Jeremy Irons in The Mission
(National Film Archive, London)

David today
(National Film Archive, London)

David, Roland Joffe, Bruce Robinson — The Killing Fields *team*
(National Film Archive, London)

Chapter 22

Stark reality

'There are only two types of animal who roam the Hollywood jungle,' Bruce Robinson maintains. 'Those who do the fucking and those who get fucked. You just try to ensure you're one of the former for they'll shaft you in every orifice they can find, then they'll cut you open and *fuck the wound*. Of all people, David knew this. For years in Britain *he's* been the fucker, now he was certain to be the fuckee.'

Said to have settled down again after the heady post-herpes, pre-AIDS era, the three most common phrases to be heard in Hollywood are still the time-honoured 'The cheque is in the mail,' plaintive 'The Jaguar is in the garage' and invariably fraudulent 'I promise I won't come in your mouth.'

Hollywood – where the last great *Hollywood* movie was *Chinatown*, produced by Robert Evans, written by Robert Towne, directed by Roman Polanski and brought to us by Paramount Pictures, whose highest aspirations today range from *Top Gun* through endless *Beverly Hills Cops*, *Indiana Joneses* and *Friday the Thirteenths*.

Hollywood – where Elia Kazan had described Harry Cohn, Columbia's founder, as 'The biggest bug in the manure pile'. When Cohn boasted about his foolproof device for judging whether a picture was good or bad, 'If my fanny squirms, it's bad. If my fanny doesn't squirm, it's good. Just as simple as that,' Herman Mankiewitz's response was, 'Imagine, the whole world wired to Harry Cohn's ass!'

Hollywood – where a company will make a deal with an artist for a given project. That's good. When the starting date arrives, often no contracts have been prepared. That's not so good. If the artist fails to turn up on the first day of shooting, however – contract or not – the studio will sue, and *win* a breach of contract suit. Hey, that's bad. That same high-minded studio is in any case planning to deceive the artist in terms of book-keeping when the eventual profit statement is due. That's really bad. Then *they* expect to be sued, secure in the certain knowledge that the whole affair will be tied up in lawsuits for ever, while they have the use of the money, and are earning interest on it. That's wicked.

Who needs stars in Hollywood?

• David Puttnam (pre-Robert De Niro): 'I'd rather go for a non-star, not someone who's going to bring the baggage of other roles to the part . . . An awful lot of the pressure the agents rely on to get their stars in these films and get their fees paid is the social pressure that producers or directors feel to be associated with these same people. They love to sit at dinner parties with them. It's the starfucker phenomenon. If someone says a star to me, all I see are the problems – none of the advantages, only the problems. And then explaining why one person gets a trailer and someone else doesn't. I basically despise human beings who feel the necessity to be treated unlike other human beings. I can't be doing with it, can't deal with it.'

• David Puttnam (post-Robert De Niro): 'Stars aren't stars by accident. By and large they're really quite good actors. You find yourself with a star because actually that is the most talented actor you can find.'

• William Goldman (writer): 'Stars are a pain in the ass to a director. They have to be coddled. They need to be stroked. Ultimately what they do is waste time and time is the enemy of all production. As a general rule I would say if you corner every director in the world and say, "This is off the record. If you can make your next picture (and you have the same budget), but in one case you have a star and in one case you don't have a star." There may be one director in the history of the world who would rather go with a star, but for the most part none of them would want to.'

• Billy Wilder (genius): 'My aunt Lizzie learns her lines, always turns up on time and does what she is told. But who wants to pay to see my aunt Lizzie?'

Who needs writers in Hollywood – where the moving finger writes and having writ moves on, whereupon a re-writ is arranged?

• Stirling Silliphant: 'On the set, the writer is very much like a hooker who has been fucked and paid and is there on sufferance.'

• Bobbi Thompson (agent): 'Being a screenwriter is to my mind the most masochistic thing you can do. They all get treated like shit and they are raped right and left. It's sad to hear that even the most talented, sought-after writers are subject to the same shitty treatment and lack of respect as the newest beginner who is shafted on the money.'

• I.A.L. Diamond (genius): 'More directors have ruined their careers by writing their own scripts than by screwing the leading lady. And some of them have done both!'

• Alfred Hitchcock (director): 'The three most vital elements in any good film are the script, the script and the script.'

Who needs directors in Hollywood?
• Gore Vidal (writer): 'Almost anyone can do what a director does. I've worked on about 15 movies; I've done 150 live TV plays; I've done 8 plays on Broadway – I never yet saw a director who contributed anything. When I went to Cannes for *The Best Man* – there was on this banner the title in French, 'Un film de Franklin Schaffner'. Well, I just hit the ceiling. I mean, this was my play, my movie. I had helped put the thing together. I had *hired* Frank.'
• Steven Spielberg (director): 'Directing is 80 per cent communication and 20 per cent knowhow. Because if you can communicate to the people who know how to edit, know how to light, and know how to act – if you can communicate what you want so that what they're doing is giving you your vision and what you feel, that's my definition of a good director.'

Who needs sneak previews in Hollywood?
• Rob Reiner (director): 'We'd had a great response to *The Sure Thing* in St Louis. The research team told us, "Wow! The only two films that did that well were *ET* and *Gable and Lombard*." I thought, "That's just it; we're going to be somewhere between *ET* and *Gable and Lombard!*"'
• David Brown (producer): 'In my experience, a sneak preview can be a triumph and result in no one coming to see the movie.'
• Richard Rush (director): 'There's an element of self-fulfilling prophecy in research. We keep being told that the audience is teenagers, between 12 and 22, and so we keep making movies that appeal to those people. So in a sense, research is leading the industry down the garden path.'
• Brian De Palma (director): 'It's appalling that 325 people recruited from shopping malls can shake the confidence of professionals who've been working in the industry for decades.'
• Richard Brooks (director): 'Today, I hear they bring the audience in to see a picture and ask them to push a little button if they like certain scenes. How the hell are they going to get involved in a movie and push buttons at the same time? And preview cards – Columbus would still be in Spain if they waited for preview cards.'
• David Puttnam: 'I believe in previewing absolutely.'

Power breakfast, anyone? It's got to be the Bel Air Hotel. Power lunch? Le Dome on Sunset, backrooms are best – or La Serre in the Valley. Power dinner? Morton's in West Hollywood, corner Melrose and Robertson, or Spago overlooking Sunset Strip. (Wolfgang Puck features wonderful food here, but the real reason everyone goes is because it's *the* in-place to be.) Old-time power? Chasen's in Beverly Hills, corner Doheny and Beverly. Can't get a table? Short of change? No problem. Most maitre d's will take American Express, but for under $100, forget it.

How about Power hotels? The Bel Air can't be beat for the élite, Chateau Marmont is frequented by the funkies, Sunset Marquis by the rock 'n' roll megas, while Shangri-La on Santa Monica has the best view of Diane Keaton when she's in town. But while nibbling on your Quiche of Sea Bass in Lemon Juice with Cucumber, Tomato and Cilantro, or Sautéed Chicken Paupiettes stuffed with Veal and served with Madeira Mushroom sauce, consider the words of the bank manager's daughter, Patsy Puttnam, 'There's nowt for nowt.' Yep, together with that luxurious pad you may have been allocated by the studio, it's all going on the bill of your current movie.

Iain Smith swears that after landing at Los Angeles airport, palely loitering British film-makers are courteously guided to an ante-room by bronzed, smiling Californians with perfect white teeth, and tendered a swift injection of a powerful inadequacy drug, the size of the dosage varying only with the proposed length of stay.

Once upon a time the lunatics, it was whispered, were taking over the asylum. Way, way back Cagney tried it. Then Bogey. Then Alan Ladd and his 'over-the-hill gang' at Warner. Then big John Wayne himself, followed in more recent times by Dustin Hoffman, Barbra Streisand, Sydney Poitier and Steve McQueen in their First Artists venture. The keepers were laughing up their sleeves. Poor loonies! They had forgotten about the small matter of distribution, forever securely retained in the studios' clutches.

With the end of the studio contract system, the era of the agents had truly arrived: MCA, William Morris, CMA, ICM – although it was Hugh French who bust the bank with the first-ever $1-million contract for a star on a single picture, Elizabeth Taylor in *Cleopatra*. BO (Before Ovitz) each star had one basic contact with whom they dealt, who would have little or no dialogue with his counterparts in the business. At Creative Artists Agency (CAA), President Michael Ovitz and his team of Ron Meyer, Bill Haber, Rowland Perkins and Martin Baum would not only represent specific clients, but would constantly cross-collateralise their career moves; the era of 'the package' had arrived, allowing studios to abdicate responsibility for stitching together the various elements in any given project. Run like a military operation, CAA's day starts at the crack of dawn and ends when it ends, which can be dawn the following day. Considered by many to be the most powerful man in Hollywood, Ovitz has become today's Talleyrand, a modern Metternich, able to whisper in the ears of kings.

David's ballroom-dancing experience as a young boy would come in handy in the next year, as he would be constantly engaged in a series of *danses macabres* with some of Hollywood's toughest acts – Ray Stark and his Stomp, Bill Cosby's Can-Can, Victor Kaufman's Carioca, Warren Beatty's Blackbottom, Barry Diller's Dirty Dancing, Marty Ransohoff's Rock 'n' Roll – and Mike Ovitz's Entrechat, for which there is no known remedy.

For the six months before David's arrival at the studio, Columbia had been slipping badly in the box-office stakes. The total for the period was still a reasonable $291 million – however, *Karate Kid II* accounted for $110 million of that, leaving the balance of $181 million split between 13 other features: *White Nights* ($42 million), *Stand by Me* ($31 million), *Murphy's Romance* ($31 million), *Jo-Jo Dancer* ($18 million), *Armed and Dangerous* ($15 million), *A Chorus Line* ($11 million), *Care Bears II* ($8 million), *Quicksilver* ($7 million), *A Fine Mess* ($5 million), *Violets are Blue* ($4 million), *Out of Bounds* ($4 million), *American Anthem* ($4 million), and *That's Life* ($1 million).

Paramount was making everyone else look sick with $412 million, far above 1985's champion, Warners, who trailed behind in second place with $307 million. Columbia was at No. 3, but only thanks to one film, and they were being challenged by 20th Century Fox with $236 million and Disney/Touchstone with $235 million. Responsibility for restoring the Columbia lady's somewhat down-at-heel fortunes rested heavily on David's fairly slender shoulders.

The Puttnams' first plan was for David to stay on his own at the Bel Air for a month until the house Patsy had selected was ready – she had picked a furnished bungalow in Coldwater Canyon which Dudley Moore was due to vacate. When his Malibu house ran behind schedule, Dudley inconveniently opted to stay an extra month, extending David's booking at the Bel Air and delaying Patsy's arrival from Kingsmead Mill.

The first few days at the 11-acre oasis the Bel Air represented, was to David, a time out from the real world. On Saturday an Italian wedding reception was held outdoors beneath the exotic palms that lined the hotel's swan lake, in a scene reminiscent of *The Godfather*. Serenaded by a bank of violins that were sheltered in a shady balcony over-looking the celebrants, David tried hard to concentrate on the scripts that had been left for his attention, as he was regaled with a medley of 'Romantica', 'That's Amore', 'Love Letters', 'Fascination' and 'Tie a Yellow Ribbon Round the Old Oak Tree'.

The atmosphere at Columbia's Burbank studios came as a rude awakening. Balefully overlooked by a huge water-tower, flanked by administrative offices at Columbia Plaza South, and with the Pro-ducers' Building opposite housing Ray Stark, the second-floor of the barrack-like Columbia Plaza East was David's destination.

'Who are you here to see?' the doorman enquired politely.

'Nobody. I'm David Puttnam, the new start.'

'Are you sure you have the correct building? There's no one here by that name, sir.'

'I'll be in Mr McElwaine's old office.'

'Oh, that's through the doors, turn left, up the stairs, then the far end of the corridor.'

Huge black-and-white blow-ups of scenes from Columbia hits lined the corridor walls, among them *It Happened One Night*, *Mr Deeds Goes to Town*, *Gilda* and *Guess Who's Coming for Dinner*, but up and down the executive corridors, doors were shut tight. It seemed the company had been running for so long on fear and uncertainty that a conviction had become embedded that the new broom would sweep instant squeaky-clean. The whole building appeared to be in a state of siege.

Valerie was already installed and busy typing lists of the 1300 script submissions that had poured into the studios since the announcement of David's appointment. She had earlier opened the door of David's office, unprepared for the eyeball-assaulting impact of Guy McEl-waine's deep maroon period. The colour was wall-to-wall and floor-to-ceiling. Furniture consisted of four gigantic settees, festooned with what resembled skunk skin rugs. A single naked light bulb hung guiltily from the ceiling. Smoked glass covering the two corner walls ensured that not a single shaft of sunlight was able to penetrate the stygian gloom. Valerie sighed and closed the door on the funereal scene. 'David, you'll need to move somewhere else while that nightmare-on-wheels is sorted out,' she told him.

'Fine,' he replied, 'now, first things first, I'd like to speak to every-one, from executives down to the janitor.'

When all personnel were congregated in the largest screening room, David gave an inspired and inspiring speech to the bemused, de-moralized gathering. They would work as a *team*. They were going to make *great movies*. There *would* be problems. They *would* be over-come. He did *not* have all the answers. He was prepared to *listen* to those who thought they had. There would be an *open door* to his office *at all times*. There would be *monthly seminars* ('The Reel Truth') to which they would *all* be invited.

The reaction was astonishing. 'I've been here ten years,' said one studio publicist, 'and I've never even *met* the head of the studio. It was like the mountain coming to Mohammed.'

By early evening even the normally tireless Valerie was flagging. 'It's been non-stop,' she told David. 'As fast as I'm logging the scripts, more pour in.' She smiled. 'Doesn't look as if you'll be short of subjects, David.' After dinner at the Bel Air, business resumed again as the two went through the day's calls and David dictated letters of reply and began to fill his diary with appointments for the week.

In the next few days, between systematic individual meetings with every member of his executive staff, David acquired Ridley Scott's thriller, *Someone to Watch over Me*, in turnaround from MGM. He bluntly told Michael Nathanson, a 29-year-old production executive, 'You're earning far too much money for what you do. You stand out like a sore thumb.' Out of David Begelman's stable via the Guy McElwaine régime, Nathanson replied he had negotiated his salary. 'Fine,' said David, 'I'm putting you in charge of Ridley Scott's new picture. We'll see how you do.' (Three months later David told Nathanson, 'You're on my team.')

As the week progressed, David began to see that his plan to make the best of his inherited team was in some cases going to be impractical. These individuals had never pulled together – they had *fallen* together and certain members were going to have to be removed from the mix. He was horrified at the backstabbing he had to listen to, the naked animosity rife in many of the conversations.

'How has it been?' Patsy asked when he phoned.

'Ask me again in a couple of days,' David replied. 'If I told you now, you wouldn't believe it. Morale is so low it's off the chart.'

Within days of his arrival at Columbia, David received a script from director Norman Jewison, whose chequered career traipsed from the wilder shores of *Jesus Christ, Superstar* and *Rollerball* through to the relatively-modest, well-received *A Soldier's Story* and *Agnes of God*. The submission was an update of the only script ever written by H. G. Wells, *The Man Who Could Work Miracles*, intended as a Richard Pryor vehicle with a budget of $19 million. 'I said I wanted to start shooting in three months' time,' Jewison recalled, 'and must have an answer. I'd spent all that time, and at my age – 61 – you've only got so many films left in you. A week goes by. No answer. So I called my agent and asked him to get in touch with David and have him call me. He never called. Finally, a month goes by and I get a letter from David saying he didn't wish to do the film.' For David's part, he maintains he passed the script on to colleagues within days with a 'Not for me' comment to be relayed to Jewison's agent.

Jewison phoned David, incensed that it had taken a month to be turned down. 'How dare you keep me waiting!' he raged down the phone. 'Then you didn't have the courtesy to call me personally!'

David maintains that he both likes and respects Jewison, although he found both *A Soldier's Story* and *Agnes of God* dull. While not as rich as some, David did not feel inclined to extend his contract after the abuse the director gave him over the phone following the *Miracles* turndown.

'It was clear,' said Jewison, 'that David Puttnam had no interest in my future at Columbia, so I announced I was leaving.' He took with him a property entitled *Moonstruck* and promptly placed the picture with Alan Ladd Jr at MGM. With Cher and Nicolas Gage cast, the film would go on to win Jewison greater critical and commercial success than he had enjoyed for years. Could it have been a Columbia picture? 'It was never offered to me,' David declared. It was an answer that would come back to haunt him.

While this was David's first encounter with Jewison, his relationship with Dan Melnick went back to *Midnight Express*, the suspension over the shower scene, then the offer to take over as production head at Columbia in 1978. Back at Columbia with his Indieprod company after a stop-over at 20th Century Fox – and a series of worthy, but expensive flops – Melnick's contract was up after two more films.

David heartily endorsed the producer's Steve Martin vehicle, *Roxanne*, and supported the casting of Daryl Hannah. He was equally keen on his off-beat comedy/drama *Punchline*, with Sally Fields and Tom Hanks, and talked of an Oscar-qualifying run for this in late 1987. There was only one problem with Melnick's pictures, which he neatly summarized. 'They were good for everybody except Columbia, the goose laying the golden eggs for other people. Dan's 7.5 per cent of the gross was the killer. It meant a film like *Roxanne* would have to take a fortune before Columbia would see a penny.'

When it was clear there was no deal, Melnick eventually exited in a huff and joined the Rambo team at Carolco Pictures. A year later he gave his version of events to *Variety*: 'I had a contractual commitment that was running out. David indicated a strong desire to continue the relationship. It was unique. I funded my own development and then made a distribution deal which was advantageous. He said he wanted to take over the development costs. We struck a deal over the phone. Later, he called back and said, "This is embarrassing, but Fay doesn't want to make any rich production deals."'

Fay Vincent denies he was ever informed. 'David was using me,' he maintains. '*I* didn't veto Melnick's deal. I didn't know of it until after the decision was made.'

'I wouldn't want it to be implied that it was Fay's decision,' David later admitted. 'I may have told Fay, but it was my decision. It was not personal. I admire Dan Melnick. I just felt that the terms of the deal were too high to live with.'

Fay had already been exposed to an aspect of David he had not anticipated. 'We all have our foibles,' says Fay, 'but one of David's problems is he's capable of lying. They're not serious, but he does have a problem with the truth and it gets in the way.' The issue was who-chased-who.

'I'm telling everyone *you* made the approach,' David told Fay. 'It sounds better.'

'That's up to you,' Fay replied, 'but I'm not going to lie for you, David. I simply won't say how it happened. I'll say we had lunch, that's all.'

(David and I had the following somewhat surrealistic conversation in August, 1988; in an attempt to lay this one to rest:

AY: 'Fay says you somewhat bent the facts about who made the approach.'

DP: 'No. *I* didn't make it. *Tom Lewyn* did.'

AY: 'Well, he's your lawyer, after all, isn't he?'

DP: 'You'll have to talk to Tom about it.'

AY: 'Tom says you both more or less cooked it up.'

DP: '*No, no, no.* Tom approached me about Paramount out the blue. I'd never had any thoughts at all about going to that studio. When the whole thing at Paramount didn't work out, he's the one who said to Fay I might be interested. My understanding clearly is that Fay had lunch with Tom.'

AY: 'I can only tell you what Fay told me.'

DP: 'Maybe they're changing their minds, they told me they had lunch. I wasn't *unaware* they were having lunch, perfectly true. Tom speaks to me once a week. He's one of those people – he's a what's happening guy – he's an information collector. No, I don't think so, I don't think the facts bear that out. I wanted the job. Fuck me, we didn't half play hardball! Did I mind him and Dick coming over and spending a day in telling me what they could offer?'

AY: 'Fay's not denying that as soon as he heard you were available, he was interested, but he hadn't actually thought of you originally!'

DP: 'Tom, I think, maybe, as a result of the Paramount thing, having tried to broker that deal, saw there was a deal to be brokered, so maybe he saw that my turndown at Paramount was a specific one, not an absolute one, and – *yes*, he *did* tell me he was having lunch with Fay.'

AY: 'What Fay said specifically was that you said to him, "I'm telling everyone *you* made the approach"; and Fay wasn't enthralled with that idea.'

DP: 'I really don't remember. *I said that?* Well, again, all of my early conversations with Fay . . . maybe I wanted to make it *clear*, to make it *unambiguous*, that's the only thing I can think – to avoid any ambiguity. I tell you what I *might* have said was, because the question's going to be asked, we did a rehearsal of a press conference, and what I *may* have said to Fay is that if the question gets asked "who approached who?" I want to make it *unambiguously clear* that you approached me, rather than say it was a conversation with our lawyers etc. etc. I can *imagine* that')

While Bill Forsyth was in New York with actor Peter Riegert in 1983, they went to see Preston Sturges's *Sullivan's Travels* at the Regency Theatre one night. While strolling back through Columbus Circle, one of the girls in the party enthused about a marvellous novel she had just read, entitled *Housekeeping*. Bill asked to see a copy and became fascinated by the book. After several months, when he began to see the movie that could be in it he took out an option on *Housekeeping*. The author, Marilynne Robinson, visited Bill in Scotland with her family while he was shooting *Comfort and Joy*, then at the end of 1984 he began working seriously on the book. He was in correspondence by this time with Diane Keaton, who had expressed interest in working with him. She was equally enthusiastic about *Housekeeping* and an informal understanding was arrived at that she would be in it. With a script written by the spring of 1985, the hope was to start shooting that autumn. Unfortunately Bill found little interest from the majors, even with Diane's name attached to the project.

The script had champions everywhere, at Disney, Columbia and Fox, but they were in the minority. Jake Eberts thought it was too depressing and worried about the suicide in it. 'But it's at the beginning, not the end,' Bill argued. Some Norwegian oil money that was fleetingly available would have seen half the film shot in Norway and the balance in Canada. Months of fruitless negotation took place in New York with Al Clark and Robert Devereux of Virgin. John Daly at Hemdale professed to love the project, but was hard to pin down.

In January 1986 Bill at last found a home for the film, albeit an unlikely one, at Cannon. With Diane Keaton on board and a budget of $5 million, they were happy. Filming was set to begin in Canada in September and pre-production offices had been set up when a call came for Bill to meet Diane at her home. He took along the script, prepared to hold an impromptu rehearsal session. Instead Ms Keaton indicated over the course of an hour that she had changed her mind and decided not to do the movie after all.

Bill put through a call to Anthony Jones in London, who said he would try to set something else up before the news leaked to Cannon. As soon as it did, the company immediately despatched an accountant to shut down pre-production. David was contacted and the situation explained. Yes, he would pick it up, providing a budget and alternative star could be agreed, and Bill would make his next film for Columbia. ('A *commercial* subject this time, if you don't mind,' David laughed.)

There was some doubt that Cannon would let the project go because of their bumpy relationship with David, but following the refund of their $300,000 pre-production costs, they did. The name of Christine Lahti kept cropping up as a replacement actress. She was flown to Vancouver to talk to Bill and to his delight, loved the script. The incredible rescue operation complete, *Housekeeping* started shooting for Columbia Pictures on its original starting date, just six weeks after Diane Keaton walked out. It was David's first acquisition for Columbia and represented a welcome reunion with the Scottish director he admired so much. And all before he had officially started at the studio.

Only weeks after his first meeting with Ray Stark, David was startled to receive a script from the producer. 'There's just this one I want you to check out,' Stark explained. Despite this flying in the face of their 'agreement', David was the soul of tact. 'I'll get back to you quickly,' he promised. 'I'm leaving tonight, but I'll read it on the plane.'

The script turned out to be based on another relative of Stark's, Libby Holman. David phoned the producer two days later with his verdict on *Sweet Libby*: 'I've read it, Ray, and it's not for me.'

'What's wrong with it?'

'I just didn't like it. I didn't like the subject matter.'

A pause, then: 'Admittedly it needs more work, David. It needs another rewrite.'

'No, Ray, I don't think so. It's got nothing to do with a rewrite; that would be a waste of time as far as I'm concerned. It's the subject matter. I've seen this back-stage drama half a dozen times. It's *Funny Lady* all over again. I think it's out of its time.'

Another pause, this one longer.

'Well, fair enough. I don't agree with you, but at least you got back to me quickly.'

Now, just two weeks into his Columbia stint, Stark was on the line again.

'Why haven't you called me? You've been here two weeks. I thought you wanted me to help.'

'Christ,' said David, 'I've only been at the studio for 30 seconds. Give me a break, Ray. I haven't even had time to work out what my problems *are* yet. I'm living like a displaced person at the Bel Air, reading scripts all night and working all day. Sure, there'll be a lot to ask you about, but right now I'm up to my ears in it.'

'Well,' said Stark sulkily, 'I thought I'd see you every day. So what do I get instead? All you've done since our meeting is to turn down *Sweet Libby*. It's not good enough. Get over here for breakfast tomorrow morning. We've got things to talk about.'

Following a restless night at the Bel Air, David squealed his Audi to a halt in Stark's driveway, ready for the scrap he knew was in front of him. To hell with it, he thought, if I give in now I'm finished. We'll soon find out if Coke meant what they said about support. Stark's massive home, with its Henry Moore sculpture garden and enormous collection of paintings, by Braque, Magritte and Léger, reminded David of a small private museum in which breakfast was served by the keeper before the curator came down to join him.

Stark launched straight into the attack.

'Am I going to make pictures at Columbia, or am I not?'

David put down his orange juice. 'If you're asking me on principal, because you're Ray Stark, would I say yes to you, the answer is no, I won't. It depends on the script. My mandate from Coke is to go with scripts I think will work. That does not extend to anything and everything you care to send me.'

Stark got up and slammed his napkin down on the breakfast table.

'Well, fuck you, then,' he hissed. 'Think I need you?'

David got up to face him.

'I don't know whether you need me. You're acting like you do need me, but you're telling me you don't. I don't understand you; there's no logic in your position.'

'I need to know where I *am* with you.'

'I'm *telling* you – if you've got something you want to do at Columbia and you send it in and it's terrific, I'll be the first person on the phone saying, please make it. Otherwise, no.'

'Are these the rules?'

'Yes, these are the rules.'

'Well, that's not what I had in mind at all.'

'Well, it's *exactly* what I had in mind when we had our conversation about your being helpful and advising.'

After refusing an invitation to a private view, with Stark and Mike Ovitz, of the Museum of Contemporary Art – ('I'm too busy reading scripts,' said David tersely. 'You'd better get your priorities right,' Stark snapped, oblivious of the irony in his remark) – the breakfast meeting broke up amid further recriminatory remarks about Stark's access to friends in high places: clearly with no idea of the depth of feeling between the two men, David unwisely came out with, 'Your relationship with Herbert Allen bothers me.' The advantage went to Stark. Many shared years and secrets had bred staunch allies.

'I can fight my own battles,' David was haughtily informed. 'I don't need Herbert, I don't need anyone.'

That very afternoon, a second 'Ray Stark Productions' packet landed on David's desk. Inside was a novella and two scripts for a project called *Revenge*, an item owned by Columbia which Stark had decided to develop. David dutifully read through the material before departing for Europe and a meeting of film-makers. Although unimpressed, he could see that the novella, rather than the existing scripts – one each by Walter Hill and John Huston – could be made into something interesting, but only at the right price. The grapevine now has it that Walter Hill himself and his producer David Giler wanted a crack at it, but not with Ray Stark aboard. David decided to flex his Columbia muscles, and wrote to Stark.

September 16, 1986

Dear Ray,

REVENGE

I'm just off to Europe for a couple of weeks and I thought I should set down my thoughts regarding the above property.

During the past ten days I have painstakingly picked my way through the novella, the Walter Hill and the John Huston screenplays. I came to the conclusion last night that this wasn't a property that we'll be in a position to move on in the coming months. With this in mind I suggest the following:

We arrange either formally or informally for you to have a 90 day period in which to set the film up at another studio. Failing this, it will return to Columbia without any further lien and we'll be free to offer it elsewhere.

I say this because in reviewing the film it transpired that the material had been of interest some while ago to a team of film-makers whom I rate highly. There is always a chance that I can interest them in picking up the pieces and turn out a good film at a price that makes it attractive. I'm eager not to close us out of the possibility of being able to reinterest them on terms that we could live with.

The reason for all the neuroses regarding this property is that we have over $600,000 tied up in it and most of all I'd like the use of the money!

See you when I get back,
Warmest regards,
    David.

This time Stark's fury could no longer be contained. Apart from his dislike of what he saw as David's prissy way of dotting every 'i' and crossing every 't' in a welter of correspondence, the contents of this particular missive, as well as the style, enraged him. And he had heard a rumour – apparently unfounded – that the team of Alan Parker and Alan Marshall were interested in the property.

'Who *are* these jerks who want to make *Revenge* without me?' he roared down the phone.

'They specifically asked me not to say who they are,' said David.

'What do you *mean*? You can't *treat* me like this. Who *are* they?'

'I'm not going to tell you.'

The final meeting between the two men during David's Columbia reign came only weeks later, during the first week of November 1986, as Stark brushed past David's startled secretaries and barged into his office.

'I never see you –' Stark opened the conversation, which was to be brief and icy.

David had no answer. To him the breakfast and *Revenge* farrago had killed off any question of a 'deal' or 'special understanding'.

'– and it's wrong of you not to tell me who the people are who want to make *Revenge*. Why *can't* I take it elsewhere?'

'You can,' said David. 'I've already covered that in my letter, but I want it back here after the 90-day period is up so the company's got a chance to get its money out.'

David knew as he watched Stark turn on his heel and march out of his office that he had made a mortal enemy of one of the most influential players in Hollywood. Still he underestimated the truly apocalyptic nature of Stark's wrath. To David he was the Wizard of Oz after Toto has pulled away the side curtain. To many others he was nothing less than Godzilla, capable of raining down hellfire and damnation on selected denizens of his own personal Tokyo. 'If you cross Ray Stark, you'd better make sure he's dead first,' ran the legend.

So who needs Ray Stark in Hollywood?
• Bobby Littman (Hollywood agent): 'He's a brilliant film producer, like he was an agent before that, a showman in the true old-fashioned sense. He's made some darned good movies and he's been good to his friends.'
• James Bridges (director): 'My two experiences with him were quite crazed. We had such a fight over *Houdini* that I thought I could never work with him again. But I'm tempted because he gets his hands on the best material, and he's a superb producer.'
• Ex-employee: 'No one who has ever worked with him has escaped his generosity.'
• Raymond Chandler (author, commenting on Stark the agent): 'Ray Stark seems to me like a flickering light on a wall.'
• Peter Guber (producer): 'I was the Columbia baby. I was 26 years old, a punk kid from the East the first day I walked into Columbia. My pictures – *The Deep*, *Midnight Express* and *Thank God It's Friday* – did $130 million in revenue for Columbia. I had never lost a penny for the studio. I enjoyed a good relationship with the management. I thought Ray was my papa. He can be the sweetest man, the most charming to be with. But his involvement with Columbia at the time of my departure was so all-encompassing that it caused one of the most incredible, bizarre episodes of my life. I was run out.'
• Dan Melnick (producer): 'Like Richelieu, Ray doesn't like change ... Ray never forgave me for leaving the presidency (of Columbia). He turned on me for a complex variety of reasons. Leaving was a betrayal of him, of Herbert Allen, of Columbia – since all three are merged in his mind. Ray loves Herbie. His affection for Herbie is genuine. He sees him as a son.'
• Alan Hirschfield (ex-chairman Columbia): 'He's the kind of person who does take delight in playing with people's lives. This is like a game to him; he gets his kicks from it.'

David, with his four most successful releases totalling $68.2 million in net rentals – *Chariots of Fire* ($30.6 million), the disowned *Midnight Express* ($15 million), *The Killing Fields* ($14.3 million) and *The Mission* (which would go on to make $8.3 million) – had just locked horns with a producer whose top seventeen films had netted $468 million – well over a billion dollars in box-office gross.

David had no illusions that news of the tremors would reach Fay Vincent, Herbert Allen and the Coke duo in short order. So be it, was his attitude. Fuck it! Apart from refusing Stark's friendship, he knew that the worst insult he had dealt him was his refusal to be part of the community the mogul had spent his life cultivating. How *dare* David not see what a magical world this was, that had driven Stark and his friends all their lives. Some observers felt he had taken Stark's dignity away from him. David's feeling was that Stark had done that to himself years before. As far as Ray was concerned, David was no longer David, but forever 'that little prick, Puttnam'.

David still had some unfinished business to attend to before he could immerse himself in Columbia – the launch of *The Mission* in key territories. ('I think it makes me a natural for a Trivial Pursuit question,' David laughs. 'What head of a major motion-picture studio simultaneously promoted a film for a rival studio?') It opened to tremendous initial figures – first in Spain, then Paris. While *Hollywood Reporter* gave the film a glowing review after its Cannes showing, *Variety* saw it as a questionable commercial prospect. They forecast it would open well on the strength of De Niro's name, but thereafter, all bets were off. It looked as if Goldcrest would not necessarily get the overage in the US they so desperately needed, although the figures from Latin America and further European openings continued to be encouraging.

On the eve of *The Mission*'s première in Britain, David declared himself confident that the film was going to be a hit and garner Oscar nominations. Eventually, he estimated, the movie would end up with a worldwide box-office gross of between $90 and $100 million. He was erring, he added, on the cautious side. He was making the major assumption that the film would be a hit in the vital American market. Fernando Ghia was a little more sanguine. 'It's been proved over and over again,' he said, 'that some films have a different life in Europe than in America.'

'With the state it's in the industry cannot afford *The Mission* to be an elegant failure, or even an honourable failure. It *has* to be a success!' David stated, clearly *willing* the film through to his predicted figures.

'What is criminal is that *The Mission* is now having to do the very thing I always said it shouldn't have had to do, and that is salvage Goldcrest. No one film should ever have to do that.'

Jake Eberts agreed that if *The Mission* did well, it would help pay off some of the company's debt. If it failed, however, he still reckoned Goldcrest would survive. 'The running of the company is covered by existing cash flow from contracts already signed or committed to,' he pointed out. 'We are currently negotiating with several companies for additional capital, and that does *not* depend on the success of *The Mission*.'

Still the media insisted that *The Mission*'s success was absolutely crucial, if not to Goldcrest, then to that old media turkey, Britain's entire future as a maker of mass-audience films.

The Mission's openings in the States initially were in New York and Los Angeles only. Underpinned by a costly and beautifully organized Warners ad campaign, the film turned in good, but unspectacular returns. No box-office records were broken, but the hope was that favourable word-of-mouth would propel the film through to the February 1987 Oscar nominations.

The film opened in London to what are euphemistically referred to as 'mixed' reviews. 'Beautiful, roaring, stupendous froth,' the *Independent* summarized. 'Carry on up the waterfall,' echoed the *New Statesman*. 'So worked up has this country become about British cinema,' their article continued, 'that any Puttnam/Goldcrest production appears not as a mere film, but as the trailer grandly puts it, "Destined to become the motion picture of the year."' The movie was likened to a spiritual *Top Gun*, with Jesuit priests Irons and De Niro 'up there with the best of the best'.

The *Times Educational Supplement* provided no relief. 'Father Gabriel is a man without a history,' they wrote, 'miscast and far too young in the person of Jeremy Irons. Robert De Niro does what he can, and makes a good job of it, despite much of the time playing in a vacuum. Puttnam's well known desire to make films of large scale and significance is wholly admirable, as is his wish to enlighten his audience . . . but there is a sogginess at the core.'

'What does one say about a work in progress that does not make progress?' asked Nigel Andrews in the *Financial Times*. At Cannes he had reckoned the second half of the film had 'enough room for improvement to swing a cat in. Alas, the new *Mission* is no better than the old one. The further we move towards the film's curtain the unhappier it gets. The climactic scenes are clumsily staged and almost totally peripheral to the story's tension. And a symbolic coda of please-the-paying-public optimism is tacked on, as if the naked truth of man's cruelty to man, and God's mysterious aloofness to it all, were more than the world's Odeons and ABCs could bear.'

Iain Johnstone remained the film's undisputed champion, as he had from the beginning at Cannes. '*The Mission,*' he wrote this time, 'may not be beyond criticism, but it is certainly beyond compare with the vast majority of modern movies. Visionally and viscerally, it is the most powerful film of the year . . . Roland Joffe again demonstrates the passion and intelligence that he brought to *The Killing Fields.*'

Richard Barkley in the *Sunday Express* saw *The Mission* as 'an earnest epic, like an above-average lecture . . . The film is sincere and stolid as far as it goes, though notably failing to put the Indians' point of view. But in the end, it seems lofty and impersonal.' *Today* took up this theme. 'For such an epic enterprise,' William Green wrote, 'with its extraordinary jungle scenery, its grandiose themes and historical sweep, it has a strangely cold centre, a rubber soul . . . part of the problem, I suspect, is that three men, Bolt, Puttnam and Joffe – struggle to have their own kind of humanism uppermost, and their efforts cancel each other out.'

'Here comes *The Killing Fields*, take two,' Amanda Lipman in the NME wrote – perhaps not David's favourite reading after their last reviewer's dissection of that film. 'If you look carefully,' Ms Lipman pointed out, 'you might just catch a fleeting female appearance in this tale of true love . . . There's so much that's ludicrous about this pompous movie that it's hard to know where to start. Perhaps by wondering whether De Niro was suffering from some kind of brainstorm?'

Confusing as it must be for Joffe to be compared with David Lean one minute and condemned as a hack the next, honest differences of opinion will always occur, no matter how unfair and perverse they may appear.

David's meeting with Stark had taken place just weeks after a resignation that took the outside world by surprise. While Dick Gallop had appeared to be one of the key figures behind David's decision to join Columbia, Fay Vincent had in fact hinted to David from the beginning that Gallop might soon be taking up a different role within the organization. Even with this knowledge, David was taken aback to learn of his destination – Allen & Co., Inc. Did *all* roads lead to Herbert Allen? (In fact, Gallop would still report to 711 Fifth Avenue, where Allen had now moved his company. Different floor, though.)

The whole episode seemed at sinister variance with the bland harmony the double act of 'Roberto and Don' had presented. Or was the fruit simply falling close to the tree?

Chapter 23

'I Leave Here in March 1990'

David had already been sucker-punched in the few weeks he had been in office. The dealer of the blow was producer Martin ('Don't walk on me with your "Fuck-you" shoes') Ransohoff, flush from his runaway *Jagged Edge* success. Ransohoff had a three-picture pick-up deal with Columbia, the first of which, *The Big Town*, starring Matt Dillon (in his umpteenth try for stardom), Diane Lane and Tommy Lee Jones (both ditto), was already in production, greenlighted before David's appointment.

'David, I need your advice,' Marty ingratiatingly began. After the welter of administrative details that had flooded in on him since his arrival, David was frankly flattered, and a little relieved, that his advice was being sought by an actual producer.

'If I can help, I will, Marty. What's the problem?'

'OK. We've been shooting *The Big Town* for a couple of days. I think we've got a pretty good script, David, but the director and I are just not working out. I'm gonna have to replace the guy. You're a wiz with directors, how about it? Could you suggest someone who's available and help me out of this hole?'

David agreed to think about it, and took the script home with him that night to the Bel Air, for another look. There could well be a problem with the director. After an hour's reappraisal of the script – which he never had liked in the first place – he became convinced that was where the main problem lay. The story was weak, the characters not fully delineated. Even so, it could probably be sharpened up. And wasn't Robert Bolt's son Ben around, between directing *Hill Street Blues* segments?

Next day he mentioned his name to Ransohoff, who promptly clasped David's hands in his bear-like paws. 'You've got a friend for life David,' the bold Marty declared, before marching off to contact young Bolt and ultimately hire him to take over *The Big Town*.

Only later, when David related the story to a colleague, was the affair put into focus. 'Marty does this sort of thing,' he was told. 'If the picture's a hit, the credit's all down to him. If it's a flop, he'll blame you for foisting Ben Bolt on him. Either way, you can't win. And he can't lose.'

Marty already had a go-ahead for a second project at Columbia, a thriller called *Smoke*, to star Burt Reynolds and Theresa Russell. The third subject he put to Columbia, and David this time, was *Switching Channels*, an updated version of the classic *Front Page* remake, *His Girl Friday*, only set in a television station instead of a newspaper office. Marty had been hawking the property around for over a year, having unsuccessfully touted Debra Winger, Bill Murray and Dan Aykroyd for the leads in an attempt to get their agency, Mike Ovitz's CAA, interested. CAA had not bitten, probably recalling the fate of their last endeavour, *Legal Eagles*, which had surrounded the unfortunate production company, Universal, in a $38-million sea of red ink.

A textbook example of the 'package' of mismatched talents David was absolutely set against, *Legal Eagles* starred Robert Redford, Debra Winger and Daryl Hannah. Allegedly a 'comedy', and written by those well-known *Top Gun* wits, Jack Epps Jr and Jim Cash, the enterprise had been well and truly run into the ground by the further lightsome touch of director Ivan (*Ghostbusters*) Reitman. Despite this it made a fortune in commissions for CAA, who had supplied all the major talent in the picture. It also brought them a deluge of bad publicity and the loss of Debra Winger as a client.

Marty's ploy to get CAA on his side failed, as Miss Winger and Messrs Murray and Aykroyd all in turn passed on the project – as David now did when it was presented to him. His idea of a movie stamped with the logo of the Columbia lady did not include *Switching Channels*, with or without the new cast Marty had assembled of Michael Caine, Kathleen Turner and Christopher Reeve.

Infuriated, Marty arranged to have lunch with the outgoing Dick Gallop, on the eve of his joining Allen & Co. In one of the labyrinthal moves that characterises buying and selling in the entertainment business – and one that Roberto Goizueta described to Fay Vincent as 'the best acquisition in the history of Coca-Cola' – the company had purchased Embassy from Jerry Perenchio and Norman Lear, Jake Eberts' erstwhile employers. They then split this in two and sold Embassy Pictures to Dino De Laurentiis, while Embassy Home Entertainment was separately parcelled off to Nelson Entertainment. Part of the deal was that Coke would co-finance twelve pictures with Nelson over a three-year-period.

Wouldn't *Switching Channels* be an ideal first project? Marty had a truly wonderful script, Gallop was assured. Just because that *jerk* Puttnam had turned it down (he neglected to mention the rest of Hollywood), it was still a brilliant property.

Gallop agreed to refer it to Frank Biondi Jr, head of Coke's Entertainment Business Sector's TV Operations, also responsible for any Nelson co-productions undertaken. While Biondi could be seen as having swallowed Marty's bait, as far as he was concerned he genuinely liked the project. In agreeing to fund *Switching Channels*, Marty's end-run around David was complete. A project that Columbia, Coke's main movie company had turned down, would still be financed by Coca-Cola!

Thrown out the front door, Marty had sneaked in the back. It seemed that his appetite for being walked over with anyone's 'fuck-you shoes' had not increased over the years. What everyone missed in all the widespread glee over Marty's triumph was the only pertinent issue, the rights or wrongs of David's rejection. Instead of Rosalind Russell, Cary Grant and Ralph Bellamy directed by Howard Hawks in one of the most brilliant and scintillating comedies ever made, Ransohoff was offering a cast ultimately comprising Burt Reynolds (Michael Caine having defected for greater things in *Jaws 4*), Kathleen Turner and Christopher Reeve, directed by Ted (*First Blood*) Kotcheff. David's embarrassment would have been increased by being forced to have Columbia release *Switching Channels*. At least he was spared this, as Victor Kaufman at Tri-Star, anxious to develop a professional ongoing relationship with Kathleen Turner, agreed to release the picture. David and the Columbia lady would yet have the last laugh.

Although much was made of this in the press, Fay Vincent took a cooler view of the development. 'The whole strategy, after all, behind Tri-Star, was that we would have a number of places making product. When David took the job at Columbia, he saw himself as Coca-Cola's film-maker. Although it was explained to him, I think he chose not to understand that there were going to be three or four Coke film people, of which he was one. There was Victor at Tri-Star, there was the Nelson link, which to David was a pain in the ass he never understood, then there was our involvement in the Weintraub group. David resented all that, but that was his problem, not mine.'

Now it was Vincent's turn to get directly involved in the Ransohoff wrangle. 'Ransohoff called me early on and said David didn't want to make a sequel to *Jagged Edge*. He wanted to use it only as a sort of '*Jagged Edge* presents' label. I said, why didn't he put the idea of *Jagged Edge II* to Victor Kaufman or one of the other companies we were involved with. It turned out that Victor at Tri-Star was in-

terested, although it was more complicated than that, since there was
an expensive deal between Ransohoff and Columbia that he didn't
like, and if they took *Jagged Edge II* they'd have to live with what they
thought was a bad deal.'

Views of Marty Ransohoff vary widely in the Hollywood community:

Take One (Bobby Littman, Hollywood agent): 'Marty's an extremely clever man, and a brilliant businessman who caters to the
popular market. Unlike some, he puts his money where his mouth is,
often part-financing, sometimes paying for prints and ads. Marty
knows what he's doing.'

Take Two (ex-Columbia lady executive): 'He's a foul-mouthed
bully. One day, in the middle of a business meeting, he called me a
fucking cunt. My boss told him to watch his mouth, not to use that
expression about one of his staff. "Oh, it's nothing *personal*," Marty
protested.'

Take Three (Hollywood agent II): 'I'd rather do business with
Marty than a lot of others. I know exactly where I stand with him.
Even if I don't like what he's got to say, I know he's telling the truth.'

Take Four (Hollywood reporter): '*The Big Town* story's balls. If
Ben Bolt had made a better film, Marty Ransohoff would have given
credit to David. I think that part of David's problem, and it's a major
flaw, is his constant self-justification. He thinks things through in a
somewhat paranoic way, not even "someone's following me", but
"what *if* someone were following me?" He can always find some
justification for himself in something that has gone wrong.'

The Cannon Group's take-over of Britain's Thorn/EMI Screen Entertainment in May 1986 had been made before shares in Cannon
reached their highest peak of $44. When the stock-market crash in
July brought them back down to $35, most other companies quickly
began to claw back lost ground. Not Cannon. Just when they should
have been advancing again, with another ostensibly excellent quarter's
results announced, still they languished. The slide continued with the
announcement of a Securities and Exchange Committee (SEC) investigation into the company's accounting procedures. 'They keep
reporting higher earnings on pictures that nobody goes to see,' said
Gordon Crawford, a senior vice-president of Capital Guardian Research in Los Angeles. Their shares would later drop to under $3.

In October, David was asked for his views on the prospects of the
company he had fought to keep out of Britain. First emphasizing that
he would rather be wrong, for the sake of the British Film Industry,

he stated, 'I don't for one second believe that the Cannon organization as presently constituted will still exist this time next year.' Replying to what they referred to as Puttnam's 'bizarre commentary', Menahem Golan and Yoram Globus declared, 'We were amused, and decided to invite you to a gracious dinner in a year's time to review where we *both* are (meaning you and us). However, in our generosity, we are prepared to extend the date to 24 months from now.' The assumption seemed to be that they would be able to afford a 'gracious dinner' two years hence.

David's appointment of his old friend David Picker to the Columbia team as his deputy met with a mixed reception in Hollywood, now rapidly split in two camps, the pro- and anti-Puttnamites. The pros largely belonged to the creative community of writers and directors, who saw an opportunity in Puttnam's term to produce some worthwhile movies, away from the extant juvenilia that had largely overtaken Hollywood. The antis were the deal-makers and fat cats, the ones with most to lose from his espousal of rich contracts and packages. Picker's appointment flung both camps into confusion, since he was widely seen as one of the fat cats David was trying to starve. He was also viewed as a creative dinosaur, for many years out of the Hollywood mainstream. David was relying on his close friendship with Picker over the years, but would Picker guide him through the Hollywood jungle and protect him from the pygmies' blowpipes? 'He wouldn't shoot Puttnam himself,' was the widespread consensus, 'but he might not deflect the arrows.'

'He asked me to share the mandate he had from Coke, which I found irresistible,' said Picker. 'I'd determined that I never wanted to be an executive again, but what David offered me was so seductive, so intelligent and so unique I had to take it.' Picker's 'last hurrah', in fact. Picker's predecessor, Steve Sohmer, was to move into nebulous 'creative areas of movie and TV production', which would turn out to be located in the region of Bill Cosby's back pocket.

Greg Coote was sought from Australia, where he was a successful producer/exhibitor/distributor. His appointment as bicontinental creative executive was questioned by some ('OK, he knows the Aussie market. So what?'), praised by others. Columbia domestic marketing executive Bob Dingilian quickly discovered Coote's strengths. 'Talent, knack, panache, *that's* international,' he gravels in a voice that emanates from underground caverns. 'What can I tell you? Coote's a *smart* man, *real* smart.'

From Public Broadcasting Catherine Wyler, daughter of director

William Wyler, stepped in to handle Columbia's new non-fiction unit, a brainchild of David's. Lynda Myles was appointed head of European Creative Affairs to liaise with local film-makers. ('A post-mistress,' one British producer grumbled. 'You send her the script and she posts it on to David in L A.') Jim Clark, David's eyes and ears on *The Killing Fields* and Academy Award winner for his editing on that movie, was reluctantly coaxed to L A as a senior production editor on a one-year contract. ('A fixer of projects in trouble,' he later called himself.)

Ex-Ray Stark protégé John Fiedler, who had moved to Columbia from Tri-Star, was moving again at his own request, into independent production for the studio. Not announced was the main reason for his departure – the unlikelihood of his being able to work with David's new appointee, David Picker. Immediate friction at staff meetings between the two rapidly made Fiedler's position untenable.

As a gesture from the Hollywood establishment, David was invited by Mike Ovitz to address a meeting of C A A's agents early in October. Although David claims that his comments at the event were heavily distorted, what he was rumoured to have said sounded like a virtual re-run of what had already been addressed to the Coke bosses – that agency packages, big stars and exorbitant salaries were a thing of the past at Columbia Pictures. Well, the news had gone down well in Atlanta, after all, why should the reaction at C A A be any different? Then there was David's response to a remark from the floor about a 'young' 44-year-old director: 'That's indicative of the age-bias built in here,' he reportedly snapped.

Following the shock waves reverberating from the event, a meeting with Herbert Allen elicited the advice to David that he should attempt to build a better personal rapport with Ovitz. David felt his hackles rise. Why was he being *lectured*?

David played up the Coca-Cola honeymoon he was still enjoying when he disclosed that South African exhibitors had been warned that no Columbia pictures would be available to any segregated the-atres after 1 May 1987. He pointed out that Coke's decision to pull out of the country and turn its franchise over to black businessmen had preceded his action. 'What they did showed real class,' he declared. 'They were ahead of me and they've done it. I thought that was terrific.' A somewhat tight-lipped Jack Valenti, Motion Picture As-sociation of America president, put David's move into perspective, describing it as 'a responsible position, quite responsible', as he re-flected on the deadline still being a full seven months away. Unlike sanctioned areas such as investments, automobiles and construction steel, his view was that feature films and TV programming advanced the cause of opposition to apartheid by exposing the South African population to the example of a multi-racial society. In any event 85 per cent of South Africa's 400 theatres had been desegregated already, Valenti pointed out, from a figure of 8 per cent a year earlier. 'If we withdrew our pictures,' he maintained, the only people who would be hurt would be the black majority. The affluent white South Africans have VCRs. Pirates would move in quickly and they would have all the movies to see, but the blacks would be denied.'

David next put Coke's name to metaphorical use in castigating irresponsible film-makers: 'If Coca-Cola accidentally created 100 million cans of faulty coke, you know for sure the entire 100 million cans would be dropped in the Atlantic or Pacific Ocean without a second thought and irrespective of what that did to the year's profits. What do we do with a crappy movie? We double its advertising budget and hope for a big opening weekend. What has been done for the audience as they walk out of the cinema? We've alienated them. We've sold the audience a piece of junk. We took $12 away from a couple and think we've done ourselves no long-term damage.' Visions were conjured up of disillusioned couples walking around in a daze, their lives diminished, $12 lighter, and vowing never to go near a cinema again. Well, maybe.

With most of his team in place, David felt the time was right, in November 1986, for a statement of policy to the outside world. Stinging from the series of encounters with the likes of Ray Stark, Marty Ransohoff and the CAA team, he chose a showing of *The Mission* at Glen Glenn's Hollywood screening-room just 24 hours after his last meeting with Stark, to serve notice on any others who doubted the strength of his policy commitment. Although the audience was aware of his reputation for outspokenness, people had come along expecting a mild question-and-answer session after the movie and were taken aback at the vehemence with which David lashed the community.

'I'm appalled,' David began, 'by the mindset I've met everywhere in the last few weeks. In Hollywood now you're not shooting movies any more, you're shooting deals. At Columbia we're going to shift radically from pre-packaged products to in-house development. The reason we want to develop in-house is because everything starts with material. Unfortunately, what I've witnessed is that the film here starts with a book, let's say, and a star – not necessarily the right star, but a book and a star. They are brought in by an agent and that becomes what's referred to as the package.

'You're already in trouble because it's difficult to get a screenplay out of that book. It's twice as difficult when you've got a star who doesn't really want the book. What he or she wants is the role they like inside the book that would be good for them. This kind of game-playing, I promise you, will be *out* under me at Columbia.

'You start from the point of view of material and a producer. You get a screenplay, and bring in a director who loves that screenplay – not someone out of work who needs a job, not someone who will do it because you offer him two-and-a-half million dollars and 10 per cent of the rolling gross, but someone who actually loves the screenplay for the same reason you do. *Then* you develop the screenplay to the point where you and the director are happy. *Then* you cast the film.

'When you do this, it is not to a set of preconceived ideas, for how or why you might get the picture off the ground, but the right cast and right movie. These are the things we're doing, I promise you. The reason there are so many lousy films around is because of the corruption of the role of producer. Only independent producers actually prepared to *produce* will find a welcome here at Columbia.

'In the few weeks I've been here, I've had several conversations with people about the making of a movie. Among the first questions they ask is, "Who shall we get to actually produce it?" I'm absolutely *furious. This* is why you see these ludicrous three-producer, four-producer credits. The one poor soul who knows how to produce the film isn't even included. The three people are the agents or the friends of the writer, or the writer's mother, who *claim* to be producer. I find it grossly offensive and really very, very upsetting.

'We can't get away any longer with shortchanging audiences. We at Columbia are going to be far more demanding of those who work for us. We will challenge directors to direct better. We'll challenge actors and actresses to act better. We'll challenge technicians to be better. Frankly, and I include myself, I think we're all a little bit lazy; we've gotten away with not giving the audience enough. If there's been a breach of faith in the last five years between the audience and the film-maker, I have to say it's been on the side of the film-maker. Audiences have been unbelievably patient, while there's been too much carping and moaning on the part of film-makers. Audiences will turn out when a film delivers and absent themselves when it does not. On the occasions – all too many – when I've known in my heart that the film didn't really deliver, sure enough, they smelled it out and didn't come.

'We're going to make an all-out effort to woo intelligent adult audiences,' David concluded. 'Our new credo at Columbia goes like this: We're saying that audiences are people, too.'

After a few seconds of stunned silence, a hearty round of applause came from the audience. If there had been any doubts before, there were none now. What had just been declared was nothing less than total war on the existing Hollywood system.

Patsy arrived in early November to find David still in temporary office quarters at Columbia. For two months she had been worried by the increasingly negative phone calls from David and Valerie. On one occasion she had never heard her husband sound so defeated. 'This place is rotten through and through,' he had told her. 'I honestly don't know if I'm going to make a go of it.' Valerie's lowest point had come when she told Patsy, 'Don't send my trunks on just yet!' Now at Columbia she found workmen finally lifting the maroon carpet in his office and beginning to lay wood flooring. 'Excuse me, but isn't that concrete under there?' she inquired.

'Sure is.'

Patsy turned disbelievingly to David. 'They're laying a wooden floor on top of concrete? The moisture will warp the wood. This is where they make *movies*? Who's in charge around here?'

Tom McCarthy was duly located and his help enlisted. Patsy could see how David had been unable to settle. 'These clowns have had two months to sort David's office out,' she raged. 'Now *I'm* having a go – and I need your help, Tom. Let's talk materials –'

Three weeks later David was installed for the first time in Patsy's style of substantial yet homely comfort, perfectly represented by the office furniture that took its name from Papa Biedermeier and now sat serenely on wood flooring that was down to stay. Patsy had found speckled glass for the corner walls that made the room look sunny even on dull days. All his favourite pictures and mementoes were carefully in position. *Now* David could work. The domestic side was taken care of as well, with the couple's move into their furnished home high up in Coldwater Canyon, its twin orange trees flanking the swimming pool and outdoor jacuzzi that Greta Garbo and Gaylord Hauser had installed in the fifties. When Columbia offered to install a screening-room in the house, they would not hear of it. 'It would be a terrible waste of money,' Patsy said. 'We're ten minutes from the studio, where there are lots of perfectly good screening-rooms. We'll go down the hill any hour of the day or night to see a movie if a projectionist is happy to do it.'

Her first glimpse of the screening-rooms at Columbia changed her mind – not about having a screen installed in Coldwater Canyon, but the conditions under which films were viewed at one of Hollywood's major studios. 'It's unbelievable,' she told Alan Parker. 'They're all pokey little rooms, full of small, uncomfortable chairs – and using sound and projection equipment that's been out of date for years.' When Alan asked, 'Why don't you do something about it?' Patsy determined that she would. Armed with a budget, she was given one screening-room to convert to state-of-the-art perfection and comfort. 'Now we're even happier to go down the hill,' she declared on the triumphant completion of her project.

Fay Vincent could not escape a feeling of concern. 'One of the problems is, David had set himself up as this low-cost individual, then all of a sudden he spent a fortune on his office and a variety of other things. His office was elegant, if not downright opulent. He spent a *lot* of money. It was inconsistent, not with his position, neces-sarily, but I'm not sure I'd have expected it from David.

'Then he gave an interview in which he said *I'd* encouraged him to get a Rolls-Royce instead of the Audi he'd chosen. "David, why did you *say* that?" I asked him. "Well, it's better," he told me. "You can't *do* that," I replied, "you can't *lie* to the public about me. Nobody in the world is going to believe that I'd encourage you to spend money; it's just not in my nature." Then he said it was someone else who had put out the Rolls-Royce story, not him. He *should* have said, "Well, I shouldn't have done that" – but that's not David's way, as I was discovering.'

By mid-November, *with the meter now running*, David had completed a review of every item in Columbia's inventory. Of 121 projects that had been in various stages of development at the studio, 57 were to be axed. Every new script submission had been ploughed through, marked A for 'definite', B for 'further development required', C for 'I need to be convinced' and D for 'dross'. With a thin release schedule in prospect for the first half of 1987, David was open for any 'pick-ups' available. The most controversial upcoming item was *Ishtar*, green-lighted by David's predecessor and ex-Righteous Brothers agent, Guy McElwaine. (Coke had lost that lovin' feeling after taking one look at the soaring costs on the movie.)

One school of thought had it that the writing had been on the wall then for Dick Gallop, for his failure to control the excesses on *Ishtar*. Another had it that even Fay Vincent had been lucky to survive. With 108 hours of film exposed by director Elaine May on the project ('kinda long for a comedy', Robert Osborne of *Hollywood Reporter* cracked), the impending turkey had so far swallowed $40 million. Post-production was still going on, as David could hardly fail to notice, since he was the recipient of the weekly bills. 'Since I'd been told the worst was over with *Ishtar*,' he says, 'I was staggered by the post-production costs that kept coming in. The theory had been that Columbia was out of the woods when shooting had finished, but financially we weren't. The whole thing ballooned even further out of proportion in post-production, both in cash terms and in delivery terms.'

'Who gives a shit what Puttnam thinks?' Warren Beatty asked one Columbia executive. 'I certainly don't. Just tell the asshole to keep paying the bills.'

Despite his arrangement with Fay Vincent that he would have nothing to do with *Ishtar*, Beatty and Dustin Hoffman were still concerned that David would somehow or other foster a negative attitude towards the movie. An ex-Columbia executive commented, 'Beatty in effect took it out on us for hiring Puttnam. How? Just by being more difficult. He believed he couldn't trust the studio. Everybody worked for Puttnam and Puttnam was against the picture, so every decision that came from the studio he saw Puttnam influencing or controlling. I think in some respects he was right.'

Beatty turned down some of the marketing team at Columbia he had known and trusted in the past. 'I can't use you,' he told one furious executive, 'You're a Puttnam man and I think you'll always be loyal to David and not to me.'

The reaction of the Hollywood community to David's first list of movies ranged from cool to lukewarm. 'You don't feel the heat that's in Disney's Touchstone programme,' said one reporter. Many felt they detected a distinct element of the cerebral; it seemed that catering for audiences' erogenous zones would continue to be the province of Warners, Universal, Paramount, et al, and in some cases the drama of getting the movies on the screen would be at least as interesting as the movies themselves:

● *Housekeeping*: Featuring the return of David's association with Bill Forsyth. Cancelled by Cannon with six weeks to go, rescued by David.
● *Someone to Watch over Me*: An attempt at a mainstream thriller; nail-biting suspense as the question is posed – can Ridley Scott tell a straightforward, gripping story without reliance on flashy effects?
● *Vice Versa*: A simple tale of a father and son changing places, adapted by Dick Clement and Ian La Frenais from the 1940s British original which starred Roger Livesey and Anthony Newley. After almost 40 years, surely there was no other studio planning virtually the same re-make, especially a sister company?

- *Little Nikita*: A surefire heartwarmer with thrills and excitement, but could director Richard Benjamin focus on the winning elements?
- *Punchline*: Dan Melnick's last throw of the dice under his Columbia housekeeping deal. Could it be ready in time for an end-December '87 Oscar nomination run?
- *Vibes*: Dan Aykroyd and Cyndi Lauper – or was it? Dan didn't consider Cyndi a big enough name. An ultimatum for David!
- *The Big Town*: Would this one do it for Marty Ransohoff? Or Ben Bolt? Or Matt Dillon? Or Diane Lane? Or Tommy Lee Jones? Or *anybody*?

An idea that David would like to have worked out failed to take off, as Alan Parker reluctantly turned down his offer to work with him at Columbia. 'He's my best pal,' Alan explained. 'I value our friendship so much I didn't want to risk it in making films with him. The reason I came out here was because he's here, Patsy's here, Patsy's a good friend of my wife, Annie, and everybody seemed to be here. David wanted me to come and be like the old-fashioned staff director to do as many films as I could while he was at Columbia. I quite liked the idea of that, taking away the preciousness of what we do, because it does become more and more difficult each time deciding which film to make, but I chickened out. The first four things he sent me I didn't want to do, so it was obviously not going to work. And I thought it was better we remained friends.

'I stayed at Coldwater Canyon with him and Patsy for weeks while Annie got the kids organized back home and we'd never discuss the proposition. People would ask me, "Well, did you talk about it?" And I'd say, "No, we don't like to mention it to one another. We talk about everything else under the sun, except the fact I'm supposed to be doing films with him."'

A friend of both men reckons there were other reasons for Alan's decision, quite apart from the rather frugal terms that David was offering. 'It's really hard for Alan to swallow that after his two biggest successes, *Bugsy Malone* and *Midnight Express*, both made with David, he's never had a major box-office hit on his own. Even critical acclaim has often been grudging, except in France, where he's idolized. Alan really wants to be considered an artist, "An Alan Parker Film" and all that. David's often told him he's not entitled to that credit unless he's both written and directed the film, which he does do occasionally. None of his films – *Fame, Pink Floyd – The Wall, Shoot The Moon, Birdy* or *Angel Heart*, have really taken off where it matters most, in the US market. So if Alan went back to David and the film they made together was a hit, quite honestly it might destroy him.'

Anyone who knows the extent of David's involvement in *Bugsy Malone* and *Midnight Express* would take issue with the supporters of this argument. A much more likely explanation for Alan continuing to plough his own furrow is his single-minded view of auteurship.

'What will I achieve here?' was the rhetorical question David addressed to one journalist, only weeks after his arrival in Hollywood, in an interview that would come back to haunt him. 'Jarvis Astaire once told me that I have a tendency to bite the hand that feeds me. There's something in that. I like a scrap. It's a working-class thing. Screw you, I don't need any of you. I leave here in March, 1990. I have the date ringed in my calendar. If I make good movies and they don't work I will go with my head held high. I'll still be a producer. I can always go back to my day job.'

Fay Vincent was surprised and dismayed at David's decision to go public with the length of his Hollywood tenure – and with no mention of staying with the company thereafter. 'That's not our understanding,' Fay told him. 'You've made me look silly, David.'

'The truth of the matter,' David explained to another journalist, compounding the felony, 'is that the day I signed on, at least half of me was still wondering if I'd done the right thing. Which means my attitude towards losing my job, or having it taken away from me, is very different from that of the normal studio executive.'

Vincent cringed again as David pointed out that his deal with Coke did not involve bonuses tied to grosses. 'What I earn will be exactly the same whether I deliver five more *Ghostbusters* or fall flat on my face. In other words, I'm allowed to fail.' David was beginning to remind Fay of the biblical fool uttering all of his mind. 'You're a Coke executive, David,' Fay reminded him. 'Don't maintain such a high profile. You don't *have* to spell out all the options and fallbacks you've got. That's not what Roberto and Don want to hear.'

David's attitude was that he had to be his own man. He had to show he could not be bought and sold. He had always shot from the hip, why should he change now? Did Coke or anyone else think he was overawed by either the Hollywood climate or Coke's corridors of power? In David's view, being upfront about his terms would allow him to make deals without hidden agendas. His self-esteem would not allow him to appear 'affected' by Hollywood. He must never be seen to have changed his views because of the 'role' he now played. There would be no hedging of bets, no favours to return and no egos to stroke. There were other reasons, but these he would scarcely admit even to himself.

The feedback to Fay Vincent was horrendous, both from Coke in Atlanta and Herbert Allen in New York. 'He's made himself a lame duck by spelling out the three years and reporting it as if he's then leaving the company,' was the message. Universal's elder statesman Lew Wasserman phoned Coke from Hollywood. 'Puttnam was a great choice,' he told them, 'but the three-year provision is self-defeating.'

The reaction from Coke was: what on earth is Puttnam playing at? The way David told the tale, it was three and a half years, then goodbye Columbia. What about the rest of it, the understanding Fay had reached with him that their relationship would be ongoing? Why was Puttnam only telling half the story? And surely, in any case, the details of his contract were between David and Coke alone? They had assumed that Puttnam understood about corporate responsibility. No other executive shot his mouth off to the press like this.

'David's single problem,' Fay spells out, 'was his private agenda became his public agenda and that ultimately caused Coke and Herbert Allen to turn negative on him, because he either missed or miscast the subtleties of what we were trying to do. My recollection is that the difficulties related to things David *said* rather than the things David *did*. All of that press comment – he's so public and open-mouthed, he just talked too much. He wasn't careful and I don't think he really understood the significance of being part of Coca-Cola. He understood the benefit, but he never understood that when he spoke, he spoke as Coke. Every time he spoke the press all over the world would pick it up and call me, saying, what is he doing, why is he saying this? Some of the remarks were innocent, some were misquoted, but there was just *so much* of it. I think everyone agreed with his principal points, but saying it publicly was like announcing we were going to land at Normandy. Costs were too high; we were paying people too much; there was too much control by agents – it was a great strategy, but why talk about it?

'I said to him, "The problem is you talk about Hollywood this and Hollywood that – it's not *subtle*, it doesn't reflect a high quality of intellect, because there's no such thing. You and I *know* that's bullshit. Who are we talking about? We're not talking about Disney? You admire them and so do I. You're not talking about Bob Daly and Terry Semel at Warners? You're not talking about us? You're not talking about Paramount?" We went through the list and I said "Who *are* you talking about? All these generalizations aren't helpful, either about the studios *or* agents." I argued with him that he got a lot of attention and people knew what he meant, but when you really got specific, what he was saying didn't hold up.' Perhaps Fay had in mind Ezra Pound's homily that any general statement is like a cheque drawn on a bank – its value depends absolutely on what is there to meet it. It was beginning to look as if David's misfortune was an ability to speak, but insufficient judgement to discern the times to keep silent.

Fay was not the only one to resent David's blanket condemnations, reminiscent as they were to some of Joe McCarthy and his infinitely variable number of 'card-carrying Commies in the White House'. The difference was that Fay shared his dismay only with David. Others were not so subtle, and hid under a blanket of their own, that of anonymity.

'Of *course* he didn't save the British Film Industry,' said an American director. 'His trick was to make it look as if he did by taking the moral high ground. He's on the right side of all the issues in this town now, like whether to tint the movie classics and the apartheid issues in South African cinemas. But there are a lot of people who would forget the miracle and call him Sammy Glick. David knows how to *get* the best of his films, but he doesn't necessarily *make* the best. In England he is a coffee-table film-maker. He is a fixer. He buys a country house in Wiltshire and it doesn't look old enough, so he gets in the make-up department to have it antiquated. In Hollywood, even the fact he knows the word "antiquated" makes him into an intellectual.'

One scriptwriter reckoned he could see beyond David's provocative public statements. 'Publicity is his acknowledged forte. But he'll tell you things he doesn't necessarily mean. It doesn't always matter as long as you make things happen. Producers *should* lie and bullshit and do all they can to make movies.'

Another scriptwriter agreed. 'He says he is going to be a professor at Harvard and he ends up working for a soft drinks company. He says he'll ignore the youth market which everyone else is playing to, but he won't ignore it, he'll just not talk about it. The great thing about Puttnam is he says things people want to hear.'

A rival studio head joked, 'No one knows what they are doing right now – except for David Puttnam, who's *talking* as if he knows what *everybody* should be doing.'

'He shoots from the *lip*,' a columnist sniped.

'Take all his pictures,' said a rival executive, 'and between the lot they didn't take as much as *Sixteen Candles*.' (An apocryphal reference to Universal's 1984 teen success, which for the record took less that $10 million in rentals.)

David marched on regardless, blithely anticipating the inevitable answer from the creative community to his suggestion that they should take less money upfront in return for a bigger profit share, for many had been taken in already by similar promises. 'I have to say,' he admitted 'the onus is on the studios to provide the burden of proof there'll be a fair count. If you enter into a partnership you have an obligation to ensure that if things work out well for you, they work out for them too. It's up to us to spend the next twelve months proving they'll get a straight count here. Will we be all things to all men? No. Will there be calls that don't get returned and movies people think we're crazy not to make? For sure. But basically, Columbia will be a polite, decent place to work for those who do work here, and when we make a profit, that profit will be shared.'

'Can we expect a massive invasion of British talent now that you are ensconced here?' David was asked. He laughed and replied, 'I'd be surprised if that happened. This is only one studio and even if I completely swamped the place with British talent that would still be a very small blob on the overall horizon. I can't be blamed, though, if in the first few months, when staring at a pretty empty production slate, that I turn to people I know and trust. I'd be foolish not to. I'll probably get a bit of stick for what seems to be a slightly disproportionate amount – maybe a third of the material – being with people I know.'

Despite this, Jake Eberts doubted if he could do business with David in case the charge of 'crony-ism' was levelled. He could not have been more wrong. The new John Boorman film, *Hope and Glory*, initially funded by Jake's Allied Filmmakers, was enthusiastically adopted by David, who described the movie as 'an English Amarcord' after being shown the footage in October. Jake had completed his caretaker role at Goldcrest, although Brent Walker's Masterman company had not been his ideal choice of buyer for the ailing company. With a loss to the shareholders of $16 million the inglorious demise of Goldcrest was a low-key, mournful affair, as the lowering of a coffin into the ground tends to be.

Jake knew David admired the work of German director Doris Dorrie and successfully interested him in her proposed new comedy, *Me and Him*. The third property, brought by Jake in script form to Columbia in December, was a little $23.5 million item that was to be Terry Gilliam's new opus, *The Adventures of Baron Munchausen*. Agreement would be reached on this one, too. A bit further down the line, again with Jake, David rescued Simon Perry's *White Mischief* when the original backer withdrew.

By the end of 1986, David was able to look back on four months of momentous change at Columbia, wrought at considerable personal cost. His 'no exceptions' philosophy of cutting out producers' 'house-keeping deals' made him powerful enemies. Brandon Tartikoff, whom Vincent had approached for the Columbia job before David's appointment, confided: 'You did what I knew I couldn't do. You stood up to the "barons".'

In sorting through the studio files, Valerie came across a 1979 Columbia inter-office memo which caused much amusement. It ran:

'Return herewith Chariots of Fire. *I am sorry to tell you this has no viability at all in the American market-place because of style and tone as well as subject matter.*'

'Make me a copy, and have it framed,' David smilingly instructed Valerie. 'That's definitely one for the office wall.'

With the approach of Christmas, David looked at the $45,000-worth of gifts Columbia dished out each year. 'I want to stop this,' he told the Christmas gift committee. 'Let's spend $1000 on Christmas cards and give the other $44,000 to charity instead.' Despite the turmoil the suggestion caused, the idea was taken up. David's director friend Roy Battersby was one recipient of the card, which ran:

Christmas is surely one of the most evocative words in our language. For most of us it conjures up childhood, gifts, family, friends and a general sense of security and well-being. Sadly, not everyone is so fortunate, which is why we at Columbia Pictures have given, in your name, our entire Christmas gift allocation to three organizations. *One for the young, one for the old and one for the homeless.

Enjoy a very happy Christmas knowing that your generosity has made it possible for many less privileged to feel cared for at this very special time of the year.

*United Friends of the Children
The Los Angeles City Department of Aging
The Salvation Army Harbor Light Center

Underneath David had scribbled self-deprecatingly: 'This card represents my *first* small victory. Love as ever – David.' At least his sense of humour was still intact. More to the point, a year later many other studios had followed his lead.

David's Christmas generosity to Mike Ovitz was not of the same calibre. Discussing the subject of fees in Hollywood, he asked one interviewer, 'Where do they get off asking for that much? Is it just

because there's some schmuck in a a large tower in Century City
that's got the balls to ask for it?' Ovitz's Tower of Babel in Century
City somehow managed to remain standing.

Chapter 24

Greed Will Conquer All

After the Christmas respite at Kingsmead Mill, which reminded David and Patsy of what life could be like away from the machinations and intrigues that were the daily stuff of life in Hollywood, their return to Los Angeles provided a low point. When a minor domestic row flared into an angry scene, it was brought home to David how much the job was getting to him. 'I'm the wrong person for it,' he told Patsy as they sat up half the night talking. 'You're damn well not,' she replied, 'and if you pack it in now you'll be sorry for the rest of your life.'

Ironically, the zenith of David's year at Columbia arrived two weeks later, with Goizueta and Keough vying with each other to pour fulsome praise over the start he had made. The occasion was Coke's Entertainment Business Sector summit dinner, held at Santa Barbara in January 1987. 'David Puttnam had the guts, sheer guts, to say, OK, I'll do it, I'll do it my way,' Keough's panegyric began 'and it is courageous for him and his wife to leave a wonderfully comfortable cocoon and come out here, where you know every agent in town is out to get you.'

Goizueta was not to be outdone. 'David Puttnam, David Picker and the team they have assembled have taken the first steps down the road that we believe will lead to an unprecedented era of creativity at Columbia Pictures. This leadership is going to give the studio a personality, a character, a style, such as the studios had during the Golden Age of motion pictures.'

David's speech, no less resounding, was received with extraordinary enthusiasm. If progress could be measured in terms of speeches alone, David was on a roll.

David dined with Michael Ovitz at Spago in a further attempt to find a way forward. Again, there was no meeting of minds, for each found a man representing the complete opposite of their own values. On the face of it, they should have had at least one shared purpose – the making of *Ghostbusters II*. David suspected that Ovitz was having trouble putting the package together, since Bill Murray was said to have no desire to goof around again with his particular role, at least for the time being. If Ovitz needed a fall guy to cover his embarrassment, David was about to oblige in spades.

Vibes, to star Dan Aykroyd, had been set before his arrival at Columbia. David saw tests of pop songstress Cyndi Lauper and determined that she was perfect for the co-starring role of the ditsy psychic. Aykroyd took another look at the package, now consisting of an untried co-star and an unknown director, Ken Kwapis, and concluded it was all too much. Mike Ovitz conveyed his sentiments to David: 'Drop Cyndi Lauper.' David Picker put his oar in. 'We've got the best combination,' he told David. 'If Dan Aykroyd doesn't agree, he has the right to withdraw.'

David decided to write to Dan Aykroyd, something that immediately infuriated Ovitz, who felt that all overtures to his client should be made through him. A lot of David's letters are mere acknowledgements, a legacy of the English middle-class 'Thank you for having us to tea' variety. Others are filibusters, like the one Dan Aykroyd was sent. Although the sentiments are admirable, David clearly does not believe in writing a paragraph where a page will do.

11 January 1987

Dear Dan,

Although we have never met I have watched, admired and envied your talent for a number of years. As a producer I always hoped that I might find myself with a piece of material so tempting that you would drop everything esle to do it. For good or ill I was promoted (or demoted) before ever coming up with the definitive Dan Aykroyd project.

This is by way of background to the fact that one of the attractions of the Columbia job was the opportunity to work with you and your colleagues and become familiar with the area of the entertainment business which has thus far simply been a distant fascination. It's also true to say that of the dozen or so scripts that I read before I joined the company VIBES represented one of the two or three home runs. For this reason I have monitored its progress and taken it particularly seriously.

I won't bore you with a litany of my impressions of the way things have gone during the past three or four months. It certainly occurred to me that they weren't proceeding in a particularly orderly manner, but I accepted the fact that the way in which I've worked as a producer and the type of material I've worked on was so at variance to this type of situation that it was impossible to draw any day to day analogy.

The important points which have now come back to haunt us are the following: —

1. At his urging I was shown the test that Ron Howard did with Cyndi Lauper and I must say, despite initial scepticism, I was won over by her and fully understand the enthusiasm that Ron and, for that matter, everyone else seemed to express.

2. I gathered that there were problems in bringing you and Cyndi together, but my clear understanding was that these, for the most part, related to geography and the fact that she was travelling whilst you were preparing your present film, they were exacerbated by the fact that you were filming by the time she came 'off the road'.

3. Although you may well have expressed reservations early on, please believe me when I tell you that these only reached me in early December. Subsequent to this we all felt that the manner in which you met with David Picker, and subsequently with Cyndi herself, reflected highly on your attitude to the Studio, a fellow artist and the cause of professionalism in general.

4. As Mike Ovitz and I discussed on Friday the present situation has been typified to me as being some form of 'arm wrestle' between Columbia Pictures and your agency. This is not true.

5. Columbia Pictures will make a significant loss this year, as indeed it has in several of the years preceding. I have to assume that I've been brought in to alter the company's thinking and the manner in which it operates rather than ape the mistakes of the past.

Now the issue at hand!

Since arriving in my present position I have, in addition to attempting to restructure the company, only taken about half a dozen decisions which could honestly be regarded as being relevant to the on-screen quality of the material that will emerge in the Fall of next year. Most of these came about as a result of my believing in the *quality* of the individual screenplays and the fact that casting opportunities existed which could embellish the strengths of those screenplays.

The downside of all of this is the fact that I have had to swallow hard and accept that the 'insurance factor' has been diminished in some cases by going with the movie as opposed to the more obviously appealing 'package'.

At the end of the day my performance at Columbia will be judged on the basis of these decisions and I'm perfectly prepared to be flung out on my ear in the event that I'm wrong more often than I'm right.

A few examples of what I'm attempting to describe above are the preference for Tom Berenger over Richard Gere for the lead in Ridley Scott's picture. Our decision to make Bill Forsyth's film with Christine Lahti in the lead rather than wait and hope for Diane Keaton; fighting for Sidney Poitier to take on a role in LITTLE NIKITA originally written for Jack Nicholson and, as you may know, holding out for Tom Hanks to play the lead in PUNCHLINE in the face of concerns expressed by a number of thoughtful people.

In all of this I believe I have shown a general consistency. I have no idea if I'm right, but I have at least trusted my instincts, the same instincts which have brought me rightly or wrongly into my present situation. It's not a question of a lack of admiration for the talents of Richard, Diane, Jack or any number of others, it's merely fighting for who's *right* as against who's 'bankable'.

The issue involving Cyndi is admittedly rather different. Is she right for the film? Off the page the answer for me is unquestionably 'yes'. Can she act? Again for me the answer is also a conclusive yes. I thought her timing was superb and the only video test I've ever seen which similarly excited me was the one for Haing Ngor when we were seeking a lead for THE KILLING FIELDS. I'm also immensely comforted by the fact that David Picker and all the rest of my colleagues at Columbia, as well as the producers and director of VIBES enthusiastically feel the same way.

Everyone involved very much wants you to play opposite her and all of us in our different ways believe that you're right to have reservations. In fact I would be concerned if you *didn't* have reservations. Any artist, director or producer going into a movie without qualms is an idiot. Most of us feel as though we put our careers on the line every time we make a significant creative decision – that's both the nightmare and the challenge of the job. Personally, I wouldn't have it any other way.

I've told Mike that I would very much like to get together with you, but he feels that a meeting in the present climate would probably be fruitless. I have to trust his instinct.

What's important is for you to know how much everyone of us would like you to be in VIBES and for you to understand our reasoning. At the end of the day we've decided to cast Cyndi and are left hoping that you'll climb into the bath with us and take your best shot based on our tortuously considered judgement.

I'm sorry this letter is so long, but I hope that it goes some way towards encouraging you to understand how truly important every film and every decision such as this is to us. I can only reiterate what David Picker has already told you; we'll go to any reasonable lengths to make you feel comfortable and confident enough to go along with our instincts. All of us believe there's a wonderful film to be made and, without doubt, it will be a better film if you're in it.

I very much look forward to meeting you.

Warmest personal regards,

David Puttnam

Dan Aykroyd's reaction to this missive is unrecorded: he had probably read shorter scripts. In the absence of a reply, David promptly signed Jeff Goldblum for *Vibes* instead. One down, one to go.

While giving a speech at a British/American Chamber of Commerce lunch, David cited Robert Redford as a shining example of an actor who gave back to the community in the form of his Sundance Institute work. According to the *New York Post* page 6 gossip column, he then said, 'Bill Murray exemplifies an actor who makes millions off movies, but gives nothing back to his art. He's a taker.'

David denies ever mentioning Bill Murray: 'Bill's lawyer was supposedly at the lunch. This phantom figure apparently left in disgust. He never came forward and identified himself.'

An infuriated Bill Murray was reported to have snapped, 'What the hell's it got to do with him how I spend my money?' In his concern over what he saw as a blatant fabrication, David wrote to several lawyers who were present at the luncheon and asked them to testify that the Murray reference had never been made. One of those, contacted later by the *Los Angeles Times* stated that the *Post*'s comments on the luncheon were 'misconstrued' rather than 'fabricated'. The host at the affair, Nigel Sinclair, was less equivocal and described the *Post* item as 'absolute balderdash'. Other columnists contrived to report the remark as a fact and had Murray informing Michael Ovitz he would no longer be involved in *Ghostbusters II*. Wow, there goes $200 million for Columbia, ran the gossip mill: Puttnam sure made an expensive crack! Ovitz was well and truly off the hook – now no one could blame *him* for failing to put the package together!

David was sufficiently concerned to write to Bill Murray personally assuring him that he had been mis-reported. Murray replied through David Picker that he had never believed it in the first place. David also wrote to Mike Ovitz: 'Sadly, I gather that even you are tempted to give credibility to this shoddy gossip. Michael, please understand that to do so characterizes the writers of these letters, as well as myself, as liars.' No reply was received from Ovitz.

Liars? Or mistaken? At the risk of introducing another phantom figure, a few of David's colleagues are convinced that he did in fact make the remark. According to one: 'There are times, when he's nervous, that he's not a particularly good speaker. Then he often rushes his words and occasionally departs from his text and makes impromptu remarks. Of course I'm sure he doesn't *remember* saying it and I'm certain he *thinks* he didn't. I'm equally sure he *did*, and that it was a fatal mistake.'

One amused agent reckoned that if David had said it, he had in any case got it wrong. Citing the case of the other movie Murray had forced on Columbia as part of his *Ghostbusters* deal – a re-make of Somerset Maugham's *The Razor's Edge*, with Murray cast in the leading role first played by Tyrone Power – 'Bill Murray *does* give back,' he said, 'not only to the industry, but to Columbia specifically.

They may not have wanted it but in return for playing the fool in *Ghostbusters*, for only a few million more he gave them one of the year's biggest turkeys in *The Razor's Edge!*'

Over a year later *Variety* finally tracked down a witness to the lunch who was prepared to speak out. 'There was a Q and A at the end,' Tom Hansen, a Los Angeles attorney recalled, 'and someone stood up and said, "You've been very outspoken in your criticism of how highly paid many Hollywood stars are. Could you comment on that?"'

According to Hansen, Puttnam praised Robert Redford for his Sundance Institute work, before adding, 'You don't see people, for example Bill Murray, putting back any dollars from *Ghostbusters*.' Hansen confirmed he had related the incident to Mike Ovitz, while emphasizing that it was an impromptu statement rather than part of David's prepared text.

'I wasn't there,' says Fay Vincent, 'but I've had people who were there tell me *without question* he said it. I phoned him about it when I saw it in one of the papers here. He hadn't seen it and was upset and surprised. *Tough as it is*, because I have affection and regard for David, he *didn't deny saying it*, but he said the reaction was ridiculous. He called me back an hour later and said he'd talked to people who said he *hadn't* said it. I told him, 'If you tell me you didn't say it, then I believe you and I'll take that position. However, there are people who say you said it.' He may not have remembered, although I think he knew he'd mentioned Murray.

'My initial advice was that the report would cause trouble and he should call Murray. When he called me back to say it was all a misunderstanding, I said he should still call Murray. I believed him, but the issue with Murray was important. We talked about what the damage control should be.'

David had already looked at the *Ghostbusters II* package and considered hiring new cast members and cutting the costs down to a more manageable size so that more would be left for the studio. The possibility existed to sign up bright new talent for a whole new series – *Ghostbusters II, III, IV* and *V*. The suggestion was enough to infuriate Ovitz. 'He saw the very idea as a slap in the face to himself and the system,' said one observer. 'To Ovitz, this was David really throwing the gauntlet down.'

There was no containing the storm over the *Ghostbusters* sequel dispute, as David inferred that the barrage of publicity over the Bill Murray remark suited Ovitz's book. Pressure from all sides mounted on Fay Vincent.

'The sequel was a huge asset of the Coca-Cola Company,' he

explains. 'David was seen as hurting the company by causing a principal asset to be affected when it wasn't necessary. So ultimately I had
to get into that. Ovitz wouldn't deal with Puttnam and we had to get
negotiations going. Almost every single cast member, and director
Ivan Reitman, said the movie would never be made with Puttnam, as
did Ovitz. They would deal only with me. When I told David that,
his initial stand was that to give in to Ovitz was ridiculous and that his
authority was being violated. How could he be the head of Columbia
and have nothing to do with its biggest picture? I pointed out that
made it two, counting *Ishtar*. Later he calmed down and phoned me
and said of course I was right, it was wrong of him to stand in the way
of the film getting made. I hadn't wanted to go over Puttnam's head,
but I couldn't let the project die in the water. It got to be a nightmare
and caused an awful lot of trouble, because to Coke it was very
simple: it was our duty to get *Ghostbusters II* made.

'That was when Herbert Allen got into it, because while he didn't
care what David did in terms of making movies, he thought it was
wrong to hurt the company which David would be leaving anyway.
After David got pushed out of *Ghostbusters*, and I started dealing
directly with the participants, the agreement was they'd make it for
no upfront salaries. We'd all be going in on a partnership share –
Ovitz's suggestion. He got everybody to agree to that. Everyone recognized it couldn't be made costing $40–50 million.'

There were differing views over the *Ghostbusters* fracas and the
notion that Ovitz was having difficulty putting it together. 'That's an
interesting theory,' said a rival agent, 'and it's also a pile of shit.
Believe me, in Hollywood, greed will conquer all. It'll be put together,
though David might not be around to see it.'

By February it was clear that *The Mission* was grinding to a halt in the
US with rentals of just $8.3 million, adding up to a major disappoint-
ment. When Fernando Ghia went on record with his view that US
reaction represented a backlash to its victory at Cannes, David reacted
– some would say over-reacted – furiously. 'That was probably the
most asinine interview I have ever read in my entire life,' he railed. 'I
can't believe it, it's absolute madness. It's also extremely dangerous,
because if people are stupid enough to believe what he says, then that
attitude could be the death, not just of Cannes, but of every festival
around the world.'

What had crazed David, it seemed, was the possibility that he was
responsible for *The Mission*'s US failure. At least there was a measure
of artistic reward, as the film went on to be nominated for no fewer

than seven Oscars: Best Film, Best Director, Best Cinematography, Best Art Direction, Best Editing, Best Costume Design and Best Original Score; although only one award was given – to Chris Menges for Cinematography.

The creative community was next to feel his wrath, following the discovery that it was not only producers and deal-makers who had inflated ideas of their worth. 'If you have a dream to make a particular film,' he told one reporter, 'and someone is prepared to invest $20 million or even $10 million in it, there's something wrong in saying "I wish to earn $2 million to fulfil my dream" – I mean, the canon of human experience doesn't allow for that. If someone's dream is about to be realized, there is an energy and commitment that should be much more important than sitting holding the bridge of your nose and demanding $2 million. If someone came to me and said, "This is the film I've always wanted to make, but this (naming some silly figure) is the minimum fee I'll make it for," I would say, "There are five other excellent studios, here are their addresses and telephone numbers. I suggest you go and talk to them." If, in America, I come across a director who has made a film as good as Ingmar Bergman's *Fanny and Alexander*, I'm going to take him very, very seriously. But if he has never made a film half as good as that, I'd like him to accept that as a starting point in our relationship. It doesn't mean he's a diminished human being, it means that in his own eyes he's a man with a lot to learn and a long road to travel. With any luck, we as a studio can help. Sadly, an awful lot of directors don't see it that way. They see themselves as having travelled the road and now they're getting their revenge. Well, I'm not in the revenge business.

'This picture of me as some kind of St George come to slay the Hollywood dragon is extremely embarrassing. I'm no St George. I'm not an intellectual. I think I'm a reasonably thoughtful person. I read and I think, and Hollywood is probably not an environment in which a lot of people do read, and frankly not a lot of people do think.

'I was naïve. It took me a month to realize I was the kid in charge of the candy store. And what came out of recognizing that was the realization of what extreme abuse there had been in the past. If I do succeed here, other studios will follow suit and the American industry will benefit. If I fail, the industry will still survive. It's a win–win situation for them.'

In David's mind the reason for the renewed media blitz was quite clear – to let everyone know yet again exactly where he stood. Terry Semel at Warner advised him that what he was doing was self-defeating, as did his friend Jeff Berg at I C M. 'Do your good work, but keep a low profile,' was the advice from one supporter, 'but for Christ's sake, David, lighten up; it's only rock 'n' roll after all!'

'David's problem,' said one rival studio executive, 'is that he regards the press here as he did when he was an independent producer in England. There he was lionized by the press, he was quoted ad nauseum, he was the guru of the industry and no one dared to disagree with him, because he was too important. When he got here he didn't realize the depth of antipathy toward him – nothing personal, he's a likable guy – but the antipathy that would have been felt for anyone coming in. He was not an ex-agent, not an ex-lawyer, not an ex-TV producer who had come up through the ranks. He was an outsider whose commercial record in the eyes of Hollywood was insignificant. *Chariots* was a major success, but *The Killing Fields* was not, nor *Cal*, nor *Local Hero*. And *The Mission* was bombing. So, number one, he talked to the press too much, and number two, his track record was bordering on zilch. And he tries to take on Ray Stark, who's made more hit movies that David's had climaxes?

'I know people who told him he would have to get used to working with people he didn't like, because in this business you've got to do 15–20 pictures a year. If you're lucky enough to work with four or five people you actually like, that's about it. The others you may neither admire nor like, but they are film makers of consequence and turn out commercial hits. I have to slog my way through a dozen pieces of crap to get to the stuff I really want to do – but I do it. I'm highly paid to turn out a certain amount of product, and let's face it, you can't feel appassionato about everything. The trouble with David is he can't seem to separate his personal feelings from the studio interests.'

David was the recipient of the Jean Renoir Humanitarian Award on 13 February 1987, at a ceremony held in the Sportsman's Lodge in Studio City, close to his Coldwater Canyon Drive home. The award was presented by the Los Angeles Film Teachers Association – clearly distanced from sordid financial considerations – who went on to cite him as 'the best last hope we have'. After the battering he had taken since his arrival at Columbia, David was delighted to receive the honour and pointedly stated, 'There may well be, in this room, more legitimate love of cinema than exists on all the lots in Hollywood.'

Robert Radnitz spoke for most of those present as he declared, 'David is someone who understands picture-making. There are many who feel he can't succeed, but many of us feel he can. His outlook appears to say that art and entertainment are not separate.'

Frank Biondi Jr, executive vice-president of Coke's Entertainment Business Sector, and greenlighter of *Switching Channels*, caused a ripple with his announcement that a feature film entity *separate from Columbia Pictures* was being set up by Coca-Cola. He went out of his way to deny there was any particular strategy. 'It's just the other side of the Nelson joint venture,' he claimed, 'a deal done essentially by the Entertainment Business Sector as opposed to Columbia Pictures.' Although basically designed for this purpose, Biondi stated that feature production by the new entity on its own, although *not intended* at present *could not be precluded* in the future.

Fay Vincent knew that David felt the move was 'aimed' at him. 'But it wasn't,' he says. 'It had nothing to do with David. It was to do with the fact he found difficult to swallow, that he was only one star in Coke's film constellation, *not* the whole constellation.'

By April David had soldiered on, producing with his team a $269 million package of 25 features, with an average budget of under $11 million, about $4 million less than the average cost before his arrival. Several were 'pick-ups':

• *Stars and Bars* was to be produced by his ex-partner Sandy Lieberson, ostensibly as an independent movie, with Susan Richards aboard as co-producer. Pat (*Cal*) O'Connor was to direct William Boyd's screenplay. Daniel Day Lewis and Harry Dean Stanton were starring.

• Director Gregory (*El Norte*) Nava had completed *Destiny*, another leftover from Coke's Embassy deal; William Hurt, Timothy Hutton and Stockard Channing were featured.

• After viewing Jim McBride's thriller, *The Big Easy*, starring Dennis Quaid and Ellen Barkin, David bought it for Columbia release. 'It's a great asset to have creative people like Puttnam, who is a movie-maker, in charge at Columbia,' said McBride, 'and not a bunch of lawyers and accountants. We just hope he survives.'

• Island Pictures gave up the rights to Spike (*She's Gotta Have it*) Lee's *School Daze* when the budget soared past $4 million. Columbia, this time at David Picker's instigation, stepped in, guaranteeing a negative pick-up on a $6 million budget. Other executives were upset at the total control Picker gave Lee. 'You just don't hand someone who's only made a little home movie $6 million to spend,' was one comment. 'Look,' Picker said, 'we're paying for a Spike Lee movie. If you do that you have to run with the guy. There's no point in turning it into something else. Either you believe in him or you don't.'

• John Boorman's World War II memoir, *Hope and Glory* , was due for release in the autumn.

• Apart from *Ghostbusters II*, where any hope of glory was now extinguished, the only rock-solid, commercial success Columbia had in its locker was *Karate Kid III*. The series' producer, Jerry

Weintraub, had formed his own Columbia-supported Weintraub Entertainment Group (president: Guy McElwaine). If only Columbia didn't have contractual rights to the sequel, Jerry must have pondered, he could have made it entirely independently. Ah, well. Although 'set to start filming in October', for some reason it never did.

• To be produced by A & M Films was *The Beast*, starring Steven Bauer, which David described as 'Das Boot in a tank in Afghanistan'. Uberto Pasolini misunderstood David's enthusiasm for the picture after a reading of the film's simplistic, but crudely effective script. Surely David could see this was not a serious comment on war? 'Every picture doesn't have to be,' David explained. 'What we have here is a classic exploitation picture in the vein of *Midnight Express*.' Uberto had discovered the commercial side of David – there *was* a mogul in there after all!

• *Little Nikita* had been in development for three years at Columbia and was Sidney Poitier's comeback picture after a long absence from the screen. His co-star was River Phoenix, a standout in *Stand by Me*. *Nikita* had virtually completed filming and already there were glum expressions every time the film was mentioned. Why? One theory: 'It was originally conceived for Jack Nicholson as a relationship adventure. He's an agent who discovers the kid's parents are Russian moles. What happened was director Richard Benjamin and the writer fell in love with the thriller aspect of the picture and overplotted it. It became a mish-mash.'

• Jane Fonda's own production company was due to make a 'comic adventure', *Flawless*, in the fall, under a pre-existing four-year arrangement at Columbia. This was subsequently dropped and another project, *The Old Gringo*, put into production in January, 1988.

Then there was the strange, convoluted case of *Vice Versa*.

David was on the panel that granted Brian Gilbert entry into the National Film School in 1979. Brian recalls saying at the interview that British films were often misunderstood in America because British obsessions tended to be easily misunderstood. David immediately pounced on the comment. 'How do we remedy this?' he asked Brian, who replied, 'I don't know: that's what I'm here to find out.'

Three years later David met Brian again, when he came along to BAFTA with Alan Parker and Alan Marshall to view his graduation film, *The Devotee*. Brian was dumbfounded as David greeted him afterwards with, 'I want you to write and direct a movie for me.'

David had very specific ideas for what turned out to be one of the *First Love* series. He wanted Brian to take the character he had created in *The Devotee* and transfer her to another screenplay. Brian went away ecstatic – an ex-actor, he had just been handed a movie after three years' film-school study. He had to pinch himself to make sure it wasn't a dream.

The script for *Sharma and Beyond* was written in late 1982 and filmed a year later. Brian had a great deal of input from David at the script stage – long detailed hand-written notes kept arriving – then found he was left entirely on his own to shoot the movie.

When the editing was ending on *Sharma*, David approached Brian about another script he wanted him to direct, *The Frog Prince*, one of the three ex-*First Love*'s David was transferring to the big screen. With Iain Smith as producer, *The Frog Prince* was shot in Paris with a little help in the translation department from the multi-lingual Uberto Pasolini.

While trying to develop a project independently after his producer's departure for Columbia, Brian heard David had something in mind for him – a re-make of the fifties British comedy, *Vice Versa*. Brian read the script, by Dick Clement and Ian La Frenais, and was highly enthusiastic. When David asked him to come out and meet the writers, Brian thought he was being invited to Los Angeles for the weekend and took a small overnight bag. He remained in Hollywood for a year.

With everyone psychologically committed to the film by November, rumours began to circulate that another movie was in development with a virtually identical storyline. This was confirmed when Dudley Moore – transplanted from Coldwater Canyon to Malibu – announced that his new picture, *Like Father, Like Son*, was soon to start shooting. Could it be? Yes, it could. The biggest shock was *where* the development was taking place – at Victor Kaufman's Tri-Star, Columbia's sister company!

David went to see Kaufman and discovered Hollywood hardball in action. 'Why don't we put all our resources behind the one picture?' he suggested. 'There's no need,' Kaufman maintained, 'you've got a terrific script there, David. You've got nothing to worry about. Our script still has problems, and we haven't even got a director lined up. Furthermore, our treatment's different, more of a madcap romp. Yours has style, texture. But no, we can't cancel, we're committed. We even have a release date.'

David knew he could win the race by rushing *Vice Versa* through, for he had a head start of several weeks on Kaufman's film. He decided not to do that and to make the best of a bad job by negotiating with Kaufman to divide up first domestic and foreign release. Kaufman cannily snagged first US domestic release, somewhat hoisting

David on his international petard. The only crumb of comfort was that everyone knew the Tri-Star version was *so* inferior. And Dudley Moore hadn't had a hit for over a hundred years. And quality would win through in the end – wouldn't it?

As the *Vice Versa* crew began shooting, with Judge Reinhold top-cast, further rumours started. There was another version about to go into production – *18 Again*, with veteran George Burns. Then, un-believably, yet another with a similar theme – *Big*, with Tom Hanks. Suddenly *everyone* was making father and son role-reversal comedies. All that was now required was a re-release of the original *Vice Versa* and there would be five versions floating around!

One of the projects that David was most excited about came in the form of a Barry Levinson/Valerie Curtin script that Levinson was keen to direct, *Toys*. The project had been at 20th Century Fox for years, but there was no problem, David was assured – Columbia could have it on turnaround. Levinson's agents, CAA, would deal with Fox direct on the matter. David saw that *Toys* could not only make an intriguing film, with its plot about a military man who was left a toy factory, but that it had far-reaching merchandising possi-bilities. Coke were alerted and enthusiastically agreed to contribute $4 million to a joint merchandising programme intended to coincide with the film's release. Iain Smith was summoned. 'I have a task for you,' David told him, 'to executive produce *Toys*.'

Barry Diller, head of 20th Century Fox, got wind of the excitement being generated at Burbank over the project. Were they letting something go they should hold on to? Had they missed out?

Diller's relationship with David went back to his running ABC's *Movies of the Week* from a tiny office in New York. At first the two men got along reasonably well, then when Diller surfaced as head of Paramount Pictures there were a couple of minor altercations over *Bugsy Malone*. The big contretemps between the two had arisen over Warren Beatty's *Reds*, where Diller – and Beatty – felt David had deliberately depicted the Oscar awards as a David versus Goliath struggle between *Chariots of Fire* and *Reds*, with David delivering a V-sign with his catapult. ('And I did,' David admits. 'I went out of my way to get it seen in those terms. I played up the cost of *Reds*, which at the time Beatty and Diller were desperately trying to play down. I crazed both of them.')

Somewhere during the negotiations between CAA and Fox, *Toys* slipped through the cracks; Leonard Goldberg at Fox was said to be suddenly hot for the project. If there was an easier way to embarrass

David than for Fox to hold on to *Toys*, it was not readily apparent. Diller knew he had been to Atlanta and had millions from Coke. He could not help but savour the situation – the egg on David's face would be ankle-deep.

'Fox have decided not to let *Toys* go,' was the brief, unthinkable message relayed to David. Infuriated, he contacted Levinson. 'I'm going to fight this,' he told him. 'Will you get your head down with us if it comes to a showdown?' When Levinson equivocated, David was forced to go it alone. The only other things left to do were explain the situation to Coke as best he could, and let Iain Smith know the project was a non-starter.

David was impressed with Bill Cosby at their first meeting. He watched as America's biggest TV star put himself over as a professional who had more money than Croesus – and a dream to make this movie, *Leonard Part VI*, a spoof on spy pictures. Cosby had outlined his basic plot idea to screenwriter Jonathan Reynolds, involving a supercool special agent that echoed his original *I Spy* success. Leonard's antagonist was certainly to be one of the most original creations of all times, a malignant female animal-rights fanatic, who discovers a way to control the brains of animals by using a secret chemical and urge them on to commit terrorist acts. Cosby was convinced it would be a wow. 'They'll be lining up round the block for it,' he informed everyone who would listen.

He boasted to David of his terrific relationship with his audience. He was prepared to work his butt off and talk through any problems like the pro he was. There would be no requirement to pal up to him. He would not need to be stroked, schmoozed, or have his hand held. David swallowed the bait. Here was America's top-rated TV star, eager and ready to turn in the family blockbuster that would be Columbia's big Christmas picture for 1987. It was a dream on a plate. Or was it? David was highly critical of the first two drafts of the screenplay, and in the end ambivalent about the whole notion of the movie, despite the built-in insurance that Cosby represented. Temporary president Steve Sohmer had stitched the extraordinary Cosby deal together, which gave the comedian virtual control of everything on the picture, including approval of script, casting, costume, music, sets and final cut. For $5 million he was the star. For another $750,000 he was the producer. In return, Cosby awarded Sohmer one of the most meaningless and demeaning titles in movie history, 'executive producer for Mr Cosby'.

David decided he would only give the $24-million project the go-ahead if Coke themselves would agree to underwrite the movie's release. At least then, he reasoned, Columbia's liability would be limited to the film's cost, although it would remain by far the biggest item on the studio's slate. Unfortunately, his action also signalled to Cosby that David had insufficient faith in his vision and was not prepared to unequivocally back him.

When a director for the project was discussed, Cosby indicated his liking of English humour and plumped for a British director, reasoning that an American would be full of preconceived ideas of the image he wanted put across. Instead, he wanted to get away as far as possible from his TV persona – this was to be the *new* Bill Cosby. When David put forward several suggestions, Cosby selected an award-winning young commercials director, 34-year-old Paul Weiland, after viewing his tapes and meeting him in his New York brownstone.

Paul Weiland and David Puttnam had been neighbours for about five minutes in 1958, when five-year-old Paul and his family moved into the same small street in Southgate, in the very week that the Puttnams crossed town. Paul's life and career followed the track of a pinball, hitting David Puttnam buttons at various stops. He worked as a copywriter at CDP. He met David socially when he was working for the Alan Parker Film Co. and observed Alan's strong, but often schizoid relationship with David. He set up his own commercial-producing firm in the eighties and had a brief romance with Debbie Puttnam before she met Loyd.

There was an unexpected chemistry between Cosby, the black US superstar and Weiland, the white Jewish candidate. But who was this guy Sohmer schlepping around, slapping everyone on the back and repeating Cosby's slightest utterances as if they were holy grail? Paul felt he had passed the acid test of getting along with Cosby, but was that to be the highpoint of the deal? The script drafts he had seen were terrible. 'Cosby's schtick will make it work,' he was told. 'He's the funniest guy in the business. It'll be magic time.' Paul was allowed to see one live show the comedian was recording and recalls wanting to like him so much his hands were sweating. He found the show bland, and Cosby did not strike him as at all funny. He remembers stumbling into a New York street after viewing Cosby's performance in an earlier movie, *Mother, Jugs, and Speed*, close to tears. Had Cosby *ever* been funny?' He managed to analyse that on each week's television show Cosby wandered in and out, averaging 10 or 15 minutes of screen time. In a feature movie like *Leonard Part VI* he would have to be on the screen for at least 90 minutes. Paul felt like the odd man out. *He* must be wrong – or was he? His best hope was that

David would have the sense to call the whole thing off – his dearest wish was to board a plane back to London and get the hell out of it.

He was sent on a tour of Columbia executives. David Picker was welcoming for two minutes, reverted to his brusque, big-shot act for another two, then cut out. Michael Nathanson, who had assumed the role of David's blue-eyed boy, was all over Paul – but he found hardly a single enthusiast for the project outside of Nathanson and one marketing executive. Was David aware of this? Was he all that *interested*? Having shown willing and gone along with all the ballyhoo, Paul felt he was sinking into a hideous quagmire, the most expensive first film any director had yet been handed. The marketing man told Paul the project would be their biggest film ever – Cosby was a commodity millions would turn out to see; it was simply a matter of pushing all the right buttons.

David had missed his last chance to get out from under the movie at Coke's Santa Barbara dinner in January. With all the lavish compliments that had flown he was riding high. With 'Roberto and Don' present (and he referred to them as such publicly to the annoyance of Fay Vincent and possibly 'Roberto and Don' themselves), he could have taken advantage of the situation, bitten the bullet and said, 'That's all the good news. The bad news is that Cosby's script is dreadful and we just shouldn't make the picture.'

Although the impact would have been horrendous to Coke's 'relationship' with Cosby – 'Christ, he was their toy-boy,' said one Columbia executive. 'He owns half of a Coke bottling plant and has been one of their main advertisers over the years.' – David thinks he might have walked away alive at that point. Instead, he funked his opportunity.

'I didn't want to have an argument,' he says now, 'and I'd got up to $8 million from Coke to promote the movie, but $8 million worth of *advertising*. That was a mistake, the biggest mistake I made all the time I was at Columbia. *Never* make a film with a script you don't believe in on the assumption it will somehow play. It was Ken Russell and *Lisztomania* all over again, putting your life and fate in someone else's hands. I made a fundamental error. It was a fundamentally lousy idea that Cosby brought us. It was no good. It just wasn't funny. It was the same old thing – you want to believe that the 'star' knows what he's doing. The truth of the matter is he didn't.

'Under other circumstances I wouldn't be so rough with myself, but that week in Santa Barbara I had every card in my hand, and, with hindsight, I *could* have got away with stopping the picture. It would have been a bit of a shock, but that would have been it.'

Patsy could see why he shirked biting the bullet. 'He'd just been through the most horrendous four months of his life. It's the old thing of 'it'll be all right on the night', same as *Trick or Treat* or *Agatha* – and it's *never* all right. History should have taught David that it wouldn't work, but he was still stinging from all the attacks on him. He was really pleased with some of the things he'd managed to develop in spite of everything and I imagine he was thinking, "Do I really need another terrible problem at the moment?" He didn't want any more wars. His eye was off the ball.'

Despite David's agonizing, there did exist one simple and painfree alternative both to proceeding *and* cancellation, which he chose not to pursue – the wholesale transfer of the project into the eager arms of Tri-Star, where Kaufman and his film chief David Matalon were ready to pick up the baton. 'I would have been happy to have made *Leonard VI*,' Matalon confirmed. Was the thought of handing Tri-Star a potential blockbuster the real reason David decided to proceed at Columbia? 'I don't doubt that he could have transferred it, but he chose not to,' says Fay Vincent.

With shooting due to start in San Franciso in April, the ill-fated vehicle lurched along, while Cosby smarted at the slight delivered by David's seeking of insurance funding at Coke.

David installed his blunt Cockney pal, Alan Marshall – with Cosby's approval – as line producer of the project, giving him some peace of mind that Columbia's most expensive undertaking would at least move along in a workmanlike manner.

In a rash moment he said, 'The budget is completely justified for *Leonard VI*. The film could really work.' Whether he was trying to convince Paul Weiland, Alan Marshall, Bill Cosby or himself is unclear.

Chapter 25

Hollywood is Fear

One of the first disputes with Cosby was over the choice of Diahnne Abbott to play his wife in the film. Paul Weiland took his courage in both hands and turned her down as unsuitable. Sohmer was alarmed but said he would smooth it out with the star. Alan Marshall's first fight with Cosby was over the money he wanted to pay Gloria Foster, a black stage actress cast as the evil, crazed Medusa, head of the 'International Tuna' terrorist gang. With her salary cut, and his hackles high in inverse proportion, Cosby next indicated that he wanted to appoint his own black make-up assistant at a 'special salary' that Marshall calculated would add $30,000 to the normal fees over the course of the film. Noting in any case that Cosby used hardly any make-up, a fact Marshall felt was possibly germane, the special salary was resisted. Cosby backed down and came up with another choice at standard salary.

Since Cosby had clearly promised jobs to serried ranks of his friends, each turn-down was a mortal blow to his pride. Paul and Alan were putting up more suitable choices purely for the good of the film and relying on Sohmer to smooth the star's feelings. After all, they had a $24-million film on their hands with a tight shooting schedule – Cosby had indicated from the outset he was off to the Hotel Du Cap in July come hell or high water. They needed professionals to see the film through, not a bunch of 'pals' or first-timers. The feedback from Cosby, with the liaison problems apparently being swept under the carpet by Sohmer, was that he was becoming good and mad.

He wanted 90 per cent of the cast to be black, even down to his English butler. With difficulty he was persuaded that this was not appropriate casting and reluctantly allowed Tom Courtenay to be brought in. He decided to take a stand, however, over the senior-citizen Italian theatre director his teenage daughter falls for in one of the movie's convoluted sub-plots, a character named Giorgio. Perfect casting for the role, Cosby felt, was 66-year-old black veteran actor, Moses Gunn. This time David got involved, with the alarm bells ringing loud and clear from the San Francisco pre-production offices. In a letter to Cosby, he questioned the casting of Gunn. Cosby replied that it was important his daughter's Italian suitor be black. If he was white, he explained, it would look as if his antagonism towards him in the film was racist-based. The message David got from Steve Sohmer was, 'For Christ's sake, don't rock the boat.' David asked Paul what he thought. With Sohmer's siren song ringing in his ears, 'Don't upset the biggest star in the world; he's a phenomenon,' Paul replied, 'Oh, it'll be all right. We can't expect to win every battle.' And the ship sailed on.

When filming began, the pellucid logic of Gloria Foster's casting as Medusa was made clear as she proceeded, with Cosby's backing, to demand that her role be dramatically extended. She turned down many of the costumes that had been specially designed for her, would work only on 'approved' floor surfaces, and insisted on spending endless hours in make-up each morning. If her role had given her the opportunity to bring one balancing ounce of humour to the production, there would have been some compensation, but of humour there was none. As far as Paul was concerned she ruled the roost and became, 'the biggest pain in the ass on the film'.

He found Cosby himself professional and courteous, never hogging scenes and encouraging everyone else to give of their best – except Frau Foster, who was a law unto herself. Relations between Paul and Cosby were still cordial, despite the crossed lines Sohmer had allowed to slip through. The victim of these was Alan Marshall, for whom Cosby cultivated a deep and terrible loathing.

For his part, the laconic producer's concern was to steward the film through to its completion under the brief David had given him. 'The problem with *Leonard*,' he says now, 'quite apart from the awful script, was that Cosby never allowed any part of it to be changed. He was like a God and treated as one by jerks like Sohmer. But not by me. All his pals thought he could walk on water, but I wasn't impressed. A producer that doesn't even watch his own rushes? To me that's no producer at all. You can't stroll through a movie like you can a TV show. All we got was stupid talk about how they'd be lining up for the movie. The man was only interested in dollars.'

(David confirms Crosby's intractability with regard to script alterations. 'I wrote a lot of comments down for Steve Sohmer, and I got an embarrassed note back from him: "Mr Cosby has made it clear that he wants to have no further amendment to his vision". And he used the word, "vision", instead of "script").'

According to some reports, David received a call from Cosby in late April, to the effect that he could no longer work with Marshall, whom he considered a racist. He wanted him fired. *Was* he asked to fire Marshall? I asked David. Well – yes and no, take your pick: 'No. Never. The problem is, people like Cosby – and when I say people like Cosby, 99.99 per cent of people reading this book are not like Cosby, therefore they're going to find this very hard to understand – are used not just to having what they say operated on, but to being interpreted and anticipated. There's an old story they used to tell when I was working on Albert Speer's story about Eva Braun, that she was very dangerous. Without ever knowing it she would come back from a dinner party saying I think that the mayor of Hamburg is incompetent, and he would be fired, or I don't trust that man – and he might end up dead. She never knew what she was doing. Other people, probably Hitlers, know exactly what they are doing and they don't have to say things like do me a favour, bump off Andrew Yule, will you? It's the old 'tiresome priest' syndrome. So it may well be that Cosby was saying things to Sohmer, possibly, then Sohmer was couching them to me in terms that I was supposed to pick up.'

Concerned, David flew to San Francisco to pour oil on the troubled Bay waters, but found Cosby absent at his daughter's graduation, obviously expecting David to attend to matters. Dinner was spent with Paul and Alan, listening to their tales of woe. If the atmosphere had been chilly before Cosby left, it turned to ice when he returned to find Marshall still around, his head still perversely attached to his body.

'He thought', says David, 'that Marshall would either have been fired, or at the very least publicly – and that is his word, not mine – *publicly* humiliated. I'm not in the business of public humiliation, so he was asking for someone to be fired who'd done nothing wrong, or humiliated in a way I would never do to anybody, black, white, green or yellow. If I'm going to fire somebody or tell somebody off I'd do it privately, so I think what we may be talking about here is a vast culture gap.'

Cosby put up Stu Gardner, musical director of his TV show, to score the movie. After questioning his qualifications for the job, Alan contacted David. 'Let him do a couple of tracks anyway and see how he does,' was the suggestion. When this was relayed to Cosby, the sparks flew. 'I'm telling you Stu's going to score the movie,' he raged, 'and you're not going to do anything about it, Marshall.'

With two short sequences chosen for Gardner to score, Marshall, Cosby, Gardner and Weiland assembled in the small viewing theatre to watch the results. Alan knew it was bad, but was ready to counsel Gardner, 'OK, you haven't got it this time, but have another shot.' Even as the thought was passing through his mind, Crosby instantly fired Gardner. There was no chance even to say goodbye to the musician, so fast was he loaded on a plane for New York. Cosby turned to Paul Weiland and said, 'OK, do what you like with the music,' and walked out. Paul looked at Alan, who just shook his head. 'I'll get Elmer Bernstein,' he said.

Alan was never fired, but following a visit from David Picker and Michael Nathanson, he seemed to make himself diplomatically scarce for the last month of production, returning full-time when shooting was over for the final dubbing sessions.

'Racist?' Alan laughs. 'Coming from him, that's a good one, someone who's totally anti-white. Have a butchers at *Fame* – I couldn't care less what colour of skin someone's got. All we wanted was the best for Columbia to make the bloody thing work. Paul worked his backside off. I just wish David had told me at the time Cosby wanted me fired. I'd have walked out. I don't believe in staying where I'm not wanted. But he didn't, he kept it from me. I'd have gone – but I'd have told Cosby a few home truths first – and that asshole Sohmer, who stabbed everybody in the back.' (Fay Vincent has a very different view of Sohmer: 'He was very complimentary of Marshall all the way through. He said Marshall and Cosby just didn't get along. There were very bad feelings. Sohmer was trying to bridge a gap that was not bridgeable.')

David decided at the end of shooting that a little present for Cosby would be in order, something not unusual when a film wraps, but certainly on this occasion more in the nature of a peace-offering than anything else. David himself collects photographic prints and selected a magnificent study of blues singer Muddy Waters for Cosby's gift. The package was returned to David in the next mail, opened and resealed.

The word to Coca-Cola was incredibly damaging. 'He's a great producer,' Cosby told them, 'but he can't run Columbia. He's killing the studio.'

Since Ray Stark had stormed out of David's office, nary a whisper had been heard directly from that quarter. It took several months, and a meeting of Coke executives in Atlanta, for Herbert Allen to feel that an initial skirmish was called for. David detected from the animated flicker of expression on Allen's face as soon as he entered the room that a jousting session was on the agenda. The disquiet he had

felt towards Allen ever since an early meeting, when he observed the
New Yorker peel off a £20 note and hand it to Claridges bellman, had
not diminished with their subsequent meetings. While he found
Allen a basically cold personality, he had to concede that the man had
an original mind and that nothing he did was obvious. Still resistant,
despite his own enhanced circumstances, to the idea of gentlemen and
players, David's theory was that 'the rich' were different and marched
to a different drum. As far as he was concerned, the one quality that
bound Allen and Ray Stark together was their overwhelming cynicism,
which he had always interpreted as a form of despair dressed up as
sophistication. Certain types he felt instinctively attracted to; certain
types he did not – both Allen and Stark firmly belonged in the latter
category. ('The difficulty with Herbert is that he's much more complicated than is apparent,' says Fay Vincent. 'The stereotype of rem-
oteness is not accurate. He's a man who's that powerful and that
wealthy, yet he's a liberal democrat. The stereotype would be that he
was a very conservative traditional. He's not. He's been a liberal
democrat all his life and very, very liberal. The people who are
closest to him and know him the best are very loyal to him. He's a
terrific friend.')

   'David, why are you *alienating* so many people – like, for example,
Mike Ovitz?' Allen asked. 'I hear that CAA have stopped sending
scripts to the studio.'

   David detected a follow-up to Allen's original lecture. He asserted
that CAA's billings to Columbia were still running at an annual rate
of $8 million. This was alienation? 'And we've plenty of scripts without
worrying about CAA,' he told Allen.

   'You put the making of *Ghostbusters II* in jeopardy,' Allen persisted.
'You're supposed to be running the studio for Fay, but he's got to
handle this picture himself now – or it'll never get made. Ovitz won't
deal with you. Dan Aykroyd won't deal with you. Bill Murray won't
deal with you. Ivan Reitman won't deal with you – '

   'Why don't you just stop at Ovitz? Doesn't that say it all?'

   'No, it doesn't, David. These people have minds of their own.'

   'Do they? And does anybody else in Hollywood, when they'd rather
believe a gossip columnist's version of the truth rather than a dozen
lawyers?'

   'Whatever, David. The Murray remark, true or otherwise, accurately
reflects your attitude. We're not dealing with puppets, we're dealing
with real people, with talent, with egos – '

   In an effort to take the heat out of the situation, Fay Vincent
interjected, 'Look, the main thing is the project is going to go ahead.'

By this time David had his second wind. 'You've known all along,' he addressed the board, 'that what I'm mandated to do is to get Columbia back to being a sovereign state. I've always made it clear that it couldn't be a painless process.'

'Fine,' Herbert Allen agreed, 'but have some regard for prime assets of the Coca-Cola Company, like the right to do *Ghostbusters II*. You have every right to make whatever pictures you want, but you announced your retirement in three years, so you have no right to tamper with the franchises of Columbia, which includes our library, people we want to do business with in the future, sequels and the infra-structure of the company which will extend after your three years are up. Had you not announced your retirement, this would have been an entirely different subject.'

Fay was in one of the most difficult positions he had ever experienced. Of all those present, he knew as well as any how totally correct Herbert Allen was in his judgement. The crux of the whole affair was David's three-year declaration, which had made Fay look foolish in the eyes of Coca-Cola and made Coca-Cola look foolish in the eyes of the film community. And the reason David had given for his announcement had increased, rather than diminished, Fay's concern . . . After the meeting ended in agreement, David sought Keough out. 'What was that all about?' he asked. 'Oh, he's been grumbling a bit,' Keough replied, 'and I felt it was better for him to come out with it at a face-to-face meeting. You handled it very well, David.'

Although never mentioned at the meeting, an intriguing rumour was sweeping Hollywood – that David had gone to C A A's main rival, the William Morris agency, and offered them a blanket deal. The ruse had blown up in David's face, the story ran, when his offer was turned down flat and the iron door of the Hollywood establishment had clanged shut in his face. Although there was not a shred of truth in the story, it produced many a smirk of satisfaction at cocktail hours all over Hollywood. David was being squeezed out between William Morris (where Bill Cosby paid the overheads) and Mike Ovitz's C A A!

A few days later one of David's secretaries confronted him with some unusual news. According to the grapevine, he was being 'tailed'. Sure enough, a black limousine seemed to be forever behind his car wherever he went. When a colleague with whom he was travelling independently came out with the same thought, David Picker was anxiously sought out. 'If you're really worried about it, go see Lew Wasserman and ask for his advice. He's dealt with this sort of thing before.' The idea of consulting the elder statesman appealed to David on several levels. First, it would be like the British Godfather consulting the senior American version. Second, Wasserman was Wasserman – who knows what might come out of the conversation? Third, despite the monk-like existence he led, every passing day convinced him further that someone had hired a private detective to monitor his movements.

The meeting with Wasserman was a fascinating experience, but his advice boiled down to, 'Forget it. If it's true there's nothing you can do about it. If it isn't you're only going to drive yourself crazy.' As David drew away from Universal's Black Tower, he felt let down, but decided to follow Wasserman's advice and let it fizzle out, reckoning the 'tail' would in any event be dead of boredom fairly soon. And if by any chance it was one of the powerful enemies he had crossed who was footing the bill – so much the better.

David flew to Europe in May to attend the Cannes Film Festival – and straight into another storm of controversy over a speech. The occasion could scarcely have been less appropriate – a Gala Dinner to honour Sir Alec Guinness, with the Prince and Princess of Wales in attendance. Bemoaning the pessimism which he felt still plagued the British Film Industry, he beseeched the 400 diners 'not to give up' on British films. One reporter found criticism of his remarks 'heartfelt and loudly expressed' late that night in Cannes bars.

Producer Don Boyd was present, flanked by his *Aria* directors. Annoyed as he had been months earlier at what he saw as David's distancing of himself from the Goldcrest débâcle, he now found himself listening with embarrassment and rage to the man who had helped re-establish him on the British film scene. 'I have to say it was the most diabolically bad speech I'd heard from a public speaker in a long time,' he says. 'First, he hardly mentioned Alec Guinness. Then the whole attitude and atmosphere of what he had to say was patronizing. How it came over was, "*I* am the most powerful film executive in the world. What *I* have to say you have to take onboard, whether you like it or not, and if you don't, you're stupid and unrealistic." He was saying this in *France*, not *Britain*, as head of an *American* company – lecturing us at an international meeting about British parochialism!

'Then he announced his contribution to the British film scene – a film Lynda Myles had developed, *To Kill a Priest*, to be made in *France* with a *Polish* director! With a room full of British directors sitting around, it was a ridiculous political gaffe. 'We've started casting,' he went on, 'and I'm trying to get the director to *consider* British actors.' Not a word of any direct British film investment.

'It was a rambling, ill-thought-out disaster, which angered everybody there. Of the seven directors I had with me, every single one of them left *enraged*.

'Next day, however, rather in the way things are, nobody would *say* anything and I thought – fuck this, I know David well enough to let him know. I chose my moment, a round-table press conference for *Aria*. What I didn't know was that there was a reporter present and that my remarks would go round the world. I never intended that to happen. He must *so* regret that speech. He wrote a huge letter to me later explaining why he thought it was justified.'

While admitting he has given better speeches, David says he aimed many of his comments at Geoffrey Pattie, the British Government's Film Minister, in what turned out to be a successful attempt to get more funding pumped into the National Film School. Then he gave *To Kill a Priest* as an *example* of internationalism. It is perhaps ironic in view of the over-use of British talent he was accused of in Hollywood, that here he was being pilloried for its non-use.

If David's speeches had become a way of life for him, and a way of elucidating his thoughts, they had also become, for observers, a reliable guide to his current state of mind. He was going through the roughest period of his entire life and felt beset on all sides. He had a suspicion that the low-key Herbert Allen assault was but the thin end of the wedge.

David unrepentantly underlined his views at Cannes to Iain Johnstone: 'Yes, we are in danger of having what I would call "over-the-garden-wall" movies. That's to say, of riveting interest to the next-door neighbours, maybe to the street, but of less than passing interest to anybody in the town. There's a smugness creeping into British films which is worrying.'

He admitted all was not sweetness and light back in Los Angeles. 'I have to accept that I'm relatively unpopular there. It's the most important thing I had to come to terms with. It became clear within two weeks of starting the job last September that there were only two options: either to assimilate and be popular, or not.'

Ishtar opened, and quickly closed, clobbered by incredulous reviews and complete public apathy. Although the Columbia campaign was exemplary, and Warren Beatty had hand-picked the marketing people responsible – the ones that passed the 'Say Puttnam is a perfect prick 20 times' test – still he tried to lay part of the blame for the film's failure at David's feet. 'Warren will never forgive David for bad-mouthing *Reds*,' said one overlooked marketing specialist. 'Never, never, *never*. And I don't see David and Dustin wandering off into the sunset together either, no way. David never even saw *Ishtar* and says he never will, which I think is a little stiff-assed. It's all ego. Could David have got involved and tried to make peace with the two of them? I guess he could have tried, but I honestly don't think he gives a shit. It's possible to live a fairly complete life without Warren or Dustin.'

Fay Vincent has his own view of the distance David kept from *Ishtar*. 'In some respects Warren was right,' he says. 'He complained that Puttnam never helped the picture, never said he liked it, never said anything good about it. In fact, he never even saw it. Beatty was very upset by that. He didn't try to hurt the picture in any way, but after it was finished and available, they were very resentful that he hadn't taken the time to see it. How could the head of the company be distributing a huge picture that he hadn't seen? Personally, I liked the movie, I liked it a lot. The problem is you get conditioned. When a picture gets that expensive you almost want to hate it before you see it, because it's portrayed as being this sort of bloated extravagance.'

David changed his mind about a 1100-screen opening for Dan Melnick's Steve Martin/Daryl Hannah comedy, *Roxanne*, after studying the results of previews held across America. 'You pays your money and you takes your choice,' he said at the June première party for the movie, with the number of screens drastically cut back to just over 800. 'Basically, we looked at the sneaks all last weekend. It played very strongly in all the areas we thought it would and where they extended it outside into downtown locations, we were having our problems.'

This relatively light-hearted announcement over *Roxanne* covered up a major faux-pas in Fay Vincent's view: 'There were two reasons *Roxanne* lost money,' he tersely explains. 'First, it cost too much to produce; second, there was substantial overspending on its marketing. Here Dan Melnick influenced David. David made a mistake. He was new at the job. When he didn't get the result from the previews he was looking for, he panicked and decided to cut back to fewer screens. It was a *terrible* mistake. Picker, who knew more about such things, was away at the time. It wouldn't have happened if Picker had been there. The cut-back in screens hurt Columbia and hurt David's relations with theatres. The owners were furious at the lateness of the cut-back, they went crazy. There was a telegram from Puttnam, it was almost amateurish, it really hurt him. He let himself down badly in the eyes of his main customers. Melnick and Puttnam agreed on the cut-back between them. It was a bad episode.' David was unrepentant. 'It was *unquestionably* the right thing to do,' he still maintains 'and I'd do it again tomorrow.'

The Richie Valens biopic, *La Bamba*, produced a happier result when released with both Spanish and English soundtracks, a sensible nod to the growing Hispanic market. With grosses just beyond the $50 million mark, Columbia turned an extremely healthy profit on *La Bamba*. A leftover from Guy McElwaine's régime, the movie had none the less been enthusiastically supported by David, reminding him as it did of his own *That'll Be The Day*.

When he saw 40 minutes of footage from Bernardo Bertolucci's *The Last Emperor*, he was immediately captivated by it and determined to purchase the film for the US and as many other territories as were available. For producer Jeremy Thomas, the footage represented the fruits of four remarkable years of labour to finance and shoot the film, the first Western production ever to be allowed to film inside Beijing's Forbidden City.

Thomas had chosen to steer the film to David at Columbia through John Daly at Hemdale, who had guaranteed as US release through a major studio. Thomas had first met David while *Melody* was being filmed, then had worked as an editor on *Brother Can You Spare a Dime?* before branching into production himself. His notable successes over the years had been achieved with an eclectic slate of movies ranging from Jerzy Skolimowski's *The Shout* through a Nicolas Roeg series that began with the remarkable *Bad Timing*, Julian Temple's *The Great Rock 'n' Roll Swindle* and Nagisa Oshima's *Merry Christmas, Mr Lawrence* (maintaining the Eastern connection with Hara San, David's great friend from his *Melody* days, onboard as executive producer).

Still on matters Eastern – with David's long-standing connection in that country, it seemed only natural for Fuji Television of Japan to turn to him, their most trusted contact in Hollywood, to re-work *The Adventures of Chatran* for the US market. The film had emerged from a six-year series of Fuji TV documentaries, some 400,000 feet of film having been shot by zoologist Masanori Hata, then subsequently edited by Kon Ichikawa. The third-largest grosser in Japanese history (behind only *E.T.* and one other home-grown film), the chief of Fuji's film division could see that *Chatran*, with its calico stray-cat hero, animals-only cast, poetry links and Japanese musical soundtrack, required considerable anglicizing if it was to succeed in English-language countries. With Jim Clark attached to the project, the decision was made to drop large chunks of the movie and intersplice it with footage from another Fuji TV production, *Puski's Story*, about a stray dog. Narration was being penned for the 'new' *Chatran* by Mark [*Sesame Street*] Saltzman. The Ryuichi Sakamoto score was dropped, being judged 'too repetitive for an American audience'. (Sakamoto would ironically go on to win an Oscar in 1988 for his share in *The Last Emperor*'s score.)

When David appeared on CBS-TV's West 57th Street programme to discuss the impact of US movies abroad, he found himself sharing airtime with his old arch-enemies, Menahem Golan and Yoram Globus of the Cannon group. In a departure from the brief, and with the questions angled towards the hostility he had encountered in Hollywood, David gave yet another uninhibited summary of his views.

The first Goizueta heard of David's appearance was when he switched his television on. 'All of a sudden Roberto's watching television,' says Fay Vincent, 'and here's David on. Nobody had told him. Roberto called me, very concerned, because he thought any time one of our major people was going to be on national television, we should know so everyone could see it. He just *stumbled* on it. He was very upset with me because he thought I wasn't keeping track of what was going on. David hadn't told anybody here that he was going to be on, although he maintained he did. Six months before we'd talked about it, he said! It wasn't the subject matter that bothered Roberto, it just looked again as if here he was on national television and doing something very prominent and I didn't know about it. That made me very vulnerable, because the guys in Atlanta were critical of me for not knowing what was going on in my own shop. David saw it as a non-event, but I think that was just his failure to realize that he wasn't just David Puttnam, producer, he was David Puttnam, Coca-Cola. When you're on national television and you're Coca-Cola, a lot of things happen. They send out notices so that everybody in the company can watch. They treat it as a big deal.'

'Look,' David defended himself. 'I'm a free agent. I've appeared on network TV so many times both here and back in Britain I don't even think about it any more.'

'Maybe you *should* think about it,' Fay countered. 'I've told you before, that you're not an independent producer any more: you're working for the Coca-Cola Company.'

During this period it became clear to Fay that the difficulties with David were growing in size and dimension. The heat from the steady procession of complaints that had found their way to Coca-Cola was such that Fay could no longer shrug it off. The three year public announcement had been a terrible error, the real reason for which David had confided only to Fay. Regardless of what David said,

CAA's script submissions to Columbia *had* dried up; to Coke this meant the cream of CAA's talent was being offered elsewhere, to their distinct disadvantage. Their relationship with Bill Cosby, a Coke shareholder and valuable spokesman for the company, was in jeopardy. Although *Ishtar* was not David's responsibility, the perception was that he could have shown a magnanimity to the principals. Hadn't he fluffed a rare chance to bury the hatchet with all concerned? And Coke had not failed to note the *Toys* débâcle; for whatever reason it had slipped away, David appeared to have been premature in his judgement that the project was with Columbia.

Then there was Stark. Ray Stark. Raymond Otto Stark. He had many hits in the past, but were his biggest successes behind him? Damned if they were! When he had taken *The Secret of My Success* from Touchstone – who had turned it down – to Universal, the Michael J. Fox starrer had turned in over $60 million at the box-office. Could Stark *ever* be counted out?

Fay discussed his concerns with David, pointing out that anything he put in motion during the second year and a half of his tenure would scarcely be at the release stage before he left. Some form of succession had to be thought of – and quickly. 'What are you going to do at the end of the three years?' Fay asked. 'Because I can't let it go on into the third year the way you've portrayed it. We have to *solve* this problem, because if you're really going home, and leaving the company, if that's what you now think, *there's no point in staying the whole three years*. You've got to go *sooner*. At Christmas we should really sit down and decide what you're going to do.'

David's appointment of Greg Coote months earlier had been specifically made to replace Patrick Williamson and grant David access to Columbia's International Distribution set-up. At last he was able to announce, in July, a re-vamp of Columbia's marketing, with an international rather than domestic perspective. Greg Coote and Bob Dingilian were the key players in charge of the new Burbank-based Worldwide Marketing Group, set to become fully operational in time for Columbia's autumn release schedule. First on the list would come John Boorman's *Hope and Glory*, then Ridley Scott's *Someone to Watch over Me*. Global campaigns were to be the order of the day, with the new concept built on the premise that the emphasis on the worldwide push would not be at the expense of domestic marketing. David insisted that the reverse would be true, that domestic would in fact be enhanced by the move, although it would be now just one part of the process rather than the priority it had been before. As for

Patrick Williamson, he was being sent upstairs, 'promoted' in corporate-speak, to 'special assistant to Francis T. Vincent'.

Although it seemed David had what he wanted, he was still not content. The International concept had been a running bone of contention for so long that, even with the announcement made, he still had the feeling Fay Vincent was not truly behind it. Fay maintains that by now David had figured out the folly of dismantling international theatrical from video and TV. 'Once he got into the job,' says Fay, 'he realized he had been wrong and that you couldn't keep the theatrical side separate. He changed his mind and recommended we keep it together, but the problem was that when that happened it wouldn't work for him, since he had no responsibility for video or television. He didn't like the solution, because although it was the right answer, it was the wrong situation, one that denied him full control. He went along with it, though. Part of it was the need to get a different structure and different people involved. Patrick Williamson was unwilling to be in a position where he was part of Puttnam. He had no use for Puttnam and Puttnam had no use for him.'

There was a gradual deterioration in relations between Fay and David in their subsequent meetings, for David had begun to feel he was walking on constantly shifting sands. For that matter, so did Fay. The signal Fay was picking up – that David was planning to resign – was reinforced when a colleague at 711 Fifth Avenue told him, 'David really wants to leave the company. He's tired and homesick and really wants out.' 'I wish he'd told me,' was Fay's heartfelt reply. His first opportunity to talk to David was on the phone, since David had been en route from Europe when his colleague had spoken to him. Two hours were spent on the transatlantic line.

'If you really want to go, you only have to tell me, David, but you can't play around,' Fay told him. 'But if you're going to go it has ramifications in financial terms. I can't pay you as if you'd stayed. It would have to be a different economic arrangement.'

Fay was well aware that it made no sense from David's legal point of view to quit. If he did, he could wave goodbye to his $3 million golden parachute. When they met the following night in Atlanta on David's return from Europe, a lengthy meeting took place between the two. 'You misunderstood me,' David now told Fay, 'I never had any intention of resigning.' As far as Fay was concerned, two things had happened. David had talked to Tom Lewyn, who had told him that if he quit he'd get nothing. Then David had thought more about it and saw how full of defeat his gesture would be seen to be.

'You never give me a straight answer,' Fay was told. 'You turn

Jesuitical on me, answering my every question with another question. If there's something cooking on International, or anything else I ought to know about, just tell me. I'm a good soldier, Fay. If you've got bad news, tell me what it is and I'll deal with it. What I hate is your "Now you see it, now you don't" act.'

'Why don't you go through the issues, David?' Fay suggested, 'and I'll tell you the things that are really causing trouble.'

'Take your pick,' David replied, 'Stark, Ovitz, Murray –'

'Your problem is you just talk too much. I don't think you understand the complexity of Coke. You have misunderstood Goizueta and Keough's role. You tend to go to them and they keep saying, "He works for you, not us. What's he coming here for?"'

If Fay was becoming alarmed at the open dissension in prospect, there was worse to come, as David decided to lay on the line his disillusion with the whole set-up. 'Maybe you've realized now,' he said, 'that I no longer feel the same way about competitiveness. Oh, I'm competitive with myself in that I want to do what I set out to do, but I don't honestly care if another studio does better than ours –' Fay's jaw dropped – 'or if another film opens the same day and outgrosses us. It honestly doesn't bother me.'

'Oh no, David,' Fay replied, 'I can't stand that.'

Fay had already reported in detail to Goizueta and Keough all of the previous conversations he had had with David and had set up a pre-board meeting the following morning with the Coke bosses. Now that David had changed his mind about resigning, Fay told him, 'I can go on my own to Roberto and Don and bring them up to date, but it's much better if you come with me. Tell them you're unhappy. Let's get the air cleared. And Herbert will be there too.'

This threw David. 'Why Herbert?' he asked. 'He's never been part of any informal meetings before.'

'We feel he should be present at this one,' Fay replied.

'Well, I don't think it's appropriate.'

David took in Herbert Allen's sphinx-like expression as the meeting convened. 'Fay tells me you've got a few things on your mind,' Goizueta opened.

'I have,' David replied, 'I need a lot of the issues made much clearer. People seem to keep shifting their positions on certain aspects of the company, particularly International. What's said one day doesn't necessarily seem to pertain the next.'

Allen shook his head wearily, 'One of the problems, David, is that you want all this control, but you'll be gone in two years' time under the present terms of your contract.'

'What I need most of all is the assurance of your support while I'm here,' David replied.

'Support? What support?' Allen asked, suddenly finding his voice. 'I *have* been supportive. And it really doesn't matter if we support you or not, just so long as you make good movies. That's all that counts, that's all you were brought here for, David. I'll be frank; I'm against a lot of what you've been doing, because you're hurting this company and its assets. You have no right to leave us with bad relationships with all these important people. That's not fair, particularly when you're here such a short time. You're killing us with all these people who are against you. You're right on a lot of the issues, but these people are too powerful; you can't take them all on at the same time. It's too many fronts and you're not that strong. They're going to get you in the end and you won't be able to pull that off.'

As Fay Vincent mentally ticked off the multitude of high-level complaints that had found their way to Atlanta, and listened to his colleague's accusation, he knew there and then that they were approaching the final curtain in their relationship with David. With every new statement that David made Fay became convinced that he was witnessing a man unravelling. Still he was unprepared for his next assertions.

'Hollywood is a despicable place,' said David.

'If it's so despicable, why did you ask to work there?' Allen answered back.

David ignored the comment, and continued, 'The trouble with Hollywood is fear. Fear in Hollywood in general. Fear at Columbia in particular. It's a fearful company. People are fearful of their jobs.' He looked directly at Goizueta. 'Everyone at Columbia is afraid of *you*. And the Coca-Cola company.'

Goizueta's mask slipped. 'That's nonsense,' he snapped. 'The truth is just the reverse! We are always being accused of being too kind and paternalistic. *Nobody* had any reason to be fearful.'

'With respect, I think you're talking rubbish,' Herbert Allen interjected, shaking his head furiously. David turned to Keough, for whom he had developed a genuine affection.

'Look, I don't want to spend the rest of my life worrying about what you, Don, think of me. We just had a conversation this morning about a misunderstanding, for I know that Fay thought I was going to resign. So I just want to say this: I hope you like what I'm doing and I hope the company is successful, but at the end of the day, I don't care whether you *like* me or not. It's not important; it's not an issue. I would become less of a man if I looked at myself in the mirror every morning and wondered whether Don Keough still likes me. That's no way to live any kind of life.'

When David saw the hurt in Keough's face, he knew he had made a grave error. He was looking at the startled expression of someone who had probably worried about exactly what he had just described on every single rung of the corporate ladder. If Coke had any doubts before, they had none now.

'The meeting was a disaster,' Fay summarizes. 'His comment about Roberto was just *bizarre*. What we concluded was that *David* was afraid of him. One of the insights I took away from that meeting was that David simply has a problem with authority. He worried desperately about Roberto and Don and continually referred to them, not me, I guess he wasn't worried about me. By that point everybody was quite negative about David. After that meeting he really was finished.'

Although David would later maintain he had been asked at the meeting to extend his stay to five years, Fay categorically refutes this. '*Nobody* asked him to stay for five years. It's not *true*. It was exactly the *reverse*. Coke's position was he should go and how do we work that out? There may have been some conversation about being a producer, but certainly not running the studio. There was no way he could stay in that job. It was *over*.'

After the meeting Herb Allen apologized to David for his little outburst. 'Someone has to be the devil's advocate,' he shrugged. The board meeting itself went without a hitch. Frank Biondi Jr was ribbed about the rumours that he was leaving to join Viacom. After the lunch that followed the participants went their separate ways.

At a Coke budgetary meeting in August, Frank Biondi Jr confirmed the Viacom rumours and resigned, amid word that the TV sector of Coke's Entertainment Business Operations was going to be around $50 million short of their forecast, a major disappointment. Fay went off to a meeting with RCA, where an attempt was made to re-negotiate Columbia's end of the RCA/Columbia joint video deal, continuing a running dialogue that had taken place for over a year.

When Debbie arrived with Patsy's mother to spend a couple of weeks at Coldwater Canyon in mid-August, she was struck by the change in her father. In their reunions at Kingsmead Mill since he had joined Columbia, he had seemed distracted and distant. Gone was the warm, loving parent she adored. 'What's up with Dad?' Sacha had asked the previous Christmas. 'He's walking about, but he's not taking anything in.' Now in Los Angeles he seemed quiet and thoughtful. While pretending to listen to Debbie's stories of home, he would switch off completely halfway through. During the first week he came home once for lunch and they enjoyed an evening out together at the Bolshoi Ballet. Apart from that, it was business dinners every night. Debbie began to feel she might as well not be there. The only saving grace was that he did not seem to be depressed – just preoccupied. The second week that changed.

David phoned Fay Vincent on 24 August and was told by his secretary that her boss was in Atlanta. This was a precedent: Fay had never gone to Coke's headquarters before without letting him know. On 26 August, before David was due to fly to Montreal to attend a lunch in honour of Cineplex Odeon chief, Garth Drabinsky, he tried to set up a meeting with Don Keough at the event. His call was not returned.

Keough was on the top table sitting near David, and greeted him jovially enough. 'Are you free for breakfast next Thursday?' he asked. 'Good, Roberto and I will be in Los Angeles and we'll see you then.' He later departed without saying goodbye. Dick Gallop, who was seated in the middle of the room, managed to avoid David completely. On the way to the airport David had time to reflect. When Goizueta and Keough normally came to town it was a big occasion – a tour of the studio, the Oscar presentations. This time it was for *breakfast*? By the time he had flown back to Los Angeles and made his way to Coldwater Canyon, his mind was in a turmoil. Debbie had never seen her father look so cold, withdrawn and utterly exhausted. As soon as he could get to a phone, he called Fay Vincent.

'What's going on, Fay? You never told me you were going to Atlanta.'

'Didn't I? Well, something came up. You know, David,' – Fay sounded totally demoralized – 'this is a really tough business we're in, isn't it? Really tough. It's this RCA deal that kills us, really kills us . . .'

'Fay, what are you talking about? Something's wrong. What is it?'

'I'll tell you next week.'

David phoned Fay again on the afternoon of Sunday, 30 August. By this time the grapevine was buzzing with rumours.

'Fay, I've heard you're moving to Atlanta.'

'It's not true.'

'Then what is going on?'

'I can't say any more right now. I'm sorry, David.'

Patsy watched anxiously as David put the phone down. 'I've got to leave now to run Mum and Debbie to the airport,' she said.

'OK, darling, I'll come through with you to say goodbye.'

A phone call had been placed to Victor Kaufman of Tri-Star on Saturday, 29 August, from Roberto Goizueta and Don Keough at Coca-Cola. Could he fly down to Atlanta for a secret weekend meeting? 'Maybe they're going to fire me,' he reportedly thought. Coke's plan for the future was a sleight-of-hand dreamt up a year earlier, to devolve their 100 per cent ownership of the Entertainment Business Sector (including Columbia Pictures Industries and Coca-Cola Television) and 37 per cent of Tri-Star – first, by increasing their stake in Tri-Star to 80 per cent and forming a new entity, Columbia Pictures Entertainment. The second stage of the devolution process would be to distribute shares in the new company to shareholders as a one-time dividend and reduce Coke's holding to 49 per cent. 'Fizz' would thus be devolved considerably from 'show-biz', Coke's balance sheet would no longer have to take the full hit on any write-off like the $25 million on *Ishtar*, and the shares in Columbia Pictures Entertainment would be a more attractive proposition on their own, trading purely as a movie-company glamour stock. Within 48 hours all this – together with the results of the concurrent power-plays – would blow up in David's face.

Valerie was waiting when David got back at 3.45 pm to continue the day's dictation. 'Are you remembering that Andrew Yule is due at 4 pm?' she asked.

'Christ, that's all I need,' David sighed.

Chapter 26

End of the Nightmare

After spending a week in New York, I was due to fly to Los Angeles on Saturday, 30 August, to keep my initial appointment with David at Coldwater Canyon Drive. On the Friday evening I became a New York statistic. I had a pleasant dinner with Eddie Chamblee. 'Ol' Horatio Hornblower', as he calls himself, was the fifth of the late Dinah Washington's eight husbands and still plays tenor sax with his quartet each Saturday in the Village. Ten minutes after leaving Eddie, and wandering back to my hotel on Eighth Avenue and 57th Street, I was attacked and held at knife point. My assailant slashed my arm in disgust when he realized all he was going to get was my precious Sony Walkman Professional, together with some change. He ran off, leaving a shaken, bleeding wreck behind. I was incredibly lucky in two ways – first, I was alive to tell the tale; second, the tape inside the Sony, on which I had recorded the latest round of Eddie's reminiscences of Dinah, was miraculously left behind.

After some first-aid in my hotel and a report to the police, I spent a restless night, constantly aware that I had to be up at the crack of dawn for the flight to Los Angeles and that my tape recorder had to be replaced. I really felt next morning, with my head splitting and my arm still hurting, that this was not the most auspicious of starts to my Hollywood trip. On the way to the airport, when the taxi-driver asked if I had enjoyed my stay in New York, I blurted out what had happened the night before – well, he was the first person I'd had a chance to talk to since the police and the hotel's security staff, and if I hadn't told someone, I'd have felt the need to bore David Puttnam to death with the story. The taxi-driver was gracious enough to apologize profusely on behalf of New York City.

My main preoccupation was to find an identical tape recorder before the Sunday appointment. First there was the flight and the standard injection of Iain Smith's inadequacy drug at Los Angeles airport, then by the time I was checked in at the Safari Inn on West Olive in Burbank – chosen by friends to be close to both Columbia

405

Pictures and Coldwater Canyon – it was almost 6 pm. After a soothing bath I fell asleep for a couple of hours, making up to some extent for the sleepless night in New York.

On waking I took a stroll and came across Chow's Kosherama Delicatessen just across West Olive – wasn't this Ray Stark's favourite in Burbank? Never one to shirk exhaustive research, I decided to eat there and ordered Eggs Foo Yong. I called the waiter back after an incredulous examination of the dish, for I'd been given what looked like three hamburgers swimming in a thick greyish brown gravy. He patiently opened the menu and pointed to 'Eggs Foo Yong – *Kosherama Style*'. Instead of the light, fluffy dish I'd expected, the very table groaned under the collective weight. Ray, your magic spell is everywhere!

On Sunday, following another sleepless night (mainly indigestion this time), I found an identical Sony model at the nearby Glendale Galleria after wandering about to seductive spend-music for a few hours. With my headache gone and flesh wound (well, this *was* Hollywood after all) on the mend, I felt ready after a settling lunch (*not* at Chow's) to meet the head of Columbia Pictures.

As the taxi wound its way up Coldwater Canyon, I reflected on the interviews I'd already carried out back in Britain. Most were with associates who had obviously tempered their comments for either 'I'd still like to work with him again', or 'I'd still like to work in the British film industry again' reasons, for David's influence went far beyond films. He was director of a radio and TV station, knew the heads of both Channel 4 and BBC 2 television, the editors of various important daily and Sunday newspapers and the head of publishing houses (including my own stamping ground, Penguin) – in fact, a regular Ray Stark of his own patch!

I tried to collect my thoughts on David and his body of work as the taxi continued on its way. I saw everything before *Chariots of Fire* as the young man finding his feet. *Melody* had got him into the world of cinema; *The Pied Piper* and the Ken Russell experiences had taught him valuable lessons; *That'll be the Day* and *Stardust* were the necessary autobiographicals everyone should get out of the way at the first opportunity. The early documentaries were there to fill the gaps between the features and to cover overheads. Both *Bugsy Malone* and *Midnight Express* were really Alan Parker/Alan Marshall collaborations; the first David found finance for, the second provided him with finance through the Casablanca deal.

I had watched *Chariots* again recently and been impressed by it. If a little dry, dusty and manipulative, it was still a film which earned high marks in every department. Colin Welland's script ('It's only a race'. 'If I can't win, I won't run.' 'If you don't run, you can't win!'); the impeccable acting by Ian Charleson and Ben Cross – Charleson in particular and the simple, eloquent passion he injected into Welland's line, 'When I run, I feel His pleasure'; together with sterling support from Ian Holm, Nigel Havers, Sir John Gielgud and Lindsay Anderson. Thanks to David, the editor and cinematographer, the film looked terrific and hung together beautifully (Pauline Kael's 'flung together in desperation in the cutting-room' I thought patently inappropriate).

Vangelis's score, while undeniably out of its time, was dramatically effective, developing some interesting variations on the main theme which lent colour and shade to several scenes. On top of them all, however, Hugh Hudson must be singled out for the major credit. This is not to subscribe to the Cahiers du Cinema school, but in the case of *Chariots*, the director's influence can be both seen and felt throughout.

Although David places great store on the music – ('When you're in post production, the composer becomes vastly important. I've seen *Chariots of Fire* without a score and can speak with great authority: I don't think it would have won the Academy Award or very much else without Vangelis.') – I found the most effective scenes in the film were the ones without musical accompaniment: Abraham's enrolment at Cambridge ('*He* won't be singing in the Chapel choir'); the half-notes in the anti-Semitic exchanges between Gielgud and Anderson (Gielgud's nostril-bristling, Anderson's weary cynicism); the beautifully-shot ensemble scene where Liddell is summoned before the Prince of Wales, Lord Cadogan, Lord Birkenham et al.

While I felt Hugh's next work in *Greystoke* confirmed the promise of *Chariots*, Pauline Kael remained no great admirer. To Hugh's notion that *Greystoke* was about 'how society lives, halfway between the apes and the angels, aspiring to go up yet coming down there, and about self-discovery, lost innocence, evolution, coming to terms with evil, the use and abuse of the earth, and the delicate balance between our moral and physical beings,' her pert put-down was, 'This man has too much on his mind to put together an exciting adventure movie.' Like most movie people, Hugh should let the movies speak for themselves. As he was later to say about David: 'There's a huge canvas up there on the screen to fill with whatever messages he wants to put across. *That's* the space he should have filled; not all these newspaper columns.'

I thought *Local Hero* was a 'nice' film which almost won me over

– in fact, without being so damned grudging, it *did* win me over by the end, but only after I'd battled my way through its determinedly fey whimsy. Now that I know how it was made, I could never understand anyone going into a film with a script twice the required length on a 'shoot anything and see which bits work' basis. Alfred Hitchcock would have choked on his storyboards! Nor did Hitch's rather too unglamorous method, smacking of the confident craftsman who knew his trade, ring any bells for the Puttnam/Joffe team as they embarked on the four hours of footage subsequently melted down to the final cut of *The Killing Fields*, although Roland claims to be a storyboard man. I believe Jim Clark really earned his Oscar on this one.

The Mission, on the other hand, had not worked at all, killed stone dead by the misguided casting of the lightweight Jeremy Irons. David and Roland would have been better either going with the cliché of the old man/young man, or getting someone more down-to-earth than Irons. Roland Joffe never got more than a tentative hold on the main theme, which seemed simplified and sanitized almost out of existence. Robert Bolt told me, 'It turned out to be not what I would have liked. The Jesuits were all on the one side and the others were all on the other; it was over-simplified. I didn't want it to be so clean-cut.' He conceded that perhaps his original approach had been a bit too subtle, and graciously excused Roland's simplifications and pious appliquéd embellishments, entertainingly contrasting production problems on even the most successful of his films with the help he had from David on *The Mission*: 'When Fred Zinnemann, a lovely man, was in the middle of *A Man for All Seasons*, Columbia took a look at it and wanted to stop it. Fred decided to call their bluff. "Fine, do that," he told them, "I know someone else who'll take it off your hands." "OK," they said, "finish it, but *be quick!*"'

'Most people you're making a movie with you're automatically fighting – not David. You feel David's an ally, not an enemy. After my stroke, when I was just getting better again,' – and with Sarah back and devotedly nursing the man she had left, but never stopped loving – 'I met Sam Spiegel one day in a lift. "Hello," I said. His hand was outstretched, then he looked at me, saw I'd been ill, put his hand down and hurried away. He was afraid of anyone who was sick. David never reacted like that for a moment. He's a lovely man, I cannot tell you what a comfort he was. He's one of those people who makes a decision and that's it. Like the Scots, his word is his bond.'

David had cleverly chosen his original pitch to Fernando Ghia when he mentioned Roland in the same breath as David Lean, ac- curately judging how that would resonate with Ghia's conception of what could be wrought from his long-treasured property, for Bolt and Lean's collaborations had ranged from the Sam Spiegel-produced *Lawrence of Arabia* through *Dr Zhivago* and *Ryan's Daughter*, the zenith of Sarah Miles' career. When Lean and Spiegel were the missing elements on *Lady Caroline Lamb*, being replaced by Robert and Fernando Ghia, the resultant embarrassment unfortunately brought about the nadir of Sarah Miles' career. The only one to profit from *Lady Caroline Lamb* was our old friend, now sadly the late Nat Cohen, who had a £250,000 equity investment in the picture that was astutely covered by overseas pre-sales. Nat was then able to book the film into the ABC cinema chain he ran in Britain – truly it's an ill wind that blows nobody any good! 'Nat was the most mogulish mogul of them all,' Bobby Littman summed up.

As for the *First Loves*, is David *serious* when he includes them in the '29' *films* he has produced, neatly doubling his credits? For sure, there was some good work amongst them, notably from director Roy Battersby with *Winter Flight* and *Mr Love*, and many new writers and directors had their first chances. *Cal* was another 'nice' little picture, nothing more, but unique in the canon of David's movies in that it centred round a heterosexual relationship. When I commented on the homophilic aspects of many of David's movies to one of his friends and colleagues, I received a thought-provoking reply: 'David and women are a whole complex subject. This industry is full of men who fancy themselves with women. David's unique in that he charms men as well. Others can't be bothered. When David's making a film, the director in effect becomes his mistress. There's homo-eroticism, buddies, in all Puttnam movies. That's because he had a very happy childhood with lots of other boys and he wants to relive that in his movies. He's like the writer who spends his whole life trying to figure out what happened in the first 16 years, trying to recapture that simplicity and innocence. That's the root of his interest in the friendship of male bonding.'

In the months leading up to this first meeting with David I had notched up a large number of NFA (Not For Attribution) quotes from various industry and media figures. One had echoed Don Boyd's criticism of David's distancing himself from Goldcrest's difficulties. 'A fortune of Goldcrest's money was poured into Lynda Myles' so-called *First Love* "sequels", love stories of our time, abandoned with over 70 scripts written and down the drain. Towards the end David talked as if he was just a producer who'd been done over by James Lee, but he wasn't, he was on the board and he can't wash his hands of that. David doesn't have that sense of corporate responsibility.'

A reporter told me, 'When you meet him, you'll find that he's so incredibly open. If he feels depressed, he's going to tell you he's depressed. If you happen to be interviewing him that day, you'll get the whole story.'

A director: 'One of the worries that David has is, "why do I keep losing my directors?" Their first film with David has been their best film, then they feel they don't need this guy around. It's their mistake and David's tragedy.'

A reporter: 'He would like to be an intellectual, but knows he isn't one. He would like to have enough intellectuality to defend himself against attacks. The people he feels threatened by – film academists – aren't worth the effort, if he only knew it. Alan Parker's approach is best – "You're a load of wankers," but David is conciliatory. I was there when an Oxford philosopher lady turned to him exasperatedly one day and said, "David, the trouble with you is, you're *so* stupid." He puts up with that because of the mystique universities hold for him. His version of a university as this place where people go and think up there in the clouds somewhere, is a total fantasy. What David would find if he took a closer look would be that all the dons and academics would give their eye-teeth to swap places with him. "I'm a teacher, I teach" – he should get himself out of all that crap. He's been so burdened by all that, just like De Niro in *The Mission*. He should let someone cut all that junk he's carrying away.'

A colleague: 'David's not emotionally sophisticated, he's not gone through an enormous amount of emotional experiences. He has a safe marriage, a very few friends, a lot of relationships. That's why his films are hollow at the centre; they don't have the emotional resonance.'

A director: 'David gets by on good grass-roots street-wise savvy. He comes to meetings, picks up, like all very bright people, who's who in the room, delivers his piece and leaves. He intervenes so cleverly, so strategically and so wisely in an industry which is crowded with dead wood, people you wouldn't be seen dead with. David weaves with tremendous dexterity through it all.'

A scriptwriter: 'Tony Smith of the BFI and Shirley Williams went to see *Chariots of Fire*. Then Tony went to David and said that Shirley was very moved by the film, that this is what the SDP was all about, this is how she viewed the SDP. There was a special screening of the movie arranged for other party members, then the notion fizzled out. When David joined the party, everyone was predicting Minister of Culture for David if they got in. It was all soft, nothing deep. Ultimately he's an advertising executive who got into the movies

– one never gets away from that. If you are an advertising executive, per se, you cannot be a profound film producer. Looking at David's films, it is possible to believe he's only ever read three books – *The Ovaltiney Annual of 1949*, with their games for boys and little fairisle-sweatered heroes, Vance Packard's *The Hidden Persuaders* and Dale Carnegie's *How to Make Friends and Influence People.*'

After being dropped, in blinding sunshine, half-way up the steep drive leading to David's house, I entered the side gate and made for what I took to be the main door, which was lying open. When there was no answer to the doorbell, I wandered through the house and found David coming through from the swimming pool in the garden, where he had been working with Valerie. 'Andrew!' he greeted me, with outstretched arm and a big smile. 'Come on and sit by the pool, it's beautiful outside.'

We chatted easily as we strolled between the orange trees that stood near the pool, and sat beneath the parasols. Although we were high up in Coldwater Canyon, we could still hear a distant muted buzz from the traffic in Studio City a mile or so down the twisting road. David looked relaxed in open-necked short-sleeved shirt and casual cotton slacks, and showed hardly any sign of the enormous strain he was under, other than an occasional tug at his pepper-and-salt beard. Throughout those first 15 minutes his Aegean blue eyes seldom left me; I could sense his curiosity and even then a slight combative nuance: what was this guy all about? At the bottom line, was I good news or bad news? For my part I felt I was no news, although I almost had been back in New York.

I had seen both *La Bamba* and *The Big Easy* in New York and enjoyed them both, I told him. He sang the praises of Esai Morales, who had played the role of Ritchie Valens' brother. I suggested he sign up Dennis Quaid quickly, a future star if ever I saw one. He smilingly replied he had tried to do that very thing at lunchtime. Valerie brought some tea and gave him some letters to sign before she left. 'Half-day today, love?' David joked.

Within the next 10 minutes we got some important points out of the way. It was my book, I must write what I like, David replied to my question about any degree of control over the final manuscript. 'I believe at the end of the day,' he told me, 'if anyone assesses who or what I am, it only has any value in terms of its effect on other people's lives. I'm not a director. I'm not a writer, the impact of my life is its impact on other people's lives. You know what I'm saying? I'm a conduit and I'm very, very aware of that and perfectly proud of it, incidentally. I would like to be judged by what I've meant to others. Does Bill Forsyth regard me as someone who's important in his life? I mean that in the *best* sense. Does Alan Parker? Does Michael Apted? Does Roland Joffe? – Am I someone who, by and large, has treated them fairly, behaved honourably, delivered what I said I would deliver – not *always* possible, alas; one simply isn't always able to.

'All I would like (and I know this is going to sound horribly pretentious) is to try and set a standard of dealing and a standard of behaviour rather like the standard my father tried to instil in me, in an industry which at times skates around that. That's really what it comes down to. So if the consensus from the Bills and the Alans and Ridleys is that I have, then maybe that will encourage other people to see they don't have to lie and cheat and steal and behave as if every deal is the last deal, and that there is the potential for decency and consistency. It doesn't work all the time, but it does work. I'd like to think 90 per cent of the time I've done what I said I'd do – and, amazing beyond belief – I've made some money, I've had a very nice life and therefore you don't have to be a *gonif* to succeed.'

Reflecting again on the dichotomy inherent in the interviews I conducted before meeting David, I thought these were not unreasonable parameters. I had a feeling David had already been briefed on my movements by his English mafia and knew to whom I had spoken. The shape of the book was decided there and then.

We talked at length of his parents, his childhood and his first jobs, how he started the photographic agency, met Sandy Lieberson and broke into films. In a couple of hours he had given me an intricate word-picture of his life. Alan Parker and the scenes at Cannes. The row with Claude Whatham over the fairground scene in *That'll Be the Day*. The Ken Russell and Jacques Demy jousts. The frustration on *Agatha*. The first Hollywood tenure.

He talked about Kingsmead Mill and what it meant to him, his 'little piece of England', the shrine he had built in the garden for his father. 'Patsy was surprised how much I took to the Mill,' he told me. '"He's going to hate it, he's an urban person", friends told her. Outside of Patsy, people who think they know me really well don't know me at all. Alan Parker was one of the most vocal: it was a wank and I was just kidding myself. I just think it's illustrative of the fact I think I'm a significantly different person to the person I maybe present myself as, or as most people think I am. Kingsmead saved my life. Columbia came at the completely wrong moment when I was enjoying the Mill. I remember shortly before I left to come here, I was fishing and I thought "I must be out of my mind, what on earth am I doing?" On the other hand, the three years at Columbia spelt independence and Patsy's security. Marcia Falkender used to say to me, "You can't ever do things you want while people can attack you financially. That's the first place to go for if they're trying to cut you down to size or manipulate you, they go for the bank account. They'll work on you." She was a great advocate of me getting myself in a financially strong situation. She's a good friend, Marcia, whose public persona and reality couldn't be more different. A smashing woman, smart and brave.'

He talked about Peter Guber, his executive producer on *Midnight Express*: 'We rubbed against each other all the time, didn't get on. We get on very well now. What it boils down to is, I don't like working for anybody. The differences with Peter were a matter of style: we have totally different styles.'

He talked of Alan Parker at the time of *Bugsy Malone* and their differing views of US success: 'Alan had an obsession with *Bugsy* being successful in America. I had a huge argument with him. "I don't give a fuck," I said. "If it happens to work there, that's great, if it doesn't, it doesn't." It comes back again to ambitions. I didn't have the same obsession of cracking America as Alan had. I was far more interested in the Cannes festival and Europe, especially France, because I'd admired French movies. *Chariots of Fire* is a perfect example, not one single concession to America. Going into it, I told Patsy it was my "shit or bust" film. If it hadn't worked, I'd made up my mind I was going back into advertising. I was trying to make a film which was related to why I'd come into the industry in the first place. I'd completely lost my bearings coming off *Midnight Express* and *Foxes*. I was now just doing a job and I thought I might as well do a job in advertising. It's less strain, less stress and I could earn quite a lot of money. *Chariots* was my one last shot.'

He talked of the process of making a movie: 'The key is the second or third day. You look at the rushes, there's always a pivotal scene where you know if you can trust the director or not. Maybe you weren't on the set that day and the first take's no good, so you don't know how many takes he did (and I deliberately never look at the sheets to find out). You're *dying* in case the next take is the last one he's made, because what you're looking at is the director's standards. Has he pushed? Then oh, the relief, when take 5 is good and still he pushed on to take 6, which is better, then *still* he pushes on – to a final, wonderful take.'

David's eyes were sparkling when he said this, the film-maker in him totally to the fore. I caught a glimpse of how frustrating so much of the Columbia year must have been, removed from the actual movie-making process he clearly thrives on, reduced to a 'suit' pacing the corridors of power.

'*Then* you can relax,' he continued, 'but the terror is when you get the opposite – take 4, which is not very good, and suddenly he's moved on. That means his standards aren't as high as my standards and I'm in the shit. What I'm really looking for is someone who's better than me, because if I work with a director whose work I look at and think, "I could have done that", then we're in all sorts of trouble. Roland and I had a bumpy first week on *The Killing Fields* but by the end of the second week I knew that here was a man, who, far from being a T V director making his first feature film, was someone who I don't understand could ever have worked in television, how he accepted it and held himself in. Ridley's another example of someone who's always that much better than you expect him to be and can always surprise me. I've never felt any form of frustration in that respect, that I don't direct, although I'm sometimes slightly frustrated in my writing. I'm a good editor; I think I write decent prose, but I can't write dialogue. My own dialogue is lousy. It doesn't sing.'

By the time Patsy got back at 7 pm, we had just moved through the French windows into the main lounge, as it had turned cool in the garden with the onset of dusk. Patsy and I greeted each other and I handed over the tin of Walker's Scottish shortbread I had brought. (You can buy this in Los Angeles, but my tin was fresh from Scotland. Patsy fell upon it, as I imagine she does on any reminder of Britain.) As she opened a bottle of Chardonnay and we spread ourselves over the more-than-ample sofa and armchairs, I asked David if he had settled into Hollywood any more readily this time than he had in the seventies.

'No,' he admitted, 'I haven't. I'm the one who counts the days and Patsy,' – he looked at her and smiled – 'well, I wouldn't say she's happy here, but –'

'You're the one who has to go down the salt-mines every day,' Patsy interjected.

'That's right. I've never felt comfortable working here. It's sad, really, and I don't say that with any British chic. Mike Apted was quite right when he said that psychologically and in every other way, I'm the most international, I'm the one who's travelled the most, I know more people than any of the others and I'm certainly the one who's dealt with the most situations in my life, yet I'm the one who's found it hardest to assimilate. Most peculiar, I can't explain it.'

As the blanket of dark fell outside and we sipped the chilled wine, Patsy looked at her husband, who appeared totally relaxed, if very tired. 'Home for you has always been so terribly important,' she said. 'I think it really shows here, because, however much one tries to make wherever we're living home, you never feel that it is.'

David nodded agreement. 'It may come back to my concern with detail. I know there's an element in me which is unhealthily a control freak. I don't *ever* feel in control here, and it's not only that I don't feel it, it's that I'm *not*. No matter what you're called, chairman or producer, you're not in control here. The creative environment here denies control to anyone. There is a constant sense of turmoil, and I don't like turmoil. Some people do like it, some people are genuinely excited by the idea of change or turmoil. I'm *not*. I like order. If that was what I was working in and doing, that would be great, but the truth of the matter is that 90 per cent of my time in the past year has been an attempt to restructure. I haven't spent 15 per cent of my time doing what I really have a skill for. Someone told me that what I've done here is, without knowing it, to transfer my sense of order to Columbia Pictures. He said I'd tried to make Columbia Pictures into a movie, that it *became* my movie. Right now, he said, you're still working on the rough cut. But you know, nothing, and I mean *nothing* could give you any inkling of what I came to. It was not to be believed.'

Patsy smiled ruefully as she replenished our glasses. 'I seriously thought you'd come home, because I'd never seen you beaten by anything else before.'

As David went on to talk with disarming frankness about the tussles with Stark, Ransohoff, Cosby and the *Ishtar* skirmishes, the thought struck me that to the outside world everything in the garden at Columbia was relatively lovely. I'd come along expecting to see a man one-third of the way into his contract, revelling in the power that being the head of one of the five major studios would bring. Instead, as David related his story of the year at Columbia, I realized how thoroughly demoralized he was, but thankfully still prepared to talk his way through those difficult days with a total stranger. One of the great secrets of David's charm was being demonstrated. He was taking me totally into his confidence, as if he had divined from the first moment we met that I could be totally trusted with the information he was imparting. This was wine far headier than the Chardonnay – I felt privileged, flattered, bemused – and very grateful. I think I would probably have marched through hell for him at that moment. At the same time another part of me was posing the question: 'Why is he telling *me* all this?'

Why, I asked him, had he been so open with the community from the outset, broadcasting his plans for all to hear? That was his way, he replied. As Patsy poured the last of the wine, and I asked David to call me a cab, he replied, 'Not at all, I'll run you back to your place in Burbank. We'd ask you to stay for a bite, but Patsy and I haven't had an evening to ourselves for two weeks. Now, what's your programme for the rest of the week?' We worked out that the following day I would spend the morning interviewing Patsy, then go over to Columbia in the afternoon for another session with David. We talked non-stop on the 15-minute run to the Safari in his black Audi. Although David's enquiries about my interviews so far were casual, I sensed his mind ticking off the list and weighing up what I might have heard. He talked about one of his proudest achievements at Columbia, the setting up of a Discovery Programme to enable professionals already in the movie business to try their hand as film directors. Six live-action short films were being made by selected first-timers, budgeted at under $30,000 each. 'I like to see new people getting chances,' he told me. 'I always have.' The difference with David, it struck me, is that while others talked about it, he actually did something, even under embattled circumstances. He talked of how he had brought one of his all-time idols, Stanley Kramer, back into the Columbia fold. (Their Chernobyl project, which Catherine Wyler had initiated, was dubbed 'The Towering Reactor' by sceptical observers.)

I felt guilty that I had intruded on the Puttnams' evening, since it was now past 9 pm. As I stepped out of the Audi into the warm night air of the Valley – the change in temperature was quite startling from the top of Coldwater Canyon – I thanked David for the run home. 'Chauffeured by the head of Columbia Pictures,' I remarked, as we smilingly shook hands before I waved him off. I was half-way to my room before our meeting fell into perspective. In the same way that I had felt compelled to blurt out my story to the taxi-driver in New York, David and Patsy had just let their hair down with me. And I had been the victim of a light skirmish compared to the year of billy-clubbing, back-stabbing, bludgeoning and non-stop bayoneting that David had just endured.

In fact, David's reign at Columbia was effectively over. Victor Kaufman, at 44, was about to be installed as the new head of the entertainment colossus that Coke was to create. As he flew back to New York from Atlanta, his head must have been spinning. The legal counsel who had hung in through the David Begelman difficulties in the seventies had been well rewarded by Ray Stark and Herbert Allen for his pains. He was about to step into the shoes of the man who had once declined to fire him, Francis T. 'Fay' Vincent.

Next morning I met Patsy again after breakfast at Coldwater Canyon. 'It's the first time I've been interviewed,' she told me, as she obediently let a tea-bag settle in the mug she brought me from the kitchen. Listening to Patsy confirmed what I had already gathered, that she was the fountain-head from which David drew succour, comfort and refreshment. She had drawn the moral guidelines in their marriage and steered her husband with infinite style and compassion through their rough patches. If David was the driver, Patsy was the navigator.

Then there was Patsy the cheer-leader. Without a scrap of make-up on her face, her cerulean eyes lit up and her cheeks glowed radiantly as she spoke of her husband and his achievements. She sat comfortably on a big floral cotton-covered armchair opposite me in the comfortable den, clad in a loose-fitting linen top and skirt, one bare leg tucked under her, a sandal dangling from her foot. The room was still cool and airy in the lull before the 110 degrees of oppressive heat that would build up by early afternoon. Flicking her fine shoulder-length blond hair back from her eyes every now and again and forever engaged in a Marcel Marceau mime show with her hands to illustrate any point she was making, Patsy talked.

Of her first meeting with David in the school yard at Minchenden: 'I couldn't imagine he was talking to me. I thought it was my friend, Sonia. Apart from having the wrong colour of uniform, the shirt I was wearing had shrunk in the wash. I felt a mess.'

Of their early struggles and pain: 'My loss of identity was in danger of becoming permanent. We got together again just in time.'

Of the turning point after the madness: 'David became a very warm person and helped to free me. I could finally show my emotions, but it took a long time.'

Of what keeps David driven: 'He wants to *show* anyone who underestimates him how wrong they were. He wants to please me and our parents more than anything else in the world. After Demy he just felt he could never trust anyone again. If he's going to go down in future, he vowed, it will be his doing, and not someone else's cock-up. At the same time he realized that our failures teach us more than our successes.'

Of David's motivations: 'It's anger, there's *always* the anger. The Cannon thing, watching as they were welcomed by people who should have known better. Warners' rejection of his little $6 million *Stars and Bars*. They should have done it anyway, even if they hated it.

They *owed* it to him. Once again cap in hand, talking to people half his age. "I am *fucked* if I'm going to do this any more," he told me.'

Of David's personal and private faces: 'He's unbelievably warm, terribly affectionate. He hugs, touches, shows it. He's always been a warm, huggy person. I've always loved the warmth of David and his family. He puts on a mask for people outside; he's a *totally different* person when he's outside, when he shuts that door. He worries about how much he only basically loves a handful of people; he thinks there's something wrong with him. His father was the same. However much he likes others – in the end, there's only family. And the older he gets the worse he's getting. It's a good thing, but also a bad thing. He sees that as a weakness in himself. It goes beyond what most people feel. He might be hurt by it, but it will never change him. It's his Achilles' heel. He's always been terrified that the one way to get to him would be through me, that's why he always kept that card up his sleeve until now.'

Of David's father: 'When he was out in the world, he saw more and more what his father had achieved. He met people who knew him and realized, "God, this man had a whole set of fans for his work!" Until he went out there, he didn't know that.'

Of David's vindictive side: 'Often, what sets it off is other people getting the blame. In Ed Victor's case, he made it look as if David's secretary, Lynda, was lying. She was the one who was there; Lynda had to put up with it. From incidents like that David carries a list in his head that's ineradicable.'

Of the Harvard idea: 'It was to do with how he felt coming off *The Killing Fields*, not the Enigma situation. He felt he had to take stock of his life.'

Of what attracts David to a project: 'It's always the same. Some little idea that could be summed up on the back of a postage stamp. Whenever he deviates from that, there's trouble – as there was with *Agatha*. There was just no *reason* for that movie. We had a hell of a fight over that one.'

Of the Columbia deal: 'I told him, "Look, David, do you really want to look back in 10 years time and with four or five more pictures under your belt and recall that you once turned down an offer to run a Hollywood studio?" That started it, then when he thought there was a possibility of Columbia working: "I'm free if I do this, I really can do what I want afterwards. I *could* become a teacher, or whatever else I decide." First it's the anger, then he has to justify himself. Then there's the trap! *What if* I really could beat the system?'

Of his first few months at Columbia: 'There's so many people here prepared to lick ass and stir the pot. Every day he rang me when he first arrived, it was terrible. "It'll be all right, David, you can do it," I told him; "it's just that you can't see the wood for the trees." I've never heard him like that before. Then that débâcle with his office! Of all the things that could have helped him, that was it. When he's got everything laid down and organized, with every last drawing-pin perfectly placed, *then* he can work. He needs this perfect order before his brain can function. If he doesn't have that he's not at the starting point to work. World War III could be going on outside, but his room has to be perfect.'

Of the moments of despair: 'Twice we sat up and talked all night. He wanted to go home; he wasn't just running a studio, he was changing a studio, and it wasn't working. A sneak was leaking stories, he never knew who. Agents were all trying to trip him up. He was going to bed and dreaming of work. All the cards were stacked against him. Each time we got over it and things ironed themselves out for another week or so before the next upset.'

Of the different versions of the same tale: 'So many stories get distorted here, like the *Jagged Edge* sequel. Yes, David turned down Ransohoff's script – it was appalling! A wonderful idea, he thought, to make a sequel, but the script was *shit*.'

After a light lunch with Patsy, I left for Burbank studios and Columbia, where the cab took me right inside, past the famous New York street permanently erected on the lot, through to Columbia Plaza East. On the building directly opposite I noted, 'Ray Stark Productions'.

'Who do you wish to see, sir?' I was asked by the security man at the door.

'David Puttnam,' I replied.

'Puttnam, Puttnam, Puttnam . . .' he muttered, thumbing through the little directory he had in front of him, 'we don't seem to have anyone by that name here.'

'You must have,' I told him, 'because his name's on the car park nearest the entrance.'

'Oh, *that* Mr Puttnam. You mean the boss! Come on, I'll show you where to go.' On the way upstairs I passed the same black-and-white blow-ups that David had first seen over a year ago. He had added one of young Mark Lester (the star of *Melody*) in his begging-bowl scene from *Oliver!* Not an inappropriate symbol of David's pre-Columbia career, I thought. So did he, as it turned out.

Minutes later I was seated in David's outer office, while the shifts changed on his two assistant secretaries to Valerie (one came in early and worked until mid-afternoon, the other until evening). Inside

Valerie's little office the phone was going non-stop; I listened as she handled every call with practised ease. She looked cool, crisp, unflustered and totally competent. After a few minutes David came out, looking smart in a beige suit, with a white shirt and green-striped tie. 'Come on in, lovey,' he told me. I noted the beautiful Biedermeier furniture, the dozens of photographs and mementoes which adorned the walls and tables, the clean, airy look of the room. Patsy's touch was unmistakable. Between calls and meetings, where I was just invited to hang around and sit in, I managed to log a couple more hours of interviews with David. He gave me a tape of Bill Rowe discussing the editing of *The Mission* on a radio programme. I toured the corridors and was introduced to Michael Nathanson, Fred Bernstein, Stanley Robinson, Lyndsey Posner and several more of David's colleagues. The message they all gave was the same: David had inspired them; they were proud of the movies they were making; he had showed them that there was a *better* way of doing things. At 5 pm David took a call from Fay Vincent in New York. 'There's going to be an announcement in the *Wall Street Journal* tomorrow morning,' Fay told him, 'that'll clarify what's happening.'

'No details, Fay?'

'No details, David.'

Around 6.30 pm David said, 'Look, I don't know what plans you've made for this evening, but Patsy and I are going to watch a new movie soon downstairs and then have dinner. Can you join us?' I replied that I would be delighted and what was the movie? 'Something called *Devil in the Flesh*, directed by Marco Bellocchio,' David replied. 'Orion have sent it over. We've heard it's quite good. And we'll be seeing it in the preview theatre Patsy's done up.'

By 7.30 pm, those at Columbia interested in seeing *Devil in the Flesh* were gathered in the little state-of-the-art studio. As soon as David, Patsy and I had sat down, the picture rolled. David sat on the extreme left of the back row (there were only ten or twelve rows, each six seats wide), with Patsy in the middle and me on the right. You could tell from the smell of the swivel leather armchairs that masqueraded as cinema seats, and by the way they creaked every time someone moved, just how new they were. *Devil in the Flesh* started off with one of the longest establishing shots in history, then slowed down, as it told the love story of a wild child and the student who becomes infatuated with her. An hour and a half into the picture, with chairs creaking all around us, the heroine unzipped the student's pants and popped something in her mouth. *Devil in the Flesh* is apparently the first 'mainstream' film to feature on-screen fellatio. The leather chairs will be fine once they're worn in, but even their symphonic creaking ceased in embarrassment at this point. I could sense the unspoken question – who recommended *this*?

David had sat throughout the performance with his feet vandalistically perched on the back of the black leather armchair in front of him. I was put in mind of David as a teenager, his foot jammed in the exit doors of cinemas showing X-rated movies. What goes around comes around. 'All persons are puzzles,' Emerson recorded in his journals, 'until at last we find in some word or act the boy and the man . . . straightway all past words and actions lie in light before us.' What we had here was either a throwback to David the vandal, or David exercising his droit de seigneur at Columbia – or a mixture of both. Screw you, everybody. *All* past words and notions illuminated? Hardly. That would come eight months later, during an interview with Fay Vincent.

David suggested we skip the rest of the picture and go out for a meal instead. I agreed, figuring I could always see the rest of *Devil in the Flesh* some other time, for review purposes only, of course. We dined Italian, and as I followed David and Patsy through to the quiet at the back of the restaurant, all eyes were on us. 'Who's that guy with Puttnam?' I heard one group mutter. I felt like the new kid in town. It was perhaps as well I didn't catch the rest of the conversation, which, probably went along the lines of, 'Oh, he'll be another of his Limey imports.'

Even so, we had a nice meal of pizza and parma ham, while David put me through a couple of hoops in the way that he does. In the afternoon, it had been 'name the film this music comes from'. It took me three guesses to get *Brief Encounter* before I asked him to turn off the background music lest my super-sensitive Sony ended up with a stereo version of Rachmaninoff's Piano Concerto No 2 instead of a David Puttnam interview. At dinner he was telling us of this Scottish newscaster who owned a piece of land near where *Local Hero* had been shot. 'Sandy Gall?' I asked. 'How did you know?' he softly snapped, piercing me with his Aegeans. 'I didn't,' I replied, 'he's the only Scottish newscaster who sprang to mind.' The answer seemed to please David; I hadn't actually *known*. Are you getting the feeling that the combative side was developing from both our points of view? So was I.

David seemed fairly preoccupied and restless throughout most of the meal. 'David, what *is* it?' Patsy asked at one point clearly exasperated. 'Nothing, Billy,' he replied. 'Well, there's a call I have to make later tonight, and generally all that's going on, I suppose.' We arranged to meet again on Wednesday for breakfast, followed by another interview with Patsy in the morning, then a further session with David at Columbia before my flight back that night. (Jake Eberts had given me two tickets for the *Hope and Glory* première at London's Odeon, Leicester Square on Thursday, 3 September.)

On Tuesday I picked up my copy of the *Los Angeles Times* on the way into Columbia. On the front page of the Business section, the headline ran 'Coke to Combine Columbia, Tri-Star, TV film Holdings.'

'In a dramatic move,' wrote Kathryn Harris, 'that will create a $2 billion entertainment company, Coca-Cola is expected to announce today that it will combine its entertainment holdings – including Columbia Pictures, Coca-Cola Television and a one-third stake in Tri-Star Pictures – in one company under Tri-Star Chairman Victor A. Kaufman.

'Although Coca-Cola would initially hold 70 per cent or more of the combined company, the Atlanta-based soft-drink company intends to reduce its stake to about 49 per cent and distribute the remainder to Coca-Cola shareholders, two Wall Street sources said Thursday.

'Sources were unwilling to predict whether both Tri-Star and Columbia would survive as separate movie-making entities, but one Wall Street executive contended that the combination would result in a stronger company with improved chances of producing hits, which – let's fact it – they haven't been doing for the last couple of years.

'No name has been selected for the combined companies, the sources said, but one executive said that "the Columbia name will be in there".

'The decision appears to be a triumph for Kaufman, a 44-year-old lawyer who left Columbia to run Tri-Star in 1982 . . . Neither Kaufman nor Columbia Chairman Francis T. Vincent Jr., 49, could be reached for comment late Monday.

'Sources said, however, that Vincent is expected to remain with Coca-Cola as an executive vice president, concentrating on the parent firm's 49 per cent-owned bottling operation, Coca-Cola Enterprises.'

That whole day at the studio, little else was discussed. There had been not a single mention of David in *The Times*' story. How must he be feeling, I wondered? Strangely, when we did meet – just for a few moments – he looked refreshed, confident, and totally on top of his game. The man was a walking contradiction.

I wandered over to the commissary for lunch, through the New York street, every doorway of which looked eerily familiar. It seemed to symbolize the tinseltown unreality of the drama currently being enacted, and highlighted the often slender margin – a word, a gesture, a phrase – that separate illusion or delusion, from truth. What is one to make of a *real* traffic accident in a *fake* street witnessed by *actors*?

I had cocktails that evening with one set of old mates, a couple who run their own small movie production company making TV programmes, and a new set, a veritable L A film-buff club of Gareth, Lenson and Ray. All the talk in town that night, as in Columbia during the day, was of the developments at Coke and David's future.

I kept my appointment with David at the designated delicatessen for breakfast, at 8.30 am on Wednesday. As I sat there waiting for his arrival, I saw several of the Columbia executives to whom I had spoken seated round the restaurant, anxiously studying their copies of the daily trades I had read earlier. 'Tri-Star and Coke joins forces in $3 billion Columbia venture,' the *Hollywood Reporter*'s headline ran:

> It'll be the 'reel' thing for Coca-Cola's Entertainment Business Sector when Coke combines its Entertainment Business Sector (EBS) operations with Tri-Star Pictures to form the $3 billion Columbia Pictures Entertainment Inc. According to Coke president/CEO Donald Keough, the new combined entity should be in place by January, 1988, with Victor Kaufman, current chairman of Tri-Star, as its president and chief executive officer . . .
>
> 'All production activity currently under way will continue during the transition,' Keough said. 'Any (future activity) will be under review. During the (expected 90-day) interim, all offices will operate via a committee composed of me, Kaufman and others.'
>
> Reaction from Hollywood and New York was swift. 'It was a shock to me and a shock to people higher than me . . . Nobody had an inkling,' said one highly placed Columbia staffer when informed of the deal. Others at Tri-Star indicated they had 'heard rumors' for months, but were surprised that the deal had fallen in place at this time. 'I read it in the papers, like everyone else,' said one.
>
> Sources said that even the likes of Columbia Pictures chairman David Puttnam and David Picker, the company's president, had no idea that a Tri-Star deal was imminent. Puttnam could not be reached for comment at press time.

As David entered the busy restaurant, he waved at me with his own copy of the paper, and made towards my table. On his way over, he was stopped several times by concerned colleagues. 'What's it mean?' one asked him. 'No idea,' David replied with a nonchalant shrug. My impression was that I was seeing a man under pressure behaving superbly well. 'I know as much as you do,' David concluded, 'just what I read in the papers. See you later.'

He sat down opposite me and ordered an omelette, tea and toast. 'Can't get a moment's peace,' he beamed at me. 'What's up, Andrew?'

'Nothing,' I replied, 'except this desperate news. They're even giving out assurances now that they'll definitely keep the Columbia name.'

'We can't put anything past them,' said David. 'I expect I'll be hearing all about it at tomorrow's breakfast meeting at the Bel Air with Goizueta and Keough. Look, why not spend the morning at Columbia with me now? I'll phone Patsy and tell her you'll be over this afternoon instead. You can meet quite a few people you haven't yet spoken to and get the general reaction to this. Now – when are you coming back to LA? If you let me know well in advance, I'll get interviews set up for you with anybody else you want to meet.'

We discussed this further on the drive to Columbia and agreed that a return trip at the end of October would be good for both of us. The morning at the studio was like a wake, with the news now thoroughly sunk in. Everyone I spoke to felt the dreadful uncertainty that Coke's decision to remove Fay Vincent and have Victor Kaufman run the show must bring. What about David? What about their future? For them the nightmare was just beginning.

One of Valerie's secretaries, Betty, jokingly asked me if I had anything to do with Coke's plans. 'Well, if you didn't, Andrew,' she joshed, 'you sure have an uncanny sense of timing!' After spending several more hours with Patsy in the afternoon, I waved goodbye and sped towards the airport in the Columbia limousine Valerie had thoughtfully conjured up, still marvelling at the new-found strength and composure that had galvanized David.

What I didn't know was that he and Patsy had been awakened at 6.30 am the previous morning, Tuesday, 1 September, by a call from Tom Lewyn in New York. He had studied the Wall Street Journal 'leak' on Coke's plans. 'This action of Coke breaches your contract,' he told David. 'You can walk away with your $3 million.' David and Patsy had hugged each other with delight and danced round the bedroom. For them the nightmare was over.

Chapter 27

The worst thing about the David Puttnam Columbia business is that I have to read the piece in the paper about the article in the magazine about the stuff I already knew anyway and which I wasn't particularly interested in in the first place ..

'*What's all this* shit *about* Poland'

Breakfast at the Bel Air with the Coke bosses and Fay Vincent on Thursday, 3 September, was a low-key affair, although the visit began somewhat disconcertingly. David had arranged to meet Fay first in his room at the Bel Air, before going down to breakfast to join Goizueta and Keough. As soon as David parked his car prior to crossing the bridge over the Bel Air's swan lake, one of Goizueta's assistants, whom David recognized, approached.

'You're to go straight through to breakfast, sir,' David was told.

'But I've arranged to meet Mr Vincent first.'

The messenger was polite, but firm. 'Mr Vincent will be making his own way, sir. It's no problem.' He then proceeded to frogmarch David through to the breakfast meeting.

'We planned this a long time ago,' David was told as the meal proceeded. 'We wanted to do it last year, but missed the 60-day regulatory period. There's no reason the move should particularly affect you, but we've given the running of the show to Victor and you'll have to sort it out with him how you're going to work together.' That Columbia and Tri-Star would be run as two separate companies was repeatedly stressed. There was no reason for any of David's staff to feel in danger, although there could be 'a little rationalization in the service areas'. David was told, 'It's your job to make everyone feel comfortable.'

'You know what they're saying all over town?' David asked. 'That Ray Stark's behind all this.' Goizueta and Keough dismissed this suggestion with roars of laughter.

Later that day David found himself 'door-stepped' by a reporter from the *Los Angeles Daily News*. Since the vast majority of his staff lived in the Valley, where the *News* had its widest circulation, he proceeded to give a bullish version of their futures along the lines of the assurances he had just received. As for himself, he claimed that Coke had given him 'a massive vote of confidence', adding, 'The only stress you come under is that in an environment in which people

426

prefer to think the worst rather than the best, immediately there is a sense that the sharks start circling. In this particular instance, if the sharks are out there, they're going to be miserably disappointed over the fact there's no blood.'

He brushed off the fact that he had first read of Coke's plan in the papers: 'I come from a non-corporate background,' he explained. 'I am a film producer. If someone explained the Coke deal to me in detail, I wouldn't have understood it. I can now see – even I can see – that from Coca-Cola's point of view, it's an extremely good move. It makes absolute financial sense. It's very much my job to carry back to the staff the assurances I've been given by Goizueta and Keough. And I absolutely accept those assurances. I don't think I'm being naïve. I've known Roberto and Don for a little over a year and they've been consistent.'

The validity of Coke's assurances was questioned immediately by many in Los Angeles. 'It depends what David means by *consistent*,' said one reporter. 'If they act *consistent* with their winery performance, they'd better look out at Columbia. They bought the wineries, then sold them off when they couldn't make them pay. The workers were all told, "Go home, folks. Sleep in your beds, secure in the knowledge that your jobs are safe." The next day when they reported for work, Coke had locked them out! Coke are paranoid about Los Angeles. It's an area where, ethnically, they should be No. 1, but they're not. They used to be, but Pepsi have them licked now. It used to be a big thing for graduates to get a job in Coke's big, beautiful boat-shaped LA plant. Not any more.'

Although David had his assurance from Tom Lewyn that in principle Coke had breached his contract, a formal approach to Coke on this vital topic had not yet been made. As for his staff, David was not unaware of the industry norm that large quantities of what Cockney Terence Donovan would define as 'claret' invariably flows along movie-executive corridors in the event of a Hollywood chieftain's exit.

David wrote to Don Keough after the meeting at the Bel Air in a strange, confused mixture of the obsequious and naïve ('I wanted to write and thank you, Roberto and Fay, for taking time out of what must have been a horrendously pressured week to meet with me . . . I was delighted to be able to carry back to the studio your broadly encouraging words with respect to the future, and I doubt if I can adequately express the sense of relief they engendered among the staff'), the unctuously humble ('Believe me, I have done my best to use yesterday's meeting, and the personal and corporate assurances you were able to give, to calm matters and alleviate fears, but frankly I have no experience in this area and I'm concerned that I'm seriously out of my depth'), and the frankly pleading ('Please stay in touch. I specifically need your personal help in ensuring that by energetically carrying out your instructions I don't find myself endangering my personal or professional reputation').

Keough may well have been a little surprised at David's pious stance in view of Coke's supreme arrogance in allowing him to read of Victor Kaufman's ascendancy, and the small matter of the breaking of his contract, in the newspapers, just like millions of others. What had happened to the two-gun kid? David's letter was unanswered.

David quickly reached the conclusion that it would be untenable to sit out Coke's proposed 90-day moratorium period, and indicated that by a deadline of 12 October he would expect to know what his new budget allocation was to be. If this proved unsatisfactory, he would have the choice under the terms of his contract to reject the proposal. This he said he was reluctant to do, due to his deep sense of obligation to those colleagues he had brought to Columbia and were therefore tied to his personal fortunes.

'What obsessed me in the next two weeks,' he later confided, 'was how to get out elegantly, to take advantage of what had happened to get myself out as nicely as possible. I had to play a slight double game. I had to be one person at the office, while I talked to Tom Lewyn every day about the extrication process.'

When Victor Kaufman noted David's new D-date, he decided to do a bit of pre-empting of his own. In a move perfectly calculated to bring the swiftest reaction possible, he announced, on Wednesday, 9 September the return of Patrick Williamson to run Columbia's International Distribution set-up. David rose immediately to the bait through his lawyer. 'There's no point in taking six weeks for something that can be sorted out in a week,' Tom Lewyn told Kaufman, who hastened to agree. A meeting with David on Friday, 11 September was set, when he would be on his way to Toronto to address the Trade Forum at their Festival of Festivals.

According to David, the meeting opened with an almost ritual exchange of unpleasantries. First he harangued Kaufman about bringing Williamson back. Kaufman was all innocence, and had a complaint of his own, that David should not have commented to the *LA Daily News* on the future of the Columbia staff. 'You'd have been better saying nothing,' he told him. 'I was only repeating what Coke had said,' David retorted. 'I was only doing the job they should have done.'

With these preliminaries out of the way, the nitty-gritty began. 'I know you can't live with my existing contract,' David claims to have told Kaufman, 'but I'll continue if you give me a smaller stockade with higher walls.' (David says he had in mind a $23 million ceiling instead of the $30 million in his contract.)

Kaufman replied, per David, that since the new company was about to prepare a public stock offering, it simply would not do for them to have a CEO who only had 18 months to go. The nature of his autonomy, rather than a lower ceiling, was the other major problem. And Kaufman intended to go back to big-star projects and packages. Was he trying to tell David something?

David says he then told Kaufman he would resign and maintains he extracted a promise from him that there would be no staff changes 'in the foreseeable future' and that all executives would get the opportunity 'to prove their worth'. David later stressed to Will Tusher at *Variety* that he believed these were not meaningless promises, since they were specifically sought by him as a quid pro quo for what was in effect the nub of the meeting – in David's terminology, his 'voluntary agreement to expeditiously remove himself from the scene'. (Curiously, in David Picker's account of why David had fallen out with Ray Stark, he claimed that 'Ray works on the basis of quid pro quo, but there are no quid pro quos in the world of David Puttnam.')

There was a sting in the tail. 'You won't be writing any more letters, will you?' Kaufman asked. 'Don Keough was irritated that you wrote to him about his promises concerning the staff. He felt you overstated the case.' This immediately deflated David. If Keough had a complaint, why was he making it through Kaufman instead of directly to him? When he got up to go, a gnawing sensation had begun to take hold in the pit of his stomach.

'Can I tell Roberto and Don you're leaving?' Kaufman asked.

'Of course.'

'Fine. I really should tell Herbert Allen as well.'

'I'd rather you didn't.'

'Well, it would be very difficult not to –'

'If you tell him,' David conceded, 'you mustn't tell another soul. If you start talking to people, so will I.'

In his speech at Toronto on Sunday, 13 September, with his 'resignation' handed in to Kaufman, David kept up the double game. He had a 'big' decision to make regarding his future at Columbia, he told his audience. 'Is it fair,' he agonized, 'to put the studio through the same thing 18 months from now it has just gone through?'

On Wednesday, 16 September, with David back in Los Angeles, a

call from Tom Lewyn in New York at 1.30 pm confirmed that settlement negotiations were satisfactorily completed with the Coca-Cola
Company – the $3 million golden parachute was fully open. Later in
the afternoon, at 5 pm, word came that the story of David's departure
had been leaked to the *Wall Street Journal* and would appear the
following day. Infuriated by this breach of faith, David decided to
announce his departure at The Reel Truth seminar already due to
take place at the studio that evening. A showing of Ridley Scott's
Someone to Watch over Me was lined up, together with a presentation
to Frank Capra that would be accepted by his son. David arranged for
a call to be put through to Will Tusher at *Variety*. 'If you're ever
going to come, make it tonight,' Tusher was told, 'and hold the
presses for a story.'

After *Someone to Watch over Me* was shown, about which David
declared himself 'unbelievably proud', Ridley Scott spoke for a while
about the making of the film. A touching tribute to Frank Capra
followed before David broke the news of his 'resignation'.

'When we originally organized tonight,' he told his audience of
200, 'I was going to give you a rather odd speech about what we'd
achieved and how it wasn't nearly enough and what a lot more we had
to achieve. I guess both are true. But the last few weeks have been
trying, very difficult. Life's like that sometimes, it's been a bit like
trying to gather yourself together after Pearl Harbour. Anyway, the
upshoot of all this is, there's a piece going to appear tomorrow and I
wanted to read this to you first if I may:

'"The Entertainment Business Sector of the Coca-Cola Co. an-
nounced today that David Puttnam, chairman and chief executive of
Columbia Pictures, a division of the Entertainment Business Sector
unit and Victor Kaufman, chairman and chief executive of Tri-Star
Pictures Inc., have met concerning Mr Puttnam's relationship with
Columbia following the anticipated combination of the Entertainment
Business Sector with Tri-Star. During that meeting Messrs Puttnam
and Kaufman agreed that in view of the anticipated combination and
Mr Puttnam's original and irrevocable decision to vacate his post no
later than the summer of 1989, it would be in the company's best
interest to plan for an orderly transition now. Both men stated that in
their view this approach would probably facilitate the organization's
long-term goals and allow a settled structure for the newly combined
company. Accordingly Mr Puttnam will remain as chief executive
officer until the consummation of the combination and will shortly
afterwards relinquish his position . . ."'

As David spoke, the video cameras recording the event panned over the shocked, tearful faces of many in the audience as the words 'relinquish his position' echoed through the small theatre.

'Well,' David continued, 'this is not – obviously, I hope it's not – thrilling for you. I'm not delighted, but it's correct, what the statement says is absolutely accurate. I came to the conclusion at the weekend that it's not right in any way, shape or form to put you all through three months of uncertainty while this particular situation gets sorted out, and put you through the entire thing again in 16 or 17 months when I go back to England. And I think it's sensible and correct – I mean obviously, I'm sick to my stomach, because one thing when I came over here I didn't reckon on was, thanks to Frank Capra and all of you, falling in love with the Columbia lady. That was never part of my plans. So it's a bad day. What is most important is this studio, and that it continues into the future. For me this studio is – and it's not a joke, sadly – a bit like Poland. An awful lot of people over the years have felt they've owned it and it continually gets knocked backwards and forwards and sideways by continuous invading forces. Victor has his own opportunity, a real opportunity, to stop that happening ever again. And in order to consolidate the studio and make it work and make it prosperous and make it all the things that you and I would want it to be, he needs time and a very clear run, and it's up to all of us to give him that.

'I've had the most wonderful year,' David concluded. 'Three months ago, I was wondering really if I'd ever made the right decision, but in the last few months it's got fabulous, and Patsy and I will take home a bunchful of memories we'll never ever be able to forget or thank you enough for.'

If he had not beaten Laura Landro to the punch at the *Wall Street Journal*, the world would have heard the news first from their pointed headline, 'Columbia Asks Puttnam To Leave Post.'

'While Hollywood is notorious for the revolving doors in its executive suites,' Ms Landro observed, 'Mr Puttnam's imminent departure marks the shortest tenure of a major studio chief in recent history . . . Dozens of projects he put into development may never see the light of day. Moreover, numerous executives hired by Mr Puttnam, mostly British and Australian colleagues, may lose their jobs under a new studio boss.' David furiously described Landro's article as 'false from top to bottom. At no point was I asked to resign – ever. It's categorically incorrect, and it's documentarily incorrect.'

When I spoke to Patsy on the phone the night after David's dramatic 'Reel Truth' resignation speech, she explained what an emotional event it had been. 'And you know what David said to me? That if there was one person in the world he wishes could have been there to see the reaction, it was you, Andrew. But it's on tape, so at least you'll be able to watch that.'

Victor Kaufman phoned David next day and angrily expressed his displeasure at the 'Variety' leak. More importantly, he had one key question for David. 'What's all this *shit* about *Poland?*' he yelled.

When David travelled to the Tokyo Film Festival in late September, he was uncharacteristically described as 'the Festival Buddah'. ('I'm not going to say a word,' was the only statement he made, 'about *anything.*') In another uncharacteristic departure, he indulged himself one night with Alan Parker, who was serving as a jury member at the Festival, during a visit to Tokyo's red-light area, Roppongi. The extent of this was the downing by both men of fairly liberal helpings of saki. ('I've never seen him drink so much in all my life,' says Alan. 'He hasn't got that outlet. He's very disciplined in that area. It's always me that used to stuff the kirs down for an instant personality change.')

Before travelling back to Los Angeles he spent a few days in London and invited Debbie and Loyd along to dinner with Cineplex-Odeon chief Garth Drabinsky. Debbie was dreading the occasion, for the picture she now carried of her father was of the careworn, frazzled individual he had turned into during the year at Columbia. To her surprise, he appeared totally relaxed and cheerful, pressing upon her a multitude of sweet and silly souvenirs he had purchased on his Hong-Kong stopover. There was no business discussed at all at the dinner, which was a joyous, lighthearted affair. Afterwards Debbie exclaimed happily to Loyd, 'Thank God, my dad's been given back to me.'

David was even then carrying a bug he had caught in the East, which manifested itself first with flu-like symptoms that proved impossible to shake off. The doctor in Los Angeles diagnosed mononucleosis, and recommended complete rest.

After several weeks of silence, the many admirers of Ray Stark could keep quiet no longer. While Ray modestly denied newspaper claims that he was a 'power guy', a 'major studio executive' contended that David had made an enormous error in dismissing Stark as 'a relic'. 'It was a matter of respect,' he declared. 'Ray wanted respect for his body of work and David wasn't willing to give it.'

'Ray was angry, not just for himself, but for the community,' an associate claimed. Another added that Stark had found Puttnam 'too callow' to appreciate the irony in his own pronouncements. 'Ray would say, "when I was David Puttnam's age, I wasn't producing *The Mission* for $28 million and then complaining that the studios let me spend the money."'

'There had been a sense of depletion and disappointment,' one of Stark's friends admitted, referring to the producer's years of agonizing failures – *Sylvester*, *The Survivors*, *The Slugger's Wife*, *Violets Are Blue*, *Amazing Grace* and *Chuck* and *Brighton Beach Memoirs* – 'but to come back like this is really amazing.' (Apart from the $65-million grosser, *The Secret of My Success*, Stark had enjoyed two small hits on Tri-Star during the year, *Peggy Sue Got Married* and *Nothing in Common*.) 'I told Ray at one point, "You have had the ultimate revenge. You've done three pictures away from Columbia and they've all been hits. Why don't you relax?"'

'I adore Ray,' said fellow-septuagenarian David Brown (of the Brown/Zanuck *Jaws/Sting/Cocoon* team). 'He's been through all the onerous things that all of us endure. Presenting projects to people of one-third our age and one-eighth our experience. But he's never been defeated. He's never become cynical.' (If he hasn't his associates have. When Don Safran, Stark's assistant, was told that a Puttnam biography was in the works, the sarcasm was thick on the ground. 'Are you sure there's enough in Puttnam for a whole book?' he sneered.)

Victor Kaufman – said to be already struggling to keep up with Ray's constant phone calls – took time off to deliver his encomium. 'Ray has always been a great adviser to me,' he asserted. 'I've talked with him as a friend, and he's taught me a lot about people.'

Coke chose at this stage to reveal that Stark had been quietly under contract as a consultant to Columbia for the last five years, but fervently denied that Stark had carried out any manoeuvring behind the scenes to effect anyone's removal. 'It is really off the wall,' said a spokesman, 'for anyone to tell you that Ray Stark or anyone else in Hollywood had anything to do with Fay Vincent's change of assignment.' How about David Puttnam's removal? There was no comment on this from Coke.

David and I met again on a brilliantly clear and sunny Saturday morning, back in Coldwater Canyon, at the end of October. Sacha was visiting for a few days, 'hanging out with his Dad' and looking for material for Midnight, the rock group in which he played guitar. David had already made a temporary recovery before the illness had struck again. His doctor had warned him that this could be the pattern until the virus burnt itself out, and that undue strain would only serve to shorten the time between the attacks and make them more acute. He looked wasted with fatigue.

Together we watched the rushes from the Paris location shoot of *To Kill a Priest*, then after a cup of tea and a chat (I kidded him about his 'Buddah' appellation at the Tokyo Festival), I left, arranging to return the following afternoon. On Sunday at 5 pm, he was still saying goodbye to his lunch guests, and seemed to have taken on a new lease of life. I said hello to Sandy Lieberson, whom I had already met in London. 'I remember you as taller,' I told him. 'I *am* taller,' he grinned. I shook hands with Alan Parker and confirmed my appointment for Tuesday at Orion. I mentioned that *Angel Heart* had just opened in London to very strong figures, adding to the excellent take in France and Germany. He acknowledged this somewhat ruefully, as if to say, 'Great! So why didn't they buy it over here?' Jim Clark was there, and I arranged there and then to see him at Columbia later in the week. Also present was Judy Scott-Fox, who had been Alan's agent for years. I heard later they had been talking divorce.

David talked at length that night about his plans for the immediate future. He was to spend the months ahead, until April 1988, in Los Angeles, overseeing the release of the movies made so far. Then, most likely, there would be a return to independent production, when he looked forward to 'knocking the spots off my competitors'. He ruminated on the role of a producer: 'Someone in France decided film was a director's medium.' A shrug. 'And with the gleeful participation of directors, the press swallowed it. This puts me in a difficult position vis-à-vis me and Roland and Alan. It'll be a real problem for Roland if his next film doesn't work on his own, which is what happened with Alan. Alan's obsession with working with me would be to do a film that would be the biggest hit since he's had with *Midnight Express*. He'd really be fucked, because people would say he's fine when he's working with Puttnam. And that would really kill him.'

When the subject got round to the delicate subject of his demise at Columbia, the mood grew darker. 'Maybe what divides me from the likes of Ray Stark,' he mused, 'is my being prepared to be judged by history and his not being prepared for this, doing absolutely everything he can to distort the record. Maybe that's an area that divides people, one of the great dividing lines. Because I've always been, rightly or wrongly – maybe wrongly – totally comfortable with the idea that in the long run, when my contributions are added up and assessed, I'll come out looking good, or certainly on the right side.

I've been absolutely confident about that always, whereas someone like Stark – he needs to have these little day-to-day victories.'

Over a supper of cold lamb salad, wine and coffee, we fixed the agenda for the week ahead. Basically, I would be spending every morning at Columbia, with appointments fixed elsewhere each afternoon. This time I insisted on finding my own way back to my hotel in Burbank.

On Tuesday I met Alan Parker at Orion's Century City offices. While we were talking, Hugh Hudson, whom I was due to see the following day, popped in to introduce himself, along with Mike Medavoy, head of production at Orion. Mike offered a few quick bon mots ('A lot of what David had to say was true, but it wasn't his place to say it. I told him, there's no need to make pronouncements – go and do it') and exited in a trail of expensive cigar smoke. At Orion's reception later I bumped into *The Big Easy*'s director, Jim McBride, who introduced himself and chatted for a while. 'David Puttnam? He's my hero. He saved *The Big Easy*,' he beamed.

Alan Parker was temporarily occupying Eric Pleskow's office while he worked on the preparation of his new film, *Mississippi Burning*. 'What do you like best about me?' he had once asked his friend. 'Your devastating honesty,' David had replied.

'He's my best buddy,' Alan told me. 'We phone each other pretty well every day. I'm like a nagging mother; if he doesn't phone I get irritable. In the end, what I like doing with him most is laughing and slagging each other off, not taking ourselves seriously. In the latter years he's done that far too much. All I ever did was try to redress the balance, because I do think we're a couple of lucky yobbos, him from Southgate and me from Islington. We've had this fantastic privilege, this wonderful opportunity to make movies. What we say we should say with our films, up there on the screen.

'*That's* what David should have done, but in order to justify why he was doing the Columbia job, he had to turn it into a crusade. It was the only way he could get that little extra dignity out of doing it. Then he made the mistake of conducting the debate in the press. And when he's doing an interview, he's so zealous about what he believes in, he's no longer talking to a journalist, but someone who has to be convinced. The problem is that you're not talking to one person, you're talking to the thousands of people who are going to read it. He could never make that differentiation.

'I can't imagine why David would want to take Ray Stark on at the beginning. In the early days, Ray always admired David; he said he was one of the only producers he ever had any time for. And in a way

I think David quite admired Ray and what he stood for, as a very powerful producer of the old school, a very powerful man. The house-keeping clearout was to get rid of a whole lot of people who shouldn't have been there, but not Ray. He might have had the most expensive deal, but it turned out to be a very costly error. It'll take a while before David acknowledges that, in the tactical way he went about achieving his aims, what happened to him was his own fault.'

Hugh Hudson gave an equally intriguing interview next day, when he gave his side of the *Chariots of Fire* and *Greystoke* controversies. Not, I would imagine, an easy man to get to know – as others had indeed pointed out – there was still something extraordinarily likable about the tall, aristocratic Hudson, and something very touching about the affection still obvious despite his criticisms of David. He saw a parallel between recent developments and his being left holding the *Greystoke* baby.

'He's done it again,' Hugh told me, 'walking out of Columbia. You could argue that he's left a lot of people in the lurch. A lot of people who brought their films to him; you could argue now they'll never get made. Because *he* feels uncomfortable, because *he's* not prepared to go on; that's fine for *him*, but what about all the other people he's left in a very uncomfortable position? And David's making a tremendous amount of money – he hasn't sacrificed the money by leaving – but all those people who had their hopes pinned on him have been sacrificed. He hung himself, by not being the diplomat he was as a producer, by being arrogant and self-righteous. In a way he came here hating it, he came for all the wrong reasons. He came to take revenge and make a pile of money. Money had never been his motivation in the past, only power. He wishes he could direct films. The memory of his father drives him forward. He considers his father was an artist and wishes he could be one. But he likes power and control and now he needs money. So that's become part of the equation, and it sits badly with him.

'"The gardener gets more pleasure from the Mill than I do," he's said. You could say that subconsciously he engineered his demise without sacrificing the bread – because he's a real fast-footer. The things I say may sound harsh, but I'm trying to be the devil's advocate. There will be many others who won't have this voice through you and will be feeling hard done by, who would cast a very harsh judgement on him for leaving after a year.

'Why immediately upset Ray Stark, a man who's been making movies here for thirty years? It was completely self-destructive to do that, immediately inflammatory. So who gives diddlyshit? But he understands that the people he's brought to Columbia have value, and he brought their dreams to fruition, then allowed them to evaporate for his own *amour propre*. He talked too much. If you want to eat at the table again, you mustn't criticize the food unless you're the chef. You've got to *own* the restaurant to criticize the food and nowadays nobody owns the store, only corporations. He was only another puppet, but he thought he wasn't. Vanity, vanity, all is vanity. It brings everybody down in the end.'

For a moment Hugh looked up at me from his doodling and broke into a craggy smile. 'Nevertheless,' he qualified, 'I'm fond of him and we're speaking again. I rang him up two days before he left Columbia and said, "This is ridiculous, we must get together." We met for lunch. There's an umbilical cord between the two of us. We're discussing the possibility of getting together on a film,' – here he laughed – 'that's got a lot of special effects in it, like the ones he claimed put him off doing *Greystoke*. Of course you *have* to change, otherwise you're fucked.'

Chapter 28

Some Porsches

During the week I got to know Columbia well, heading almost every day through the New York street to the commissary. This time there was anger and hurt among the staff at David's departure. One or two gave me what they called the 'inside story' of events, but these were wildly conflicting. Did Ray Stark and Herbert Allen have anything to do with it? 'Absolutely not, that's a ridiculous suggestion.' 'Of course they did. These guys are so incredibly powerful.' Equally conflicting were their views on their boss's conduct, together with one hefty sideswipe at their new boss.

- 'You won't find one person in this building with a word to say against him.'
- 'David was a minnow who thought he was a piranha.'
- 'David should have taken the cotton wool out of our ears and stuffed it in his mouth. He should have listened first instead of sounding off.'
- 'It's a damned shame. He had just gotten started. We were all rooting for him. Victor has perpetuated the myth of Tri-Star being successful. They've never had a real hit since they were founded, except for *Rambo*, and they only acted as distributors for Carolco. If you count that as a credit, the fact that Victor picked it up – and it *was* enormously successful – you should also bear in mind the many, many disastrous pick-ups, like *Space Vampires* from Cannon, *Supergirl* and *Santa Claus* from the Salkinds. These films represented millions down the tubes. And *this* is the guy who's come out on top?'

Jim Clark was already looking forward to going home, his time as David's 'product fixer' almost over. 'It started off more interesting than it ended up,' he told me. 'The Cosby movie? I've spent a great deal of time on it, to very little avail. That aspect of the job, which I was aware of when I took it, I didn't particularly enjoy. I kept saying I'd rather make my own mess than clear up someone else's.

'It was my job to see all the rushes of current films shooting and report to David if I found anything wrong. Another unenviable task;

it's extremely boring sitting through everyone else's rushes. When you do spot mistakes or something you're unhappy with, it's quite difficult to do anything about them because nobody likes negative reports, so you find yourself constantly giving bad news instead of good, since there's no need to give the good news. On *Leonard VI* I kept reporting that it wasn't funny, but I don't know if the reports ever got back. I said it was fine visually, but it wasn't funny.' Jim brightened up when I asked him about the Japanese *Chatran*, shortly to be retitled *Milos and Otis*. 'It should do very well in the children's market,' he said. 'It's an exemplary children's film.'

Despite the somewhat disappointing year he had gone through at Columbia, Jim saw the effect David had had on the personnel there. 'They respected him enormously,' he said. 'He really inspired people. It was the side of David that is a crusader that got him into trouble with the establishment. He wanted to change the nature of things and there are so many people here who, in a sense quite rightly, were offended by a foreigner, an Englishman, coming over and telling them how to run their business. That side of David – his zealous, crusading side – does occasionally get the better of him and makes him say or do things that are probably better left unsaid. However, among the people who worked here, when he resigned, I've never seen such a display of public emotion.'

Further down the corridor I spoke with Fred Bernstein, David's worldwide head of production. 'I would have to guess this has been the worst year of his life', he said. 'In his professional life, maybe it's Dickens's worst of times and best of times. He is the most opinionated man I've ever met; he is also the most self-assured man in his right to be wrong in his opinion. I really think he doesn't care. Most of us are very cautious about rendering our opinions, because invariably our opinions are a reflection of ourselves. David doesn't care, right or wrong. He puts himself on the line every day and it staggers people.'

I asked Fred how he felt about David's public pronouncements. 'There was a couple of times I winced,' he admitted. 'I would have done it differently, but you've got to look at the whole record. David Puttnam never got anywhere biting his tongue. He truly believed there is a malaise in this industry and he wasn't going to play the game. Could he have played the game and lasted longer? Maybe. That might not have been true to his own spirit. I think David made a fatal mistake and it wasn't that he talked too much, that's David. The mistake was to take the management of the Coca-Cola company at total face value. You do it, we'll back you up. He didn't expect them to kow-tow to the Hollywood pressures and obviously they did. I don't believe the Coke transaction is anything to do with David Puttnam; it had to do with a big bowl of wax. David was a detail. They wanted to do this transaction and David became a problem and they simply decided they couldn't have the two guys. Victor wants it, and David was leaving anyway.'

Compared to the last time I had gone the rounds of Columbia's offices, the blinkers were off as far as the product was concerned. *Little Nikita* and *Leonard Part VI*, even at this stage, were acknowledged disasters. *Pulse* was David Picker's utter folly, an idiotic, laughable horror film. Spike Lee should never have been handed $6 million for *School Daze*. *Zelly and Me* drew either blank stares or the comment, 'a home movie'. *Punchline*? Good movie, great performances by Sally Fields and Tom Hanks, but could be a difficult sell. Oscar nominations for *Punchline*? Maybe next time, not this year. *The Beast*? Good 'B' war film in the Sam Fuller mould. *Someone to Watch over Me*? Should have been better. *Housekeeping*? Brilliant, but totally uncommercial. *Vibes*? A faint chance of being a good summer picture. *Stars and Bars*? Misfire, not funny. *Hope and Glory*? Quality film, tough sell, might just make it in the end. *Last Emperor*? Dazzling, unknown quantity commercially. Pride in the product? Still yes, for the most part, but there was an element of realism creeping in that had been absent before.

Since David had announced his departure, several names had been mooted as his likely successor, notably Frank Price, now an independent since his release from Universal following the summer 1986 disaster of *Howard the Duck*. (Why is it movie bosses are only remembered for their failures and the hits that get away? Price had a major hit with *Out of Africa* in the same Universal season. At Columbia he was responsible for the brilliant *Tootsie* and the hugely successful *Ghostbusters*. But he'll always be chiefly regarded as the guy who wouldn't take *E.T.*'s calls at Columbia.)

On Wednesday, 28 October the uncertainty over David's successor was ended, with *Hollywood Reporter*'s headline, 'New Day Dawns At Columbia.' David's post of chairman of the studio was being eliminated. Taking his place, but on a somewhat lower rung, as president, was Dawn Steel, the current production president at Paramount Pictures. 'This is a job of a lifetime,' said Ms Steel. 'This is the head of a studio. How could I turn it down? The fact of the matter is they made me an offer I couldn't refuse.' (The other fact of the matter is that Paramount executives could look forward to relief from exposure to Ms Steel's well-known temper.) Also announced was David Picker's return to independent production in New York, producing for Columbia, and serving as a 'consultant' to Victor Kaufman. Once again Betty pointed out the newspaper headline to me reprovingly. 'Andrew, are you *sure* this is nothing to do with you?' she asked. 'For every time you come here . . .'

At the end of the week Valerie presented me with a copy of 'The Reel Truth' video Patsy had promised, which I viewed in David's office before I left. Back home I would study it again, for even at that first viewing, I was struck by a false note that seemed to permeate the proceedings. At the time, I couldn't put my finger on what it was.

On the last day I was invited by musical genius Quincy Jones to have lunch with him at his beautiful Bel Air home. Thirty years ago Quincy had recorded Dinah Washington, whose biography I intended to write in the future. When I arrived, Quincy had just come off a 45-minute phone call from Michael Jackson in Hong-Kong, so was naturally full of Michael's observations and concerns. During the next three hours we talked of his early days at Mercury Records with Dinah, through whose encouragement Quincy became the first black A and R man of a major record company at the age of 23. It was only later I realized that I must be the first person ever to interview Quincy who pressed the pause button on his tape recorder every time Michael Jackson's name was mentioned.

'Man, Dinah was a trip,' he told me, as he regaled me with tales of their adventures together. Quincy, the whole visit was a trip.

The roll-out of David's movie slate reminded the industry that this was the first time ever a studio head had left before a single film of his had been released. True, Marty Ransohoff's *The Big Town*, to which David had contributed the director, had taken less than $2 million at the box-office against a $17 million cost, but no one seriously claimed this was part of David's output. He says he was chary about releasing *Someone to Watch over Me* only a few short weeks after Paramount's *Fatal Attraction* had hit the market, but allowed his judgement to be overruled by his marketing people. Many felt the film was a non-starter in any case, including Tom Matthews at Box Office, who described it as 'gorgeous-looking, but dull and empty'. Ridley Scott's 'Give me a disco and I'll give you Dante's Inferno' had once again prevailed over pacing, character motivation and plot. At a cost of almost $17 million to Columbia, the movie faltered at $10 million box-office gross, a net return to the studio from the US theatrical release of around $4 million.

Regrettably, Bill Forsyth's beautiful *Housekeeping* was next to take a box-office tumble, grossing just over a meagre $1 million on a budget of $6.5 million. Despite dazzling reviews, among the best of Bill's career (one critic described the move as being 'as close to perfection as it is possible to get'), it seemed that exquisite delicacy of touch was not enough to fan the film out to a wide audience. David had described the movie to me before its opening as 'a gem, an absolute gem'. He was right then and he's right now. *Housekeeping* is a film that will surely come to be appreciated more and more as the years go by, and will stand as a watershed in Bill Forsyth's career.

All eyes were on Tri-Star as they released their father/son role-reversal saga, *Like Father, Like Son*, while Brian Gilbert was still knee-deep in the post-production process on *Vice Versa* at Columbia. The critical reaction to the effort Kaufman rushed through was terrible, *Variety* describing it as a 'messy, repetitive role reversal comedy . . . strictly sit com stuff . . . sloppy directing and choppy editing.' One week later the film took in over $7 million at the box office in its first weekend and went on to gross a very respectable $35 million total. The old Hollywood adage, 'Do you want it quick, or do you want it good?' had once more been stood on its head. Apart from the previous tenant of Coldwater Canyon Drive, Dudley Moore, credit for bringing the crowds in went to Kirk Cameron, a 'teen heartthrob' from T V's *Growing Pains*, playing Dudley's son. The vexed word at Columbia was that Kaufman had spent a fortune to push the film, and anxiety about the prospects for *Vice Versa*, with an identical plot, was now raised. At least it would be next out of the box, for although postponed from a December 1987 opening to spring 1988, it was still ahead of George Burns' *18 Again* and Tom Hanks' *Big*. By that time the hope was that *Like Father, Like Son* would be forgotten.

The first bright spark on both the critical and commercial horizons was John Boorman's *Hope and Glory*. The film had a tremendous amount going for it, enough even to survive a jarring switch of locations halfway through. The slow roll-out Columbia gave the film was generally seen as appropriate, allowing as it did for good word-of-mouth to get around.

The second ray of hope was provided by David's other pick-up. *Variety* previewed Jeremy Thomas's production of Bernardo Bertolucci's *The Last Emperor* as 'a film of unique, quite unsurpassed visual splendour.' They paid special tribute to producer Jeremy Thomas for the 'enormous, impressive job he pulled off . . . in organizing such an ambitious production . . . without upfront involvement of any major studio.' The film went on to open to further hugely enthusiastic reviews and brisk business. By Christmas 1987 it was playing at 94 cinemas and taking $1 million a week. As with *Hope and Glory*, the plan was to go wider with the announcements of the Oscar nominations.

All the post-production resources at Columbia's command were poured into making *Leonard VI* work. Choruses of frogs croaked on cue, lobsters leapt, turkeys trotted and fish flew, as Paul Weiland anxiously assembled the first cut of the film back in London. When Bill Cosby heard that David Picker was flying over for a viewing, he banned him from seeing the film. Under his contract, no Columbia executive was allowed to pre-empt his first viewing. He was so pleased after seeing it that he insisted on a third credit. As well as producer and star, he now claimed Original Story. 'It will take a hundred million dollars,' a punch-drunk Paul Weiland was told. The same message was relayed by the comedian to Fay Vincent in New York and Don Keough in Atlanta. As far as Paul was concerned, the film had no heart, no soul, and an unsympathetic star.

Two audience previews were held, neither of which Cosby attended. After the first went badly, doubts and not a little panic began to spread. Why wasn't Cosby funny? Editor Gerry Hamblin was blamed. Hadn't he cut away too fast from Cosby? ('We did that to get off him because he wasn't funny,' says Paul.) 'You should let the camera linger on him, let him wait for the laugh like he does on TV, let him burn,' they were told. After Hamblin had dutifully reassembled every scene, a new preview was set for San Bernardino. 'David hugged me, put his arm around me after this,' says Paul, 'in *commiseration*. I was *broken*. The audience *hated* it. You could *feel* the hatred. Jesus Christ, a rainbow trout got a bigger laugh than the great God Cosby!'

If there was despondency among the Columbia production executives about the film, the marketing men still set about its promotion as if they existed in another dimension – one in which only hit movies exist. Integrally built into *Leonard* were crateloads of on-screen Coke, together with other 'product placements' like Porsche cars. 'This is a whole new ball of wax,' a marketing head enthused. 'We devised a couple of premium items and placed them in the film, products you can only get with the purchase of Coca-Cola. Seven or eight characters from the film will appear on collectable badges, T-shirts and mugs. A Porsche was featured, so apart from in-store displays, we plan to give away some Porsches as well.' It seemed the always tenuous hold on reality in Hollywood had completely snapped. In the jargon of ad-speak, 'some Porsches' will forever be immortalized, as will the 'synergistic' *Leonard*/Coke advertising campaign on which the company was estimated to be blowing upwards of $15-$20 million. Marcio Moreira of McCann-Ericson Worldwide, the agency responsible for handling the blitz, declared the strategy had 'created new energy and excitement in the studio.' Sure. And record billings too! If the final figures were to be believed, Columbia and Coke between them had more than $40 million wrapped up in *Leonard VI*.

With the film due to open in December, Cosby had a change of mind regarding the film's prospects, after studying the results of the two previews and listening to his wife's advice. She hated it. Even after a final, panic-induced re-cut by Jim Clark, it was clear the film was going nowhere. On the eve of the movie's opening, Cosby decided to disown the project, and flush Coke's advertising campaign down the toilet – Porsches, placements and all. Viewers of Larry King's TV chat show were startled to hear Cosby say, 'It took an awful lot, Larry, to come on this show and say to people, "Look, I don't know if this product is good enough".' Humble pie? Not a bit of it. 'It's not my picture,' he hastily added – despite the fact that his name was in the hoardings three times over.

'Puttnam asked for the director,' he enlarged later. 'Puttnam asked for the line producer, who then went on and hired people. Puttnam calls me and says, "Listen, you're a partner on this", and I find I'm not really a partner, man. I think part of the problem was that these people came from England and in a way were saying, "We understand he's very big in America, but we have to have our control." '

'Perhaps no studio,' *Variety* wrote, 'deserves two *Ishtars* in a single year, but Columbia has turned the trick, with *Leonard Part VI* opening as its Christmas release. Bill Cosby is right to be embarrassed by this dud, but the result can't have come as a total surprise to him, since he wrote the story and produced it.'

Public reaction supported this view seven days later as 1142 theatres reported a rock-bottom $1153 average for the opening weekend. (For the record, *Ishtar* opened at the same number of cinemas and took $3803 average – and that was a *disaster*.) The total US take came to less than $5 million.

Paul Weiland's recollection of Cosby is still far from totally negative, for the relationship between the two had survived all the vicissitudes on the film. 'Bill's a big baby,' Paul maintains, 'who needs to be cuddled and mothered. And he's got all the normal hang-ups, although in his case they're *billionized* because of the enormous power he wields. He's got a huge ego and is paranoid about two main items, Eddie Murphy – and critics. The reviews must have crucified him.'

Paul felt seduced and abandoned – in a sense the sacrificial goat. 'I'd been drawn into making a *product*,' he groaned. 'not a *movie*. Christ, I make *product* commercials all the time. The last thing I needed was a mega-budget *product*. What I could have used for a first Hollywood film was something smaller, controllable, and if it had bombed, it would have been my fault. Instead, I was made caretaker over a fucking disaster. The ship was going down and there was little me trying to plug up this hole. It must be the biggest first film any director's ever been given. 'Are you sure this is right, David?' I kept asking him. Even Alan Parker told me, 'Take it, Paul, you can't fail.' In the end I believed them. I should have followed my own judgement instead. Puttnam and Marshall certainly should have known better. It would have helped if one of them had just said it was dreadful.

'Am I angry with David Puttnam? To a degree. He gets people wrong. His character assessments are sometimes way off. Nathanson's friendship suddenly cooled when the shit hit the fan. "You've done a brilliant job no matter what happens with the movie," David told me after the first preview. "You're making me look smart," he wrote to me later. But then his associates withdrew all their support and left me on my own.

'I'd like to work with him again on a one-to-one basis, that would be brilliant. To sit down with him and go through ideas, to be his friend, like Roland and all the others must have done, that would be great. But to have him as an executive, was a total – I mean, it wasn't working with *David Puttnam*. He's a very honourable man, and on the other hand, he's *not* so honourable. He's a bit of an enigma.'

When Cosby announced in a huff that his next film would be made with Warners, one Columbia executive dryly commented, 'Don't dress for it.'

A bizarre encounter took place one night in November in Giardino's Restaurant on 3rd Street, west of Doheny in Beverly Hills, where David and Patsy had arranged to meet Columbia's business affairs lady, Lyndsey Posner, for dinner. When Lyndsey arrived first, she found their table was close to another occupied by Ray Stark and Barry Diller. Shortly after she had arranged for a diplomatic change, David and Patsy arrived.

When the threesome were halfway through their meal, Stark and Diller got up, passed their table in silence and left the restaurant. A moment later David, Patsy and Lyndsey were treated to the spectacle of Ray Stark squinting through the glass doors at them. When he saw he had been spotted, the indomitable Ray was not to be defeated. He promptly re-entered the dining room and strode up to address two men seated at a table next to the group. The diners looked totally perplexed. Obviously, they knew who Stark was, but appeared to have no idea just why they were being so honoured. After a few minutes of this charade, Stark turned from their table.

'Oh, David,' he laughed, 'I nearly walked straight past you.'

'Yes, Ray,' David replied quietly, without looking up, 'and that's how I want it to be. Let's leave it that way, shall we?'

Stark scowled, thoroughly discomfited. This wasn't the line he'd expected. 'Yes, but –' he stammered, 'I wanted to let you *know* I'd walked past you and didn't acknowledge you. I did it *deliberately*!'

It was Lyndsey's turn. 'We *know*, Ray,' she cooed, 'but you had to come back and tell us, didn't you?'

He glared at her for a moment, then at David and Patsy, the veins on his forehead pulsing. Where, oh where, was Neil Simon with that perfect exit line? Stark was left to stumble towards the door, having shot himself neatly in both feet.

'We can't believe it,' said the two men he'd been addressing, 'we've never actually spoken to Mr Stark before.'

'You're lucky,' said David, smiling at his companions.

As they had gone into their little dance of joy after that first reassuring phone call from Tom Lewyn in September, David and Patsy's thoughts regarding the fate of the executive team at Columbia were banished, if only for a few carefree seconds. Coke's assurances and the later promises David thought he had extracted from Victor Kaufman were still ringing in his ears in early December, despite the departures of David Picker and, later, Greg Coote. David and Patsy had consulted a psychic specializing in 'astral plane' projection just a week earlier. When a dreadful time ahead was predicted, they thought the seer must be a little late with the news. Surely, they were through the worst? Then the wholesale slaughter began.

'Axe Falls At Columbia Pictures,' ran *Variety*'s headline, as they went on to list a 'massive first wave of anticipated firings . . . Columbia reverberated with shock and apprehension over the wholesale pay-roll lopping . . . Executive suites from one corridor to another were swept out . . . Despite the claim that Columbia is divesting itself of "superfluous employees" there was no doubt that almost all personnel fingerprints left by Puttnam are being – or appear to be – being systematically erased.'

Two days later, *Hollywood Reporter* noted, 'Another round of firings at Columbia Pictures resulted in a clean sweep of the studio's creative production staff both in New York and London. The terminations, which come on the heels of ongoing firings at headquarters in Burbank, signal the virtual disbandment of production operations . . .'

A week later *Variety* provided an update, revealing that as many as 500 of the new Columbia Pictures Entertainment's 3500 employees were being dismissed in a restructuring that would aim to reduce overhead costs by $40 million annually. The key expression used for the cut-back was '*to the bone*' – in total and painful contrast to Goizueta and Keough's 'little rationalisation' in the service areas.

At least the blood bath ended the uncertainty for the many Columbia personnel either recruited by David or judged by Victor Kaufman to have found favour with him. And hadn't Kaufman proved himself a master of timing? Merry Christmas, guys!

In the same week as the slaughter of the innocents, Ray Stark had a cheerier Christmas message – a $236-million slate of 18 features ready to roll, of which 10 so far were either at Columbia or Tri-Star. *Annie II* was going ahead. *Revenge* was with New World at a budget of $12 million (this was boosted to $20 million later and turned into a co-production with Columbia). *Sweet Libby* was being made for Home Box Office. Stark's president of production Doreen Bergeson was in ebullient mood on the regained rapport the company had struck with Columbia. 'I think we'll put about eight projects into development with them,' she trumpeted, 'starting right away. We're going to be doing a lot of business with Columbia.' Right *on*, Ray!

In the movie *Broadcast News*, William Hurt plays a newscaster shown interviewing a rape victim on film. Towards the end of the interview, there is a close-up of Hurt brushing a stray tear from his cheek. Only later is it discovered that the newscaster had the tear-stained reaction separately filmed after the interview, then spliced in for maximum emotional voltage. If life imitates art, this is the flip side of what David perpetrated on his 'Reel Truth' audience with his 'resignation' speech. Flip in more ways than one, for instead of planting the tear on his own cheek – he was *totally* in control – he planted it on the cheeks of his audience, and captured the emotional reaction for posterity with a bank of zooming, panning cameras.

Although David modestly claims that as a producer he can neither write a good enough script nor direct a movie, here he had done exactly that, with a supporting cast of 200. Instead of pressing every single patently loaded emotional button (Falling in love with the Columbia lady . . . the most wonderful year . . . it's got fabulous . . . bunch of memories), why couldn't he just have told them the truth – that he was off back to England with $3 million in cash and Coke shares and that, yes, if it hadn't been for his posturing they would still be reporting to him and not left to Victor Kaufman's tender mercies.

Maybe then his audience would have loved him less.

Of course David was going through a dreadful time; on this there was no dispute, whether or not he had brought it upon himself. He *needed* the approbation of his Columbia colleagues, and the wave of emotion and love that washed over and soothed him. And if the price was a manipulative tug on the heartstrings, what of it? David wanted the best of all possible worlds, the cash *and* the kudos. Cry for me, Columbia, on cue and on video.

When the *Sunday Times* published its year-end list of 'Risers and Fallers', David had close connections with every one in the Hollywood section. One 'Riser' was Ridley Scott's brother Tony, who had directed two of the biggest hits of the year, *Top Gun* and *Beverly Hills Cop II*. David had begged Tony not to undertake the Cop sequel after arguing that one 'sell-out' was enough. The second 'Riser' was Adrian Lyne, with whom David had fallen out after *Foxes* back in the seventies. The *Times* described Lyne as 'Hollywood's hottest director' after the phenomenon *Fatal Attraction* had become.

In the 'Fallers' section were the 'Go-Go boys', Menahem Golan and Yoram Globus of Cannon, rescued, according to the *Times*, 'by a Madrid property company to avoid bankruptcy'. (The SEC report had earlier roundly condemned the accounting policies by which they had appeared to make constantly rising profits). David's intuition that their take-over of Thorn-EMI's Screen Entertainment in Britain would be a disaster had quickly proved correct. The film library had been parcelled off to Jerry Weintraub, many ABC and Classic cinemas had been sold to real estate developers, the promised flood of investment in the industry had never taken place, and despite their protestations, Elstree Studios was facing the axe.

Fate makes strange bedfellows, for the occupant of the other 'Fallers' berth was David Terence Puttnam himself.

Chapter 29

'There's no creative community'

Which had come first, the Coke plan or the decision that David was leaving? 'The *thought process* was that David was going to go,' Fay Vincent recalls. 'The first *issue* was, what does Coke do with its entertainment operations? You either have to put more money in or you have to stay where you are, or get out. My argument was that to get into the nineties you're going to have to make a much bigger investment. That didn't seem to be very attractive to the people in Atlanta, because they have a huge soft-drink business and to build entertainment to where it's competitive with soft drink wasn't on the cards. So the first *judgement* had nothing to do with David. It was time to get Coke's entertainment division in a different position.

'Point two was what we did about it, and I came up with the scheme to spin off half the business to Coke's shareholders and get Columbia into a position where it was not a wholly-owned division of Coke and they'd get back all the money they'd invested in it. Financially, it turned out to be a very good deal, but David *could* have stayed on to run Columbia through all that.

'The *coincidence* was that while Coke were making these strategic moves, David's problems were also coming to a head. So having decided we were going to put all of entertainment together, and have Victor be the chief executive, then the question of David became very clear. David could not work with Victor, and Coke and all the other powers recognized that Puttnam would have to go. It was inevitable. Once that whole series of transactions occurred, David would leave.

'Ray, I'm sure, was out trying to do Puttnam in very early on, but he couldn't have done it if Puttnam hadn't co-operated so well, because Ray went after a lot of things around here over the years, without success. Puttnam just made it easy for him by giving him so much ammunition.'

Back in Hollywood after a holiday with David in Thailand and a spell on safari in South Africa, Patsy now appeared to be enjoying life, despite the resolution of the fight. Now she could see where their trust had been misplaced. Surprisingly, it was not the big stars or agents that drew her fire one overcast February morning in Los Angeles – but the creative community.

'They used everything to trip David up,' she told me. 'Take the Edith Wharton stories. I'd been at him for years, saying they'd make wonderful films. I kept banging on about them. At the right price, I felt, they could be extraordinary for the *Room with a View* market. So here's an example of how David wanted to try and build the studio up. He went to Tina Rathborne, after supporting *Zelly and Me*; how would she feel about tackling an Edith Wharton story? She knew and loved *Age of Innocence*, as it turned out. Meantime, Lyndsey Posner had been working for three months to get the rights to the books, through an agent that David knows. When David was out of town in Atlanta, for *one* day, the agent phoned Columbia. He had to have David's offer *that day* or the rights were going elsewhere. David Picker didn't know what it was all about, he hadn't been told, and Lyndsey was away, so we missed the deadline. Who got the rights? Martin Scorsese. Nobody had even *heard* of Edith Wharton until then. David said he'd never speak to that agent again. And do you want to know what's funny? Scorsese in the end let the rights go! It was about the same as the *Toys* saga, which I've just heard is no longer going ahead at Fox, another perfect example. As soon as David showed interest, they wanted it. Creative community? There's *no* creative community.

'Greg Nava, who'd only made *El Norte* before, made *Destiny* for us. God, you should have heard him: David did this for me, David did that for me. $800,000 he got for *Destiny*. When David asked him what he wanted to do next, oh, he was off elsewhere – for $1.1 million. For $300,000 he went with someone else! And he's already got screwed! There's just so much *greed*, you can't *build* anything. Someone who owes everything to you, they'll sell out for $300,000. Fuck them – they're not worth it. It's *impossible* to deal with that. David wanted to nurture people, do it from within, but you can't do it with that society. They say nobody supports them, but nobody supports them because they don't give any loyalty.'

Patsy sat curled up in a chair, a mug of coffee cupped in her hands. Now she smiled. 'Looking back, it's wonderful,' she said. 'Now that all the rage, the cynicism, the betrayal is over, it's wonderful. I can now look and say, he did it for a year, a year and a half. He's come away with all his money in a year and a bit instead of three years. "We're a year and a half ahead," he told me, "now we can get on with whatever we want to do." It's the first time he's shown that cynicism; he's never had it before. And the enjoyment of Thailand, on holiday *free* from Columbia! We've been on holiday before, but it wasn't as sweet as a *paid* holiday. It was another way of saying, "You didn't *really* get me! I came out ahead!" Because he needs to feel that, however disappointed he was. Jim Clark told him he'd never have survived through three years at the rate he was going, burning himself out. He would have had a heart attack, never mind mononucleosis. So he has to weigh one year's satisfaction against three. And Goizueta and Keough are already working hard to mend the bridges. David's not someone they don't want to get on with.

'Yes, he's got decisions to make. The role of executive producer, that's not open to him. It doesn't work for him. If he's going to stay in the film industry, he'll either have to line-produce, or set up his own mini-Columbia. I used to fantasize that when David was finished at Columbia, his relationship with them would be so good they'd say, "Whatever he wants to do, we'll follow him" – like going back to Europe and opening a European film-making studio with their money.'

The irony of Patsy's last remark remains stuck in my throat, for wasn't this one of the things Fay Vincent had in mind from the beginning?

Later that same day I had lunch with Marion Rosenberg, an agent and great admirer of David, whom she has known since his *Melody* days. 'David's totally unlike other people in the business,' she told me. 'Daryl Hannah's my client and has always refused to do commercials. Without our knowing anything about it, Columbia came up with this idea of doing a television commercial showing scenes from *Roxanne* and, separately, people drinking Diet Coke. The slogan was, 'If you want to have fun at a theatre this summer, see *Roxanne*, drink Diet Coke'. This was deemed by us, reasonably enough, I think, to be a commercial for Diet Coke. Daryl was very upset; she'd turned down so many and now people were phoning up and saying, "I thought your girl didn't do commercials?" Amidst all the threats of lawsuits and stuff, David was just amazing. He finessed it to the point where we were able to make a settlement. Columbia gave Daryl some money which she's given to charity. One of the things David did wrong, though, was serious. He knocked this town and he shouldn't have. He seemed to have just no sense of tactics; everyone was astonished. A lot of support he had at the beginning quickly cooled. The consensus is that if David had just done his job, he could have *owned* the place.'

Another friend had reservations about David's choice of executives at Columbia. 'None of them came from the mainstream pool that moves sideways and occasionally marginally up and down – "Get me so-and-so on the phone, where is he now? Wasn't he at Paramount?" – that group. The bottom line is, it doesn't really matter what they are, they're all pretty efficient at what they do and if they didn't have power at one place, they're not going to have it at the other place. But they do perform a function and David, I believe by design, never hooked into any of those people. He chose people who had not done these jobs before, with the exception of David Picker, which was also an odd choice; he was *Old* Hollywood.

'It's hard to go for what's positive about David Puttnam without emphasizing what's wrong with the rest of the business. You can't look at this business as a pimple on some corporate map and say, "That's our movie division". It's the only business you can't look at as a division. If it's not functioning on its own, or generating its own power or feeding off itself, it can't exist. Ever since big business got in, the whole concept of the movie industry has changed. Coke, Kinney, Transamerica, Gulf and Western – there's always somebody above the studio who has to be answered to. The studio bosses are forever looking over their shoulders.'

A second agent was less flattering, and very specific in his criticism. 'David was never *there*,' he maintained. 'He was always at a film festival or a sales conference or abroad somewhere. It was always, "I'm going away, but I'll be back, we'll talk then." You can't do that in this town, not when you're the head of a studio. You've got to be there every single day. You can't go to film festivals. It was OK for Sherry Lansing to do that as the "head" of Fox, she was *hired* to do that, and never given any power. She was the mouthpiece, she was pretty, everybody liked her and it enabled Fox to say, "Look every-body, we've got a woman president". But David should have been there every day, *doing* it. After a while you pitch a project to Columbia and they say, David's away for two weeks, so you say, OK, I'll take it to Ned Tanen or Jeff Katzenberg or Mike Medavoy. It has a lot to do with staying on top of relationships, having access to the right informa-tion. You don't do that by being at a film festival in Sri Lanka. He turned himself into the Sherry Lansing of Columbia.'

A producer agreed with this observation. 'He didn't have time to return phone calls, but he had time to give every interview and speech. He attended every film festival that invited him.'

'Part of my agreement with Coke was to internationalize the com-pany,' David protested. 'The first time I told Don Keough I was going to get on the road, he said, "Thank God. Frank Price's idea of a trip was to the beach!".'

David was infuriated when Victor Kaufman announced that the newly-formed Columbia Pictures Entertainment was writing off a staggering $105 million post-tax on a slate of 12 of his movies. 'They're doing nothing with the films,' he raged, 'they intend to do nothing with them, and then they turn around and say the films have no value. It's transparent, it's ridiculous, and unfortunately it's the filmmakers who will suffer most from it.' Financial analysts recognized Columbia's write-downs as all-too-familiar normal procedure in any studio shake-up, with all losses conveniently shunted into the old régime. Any business the movies did subsequently generate would be money from home.

Kaufman's public claim that Columbia would be taking a 'considerable loss' on *Hope and Glory* was one for which he would later profusely apologize to John Boorman, never a director to take statements of this nature lying down. Another Columbia executive described *The Last Emperor*'s acquisition as a 'dumb deal' and the movie itself as 'a huge-budget art-house film. You're condemned to a loss. You have to support it or you're seen as an enemy of the arts.'

Columbia had appeared to support *The Last Emperor* in fairly regal style, beginning with its carefully-structured release in November, when it opened in five cinemas to take an encouraging $30,000 per cinema. The strategy was to roll the movie out slowly, conserving its strength for the February Oscar nominations, a plan that was only too familiar to David, who had benefited from the same decision by Warner as far back as *Chariots of Fire*. By Christmas *The Last Emperor* had spread out to a still modest 94 theatres, bringing the per-screen average down to a less glowing $8000, tending to confirm Columbia's suspicion that without Oscar nominations or awards, the movie would die in the sticks. To their credit, when nine Oscar nominations were announced, *The Last Emperor* was showing in 377 cinemas, although by this time the average was down to a none-too-bright $4000 per cinema.

One week before the Awards, *The Last Emperor* was on its last pre-Oscar legs in every sense with screens up to 460 and the average take down to under $2000. Following the film's triumph on the Oscars night of 11 April, when it made an astonishing sweep of the board and won in every single nominated category, Columbia – arguably one week late – jumped the screens up to 882 and spent millions of dollars on an advertising blitz. The results were disappointing. 'The film

plays well in major markets,' said distribution executive James Spitz,
'but in the smaller markets the urgency to see the picture is just not
there, even with the panache and cachet of nine Academy Awards.' In
other words – nix from the stix, which had been the studio's feeling
all along.

'There was every opportunity for a good distributor to make a lot
of money out of the film,' David had asserted as Kaufman made his
write-down. Although producer Jeremy Thomas was initially critical of
Columbia's handling of the film, he conceded his satisfaction with
their efforts in the end. It's an age-old argument – throw the film
on the mass market and if it doesn't click quickly, it's yanked for ever. Roll
it out slow, and you're not giving the movie enough exposure – you're
damned if you do and you're damned if you don't. The treasure for
The Last Emperor at the end of its US run looked like $44 million, a
fairly commendable haul by any standards. Columbia should have
more such 'dumb deals'.

With its Oscar tally bettered only by *Ben Hur*, with 11 wins in
1960, and *West Side Story*'s 10 in 1962, the Awards night should
really have been dubbed '*The Last Emperor*'s Picture Show'. Bernardo
Bertolucci was jubilant. 'Two hours ago,' he exclaimed, 'I said nine
nominations. Now I can say nine Oscars.' When one reporter asked
Jeremy Thomas why not a single award-winner had mentioned the
name of David Puttnam in their acceptance speeches, he replied, 'I
don't understand the question.' Then he was asked directly why he
had not thanked Puttnam. 'There was no reason to,' he said. 'This is
not an award for David Puttnam. He didn't produce the film. I did.'
After his years of patient struggle to bring Bertolucci's vision to the
screen, Jeremy's reaction was understandable, and perhaps made, at
least in part, on behalf of the other low-profilers working away in the
British Film Industry. And after all, David's 1982 triumph had never
been regarded as 'Alan Ladd Jr's *Chariots of Fire*', although Laddie
had performed exactly the same function in that film's US release as
David had with *The Last Emperor* at Columbia.

Equally understandable, if somewhat more predictable, was David's
reaction to the Awards. His joy apparently undiluted by murmurings
that he had bought the Awards rather than produced them, and *Hope
and Glory* being overlooked despite four nominations, he managed to
make every barbed line count. There was one for the Coca-Cola
company: 'I was asked to join Columbia to give the studio some
prestige, and I have to believe the Coke people are proud tonight.'
There was one for Hollywood: 'We tried to make the studio international, and tonight 12 of the Awards went overseas.' There was one

for Columbia: 'At every studio there's an obligation to distribute their films with as much effort as went into making them.' Then there was a somewhat self-serving nod to Fay Vincent, 'who has suffered more than anyone in this whole mish-mash': 'I'd like to think this begins to vindicate the decision he made to bring me to the studio.' (Missing was any word of congratulation for Norman Jewison, whose *Moonstruck* had garnered three Oscars for MGM.)

Fay Vincent was somewhat more sanguine about the outcome when I asked for his feelings on the Awards and David's reaction to them. 'I think David should feel very proud,' he murmured, 'and I'm happy for myself because it's another Columbia award to add to the others in my 10 years. The fact is, though, it doesn't matter. The chapter's over; he's out; it's all history and all that matters is the future.'

The continuing roll-out of David's own production slate seemed to fully justify Kaufman's decision to write off the films' costs, despite David's claim that the action represented a 'self-fulfilling prophecy'. *Variety*'s reviews and the films' grosses told their own story:

- *Zelly and Me*: 'This precious story . . . will be as off-putting to some people as it will be moving to others.' The film cost $2.3 million to make and took precisely $55,000 gross.
- *School Daze*: 'A loosely-connected series of musical set pieces . . . the film is a hybrid of forms and styles that never comes together in a coherent whole.' I was with David in Los Angeles the Monday after the movie's opening weekend and when we checked the figures David declared that the $7000 per cinema average take was better than he had expected. At a cost of $5.5 million, the film grossed a good-for-its-budget $14 million. Still director Spike Lee would claim the film had been mishandled by the new Columbia régime. Although Victor Kaufman had approached him for his new film, he announced that under no circumstances would he work with Columbia or Tri-Star again. 'All of Puttnam's films,' he declared, 'have been treated like illegitimate stepchildren.'
- *Little Nikita*: '. . . never really materializes as a taut espionage thriller and winds up as an unsatisfying execution of a clever premise . . . narrative unravels in the latter third of the film as chaotic and jumbled action takes over completely.' Sydney Poitier's comeback film cost $15 million to produce and grossed a meagre $1.7 million.
- *Stars and Bars*: 'In David Puttnam's film legacy *Stars and Bars* represents a major faux pas. Unfunny mix of farce and misdirected satire has no conceivable audience apart from undiscriminating pay cable viewers . . . pic self-destructs rapidly. Helmer Pat O'Connor

evidences no feel for comedy, having the cast overact unmercifully. Daniel Day Lewis is downright embarrassing.' *Village Voice* chipped in with 'The luckless *Stars and Bars* just lays there, gross and depressing . . . David Puttnam . . . who commissioned the movie, must have thought the subject foolproof – a fish out of water comedy with something real to say about America. In the 18th century, people were tarred and feathered for less – now they get the golden parachute. Who says the Yanks haven't been civilized?' Cost: $8 million; Gross: $100,000.

- *A Time of Destiny*: 'A heavy-handed melodrama . . . stumbles awkwardly over a stiff, conventional screenplay laden with tedious and lachrymose plot.' Cost: $9.5 million; Gross: $1.2 million.

Normally a distributor stops reporting films' grosses when they have reached a certain level, but this much Columbia was not prepared to do, apparently determined that maximum mortification should be generated. *Variety* was constrained to note in late June that, 'for some reason, distrib continued to report embarrassing figures for some of its major releases: *Stars and Bars* made $3599 in six theatres; *A Time of Destiny* had a date with $1758 in seven foxholes and *Zelly and Me* did all of $241 in four situations.' By the following week, Columbia seemed to realize they were making a bigger ass of themselves than anyone else and did the decent, sensible thing, reporting no further figures on the three films.

The hopes that lay in Brian Gilbert's switched father/son saga were also to be cruelly dashed. '*Vice Versa* doesn't even have the pep of *Like Father Like Son*,' wrote David Edelstein in *Village Voice*. 'It's drably tasteful . . . a lame affair.' *Variety* might have put it, 'Village Voice Vetoes *Vice Versa*.' One ex-Columbia executive now felt able to talk freely about the first time he saw the movie: 'David was talking as if Brian had worked a miracle, the new Capra, all that. It scared the living daylights out of me when I saw the film, because I thought, well, either I'm losing my marbles or – it just *wasn't funny*. I said to myself, "What the fuck is going on?" It was like in advertising agencies when they *have* to believe in their product, the power of positive thinking, mass hysteria. There was an element of that in David's reign.' At a cost of $13 million, box-office gross came to the same, a net return to Columbia of $5 million, not even enough to cover the marketing costs.

Even after these reviews and box-office figures, David kept up the attack on the new Columbia régime. 'They are strangling my pictures at birth,' he still claimed. 'They're making absolutely sure the slate doesn't make money. They can deny it, but I'm saying it.' Dawn Steel felt constrained to issue a cool rebuff. 'Columbia Pictures and David Puttnam have one thing in common,' she averred, 'a need, desire and obligation for the pictures made during his administration, to succeed.'

Several films that David left in the can have interesting potential, perhaps none more so than Terry Gilliam's *The Adventures of Baron Munchausen*. Will the teller of tall tales ride to the rescue of David's beleaguered slate? Only time will tell.

And what of the movie David had turned away – Marty Ransohoff's *Switching Channels*? In the same week that Edelstein flattened *Vice Versa*, he was one of the many critics who also pounded Marty's movie. 'There is nothing particularly wrong with *Switching Channels*, except it has no taste and no bite,' he wrote. 'A flop on style alone, it moves with the bleary desperation of bad dinner theatre.' Tri-Star's release of the movie had Victor Kaufman licking his wounds with a puny $8.5 million gross, $3 million net, possibly enough to defray half the movie's marketing costs.

The close on $80 million gross of Norman Jewison's *Moonstruck* re-opened the original question: could this have been a Columbia movie? It would certainly have sweetened the pot considerably, although no one would suggest that rejecting a Norman Jewison project was tantamount to turning down a fortune. Good film-maker that he is, Jewison's last real hit is lost in the mists of time. Despite David's earlier assertion, made at several stages since the film had opened to dazzling reviews, that neither he nor Columbia were offered the picture, *Variety* provided 'an update' on the subject in May 1988. 'I'm now told the studio read *Moonstruck*,' David at first admitted. 'I don't know if the studio did. I certainly didn't. I mean, it certainly wasn't submitted to David Puttnam.'

Norman Jewison was equally adamant that it was. 'I submitted it to Columbia to David Puttnam's attention,' he insisted. Then he dropped his bombshell. He had proof – in the form of an actual rejection letter from David himself. *Variety* contacted David for a *third* time.

'I've got one thing to clear up,' he now said, 'because I did some checking up on my own. While I was at Columbia, we did turn down a film called *Moonglow*, which did eventually become *Moonstruck*. ['It was called a lot of things,' Jewison acknowledged, 'and at one time it was called *Moonglow*.'] The letter I sent out to Larry Auerbach, Jewison's agent, was the 6th of September, which means it was at the end of the first week I was there. As we got 4000 scripts in, and as I'd done nothing but read in the previous few months – I only read scripts – it could have been one of the ones I read, I have no idea. In the letter I sent, it sounds as though I did. I said, "I'm pretty sure in my own mind that this is the one decision I'm going to regret and at least half of me hopes I will regret it." It's an unusual letter, the only one like that I wrote. It sounds to me as though I must have been right on the edge.' It sounded to a lot of others as if David – to borrow from one of his cricketing expressions – had been fairly and squarely caught out.

When David gave his account of what many regarded as the original seed of his downfall – the three-year declaration – as ever, it provided only a tantalizing, half-revealing glimpse into his motivation that managed by the same token to be half-concealing. 'I had to deal with this sense of selling out,' he claimed in the same interview with *Variety*. 'I'd said a lot of stuff in my life about not wanting to go back to Hollywood. For the sake of my own dignity, I had to time-cap it. It was very, very important to my dignity that I hung on to this three-year notion. There was a 50-50 chance I'd never even complete the three years. In effect, I was saying, "You can't fire me, I'm already leaving."'

The astonishing reason that David had given Fay Vincent *18 months earlier*, tells the *whole* story. 'David's real problem from day one was that he was very frightened of failure,' Fay reveals. 'He said it was *psychological*. He was very, very worried about failing and he wanted to make it clear to everyone that he was leaving. It was all caught up in his own psyche. He felt that by telling everybody that he was leaving in 1990, that no matter what might happen, that was *it*. If he'd put over my view that he was going to continue at Columbia *after* the three years – and that hadn't happened – then it would be perceived that he had been fired. So he was anxious about that and defensive from the outset. The point here is that David was saying he can't have a superior officer. It was just too *terrifying* for him to think about *failure*. The fact is he got into a mess very quickly. The moment he made that declaration about having his date circled made it appear that that was the day he was leaving the company completely.'

'When I shook hands with Fay Vincent and Dick Gallop in New York,' David continued in his *Variety* statement, 'something in my heart of hearts told me I should not be shaking hands with them. Really, what I would like to have done is got out of that room without having made a final commitment. But every little thing I had asked for had been agreed to. And I had no cause to procrastinate and they said, "We've got a deal." I guess what I'm trying to say to you is, all things being equal, if I hadn't shaken hands at that moment, I would have picked up the phone and called Fay Vincent and said, "Look, I'm making a mistake and I suspect you're making a mistake." But we had shaken hands. And I felt obligated to Fay.'

Fay smiled ruefully as he talked about David's account. 'All he had to do was tell us,' he said. 'I'd have been disappointed, but it would not have been unsurmountable. It ties in with his terrific insecurity and his belief he was going to fail, and says to you from the outset David probably understood he was in over his head. He wanted the money, but he recognized he was taking a terrific risk with his own standing and his own career and that really says, "I shouldn't have taken the job, because I don't think I can *do* it properly." If he'd said that to me, I'd have said, "Then don't *take* the job; we'll give it to someone else." But he told me he could do it. In fact, he told me he was very excited about it.'

Since Dick Gallop had been involved with Fay Vincent in the negotiations that brought David to Columbia, David cited him to confirm that the subject of making money had never come up at this stage. 'It *was* made clear to him from day one,' said Gallop, 'and he accepted the fact that Columbia is a profit-making venture. There was no question – through direct conversations at our meeting – that making popular pictures and making the studio money was the essence of the assignment.'

When David demurred on this, allowing only that the idea of making money was 'implicit' in their discussions, Gallop came thundering back. 'It was *explicit*,' he insisted, 'absolutely explicit.'

Fay Vincent agrees with Gallop's recollection: 'Of course it was explicit,' he confirms. 'After he started there was one great moment when David said, "We'll have the number-one record in box-office results in 1988." I said, "*That's* the kind of thing I want to hear!"' He and Coote suggested that we have our next distributors' meeting in Paris and take the whole group over as a treat if we reached number one. I gladly agreed. But that illustrates the schizophrenia in David's mind. On the one hand, I think he felt he had the ability and knew how to make pictures. On the other, there was this terrific insecurity and concern that he was going to fail.

'David didn't want to be put in the position where some day he could be fired. He had a tremendous anxiety about working for somebody who could fire him. He'd never done that before. I think the fear of being fired was really the thing that I missed completely. It explains the three-year thing, going public, circling the date in his diary, all of that. When he said that everybody was frightened of Roberto, he meant that *he* was frightened of Roberto. He was afraid that one day they were going to call him up and say, "You're out," and sure enough . . .'

When David violently objected to Fay's bracketing of his departure with the firings of McElwaine and Price, Fay conceded that, of course, he had not been present at the fateful meeting with Kaufman. 'I knew about McElwaine and Price, since I was directly involved,' he told me. 'When Coke told me of the reconstruction, I knew it was their intention to fire David, I knew that he was not going to survive under Victor. David would go, he and Victor were not compatible, Victor was going the Ray Stark route, they wouldn't mesh. The problem is the word "fired" – people never use the word. I never used it to McElwaine or Price, I just said, "I think it would be better if you left," and I'm sure that's what Victor and David talked about. I think *Victor* would say, "I fired David Puttnam." It's a *semantics* problem, not a *substance* problem. The substance is that when the decision was made to put Victor in charge, everybody knew David was going to leave. However you characterize it, he was no longer going to run the studio, and that's what happened.

'The ultimate problem, had to do more with the cumulative effect of all those things stacked against him. The effect of Ovitz, Stark, Murray, Aykroyd, Beatty, Cosby – it got to be a long list. I've thought about it and I think there's a big difference between being a producer and being head of a studio. As a producer you can fight with people, that's how you live. It's your product and there is no long-term, it's just *you*. If you don't want to deal with Beatty ever again or with Murray or with Ovitz, fine. Running a studio is different, because it's all about relationships. It's an entirely different set-up.

'And Columbia wasn't just any studio, but one owned by Coca-Cola, with a worldwide image to keep up. I think that probably David and I completely misjudged the circumstances when he came in. Looking back, I don't think I spent enough time coaching him. I assumed he knew a lot more than he did. I bear some of the re-sponsibility and he bears some too.'

In February I talked to Roland Joffe as he relaxed by the side of the pool in his Beverly Hills home, fresh from an early-morning tennis work-out. 'David's got this ineffable gaiety,' he told me. 'There's an immense *zest* inside David just for living. And he's like an anteater, constantly rooting around, sniffing out little bits, morsels, collecting newspaper-cuttings, phrases, quotes, all random, but for David a means of understanding the world. The key to really understanding David is to see him as a London kid who, through innate curiosity, discovered that the world was available. In another century, he'd have been a privateer. He'd have run away from home; he'd have been floating about in the Spanish Main, knocking off Spanish galleons, pinching gold, coming back – but he'd have subsumed all the cultures he'd bumped into. And his ship would have been elegantly British, with Union Jacks all over it and stuffed with goodies from all over the world.

'The *same* David does one extraordinarily dangerous thing in that he uses other human beings as examples. It's the least likable part of his nature. He did it in this town. It's not a side of David I approve of.'

Roland next inadvertently anticipated Fay Vincent's words to me four months later in New York, in a parallel from his own experience. 'What was happening to Sydney Schanberg in Cambodia,' he told me, 'was something that happens to people at different times in their lives. Sydney was coming to terms with what it means to be Sydney Schanberg. Like a lot of men in his position, Sydney's career was made up of compensations, his way of coping with the difficult world he had inside him as well as the world he found outside. That's a clue to David, too.'

Fay's later comment closely echoed this: 'I think David's reached a very serious level,' he said. 'He's hurt pretty badly. One of the things he's lost in this process is in terms of character and standing. He came over as a class act and a lot of things have hurt that. He's come face-to-face with himself.'

Face-to-face or not, David continued to rail against the slings and arrows that were part and parcel of the outrageous Columbia fortune he had carried home. 'I'm 47 years old and nobody ever asked me to leave anything,' he insisted to *Variety*. 'If anyone says I was asked to leave, there will be a lawsuit the next morning.' Although earlier in the year he had quipped that Coke had 'bottled Fay Vincent', David clearly did not accept that he himself had been ever-so-neatly canned.

Chapter 30

What Makes David Run?

After less than a year at Coca-Cola bottling, Fay Vincent left to rejoin his original law firm of Caplin and Drysdale. To many he was seen as the main casualty of the Coke business plan; Fay doesn't see it that way at all. 'I'd been doing the job for 10 years,' he told me, as he sat comfortably in his new office 30 floors above East 53rd Street in midtown Manhattan, 'and I'm not really an entertainment person. Victor views himself as a creative person; he likes to get involved with casting, reading the scripts, as a producer. I went the other way. What I did was build the company up; the earnings were very good, the stock went up and people made a lot of money. I hired people. Some did well, some didn't. I didn't interfere. Frank Price would argue that I did, but Puttnam and others will tell you that I didn't. I know a lot about finance and acquisitions and we built the biggest company, the most profitable entertainment company in the business in 1986, but the fact is that from my point of view it was a job I was becoming tired of. So my move out of entertainment wasn't totally unexpected, since I'd been saying I'd like to do something else.

'I *still* think David was the right choice. The cynics say the only way to tell is to look at the movies. In fact, they haven't been terrific and I think the opposition would say he was the wrong choice on every count. He didn't make good movies; caused a lot of trouble in the community; he hurt the company; he hurt me. On what score was he the right choice? I'd say he was a terrific experiment in that he had a lot of talent and you can't judge somebody by the first year in the job. Most of the people I've watched had beginnings that were not spectacular.

'Victor is very able, smart and talented and has a very big job to do in a difficult situation. He's very different from me, too, in that he's closer to Ray, and Ray is much more involved in the company again. He's back to being a very influential and significant factor in Columbia.' This put Fay in mind of an incident in his relationship with

Stark. 'He talks to people in my position four, five times a day when relationships are good. He's on the phone *constantly*. Years ago he called and wanted to speak to me, but I was on the phone and my secretary said I would call him back. On this occasion I was busy and I didn't call him right back. He called again, and again I was on the phone. He got upset and said I was to call him right back. The third time he called he said he was at the airport on a pay phone and he was running out of change and it was urgent. I excused myself from the meeting I was in and took the call. He was mad at me for something and went on and on and on, then after about two minutes he said, "Wait a minute, there's a call coming in on the other line, *hold on*!" I think that explains Ray.'

When I mentioned Stark's current rejuvenation and box-office success with *Biloxi Blues*, Fay smiled. 'Lots of people thought he was finished,' he told me, as he puffed contentedly on his pipe. 'He fooled us all!'

Back in 1984 David had composed a witty and trenchant introduction to a collection of Alan Parker's cartoons:

> Attempting to come up with a rational explanation of why I had tolerated (and even enjoyed) the past dozen years of humiliation, I turned to the dictionary to find:
>> Masochism: form of perversion in which person derives pleasure from his own pain or humiliation (opp: sadism; (colloq.) enjoyment in what appears to be painful or tiresome.)
>
> However, even this doesn't adequately explain why I continue to open the familiar, cream Pinewood-stamped envelopes with anticipation rather than dread. Worse still, finding that the current Screen cartoon spotlights someone else's torment, merely sets me wondering if I'm working hard enough, or if I've offended Alan in some way. In fact, all the symptoms of:
>
> Paranoia: mental derangement with delusions of grandeur, persecution, etc.
>
> For the sake of my continuing sanity, long may I drink from my friend's poisoned chalice!

Sadly, the friendship is now over. Late in 1987 Alan did the unthinkable, the utterly unacceptable – he switched agencies and signed with Mike Ovitz's CAA, an action that David sees as the ultimate betrayal, and the unkindest cut of all. Alan had crossed the line that David carries in his head. If there is no going back, it will be a pity for both men. For David, the loss of his best friend will be yet another price he has paid for his sojourn in Babylon. Alan shrugged off the situation with the casual air of one resigned to losing something irretrievably precious. 'He's warm, charming, concerned, helpful and unbelievably generous,' he railed, 'and he's cold, callous spiteful, selfish and mean. I know more about him than anybody and I know *nothing* about him!'

David gave me his farewell address to Hollywood on the eve of his departure in April 1988. Although there is no doubt his views are sincerely held, equally David has put himself in the invidious position of one to whom the only good news is bad news. 'I believe Hollywood is facing ruin eventually,' he said, 'but unfortunately it keeps having these series of comebacks when business is up, and the underlying cancer, which I sincerely believe is there, isn't being addressed. The patient keeps on showing signs of recovery. This, plus the tremendous comforts created by the people who are for the most part in power. No one is addressing the cancer, which is costs. From 1982 to 1986 costs rose 63 per cent against a Consumer Price Index of 13 per cent – five times as fast. The average cost of a movie now is $19.7 million. You know what I think sums up the present situation? At the end of all the bloodletting in the 1914/18 war, T.E. Lawrence observed the political manoeuvring and the manipulation that we now refer to as the Versailles Treaty. As he put it at the time, "When the new world dawned, the old men came out again and took from us our victory. Then they re-made it in the likeness of the former world we knew." What ever gets changed without shouting taking place? I was misled – I was led to believe that the situation at Columbia was desperate. Clearly Coke didn't feel it was as desperate as all that, or as they said it was.'

Not content with being merely the California Cassandra, a few days later he delivered another farewell, this time to America itself, at a USC Law Symposium. 'As I see it,' he declared, 'the US is in genuine danger of becoming the lost land ... There is a disillusionment wafting through the heady winds of the American dream, as more and more people come to feel that they've had the experience, but somehow, somewhere, missed out in the meaning of it. It's as if there was a vision gap. Prosperity had bred contentment, but not enough to overcome this sense of drift. Something far less tangible than deficit assails the national spirit. Many Americans are concerned at the growth of influence peddling ... These same citizens watched in dismay as inside traders took over Wall Street. They rightly question a system which allows the transformation, by greed and technology, of their stock exchange into a market place which functions much more like a casino than a financial institution.

'Reeling under the implications of problems of government and finance, some Americans turned to institutionalized faith for help, that's until they discovered that a new generation of religious leaders had merely set up profitable Disneylands, built in the name of Jesus.

'While all this was happening, American's saw their place in the traditional world markets decline, as their interest was distracted from opportunities overseas; thus confirming the belief that in time of crisis there invariably looms in this country a very real form of parochialism.'

David had learned the hard way the Great American Truth: Payback's a *bitch*. Ray Stark responded to his prognosis in his usual irrepressible manner. 'How could he say the American dream is dead?' he asked. 'He spent one year here and left with millions of dollars. Only in America!'

In Britain the reaction to David's homecoming was a muted one. With another 10 years under his belt, Brian Duffy felt he could see where his friend had gone wrong: 'David had worked the reviewers and press in this country brilliantly, and got them on his side. In the end, they started writing eulogies to him and he started believing their crap. He thought all he had to do was repeat the performance in America, but nobody there wanted to know that some smart-arsed Englishman was going to show them how to play jazz or save money. What they wanted from David was his brilliance at promoting. If he'd kept to that, he'd have promoted people's salaries and promoted the industry, but he had read the drivel these half-wits in this country had poured on him and swallowed it. He set up his own downfall in believing he could walk on water.'

Alan Yentob at the BBC was another supporter who had watched in dismay. 'The surprise was that David wasn't tactical,' he told me. 'There was a sense of holier-than-thou. He was self-righteous, a bit pompous. He would make these long speeches and give the impression he was the only person who'd ever made a movie. You *have* to be tactical. Maybe he should have tried to let some of these popular films happen and *then* made the films he wanted to make as well. Then what he didn't reckon on was the revenge of Columbia. The wrath of Hollywood has just been merciless on him. It was *unprecedented* the way they went for him. What they did – it was almost *crucifying* him. Hopefully, when he's rehabilitated, he'll be able to look back on it as a pretty extraordinary experience. In the end, I don't think it's been that damaging to him. It may teach him some lessons. It's just hurt him, but he's got to come back and get on with it.'

Terence Donovan saw David's Hollywood episode as just the latest instalment in his career. 'It's an industry where the square-root of punishment is very high,' he said. 'The more successful you get, the more they loathe you. David hasn't got what he's got the easy route, lesser men would have given up. What's happened describes the nature of the weasels in Hollywood and Atlanta more than it describes David. In his career there's certainly been lots of gruesome. I hope later things will get less gruesome, but I suspect it won't, because film-making as a craft has got so much gruesome built into it. But to me it doesn't matter terribly in life what happens, it's how you *react* to it. You've got to *keep going*. And David will keep going.'

If David is deep in many ways, he can be incredibly shallow in others. In one conversation we had, I asked him if he thought he had a big ego. 'It's a very unusual ego,' he hedged, 'therefore it's hard to say whether it's big or small.'

'Is there a difference between having a big ego and being egotistical?' I persisted. 'Yes,' he replied, feeling himself now on surer ground, 'and I'd certainly go along with the idea that I've got a big ego. You couldn't do my job without it.'

I asked him how this manifested itself in his dealing with other people. 'I'm obsessed with being understood for what I am,' he said, 'and not for what other people judge me as. A useful quality, but very un-American, is my acceptance of the irresolution of life: that there are no answers, only questions. I understand the complexities of paradox.'

Did he accept, therefore, the ambivalence of success, and how would he define it? 'I absolutely accept it. I can't, for example, fully rationalize why being successful should make my life in the country-side more difficult.'

I had expected a somewhat deeper dissertation; but David was already off on a different, but clearly countryside-related tack: 'Something I find hard to deal with, because I don't have any, is envy. I find it an extraordinarily difficult emotion to comprehend. I come up against it a lot. What happens, tragically, is that it distances you from people. I genuinely believe that my career has been built on what I've done. I don't think it's a career of shadows. I'm a product of a lot of products and so I've defined myself. It always annoys me, the fact that I've made some good films, which have been successful films, and I had to pay a price for that. That seems wrong to me.

'When people are envious of me and react negatively, what are they envious of? The fact that I've made successful movies? Enough successful movies to have been able to afford the things I've been able to afford and to have the life I've had? Several friends of mine have a problem with how happy my marriage is. They think it's unjust; they think it's wrong; that I don't deserve this charmed life. They could deal with me being successful if my marriage was on the rocks, or, God forbid, if I'd had personal tragedies in my life. I think what irritates people is the idea of someone who's successful, well-known and extraordinarily happy. I reckon that says something about the people it rankles, not me.'

I was genuinely interested to hear David's answer to my next question, 'If you could choose a director, *anyone*, living or dead, to film the story of your life, who would it be?' Would he pick Kazan? Wilder? Bob *Rafelson*? *David Lynch*? *Jonathan Demme*??

'Brian Gilbert,' came the astonishing reply. 'I'd feel comfortable with Brian. He's absolutely a humanist, he would get on film those things that are important to me. Yes, Brian's middle-class humanism would tie in very well with what I think are my best qualities. I'd know I was in good hands and I know I'd like the film. Alan would end up making Alan's film, so would Rolie. With Brian it would be a film about me and I'd know it would be affectionate.' (I'd met Brian and he's an enormously likeable, bluff character who I'm sure will go on to become a first-class director, once he cuts loose from his moorings.) However, based on *The Frog Prince* and the 'drably tasteful' *Vice Versa*, the choice seemed to be incredibly revealing. David clearly defined 'good hands' as 'safe hands'.

'You wouldn't go with someone who would bring out more of your undercurrents, for example?' I asked. 'Or haven't you got any?'

'No,' David replied, very positively, 'because I'm sure that whatever undercurrents I have, Brian probably shares. I'm sure he does. He's a complex man, conflicted to a degree. He loved this last year in America, but hated being away from his family. Yes, it's absolutely the right choice.'

I was left to reflect that David's simplistic notion of human conflict was having to live in the country and work in the town, or enjoying a year in America while still missing your family. A bit superficial, a little on the thin side. Or was he being disingenuous?

The speeches of Ray Stark, Mike Ovitz and all the studio heads combined would still make only a slim volume, where David would be deep into his second or third tome . . . Why? Has David got so much more to say, or is he simply ambitious in a different direction?

His statesmanlike utterances, whether borrowed or otherwise, seem to indicate a move into politics (more difficult now with the collapse of the SDP, but not impossible), the conservation arena, or a combination of the two. Whichever he chooses, he would do well to heed the admonition that speeches measured by the hour also tend to die with the hour.

'My biggest single problem,' David admitted, 'is that I'm not in show business and deep down there's a bit of me that despises show business. I'm interested in what's behind the clown in the circus, what the clown's thinking, but I'm not interested in the clown himself and all that razzmatazz. I think a lot of people find me a rather mean-spirited person in that respect. I've never joined the Variety Club; I hate all that "here we are again" stuff; I find it awful. Sincerely embarrassing. That's why the role I've cast myself in is quite deliberately a role that – I've never said this before, never even thought of it before – while I went along with my dad's wishes that I didn't go into Fleet Street, maybe in the end I'm a journalist and there's a part of me that still thinks like a journalist or biographer.'

It was back to Emerson and his journals: 'until at last we find in some word or act the boy and the man . . . Straightway all past words and actions lie in light before us!' The basic conflict in David lay exposed – and the reason the Hollywood trip had been doomed from the beginning. For millions of dollars he had blithely sacrificed himself and his ideals. The producer of films dealing with men in moral crises had turned himself into *a man in moral crisis*. A man who loathed razzmatazz had surrendered – indeed, offered himself – to the tinsel capital of the world.

To make his joining them palatable, David portrayed the benighted Coca-Cola company and its officers as an uneasy amalgam of the Friends of the Earth and Brothers of the Cross, with a touch of Amnesty International thrown in for good measure. Never could they simply be, with all the cant stripped away, an enormous multinational soft drinks firm run by salaried executives responsible to their shareholders and watch committees, attempting day by day to turn a buck. If this was all they were, why on earth would David ally himself with such an enterprise? Three million reasons suggest themselves, but provide no acceptable scenario for David to present to the world in order to justify his second descent into the lower depths. No, it had to be a crusade, just as his leaving had to be portrayed as martyrdom. (He put to me the comparison of the 'man alone' deserted by the townspeople and even his bride-to-be, as portrayed by Gary Cooper in *High Noon*. But didn't the townspeople finally rally round Gary? Ah, but that was in another, more idealized galaxy.)

Along with his 'fuck-you' money, David wanted to be seen and heard and respected. The pity of it is that he had not yet learned to differentiate between attention and respect. The community itself had been bothering him for years. He had been constantly told. 'This is the price, take it or leave.' The 'other guy' had got the better of him all the time. David had paid all these dues, now he wanted them back – both emotionally and financially. He wanted to get *even*.

Then there was the second conflict – the guilt of uninvolvement. There are few film-makers in the world today who have the inclination to make the sort of movies David does, and we should be grateful there are some left. On the other hand, life would be tedious if we were fed nothing but a steady diet of Puttnam films. Fay Vincent, being the decent and honourable man that he is, may still think he was the right person for the Columbia job, or at least the 'terrific experiment' he claims. This could be disputed. Just as in the so-called 'Golden Age', studios today are obliged to turn out a cross-section of movies that will appeal to the broad public – comedy, adventure, romance, drama, thriller – since most people go to the cinema to be entertained. The studios are in show-*business* and have an obligation to their shareholders to make money. Some will choose to make endless *Rambo*s and *Friday the Thirteenth*s, others will not. Now and again a thoughtful, serious movie provides a welcome change of pace, and as an independent producer David will hone and polish his contribution to this oeuvre as close to perfection as he can, through his tremendous personal enthusiasm. Others can pursue this course and still manage to find enthusiasm left over for the lightweight material. *Not David*. Faced with a *Leonard VI*, David has no idea how to approach the project, doesn't want to know anything about it and is able to do next to nothing in order to make it better. For sure, he'll go through the motions, but basically he has no real enthusiasm for the kind of lightweight material that comedy to him embodies. Bill Forsyth could bring off a *Local Hero* for his producer, but nothing could save the mismatched talent David cast on *Stars and Bars*. So what do 'Puttnam's illegitimate stepchildren', as Spike Lee would have it, *really* constitute? Aren't they just as much the neglected *Leonard*s and aborted *Stars and Bars* on the slate – films where he could have said, 'It's no good as it is, but here's how we could make it better' – as the movies to which Lee refers?

Instead of flagellating *himself* for his guilt, he had picked on what he saw as the worst elements in the community – costs, deals and individuals – and excoriated them instead. Mercilessly. While every stroke of the verbal whip had made him feel that much less compromised, there was still no escaping his own responsibility, the damned spot that refused to budge. Knowing he was basically there under false pretences, for all the worst reasons, his self-righteousness was an almighty din to cover the voice of his guilt.

In Europe, people will listen to criticisms, or what David would call his 'debate'. And some will say, 'Well, we don't like it, but maybe we should listen. He's not saying things we want to hear but we could learn from it.' In America, where latent xenophobia is endemic, especially against Britons with a tendency to shoot their mouths off, the response was short and sharp: 'Fuck *you*, David.'

The final element that blew this explosive confusion of emotions sky-high was the dread David had been carrying about for years hidden deep within his subconscious – a neurotic, haunting fear of failure. Only he knew at what frightening a cost he had succeeded; to fail would be something too awful to contemplate. This was the secret that David had to deal with in Hollywood, the secret that illuminates his every action there.

'With every triumph,' said one detractor, 'there are a thousand small betrayals in his wake.' In David's case, a failure to behave in a predictable manner might account for this impression, for he creates an agenda for himself that is doomed to fail. When too many people are owed or promised favours, each shortfall or non-delivery constitutes a betrayal.

If David has been finally brought face to face with himself, he has not yet reached a stage where he can admit it. For the moment the possibility that the Hollywood débâcle was of his own making is utterly precluded from his consciousness. What Fay Vincent sees as David's 'problem with the truth' reflects nothing more than the falsehoods we all create in our lives as a kind of binding agent to hold the flimsy structure of our existence together. In David's case, the process lies buried in a deep mistrust of himself. Can he ever live up to his father's ideals? For that matter, can he ever live up to Patsy's ideals? Or, to use a movie cliché, will it forever be 'one last bank heist' before he can 'go straight'? The Columbia heist had certainly produced the money, but at a shattering emotional cost.

Another 'welcome home' to Britain came in the form of the now-obligatory brush with the gutter press that many celebrities have to endure. Of more concern were David's plans for the future and the rebuilding of his shattered image in the wake of the Hollywood misadventure. A $50 million slate of features was soon to be launched, with backing from an international consortium including Warner in America and Japan's Fuji-Sankei. Possible projects encompass a distinct shelf-clearing element in explorer Ernest Shackleton's story and *October Circle*. A new addition is *Thumbs Up*, Jim Brady's account of life following the assassin's bullet in the head he suffered in the attempt on Ronald Reagan's life. David describes *Memphis Belle*, the story of a World War II B-52 squadron's 25th bombing mission, as a sort of 'thinking man's *Top Gun*' with many of the same elements that first excited him about *Chariots Of Fire*. Then there's *Gabriela*, where the central character is a woman. Since the female experience has been very much the dark continent until now in the Puttnam pantheon, I referred to it as an unusual project for him. 'Not really,' he claimed.

'But we don't have women in Puttnam films,' I pointed out. 'What's going on here?'

'We're going to change all that,' he laughingly replied. 'I'm really embarrassed. The only excuse is that I've got a problem with characters whose motivations I don't understand. So because I can never understand women . . .'

He talked enthusiastically of his chairmanship of the National Film School, an organization he has supported, both in terms of teaching and fund-raising activities, since the mid-seventies. David may be a wonderfully enthusiastic film producer, but his eyes light up every time he talks of his Film School work. The jibes that he does it for the purposes of personal glorification are surely unjust. Any glory that does accrue – and his CBE was seen in this light – will be as a *consequence* of his actions, not the driving force *behind* them.

Patsy perhaps provided a glimpse into the future. 'I'd like to see him take a bigger role in CPRE and the whole conservation issue,' she told me. 'I think he's a visionary in many ways and the ecology has to come first in all of our lives. I don't want him to give up on film-making, but it's possible he could run in parallel with that. He could bring some real wisdom to the ecology debate. I think it's the standpoint, the platform to be on, and if anybody could do it, he could. Perhaps you can't juggle the two balls, but I think it is *the* major subject of the end of the 20th century and I would very much encourage him to get involved in that.'

With Patsy's help, and a new, mature outlook that will evolve when he is finally able to objectively assess the last couple of years, David could well handle both. Hollywood saw the worst of the man. The best can be found in the aspirations inherent in a letter he wrote to the crew of *The Killing Fields* on 6 May 1983:

> On Sunday we all start to make a very difficult but worthwhile film. It is by far and away the most ambitious that I have ever attempted to produce, and it will, by the time we get through, have thoroughly tested us all. I'm sure that, like me, you constantly get asked what movies you've worked on. I always *hope* that the one I'm presently working on will instantly top the list when answering that question. All too often it doesn't work out that way. However, by nature, by sheer scope and theme, *The Killing Fields* is one of those few movies by which all our careers will undoubtedly be judged.
>
> Roland and I found a speech of President Kennedy's this week in which he said, 'I realize that the pursuit of peace is not as dramatic as the pursuit of war. And frequently the words of the pursuer fall on deaf ears. But we have no more urgent task.' Those words, spoken twenty years ago, have never been more relevant. We have a unique opportunity with this film to make our contribution. In the years to come, it is my honest belief that *The Killing Fields* will be the very first we mention in explaining and justifying the way we spent the best and most difficult years of our lives.
>
> For my part, I'll always be around to help if things go ugly. But in the final analysis all I can do is stand back, support Roland to the hilt and hope that luck and good sense run with us. All the best to all of us. This story deserves to be told and told well. If we pull that off then every form of possible reward will undoubtedly follow, and we will deserve it.
>
> David Puttnam

Although the 'blitz baby' has come a long way, he still has a long way to go. The direction he takes will indicate whether the expediency that has so often been David's prime motivation has finally been overcome. The emotional and psychological catharsis that will yet emerge from the Columbia adventure will be a painful, but ultimately a learning and healing process. One thing is certain; this is a man, for all his human failings, *never* to be underestimated.

Index

NOTE: This index is intended to give general reference to the life of David Puttnam; films which directly concerned him and his work; people with whom he worked and/or were his personal friends; and companies in or with which he was directly involved.